CAT
INTERACTIVE TEXT

Introductory
Paper 1

Recording Financial Transactions

> BPP is the **official provider** of training materials for the ACCA's CAT qualification. This Interactive Text forms part of a suite of learning tools, which also includes CD-ROMs for tuition and computer based assessment, and the innovative, internet-based 'virtual campus'.
>
> This text has been specifically written to the **current syllabus** and Teaching Guide.
>
> - Clear language and presentation
>
> - Plenty of activities, examples and quizzes to demonstrate and practise techniques
>
> - Syllabus and teaching guide
>
> - A new question and answer bank prepared by BPP authors.
>
> **FOR DECEMBER 2005 AND JUNE 2006 EXAMS**

First edition 2003
Third edition June 2005

ISBN 0 7517 2300 2 (Previous edition 0 7517 1647 2)

British Library Cataloguing-in-Publication Data
A catalogue record for this book
is available from the British Library

Published by

BPP Professional Education
Aldine House, Aldine Place
London W12 8AW

www.bpp.com

Printed in Great Britain by WM Print
Frederick Street
Walsall
West Midlands
WS2 9NE

All our rights reserved. No part of this publication may be reproduced, stored in a retrieval system or transmitted, in any form or by any means, electronic, mechanical, photocopying, recording or otherwise, without the prior written permission of BPP Professional Education.

We are grateful to the Association of Chartered Certified Accountants for permission to reproduce the syllabus, teaching guide, past examination questions and Pilot Paper questions of which the Association holds the copyright. The answers have been prepared by BPP Professional Education.

©

BPP Professional Education
2005

Contents

Page

INTRODUCTION
How to use this Interactive Text – Syllabus – Study Session – Approach to examining the syllabus – Computer based examinations (v)

PART A: INTRODUCTION TO TRANSACTION ACCOUNTING

1	Business transactions and documentation	3
2	Assets, liabilities and the accounting equation	33
3	Balance sheet and profit and loss account	47
4	Recording, summarising and posting transactions	58
5	Completing ledger accounts	91

PART B: RECORDING AND ACCOUNTING FOR CASH TRANSACTIONS

6	Receiving and checking money	123
7	Banking monies received	142
8	Recording monies received	164
9	Authorising and making payments	177
10	Recording payments	205
11	Maintaining petty cash records	223
12	Bank reconciliations	258

PART C: RECORDING AND ACCOUNTING FOR CREDIT TRANSACTIONS

13	Sales and sales returns day books	273
14	The sales ledger	293
15	Purchase and purchase returns day books	318
16	The purchase ledger	342
17	Control accounts	357

PART D: PAYROLL

18	Recording payroll transactions	367

QUESTION BANK 405

ANSWER BANK 415

LIST OF KEY TERMS 437

INDEX 439

ORDER FORM

REVIEW FORM & FREE PRIZE DRAW

HOW TO USE THIS INTERACTIVE TEXT

Aim of this Interactive Text

> To provide the knowledge and practice to help you succeed in the examination for Paper 1 *Recording Financial Transactions*

To pass the examination you need a thorough understanding in all areas covered by the syllabus and teaching guide.

Recommended approach

(a) To pass you need to be able to answer questions on **everything** specified by the syllabus and teaching guide. Read the text very carefully and do not skip any of it.

(b) Learning is an **active** process. Do **all** the activities as you work through the text so you can be sure you really understand what you have read.

(c) After you have covered the material in the Interactive Text, work through the **Question Bank**, checking your answers carefully against the **Answer Bank**.

(d) Before you take the exam, check that you still remember the material using the following quick revision plan.

   (i) Read through the **chapter topic list** at the beginning of each chapter. Are there any gaps in your knowledge? If so, study the section again.

   (ii) Read and learn the **key terms**.

   (iii) Look at the **exam alerts**. These show the ways in which topics might be examined.

   (iv) Read and learn the **key learning points**, which are a summary of each chapter.

   (v) Do the **quick quizzes** again. If you know what you're doing, they shouldn't take long.

This approach is only a suggestion. You or your college may well adapt it to suit your needs.

Remember this is a **practical** course.

(a) Try to relate the material to your experience in the workplace or any other work experience you may have had.

(b) Try to make as many links as you can to other papers at the Introductory and Intermediate level.

Syllabus

SYLLABUS

Introduction

This booklet contains the Study Guide for ACCA's Certified Accounting Technician Paper 1 (GBR): Recording Financial Transactions.

The Study Guide is designed to help you plan your studies and to provide more detailed interpretation of the syllabus for ACCA's Certified Accounting Technician examinations. It contains both the Syllabus and the Study Sessions for the paper, which you can follow when preparing for the examination.

The Syllabus outlines the content of the paper and how that content is examined. The Study Sessions take the syllabus and expand it into teaching or study sessions of similar length. These sessions indicate what the examiner expects of candidates for each part of the syllabus, and therefore gives you guidance in the skills you are expected to demonstrate in the examinations. The time to complete each session will vary according to your individual capabilities and the time you have available to study. Tuition providers offering face-to-face tuition are recommended to design courses with a minimum of two hours tuition per study session. However, repeated coverage of the material is vital to ensure your understanding and recall of the subject. Be sure to practice past examination questions to consolidate your knowledge and read your *student accountant* magazine regularly.

If you have any queries concerning the study guide, please direct them to:

Education Department
ACCA 29 Lincoln's Inn Fields London WC2A 3EE United Kingdom
tel: +44 (0)20 7396 5891/2 fax: +44 (0)20 7396 5968
e-mail: info@accaglobal.com

Additional information can be accessed on the ACCA website at:
www.accaglobal.com

© The Association of Chartered Certified Accountants
May 2004

ABOUT ACCA
ACCA is the largest and fastest-growing international accounting body, with over 320,000 students and members in 160 countries. ACCA has an extensive network of 70 staffed offices and other centres around the world.

Recording Financial Transactions (GBR)

AIMS
To develop knowledge and understanding of the operational aspects of maintaining accounting records and procedures relating to invoicing, receipts and payments, recording income and expenditure, the preparation of ledger accounts and the preparation of an initial trial balance.

OBJECTIVES
On completion of this paper, candidates should be able to:
- distinguish between types of business transactions and documentation, recognising relevant basic business law and data protection legislation
- prepare basic ledger accounts under the double entry system
- record income and receipts from credit customers
- explain and account for bad debts
- record purchases, expenditure, and payments to suppliers
- account for banking transactions
- maintain general cash and petty cash records
- produce bank reconciliation statements
- record payroll transactions
- prepare and reconcile control accounts
- prepare an initial trial balance identifying and correcting errors using journal entries.

POSITION OF THE PAPER IN THE OVERALL SYLLABUS
No prior knowledge is required before commencing study for Paper 1. This paper provides the basic techniques required to enable candidates to prepare financial statements for various enterprises at a later stage. Candidates will, therefore, need a sound knowledge of the methods and techniques introduced in this paper to ensure they can employ them in later papers. The methods used in this paper are extended in Paper 3, *Maintaining Financial Records* and further developed in Paper 6, *Drafting Financial Statements*.

SYLLABUS CONTENT

1 **Business transactions and documentation**
   (a) Types of business transactions
       (i) sales
       (ii) purchases
       (iii) receipts
       (iv) payments
       (v) petty cash
       (vi) payroll
   (b) Types of business documentation
       (i) quotation
       (ii) sales and purchase orders
       (iii) delivery note
       (iv) invoice
       (v) credit note
       (vi) debit note
       (vii) statement
       (viii) remittance advice
       (ix) receipt
       (x) internal cheque requisition
       (xi) petty cash claim
       (xii) payslip
   (c) Basic law and business policies
       (i) contract law
       (ii) Sale of Goods Act
       (iii) document retention policies
       (iv) data protection law

2 **Double entry bookkeeping**
   (a) Double entry transactions
       (i) nature and function of primary records
       (ii) types of ledger accounts
       (iii) posting by means of double entry
       (iv) balancing-off ledger accounts
   (b) Classification of expenditure
       (i) capital
       (ii) revenue
   (c) The accounting equation

3 **Banking and petty cash**
   (a) Sources of funds and documentation
       (i) types of receipts / payments: cash, cheque, standing orders and direct debits, credit card, debit card and BACS
       (ii) supporting information: invoice, credit note, remittance advice and statement
       (iii) unusual features: wrongly completed cheques, out-of-date cheques, credit and debit card limits exceeded and disagreement with / insufficient supporting documentation

Syllabus

Recording Financial Transactions (GBR)

- (b) Banking monies received
    - (i) banking documentation: paying-in slips, credit and debit card documentation
    - (ii) methods of handling and storing money, including security aspects
- (c) Recording payments and monies received
    - (i) manual cash book
    - (ii) manual general ledger and sales ledger
    - (iii) computerised records
- (d) Authorising and making payments
    - (i) documentation: cheque requisitions
    - (ii) authorisation
- (e) Maintaining petty cash records
    - (i) documentation: petty cash claims
    - (ii) authorisation
    - (iii) security of cash
    - (iv) queries: unauthorised claims for payment, insufficient supporting evidence, claims exceeding authorised limit
    - (v) manual petty cash book
    - (vi) imprest and non-imprest methods
    - (vii) reconciliation of petty cash book to cash in hand

4 Sales and sales records
- (a) Sales and sales returns
    - (i) source documents
    - (ii) invoices and credit notes
    - (iii) general principles of VAT
    - (iv) types of discount
    - (v) methods of coding data
    - (vi) sales day book
    - (vii) sales returns day book
    - (viii) authorisation
- (b) Recording sales
    - (i) manual general ledger
    - (ii) manual sales ledger
    - (iii) computerised ledgers
    - (iv) statements
    - (v) aged debtors analysis
    - (vi) communication with customers (orally and in writing)
    - (vii) credit limits
    - (viii) bad debts

5 Purchases and purchase records
- (a) Purchases and purchase returns
    - (i) ordering systems: Internet, verbal, written
    - (ii) source documents
    - (iii) suppliers' invoices and credit notes
    - (iv) types of discount
    - (v) methods of coding data
    - (vi) purchase day book
    - (vii) purchase returns day book
- (b) Recording purchases
    - (i) manual general ledger
    - (ii) manual purchase ledger
    - (iii) computerised ledgers
    - (iv) statements
    - (v) aged creditor analysis
    - (vi) communication with suppliers: (orally and in writing), incorrect calculations, non-delivery of goods charged, duplication of invoices and incorrect discounts

6 Payroll
- (a) Recording payroll transactions
    - (i) documentation: payslips
    - (ii) authorisation
    - (iii) payment methods: cash, cheques, automated payments
    - (iv) queries
    - (v) security and control
    - (vi) cash book
    - (vii) general ledger

7 Control accounts and the initial trial balance
- (a) Bank reconciliations
    - (i) general bank services and operation of bank clearing system
    - (ii) function and form of banking documentation
    - (iii) bank reconciliation statement
- (b) Control accounts
    - (i) different types of errors
    - (ii) correction of errors (including journals)
    - (iii) reconciliation of control account with ledger: sales ledger, purchase ledger

Recording Financial Transactions (GBR)

(c) The trial balance
- (i) initial trial balance
- (ii) identification of errors
- (iii) suspense accounts

EXCLUDED TOPICS

The following topics are specifically excluded from Paper 1:
- detailed knowledge of VAT
- specific and general provisions for doubtful debts
- foreign currency transactions
- use of PAYE tax and NIC tables.

KEY AREAS OF THE SYLLABUS

The key topic areas are as follows:
- sales
- purchases
- receipts
- payments
- petty cash
- bank reconciliations
- control accounts
- the trial balance.

APPROACH TO EXAMINING THE SYLLABUS

The examination is a two-hour paper. It can be taken as a written paper or as a computer based exam. Assessment will be based on multiple choice questions covering the breadth of the syllabus, testing that candidates have acquired the necessary knowledge of the areas identified above.

	No. of marks
50 multiple choice questions:	100

RELEVANT TEXTS

There are a number of sources from which you can obtain a series of materials written for the ACCA CAT examinations. These are listed below:

BPP – ACCA's official CAT publisher
Contact number: +44 (0)20 8740 2211
Website: www.bpp.com

FTC Foulks Lynch
Contact number: +44 (0)118 989 0629
Website: www.financial-training.com/new/foulkslynch

Candidates may also find the following texts useful:

Wood, Frank and Robinson, Sheila. *Bookkeeping and Accounts* (Pitman Publishing: 4th edition) – Sections 1, 2 and 3
ISBN: 0273646192

Cox, David and Fardon, Michael. *Cash and Credit Accounting – NVQ Level 2 Accounting* (Osborne Books) – This is a tutorial and workbook. ISBN: 1872962033

Whitehead, Geoffrey. *Bookkeeping* (Made Simple Books, Butterworth & Heinemann) – Chapters 1-10

Wider reading is also desirable, especially regular study of relevant articles in ACCA's *student accountant* magazine.

Recording Financial Transactions (GBR)

STUDY SESSIONS

1. **Types of business transactions and types of business documentation**
   (a) Identify the main types of transactions that a business is likely to undertake e.g. sales, purchases, payments, receipts, cash and bank, and payroll
   (b) Define a simple contract in accordance with contract law
   (c) Identify the main provisions of a Sale of Goods Act or equivalent (fitness for purpose, merchantable quality, description)
   (d) Understand the importance of coding transactions correctly
   (e) Distinguish between cash and credit transactions
   (f) Identify the key personnel involved in initiating, processing and completing transactions
   (g) Understand the need for effective control over transactions
   (h) Identify the timing of various transactions e.g. daily, monthly, annually
   (i) Understand the need to document business transactions
   (j) Explain the purpose and scope of data protection law, storage and archiving policies
   (k) Distinguish between different types of business documentation e.g. quotation, sales and purchase order, delivery note, invoice, statement, credit note, debit note, remittance advice, receipt, internal payment, petty cash claim and payslip
   (l) Identify the main provisions of a Sale of Goods Act or equivalent
   (m) Outline the contents and purpose of each piece of documentation
   (n) Describe the documentation and the flow of documentation for different transactions including Internet transactions
   (o) Identify the personnel involved in preparing and authorising documents
   (p) Outline the main features of systematic recording and filing of documents and data in manual and computerised systems

2. **The duality of transactions and the double entry system**
   (a) Understand the nature and function of books of prime entry
   (b) Recognise the duality of transactions and understand and apply the accounting equation
   (c) Explain the fundamental rules of double entry accounting and debits and credits
   (d) Identify the main types of ledger account
   (e) Identify and classify assets, liabilities, income and expenditure
   (f) Distinguish between capital and revenue expenditure and identify examples of each

3. **Recording business transactions in the double entry bookkeeping system**
   (a) Record a complete series of basic transactions within a double entry system
   (b) Prepare journal entries and identify the uses of the journal
   (c) Balance off ledger accounts, recording closing balances
   (d) Understand the basic functions of a computerised accounting system

4. **Banking systems and transactions**
   N.B for the purpose of answering questions, please note that a detailed understanding of UK banking legislation will not be required
   (a) Describe the relationship between a bank and its customer
   (b) Outline the working of a central bank clearing system
   (c) Recognise the obligation owed by a bank to its clients
   (d) Understand the content and format of a cheque
   (e) Prepare a cheque prior to despatch
   (f) Outline the purpose and format of paying-in documents
   (g) Describe the procedures and documentation relating to the use of credit and debit cards
   (h) Describe other services offered by banks – inter-bank transfers, payable orders, automated credit systems, standing orders, direct debits, credit transfers
   N.B foreign currency transactions are not examinable

Recording Financial Transactions (GBR)

5 **Cash handling, petty cash operations and cash security**
   (a) Describe the general procedures for dealing with cash, cheques, credit and debit card receipts and payments
   (b) Identify the documentation accompanying payments and receipts
   (c) Recognise the importance of accurately recording all payments and receipts
   (d) Identify the main ways to ensure that only authorised payments are made
   (e) Record payments and receipts in the cash book, general ledger, purchase and sales ledger (manual or computerised)
   (f) Understand procedures for banking cash receipts
   (g) Recognise the types of transaction likely to be paid out of petty cash
   (h) Account for petty cash using imprest and non-imprest methods
   (i) Exercise control over petty cash and recognise how control can be maintained – security of cash, authorised personnel and reconciliations
   (j) Record petty cash claims
   (k) Describe the key procedures for ensuring safety, security and, where appropriate, confidentiality over the handling of cash and cheques
   (l) Explain the correct procedure to cope with unusual situations: wrongly completed or out of date cheques, exceeded credit limits on debit or credit cards, or discrepancies between receipts and supporting documents, unauthorised claims for payment, insufficient supporting evidence, or claims exceeding authorised limits

6 **Sales and sales records**
   (a) Identify and recognise source sales documents
   (b) Complete sales invoices and process credit notes / debit notes
   (c) Understand the general principles of VAT
   (d) Calculate VAT on transactions
   (e) Calculate and record trade and settlement discounts
   (f) Record transactions in a sales day book and a sales returns day book
   (g) Code sales and customer records and data
   (h) Recognise and describe authorisation procedures
   (i) Record sales
      (i) maintain a manual general and sales ledger
      (ii) describe a computerised sales ledger
      (iii) prepare, reconcile and understand the purpose of customer statements
   (j) Communicate efficiently and effectively with customers

7 **Credit control and bad debts**
   (a) Explain the benefits and costs of offering credit facilities to customers
   (b) Understand the purpose of and prepare an aged debt analysis
   (c) Understand the purpose of credit limits
   (d) Recognise the existence and impact of bad debts
   (e) Record the accounting treatment of bad debts

8 **Purchases and purchase records**
   (a) Identify and recognise source purchase and expenditure documents
   (b) Complete purchase invoices and process credit notes
   (c) Calculate and record trade and settlement discounts
   (d) Record transactions in a purchase day book and a purchase returns day book
   (e) Code purchases and supplier records and data
   (f) Record purchases
      (i) maintain a manual general and purchase ledger
      (ii) describe a computerised purchase ledger
      (iii) understand the purpose of and prepare an aged creditors analysis
      (iv) prepare, reconcile and understand the purpose of supplier statements
   (g) Communicate efficiently and effectively with suppliers

9 **Bank reconciliation statements**
   (a) Recognise the need to reconcile the cash book with the bank statement periodically
   (b) Identify the main reasons for any discrepancies between the cash book and the bank statement, such as errors, unanticipated receipts and payments and timing

Recording Financial Transactions (GBR)

    differences
- (c) Correct cash book errors and/or omissions
- (d) Reconcile the corrected cash book balance with the bank statement through adjustments for uncleared and uncredited cheques

10 **Payroll**
- (a) Understand payroll systems
- (b) Understand the duties of employers in relation to taxes, state benefit contributions and other deductions
- (c) Record hours worked; time sheets, clock cards
- (d) Calculate gross wages for employees paid by hour, by output (piecework) and salaried workers
- (e) Define and calculate bonuses, overtime, and commission given the details of each scheme
- (f) Describe the documentation required for recording various elements of wages and salaries
- (g) Recognise the need for payroll to be authorised and identify appropriate authorisation, security and control procedures
- (h) Make other deductions from wages - trade union subscriptions, payroll saving, pension contributions and payroll giving
- (i) Identify various methods for making payments to employees
- (j) Account for payroll costs and payroll deductions

11 **Principles of internal checks and control accounts**
- (a) Understand the need for internal checks
- (b) Complete postings to control accounts and understand the link to books of prime entry
- (c) Understand the need for individual debtors and creditors accounts and understand the link to books of prime entry
- (d) Explain the purpose of control accounts
    - (i) as a check on the accuracy of entries in the individual accounts
    - (ii) to establish a total of debtors and creditors at any time
    - (iii) to identify errors in the completion of the day book and in posting the totals from book of prime entry
    - (iv) as an internal check; the control account should be administered by someone other than the person who completes the day books
- (e) Perform a basic control account reconciliation
- (f) Identify errors which would be highlighted by performing a control account reconciliation

12 **Preparing an initial trial balance and recognising and correcting errors**
- (a) Compile an initial trial balance
- (b) Identify errors which would be highlighted by the extraction of a trial balance
- (c) Identify and explain different types of errors:
    - (i) errors of commission
    - (ii) errors of principle
    - (iii) errors of omission
    - (iv) single entry
    - (v) transposition errors
    - (vi) casting errors
- (d) Distinguish between compensating and non-compensating errors
- (e) Prepare, and explain the function of a suspense account
- (f) Correct errors using journal entries

APPROACH TO EXAMINING THE SYLLABUS

The examination is structured as follows:

	No of marks
50 multiple choice questions	100

Time allowed: 2 hours

The examination can be taken as a written paper or as a computer based examination (see page (xiv) for frequently-asked questions about computer-based examinations).

Analysis of Pilot Paper

Pilot paper

Fifty multiple choice questions covering various topics	100

COMPUTER BASED EXAMINATIONS

The Introductory level (formerly Level A) has been assessed by CBE since the introduction of the CAT qualification in 1998.

Frequently asked questions about CBEs

Q   What are the main advantages of CBEs?

A   • Examinations can be offered on a continuing basis rather than at six-monthly intervals
    • Instant feedback is provided for candidates when their results for each individual paper are displayed on the screen.

Q   Where can I take CBEs?

A   CBEs must be taken at an ACCA Approved Computer Examination Centre (See ACCA's website in the Tuition Providers' Database)

Q   How does CBE work?

A   • Questions are displayed on a monitor
    • Candidates enter their answer directly onto the computer
    • When the candidate has completed their examination, the computer automatically marks the file containing the candidate's answers
    • Candidates are provided with a certificate showing their results before leaving the examination room
    • The Approved Assessment Centre returns the test disk to the ACCA (as proof of the candidate's performance)

Q   How can I practise for CBEs?

A   BPP's i-Pass CDs will offer you plenty of opportunity for question practice in a format similar to the exam, with instant feedback.

Part A
Introduction to transaction accounting

Chapter 1 Business transactions and documentation

Chapter topic list

1 Types of business transaction
2 Documenting business transactions
3 Invoices and credit notes
4 Discounts, rebates and allowances
5 VAT (Value Added Tax)
6 Contract law
7 The Sale of Goods Act
8 Storage of information
9 Data protection

The following study sessions are covered in this chapter

			Syllabus reference
1	(a)	Identify the main types of transactions that a business is likely to undertake eg, sales, purchases, payments, receipts, cash and bank and payroll	1a
	(b)	Define a simple contract in accordance with contract law	1c
	(c)	Identify the main provisions of a Sale of Goods Act or equivalent (fitness for purpose, merchantable quality, description)	1c
	(e)	Distinguish between cash and credit transactions	1a
	(i)	Understand the need to document business transactions	1b
	(j)	Explain the purpose and scope of data protection law, storage and archiving policies	1c
	(k)	Distinguish between different types of business documentation	1b
	(l)	Identify the main provisions of a Sale of Goods Act or equivalent	1c
	(m)	Outline the contents and purpose of each piece of documentation	1b
	(n)	Describe the documentation and the flow of documentation for different transactions including Internet transactions	1b
6	(a)	Identify and recognise source sales documents	4a
	(b)	Complete sales invoices and process credit notes/debit notes	4a
	(e)	Calculate and record trade and settlement discounts	4a
8	(a)	Identify and recognise source purchase and expenditure documents	5a
	(b)	Complete purchase invoices an process credit notes	5a
	(c)	Calculate and record trade and settlement discounts	5a

Part A: Introduction to transaction accounting

1 TYPES OF BUSINESS TRANSACTION

Businesses

1.1 In your studies for the ACCA Accounting Technician qualification, and specifically for this paper on transaction accounting, you will be concerned with **business** transactions. There is no one definition of a business, although we all know more or less what it is. Broadly speaking it is a **commercial** organisation, large or small, which exists to make money or profits for its owners. It may make this money by manufacturing and/or selling goods or services.

Business transactions

1.2 Wherever property changes hands there has been a **business transaction**. The main types of business transactions are **sales** and **purchases**.

1.3 Sales and purchases occur in two different ways, by cash or on credit.

(a) A **sale** takes place at one of two points in time.

(i) **Cash sales**. If the sale is for cash, the sale occurs when goods or services are given in exchange for immediate payment, in notes and coins, or by cheque or plastic card.

(ii) **Credit sales** (goods are ordered and delivered before payment is received). If it is on credit, the sale occurs when the business sends out an invoice for the goods or services supplied; cash is received later.

(b) A **purchase** also takes place at one of two points in time.

(i) **Purchases for cash**. If the goods are paid for in cash then the purchase occurs when the goods and cash exchange hands.

(ii) **Purchases on credit**. If the goods are bought on credit, the purchase normally occurs when the business receives the goods, accompanied by an invoice from the supplier. Cash is paid later.

> **KEY TERMS**
>
> A **cash transaction** is one where the buyer pays cash to the seller at the time the goods or services are transferred.
>
> A **credit transaction** is a sale or a purchase which occurs some time **earlier** than cash is received or paid.

1.4 With credit transactions, the **point in time when a sale or purchase is recognised in the accounts of the business** is *not* the same as **the point in time when cash is eventually received or paid** for the sale or purchase. There is a **gap** in time between the sale or purchase and the eventual cash settlement. (It is possible that something might happen during that time which results in the amount of cash eventually paid (if any) being different from the original value of the sale or purchase on the invoice.)

1.5 There are other types of business transaction which need to be recorded.

- **Payment of wages**
- **Borrowing money**
- Offering a **discount**

1: Business transactions and documentation

1.6 The simplest form of business transaction is a **cash transaction**.

2 DOCUMENTING BUSINESS TRANSACTIONS

External documentation

2.1 It is usual to record a business transaction on a **document**. The amount of documentation required will vary depending on the type of transaction and the people involved.

   (a) If you buy a **small item** from a market stall and pay cash, it is unlikely that any documents would change hands unless you ask for a receipt.

   (b) By contrast, if you have a **central heating system** installed, the paperwork involved can include the following. (This is summarised in the diagram on page 6.)

   (i) First of all you get in touch with the central heating company either by phone, or by **letter of enquiry**.

   (ii) The central heating company will probably send round a sales engineer, at an agreed time, to visit you. The sales engineer will take a look at your residence and estimate how much work needs to be done.

   You will eventually receive a **quotation** detailing the price.

   (iii) Merely asking for a quotation does not commit you to anything. Should you wish to proceed with the quotation, the next thing you might do is **send a letter accepting the quotation**. You may, on the other hand, be required to sign a more formal **sales order document**, which you will return to the company.

   You should receive an **acknowledgement**.

   (iv) The **sales order** you have signed will be used by the central heating company as evidence of what you require. It gives them the 'go-ahead' to prepare and carry out the work.

   (v) A great deal of **internal documentation** will then be prepared. A record must be kept of the process of the installation and its costs. Also, the company might keep other documents. We will look at internal documentation in Paragraph 2.4 below.

   (vi) Your central heating system has now been installed. The central heating staff will ask you to sign a **delivery note**.

   (vii) The delivery note will be evidence to the company that the job has been completed. This is then taken to the accounts department for review. Eventually you will be sent a **bill or invoice**.

   If you are charged too much, you will in due course receive a **credit note**.

   (viii) At the end of the agreed period of credit that the company has allowed you, you will pay the invoice by **cheque**.

   (ix) The company, on receipt of your cheque, will ensure that it is banked, and recorded in the internal **books of account**.

Part A: Introduction to transaction accounting

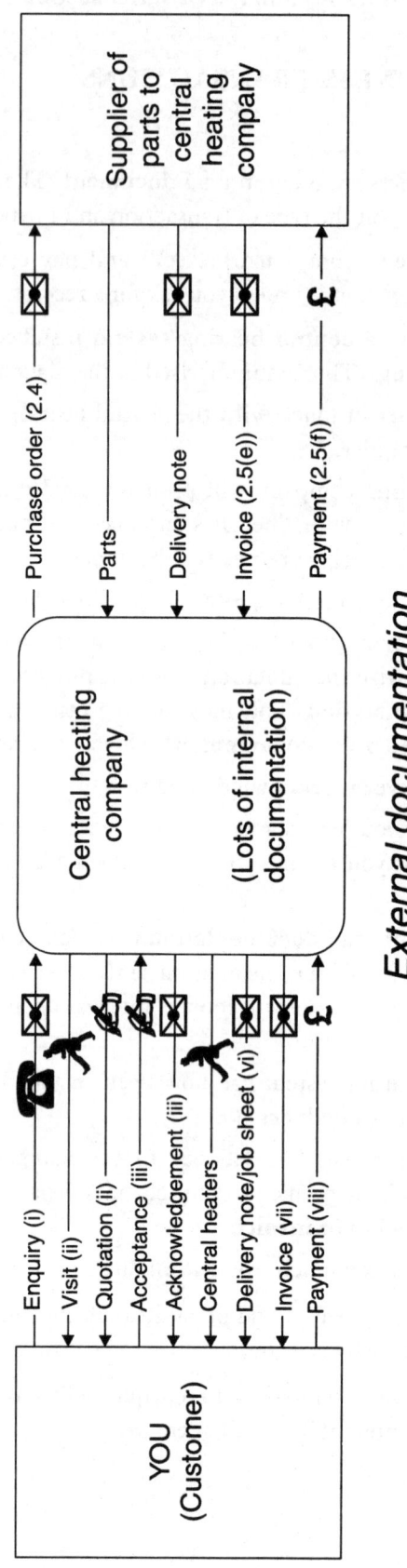

2.2 The above diagram gives a picture of the **external documentation** involved. We will not examine what happens inside the central heating company yet, but just look at the system as a whole.

2.3 In this one business transaction, then, there has already been a large amount of **paperwork**. It is quite possible that some of this paperwork will not be paperwork at all. It might be automated, and the majority of the transactions will be carried out by **computer**. No matter, **the principles are the same**.

Activity 1.1

(a) A friend of yours who has no knowledge of accounting matters has asked you to explain the difference between a cash transaction and a credit transaction. What would you say to him?

(b) State what documentation you would expect to change hands in the following circumstances.

    (i) You buy a CD from a shop, paying cash
    (ii) You have double glazing installed

Internal documentation

2.4 Internal documents needed would include **purchase orders**, if some parts had to be purchased from other suppliers. A similar set of documents to the ones described above, but this time between the central heating company and its suppliers, would then be necessary.

2.5 In addition there will be several other internal documents.

(a) **Stock lists,** to check that all the parts for the central heating system are available. Each part will be identified by its own specific code number.

(b) **Supplier lists,** to trace from the code numbers of the parts which supplier manufactures which item of stock.

(c) **Staff schedules**. The central heating company's engineers will travel from job to job, and it is thus probable that the right mix of qualified staff must be booked. They will record the actual hours they spend on a **timesheet**.

(d) **Goods received notes.** When the parts ordered have been received, a goods received note might be raised by the goods inwards section to notify other sections that the parts have been received.

(e) **Invoices.** The company will receive an invoice from its supplier which will be used to update the company's accounting records. A **credit note** may be required.

(f) **Cheques.** The company will eventually pay the supplier by cheque.

(g) **Expense claims.** Employees may incur expenses which need to be reimbursed.

2.6 Are more documents involved? Plenty! This is for several reasons.

(a) Yours will not have been the only central heating system installed. The organisation will have hundreds of transactions to schedule, to keep track of, to account for and to keep on a list of **who owes it money**.

(b) The central heating company might also need a list of people **to whom it owes money** (the suppliers of parts for example).

(c) The central heating company needs to ensure that it has enough **cash at the right times** to pay its bills, and to pay its employees.

(d) Comparing what it earns with what it costs is important, as the company hopes to make a **profit**.

Part A: Introduction to transaction accounting

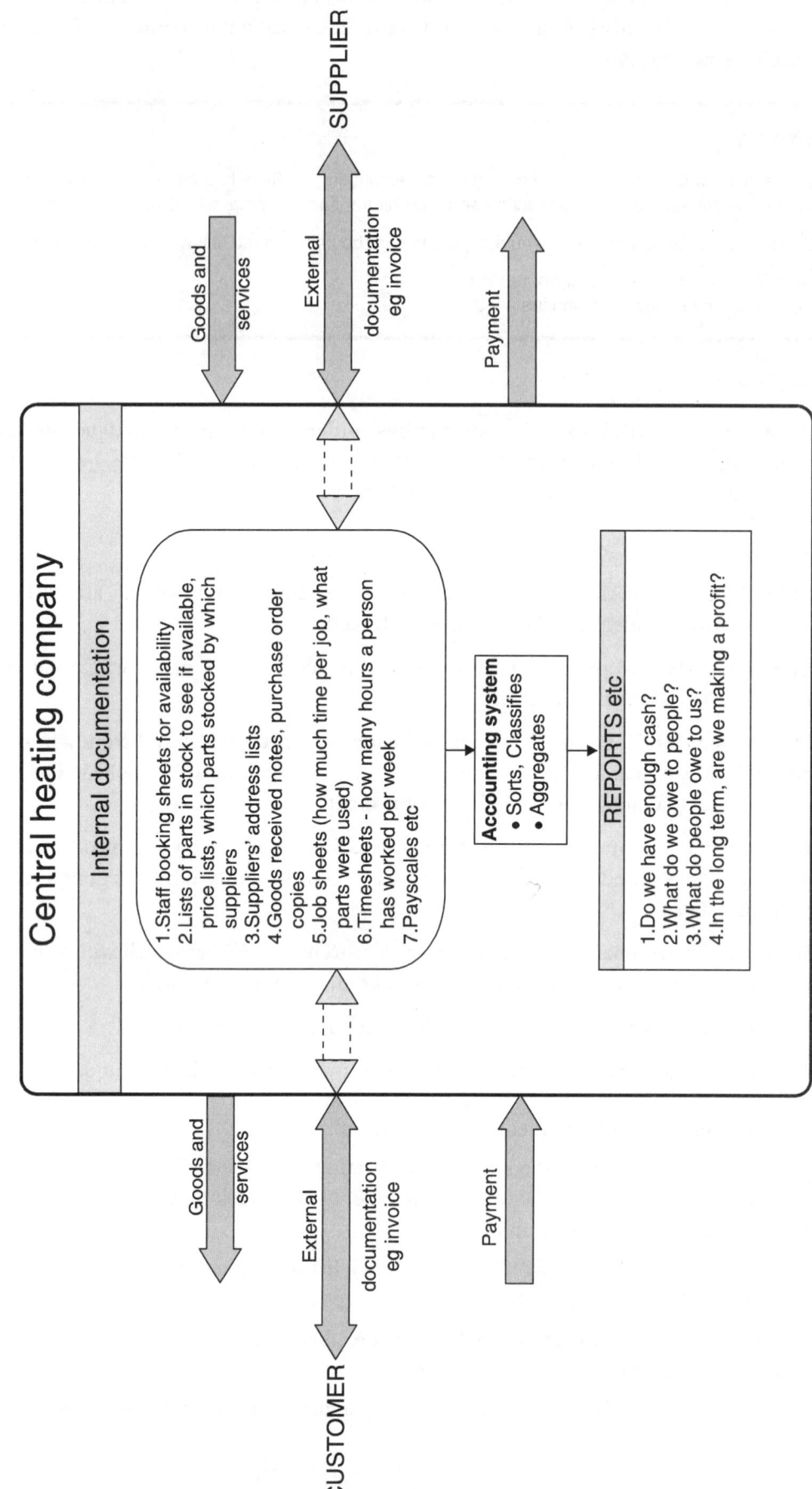

1: Business transactions and documentation

2.7 The diagram on the previous page summarises the internal documentation required by the central heating company. What does the accounting system actually do?

> **KEY TERM**
>
> The purpose of the **accounting system** is to **record**, **summarise** and **present** the information contained in the documentation generated by transactions.

2.8 In the case of the central heating company, this would entail the following.

(a) The workers who installed the central heating system will expect to be paid. If they are paid an hourly rate, then the total number of hours they work in a period must be aggregated.

> This is the job of the **payroll system**, and is covered in Part D of this Interactive Text.

(b) At defined periods the accounting system produces the following lists.
- Those who owe the firm money (debtors)
- Those to whom the company owes money (creditors)

> This is the job of the **sales ledger** and **purchase** (or **bought**) **ledger** systems, and is covered in Part C of this Interactive Text.

(c) The accounting system will keep track of the business's resources of **cash**, and the funds in the bank account.

> This is covered in Part B of this Interactive Text.

(d) Finally, the accounting system will be used to provide periodic information to management (covered in the later stages of your studies).

2.9 In this chapter we will concentrate on two very important types of document, **invoices** and **credit notes**, as examples of the sort of accounting information contained in business documentation.

3 INVOICES AND CREDIT NOTES

3.1 As an example of the importance of documents in organisations, let us examine the use of the **invoice**. Documents, as we have seen, are created when contact is made between customer and supplier.

(a) **Sales order:** a customer writes out an order or signs an order for goods or services he wishes to buy.

(b) **Purchase order:** a business places an order with another business for the purchase of goods or services, such as material supplies.

The invoice

3.2 **Invoices** are created when there is a sale or a purchase. Remember that what is a **sale** to one business is a **purchase** to the individual or business in receipt of the goods. The details on the invoice should agree with what was on the purchase/sales order.

Part A: Introduction to transaction accounting

> **KEY TERM**
>
> An **invoice** is a demand for payment

3.3 Three different uses of the invoice can be described.

Transaction	Example	Document best described as
A transaction is **settled immediately in cash**, with the invoice created as evidence of expense/receipt of payment	Manager paying cash for a business meal in a restaurant	Receipt: invoice marked by restaurant as 'paid with thanks'
An invoice is sent from seller to buyer, and is **paid on receipt of the goods** using cheque or cash	Delivery of new car to company	Cash on delivery (COD) invoice
An invoice is sent after goods have been delivered, with request to **pay within a certain time**	Delivery of raw materials from long-standing supplier on usual credit terms	Credit invoice

3.4 Although you may find it helpful to think of the receipt, the COD invoice and the credit invoice, you will find that usually people refer only to **receipts** (for cash transactions, such as buying a newspaper) and **invoices** (for credit transactions). Remember, however, that not all documents described as invoices are invoices on **credit terms** - they may need to be settled immediately.

What does an invoice show?

3.5 The invoice below is a fairly typical example of a demand for payment from a seller (Chippies Ltd) to a purchaser (Table Tops Ltd).

(a) Name and address of the seller
(b) Name and address of the purchaser
(c) Invoice number (so that the business can keep track of all the invoices it sends out)
(d) Date of the transaction
(e) Description of what is being sold
(f) Quantity and unit price of what has been sold (30 tables at £250 a table)
(g) Total amount of the invoice including (in the UK) any details of VAT
(h) The tax point for VAT purposes (see Section 5 of this chapter)

1: Business transactions and documentation

```
                    CHIPPIES LTD  (a)
                       Wood House
                      Richmans Road
                     LONDON SE1N 5AB
```

Invoice Number: 123456 (c)
Date: 01/08/X7 (d)
Tax Point: 01/08/X7 (h)
Account Number: 3365

INVOICE

DELIVER TO	INVOICE TO:	
Table Tops Ltd	Same address	Telephone Number 0171 123 4567
112 Peters Square		VAT Registration Number 457 4635 19
Weyford		Northern Bank plc Code 20-25-42
Kent CR2 2TA (b)		Account Number 957023

Item Code	Description	Quantity	Unit Price £	Net Amount £
Your order number: 2490				
13579A	Tables (e)	30 (f)	250.00	7,500.00
	Delivery	1	100.00	100.00
			SALES VALUE:	7,600.00
			VAT AT 17.5%:	1,330.00
			AMOUNT PAYABLE:	8,930.00 (g)

3.6 Points to note about the invoice shown above include the following.

(a) **Delivery address.** Businesses sometimes want goods delivered to somewhere other than their own premises.

(b) **Referencing.** A business usually keeps a record of its orders, just as it does of its sales. In this case, Table Tops Ltd's order number was 2490. Chippies Ltd puts the order number on the invoice so that Table Tops Ltd can quickly see which order the invoice relates to.

(c) **Unit price.** In our example, tables were £250.00 each, but sometimes goods are sold in batches of, say, 20. If that is the case, then something like '£6 for 20' will be put in the unit price column. The amount of the invoice is calculated in the usual way.

Other information often found on invoices

3.7 Sometimes, the **date by which payment is due**, and other terms of sale, are shown on the invoice. 'Net 30 days' means that payment is due 30 days after the date of delivery.

3.8 'FOB' stands for '**free on board**', and may be found on import or export invoices. 'FOB shipping point' means that the supplier pays all costs of carriage (shipping, insurance and freight for example) up to the point of shipping but the customer will have to pay any subsequent carriage costs.

11

Part A: Introduction to transaction accounting

3.9 Two other phrases you may find on an invoice are as follows.

(a) **Ex works**. This means that the price excludes the cost of delivery.

(b) **E & O E**. This stands for 'errors and omissions excepted', meaning that the supplier reserves the right to make alterations to the details as shown on the invoice should any prove at a later date to be incorrect.

Invoice copies

3.10 Invoice forms for different businesses will be designed in different ways, although they all show the same sort of information. Another thing they have in common is that there are usually **several copies of the invoice**.

3.11 Businesses may use as many as four **copies of an invoice**, often as follows.

Copy	Location	Purpose of invoice copy
1	Sent to the **purchaser**	Request to pay for the goods, as we have seen.
2	Kept as a **file copy**	Partly to keep records straight, and partly so that the business can prove it made out the invoice in the first place. (In a large business, both the sales and accounts departments may keep copy sales invoices.)
3	**Delivery note** sent to customer for signature, and then retained by seller	Whoever delivers the goods to the purchaser asks the purchaser to sign the note as proof that the goods have actually been delivered. The delivery note is then brought back to the supplier's business and matched with the file copy as proof of the validity of the sale.
4	**Advice note** signed and kept by purchaser	Rather like the delivery note, this goes with the goods but instead of being brought back to the supplier, it is left with the purchaser. (The purchaser's storekeeper uses it as a checklist to make sure that the goods being delivered are the same as those on the invoice.)

Note that either copy 3 or copy 4 may be used by the selling business as a 'picking list' for an order, so it can be sure it packs up the required quantities.

Sales order sets

3.12 Another common approach is to use multi-part **sales order sets** so the seller can keep track of the order.

Copy	Location	Purpose of sales order copy
1	Sent to customer	Confirming order
2	Sent to warehouse	Arranging delivery to customer
3	Kept in sales dept	Dealing with customer queries
4	Passed to 'accounts'	Raising an invoice
5	Sent with goods	Acting as advice note for customer to keep
6	Sent with goods	Acting as delivery note - signed by customer and retained by seller
7	Kept in warehouse	Dealing with customer queries

1: Business transactions and documentation

3.13 Multi-part **purchase order sets** follow the same pattern so the purchaser can keep track of his order.

Copy	Location	Purpose of purchase order copy
1	Sent to supplier	To place, or confirm an earlier telephone, order
2	Kept in purchasing department *or* warehouse	For reference, and to compare with supplier's advice and delivery notes
3	Accounts department	To match against invoice and goods received note when delivered

Activity 1.2

(a) A multi-part sales order set completed on receipt of a customer order may have as many as seven copies. State the possible destination and purpose of each copy.

(b) A multi-part purchase order set generally consists of only three copies. State the usual purpose and destination of each copy.

The credit note

KEY TERM

A **credit note** is used by a seller to cancel part or all of previously issued invoice(s).

3.14 A seller might sometimes give the purchaser a **credit note**, so that the total amount payable to the seller is the value of the unpaid invoice **minus** the amount of the credit note.

3.15 Credit notes can be treated like **negative invoices**. They should be matched with the seller's invoices and when the invoices to the seller are paid, the cheque should be made up for the value of the invoices **minus** the credit notes.

3.16 EXAMPLE: INVOICE AND CREDIT NOTE

Table Tops Ltd has received an invoice from its supplier, Paperchase Ltd, for office stationery. There has been some dispute with the supplier about the goods, and the supplier has issued a credit note. The invoice and credit note are held in the accounts department's file of unpaid invoices, and are as shown on page 15.

If the accounts department prepares a cheque for payment on 24 April 20X7, the amount of the cheque will be £470 less £117.50 = £352.50.

The cheque counterfoil could include a note of the invoice number (123678) and credit note number (2045). Both the invoice and credit note should be stamped, PAID and CLAIMED respectively, with the date of payment (24/4/X7).

Part A: Introduction to transaction accounting

3.17 Some other documents are sometimes used in connection with sales and purchases.

Document	Purpose
Debit note	A debit note is issued by a customer to a supplier as a means of formally requesting a credit note.
	A supplier might also issue a **debit note** instead of an invoice in order to adjust upwards the amount of an invoice already issued.
Goods received note (GRNs)	Goods received note**s** (GRNs) are filled in to record a receipt of goods, most commonly in a warehouse. They may be used instead of or in addition to suppliers' advice notes. Often the accounts department will want to see the relevant GRN before paying a supplier's invoice. Even where GRNs are not routinely used, the details of a consignment from a supplier which arrives without an advice note must always be recorded.

Proforma invoices

3.18 When a customer does not want credit and/or wishes to pay in advance for goods, he may request a **proforma invoice** from the supplier.

(a) This will show all the details of the sale as we have seen on invoices above, but will not be entered into the seller's books of account - it is a dummy invoice.

(b) The customer will create a cheque or get the cash to pay the proforma invoice.

(c) When the seller receives the cash or cheque it creates a real invoice which is recorded as normal. Because it is paid immediately the invoice is effectively a COD (cash on delivery) invoice.

3.19 Proforma invoices are vital for a **seller** who cannot settle in advance of despatch but which has customers who do not want credit and need an 'invoice' against which to raise payment (and because their procedures do not permit payment except against invoice).

3.20 Many **importing buyers** (ie buyers who require goods from a seller overseas) require proforma invoices so that payment (often by bank transfer) and export/import documentation can be prepared for despatch. **Buyers** whose credit is not good also have little choice but to pay against proforma invoices.

E-commerce

3.21 Internet trading cuts across many of the traditional documentation flows and takes out the time factor.

3.22 Customers can go online, select the goods they want and pay for them all with a series of clicks. For instance, if you purchase an airline ticket online, you receive an e-ticket which prints out on your printer. The seller may print out a copy at his end or he may not need to – your purchase is already recorded in his sales ledger.

3.23 The growth of e-commerce has increased the volume of transactions made using credit and debit cards.

PAPERCHASE SUPPLIES LTD
15 Great Way
Hending
Kent KN5 3TX

INVOICE

Invoice Number: 123678
Date: 25th March 20X7
Tax Point: 25/03/X7
Account Number: B138

Attention: J Smith
Table Tops Ltd
112 Peters Square
Weyford
Kent CR2 2TA

AUTHORISED JS 25/3/X7 Credit to follow

Quantity	Code	Description	Unit Price £	Net Amount £
200	X12345Y	Ring Binders	2.00	400.00

TOTAL GOODS: 400.00
VAT AT 17.5%: 70.00
AMOUNT PAYABLE: 470.00
TERMS: 30 Days Net

VAT Registration Number 345 7654 32

PAPERCHASE SUPPLIES LTD
15 Great Way
Hending
Kent KN5 3TX

CREDIT NOTE

Credit Note Number: 2045
Date: 6 April 20X7
Tax Point: 06/04/X7
Account Number: B138

Attention: J Smith
Table Tops Ltd
112 Peters Square
Weyford
Kent CR2 2TA

AUTHORISED JS 6/4/X7

Quantity	Code	Description	Unit Price £	Net Amount £
50	X12345Y	Ring Binders	2.00	100.00

TOTAL GOODS: 100.00
VAT AT 17.5%: 17.50
AMOUNT PAYABLE: 117.50

VAT Registration Number 345 7654 32

Part A: Introduction to transaction accounting

4 DISCOUNTS, REBATES AND ALLOWANCES

KEY TERM

A **discount** is a reduction in the price of goods below the amount at which those goods would normally be sold to other customers of the supplier.

Types of discount

4.1 There are two types of discount.

Type of discount	Description	Timing	Status
Trade discount	A reduction in the **cost of goods** owing to the nature of the trading transaction. It usually results from buying goods in bulk. For example (a) A customer might be quoted £1 per unit for a particular item, but a lower price of 95 pence per unit if 100 units or more are purchased at a time. (b) An important or regular customer might be offered a discount on all the goods he buys, regardless of the size of each order, because his total purchases over time are so large. Customers who receive trade discounts are often other business customers, but not always.	Given on supplier's invoice	Permanent
Cash (or settlement) discount	A reduction in the **amount payable** to the supplier, in return for immediate or very early payment in cash, rather than purchase on credit. For example, a supplier might charge £1,000 for goods, but offer a cash discount of 10% if the goods are paid for immediately in cash or 5% if they are paid for within 7 days of the invoice date. Payment of the full amount is due within 30 days. In this case the invoice would show '10% 0 days, 5% 7 days, net 30 days', indicating these terms.	Given for immediate or very prompt payment	Withdrawn if payment not received within time period indicated

4.2 The distinction between trade and cash discounts is important as they are accounted for differently.

4.3 EXAMPLE: DISCOUNTS

Ginger trades widely in her district. In particular, she has three suppliers.

(a) Scary is in the same business as Ginger and offers 5% trade discount.

(b) Posh offers a trade discount of 7% on amounts in excess of £100 (ie the trade discount does not apply to the first £100).

(c) Sporty offers a 10% cash discount for immediate payment or a 5% cash discount for all items paid for within 30 days of purchase.

In January 20X7, Ginger makes purchases of goods worth the following amounts before discounts have been deducted.

(a) From Scary: £400
(b) From Posh: £700
(c) From Sporty: £350 cash
                  £700 to be paid on 14.1.X7 for goods purchased on 3.1.X7

Calculate how much Ginger has received as discounts in January. How much were trade and cash discounts?

4.4 SOLUTION

		£	
From Scary	£400 × 5%	20	Trade
From Posh	(£700 − £100) × 7%	42	Trade
From Sporty	£350 × 10%	35	Cash: immediate
	£700 × 5%	35	Cash: prompt
		132	

Accounting for trade discounts

KEY TERM

A **trade discount** is a reduction in the amount of money demanded from a customer.

4.5 If a trade discount is **received** by a business for goods purchased from a supplier, the **amount of money demanded from the business** by the supplier will be **net** of discount (ie it will be the normal sales value less the discount).

Similarly, if a trade discount is **allowed** by a business for goods sold to a customer, the amount of money demanded by the business will be after deduction of the discount.

Accounting for cash discounts

KEY TERM

A **cash discount** is an optional reduction in the amount of money payable by a customer.

Cash discounts received

4.6 Taking advantage of a cash discount is a matter of **financing policy**, not of **trading policy**. This is because the discount is **optional**.

Part A: Introduction to transaction accounting

4.7 EXAMPLE: OPTIONAL CASH DISCOUNTS RECEIVED

Company A buys goods from Company B, on the understanding that A will be allowed a period of credit before having to pay for the goods.

Date of sale: 1 July 20X7

Credit period allowed: 30 days

Invoice price of the goods (the invoice will be issued at this price when the goods are delivered): £2,000

Cash discount offered: 4% for immediate payment

Company A has the choice of doing one of the following.

(a) Holding on to the £2,000 for 30 days and then paying the full amount
(b) Paying £2,000 less 4% (a total of £1,920) now

This is a financing decision about whether it is worthwhile for Company A to save £80 by paying its debts sooner, or whether it can employ its cash more usefully for 30 days and pay the debt at the latest acceptable moment.

Assume that if Company A pays now, its bank account would go overdrawn for a month. The bank would charge an overdraft fee of £50 together with interest of 1.6% per month (also charged on the overdraft fee). A currently has £150 in the bank (and has an agreed overdraft facility). Assuming no other transactions, what should Company A do? Work it out before looking at the solution.

4.8 SOLUTION

Company A pays now, so the bank account will be as follows.

		£
Funds		150.00
Less:	payment	(1,920.00)
	overdraft fee	(50.00)
Overdraft		(1,820.00)
Interest (1.6% × £1,820) added at end of the month		29.12

Whereas the discount is worth £80, bank charges and interest of £79.12 (£50 + £29.12) will be incurred. However, the amount of the discount is still worth more than the bank charges by 88p. Company A should therefore take advantage of the discount offered by Company B.

Cash discounts allowed

4.9 The same principle is applied in **accounting for cash discounts given** (allowed) to customers. Goods are sold at a trade price, and the offer of a cash discount on that price is a matter of **financing policy** for the selling business and not a matter of trading policy.

4.10 Allowing cash discounts to customers, as opposed to receiving discounts from suppliers, is subject to similar considerations.

(a) It may be worth your while to **receive an amount of cash now,** as you can earn more in **interest** on it than you would lose by offering the discount.

(b) If you are in a **precarious financial position,** your bank manager might be happier to see the money now rather than later (and you might save money on overdraft interest and bank charges).

(c) You may be concerned that the **customer's own financial position** is insecure. Accepting cash now, rather than more later, means that at least the money is securely yours.

Activity 1.3

Payquick Ltd purchases goods with a list price of £22,000. The supplier offers a 10% trade discount, and a 2½% cash discount for payment within 20 days.

Tasks

Note. Ignore VAT.

(a) Calculate the amount Payquick Ltd will have to pay if it delays longer than 20 days before paying.
(b) Calculate the amount the company will pay if it pays within 20 days.

4.11 Businesses may be offered other kinds of 'discounts' as incentives, to encourage them to buy in bulk or to stop them buying from other businesses. **Rebates** and **allowances** do not affect the cash function to a great extent and they are only mentioned briefly here.

(a) An example of a **rebate** is where the gas company will lower its overall tariff for customers who use over a certain number of units per year. The rebate will be given in one of the following forms.

(i) A reduction in the bills for the following year
(ii) A cheque for the calculated rebate amount

(b) An example of an **allowance** is where, if a certain number of units are ordered at one time, then a few extra units are given free of charge. For instance, if a record shop orders 50 compact discs, then another five may be sent **free of charge.**

5 VAT (VALUE ADDED TAX)

5.1 Many business transactions involve VAT (Value Added Tax), and most invoices, like the one shown earlier, show any VAT charged separately.

KEY TERMS

- **VAT** is a tax levied on the sale of goods and services. It is administered by HM Customs & Excise, but most of the work of collecting the tax falls on VAT-registered businesses, which hand the tax they collect over to the authorities.

- **Output tax**: VAT charged on goods and services sold by a business (that is, the business 'output').

- **Input tax**: VAT paid on goods and services bought in by a business.

5.2 VAT is charged by all members of the European Union (EU), though at different rates. Some countries, for example, charge 5% for some kinds of product and 10% on others.

5.3 In the UK there are three main rates of VAT.

(a) **Standard rate.** This is 17½% of the value of the goods. So, if you sell a standard rated item for £100, you must also charge £17.50 VAT. So the total paid by your customer will be £117.50. (Note that the prices you pay in shops generally **include** VAT.)

Part A: Introduction to transaction accounting

(b) **Lower rate.** This is 5% and is charged on **domestic** fuel and power (gas and electricity) and the installation of energy saving materials and home security goods.

(c) **Zero-rate.** This is 0%.

Exam alert

If an exam question includes VAT, this will **always** be at the standard rate of 17½%.

Not all goods and services have VAT on them. **Exempt items** are not part of the VAT system.

Calculating VAT

5.4 If a product has a **net price** of £120 and VAT is to be added, then the VAT is 17½% of £120.

$$\text{VAT} = £120 \times 17.5/100$$
$$= £21$$

5.5 The **gross price** of the product is therefore £120 + £21 = £141. **It is always true that gross price = net price + VAT.**

	£
Purchaser pays gross price	141
Customs and Excise take VAT	(21)
Seller keeps net price	120

5.6 If you are given the gross price of a product (say £282), then the VAT which it includes is 17.5/117.5 (or 7/47).

$$£282 \times 17.5/117.5 = £42$$

Therefore the net price must be £282 − £42 = £240. (To double check, 17.5% of £240 is £42.)

Activity 1.4

The gross price of product A is £705 and the net price of product B is £480. What is the VAT charged on each product?

Input and output VAT

5.7 Usually output VAT (on sales) exceeds input VAT (on purchases). The excess is paid over to Customs & Excise. If output VAT is less than input VAT in a period, Customs & Excise will refund the difference to the business. In other words, if a business pays out more in VAT than it receives from customers it will be paid back the difference.

Output tax received	Input tax paid	Total	Treatment
£1,000	£(900)	£100 received	Pay to C&E
£900	£(1,000)	£(100) paid	Refund from C&E

5.8 **EXAMPLE: INPUT AND OUTPUT TAX**

A company sells goods for £35,250 including VAT in a quarter (three months of a year). It buys goods for £32,900 including VAT. What amount will it pay to or receive from HM Customs & Excise for the quarter?

5.9 SOLUTION

Output tax

		£
£35,250 × $\frac{17.5}{117.5}$ =		5,250

Input tax

£32,900 × $\frac{17.5}{117.5}$ =		4,900

Tax **payable**   350

Some practical aspects of VAT

Administrative time

5.10 VAT affects a large proportion of businesses in the UK (and in other European countries) and it is something that a business will have to spend quite a lot of time administering. There are several reasons for this.

(a) Most businesses account to HM Customs & Excise for their transactions involving VAT **every quarter**. There is a special scheme which allows accounting on an annual basis but normally, every quarter, someone will have to work out the VAT position of the business.

(b) All transactions involving VAT will have to show **separately** the net price, VAT and the gross price. This increases the **time taken to record** the transactions of the business.

(c) Accounting for VAT will have an effect on **cash flow**, whether the business is a net payer of VAT or a net receiver.

(d) Failure to comply with all the rules relating to VAT will lead to **large penalties**. HM Customs & Excise has far more wide-ranging and punishing powers than the Inland Revenue.

Discounts and VAT

5.11 If a **cash discount** is offered for prompt payment, VAT is computed on the amount **after** deducting the discount (at the highest rate offered), even if the discount is not taken.

Activity 1.5

For Activity 1.3 above calculate the VAT payable for (a) and (b) if VAT was charged at the standard rate.

Credit cards

5.12 If a trader charges **different prices** for payment by credit cards from payment by other means, the VAT due on each standard rated sale is the full amount paid × 7/47.

Non-deductible inputs

5.13 There are some circumstances in which traders are not allowed to reclaim VAT paid on their inputs. In such cases, the trader must bear the cost of VAT and account for it

Part A: Introduction to transaction accounting

accordingly (see Chapter 4). The most important of these are **non-deductible** inputs, eg motor cars.

Documentation and VAT

5.14 We have already looked at invoices and some other documentation. There are special rules relating to the content of an invoice if it is to be used as a proof of purchase (or sale) for reclaiming VAT - a **VAT invoice**.

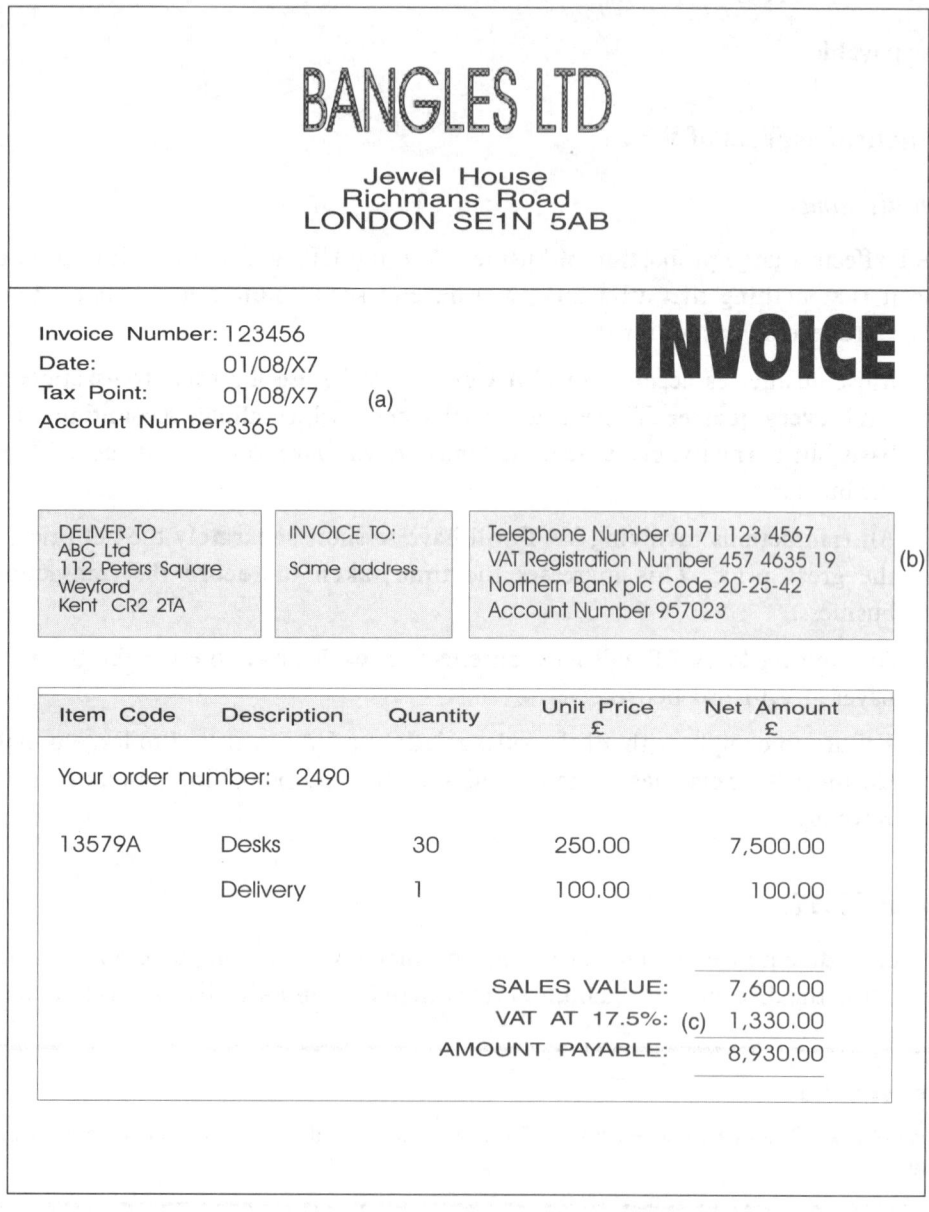

5.15 Note the following contents which are necessary for the invoice to be a 'VAT invoice'.

(a) **Tax point**. This determines when the transaction has taken place for VAT purposes. It is normally the invoice date. Note that, for cash transactions, the tax point for VAT purposes is the date the transaction took place.

(b) **VAT registration number** of the supplier. This is to prove to HM Customs & Excise that the purchase was from a real supplier of standard rated goods.

(c) **VAT rate**. The correct rate must be applied to each type of goods. If the goods are zero-rated then the rate would be shown as 0%.

The VAT return

5.16 Where a business is registered for VAT, it has to complete a **VAT return**. Generally, the return is prepared every quarter, although there is an option to complete it every month.

5.17 A VAT return is pictured below to **give you an overview**.

> **Exam alert**
> The Teaching Guide states that students should be aware of the **use and purpose** of this form. Detailed knowledge of the form of a UK VAT return is **not** required.

Value Added Tax Return
For the period
01 07 X5 to 30 09 X5

For Official Use

Registration number: 212 7924 36
Period: 09 X5

You could be liable to a financial penalty if your completed return and all the VAT payable are not received by the due date.

BERNINI PLC
1 LONG LANE
ANYTOWN
AN4 5QP

Due date: 31 10 X5

For Official Use

Your VAT Office telephone number is 0123-4567

Before you fill in this form please read the notes on the back and the VAT Leaflet "Filling in your VAT return".
Fill in all boxes clearly in ink, and write 'none' where necessary. Don't put a dash or leave any box blank. If there are no pence write "00" in the pence column. Do not enter more than one amount in any box.

For official use		£	p
	VAT due in this period on sales and other outputs	1	
	VAT due in this period on acquisitions from other EC Member States	2	
	Total VAT due (the sum of boxes 1 and 2)	3	
	VAT reclaimed in this period on purchases and other inputs (including acquisitions from the EC)	4	
	Net VAT to be paid to Customs or reclaimed by you (Difference between boxes 3 and 4)	5	
	Total value of sales and all other outputs excluding any VAT. Include your box 8 figure	6	00
	Total value of purchases and all other inputs excluding any VAT. Include your box 9 figure	7	00
	Total value of all supplies of goods and related services, excluding any VAT, to other EC Member States	8	00
	Total value of all acquisitions of goods and related services, excluding any VAT, from other EC Member States	9	00

Retail schemes. If you have used any of the schemes in the period covered by this return, enter the relevant letter(s) in this box.

If you are enclosing a payment please tick this box.

DECLARATION: You, or someone on your behalf, must sign below.

I, ... declare that the
(Full name of signatory in BLOCK LETTERS)
information given above is true and complete.

Signature .... Date .... 20 ......

A false declaration can result in prosecution.

Part A: Introduction to transaction accounting

6 CONTRACT LAW

6.1 We will now look at those aspects of law and regulation which apply to business records and transactions, starting with **contract law**.

6.2 **What is a contract?**

A contract is a legally binding agreement. In all areas of life we make contracts. If you buy or sell a house, a contract is made and 'exchanged'. When you start a job, you will probably have a contract of employment. When you go into a shop and buy something, you have entered into an agreement with the shopkeeper – you agree that the shopkeeper will give you the goods and you will give him or her the money.

6.3 Under contract law, the money that you give in exchange for the goods is referred to as the '**consideration**'. For a contract to take place, there must be **agreement** between the parties. This requires an **offer** made by one party, **acceptance** by the other party and some **consideration** passing between them. A price label displayed in a shop is an invitation to the customer to make an offer, which the shop can either accept or reject.

6.4 The example of a shop illustrates an important point about contracts. They do not have to be written. They do not even have to be spoken. A customer picking up something in a supermarket and walking to the checkout is making an offer to the shop, and that offer is **implied** by his behaviour.

6.5 Any business buying and selling goods is continually making and discharging (completing) contracts. Probably none of the parties involved give much thought to the legal aspect of what they are doing **until something goes wrong**.

6.6 When one party to a contract fails to carry out his part of the agreement, the other party can take legal action against him for **breach of contract**. So if a business has a debtor who is failing to pay, they can take him to court.

6.7 Where one party makes a misrepresentation to the other, the contract is considered **void**. For example, A sells goods to B, who sells them on to C. B then fails to pay A for the goods and disappears without trace. If A can demonstrate that he was genuinely mistaken as to the identity of B and would not have dealt with him had he known who B really was, then A can recover the goods which were subject to the original contract from C. This is because the law takes the view in such a situation that the original contract between A and B was no contract at all. Therefore C, who was an innocent third party acting in good faith, has to return the goods to A and either bear the loss or find and sue B.

Activity 1.6

You pick up something in a department store which is priced at £24. When the assistant scans it, the price appears as £26. You tell her that, as it was marked at £24, the store is legally obliged to sell it to you at that price. Are you correct?

7 THE SALE OF GOODS ACT

7.1 Contracts for the sale of goods are additionally subject to specific legislation. In the UK this is the Sale of Goods Act 1979, extended by the Supply of Goods and Services Act 1982 to cover contracts for the supply of services. The emphasis in this legislation is on protecting the rights of the consumer.

7.2 The main provisions are as follows:

- The goods must be **in existence** and must be able to be specified before a contract can be made. Property (ownership) cannot pass from seller to buyer unless, or until, the goods exist as specific or **ascertained** goods.

- If the price for the goods is not determined by the contract then a **reasonable price** must be paid.

- Performance (delivery of the goods) must be tendered at a reasonable time.

- The seller must have the **right to sell** the goods.

- In a sale by description, the goods must **match the description** given.

- Goods must be of **satisfactory quality**. They must meet the standard that a reasonable person would regard as satisfactory.

- If the seller knows the purpose for which the goods are being bought, it is an implied condition that the goods are reasonably **fit for the purpose**.

- The property in goods passes from seller to buyer when the parties intend that it shall pass. Goods are generally at the **buyer's risk** from the time that property passes. This means that, from this point on, any loss or damage to the goods is the buyer's loss. In practice, many contracts for the supply of goods contain a '**retention of title**' or '**Romalpa**' clause, stating that the title to the goods remains with the seller until the contract price is paid.

- A person not owning goods cannot in general transfer title to a buyer. A number of exceptions to this are specified to protect the innocent buyer.

- Once the buyer has accepted the goods, he cannot later reject them.

- An unpaid seller of goods may be able to retrieve the goods even if title has passed to the buyer. If this fails, he may sue the buyer.

7.3 These provisions are important for a seller in determining when revenue can be **recognised** (included in the accounts).

7.4 Revenue from the sale of goods should only be recognised when *all* these conditions are satisfied.

- The enterprise has transferred the **significant risks and rewards** of ownership of the goods to the buyer

- The enterprise has **no continuing managerial involvement** with the goods

- The amount of revenue can be **measured reliably**

- It is probable that the **economic benefits** associated with the transaction will flow to the enterprise

- The **costs incurred** in respect of the transaction can be measured reliably

7.5 If **significant risks and rewards** remain with the seller, then the transaction is not a sale. So an enterprise which sells goods under a **Romalpa** clause cannot recognise the revenue in its accounts until it has received payment.

Part A: Introduction to transaction accounting

8 STORAGE OF INFORMATION

8.1 Business transactions give rise to large amounts of paperwork, which must be properly handled in order to ensure both security and the availability of information.

8.2 There is a constant **demand for information within the organisation**, particularly from managers, who may request information of the following kinds.

(a) **Records of past and current transactions**, which must be stored pending confirmation, or for later analysis.

(b) **Information about past trends and current operations** on which to base planning and decision-making. For example, the past rate at which raw materials were consumed by a production process would dictate the frequency and amount of stock orders in the future.

(c) **Routine transaction information** on which to base current operations and decisions (for example, the information on a customer order dictates how many items, and of what sort, must be supplied from stock, and what delivery and payment arrangements should be made).

(d) **Information about performance** to compare with plans, budgets and forecasts for the purposes of control (checking for and correcting errors and shortcomings).

8.3 **People and groups outside the organisation** who are entitled to information, include the following.

(a) **Others involved in the business's transactions**: customers, suppliers, or sub-contractors, who require instructions, requests, contracts and so on.

(b) Parties interested in the financial performance of the organisation: the owners (shareholders), **investors** and **creditors** (those to whom the firm owes money, such as banks).

(c) **Outside agencies requiring information for surveys, or for their own activities**. The Department of Trade and Industry requires company accounts to be filed; returns have to be made to the Inland Revenue for the purposes of assessing tax and National Insurance contributions; Value Added Tax (VAT) is administered by the Excise authorities; and so on.

(d) **Regulatory bodies**. Non-financial information has to be supplied on working practices to the Health and Safety Executive; on employees to the Training Commission and its agencies; on new building works to local government planning departments; and so on.

8.4 Information **exchanged on a more specific personal or interpersonal level** may include the following.

(a) **Details relevant to enquiries or complaints** from clients, customers, colleagues or other parties, including introductions, explanations, apologies and answers to questions.

(b) **Information supplied to the organisation about an employee**:

- Which he supplies about himself in an interview, on a job application form or curriculum vitae; and
- For the organisation's records.

(c) **Information supplied to employees about the organisation**, its activities and methods, and about their own place in the system. For example, an 'induction' course

1: Business transactions and documentation

or training manual; a memorandum sent to members of staff with instructions, warnings, or encouragement; a staff meeting to discuss 'how things are going'.

8.5 In an Accounts Department, the main types of information which therefore require handling and storage are as follows.

(a) **Incoming correspondence**: letters, e-mails, memos, reports and other documents directed from people outside the organisation and department to those within it. These need to be stored and managed for the purposes of action (reply, transaction), analysis, confirmation and so on.

(b) **Outgoing correspondence**: similar messages generated by the department and flowing outwards. Copies of these need to be stored and managed as evidence and confirmation of what has been sent.

(c) **Financial records** prepared or received in the course of transactions and reporting. These require storage and management for the purposes of planning and control, and to comply with the accountability requirements of external agencies (eg the DTI, the Inland Revenue, Customs and Excise) and legislation (eg the Companies Acts).

Retention policy

8.6 Files of data may be **temporary, permanent, active,** and **non-active.**

(a) **Master files** and **reference files** are usually **permanent**, which means that they are never thrown away or scrapped. They will be **updated** from time to time, and so the information on the file might change, but the file itself will continue to exist.

(b) A **temporary** or **transitory file** is one that is eventually scrapped. Many **transaction files** are held for a very short time, until the transaction records have been processed, but are then thrown away. Other transaction files are permanent (for example a cash book) or are held for a considerable length of time before being scrapped.

(c) An **active file** is one that is frequently used, for example, sales invoice files relating to the current financial year, or correspondence files relating to current customers and suppliers.

(d) A **non-active file** is one that is no longer used on a day-to-day basis. For example, files that contain information relating to customers and suppliers who are no longer current, and purchase invoices relating to previous financial periods. **Semi-active files** are those that contain information that is still active, but are on their way to becoming inactive, for example, as a contract nears completion, it will not be used so frequently, but should be kept on hand for reference if so needed.

8.7 When information contained within files is no longer needed on a daily basis, it is not automatically thrown away (as you may be forgiven for thinking). It is generally dealt with in one of the following ways.

(a) **Microfilmed or microfiched** (as discussed earlier) for long-term storage

(b) Retained in its original form and stored elsewhere (this is generally known as **archiving**) for a certain period of time

(c) **Securely destroyed**

8.8 Imagine how distressed you would be if you needed to refer to a legal document that had been filed some years ago, and you found out that it had been thrown away by a filing clerk during the latest office spring-clean! (Alternatively, imagine trying to find an urgently

Part A: Introduction to transaction accounting

needed current file, with *all* the paperwork of the organisation's history still in the active filing system!)

8.9 In order to streamline the system, information which is no longer current, but which may need to be referred to at some point in the future, should be given a revised **status**: no longer active, but semi-active; no longer semi-active, but non-active – in which case, a prime candidate for the **archive**!

> **KEY TERM**
>
> A **retention policy** sets down for how long different kinds of information are retained

8.10 **Retention periods** vary. Under **The Companies Acts**, documents concerned with the legal establishment of the organisation will have to be kept permanently, as will the annual accounts. Simple legal contracts will have to be kept for six years, and more important sealed ones for twelve. Other documents may be kept at the organisation's discretion but the principle overall is: if you think you might need it, for as long as you might need it – keep it!

9 DATA PROTECTION

9.1 Storage of information is now regulated by the Data Protection legislation, which is concerned with storage of information about individuals. In a business, the department most likely to be affected by these regulations is Personnel or Human Resources.

The Data Protection Act 1998

9.2 Especially with the advent of computer records systems, fears have arisen with regard to:

- Access to personal information by unauthorised parties

- The likelihood that an individual could be harmed by the existence of computerised data about him or her which was inaccurate or misleading, and which could be transferred to unauthorised third parties at high speed and little cost

- The possibility that personal information could be used for purposes other than those for which it was requested and disclosed.

The Data Protection Acts (first in 1984, replaced in 1998) address these concerns.

9.3 The legislation is an attempt to afford some measure of protection to the individual. It covers data about **individuals** – not corporate bodies – and data which are processed **mechanically** (which includes any 'equipment operated automatically in response to the instructions given for that purpose', not just computers) and **manually** (a new development in the 1998 Act) – as long as the manually created records can be systematically used to access data about the individual.

1: Business transactions and documentation

> **KEY TERMS**
>
> **Personal data** are information about a living individual, including facts and expressions of opinion about him or her. Data about other organisations are not personal, unless they contain data about their members. The individual must be identifiable from the data, whether by name, or by code number (say, an employment number).
>
> **Data controllers** (formally known as data users) are organisations or individuals who control the contents of files of personal data and the use of personal data which are processed (or intended to be processed) automatically.

9.4 Data controllers and computer bureaux have to register with the Data Protection Commissioner. Data controllers must limit the use of personal data to the uses which are registered, and must abide by Data Protection Principles (discussed below).

9.5 The 1998 Act establishes the following rights for data subjects.

(a) A data subject may seek compensation through the courts for damage and any associated distress caused by:

   (i) the loss, destruction or unauthorised disclosure of data about himself or herself; or by

   (ii) inaccurate data about himself or herself.

(b) A data subject may apply to the courts or to the Registrar for inaccurate data to be put right or even wiped off the file.

(c) A data subject may obtain access to personal data of which he or she is the subject.

(d) A data subject is entitled to know the purposes for which data is collected and processed, the recipients to whom it may be disclosed and (in some cases) the source of the data.

Data Protection Principles

(1) The information to be contained in personal data shall be obtained, and personal data shall be processed, fairly and lawfully. (In particular, information must not be obtained by deception.)

(2) Personal data shall be held only for one or more specified (registered) and lawful purposes.

(3) Personal data shall be adequate, relevant and not excessive in relation to its purpose or purposes.

(4) Personal data shall be accurate and, where necessary, kept up to date. ('Accurate' means correct and not misleading as to any matter of *fact*. An *opinion* cannot be challenged.)

(5) Personal data shall not be kept for longer than is necessary for its purpose or purposes.

(6) An individual shall be entitled:

   (i) to be informed by any data controller whether he/she holds personal data of which that individual is the subject;

   (ii) to be informed of the purpose or purposes for which personal data is held;

   (iii) to have access to any such data held by a data controller; and

   (iv) where appropriate, to have such data corrected or erased.

> (7) Appropriate security measures shall be taken against unauthorised access to, or alteration, disclosure or destruction of, personal data and against accidental loss or destruction of personal data. The prime responsibility for creating and putting into practice a security policy rests with the data controller.
>
> (8) Data may not be exported outside the European Economic Area, except to countries where the rights of data subjects can be adequately protected.

9.6 There are some important **exemptions** from the Acts.

(a) **Unconditional exemptions**: personal data which are essential to national security, required to be made public by law, or concerned only with the data user's personal, family or household affairs;

(b) **Conditional exemptions**, including:

(i) personal data held for payroll and pensions;

(ii) data held by unincorporated members' clubs, relating only to club members; and

(iii) data held only for distribution of articles or information to the data subjects (say, for mailshot advertising) and consisting only of their names and addresses or other particulars necessary for the distribution.

(c) **Exemptions from the 'subject access' provisions only**, including: data held for the prevention or detection of crime, or assessment or collection of tax; data to which legal professional privilege could be claimed (for example, that held by a solicitor); data held solely for statistical or research purposes.

(d) A **special exemption for word processing operations** performed only for the purpose of preparing the text of documents. If a manager writes reports on his employees for disclosure to third parties using his computer as a word processor, he will not as a result become a data user. If, however, he intends to use the stored data as a source of information about the individual and can extract the information automatically, he must register as a data user.

Key learning points

- Business transactions are of two main types: cash and credit.
- Invoices and credit notes are important documents which must contain specific information.
- There are two kinds of discount.
    - **Trade discount**: a reduction in the cost of goods
    - **Cash (or settlement) discount**: a reduction in the amount payable to the supplier
- VAT rules can be quite complex but the following are the main points to remember.
    - **Output VAT** is charged on sales and **input VAT** is incurred on purchases
    - **VAT invoices** must contain specific pieces of information
- Business transactions are subject to
    - **Contract law**
    - **Sale of Goods Act**
- Under the **Sale of Goods Act** goods must be
    - of satisfactory quality
    - fit for the purpose
- A company's **retention policy** sets down how long different kinds of information are retained
- Information stored about individuals is regulated by the **Data Protection Act**

1: Business transactions and documentation

Quick quiz

1. What type of document would a business raise to give a customer a price for something?
2. Why should a business raise a goods received note?
3. What is an invoice?
4. What information is usually shown on an invoice?
5. What does E&OE on an invoice mean?
6. What is input tax and what is output tax?
7. What is a VAT 'tax point'?
8. If goods are sold under a 'retention of title' clause, when is the sale considered to have taken place?

Answers to quick quiz

1. A quotation.
2. A GRN acts as notification that the goods have been received (complete and in good condition) and it can be used to input the information into the business's accounting system.
3. An invoice is a demand for payment.
4.
   (a) Name and address of the seller
   (b) Name and address of the purchaser
   (c) Invoice number, so that the business can keep track of all the invoices it sends out
   (d) Date of the transaction
   (e) Description of what is being sold
   (f) Quantity and unit price of what has been sold
   (g) Total amount of the invoice including any details of VAT
   (h) The tax point for VAT purposes
5. Errors and omissions excepted, ie the supplier can alter any incorrect details on the invoice.
6. Input tax is VAT paid on purchases and output tax is VAT charged on sales.
7. A 'tax point' determines the date a transaction has taken place for VAT purposes.
8. When payment is received.

Answers to activities

Answer 1.1

(a) In a cash transaction you pay cash for the goods at the time they are supplied. In a credit transaction you do not pay until some time after the goods have been supplied.

(b) (i) It is usual for shops to provide a **till receipt**, although the customer does not always take it or retain it. This is the only piece of business documentation that would need to change hands.

   (ii) This is a **much more complicated** transaction, and is likely to involve the following documents.

   (1) A letter of enquiry
   (2) A quotation
   (3) An order
   (4) An order acknowledgement
   (5) A delivery note
   (6) An invoice

   The quotation or the order acknowledgement might include details of the supplier's terms and conditions of business. If any part of the work is unsatisfactory, or if the firm overcharges, a credit note may also be issued.

Part A: Introduction to transaction accounting

Answer 1.2

(a) The copies of the sales order set may be distributed as follows.

    (i) The top copy might be sent to the **customer** to confirm the order.

    (ii) A copy must be passed from the sales department to the **warehouse** or production department so that delivery can be arranged.

    (iii) Another copy might be kept in the **sales department** to help deal with customer queries.

    (iv) Another copy would be passed to **accounts** as a means of requesting accounts to 'raise' (ie produce) an invoice.

    (v) One copy can be used as a **delivery note** and another as an **advice note**. The delivery note might be returned to accounts to be matched with the invoice to ensure that the invoice is not sent out until the goods have been delivered.

    (vi) A copy might be kept in the warehouse for the **warehouse records**, in case of a query.

(b) The parts of a purchase order set might be used as follows.

    (i) The top copy is sent to the **supplier**, possibly to confirm a telephone order.

    (ii) A copy is kept by the **department placing the order** for reference and possibly to be compared with the supplier's delivery note. (Alternatively, a copy may go to the warehouse for checking against the delivery note.)

    (iii) Another copy may be given to the **accounts department** to be matched with the supplier's invoice when it comes in.

Answer 1.3

	£
List price	22,000
Less 10% trade discount	2,200
	19,800
Less 2½% cash discount (£19,800 × 2½%)	495
	19,305

(a) If Payquick Ltd pays after 20 days it will receive only the trade discount. The company will therefore pay £19,800.

(b) If payment is made within 20 days, the company will be able to take advantage of the cash discount and pay only £19,305.

Note. The cash discount is calculated as a percentage of the list price **net of trade discount**.

Answer 1.4

(a) VAT for product A = 17.5/117.5 × £705 = £105. (So net price was £705 – £105 = £600.)

(b) VAT for product B = 0.175 × £480 = £84. (So gross price was £480 + £84 = £564.)

Answer 1.5

The VAT is calculated as if **all discounts** are taken, so the VAT is the same for both (a) and (b), ie 17½% × £19,305 = £3,378.37.

Answer 1.6

No, you are not correct. The price label in the store is an 'invitation to treat' (invitation to make an offer). Your proposal to pay £24 is the offer. There is no acceptance from the store, so no contract has been made.

Chapter 2   Assets, liabilities and the accounting equation

Chapter topic list

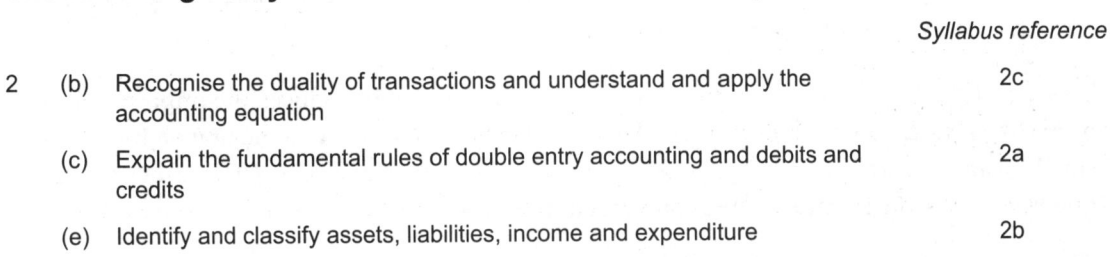

1. Introduction: accounting fundamentals
2. What is a business?
3. Assets and liabilities
4. A business is separate from its owner(s)
5. The accounting equation
6. Creditors and debtors
7. Double entry bookkeeping

The following study sessions are covered in this chapter

			Syllabus reference
2	(b)	Recognise the duality of transactions and understand and apply the accounting equation	2c
	(c)	Explain the fundamental rules of double entry accounting and debits and credits	2a
	(e)	Identify and classify assets, liabilities, income and expenditure	2b

Part A: Introduction to transaction accounting

1 INTRODUCTION: ACCOUNTING FUNDAMENTALS

1.1 The purpose of Chapters 1 to 5 of this Interactive Text is to introduce the **fundamentals of accounting**, particularly the principles of **double entry bookkeeping**. It is essential that you understand the topics discussed in the next few chapters, as they form a basis for your studies of **financial accounting** at all levels.

> **Exam alert**
> Double entry transactions were tested in many of the multiple choice questions on the Pilot Paper. Without a thorough grasp of double entry and the basics of accounting you will not be able to understand the practical aspects of cash, credit and payroll transactions covered in Parts B to D of this Interactive Text.

2 WHAT IS A BUSINESS?

2.1 Before tackling the nuts and bolts of accounting, it is worth considering what we mean when we talk about a **business**. Some ideas are listed below.

(a) A business is a commercial or industrial concern which exists to **deal in the** manufacture, resale or **supply of goods and services**.

(b) A business is an organisation which uses **economic resources** to create goods or services which customers will buy.

(c) A business is an organisation **providing jobs** for people to work in.

(d) A business invests money in resources (eg it buys buildings, it pays employees) in order to make even **more money for its owners**.

2.2 This last definition - investing money to make more money - introduces the important idea of **profit**. Business enterprises vary in character, size and complexity. They range from very small businesses (the local shopkeeper or plumber) to very large ones (ICI). However the **objective of earning profit** is common to all of them.

> **KEY TERM**
> **Profit** is the excess of income over expenditure. When expenditure exceeds income, the business is running at a **loss**.

2.3 One of the jobs of an accountant is to **measure** income, expenditure and profit. This is not always straightforward. It can be an inexact science, although the accounting fundamentals of **double entry bookkeeping** make sure that there is a firm set of principles underlying everything an accountant does.

2.4 Learning how to account for a business involves building up a clear picture of what a business consists of. We shall start with what a business **owns** and what it **owes** - its **assets** and **liabilities**.

3 ASSETS AND LIABILITIES

Assets

> **KEY TERM**
>
> An **asset** is something valuable which a business owns or has the use of.

3.1 Examples of assets are factories, office buildings, warehouses, delivery vans, lorries, plant and machinery, computer equipment, office furniture, cash, goods held in store awaiting sale to customers, and raw materials and components held in store by a manufacturing business for use in production.

Fixed and current assets

3.2 Some assets are held and used in operations for a **long time**. An office building can be occupied by administrative staff for years. Similarly, a machine has a productive life of many years before it wears out. These are usually referred to as **fixed assets**.

3.3 Other assets are held for only a **short time**. The owner of a newsagent's shop, for example, has to sell his newspapers on the same day that he gets them, and weekly newspapers and monthly magazines also have a short shelf life. The more quickly a business can sell the goods it has in store, the more profit it is likely to make. We usually call these **current assets.**

Liabilities

> **KEY TERM**
>
> A **liability** is something which is owed to somebody else.

3.4 'Liabilities' is the accounting term for the debts of a business. Debts are owed to **creditors**. Here are some examples of liabilities.

Liability	Description
A **bank loan** or **bank overdraft**	The **liability** is the amount which is eventually repaid to the **bank**.
Amounts owed to **suppliers** for goods purchased but not yet paid for	A boat builder buys some timber on credit from a **timber merchant**, and so the boat builder does not have to pay for the timber until some time after it has been delivered. Until the boat builder pays what he owes, the timber merchant will be his **creditor** for the amount owed.
Taxation owed to the **government**	A business pays tax on its profits, but there is a gap in time between when a business earns its profits (and becomes liable to pay tax) and the time when the tax bill is eventually paid. The **government** is the business's **creditor** during this time.

Part A: Introduction to transaction accounting

4 A BUSINESS IS SEPARATE FROM ITS OWNER(S)

4.1 So far we have spoken of assets and liabilities 'of a business'. We shall see that, in accounting terms, a business is **always a separate entity from its owner(s)**. There are two aspects to this question: the strict legal position and the convention adopted by accountants.

The legal position

4.2 Many businesses are carried on in the form of **limited companies**. The owners of a limited company are its **shareholders**, who may be few in number (a small, family-owned company) or very numerous (a large public company with shares quoted on the Stock Exchange).

4.3 The **law recognises a company as a legal entity, quite separate from its owners**.

   (a) A company may, in its own name, acquire assets, incur debts, and enter into contracts.

   (b) If a company **owns** less than it **owes** (its assets are not enough to meet its liabilities), the company as a separate entity might become 'bankrupt', but the owners of the company would not usually be required to pay the debts from their own private resources. The company's debts are not debts of the shareholders, but of the company.

   This is **limited liability**. The liability of shareholders to the company is **limited** to the amount they 'put in' to the company (how much the company asks for their shares on issue).

4.4 The case is different, in law, when a business is carried on, not by a company, but by an individual (a **sole trader**) or by a group of individuals (a **partnership**). Suppose that Audrey Roberts sets herself up in business as a hairdresser trading under the business name 'Hair by Audrey'. The law recognises no distinction between Audrey, the individual, and the business known as 'Hair by Audrey'. Any debts of the business which cannot be met from business assets must be met from Audrey's private resources.

4.5 The **law recognises no distinction between the business of a sole trader or partnership and its owner(s)**.

Activity 2.1

Distinguish between the terms 'entity', 'business', 'company' and 'firm'.

The accounting convention

4.6 The crucial point to grasp, however, is that **a business must always be treated as a separate entity from its owners when preparing accounts**. This applies whether or not the business is recognised in law as a separate entity, so it applies whether the business is carried on by a company, a sole trader or by a partnership.

Activity 2.2

Fill in the missing words to make sure you understand the concept of the business as a separate entity and how the law differs from accounting practice.

A business is a _____ entity, distinct from its _____ . This applies to _____ businesses. However, the law only recognises a _____ as a legal entity separate from its _____ . The liability of shareholders to the company is _____ to the amount the company asks them to pay for their shares.

5 THE ACCOUNTING EQUATION

5.1 A business is a separate entity from its owners.

- The business can owe money to, or be owed money by, its owners.
- The assets and liabilities of the business are separate from those of the owners.

This is the basis of a fundamental rule of accounting, which is that **the assets and liabilities of a business must always be equal** (**the accounting equation**). Let's demonstrate this with an example, which we will build up during this chapter.

5.2 EXAMPLE: THE ACCOUNTING EQUATION

On 1 July 20X7, Neelim Sultan decides to open up a flower stall in the market, to sell flowers and potted plants. She has £2,500 to put into her business.

When the business is set up, an 'accountant's picture' can be drawn of what it **owns** and what it **owes**. The business begins by **owning** the cash that Neelim has put into it, £2,500. Does it **owe** anything? The answer is **yes**.

The business is a separate entity in accounting terms. It has obtained its **assets**, in this example cash, from its owner, Neelim Sultan. **It therefore owes this amount of money to its owner.** If Neelim changed her mind and decided not to go into business after all, the business would be dissolved by the 'repayment' of the cash by the business to Neelim.

5.3 The money put into a business by its owners is **capital**. As long as that money is invested, **accountants will treat the capital as money owed to the proprietor by the business**.

> **KEY TERM**
>
> **Capital** is an investment of money (funds) with the intention of earning a return. A business proprietor invests capital with the intention of earning **profit**. The business owes the capital and the profit to the proprietor.

5.4 Capital invested is therefore a form of **liability**. Adapting this to the idea that liabilities and assets are always equal amounts, we can state the accounting equation as follows.

> **THE ACCOUNTING EQUATION 1**
>
> Assets = Capital + Liabilities

5.5 For Neelim Sultan, as at 1 July 20X7

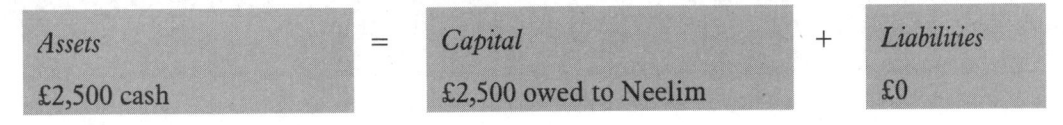

Assets	=	Capital	+	Liabilities
£2,500 cash		£2,500 owed to Neelim		£0

5.6 EXAMPLE CONTINUED: DIFFERENT ASSETS

Neelim Sultan purchases a market stall from Sanjay Patel for £1,800.

She also purchases some flowers and potted plants from a trader in the New Covent Garden wholesale market, at a cost of £650.

Part A: Introduction to transaction accounting

This leaves £50 in cash, after paying for the stall and goods for resale, out of the original £2,500. She is now ready for her first day of market trading on 3 July 20X7. How does the accounting equation look now?

5.7 SOLUTION

The assets and liabilities of the business have now altered, and at 3 July, before trading begins, the state of her business is as follows.

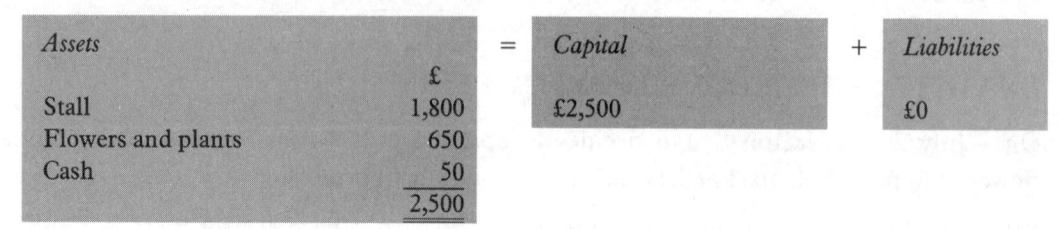

Assets	£	=	Capital	+	Liabilities
Stall	1,800		£2,500		£0
Flowers and plants	650				
Cash	50				
	2,500				

5.8 EXAMPLE CONTINUED: PROFIT INTRODUCED

On 3 July Neelim has a very successful day. She sells all of her flowers and plants, for £900 cash.

Since Neelim has sold goods costing £650 to earn revenue of £900, we can say that she has earned a **profit** of £(900 − 650) = £250 on the day's trading. How do we reflect this in the accounting equation?

5.9 SOLUTION

Profit, like capital, belongs to the owners of a business. It's why they invested in the first place. In this case, the £250 belongs to Neelim Sultan. However, so long as the **business retains the profits, and does not pay anything out to its owners, the retained profits are accounted for as an addition to the proprietor's capital:** they become part of that capital.

Assets	£	=	Capital	£	+	Liabilities
Stall	1,800		Capital introduced	2,500		
Flowers and plants	0		Retained profit	250		
Cash (50 + 900)	950			2,750		£0
	2,750					

5.10 So we could expand the accounting equation as follows.

THE ACCOUNTING EQUATION 2

Assets = (Capital introduced + Retained profits) + Liabilities

Increase in net assets

KEY TERM

Net assets = Total assets − Total liabilities

2: Assets, liabilities and the accounting equation

5.11 We can re-arrange the accounting equation to help us to calculate the total capital balance, which we have seen is the sum of capital introduced plus retained profit.

Assets – Liabilities	=	Capital
Net assets	=	Capital

5.12 At the beginning and then at the end of 3 July 20X7 Neelim Sultan's financial position was as follows.

	Net assets	=		*Capital*
(a) At the beginning of the day:	£(2,500 – 0)	=		£2,500
(b) At the end of the day:	£(2,750 – 0)	=		£2,750
Increase in net assets	250	= Retained profit for day		250

5.13 We can now state various principles.

(a) At any point in time, a business's **net assets** represent the **capital introduced** by the owner plus the business's **retained profit** to that point in time.

(b) At a later point in time, the **increase** in the business's net assets represents the additional **profit made** in the intervening period.

(c) **Total** net assets at that later point represent the capital introduced by the owner plus the business's **increased** retained profit.

For example

		£m				£m
1 Jan	Net assets	170	= Capital introduced	20	+ Retained profit	150
1 Jan-31 Dec	Increase in net assets	34	=		Profit made in year	34
31 Dec	Total net assets	204	= Capital introduced	20	+ Total retained profit	184

Drawings

> **KEY TERM**
>
> **Drawings** are amounts of money taken out of a business by its owner.

5.14 EXAMPLE CONTINUED: DRAWINGS

Since Neelim Sultan has made a profit of £250 from her first day's work, she feels justified in drawing some of the profits out of the business, for living expenses. Neelim decides to pay herself £180, in what she thinks of as 'wages', as a fair reward for her day's work.

As she is the business's **owner**, the £180 is **not** an expense to be deducted before the figure of profit is arrived at. In other words, it would be **incorrect** to calculate the profit earned by the business as follows.

	£
Profit on sale of flowers etc	250
Less 'wages' paid to Neelim as drawings	180
Profit earned by business (incorrect)	70

This is because **any amounts paid by a business to its proprietor are treated by accountants as withdrawals of profit (drawings)**, and not as expenses incurred by the business. In the case of Neelim's business, the true position is that the profit **earned** is the £250 surplus on sale of flowers, but the profit **retained** in the business is £(250 – 180) = £70.

Part A: Introduction to transaction accounting

	£
Profit earned by business	250
Less profit withdrawn by Neelim	180
Profit retained in the business	70

The drawings are taken in cash, and so the business loses £180 of its cash assets. After the drawings have been made, the accounting equation would be restated.

Assets	£	=	Capital	£	+	Liabilities
Stall	1,800		Capital introduced	2,500		
Flowers and plants	0		Profit earned	250		
Cash £(950 – 180)	770		Less drawings	(180)		
	2,570			2,570		£0

The increase in net assets since trading operations began is now only £(2,570 – 2,500) = £70, which is the amount of the retained profits.

5.15 So **profits are capital as long as they are retained in the business**. When they are paid out as drawings, the business suffers a **reduction in capital**.

5.16 We can therefore restate the accounting equation again.

THE ACCOUNTING EQUATION 3

Assets = Capital introduced + (Earned profit – Drawings) + Liabilities

---

5.17 These examples have illustrated that the basic equation (Assets = Capital + Liabilities) always holds good. Any transaction affecting the business has a **dual effect** as shown in the table below.

	Asset	=	Capital	+	Liabilities
	Increase		Increase		
or	Increase				Increase
or			Increase		Decrease
or			Decrease		Increase
or	Decrease		Decrease		
or	Decrease				Decrease

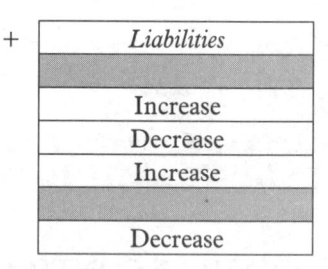

Activity 2.3

Consider each of the transactions below, and mark on the grid which area will be increased and which decreased by the transaction. We have done the first one for you.

(a) The bank tells the business it no longer owes the bank £100 in bank charges.
(b) The business finds it has been overcharged £50 for some furniture it bought on credit.
(c) A gas bill of £200 is received by the business.
(d) The owner withdraws £500 from the business.
(e) Cash is introduced into the business by its owner.
(f) A car is bought by the business, for payment in 1 month's time.

Transaction	=	Assets	=	Capital	+	Liabilities
a				Increase		Decrease
b						
c						
d						
e						
f						

6 CREDITORS AND DEBTORS

Credit transactions

6.1 We have been concentrating on **capital** (including profits) and **assets** (cash, goods for resale, fixed assets). We shall now look at two important items which arise when goods and services are purchased or sold as part of a **credit transaction: debtors and creditors**.

Creditors

> **KEY TERMS**
>
> - A **creditor** is a person from whom a business has **purchased** items and to whom a business **owes** money. A creditor is a **liability** of the business.
> - A **trade creditor** is a person to whom a business owes money for debts incurred in the course of trading operations. The term might refer to debts still outstanding which arise from the purchase from suppliers of materials, components or goods for resale.

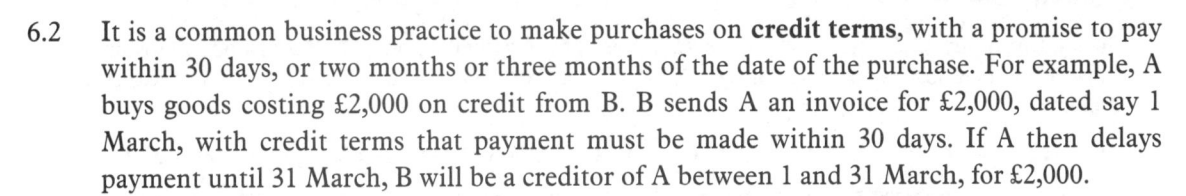

6.2 It is a common business practice to make purchases on **credit terms**, with a promise to pay within 30 days, or two months or three months of the date of the purchase. For example, A buys goods costing £2,000 on credit from B. B sends A an invoice for £2,000, dated say 1 March, with credit terms that payment must be made within 30 days. If A then delays payment until 31 March, B will be a creditor of A between 1 and 31 March, for £2,000.

We will be looking at **invoices** in a great deal more detail in later chapters.

Debtors

> **KEY TERMS**
>
> - A **debtor** is a person to whom the business has **sold** items and by whom the business is **owed** money. A debtor is an **asset** of a business (the right to receive payment is owned by the business).
> - A **trade debtor** is a person who owes the business money for debts incurred in the course of trading operations ie because the business has sold its goods or services.

6.3 Just as a business might buy goods on credit, so too might it sell goods to customers on credit. For example, C sells goods on credit to D for £6,000 on terms that payment is due within two months of the invoice date, 1 October. If D does not pay the £6,000 until 30 November, D will be a debtor of C for £6,000 from 1 October until 30 November.

Part A: Introduction to transaction accounting

6.4 This should serve as a useful summary.

CREDIT TRANSACTIONS	
SALES by the business to a customer	PURCHASES by the business from a supplier
↓ creates a DEBTOR (a customer who owes money to the business)	↓ creates a CREDITOR (a supplier who is owed money by the business)
↓ recorded as an ASSET of the business	↓ recorded as a LIABILITY of the business
↓ settled when the business RECEIVES CASH	↓ settled when the business PAYS CASH

Activity 2.4

Jackie Dixon has £2,500 of capital invested in her business. Of this, only £1,750 has been provided by herself, the balance being provided by a loan of £750 from Barry Grant. What are the implications of this for the accounting equation?

Hint. The answer is not necessarily clear cut. There are different ways of looking at Barry's investment.

7 DOUBLE ENTRY BOOKKEEPING

Exam alert
You will always be asked to demonstrate your knowledge of double entry bookkeeping both in the Paper 1 exam and in your later studies.

7.1 We know that, since the **total of liabilities plus capital is always equal to total assets**, any transaction has a **dual effect** - if it changes the amount of total assets it also changes the total liabilities plus capital, and *vice versa*. Alternatively, a transaction might use up assets of a certain value to obtain other assets of the same value. For example, if a business pays £50 in cash for some goods, its total assets will be unchanged, but as the amount of cash falls by £50, the value of goods in stock rises by £50.

7.2 We can say then that there are two sides to every business transaction. Out of this concept has developed the system of accounting known as the 'double entry' system of bookkeeping, so called because every transaction is recorded twice in the accounts.

2: Assets, liabilities and the accounting equation

> **KEY TERM**
>
> **Double entry bookkeeping** is the system of accounting which reflects the fact that:
>
> - every financial transaction gives rise to two accounting entries, one a debit and the other a credit, and so
> - the total value of **debit entries** is therefore always equal at any time to the total value of **credit entries**.

7.3 Each asset, liability, item of expense or item of income has a **ledger account** in which debits and credits are made. Which account receives the credit entry and which the debit depends on the nature of the transaction.

7.4 Below is a summary. We shall look at double entry in detail in Chapter 4.

DEBIT To own/have ↓	CREDIT To owe ↓
AN ASSET INCREASES eg new office furniture	AN ASSET DECREASES eg pay out cash
CAPITAL/ A LIABILITY DECREASES eg pay a creditor	CAPITAL/A LIABILITY INCREASES eg buy goods on credit
INCOME DECREASES eg cancel a sale	INCOME INCREASES eg make a sale
AN EXPENSE INCREASES eg incur advertising costs	AN EXPENSE DECREASES eg cancel a purchase
Left hand side	Right hand side

Activity 2.5

Try to explain the dual effects of each of the following transactions.

(a) A business receives a loan of £5,000 from its bank
(b) A business pays £800 cash to purchase a stock of goods for resale
(c) The proprietor of a business removes £50 from the till to buy her husband a birthday present
(d) A business sells goods costing £300 at a profit of £140
(e) A business repays a £5,000 bank loan, plus interest of £270

Part A: Introduction to transaction accounting

> **Key learning points**
>
> - It is vital that you acquire a thorough understanding of the **principles of double entry bookkeeping.** These principles, outlined in this chapter and developed in Chapter 4, apply to both cash and credit transactions.
> - A **business** may be defined in various ways. Its purpose is to make a **profit** for its owner(s).
> - **Profit** is the excess of income over expenditure.
> - A business **owns assets** and **owes liabilities**.
> - For accounting purposes it is important to keep business assets and liabilities **separate** from the personal assets and liabilities of the proprietor(s).
> - **Assets** are items belonging to a business and used in the running of the business. They may be **fixed** (such as machinery or office premises), or **current** (such as stock, debtors and cash).
> - **Liabilities** are sums of money owed by a business to outsiders such as a bank or a trade creditor.
> - **Assets = Capital + Liabilities** (the accounting equation).
> - Double entry book-keeping requires that every transaction has two accounting entries, a **debit** and a **credit.**

Quick quiz

1. What is a business's prime objective?
2. Define profit.
3. What is an asset?
4. What is a liability?
5. How does the accounting view of the relationship between a business and its owner differ from the strictly legal view?
6. State the basic accounting equation.
7. What is capital?
8. What are drawings? Where do they fit in the accounting equation?
9. What is the main difference between a cash and a credit transaction?
10. What is a creditor? What is a debtor?
11. Define double entry book-keeping.

Answers to quick quiz

1. A business's prime objective is earning a profit.
2. Profit is the excess of income over expenditure.
3. An asset is something valuable which a business owns or has the use of.
4. A liability is something which is owed to someone else.
5. In accounting a business is always treated as a separate entity from its owners, even though in law there is not always a distinction (in the cases of a sole trader and a partnership).
6. Assets = Capital + Liabilities.
7. Capital is the investment of funds with the intention of earning a profit.
8. Drawings are the amounts of money taken out of a business by its owner. In the accounting equation drawings are a reduction of capital.
9. The main difference between a cash and a credit transaction is simply a matter of time - cash changes hands immediately in a cash transaction, whereas in a credit one it changes hands some time after the initial sale/purchase takes place.

2: Assets, liabilities and the accounting equation

10 A creditor is a person from whom a business has purchased items and to whom it owes money. A debtor is a person to whom the business has sold items and by whom it is owed money.

11 Double entry book-keeping is a system of accounting which reflects the fact that every financial transaction gives rise to two equal accounting entries, a debit and a credit.

Answers to activities

Answer 2.1

An **enterprise** is the most general term, referring to just about any organisation in which people join together to achieve a common end. In the context of accounting it can refer to a multinational conglomerate, a small club, a local authority and so on.

A **business** is also a very general term, but it does not extend as widely as the term 'enterprise', eg it would not include a charity or a local authority. Any organisation existing to trade and make a profit could be called a business.

A **company** is an enterprise constituted in a particular legal form, usually involving limited liability for its members. Companies need not be businesses, for example, many charities are constituted as companies.

A **firm** is a much vaguer term. It is sometimes used loosely in the sense of a business or a company. Some writers, more usefully, try to restrict its meaning to that of an unincorporated business (ie a business not constituted as a company, for example a partnership).

Answer 2.2

The missing words are

Separate, owners, all, company, owners, limited.

Answer 2.3

Transaction	Assets	=	Capital	+	Liabilities
(a)		=	Increase	+	Decrease
(b)	Decrease	=		+	Decrease
(c)		=	Decrease	+	Increase
(d)	Decrease	=	Decrease	+	
(e)	Increase	=	Increase	+	
(f)	Increase	=		+	Increase

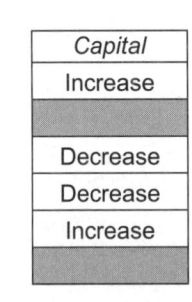

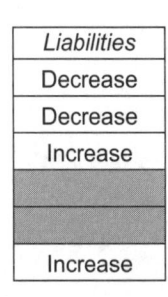

Answer 2.4

We have assets of £2,500 (cash), balanced by liabilities of £2,500 (the amounts owed by the business to Jackie and Barry).

- The £1,750 owed to Jackie clearly falls into the special category of liability labelled **capital**, because it is a sum owed to the proprietor of the business.

- To classify the £750 owed to Barry, we would need to know more about the **terms of his agreement** with Jackie.

- If they have effectively gone into **partnership**, sharing the risks and rewards of the business, then Barry is a proprietor too and the £750 is 'capital' in the sense that Jackie's £1,750 is.

- If Barry has no share in the profits of the business, and can expect only a repayment of his 'loan' plus some interest, the amount of £750 should be classified under **liabilities**.

Part A: Introduction to transaction accounting

Answer 2.5

(a) Assets (cash) increase by £5,000, liabilities (amount owed to the bank) increase by £5,000.

(b) Assets (cash) decrease by £800, assets (stock) increase by £800.

(c) Assets (cash) decrease by £50, capital decreases by £50 (the proprietor has taken £50 drawings for her personal use. In effect, the business has repaid her part of the amount it owed).

(d) Assets (cash) increase by £440, assets (stock) decrease by £300, capital (the profit earned for the proprietor) increases by £140.

(e) Assets (cash) decrease by £5,270, liabilities (the bank loan) decrease by £5,000, capital decreases by £270 (the proprietor has made a 'loss' of £270 on the transaction).

Chapter 3 Balance sheet and profit and loss account

Chapter topic list

1. Introduction to financial statements
2. The balance sheet
3. Fixed assets
4. Current assets
5. Liabilities
6. The profit and loss account
7. Capital and revenue expenditure

The following study sessions are covered in this chapter

			Syllabus reference
1	(h)	Identify the timing of various transactions eg daily monthly annually	1a
2	(f)	Distinguish between capital and revenue expenditure and identify examples of each	2b

Part A: Introduction to transaction accounting

1 INTRODUCTION TO FINANCIAL STATEMENTS

1.1 In Chapter 2 you were introduced to the idea of the accounting equation. If you understand this, you should have little difficulty in getting to grips with the **balance sheet** and **profit and loss account**.

> **Exam alert**
> Preparation of the balance sheet and profit and loss account is outside the syllabus. However, you are required to distinguish between capital and revenue expenditure, and an understanding of the balance sheet and profit and loss account will help make this distinction clear.

1.2 While transaction processing will go on as a continuous process, most enterprises will produce **monthly** financial statements. The monthly procedure will involve reconciling debtors and creditors ledgers, sending out customer statements and reconciling the bank account. Then a trial balance will be taken out and the balance sheet and profit and loss account produced. This procedure will also be followed at the **year end.**

2 THE BALANCE SHEET

> **KEY TERM**
> A **balance sheet** is a statement of the assets, liabilities and capital of a business at a given moment in time. It is like a 'snapshot' photograph, since it captures on paper a still image, frozen at a single moment in time, of something which is dynamic and continually changing. Typically, a balance sheet is prepared to show the assets, liabilities and capital as at the **end** of the accounting period to which the financial statements relate.

2.1 A **balance sheet** is therefore very similar to the **accounting equation**.

Assets = Capital introduced + Retained profit − Liabilities

In fact, there are only two differences between a balance sheet and the accounting equation which are as follows.

- The manner or **format** in which the assets and liabilities are presented
- The extra **detail** which is usually contained in a balance sheet

2.2 A balance sheet is divided into two halves, usually showing **capital** in one half and **net assets** (ie assets less liabilities) in the other.

NAME OF BUSINESS
BALANCE SHEET AS AT (DATE)

	£
Assets	X
Less liabilities	X
Net assets	X
Capital	X

The total value in one half of the balance sheet will equal the total value in the other half. You should readily understand this from the **accounting equation**.

2.3 For many businesses, the way in which assets and liabilities are categorised and presented in a balance sheet is a matter of choice, and you may come across different formats. (For limited companies, the form of the balance sheet is closely defined by the Companies Act.) The format below should help you see how a typical balance sheet is compiled. It is a simplified version of the format prescribed for limited companies.

XYZ
BALANCE SHEET AS AT 31 DECEMBER 20X7

	£	£
Fixed assets		
Land and buildings	X	
Plant and machinery	X	
Fixtures and fittings	X	
		X
Current assets		
Stock	X	
Debtors	X	
Cash at bank and in hand	X	
	A	
Current liabilities		
Bank overdraft	X	
Trade creditors	X	
	B	
Net current assets (A – B)		X
Long-term liabilities		(X)
Net assets		C
Capital		
Proprietor's capital		X
Retained profits (including previous and current year profits)		X
		C

3 FIXED ASSETS

3.1 Assets in the balance sheet are divided into **fixed** and **current** assets, as we saw in Chapter 2.

> **KEY TERM**
>
> A **fixed asset** is an asset acquired for use within the business (rather than for selling to a customer), with a view to earning income or making profits from its use, either directly or indirectly, over more than one accounting period.

3.2 Examples of fixed assets may be production machinery in a manufacturing company, furniture for a hotel, or testing machinery and ramps in a garage.

Part A: Introduction to transaction accounting

4 CURRENT ASSETS

> **KEY TERM**
>
> **Current assets** are either:
> - items owned by the business with the intention of turning them into cash within one year (stocks of goods, and debtors); or
> - cash, including money in the bank, owned by the business.
>
> Assets are 'current' in the sense that they are continually flowing through the business.

4.1 Cars are current assets for a car trader as these are continually flowing through business and are being bought with the view of immediate resale. Vans are, however, fixed assets for a delivery firm as these are used within the business for more than one accounting period for earning income and are not intended for sale to customers.

Example: Turning stock and debtors into cash within one year

4.2 Cash is used to buy goods which are sold. Sales on credit create debtors, but eventually cash is earned from the sales. Some, perhaps most, of the cash will then be used to replenish stocks.

4.3 The transactions described above could be shown as a **cash cycle**.

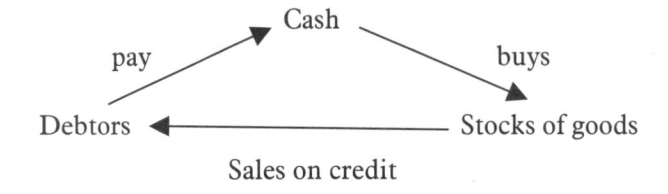

```
              Cash
       pay  ↗      ↘  buys
     Debtors  ←——————  Stocks of goods
                Sales on credit
```

5 LIABILITIES

5.1 In the case of liabilities, the main categories are as follows.
- **Current** liabilities
- **Long-term** liabilities

Current liabilities

> **KEY TERM**
>
> **Current liabilities** are debts of the business that must be paid within a fairly short period of time (by convention, within one year).

5.2 Examples of current liabilities include **loans** repayable in one year, **bank overdrafts**, **trade creditors** and **taxation payable**.

3: Balance sheet and profit and loss account

Activity 3.1

Try to classify the following items as long-term assets ('fixed assets'), short-term assets ('current assets') or liabilities.

(a) A PC used in the accounts department of a retail store
(b) A PC on sale in an office equipment shop
(c) Wages due to be paid to staff at the end of the week
(d) A van for sale in a motor dealer's showroom
(e) A delivery van used in a grocer's business
(f) An amount owing to a bank for a loan for the acquisition of a van, to be repaid over 9 months

Long-term liabilities

> **KEY TERM**
>
> **Long-term liabilities** are debts which are not payable within the 'short term' and so any liability which is not current must be long-term. Just as 'short-term' by convention means one year or less, 'long-term' means more than one year.

5.3 Examples of long-term liabilities are bank or venture capital fund loans **repayable after more than one year**.

Capital

5.4 The make-up of the 'capital' section of the balance sheet will vary, depending on the legal nature of the business. It will include **amounts invested** by the owner(s) in the business, plus **profits earned and retained** by the business. In the case of a limited company, amounts invested by the owners are in the form of **share capital**: this means that each investor contributes a sum of money to purchase a share in the overall ownership of the company.

6 THE PROFIT AND LOSS ACCOUNT

> **KEY TERM**
>
> The **profit and loss account** is a statement which matches the **revenue** earned in a period with the **costs** incurred in earning it. It is usual to distinguish between a **gross profit** (sales revenue less the cost of goods sold) and a **net profit** (being the gross profit less the expenses of selling, distribution, administration etc). If costs exceed revenue the business has made a **loss**.

6.1 Any organisation needs income (or revenue) from one or more sources. A **business** will **sell** its **goods or services** to **customers** in exchange for **cash**.

6.2 The income generated will be used to finance the activities of the business which incur **costs**: purchasing raw materials for use in manufacturing goods, purchasing ready-made goods for onward sale, purchasing equipment, paying expenses such as staff salaries, stationery, lighting and heating, rent and so on.

Part A: Introduction to transaction accounting

6.3 **Revenue** less **costs** result in a **profit or loss**. Periodically the organisation will prepare a **trading and profit and loss account**.

The trading, profit and loss account

6.4 Many businesses try to distinguish between a **gross profit** earned on trading, and a **net profit**. They therefore prepare a statement called a **trading, profit and loss account**.

(a) In the first part of the statement (the **trading account**) revenue from selling goods and services is compared with direct costs of acquiring, producing or supplying the goods sold to arrive at a **gross profit figure**.

(b) From this, deductions are made in the second half of the statement (the **profit and loss account**) in respect of indirect costs (overheads) to arrive at a **net profit figure**.

6.5 As with the balance sheet earlier in this chapter, it may help you to focus on the content of the profit and loss account if you have an example in front of you. The specimen below is based on a format prescribed for limited companies. As usual, other entities have greater flexibility in presentation.

XYZ
TRADING, PROFIT AND LOSS ACCOUNT
FOR THE YEAR ENDED 31 DECEMBER 20X7

	£	£
Sales (or turnover for a limited company)		X
Cost of sales		X
Gross profit		X
Selling costs	X	
Distribution costs	X	
Administration expenses	X	
		X
Profit retained for the current year		X

The trading account

> **KEY TERMS**
> - The **trading account** shows the gross profit for the accounting period.
> - **Gross profit** is the difference between:
>   ○ the value of sales; and
>   ○ the purchase cost or production cost of the goods sold.

The profit and loss account

> **KEY TERMS**
> - The **profit and loss account** shows the net profit of the business.
> - The **net profit** is:
>   ○ the gross profit **plus** any other income from sources other than the sale of goods and **minus** other 'overhead' expenses of the business which are not included in the cost of goods sold, mainly selling, distribution and administration expenses.

6.6 Typical expenses falling into the **overhead category** are as follows.

Overhead expenses	Include
Selling	Salaries of a sales director and sales management Salaries and commissions of salesmen Travelling and entertainment expenses of salesmen Marketing costs (eg advertising and sales promotion expenses) Discounts allowed to customers for early payment of their debts
Distribution	The costs of getting goods to customers, such as the costs of running and maintaining delivery vans
Administration	The expenses of providing management and administration for the business, eg rent and rates, insurance, stationery and postage

7 CAPITAL AND REVENUE EXPENDITURE

KEY TERMS

- **Capital expenditure** is expenditure which results in the acquisition of fixed assets, or an improvement in their earning capacity.
    - Capital expenditure on fixed assets results in the appearance of a fixed asset in the **balance sheet** of the business.
    - Capital expenditure is **not** charged as an expense in the **profit and loss account**.

- **Revenue expenditure** is expenditure which is incurred either:
    - for the purpose of the trade of the business, including expenditure classified as selling and distribution expenses, administration expenses and finance charges; or
    - to maintain the existing earning capacity of fixed assets, eg repairs to fixed assets.

Revenue expenditure is shown in the **profit and loss account of a period**, provided that it relates to the trading activity and sales of that particular period. If it carries over into the next period, revenue expenditure would appear as a **current asset** in the balance sheet.

7.1 EXAMPLE: REVENUE EXPENDITURE

If a business buys ten widgets for £200 (£20 each) and sells eight of them during an accounting period, it will have two widgets left at the end of the period. The full £200 is **revenue expenditure** but only (8 × £20) = £160 is a cost of goods sold during the period. The remaining £40 (cost of two units) will be included in the **balance sheet** in the stock of goods held - as a **current asset** valued at £40.

Part A: Introduction to transaction accounting

Capital income and revenue income

> **KEY TERMS**
>
> - **Capital income** is the proceeds from the sale of non-trading assets (ie proceeds from the sale of fixed assets). The profits (or losses) from the sale of fixed assets are included in the **profit and loss account** of a business, for the accounting period in which the sale takes place.
>
> - **Revenue income** is income derived from:
>   - the sale of trading assets, such as goods bought or made for resale; or
>   - rent, interest and dividends received from fixed assets held by the business.
>
>   Revenue income appears in the **profit and loss account**.

Additional capital, additional loans and the repayment of existing loans

7.2 The categorisation of capital and revenue items given above does not mention raising additional capital from the owner of the business, or raising and repaying loans. These are transactions which have one of the following results.

(a) Add to the cash **assets** of the business, with a corresponding addition to **capital** or a **liability**

(b) On repayment, reduce the **liabilities** (loan) and the **assets** (cash) of the business

From your understanding of the accounting equation, you should see that these transactions would be reported through the balance sheet, **not** the profit and loss account.

Why is the distinction between capital and revenue items important?

7.3 Since **revenue expenditure** and **capital expenditure** are accounted for in different ways (in the **profit and loss account** and **balance sheet** respectively), the correct and consistent calculation of profit for any accounting period depends on the correct and consistent classification of items as revenue or capital. Failure to classify items correctly will lead to the production of misleading profit figures.

Activity 3.2

Complete the missing words to ensure you fully understand the difference between capital and revenue items.

Revenue expenditure results from the purchase of goods and services that will either:

(a) be _____ fully in the accounting period in which they are _____, and so be a cost or expense in the trading, profit and loss account

(b) result in a _____ asset as at the end of the accounting period (because the goods or services have not yet been consumed or made use of)

Capital expenditure results in the purchase or improvement of _____ assets, which are assets that will provide benefits to the business in more than _____ accounting period, and which are not acquired with a view to being resold in the normal course of trade. The cost of purchased fixed assets is not charged to the trading, profit and loss account of the period in which the purchase occurs.

Activity 3.3

State whether each of the following items should be classified as 'capital' or 'revenue' expenditure or income for the purpose of preparing the trading, profit and loss account and the balance sheet of the business.

(a) Purchase of leasehold premises

(b) Solicitors' fees in connection with the purchase of leasehold premises

(c) Costs of adding extra storage capacity to a mainframe computer used by the business

(d) Computer repair and maintenance costs

(e) Profit on the sale of an office building

(f) Revenue from sales by credit card

(g) Cost of new machinery

(h) Customs duty charged on the machinery when imported into the country

(i) 'Carriage' costs of transporting the new machinery from the supplier's factory to the premises of the business purchasing the machinery

(j) Cost of installing the new machinery in the premises of the business

(k) Wages of the machine operators

Key learning points

- The purpose of this chapter has been to introduce in broad outline the characteristics of the balance sheet and the trading, profit and loss account.
- A **balance sheet** is a statement of the financial position of a business at a given moment in time.
- A **trading, profit and loss account** is a financial statement showing in detail how the profit or loss of a period has been made.
- A distinction is made in the balance sheet between **long-term liabilities** and **current liabilities**, and between **fixed assets** and **current assets**.
- **Fixed assets** are those acquired for long-term use within the business.
- 'Current' means 'within one year'. **Current assets** are expected to be converted into cash within one year. **Current liabilities** are debts which are payable within one year.
- An important distinction is made between **capital** and **revenue** items. If these are not identified correctly, then the resulting **profit figure** will be wrong and misleading.

Part A: Introduction to transaction accounting

Quick quiz

1. What is a balance sheet?
2. How long does a business keep a fixed asset?
3. What are current liabilities?
4. Is a bank overdraft a current liability?
5. What will be included in the 'capital' section of a company balance sheet?
6. What is a profit and loss account?
7. Distinguish between the trading account and the profit and loss account.
8. Distinguish between capital expenditure and revenue expenditure.

Answers to quick quiz

1. A balance sheet is a listing of asset and liability balances on a certain date. The balance sheet gives a 'snapshot' of the net worth of the company at a single point in time.
2. At least one accounting period and usually several.
3. Amounts owed which must be paid soon, usually within one year.
4. Yes, usually, because it is repayable on demand (in theory at least).
5. Share capital plus retained profits.
6. A profit and loss account matches revenue with the costs incurred in earning it.
7. The trading account shows the gross profit; the profit and loss account shows net profit (gross profit plus non-trading income, less overhead expenses).
8. Capital expenditure results in a fixed asset appearing on the balance sheet. Revenue expenditure is trading expenditure or expenditure in maintaining fixed assets, which appears in the profit and loss account.

Answers to activities

Answer 3.1

(a) Fixed asset
(b) Current asset
(c) Current liability
(d) Current asset
(e) Fixed asset
(f) Current liability

Note that the same item can be categorised differently in different businesses.

Answer 3.2

The missing words are: used, purchased, current, fixed, one.

Answer 3.3

(a) Capital expenditure

(b) The legal fees associated with the purchase of a property may be added to the purchase price and classified as capital expenditure

(c) Capital expenditure (enhancing an existing fixed asset)

(d) Revenue expenditure

3: Balance sheet and profit and loss account

(e) Capital income (net of the costs of sale)

(f) Revenue income

(g) Capital expenditure

(h) If customs duties are borne by the purchaser of the fixed asset, they may be added to the cost of the machinery and classified as capital expenditure

(i) Similarly, if carriage costs are paid for by the purchaser of the fixed asset, they may be included in the cost of the fixed asset and classified as capital expenditure

(j) Installation costs of a fixed asset are also added to the fixed asset's cost and classified as capital expenditure

(k) Revenue expenditure

Chapter 4 Recording, summarising and posting transactions

Chapter topic list

1. Recording business transactions: an overview
2. The sales day book
3. The purchase day book
4. The cash book
5. The general ledger
6. Double entry bookkeeping
7. Posting from the day books
8. The sales ledger
9. The purchase ledger
10. Control accounts
11. Accounting for VAT

The following study sessions are covered in this chapter

			Syllabus reference
1	(f)	Identify the key personnel involved in initiating, processing and completing transactions	1a
	(g)	Understand the need for effective control over transactions	1a
	(o)	Identify the personnel involved in preparing and authorising documents	1b
2	(a)	Understand the nature and function of books of prime entry	2a
	(d)	Identify the main types of ledger account	2a
3	(a)	Record a complete series of basic transactions within a double entry system	2a
6	(c)	Understand the general principles of VAT	4a
	(d)	Calculate VAT on transactions	4a

4: Recording, summarising and posting transactions

1 RECORDING BUSINESS TRANSACTIONS: AN OVERVIEW

Source documents

> **KEY TERM**
>
> **Source documents** are the source of all the information recorded by a business.

1.1 In the previous chapter we looked at the source documents which relate to sales and purchases (invoices and credit notes). Here are some other source documents.

- Petty cash vouchers
- Cheques received
- Cheque stubs (for cheques paid out)
- Wages, salary and PAYE records

These are described in Parts B and D of this Interactive Text.

Recording source documents

1.2 During the course of its business, a company sends out and receives many source documents. The details on these source documents need to be recorded, otherwise the business might forget to ask for some money, or forget to pay some, or even accidentally pay something twice. In other words, it needs to **keep records of source documents** - of transactions - so that it can keep tabs on what is going on.

1.3 Such records are made in **books of prime entry**.

> **KEY TERM**
>
> **Books of prime entry** form the record of all the documented transactions sent and received by the company. They are as follows.
>
> | Book of prime entry | Documents recorded | Summarised and posted to |
> |---|---|---|
> | Sales day book | Sales invoices, credit notes sent | Sales ledger/control account |
> | Sale returns day book | Sales returns, credit notes | Sales ledger/returns control a/c |
> | Purchase day book | Purchase invoices, credit notes received | Purchases ledger/control account |
> | Purchase returns day book | Purchase returns, credit notes received | Purchase ledger/ returns control a/c |
> | Cash book | Cash paid and received | General ledger |
> | Petty cash book | Notes and coin paid and received | General ledger |
> | Journal | Adjustments | General ledger |

Sales returns and purchase returns could be shown as bracketed figures in the sale day book and purchase day book respectively, instead of in separate books of prime entry.

Activity 4.1

State which books of prime entry the following transactions would be entered into.

(a) Your business pays A Brown (a supplier) £450
(b) You send D Smith (a customer) an invoice for £650

Part A: Introduction to transaction accounting

(c) You receive an invoice from A Brown for £300
(d) You pay D Smith £500
(e) F Jones (a customer) returns goods to the value of £250
(f) You return goods to J Green to the value of £504
(g) F Jones pays you £500

1.4 The **cash book** and **petty cash** book are covered in depth in Part B and the sales and purchase day books in Part C. However, they are introduced here, along with the **journal** (in Chapter 5), to enable you to understand the full system of recording, summarising, posting and presenting transactions.

Summarising source documents

1.5 Due to the volume of source documents, and the fact that they come from and are sent to a very large number of suppliers and customers, it is vital that the information in them is **summarised.** This is done in two ways.

Need for summary	Ledger used
Summaries need to be kept of all the transactions undertaken with an **individual** supplier or customer - invoices, credit notes, cash - so that a net amount due or owed can be calculated.	**Sales ledger** **Purchase ledger**
Summaries need to be kept of **all** the transactions undertaken with all suppliers and customers, so a total for debtors and a total for creditors can be calculated.	**General ledger** (a) Sales ledger control account (b) Purchase ledger control account

1.6 We will be looking at these in more detail later in this chapter, and in Part C.

Posting the ledgers

1.7 The diagram on page 61 shows how items are **posted** to (**entered in**) the ledgers, ultimately to arrive at the financial statements. Don't worry that some of the terms are unfamiliar currently - you will be able to trace through what is going on when you have completed this chapter.

> **Exam alert**
> A great deal of the material covered in this chapter could appear in various forms in the exam. For example you could be tested on this area as part of a 'business transactions', 'double entry', 'cash handling' or 'credit transactions' question. You must understand all the principles laid out in this chapter.

Personnel

1.8 In a small company there may be just one or two people dealing with all of the accounting transactions.

In a large company there will be a greater volume of transactions and larger sums of money involved. There will be a need for **separation of duties** for security purposes as well as to meet the demands of the workload.

4: Recording, summarising and posting transactions

A typical accounts department would have:

(a) A sales ledger controller

(b) A credit controller, responsible for collecting amounts owed. (These two functions may be combined.)

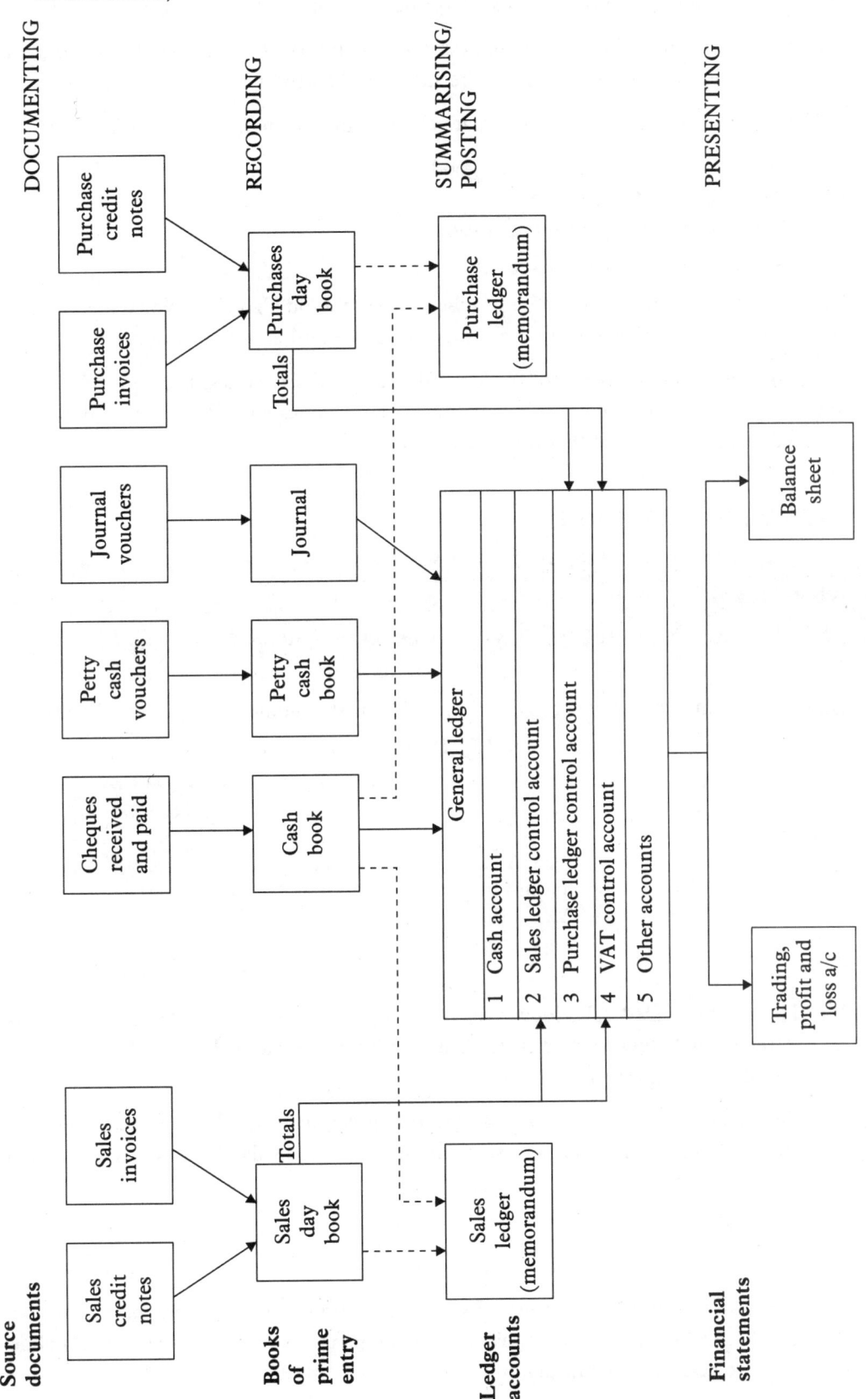

DOCUMENTING (Source documents)	Purchase credit notes; Purchase invoices; Journal vouchers; Petty cash vouchers; Cheques received and paid; Sales invoices; Sales credit notes
RECORDING (Books of prime entry)	Purchases day book; Journal; Petty cash book; Cash book; Sales day book
SUMMARISING/POSTING (Ledger accounts)	Purchase ledger (memorandum); General ledger (1 Cash account, 2 Sales ledger control account, 3 Purchase ledger control account, 4 VAT control account, 5 Other accounts); Sales ledger (memorandum)
PRESENTING (Financial statements)	Balance sheet; Trading, profit and loss a/c

- - - - ▶ Posting of individual amounts in memorandum personal accounts

Part A: Introduction to transaction accounting

(c) A purchase ledger (or bought ledger) controller

(d) An assistant accountant, or similar who will oversee the general ledger

(e) A payroll controller, if it is a large payroll

(f) An accountant, who will oversee all of the functions and prepare the accounts

Petty cash will probably be handled by the bought ledger controller or the assistant accountant, but payments will have to be authorised by the accountant.

The bought ledger controller will prepare cheques for payment after checking that:

(a) There is a purchase order for the goods
(b) The correct goods were received
(c) They were received in good conditions
(d) The invoice is correct.

Ideally, the person who placed the purchase order should sign the invoice to authorise it for payment. Only certain people in the company will be authorised to issue purchase orders.

Although the bought ledger controller will prepare the cheques, they are unlikely to be a signatory, and certainly not a sole signatory. The cheques will be signed by the accountant, who will check for himself that they are correct.

2 THE SALES DAY BOOK

> **KEY TERM**
>
> The **sales day book** is a list of all invoices sent out to **customers** each day.

2.1 An extract from a sales day book, ignoring VAT for the moment, might look like this.

SALES DAY BOOK

Date 20X7	Invoice number (2)	Customer	Sales ledger ref. (1)	Total amount invoiced £
Jan 10	247	Jones & Co	SL14	105.00
	248	Smith Ltd	SL 8	86.40
	249	Alex & Co	SL 6	31.80
	250	Enor College	SL 9	1,264.60
				1,487.80

(1) The column called 'sales ledger ref.' is a reference to a page for the individual customer in the **sales ledger**. It means, for example, that the sale to Jones & Co for £105 is also recorded on page 14 of the sales ledger.

(2) The invoice number is the **unique number** given to each sales invoice by the business's sales system. Listing them out sequentially in the sales day book helps us to see that all the invoices are included.

Sales analysis

2.2 Most businesses 'analyse' their sales. For example, suppose that the business sells boots and shoes, and that the sale to Smith was entirely boots, the sale to Alex was entirely shoes, and the other two sales were a mixture of both.

2.3 Then the sales day book might look like this.

SALES DAY BOOK

Date 20X7	Invoice	Customer	Sales ledger ref.	Total amount invoiced £	Boot sales £	Shoe sales £
Jan 10	247	Jones & Co	SL 14	105.00	60.00	45.00
	248	Smith Ltd	SL 8	86.40	86.40	
	249	Alex & Co	SL 6	31.80		31.80
	250	Enor College	SL 9	1,264.60	800.30	464.30
				1,487.80	946.70	541.10

This sort of analysis gives the managers of the business useful information which helps them to decide how best to run the business.

The sales returns day book

> **KEY TERM**
>
> When customers return goods for some reason, the returns are recorded in the **sales returns day book**.

2.4 An extract from the sales returns day book might look like this.

SALES RETURNS DAY BOOK

Date 20X7	Customer and goods	Sales ledger ref.	Amount £
30 April	Owen Plenty		
	3 pairs 'Texas' boots	SL 82	135.00

2.5 Not all sales returns day books analyse what goods were returned, but it makes sense to keep as complete a record as possible.

2.6 Sales returns could alternatively be shown as **bracketed figures in the sales day book,** so that a sales returns day book would not be needed.

Part A: Introduction to transaction accounting

3 THE PURCHASE DAY BOOK

> **KEY TERM**
>
> The **purchase day book** is the record of all the invoices received from **suppliers**.

3.1 An extract from a purchase day book might look like this (again, we have ignored VAT).

PURCHASE DAY BOOK

Date 20X7	Supplier (2)	Purchase ledger ref. (1)	Total amount invoiced £	Purchases (3) £	Expenses £
Mar 15	Cook & Co	PL 31	315.00	315.00	
	W Butler	PL 46	29.40	29.40	
	EEB	PL 42	116.80		116.80
	Show Fair Ltd	PL 12	100.00	100.00	
			561.20	444.40	116.80

(1) The 'purchase ledger ref.' is a reference to a page for the individual supplier in the purchase ledger. Again, we will see the purpose of this later in the chapter.

(2) There is no 'invoice number' column, because the purchase day book records **other people's invoices**, which have all sorts of different numbers. Sometimes, however, a purchase day book may allocate an internal number to an invoice.

(3) Like the sales day book, the purchase day book analyses the invoices which have been sent in. In this example, three of the invoices related to goods which the business intends to re-sell (called simply 'purchases') and the fourth invoice was an electricity bill.

The purchase returns day book

> **KEY TERM**
>
> The **purchase returns day book** is kept to record credit notes received in respect of goods which the business sends back to its suppliers.

3.2 The business might expect a credit note from the supplier. In the meantime, however, it might issue a debit note to the supplier, indicating the amount by which the business expects its total debt to the supplier to be reduced.

An extract from the purchase returns day book might look like this.

PURCHASE RETURNS DAY BOOK

Date 20X7	Supplier and goods	Purchase ledger ref.	Amount £
29 April	Boxes Ltd 300 cardboard boxes	PL 123	46.60

3.3 Again, purchase returns could be shown as **bracketed figures** in the purchase day book.

4 THE CASH BOOK

> **KEY TERM**
>
> The **cash book** is a book of prime entry, used to keep a cumulative record of money received and money paid out by the business via its bank account.

4.1 This could be money received **on the business premises** in notes, coins and cheques which are subsequently banked. There are also receipts and payments made by bank transfer, standing order, direct debit, BACS and, in the case of bank interest and charges, directly by the bank.

4.2 In its simplest form, a cash book consists of a single page divided into two halves by a vertical line. The left hand side of the page (the **debit** side) is used to record amounts of monies **received** by the business, while the right hand side (the **credit** side) is used to record **payments** of monies by the business. Periodically (perhaps once a month) the entries in the book are totalled and the **balance of cash** available to the business is determined.

4.3 It is usual to maintain one main cash book to record the amounts received and paid through the **business bank account**. The 'cash' referred to in the title of the book will therefore consist normally of cheques, rather than notes and coins, depending on the nature of the business. But most businesses need a supply of notes and coins to pay for small everyday expenses such as postage, tea and coffee and so on. These amounts are usually recorded in a separate book of prime entry called a **petty cash book**. We will look at the petty cash book in Chapter 11.

4.4 The simplified form of the cash book described above would very seldom be found in practice because it would not give enough detail about the nature of each receipt and payment. Most businesses instead use an **analysed cash book**. In this format each payment is recorded on the right hand side of the page not only in a single 'total' column, but also in one of a number of other columns with suitable headings such as 'Suppliers', 'Wages' and so on. Similarly, the left hand side of the page has columns in which cash receipts are analysed as 'Customers', 'Cash sales' and so on. One part of the cash book is used to record **receipts of cash**, and another part is used to **record payments**.

4.5 The best way to see how the cash book works is to follow through an example. Note that in this example we are continuing to ignore VAT.

4.6 EXAMPLE: CASH BOOK

At the beginning of 1 September, Warren Miles had £900 in the bank. During 1 September 20X7, Warren Miles had the following receipts and payments.

(a) Cash sale: receipt of £80
(b) Payment from credit customer Anna: £400 less discount allowed £20
(c) Payment from credit customer Milly: £720
(d) Payment from credit customer Egg: £1,000 less discount allowed £40
(e) Cash sale: receipt of £150
(f) Cash received for sale of machine: £200
(g) Payment to supplier Ferdie: £130 less discount received £10
(h) Payment to supplier Kiera: £330 less discount received £20
(i) Payment of telephone bill: £400

Part A: Introduction to transaction accounting

(j) Payment of gas bill: £280
(k) Payment of £1,500 to Joe for new plant and machinery

If you look through these transactions, you will see that six of them are receipts and five of them are payments.

4.7 SOLUTION

The cash book for Warren Miles would be as follows. Do not worry too much about the details at the moment - we will follow them through later on in this text.

4.8 Receipts and payments are listed out on either side of the cash book - **receipts** on the **left** (debit **asset**) and **payments** on the **right** (credit **asset**).

Both sides have columns for these details.

- Date
- Narrative
- Reference
- Total

Each side has a number of **columns for further analysis** - receipts from debtors, cash sales and other receipts, payments to creditors, expenses and fixed assets for payments.

Balancing the cash book

4.9 At the beginning of the day there is a debit **opening balance** of £900. During the day, the total receipts and payments were as follows.

4: Recording, summarising and posting transactions

WARREN MILES: CASH BOOK

RECEIPTS

Date 20X7	Narrative	Ref	Discount allowed	Total	Receipts from debtors	Cash sales	Other
01-Sep	Balance b/d			900.00			
	(a) Cash sale			80.00		80.00	
	(b) Debtor pays: Anna	SL96	20.00	380.00	380.00		
	(c) Debtor pays: Milly	SL632		720.00	720.00		
	(d) Debtor pays: Egg	SL501	40.00	960.00	960.00		
	(e) Cash sale			150.00		150.00	
	(f) Fixed asset sale			200.00			200.00
			60.00	3,390.00	2,060.00	230.00	200.00
				780.00			
02-Sep	Balance b/d			780.00			

PAYMENTS

Date 20X7	Narrative	Ref	Discount received	Total	Payments to creditors	Expenses	Fixed assets
01-Sep	(g) Creditor paid: Ferdie	PL543	10.00 *	120.00	120.00		
	(h) Creditor paid: Kiera	PL76	20.00 *	310.00	310.00		
	(i) Telephone expense			400.00		400.00	
	(j) Gas expense			280.00		280.00	
	(k) Plant & machinery purchase			1,500.00			1,500.00
			30.00	2,610.00	430.00	680.00	1,500.00
	Balance c/d			780.00			
				3,390.00	430.00	680.00	1,500.00

* Discount received: see also Chapter 10 Sections 2.4 and 2.5 and Chapter 16 Section 2.6

Part A: Introduction to transaction accounting

	£
Opening balance	900
Receipts	2,490
	3,390
Payments	(2,610)
Closing balance	780

The **closing balance** of £780 represents the excess of receipts over payments. It means that Warren Miles still has cash available at the end of the day, so he 'carries it down' at the end of 1 September from the payments side of the cash book, and 'brings it down' at the beginning of 2 September to the receipts side of the cash book. Accountants generally use the terminology 'balance brought down' or 'balance b/d' and 'balance carried down' or 'balance c/d' instead of 'opening balance' and 'closing balance'.

Balance b/d	Balance brought down	Opening balance
Balance c/d	Balance carried down	Closing balance

Discounts

4.10 The discount allowed column on Warren Miles's cash receipts page shows **how cash discounts are recorded**.

(a) Discounts allowed on sales are shown in a separate column which has nothing to do with the actual monies received, it is a **memorandum** column.

(b) The discount allowed column is required to show why the **full amount of a debt** has not been received from a customer.

(c) A list of the debts owed to the company will be recorded in the **sales ledger**. The individual discounts allowed will be posted to these individual's ledger accounts, thus clearing the **total** debt.

4.11 EXAMPLE

Katy buys goods from Nick for £1,200. She will receive a discount if she pays within two weeks. Show the accounting entries in the cash book and receivables ledger in Nick's accounting records.

4.12 SOLUTION

In Nick's cash book the actual cash received will be part of the double entry with the discount recorded in the memorandum column in the cash book.

The memorandum column is helpful in explaining why the total debt is not received in full.

The discount will, however, be posted in the debtors' account in the nominal ledger thus clearing the whole debt.

	£	£
DEBIT Debtors	1200	
CREDIT Sales		1200

Being sale for £1,200 to Katy

	£	£
DEBIT Cash	1100	
CREDIT Debtors		1100

Being cash received from Katy

	£	£
DEBIT Discount allowed	100	
CREDIT Debtors		100

Being discount allowed in final settlement

Bank statements

4.13 Weekly or monthly, a business will receive a **bank statement**. Bank statements should be used to check that the amount shown as a balance in the cash book agrees with the amount on the bank statement, and that no cash has 'gone missing'. A business should reconcile its cash book with the bank statement. The reconciliation of the cash book with the bank statement is the subject of Chapter 12.

Activity 4.2

Which of the following will *not* be entered in the cash book?

(a) Cheque received
(b) Payment to sales ledger customers
(c) Supplier's invoice
(d) Credit note
(e) Debit note
(f) Bank charges debited to the bank account
(g) Overdraft interest debited to the bank account
(h) Payment for a fixed asset purchased on credit
(i) Refund received from a supplier
(j) Depreciation

Petty cash book

4.14 Most businesses keep a small amount of cash on the premises to make occasional **small payments in cash** - eg to pay the milkman, to buy a few postage stamps, or to pay for some bus or taxi fares. This is often called the **cash float**. It can also be the resting place for occasional small receipts, eg cash paid by a visitor to make a phone call.

KEY TERM

The **petty cash book** is the book of prime entry which keeps a cumulative record of the small amounts of cash received into and paid out of the cash float.

4.15 There are usually more payments than receipts, and petty cash must be 'topped-up' with cash from the business bank account. We will see how this is done in Chapter 11.

5 THE GENERAL LEDGER

KEY TERM

The **general ledger** is the accounting record which summarises the financial affairs of a business. It contains details of assets, liabilities and capital, income and expenditure and so profit and loss. It consists of a large number of different **ledger accounts**, each account having its own purpose or 'name' and an identity or code. Another name for the general ledger is the **nominal ledger**.

Part A: Introduction to transaction accounting

5.1 Transactions are **posted** to accounts in the general ledger from the books of prime entry.

> **KEY TERM**
>
> **Posting** means to enter transactions in ledger accounts in the general ledger from books of prime entry. Often this is done in total (ie all sales invoices in the sales day book for a day are added up and the total is posted to the total debtors account) but individual transactions are also posted (eg fixed assets).

5.2 Examples of ledger accounts in the general ledger include the following.

Ledger account	Fixed asset	Current asset	Current liability	Long-term liability	Capital	Expense	Income
Plant and machinery at cost	✓						
Motor vehicles at cost	✓						
Proprietor's capital					✓		
Stocks: raw materials		✓					
Stocks: finished goods		✓					
Total debtors		✓					
Total creditors			✓				
Wages and salaries						✓	
Rent and rates						✓	
Advertising expenses						✓	
Bank charges						✓	
Motor expenses						✓	
Telephone expenses						✓	
Sales							✓
Cash		✓					
Bank overdraft			✓				
Bank loan				✓			

The format of a ledger account

5.3 If a ledger account were to be kept in an actual book rather than as a computer record, its **format** might be as follows.

ADVERTISING EXPENSES

Date	Narrative	Ref.	£	Date	Narrative	Ref.	£
20X7							
15 April	JFK Agency for quarter to 31 March	PL 348	2,500				

Only one entry in the account is shown here, because the example is introduced simply to illustrate the general format of a ledger account.

There are two sides to the account, and an account heading on top, and so it is convenient to think in terms of 'T' accounts.

(a) On top of the account is its name
(b) There is a left hand side, or **debit** side
(c) There is a right hand side, or **credit** side

NAME OF ACCOUNT

DEBIT SIDE	£	CREDIT SIDE	£

5.4 We have already seen this with Warren Miles's cash book. We will now go on to use the cash book to demonstrate double-entry.

6 DOUBLE ENTRY BOOK-KEEPING

6.1 In Chapter 2 we saw that double entry book-keeping allowed us to keep the accounting equation always in balance, because **every financial transaction gives rise to two accounting entries, one a debit and the other a credit**.

DEBIT To own/have ↓	CREDIT To owe ↓
AN ASSET INCREASES eg new office furniture	AN ASSET DECREASES eg pay out cash
CAPITAL/ A LIABILITY DECREASES eg pay a creditor	CAPITAL/A LIABILITY INCREASES eg buy goods on credit
INCOME DECREASES eg cancel a sale	INCOME INCREASES eg make a sale
AN EXPENSE INCREASES eg incur advertising costs	AN EXPENSE DECREASES eg cancel a purchase
Left hand side	Right hand side

Cash transactions: double entry

6.2 Students coming to the subject for the first time often have difficulty in knowing where to begin. A good starting point is the cash book, which is simply the book of prime entry for the general ledger cash account in which receipts and payments of cash are recorded.

Remember that the **cash book** is a book of prime entry while the **cash account** is the ledger account in the general ledger. It is the cash account which is part of the double entry system.

Book of prime entry		Ledger account in general ledger
Cash book	Summary posted to	Cash account

In practice many businesses using a computerised accounts system have an integrated cash book which means that it is both a book of prime entry **and** a ledger account.

6.3 The rule to remember about the cash account is as follows.

(a) A **cash payment** is a **credit entry** in the cash account. Here the **asset** (cash) **is decreasing**. Cash may be paid out, for example, to pay an expense (such as rates) or to purchase an asset (such as a machine). The **matching debit entry** is therefore made in the appropriate **expense** account or **asset** account.

Part A: Introduction to transaction accounting

(b) A **cash receipt** is a **debit entry** in the cash account. Here the **asset** (cash) **is increasing**. Cash might be received, for example, by a retailer who makes a cash sale. The **matching credit entry** would then be made in the **sales** account.

Cash transactions	DR	CR
Sell goods for cash	Cash	Sales
Buy goods for cash	Purchases	Cash

6.4 EXAMPLE: DOUBLE ENTRY FOR CASH TRANSACTIONS

In the cash book of a business, the following transactions have been recorded.

(a) A cash sale (ie a receipt) of £2
(b) Payment of a rent bill totalling £150
(c) Buying some goods for cash at £100
(d) Buying some shelves for cash at £200

How would these four transactions be posted to the ledger accounts? For that matter, which ledger accounts should they be posted to? Don't forget that each transaction will be posted twice, in accordance with the rule of double entry.

6.5 SOLUTION

(a) The two sides of the transaction are
  (i) cash is received (**debit** entry in the cash account)
  (ii) sales increase by £2 (**credit** entry in the sales account)

CASH ACCOUNT

	£		£
Sales a/c	2		

SALES ACCOUNT

	£		£
		Cash a/c	2

(Note how the entry in the cash account is cross-referenced to the sales account and vice-versa. This enables a person looking at one of the accounts to trace where the other half of the double entry can be found.)

(b) The two sides of the transaction are
  (i) cash is paid (**credit** entry in the cash account)
  (ii) rent expense increases by £150 (**debit** entry in the rent account)

CASH ACCOUNT

	£		£
		Rent a/c	150

RENT ACCOUNT

	£		£
Cash a/c	150		

4: Recording, summarising and posting transactions

(c) The two sides of the transaction are
   (i) cash is paid (**credit** entry in the cash account)
   (ii) purchases increase by £100 (**debit** entry in the purchases account)

CASH ACCOUNT

	£		£
		Purchases a/c	100

PURCHASES ACCOUNT

	£		£
Cash a/c	100		

(d) The two sides of the transaction are
   (i) cash is paid (**credit** entry in the cash account)
   (ii) assets - in this case, shelves - increase by £200 (**debit** entry in shelves account)

CASH ACCOUNT

	£		£
		Shelves a/c	200

SHELVES (ASSET) ACCOUNT

	£		£
Cash a/c	200		

If all four of these transactions related to the same business, the **summary cash account** of that business would end up looking as follows.

CASH ACCOUNT

	£		£
Sales a/c	2	Rent a/c	150
		Purchases a/c	100
		Shelves a/c	200

Activity 4.3

In the cash book of a business, the following transactions are recorded on 7 April 20X7.

(a) A cash sale (ie a receipt) of £60
(b) Payment of a rent bill totalling £4,500
(c) Buying some goods for cash at £3,000
(d) Buying some shelves for cash at £6,000

Task

Draw the appropriate ledger ('T') accounts and show how these four transactions would be posted to them.

Credit transactions: double entry

6.6 Not all transactions are settled immediately in cash. A business might purchase goods from its suppliers on **credit terms**, so that the suppliers would be **creditors** of the business until settlement was made in cash. Equally, the business might grant credit terms to its customers who would then be **debtors** of the business. Clearly no entries can be made in the cash book

Part A: Introduction to transaction accounting

when a credit transaction occurs, because initially no cash has been received or paid. Where then can the details of the transactions be entered?

6.7 The solution to this problem is to use **ledger accounts for debtors and creditors.**

CREDIT TRANSACTIONS	DR	CR
Sell goods on credit terms	Debtors	Sales
Receive cash from debtor	Cash	Debtor
Net effect = cash transaction	Cash	Sales
Buy goods on credit terms	Purchases	Creditors
Pay cash to creditor	Creditors	Cash
Net effect = cash transaction	Purchases	Cash

The net effect in the ledger accounts is the same as for a cash transaction - the only difference is that there has been a time delay during which the debtor/creditor accounts have been used.

6.8 EXAMPLE: CREDIT TRANSACTIONS

Recorded in the sales day book and the purchase day book are the following transactions.

(a) The business sells goods on credit to a customer Mr A for £2,000.
(b) The business buys goods on credit from a supplier B Ltd for £100.

How and where are these transactions posted in the ledger accounts?

6.9 SOLUTION

(a)

DEBTORS ACCOUNT

	£		£
Sales a/c	2,000		

SALES ACCOUNT

	£		£
		Debtors account (Mr A)	2,000

(b)

CREDITORS ACCOUNT

	£		£
		Purchases a/c	100

PURCHASES ACCOUNT

	£		£
Creditors a/c (B Ltd)	100		

6.10 EXAMPLE CONTINUED: WHEN CASH IS PAID TO CREDITORS OR BY DEBTORS

Suppose that, in the example above, the business paid £100 to B Ltd one month after the goods were acquired. The two sides of this new transaction are

(a) cash is paid (**credit** entry in the cash account)
(b) the amount owing to creditors is reduced (**debit** entry in the creditors account)

CASH ACCOUNT

	£		£
		Creditors a/c (B Ltd)	100

CREDITORS ACCOUNT

	£		£
Cash a/c	100		

6.11 If we now bring together the two parts of this example, the original purchase of goods on credit and the eventual settlement in cash, we find that the accounts appear as follows.

CASH ACCOUNT

	£		£
		Creditors a/c	100

PURCHASES ACCOUNT

	£		£
Creditors a/c	100		

CREDITORS ACCOUNT

	£		£
Cash a/c	100	Purchases a/c	100

6.12 The **two entries in the creditors account cancel each other out**, indicating that no money is owing to creditors any more. We are left with a credit entry of £100 in the cash account and a debit entry of £100 in the purchases account. These are exactly the entries which would have been made to record a **cash** purchase of £100. This is what we would expect: after the business has paid off its creditors it is in exactly the position of a business which has made cash purchases of £100, and the accounting records reflect this similarity.

6.13 Similar reasoning applies when a **customer settles his debt**. In the example above when Mr A pays his debt of £2,000 the two sides of the transaction are

(a) cash is received (debit entry in the cash account)
(b) the amount owed by debtors is reduced (credit entry in the debtors account)

CASH ACCOUNT

	£		£
Debtors a/c (Mr A)	2,000		

Part A: Introduction to transaction accounting

DEBTORS ACCOUNT

	£		£
		Cash a/c	2,000

The accounts recording this sale to, and payment by, Mr A now appear as follows.

CASH ACCOUNT

	£		£
Debtors a/c	2,000		

SALES ACCOUNT

	£		£
		Debtors a/c	2,000

DEBTORS ACCOUNT

	£		£
Sales a/c	2,000	Cash a/c	2,000

6.14 The **two entries in the debtors account cancel each other out**, while the entries in the cash account and sales account reflect the same position as if the sale had been made for cash.

Activity 4.4

Identify the debit and credit entries in the following transactions.

(a) Bought a machine on credit from A, cost £8,000
(b) Bought goods on credit from B, cost £500
(c) Sold goods on credit to C, value £1,200
(d) Paid D (a creditor) £300
(e) Collected £180 from E, a debtor
(f) Paid wages £4,000
(g) Received rent bill of £700 from landlord G
(h) Paid rent of £700 to landlord G
(i) Paid insurance premium £90

Activity 4.5

Your business, which is not registered for VAT, has the following transactions.

(a) The sale of goods on credit
(b) Credit notes to credit customers upon the return of faulty goods
(c) Daily cash takings paid into the bank

Task

For each transaction identify clearly the following.

(a) The original document(s)
(b) The book of prime entry for the transaction
(c) The way in which the data will be incorporated into the double entry system

7 POSTING FROM THE DAY BOOKS

Sales day book to total debtors account

7.1 In Paragraph 2.3 we used the following example of four transactions entered into the sales day book.

SALES DAY BOOK

Date 20X7	Invoice	Customer	Sales ledger ref.	Total amount invoiced £	Boot sales £	Shoe sales £
Jan 10	247	Jones & Co	SL 14	105.00	60.00	45.00
	248	Smith Ltd	SL 8	86.40	86.40	
	249	Alex & Co	SL 6	31.80		31.80
	250	Enor College	SL 9	1,264.60	800.30	464.30
				1,487.80	946.70	541.10

7.2 How do we post these transactions to the general ledger, and which accounts do we use in the general ledger?

7.3 We would post the total of the **total amount invoiced column** to the **debit** side of the **total debtors account** (often called the **sales ledger control account**). The **credit** entries would be to the different **sales accounts,** in this case, boot sales and shoe sales.

TOTAL DEBTORS ACCOUNT

	£		£
Boot sales	946.70		
Shoes sales	541.10		
	1,487.80		

BOOT SALES

	£		£
		Total debtors	946.70

SHOE SALES

	£		£
		Total debtors	541.10

7.4 That is why the analysis of sales is kept. Exactly the same reasoning lies behind the analyses kept in other books of prime entry.

7.5 So how do we know how much we are owed by individual debtors? The answer is that we keep two sets of accounts running in parallel - the **total debtors account** in the general ledger and the memorandum **sales ledger** (individual debtor accounts). **Only the total debtors account is actually part of the double-entry system,** but **individual** debtors' transactions are posted to the sales ledger from the sales day book.

Part A: Introduction to transaction accounting

Purchases day book to total creditors account

7.6 Here is the page of the purchases day book which we saw in Paragraph 3.1.

PURCHASE DAY BOOK

Date 20X7	Supplier	Purchase ledger ref.)	Total amount invoiced £	Purchases £	Expenses £
Mar 15	Cook & Co	PL 31	315.00	315.00	
	W Butler	PL 46	29.40	29.40	
	EEB	PL 42	116.80		116.80
	Show Fair Ltd	PL 12	100.00	100.00	
			561.20	444.40	116.80

7.7 This time we will post the total of the **total amount invoiced** column to the **credit** side of the **total creditors account** (or purchase ledger control account) in the general ledger. The **debit** entries are to the different expense accounts, in this case purchases and electricity.

TOTAL CREDITORS ACCOUNT

	£		£
		Purchases	444.40
		Electricity	116.80
			561.20

PURCHASES

	£		£
Total creditors	444.40		

ELECTRICITY

	£		£
Total creditors	116.80		

7.8 Again, we keep a separate record of how much we owe individual creditors by keeping two sets of accounts running in parallel - the **total creditors account** in the general ledger, part of the double-entry system, and the memorandum **purchase ledger** (individual creditors' accounts). Individual creditors' transactions are entered in their purchase ledger account from the purchase day book.

7.9 **Section summary**

CREDIT TRANSACTIONS	DR		CR	
	Memorandum	*General ledger**	*General ledger**	*Memorandum*
Sell goods to Enor College	Sales ledger: Enor College	Total debtors a/c	Sales	-
Receive cash from Enor College	-	Cash a/c	Total debtors a/c	Sales ledger: Enor College
Buy goods from Cook & Co	-	Purchases	Total creditors a/c	Purchase ledger: Cook & Co
Pay cash to Cook & Co	Purchase ledger: Cook & Co	Total creditors a/c	Cash a/c	-

*Individual transactions included in **totals** posted from books of prime entry.

4: Recording, summarising and posting transactions

7.10 In the next three sections of this chapter we shall look at the sales and purchase ledgers, and the total accounts, in more detail.

8 THE SALES LEDGER

Impersonal accounts and personal accounts

8.1 Accounts in the general ledger (ledger accounts) relate to types of income, expense, asset, liability - rent, rates, sales, debtors, creditors etc - rather than to the person to whom the money is paid or from whom it is received. They are therefore called **impersonal accounts**. However, there is also a need for **personal accounts**, most commonly for debtors and creditors, and these are contained in the sales ledger and purchase ledger.

> **KEY TERM**
>
> **Personal accounts** include details of transactions which have already been summarised in ledger accounts (eg sales invoices are recorded in sales and total debtors, payments to creditors in the cash and total creditors accounts). **The personal accounts do not therefore form part of the double entry system**, as otherwise transactions would be recorded twice over (ie two debits and two credits for each transaction). They are **memorandum** accounts only.

Personal accounts in the sales ledger

> **KEY TERM**
>
> The **sales ledger** consists of a number of personal **debtor** accounts. They are separate accounts for each individual customer, and they enable a business to keep a continuous record of how much a debtor owes the business at any time. The sales ledger is often also known as the **debtors ledger**.

8.2 The **sales day book** provides a chronological record of invoices sent out by a business to credit customers. For many businesses, this might involve very large numbers of invoices per day or per week. The same customer might appear in several different places in the sales day book, for purchases he has made on credit at different times. So at any point in time, a customer may owe money on several unpaid invoices.

8.3 In addition to keeping a chronological record of invoices, a business should also keep a record of how much money each individual credit customer owes, and what this total debt consists of. The need for a **personal account for each customer** is therefore a practical one.

(a) A customer might **telephone**, and ask how much he currently owes. Staff must be able to tell him.

(b) It is a common practice to send out **statements** to credit customers at the end of each month, showing how much they still owe, and itemising new invoices sent out and payments received during the month.

(c) The managers of the business will want to keep a check on the **credit position** of an individual customer, and to ensure that no customer is exceeding his credit limit by purchasing more goods.

Part A: Introduction to transaction accounting

(d) Most important is the need to **match payments received against debts owed**. If a customer makes a payment, the business must be able to set off the payment against the customer's debt and establish how much he still owes on balance.

8.4 Sales ledger accounts are written up as follows.

(a) When individual entries are made in the sales day book (invoices sent out), they are subsequently also made in the **debit side** of the relevant customer account in the sales ledger.

(b) Similarly, when individual entries are made in the cash book (payments received), or in the sales returns day book, they are also made in the **credit side** of the relevant customer account.

8.5 Each customer account is given a reference or code number, and it is that reference which is the 'sales ledger folio' in the **sales day book** and the **cash book**. Amounts are **entered** from the sales day book and the cash book into the sales ledger.

8.6 Here is an example of how a sales ledger account is laid out.

ENOR COLLEGE   A/c no: SL 9

		£			£
10.1.X7	Balance b/d	250.00			
10.1.X7	Sales - SDB 48				
	(invoice no 250)	1,264.60	10.1.X7	Balance c/d	1,514.60
		1,514.60			1,514.60
11.1.X7	Balance b/d	1,514.60			

8.7 The debit side of this personal account, then, shows amounts owed by Enor College. When Enor pays some of the money it owes it will be recorded in the cash book (receipts) and this receipt will subsequently be posted individually to the **credit** side of the personal account, the **credit** side of the total debtors account (as part of a total) and the **debit** side of the cash account (as part of a total). For example, if the college paid £250 on 10.1.X7, it would appear as follows.

ENOR COLLEGE   A/c no: SL 9

		£			£
10.1.X7	Balance b/d	250.00	10.1.X7	Cash	250.00
10.1.X7	Sales - SDB 48				
	(invoice no 250)	1,264.60	10.1.X7	Balance c/d	1,264.60
		1,514.60			1,514.60
11.1.X7	Balance b/d	1,264.60			

The opening balance owed by Enor College on 11.1.X7 is now £1,264.60 instead of £1,514.60, because of the £250 receipt which came in on 10.1.X7.

8.8 The sales ledger is covered in more detail in Part C of this Text on credit transactions.

9 THE PURCHASE LEDGER

KEY TERM

The **purchase ledger**, like the sales ledger, consists of a number of **personal creditor accounts**. These are separate accounts for each individual supplier, and they enable a business to keep a continuous record of how much it owes each supplier at any time. The purchase ledger is often known as the **bought ledger** or the **creditors ledger**.

4: Recording, summarising and posting transactions

9.1 After transactions are recorded in the purchase day book, cash book, or purchase returns day book - ie after entries are made in the books of prime entry - they are also entered in the relevant supplier account in the purchase ledger. The **double entry posting,** however, is to the **total creditors account** and the **cash account**.

9.2 Here is an example of how a purchase ledger personal account is laid out.

	COOK & CO			A/c no: PL 31
	£			£
15.3.X7 Balance c/d	515.00	15.3.X7	Balance b/d	200.00
		15.3.X7	Invoice received PDB 37	315.00
	515.00			515.00
		16 3.X7	Balance b/d	515.00

9.3 The credit side of this personal account, then, shows amounts owing to Cook & Co. If the business paid Cook & Co some money, it would be entered into the cash book (payments) and subsequently be entered individually into the **debit** side of the personal account, and posted to the **debit** side of the total creditors account (as part of a total) and the **credit** side of the cash account (as part of a total). For example, if the business paid Cook & Co £100 on 15 March 20X7, it would appear as follows.

	COOK & CO			A/c no: PL 31
	£			£
15.3.X7 Cash	100.00	15.3.X7	Balance b/d	200.00
15.3.X7 Balance c/d	415.00	15.3.X7	Invoice received PDB 37	315.00
	515.00			515.00
		16.3.X7	Balance b/d	415.00

9.4 The opening balance owed to Cook & Co on 16.3.X7 is now £415.00 instead of £515.00 because of the £100 payment made during 15.3.X7.

9.5 The purchase ledger is covered in more detail in Part C of this text on credit transactions.

10 CONTROL ACCOUNTS

10.1 So far we have talked about the total debtors and the total creditors accounts being part of the double entry system in the general ledger, and effectively duplicating the entries to the sales ledger and purchase ledger respectively. So why do we need them? The answer is that they act as **control accounts.**

KEY TERMS

- A **control account** is an account in the general ledger in which a record is kept of the **total** value of a number of similar but individual items. Control accounts are used chiefly for debtors and creditors. **They should agree with the total of the individual balances** and act as a check to ensure that all transactions have been recorded correctly in the individual ledger accounts.

- The **sales ledger control account** (also known as the **total debtors account**) is a control account in which records are kept of transactions involving all debtors **in total**. It is posted with **totals** from the **sales day book** and the **cash book**. The balance on the total debtors account at any time will be the total amount due to the business at that time from its debtors, and will agree with the total of the sales ledger accounts.

Part A: Introduction to transaction accounting

> - The **purchase ledger control account** (also known as the **total creditors account**) is an account in which records are kept of transactions involving all creditors **in total**, being posted with **totals** from the **purchase day book** and the **cash book**. The balance on the total creditors account at any time will be the total amount owed by the business at that time to its creditors, and will agree with the total of the purchase ledger accounts.

10.2 Note that it is the **control account balances** which will appear in the **final accounts** of the business. The sales ledger and purchase ledger act as memoranda for the list of individual account balances.

10.3 Although control accounts are used mainly in accounting for debtors and creditors, they can also be kept for other items, such as **stocks** of goods, **wages and salaries** and **VAT**. The same principles apply to all the other control accounts in the general ledger.

10.4 Control accounts are covered in more detail in Chapter 17.

10.5 **Section summary**

Control accounts	Posted from	With	Agrees with	Part of general ledger double entry?
Debtors control a/c	Sales day book Sales returns day book Cash book	Totals	Sales ledger balances in total	✓
Creditors control a/c	Purchase day book Purchase returns day book Cash book	Totals	Purchase ledger balances in total	✓

Memorandum accounts	Posted from	With	Agrees with	Part of general ledger double entry?
Sales ledger	As for control a/c	Individual transactions	Debtors control a/c	✗
Purchase ledger	As for control a/c	Individual transactions	Creditors control a/c	✗

Activity 4.6

Sally Webster runs her own business as a sole trader. She has adopted an integrated manual system of accounting and has divided up the various accounts to form a Cash Book, a Sales Ledger, a Purchases Ledger (all of which are part of the double entry) and a General Ledger. The following transactions take place.

(a) R Sullivan, the landlord, is paid £2,300 rent by cheque. The liability had not previously been accounted for.

(b) £395 of goods are sold to L Battersby on credit.

(c) A credit note for £85 is issued to B Turpin for goods returned.

(d) £2,345 of goods are purchased for resale from Gilroy Ltd on credit.

4: Recording, summarising and posting transactions

(e) Equipment costing £12,500 is purchased by the business by cheque.

(f) An invoice for £86 is received being the installation charge for the equipment. A cheque is issued for this amount.

(g) The £2,345 owing to Gilroy Ltd is paid by cheque.

Task

For each transaction identify the following clearly.

(a) The name of the account to be debited.
(b) The ledger in which the account to be debited is located.
(c) The name of the account to be credited.
(d) The ledger in which the account to be credited is located.

Activity 4.7

(a) Name **five** accounts which may be found in the general ledger.
(b) Explain what **control accounts** are and what they are used for.

---

11 ACCOUNTING FOR VAT

11.1 The topic of VAT was introduced in Chapter 1 of this text. Now that you know about double entry and the books of prime entry, it is appropriate to outline how VAT is accounted for.

> **Exam alert**
>
> Your syllabus and Teaching Guide refer to a 'sales tax', of which VAT, in the UK, is an example.

Profit and loss account

11.2 A business does not keep the output VAT it charges - it pays it back to Customs & Excise. It therefore follows that its **records of sales should not include VAT.**

11.3 EXAMPLE: ACCOUNTING FOR OUTPUT VAT

If a business sells goods for £600 + £105 VAT, ie for £705 gross price, the sales account should only record the £600 excluding VAT. The accounting entries for the sale would be as follows.

DEBIT	Cash **or** trade debtors	£705	
CREDIT	Sales		£600
CREDIT	VAT account (output VAT)		£105

11.4 Similarly, the business does not want to show input VAT paid on purchases as a cost of the business - it must reclaim it from C&E. However, the cost of purchases in the profit and loss account may or may not include the 'input' VAT paid, depending on whether or not the input VAT is recoverable.

(a) If input VAT is **recoverable**, the cost of purchases should exclude the VAT. For example, if a business purchases goods on credit for £400 + recoverable VAT £70, the transaction would be recorded as follows.

DEBIT	Purchases	£400	
DEBIT	VAT account (input VAT)	£70	
CREDIT	Trade creditors		£470

Part A: Introduction to transaction accounting

(b) If the input VAT is **not recoverable**, the cost of purchases must include the tax, because it is the business itself which must bear the cost of the tax.

DEBIT	Purchases	£470
CREDIT	Trade creditors	£470

When is VAT accounted for?

11.5 VAT is accounted for **when it first arises** - when recording **credit purchases/sales in credit transactions**, and when recording **cash received or paid in cash transactions**.

VAT in credit transactions

11.6 When a business makes a credit sale the total amount invoiced, including VAT, will be recorded in the **sales day book**. The analysis columns will then separate the VAT from the sales income of the business as follows.

Date	Total	Sales income	VAT
	£	£	£
A Detter and Sons	235	200	35

11.7 When a business is invoiced by a supplier the total amount payable, including VAT, will be recorded in the **purchase day book**. The analysis columns will then separate the recoverable input VAT from the purchase cost to the business as follows.

Date	Total	Purchase cost	VAT
	£	£	£
A Splier (Merchants)	188	160	28

11.8 When debtors pay what they owe, or creditors are paid, there is no need then to show the VAT in an analysis column of the cash book, because input and output VAT were recorded when the sale or purchase was made, not when the debt is settled.

VAT in cash transactions

11.9 VAT charged on **cash sales** or VAT paid on **cash purchases will be analysed in a separate column of the cash book**. This is because output VAT, having just arisen from the cash sale, must be credited to the VAT account. Similarly, input VAT paid on cash purchases, having just arisen, must be debited to the VAT account.

11.10 For example, the cash book for Warren Miles which we saw in Section 4 of this chapter would be written up as shown on page 86 if items (a), (e) and new item (l) were cash transactions involving VAT.

The VAT account

11.11 The VAT paid to or recovered from the authorities each quarter is the **balance on the VAT account**. This is a control account to which these items are posted.

- The total input VAT in the purchases day book (**debit**)
- The total output VAT in the sales day book (**credit**)
- VAT on cash sales (**credit**)
- VAT on cash purchases (**debit**)

For example, if Warren Miles is invoiced for input VAT of £175 and charges VAT of £450 on his credit sales on 1 September 20X7, his VAT account would be as follows.

VAT ACCOUNT

	£		£
Purchase day book (input VAT)	175.00	Sales day book (output VAT invoiced)	450.00
Cash (input VAT on cash purchases)	14.44	Cash (output VAT on cash sales)	34.25
Balance c/d (owed to Customs & Excise)	294.81		
	484.25		484.25

11.12 Payments to or refunds from Customs and Excise do not coincide with the end of the accounting period of a business, and so at the balance sheet date there will be a balance on the VAT account. The balance is usually for an amount **payable to** Customs and Excise, ie an outstanding creditor for VAT. Occasionally, a business will be **owed money** back by Customs and Excise, and the VAT refund due will be an amount **receivable from** Customs and Excise.

Exam alert

Unless you are told otherwise you should make the following postings for VAT transactions.

CREDIT TRANSACTIONS	DR		CR	
	Memorandum	*General ledger*	*General ledger*	*Memorandum*
Sell goods on credit	Sales ledger 117.50	Total debtors 117.50	Sales 100.00 VAT 17.50	-
Receive cash in settlement	-	Cash 117.50	Total debtors 117.50	Sales ledger 117.50
Buy goods on credit	-	Purchases 100.00 VAT 17.50	Total creditors 117.50	Purchase ledger 117.50
Pay cash in settlement	Purchase ledger 117.50	Total creditors 117.50	Cash 117.50	-
CASH TRANSACTIONS				
Sell goods for cash	-	Cash 117.50	Sales 100.00 VAT 17.50	-
Buy goods for cash	-	Purchases 100.00 VAT 17.50	Cash 117.50	-

Part A: Introduction to transaction accounting

WARREN MILES: CASH BOOK

RECEIPTS

Date 20X7	Narrative		Discount allowed	Total	Output VAT on cash sales	Receipts from debtors	Cash sales	Other
01-Sep	Balance b/d			900.00				
	(a) Cash sale			80.00	11.91		68.09	
	(b) Debtor pays: Anna	SL96	20.00	380.00		380.00		
	(c) Debtor pays: Milly	SL632	40.00	720.00		720.00		
	(d) Debtor pays: Egg	SL501		960.00		960.00		
	(e) Cash sale			150.00	22.34		127.66	
	(f) Fixed asset sale			200.00				200.00
			60.00	3,390.00	34.25	2,060.00	195.75	200.00

02-Sep	Balance b/d	683.00

PAYMENTS

Date 20X7	Narrative		Discount received	Total	Input VAT on cash purchases	Payments to creditors	Expenses	Fixed assets
01-Sep	(g) Creditor paid: Ferdie	PL543	10.00	120.00		120.00		
	(h) Creditor paid: Kiera	PL76	20.00	310.00		310.00		
	(i) Telephone expense			400.00			400.00	
	(j) Gas expense			280.00			280.00	
	(k) Plant & machinery purchase			1,500.00				1,500.00
	(l) Cash purchase: Stationery			97.00	14.44		82.56	
			30.00	2,707.00	14.44	430.00	762.56	1,500.00
	Balance c/d			683.00				
				3,390.00	14.44	430.00	762.56	1,500.00

Key learning points

- Business transactions are initially recorded on source documents. Records of the details on these documents are made in books of prime entry.
- The main **books of prime entry** are as follows.
  - Sales day book
  - Purchase day book
  - Journal
  - Cash book
  - Petty cash book
- Most accounts are contained in the **general ledger** (or **nominal ledger**).
- The rules of double entry state that every financial transaction gives rise to **two accounting entries**, one a **debit**, the other a **credit**. It is vital that you understand this principle.
- A **debit** is one of the following.
  - An increase in an asset
  - An increase in an expense
  - A decrease in a liability
- A **credit** is one of the following.
  - An increase in a liability
  - An increase in income
  - A decrease in an asset
- The accounts in the general ledger are **impersonal accounts**. There are also **personal accounts** for debtors and creditors and these are contained in the sales ledger and purchase ledger.
- A **control account** is an account in the general ledger in which a record is kept of the total value of a number of similar but individual items.
  - A **debtors control account** is an account in which records are kept of transactions involving all debtors in total. It is posted with totals from the sales day book and the cash book.
  - A **creditors control account** is an account in which records are kept of transactions involving all creditors in total, being posted with totals from the purchases daybook and the cash book.

Quick quiz

1. What are books of prime entry?
2. What is recorded in the sales day book?
3. Does a debit entry on an asset account increase or decrease the asset?
4. What is the double entry when goods are sold for cash?
5. What is the double entry when goods are purchased on credit?
6. Personal accounts form part of the double entry system. True or false?
7. How do control accounts act as a check?
8. What is the double entry for goods sold on credit which are standard-rated for VAT and whose price excluding VAT is £100?

Answers to quick quiz

1. The books of prime entry record all the documented transactions undertaken by the company.
2. The sales day book records the list of invoices sent out to customers each day.
3. It increases the asset balance.
4. *Debit* Cash, *Credit* Sales.
5. *Debit* Purchases, *Credit* Creditors account.
6. False. They are memoranda accounts only.

Part A: Introduction to transaction accounting

7   Control accounts should agree with the total of the individual balances of debtors or creditors to show all transactions have been recorded correctly.

8   *Debit* Trade debtors £117.50, *Credit* Sales £100.00, *Credit* VAT £17.50.

Answers to activities

Answer 4.1

(a) Cash book
(b) Sales day book
(c) Purchase day book
(d) Cash book
(e) Sales returns day book
(f) Purchase returns day book
(g) Cash book

Answer 4.2

Tutorial note. The cash book records money received and money paid. If something does not involve money coming into or going out of the business, it will not result in an entry in the cash book. The following will *not* be entered in the cash book.

(c) Supplier's invoice
(d) Credit note
(e) Debit note
(j) Depreciation

A cheque received (a) and a payment to sales ledger customers (b) comprise a receipt and a payment respectively. But receiving a supplier's invoice (c) is not a receipt or payment of money: the invoice establishes a debt, which might not be paid until some time later. Similarly, issuing (d) a credit note or (e) a debit note does not involve money changing hands. Bank charges (f) and overdraft interest (g) are both paid (by the business, to the bank) when debited to the bank account, and these need to be recorded in the cash book. A non-current asset purchased on credit will have been invoiced previously, the payment for it (h) must be recorded in the cash book. Depreciation of non-current assets (j) may be necessary, but the accounting entries for it do not involve money changing hands. A refund from a supplier (i) would be included as it is a monetary item (ie it is *not* a credit note).

Answer 4.3

(a) The two sides of the transaction are

(i) cash is received (**debit** cash account)
(ii) sales increase by £60 (**credit** sales account)

CASH ACCOUNT

		£			£
07.04.X7	Sales a/c	60			

SALES ACCOUNT

					£
			07.04.X7	Cash a/c	60

(b) The two sides of the transaction are

(i) cash is paid (**credit** cash account)
(ii) rent expense increases by £4,500 (**debit** rent account)

CASH ACCOUNT

		£			£
			07.04.X7	Rent a/c	4,500

4: Recording, summarising and posting transactions

RENT ACCOUNT

		£		£
07.04.X7	Cash a/c	4,500		

Tutorial note. This assumes that no rent liability had previously been recognised. If the expense had been posted already, the debit posting would be made to the creditors account.

(c) The two sides of the transaction are
  (i) cash is paid (**credit** cash account)
  (ii) purchases increase by £3,000 (**debit** purchases account)

CASH ACCOUNT

		£			£
			07.04.X7	Purchases a/c	3,000

PURCHASES ACCOUNT

		£		£
07.04.X7	Cash a/c	3,000		

(d) The two sides of the transaction are
  (i) cash is paid (**credit** cash account)
  (ii) assets - in this case, shelves - increase by £6,000 (**debit** shelves account)

CASH ACCOUNT

		£			£
			07.04.X7	Shelves a/c	6,000

SHELVES (ASSET) ACCOUNT

		£		£
07.04.X7	Cash a/c	6,000		

Tutorial note. If all four of these transactions related to the same business, the cash account of that business would end up looking as follows.

CASH ACCOUNT

		£			£
07.04.X7	Sales a/c	60	07.04.X7	Rent a/c	4,500
				Purchases a/c	3,000
				Shelves a/c	6,000

Answer 4.4

(a)	DEBIT	Machine account (fixed asset)	£8,000	
	CREDIT	Creditors (A)		£8,000
(b)	DEBIT	Purchases account	£500	
	CREDIT	Creditors (B)		£500
(c)	DEBIT	Debtors (C)	£1,200	
	CREDIT	Sales		£1,200
(d)	DEBIT	Creditors (D)	£300	
	CREDIT	Cash		£300
(e)	DEBIT	Cash	£180	
	CREDIT	Debtors (E)		£180
(f)	DEBIT	Wages expense	£4,000	
	CREDIT	Cash		£4,000
(g)	DEBIT	Rent expense	£700	
	CREDIT	Creditors (G)		£700

Part A: Introduction to transaction accounting

(h)	DEBIT	Creditors (G)	£700	
	CREDIT	Cash		£700
(i)	DEBIT	Insurance expense	£90	
	CREDIT	Cash		£90

Answer 4.5

		Original document	Book of prime entry	Accounts in general ledger to be posted to	
				Dr	Cr
(a)	Sale of goods on credit	Sales invoice	Sales day book	Total debtors	Sales
(b)	Allowances to credit customers	Credit note	Sales returns day book	Sales/Returns inward	Total debtors
(c)	Daily cash takings	Till rolls and/or sales invoices and receipts, bank paying-in book	Cash book	Cash	Sales

Tutorial note. All these transactions would be incorporated into the double entry system by means of periodic postings from the books of prime entry to the general ledger.

Answer 4.6

	Account to be debited	Ledger	Account to be credited	Ledger
(a)	Rent	General	Cash	Cash book
(b)	L Battersby	Sales	Sales	General
(c)	Returns inwards	General	B Turpin	Sales
(d)	Purchases	General	Gilroy Ltd	Purchases
(e)	Fixed assets	General	Bank	Cash Book
(f)	Fixed assets	General	Bank	Cash Book
(g)	Gilroy Ltd	Purchases	Bank	Cash Book

Answer 4.7

(a) Any five of the following.

  (i) Plant and machinery
  (ii) Motor vehicles
  (iii) Stocks - raw materials
  (iv) Stocks - finished goods
  (v) Total debtors
  (vi) Total creditors
  (vii) Wages and salaries
  (viii) Rent and rates
  (ix) Advertising expenses
  (x) Bank charges
  (xi) Motor expenses
  (xii) Telephone expenses
  (xiii) Sales
  (xiv) Total cash or bank overdraft

(b) A control account is an account in which a record is kept of the total value of a number of similar but individual items. They are used to **check** that the sum of the individual balances in sales and purchase ledgers is correct.

It is the control account balance which will appear in the final accounts of the business, the sales ledger and purchase ledger act as **memoranda** for the lists of individual account balances.

Chapter 5 Completing ledger accounts

Chapter topic list

1 The journal
2 The trial balance
3 Methods of coding data
4 Manual and computerised systems
5 Batch processing and control totals
6 Accounting systems
7 Accounting modules

The following study sessions are covered in this chapter

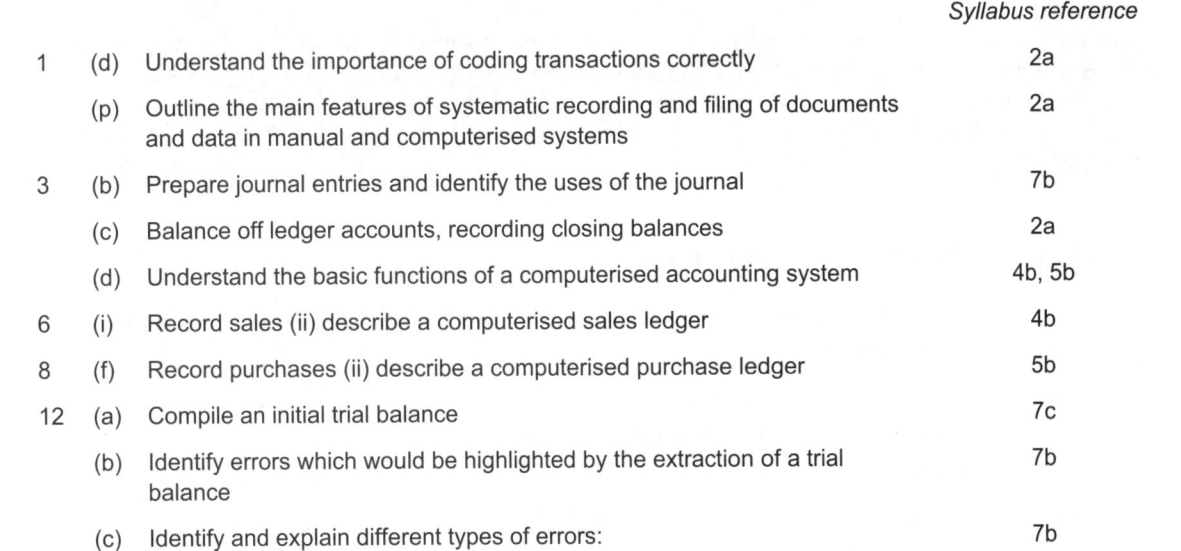

			Syllabus reference
1	(d)	Understand the importance of coding transactions correctly	2a
	(p)	Outline the main features of systematic recording and filing of documents and data in manual and computerised systems	2a
3	(b)	Prepare journal entries and identify the uses of the journal	7b
	(c)	Balance off ledger accounts, recording closing balances	2a
	(d)	Understand the basic functions of a computerised accounting system	4b, 5b
6	(i)	Record sales (ii) describe a computerised sales ledger	4b
8	(f)	Record purchases (ii) describe a computerised purchase ledger	5b
12	(a)	Compile an initial trial balance	7c
	(b)	Identify errors which would be highlighted by the extraction of a trial balance	7b
	(c)	Identify and explain different types of errors: (i) errors of commission (ii) errors or principle (iii) errors of omission (iv) single entry (v) transposition errors (vi) casting errors	7b
	(d)	Distinguish between compensating and non-compensating errors	7b
	(e)	Prepare and explain the function of a suspense account	7c
	(f)	Correct errors using journal entries	7b

Part A: Introduction to transaction accounting

1 THE JOURNAL

1.1 You should remember that one of the **books of prime entry** is the **journal**.

> **KEY TERM**
>
> The **journal** keeps a record of unusual movement between accounts. It is used to record any double entries made which do not arise from the other books of prime entry.

1.2 Whatever type of transaction is being recorded, the following shows the **format of a journal entry**.

Date	Narrative	DR	CR
		£	£
	DEBIT Account to be debited	X	
	CREDIT Account to be credited		X
	Narrative to explain the transaction		

(Remember: in due course, the ledger accounts will be written up to include the transactions listed in the journal.)

1.3 A narrative explanation **must** accompany each journal entry. It is required for audit and control, to indicate the purpose and authority of every transaction which is not first recorded in a book of prime entry.

> **Exam alert**
>
> Note that an exam question might appear to 'journalise' transactions which would not in practice be recorded in the journal at all. This is to test your understanding of double entry. For example it might give you four options, of which one (debit cash, credit debtors) is the correct entry for cash received from a debtor.

1.4 EXAMPLE: JOURNAL ENTRIES

The following is a summary of the transactions of Yve's hairdressing business of which Paul Brown is the sole proprietor.

- 1 January   Put in cash of £2,000 as capital
  Purchased brushes and combs for cash of £50
  Purchased hair driers from Z Ltd on credit for £150
- 30 January   Paid three months rent to 31 March of £300
  Collected and paid in takings of £600
- 31 January   Gave Mrs X a perm, highlights etc on credit £80.

Show the transactions by means of journal entries.

1.5 SOLUTION

JOURNAL

Date				£	£
1 January	DEBIT	Cash		2,000	
	CREDIT	Paul Brown - capital account			2,000
	Initial capital introduced				
1 January	DEBIT	Brushes and combs account		50	
	CREDIT	Cash			50
	The purchase for cash of brushes and combs as fixed assets				
1 January	DEBIT	Hair dryer account		150	
	CREDIT	Sundry creditors account *			150
	The purchase on credit of hair driers as fixed assets				
30 January	DEBIT	Rent account		300	
	CREDIT	Cash			300
	The payment of rent to 31 March				
30 January	DEBIT	Cash		600	
	CREDIT	Sales (or takings account)			600
	Cash takings				
31 January	DEBIT	Debtors account		80	
	CREDIT	Sales account (or takings account)			80
	The provision of a hair-do on credit				

*Note. Creditors who have supplied fixed assets are included amongst **sundry creditors**, as distinct from creditors who have supplied raw materials or goods for resale, who are **trade creditors**. It is quite common to have separate 'total creditors' accounts, one for trade creditors and another for sundry other creditors.

The correction of errors

1.6 The journal is most commonly used to record **corrections to errors that have been made** in writing up the general ledger accounts. Errors corrected by the journal **must be capable of correction by means of a double entry** in the ledger accounts. In other words, the error must not have caused total debits and total credits to be unequal. (When errors are made which break the rule of double entry, that debits and credits must be equal, another approach must be followed, covered in your later studies.)

Journal vouchers

1.7 Journal entries might be logged, not in a single 'book' or journal, but on a separate slip of paper, called a journal voucher.

> **KEY TERM**
>
> A **journal voucher** is used to record the equivalent of one entry in the journal.

1.8 The use of journal vouchers is fairly widespread.

(a) The **repetitive nature** of certain journal entries means vouchers can be pre-printed to standardise the narrative of such entries, and to save time in writing them out.

(b) A voucher is able to hold **more information** than a conventional journal record.

Part A: Introduction to transaction accounting

2 THE TRIAL BALANCE

2.1 If you are asked to post a list of transactions to the relevant ledger accounts, how do you check that you have posted the debit and credit entries correctly? There is no foolproof method for making sure that all entries have been posted to the correct ledger account, but a technique which shows up the more obvious mistakes is to prepare a **trial balance**.

> **KEY TERM**
>
> A **trial balance** is a list of ledger balances shown in debit and credit columns.

Collecting together the ledger accounts

2.2 Before you draw up a trial balance, you must have a **collection of ledger accounts**. These are the ledger accounts of Ian Beale, a sole trader.

CASH

	£		£
Capital - Ian Beale	7,000	Rent	3,500
Bank loan	1,000	Shop fittings	2,000
Sales	10,000	Trade creditors	5,000
Debtors	2,500	Bank loan interest	100
		Incidental expenses	1,900
		Drawings	1,500
			14,000
		Balancing figure - the amount of cash left over after payments have been made	6,500
	20,500		20,500

CAPITAL (IAN BEALE)

	£		£
		Cash	7,000

BANK LOAN

	£		£
		Cash	1,000

PURCHASES

	£		£
Trade creditors	5,000		

TRADE CREDITORS

	£		£
Cash	5,000	Purchases	5,000

RENT

	£		£
Cash	3,500		

SHOP FITTINGS

	£		£
Cash	2,000		

SALES

	£		£
		Cash	10,000
		Debtors	2,500
			12,500

DEBTORS

	£		£
Sales	2,500	Cash	2,500

BANK LOAN INTEREST

	£		£
Cash	100		

OTHER EXPENSES

	£		£
Cash	1,900		

DRAWINGS ACCOUNT

	£		£
Cash	1,500		

The first step is to 'balance' each account.

Balancing ledger accounts

2.3 At the end of an accounting period, a balance is struck on each account in turn. This means that all the **debits** on the account are totalled and so are all the **credits**.

- If the **total debits exceed the total credits** there is a **debit balance** on the account
- If the **total credits exceed the total debits** then the account has a **credit balance**

Action		Eg Ian Beale's Cash a/c
Step 1.	Calculate a total for both sides of each ledger account.	Dr £20,500, Cr £14,000
Step 2.	Deduct the lower total from the higher total.	£(20,500 – 14,000) = £6,500
Step 3.	Insert the result of Step 2 as the balance c/d on the side of the account with the lower total.	Here it will go on the credit side, because the total credits on the account are less than the total debits.

Part A: Introduction to transaction accounting

Action	Eg Ian Beale's Cash a/c
Step 4. Check that the totals on both sides of the account are now the same	Dr £20,500, Cr £(14,000 + 6,500) = £20,500
Step 5. Insert the amount of the balance c/d as the new balance b/d on the other side of the account. The new balance b/d is the balance on the account.	The balance b/d on the account is £6,500 Dr.

2.4 In our simple example, there is very little balancing to do.

(a) Both the trade creditors account and the debtors account balance off to zero.
(b) The cash account has a debit balance (the new balance b/d) of £6,500 (see above).
(c) The total on the sales account is £12,500, which is a credit balance.

Otherwise, the accounts have only one entry each, so there is no totalling to do to arrive at the balance on each account.

Collecting the balances on the ledger accounts

2.5 If the basic principle of double entry has been correctly applied throughout the period it will be found that the **credit balances equal the debit balances** in total. This can be illustrated by collecting together the balances on Ian Beale's accounts.

	Debit £	Credit £
Cash	6,500	
Capital		7,000
Bank loan		1,000
Purchases	5,000	
Trade creditors	-	-
Rent	3,500	
Shop fittings	2,000	
Sales		12,500
Debtors	-	-
Bank loan interest	100	
Other expenses	1,900	
Drawings	1,500	
	20,500	20,500

2.6 It does not matter in what order the various accounts are listed in the **trial balance**, because it is not a document that a company *has* to prepare. It is just a method used to test the accuracy of the double entry bookkeeping methods.

What if the trial balance shows unequal debit and credit balances?

2.7 If the two columns of the trial balance are not equal, there must be an **error in recording of transactions in the accounts**. A trial balance, however, will **not** disclose the following types of errors.

(a) The **complete omission** of a transaction, because neither a debit nor a credit is made

(b) Posting a debit or credit to the correct side of the ledger, but to a **wrong account** (an error of **commission**)

(c) **Compensating errors** (eg debit error of £100 is exactly cancelled by credit £100 error elsewhere)

(d) **Errors of principle** (eg cash received from debtors being debited to the total debtors account and credited to cash instead of the other way round)

(e) Errors of transposition (eg £11,729 written as £11, 279)

2.8 Once an error has been detected, it needs to be put right.

(a) If the correction **involves a double entry** in the ledger accounts, then it is done by using a **journal entry** in the journal.

(b) When the error **breaks the rule of double entry**, then it is corrected by the use of a **suspense account** as well as a journal entry.

Errors of transposition

> **KEY TERM**
>
> An **error of transposition** is when two digits in an amount are accidentally recorded the wrong way round.

2.9 For example, suppose that a sale is recorded in the sales account as £11,279, but it has been incorrectly recorded in the total debtors account as £11,729. The error is the transposition of the 7 and the 2. The consequence is that total debits will not be equal to total credits. You can often detect a transposition error by checking whether the difference between debits and credits can be divided exactly by 9. For example, £11,729 – £11,279 = £450; £450 ÷ 9 = 50.

Errors of omission

> **KEY TERM**
>
> An **error of omission** means failing to record a transaction at all, or making a debit or credit entry, but not the corresponding double entry.

2.10 Here are two examples.

(a) If a business receives an invoice from a supplier for £1,350, the transaction might be omitted from the books entirely. As a result, both the total debits and the total credits of the business will be out by £1,350.

(b) If a business receives an invoice from a supplier for £820, the purchase ledger control account might be credited, but the debit entry in the purchases account might be omitted. In this case, the total credits would not equal total debits (because total debits are £820 less than they ought to be).

Errors of principle

> **KEY TERM**
>
> An **error of principle** involves making a double entry in the belief that the transaction is being entered in the correct accounts, but subsequently finding out that the accounting entry breaks the 'rules' of an accounting principle or concept.

2.11 A typical example of such an error is to treat certain revenue expenditure incorrectly as capital expenditure.

(a) For example, repairs to a machine costing £300 should be treated as revenue expenditure, and debited to a repairs account. If, instead, the repair costs are added to the cost of the fixed asset (capital expenditure) an error of principle would have occurred. As a result, although total debits still equal total credits, the repairs account is £300 less than it should be and the cost of the fixed asset is £300 greater than it should be.

(b) Similarly, suppose that the proprietor of the business sometimes takes cash out of the till for his personal use and during a certain year these drawings amount to £1,400. The bookkeeper states that he has reduced cash sales by £1,400 so that the cash book could be made to balance. This would be an error of principle, and the result of it would be that the drawings account is understated by £1,400, and so is the total value of sales in the sales account.

Errors of commission

> **KEY TERM**
>
> **Errors of commission** are where the bookkeeper makes a mistake in carrying out his or her task of recording transactions in the accounts.

2.12 Here are two common errors of commission.

(a) **Putting a debit entry or a credit entry in the wrong account.** For example, if telephone expenses of £342 are debited to the electricity expenses account, an error of commission would have occurred. The result is that although total debits and total credits balance, telephone expenses are understated by £342 and electricity expenses are overstated by the same amount.

(b) **Errors of casting (adding up).** Suppose for example that the total daily credit sales in the sales day book of a business should add up to £79,925, but are incorrectly added up as £79,325. The total sales in the sales day book are then used to credit total sales and debit total debtors in the ledger accounts, so that total debits and total credits are still equal, although incorrect.

Compensating errors

> **KEY TERM**
>
> **Compensating errors** are errors which are, coincidentally, equal and opposite to one another.

2.13 Some errors can be corrected by **journal entries.** For example, two transposition errors of £360 might occur in extracting ledger balances, one on each side of the double entry. In the administration expenses account, £3,158 might be written instead of £3,518, while in the sundry income account, £6,483 might be written instead of £6,843. Both the debits and the credits would be £360 too low, and the mistake would not be apparent when the trial balance is cast. Consequently, compensating errors hide the fact that there are errors in the trial balance.

2.14 Some errors can be corrected by **journal entries**. The journal requires a debit and an equal credit entry for each 'transaction' - ie for each correction. This means that if total debits equal total credits before a journal entry is made then they will still be equal after the journal entry is made. This would be the case if, for example, the original error was a debit wrongly posted as a credit or *vice versa*.

2.15 Similarly, if total debits and total credits are unequal before a journal entry is made, then they will still be unequal (by the same amount) after it is made.

2.16 For example, suppose a bookkeeper accidentally posts a bill for £200 to the gas account instead of to the business rates account. A trial balance is drawn up, and total debits are £100,000 and total credits are £100,000. A journal entry is made to correct the misposting error as follows.

1.5.20X0

DEBIT	Business rates account	£200	
CREDIT	Gas account		£200

To correct a misposting of £200 from the rates account to electricity account.

2.17 After the journal has been posted, total debits will still be £100,000 and total credits will be £100,000. Total debits and totals credits are still equal.

2.18 Now suppose that, because of some error which has not yet been detected, total debits were originally £100,000 but total credits were £99,520. If the same journal correcting the £200 is put through, total debits will remain £100,000 and total credits will remain £99,520. Total debits were different by £480 *before* the journal, and they are still different by £480 *after* the journal.

2.19 This means that journals can only be used to correct errors which require both a credit and (an equal) debit adjustment. If the error cannot be corrected by journal, we use a **suspense account.**

Part A: Introduction to transaction accounting

> **KEY TERM**
>
> A **suspense account** is an account showing a balance equal to the difference in a trial balance.

2.20 A suspense account is a **temporary** account which can be opened for a number of reasons. The most common reasons are as follows.

(a) A trial balance is drawn up which does not balance (ie total debits do not equal total credits).

(b) The bookkeeper of a business knows where to post the credit side of a transaction, but does not know where to post the debit (or vice versa). For example, a cash payment might be made and must obviously be credited to cash. But the bookkeeper may not know what the payment is for, and so will not know which account to debit.

2.21 In both these cases, a temporary suspense account is opened up until the problem is sorted out. The next few paragraphs explain exactly how this works.

Use of suspense account: when the trial balance does not balance

2.22 When an error has occurred which results in an **imbalance** between total debits and total credits in the ledger accounts, the **first step** is to open a **suspense account**. For example, suppose an accountant draws up a trial balance and finds that, for some reason he cannot immediately discover, total debits exceed total credits by £207.

2.23 He knows that there is an error somewhere, but for the time being he opens a suspense account and enters a credit of £207 in it. This serves two purposes.

(a) Because the suspense account now exists, the accountant will not forget that there is an error (of £207) to be sorted out.

(b) Now that there is a credit of £207 in the suspense account, the trial balance balances.

2.24 When the cause of the £207 discrepancy is tracked down, it is corrected by means of a journal entry. For example, suppose it turned out that the accountant had accidentally failed to make a credit of £207 to purchases. The journal entry would be:

DEBIT	Suspense a/c	£207	
CREDIT	Purchases		£207

To close off suspense a/c and correct error

2.25 Whenever an error occurs which results in total debits not being equal to total credits, the first step an accountant makes is to open up a suspense account.

Activity 5.1

A trial balance does not balance and the bookkeeper posts the difference to a suspense account. He then finds the following errors which clear the suspense account when they are corrected:

(i) Opening stock had been understated by £10,000.

(ii) A credit note for £200 had been posted to sales returns but not to the debtors control account.

5: Completing ledger accounts

Tasks

(a) What was the balance on the suspense account before these errors were corrected?

(b) Show the journal which clears the balance.

2.26 EXAMPLE: TRIAL BALANCE

As at the end of 30 March 20X7, your business, Widgets Galore, has the following balances on its ledger accounts.

Accounts	Balance £
Bank loan	12,000
Cash	11,700
Capital	13,000
Rates	1,880
Trade creditors	11,200
Purchases	12,400
Sales	14,600
Sundry creditors	1,620
Debtors	12,000
Bank loan interest	1,400
Other expenses	11,020
Vehicles	2,020

During 31 March the business made the following transactions.

(a) Bought materials for £1,000, half for cash and half on credit
(b) Made £1,040 sales, £800 of which were for credit
(c) Paid wages to shop assistants of £260 in cash

You are required to draw up a trial balance showing the balances as at the end of 31 March 20X7.

2.27 SOLUTION

Step 1. Put the opening balances into a trial balance, ie decide which are debit and which are credit balances.

Account	Debit £	Credit £
Bank loan		12,000
Cash	11,700	
Capital		13,000
Rates	1,880	
Trade creditors		11,200
Purchases	12,400	
Sales		14,600
Sundry creditors		1,620
Debtors	12,000	
Bank loan interest	1,400	
Other expenses	11,020	
Vehicles	2,020	
	52,420	52,420

Part A: Introduction to transaction accounting

Step 2. Take account of the effects of the three transactions which took place on 31 March 20X7.

			£	£
(a)	DEBIT	Purchases	1,000	
	CREDIT	Cash		500
		Trade creditors		500
(b)	DEBIT	Cash	240	
		Debtors	800	
	CREDIT	Sales		1,040
(c)	DEBIT	Other expenses	260	
	CREDIT	Cash		260

Step 3. Amend the trial balance for these entries.

WIDGETS GALORE: TRIAL BALANCE AT 31 MARCH 20X7

	30-Mar-X7 DR	30-Mar-X7 CR	Transactions DR		Transactions CR		31-Mar-X7 DR	31-Mar-X7 CR
Bank loan		12,000						12,000
Cash	11,700		(b) 240		500	(a)	11,180	
					260	(c)		
Capital		13,000						13,000
Rates	1,880						1,880	
Trade creditors		11,200			500	(a)		11,700
Purchases	12,400		(a) 1,000				13,400	
Sales		14,600			1,040	(b)		15,640
Sundry creditors		1,620						1,620
Debtors	12,000		(b) 800				12,800	
Bank loan interest	1,400						1,400	
Other expenses	11,020		(c) 260				11,280	
Vehicles	2,020						2,020	
	52,420	52,420	2,300		2,300		53,960	53,960

Activity 5.2

Mr Ringo Binder commenced trading as a wholesale stationer on 1 May 20X7 with a capital of £5,000 with which he opened a bank account for his business.

During May the following transactions took place.

May	1	Bought shop fittings and fixtures for cash from Folder Fitments Ltd for £2,000
	2	Purchased goods on credit from Staple £650
	4	Sold goods on credit to Clip £700
	9	Purchased goods on credit from Green £300
	11	Sold goods on credit to Hill £580
	13	Cash sales paid intact into bank £200
	16	Received cheque from Clip in settlement of his account
	17	Purchased goods on credit from Kaye £800
	18	Sold goods on credit to Nailor £360
	19	Sent cheque to Staple in settlement of his account
	20	Paid rent by cheque £200
	21	Paid delivery expenses by cheque £50
	24	Received from Hill £200 on account
	30	Drew cheques for personal expenses £200 and assistant's wages £320
	31	Settled the account of Green

Tasks

(a) Record the foregoing in appropriate books of original entry.
(b) Post the entries to the ledger accounts.
(c) Balance the ledger accounts where necessary.
(d) Extract a trial balance at 31 May 20X7.

Tutorial note. You are not required to complete any entries in personal accounts.

3 METHODS OF CODING DATA

3.1 Each account in an accounting system has a **unique code** which is what will be used to identify the correct account for a posting (to be keyed into the computer if the system is computerised). If there were two debtors called John Smith, you could only tell their accounts apart by the fact the accounts had a different code.

3.2 Coding also saves time in copying out data because **codes are shorter** than 'longhand' descriptions. For the same reason, and also to save storage space, computer systems make use of coded data.

3.3 In accounting systems, the most obvious examples of codes are as follows.

- Customer account numbers
- Supplier account numbers
- General ledger account numbers
- Employee reference numbers
- Stock item codes

These are all codes a business sets up and applies internally. External codes which affect the business include **bank account numbers** and **bank sort codes**.

Coding in the general ledger

3.4 A general ledger will consist of a **large number of coded accounts**. For example, part of a general ledger might be as follows.

Account code	Account name
100200	Plant and machinery (cost)
100300	Motor vehicles (cost)
100201	Plant and machinery depreciation
100301	Vehicles depreciation
300000	Total debtors
400000	Total creditors
500130	Wages and salaries
500140	Rent and rates
500150	Advertising expenses
500160	Bank charges
500170	Motor expenses
500180	Telephone expenses
600000	Sales
700000	Cash

Part A: Introduction to transaction accounting

There are an example of **significant digit codes** – they incorporate some digits which describe the item being coded. For instance, fixed asset accounts begin with 1 and expense accounts begin with 5.

3.5 A business will, of course, choose its own codes for its general ledger accounts. The codes given in the above table are purely imaginary.

3.6 You will have realised by now the importance of **correct coding**. Items posted to the wrong code in the sales ledger would be debited to the wrong customers account. Items posted to the wrong account in the purchase ledger could lead to payment being sent to the wrong supplier. This will not improve relationships with customers and suppliers. Incorrect coding in the general ledger will create errors in the accounts.

Activity 5.3

A nominal ledger has the following codes.

Account code	Account name
100200	Plant and machinery
100300	Motor vehicles
300000	Total debtors
400000	Total creditors
500130	Wages and salaries
500140	Rent and rates
500150	Advertising expenses
500160	Bank charges
500170	Motor expenses
500180	Telephone expenses
600000	Sales
700000	Cash

Task

State what type of code this is. Explain your answer.

4 MANUAL AND COMPUTERISED SYSTEMS

4.1 We have looked at the way an accounting system is organised in the last few chapters. It is important to realise that all of the books of prime entry and the ledgers may be either **hand-written books** or **computer records.** Most businesses now use computers, ranging in size from one **PC** used by a one-man business to huge **mainframe computer systems used** by multi-national companies.

4.2 All computer activity can be divided into three processes.

Areas	Activity
Input	Entering data from original documents
Processing	Entering up books and ledgers and generally sorting the input information
Output	Producing any report desired by the managers of the business, including financial statements

Activity 5.4

Your friend Lou Dight believes that computerised accounting systems are more trouble than they are worth because 'you never know what is going on inside that funny box'.

Task

Explain briefly why computers might be useful in accounting.

4.3 Computerised accounting systems perform the same tasks as manual systems.

The following differences arise.

- How information is stored
- How tasks are performed
- How some package do things 'automatically'

4.4 Computerised systems store **information in computer files** rather than in a book. These files can either be viewed on screen, or printed out.

4.5 Tasks such as journal entries are performed **by accessing the function through the menu option** on screen rather than entering journals by hand. Many businesses with computerised systems require journal entries to be written manually, or at least printed out to provide an audit trail.

4.6 An **advantage of computerised systems** are that they can be instructed to perform some tasks automatically. For example to reverse a journal, or to post from the computerised cashbook to the general ledger.

5 BATCH PROCESSING AND CONTROL TOTALS

> **KEY TERM**
>
> **Batch processing** is where similar transactions are gathered into batches, and then each batch is sorted and processed by the computer.

5.1 Rather than inputting individual invoices into a computer for processing, which would be time consuming and expensive, invoices can be gathered into a **batch** and **input and processed all together**. Batches can vary in size, depending on the type and volume of transactions and on any limit imposed by the system on batch sizes. This type of processing is less time consuming than **transaction processing**, where transactions are processed individually as they arise.

> **KEY TERM**
>
> **Control totals** are used to make sure that there have been no errors when the batch is input. A control total is used to make sure that the total value of transactions input is the same as that previously calculated.

5.2 As an example, say a batch of 30 sales invoices has a manually calculated total value of £42,378.47. When the batch is input, the computer adds up the total value of the invoices input and produces a total of £42,378.47. The control totals agree and therefore no further action is required.

5.3 Should the control total **not agree** then checks would have to be carried out until the difference was found. It might be the case that an invoice had accidentally not been entered or the manual total had been incorrectly calculated.

6 ACCOUNTING SYSTEMS

6.1 Most accounting systems are computerised and anyone training to be an accountant should be able to work with them. The most important point to remember is that the **principles** of computerised accounting are the same as those of **manual accounting**. You should by now have a good grasp of these principles.

6.2 This section is about **accounting packages**. This is a rather general term, but most of us can probably name the accounting package that we use at work. An accounting package consists of several accounting **modules**, eg sales ledger, cash book. An exam question may take one of these modules and ask you to describe inputs, processing and outputs. Alternatively, you may be asked to outline the advantages of computer processing over manual processing, for example, for debtors or payroll.

6.3 A particularly useful tool for accountants is the **spreadsheet**. It is likely that you will have used a spreadsheet in your workplace.

> **Exam alert**
>
> Questions will *not* be set on the technical aspects of how computers work.

6.4 We shall assume that you know that a modern computer generally consists of a keyboard, a television-like screen, a box-like disk drive which contains all the necessary electronic components for data processing, and a printer. This is the computer hardware.

> **KEY TERM**
>
> **Computer programs** are the instructions that tell the electronics how to process data. The general term used for these is **software**.

6.5 Software is what we are concerned with in this text, and in particular 'applications software', that is packages of computer programs that carry out specific tasks.

(a) Some applications are devoted specifically to an accounting task, for example a payroll package, a fixed asset register or a stock control package.

(b) Other applications have many uses in business, including their use for accounting purposes. Examples are databases and spreadsheets.

Accounting packages

> **IMPORTANT!**
> One of the most important facts to remember about computerised accounting is that in principle, it is exactly the same as manual accounting.

6.6 Accounting functions retain the same names in computerised systems as in more traditional written records. Computerised accounting still uses the familiar ideas of day books, ledger accounts, double entry, trial balance and financial statements. The principles of working with computerised sales, purchase and nominal ledgers are exactly what would be expected in the manual methods they replace.

6.7 The only difference is that these various books of account have become invisible. Ledgers are now computer files which are held in a computer-sensible form, ready to be called upon.

Advantages

6.8 The advantages of accounting packages compared with a manual system are:

(a) The packages can be used by **non-specialists**.

(b) A large amount of **data can be processed very quickly**.

(c) Computerised systems are **more accurate** than manual systems.

(d) A computer is capable of handling and processing **large volumes** of data.

(e) Once the data has been input, computerised systems can **analyse data** rapidly to present useful control information for managers such as a trial balance or a debtors schedule.

Disadvantages

6.9 The advantages of computerised accounting system far outweigh the disadvantages, particularly for large businesses. However, the following may be identified as possible disadvantages.

(a) The initial **time and costs** involved in installing the system, training personnel and so on.

(b) The need for **security checks** to make sure that unauthorised personnel do not gain access to data files.

(c) The necessity to develop a **system of coding** (see below) and checking.

(d) **Lack of 'audit trail'**. It is not always easy to see where a mistake has been made.

(e) Possible **resistance** on the part of staff to the introduction of the system.

Coding

6.10 Computers are used more efficiently if vital information is expressed in the form of codes. For example, nominal ledger accounts will be coded individually, perhaps by means of a two-digit code: eg

00 Ordinary share capital

Part A: Introduction to transaction accounting

01 Share premium
05 Profit and loss account
15 Purchases
22 Debtors ledger control account
41 Creditors ledger control account
42 Interest
43 Dividends etc

In the same way, individual accounts must be given a unique code number in the sales ledger and purchase ledger.

6.11 EXAMPLE: CODING

When an invoice is received from a supplier (code 1234) for £3,000 for the purchase of raw materials, the transaction might be coded for input to the computer as:

	Nominal ledger			*Stock*	
Supplier Code	*Debit*	*Credit*	*Value*	*Code*	*Quantity*
1234	15	41	£3,000	56742	150

Code 15 might represent purchases and code 41 the creditors control account. This single input could be used to update the purchase ledger, the nominal ledger, and the stock ledger. The stock code may enable further analysis to be carried out, perhaps allocating the cost to a particular department or product. Thus the needs of both financial accounting and cost accounting can be fulfilled at once.

Using an accounting package

6.12 When a user begins to work with an accounting package he will usually be asked to key in a **password**. Separate passwords can be used for different parts of the system, for example for different ledgers if required. The user will then be presented with a 'menu' of options such as 'enter new data' or 'print report' or a Windows-type screen with buttons and icons. By selecting the appropriate option the user will then be guided through the actions needed to enter the data or generate the report.

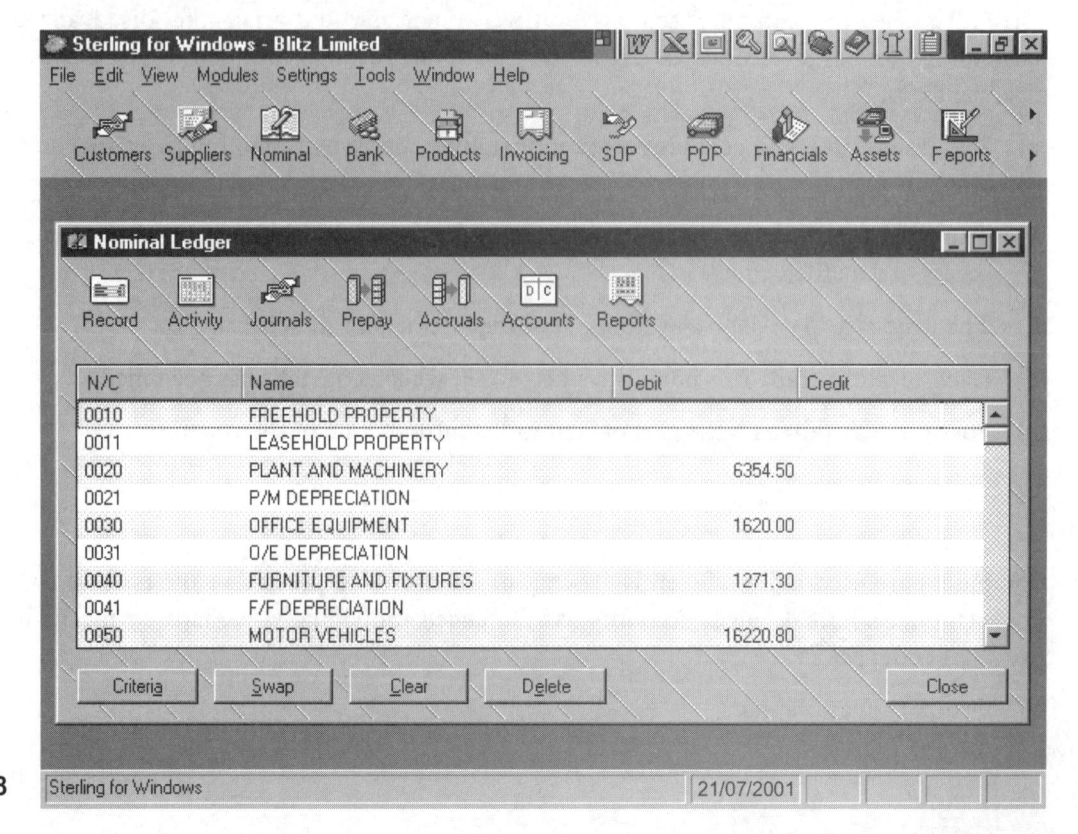

5: Completing ledger accounts

> **IMPORTANT!**
> If you are not already using one, try to get some experience between now and the exam, of using an accounting package.

Modules

> **KEY TERM**
> A **module** is a program which deals with one particular part of a business accounting system.

6.13 An accounting package will consist of several modules. A simple accounting package might consist of only one module (in which case it is called a stand-alone module), but more often it will consist of several modules. The name given to a set of several modules is a **suite**. An accounting package, therefore, might have separate modules for:

- Invoicing
- Stock
- Sales ledger
- Purchase ledger
- Nominal ledger
- Payroll
- Cash book
- Job costing
- Fixed asset register
- Report generator

and so on.

Integrated software

6.14 Each module may be integrated with the others, so that data entered in one module will be passed automatically or by simple operator request through into any other module where the data is of some relevance. For example, if there is an input into the invoicing module authorising the despatch of an invoice to a customer, there might be **automatic links**:

(a) To the sales ledger, to update the file by posting the invoice to the customer's account

(b) To the stock module, to update the stock file by:

- Reducing the quantity and value of stock in hand
- Recording the stock movement

(c) To the nominal ledger, to update the file by posting the sale to the sales account

(d) To the job costing module, to record the sales value of the job on the job cost file

(e) To the report generator, to update the sales analysis and sales totals which are on file and awaiting inclusion in management reports.

Part A: Introduction to transaction accounting

6.15 A diagram of an **integrated accounting system** is given below.

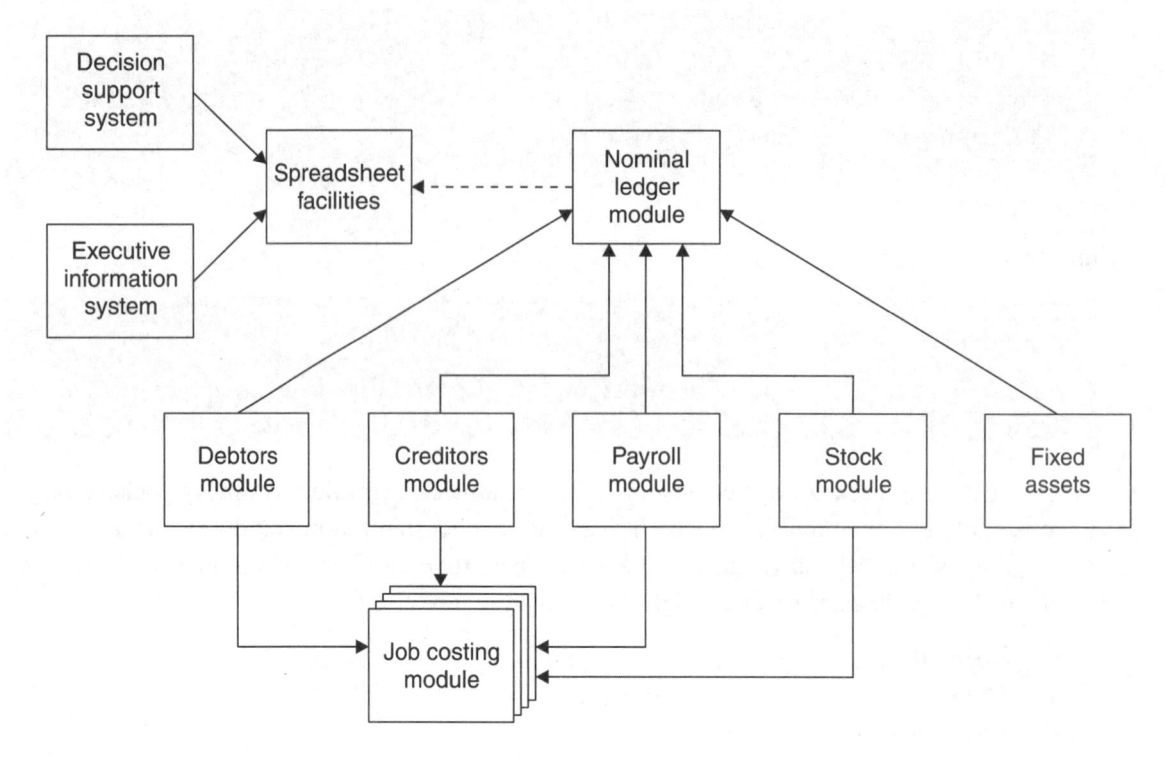

Advantages

6.16 (a) It becomes possible to make just one entry in one of the ledgers which automatically updates the others.

(b) Users can specify reports, and the software will automatically extract the required data from all the relevant files.

(c) Both of the above simplify the workload of the user, and the irritating need to constantly load and unload disks is eliminated.

Disadvantages

6.17 (a) Usually, it requires more computer memory than separate (stand-alone) systems - which means there is less space in which to store actual data.

(b) Because one program is expected to do everything, the user may find that an integrated package has fewer facilities than a set of specialised modules. In effect, an integrated package could be 'Jack of all trades but master of none'.

7 ACCOUNTING MODULES

7.1 In this section we shall look at some of the accounting modules in more detail, starting with the sales ledger.

Accounting for debtors

7.2 A computerised sales ledger will be expected to keep the sales ledger up-to-date, and also it should be able to produce certain output (eg statements, sales analysis reports, responses to file interrogations etc). The output might be produced daily (eg day book listings), monthly (eg statements), quarterly (eg sales analysis reports) or periodically (eg responses to file interrogations, or customer name and address lists printed on adhesive labels for despatching circulars or price lists).

7.3 What we need to do is to have a closer look at the forms that input, output and processing take within a sales ledger. We will begin by thinking about what data we would expect to see in a sales ledger.

Data held on a sales ledger file

7.4 The sales ledger **file** will consist of individual **records** for each customer account. Some of the data held on the record will be **standing data** (ie it will change infrequently). Typical items of standing data are:

(a) Customer account number

(b) Customer name

(c) Address

(d) Credit limit

(e) Account sales analysis code

(f) Account type (there are two different types of account - open item or balance forward - which we will look at shortly)

Each of these items is referred to as a **field** of information.

7.5 Other data held on a customer record will change as the sales ledger is updated. Such data is called **variable data**, and will include:

- Transaction data
- Transaction description (eg sale, credit note etc)
- Transaction code (eg to identify payment period allowed)
- Debits
- Credits
- Balance

7.6 The file which contains these customer records - the sales ledger - is sometimes called a **master file**. If it is updated from another file containing various transactions, then that file is called a **transactions file**. Developments in the way computers store information mean that you are not likely to see these terms much any more - people more often talk about 'databases' of information.

Activity 5.5

What is the relationship between a file, a field and a record?

Inputs to a sales ledger system

7.7 Bearing in mind what we expect to find in a sales ledger, we can say that typical data input into sales ledger system is as follows.

(a) **Amendments**

- Amendments to customer details, eg change of address or credit limit
- Insertion of new customers

Part A: Introduction to transaction accounting

- Deletion of old 'non-active' customers

(b) **Transaction data relating to:**
- Sales transactions, for invoicing
- Customer payments
- Credit notes
- Adjustments (debit or credit items)

7.8 Some computerised sales ledgers produce invoices, so that basic sales data is input into the system. But other businesses might have a specialised invoicing module, so that the sales ledger package is not expected to produce invoices. The invoice details are already available (as output from the specialised module) and are input into the sales ledger system rather than basic sales data. So the first bullet point of (b) Transaction data should read as follows.

- Sales transactions, for invoicing (if the sales ledger is expected to produce invoices) or invoice details (if already available from a specialised invoicing module).

Processing in a sales ledger system

7.9 The primary action involved in updating the sales ledger is modifying the amount outstanding on the customer's account. How the amount is modified depends on what data is being input (ie whether it is an invoice, credit note, remittance etc).

7.10 When processing starts, the balance on an account is called the *brought-forward* balance. When processing has finished, the balance on the account is called the *carried-forward* balance. These terms are often abbreviated to b/f and c/f.

7.11 What a computer does is to add or subtract whatever you tell it to from the b/f balance, and end up with a c/f balance.

	£	£
Brought forward account balance		X
Add:		
Invoice value	X	
Adjustments (+)	X	
		X
		X
Deduct:		
Credit note value	X	
Adjustments (-)	X	
Remittances	X	
		X
Carried forward account balance		X

This method of updating customer accounts is called the balance forward method.

7.12 Most systems also offer users the **open item** method of processing the data, which is much neater. Under this method, the user identifies specific invoices, and credits individual payments against specific invoices. Late payments of individual invoices can be identified and chased up. The customer's outstanding balance is the sum of the unpaid open items. The open item method follows best accounting practice, but it is more time consuming than the balance forward method.

5: Completing ledger accounts

Outputs from a sales ledger system

7.13 Typical outputs in a computerised sales ledger are as follows.

(a) **Day book listing.** A list of all transactions posted each day. This provides an audit trail - ie it is information which the auditors of the business can use when carrying out their work. Batch and control totals will be included in the listing.

(b) **Invoices** (if the package is one which is expected to produce invoices.)

(c) **Statements.** End of month statements for customers.

(d) **Aged debtors list.** Probably produced monthly.

(e) **Sales analysis reports.** These will analyse sales according to the sales analysis codes on the sales ledger file.

(f) **Debtors reminder letters.** Letters can be produced automatically to chase late payers when the due date for payment goes by without payment having been received.

(g) **Customer lists** (or perhaps a selective list). The list might be printed on to adhesive labels, for sending out customer letters or marketing material.

(h) **Responses to enquiries,** perhaps output on to a VDU screen rather than as printed copy, for fast response to customer enquiries.

(i) **Output onto disk file for other modules,** eg to the stock control module and the nominal ledger module, if these are also used by the organisation, and the package is not an integrated one.

The advantages of a computerised debtor system

7.14 The advantage of such a system, in addition to the advantages of computerised accounting generally, is its ability to assist in sales administration and marketing by means of outputs such as those listed above.

Purchase ledger

7.15 A computerised purchase ledger will certainly be expected to keep the purchase ledger up-to-date, and also it should be able to output various reports requested by the user. In fact, a computerised purchase ledger is much the same as a computerised sales ledger, except that it is a sort of mirror image as it deals with purchases rather than sales.

Activity 5.6

What sort of data would you expect to be held on a purchase ledger file?

Inputs to a purchase ledger system

7.16 Bearing in mind what we expect to see held on a purchase ledger, typical data input into a purchase ledger system is:

- Details of purchases recorded on invoices
- Details of returns to suppliers for which credit notes are received
- Details of payments to suppliers
- Adjustments

Part A: Introduction to transaction accounting

Processing in a purchase ledger system

7.17 The primary action involved in updating the purchase ledger is adjusting the amounts outstanding on the supplier accounts. These amounts will represent money owed to the suppliers. This processing is identical to updating the accounts in the sales ledger, except that the sales ledger balances are debits (debtors) and the purchase ledger balances are credits (creditors). Again, the open item approach is the best.

Outputs from a purchase ledger system

7.18 Typical outputs in a computerised purchase ledger are as follows.

(a) Lists of transactions posted - produced every time the system is run.

(b) An analysis of expenditure for nominal ledger purposes. This may be produced every time the system is run or at the end of each month.

(c) List of creditors balances together with a reconciliation between the total balance brought forward, the transactions for the month and the total balance carried forward.

(d) Copies of creditors' accounts. This may show merely the balance b/f, current transactions and the balance c/f. If complete details of all unsettled items are given, the ledger is known as an **open-ended ledger**. (This is similar to the open item or balance forward methods with a sales ledger system.)

(e) Any purchase ledger system can be used to produce details of payments to be made. For example:

- Remittance advices (usually a copy of the ledger account)
- Cheques
- Credit transfer listings

(f) Other special reports may be produced for:

- Costing purposes
- Updating records about fixed assets
- Comparisons with budget
- Aged creditors list

Nominal ledger

7.19 The nominal ledger (or general ledger) is an accounting record which summarises the financial affairs of a business. It is the nucleus of an accounting system. It contains details of assets, liabilities and capital, income and expenditure and so profit or loss. It consists of a large number of different accounts, each account having its own purpose or 'name' and an identity or code.

7.20 A nominal ledger will consist of a large number of coded accounts. For example, part of a nominal ledger might be as follows.

Account code	Account name
100200	Plant and machinery (cost)
100300	Motor vehicles (cost)
100201	Plant and machinery depreciation
100301	Vehicles depreciation
300000	Total debtors
400000	Total creditors

5: Completing ledger accounts

Account code	Account name
500130	Wages and salaries
500140	Rent and rates
500150	Advertising expenses
500160	Bank charges
500170	Motor expenses
500180	Telephone expenses
600000	Sales
700000	Cash

7.21 A business will, of course, choose its own codes for its nominal ledger accounts. The codes given in this table are just for illustration.

7.22 It is important to remember that a computerised nominal ledger works in exactly the same way as a manual nominal ledger, although there are some differences in terminology. For instance, in a manual system, the sales and debtors accounts were posted from the sales day book (not the sales ledger). But in a computerised system, the sales day book is automatically produced as part of the 'sales ledger module'. So it may *sound* as if you are posting directly from the sales ledger, but in fact the day book is part of a computerised sales ledger.

Inputs to the nominal ledger

7.23 Inputs depend on whether the accounting system is integrated or not.

(a) If the system is integrated, then as soon as data is put into the sales ledger module (or anywhere else for that matter), the relevant nominal ledger accounts are updated. There is nothing more for the system user to do.

(b) If the system is not integrated then the output from the sales ledger module (and anywhere else) has to be input into the nominal ledger. This is done by using journal entries. For instance.

DEBIT	A/c 300000	£3,000	
CREDIT	A/c 600000		£3,000

Where 600000 is the nominal ledger code for sales, and 300000 is the code for debtors.

7.24 Regardless of whether the system is integrated or not, the actual data needed by the nominal ledger package to be able to update the ledger accounts includes:

- Date
- Description
- Amount
- Account codes (sometimes called distinction codes)

Outputs from the nominal ledger

7.25 The main outputs apart from listings of individual nominal ledger accounts are:

- The trial balance
- Financial statements

Part A: Introduction to transaction accounting

Key learning points

- A **journal** keeps a record of unusual movements between accounts. The format of a journal is

Date	£	£
DEBIT Account to be debited	X	
CREDIT Account to be credited		X

  Narrative to explain the transaction

- Balances on ledger accounts can be collected in a **list of account balances**. The debit and credit balances should be **equal**.

- Each account in an accounting system has a **unique code** to identify the correct account for posting.

- You should understand the **function and importance** of the following.
  - Manual and computerised systems
  - Batch processing and control totals

- Computer **software** used in accounting may be divided into two types.
  - Dedicated accounting packages
  - General software, the uses of which include accounting amongst many others

- In principle computerised accounting is the same as manual accounting, but a computerised approach has certain advantages which you should learn thoroughly.

- An accounting package consists of a number of '**modules**' which perform all the tasks needed to maintain a normal accounting function like purchase ledger or payroll. In modern systems the modules are usually integrated with each other.

- **Reading about accounting packages is no substitute for using one.**

Quick quiz

1. Why must a journal include a narrative explanation?
2. A journal can be used to correct errors which cause the total debits and credits to be unequal. True or false?
3. What is the other name for a 'list of account balances'?
4. If the total debits in an account exceed the total credits, will there be a debit or credit balance on the account?
5. What types of error will *not* be discovered by drawing up a trial balance?
6. Which external codes will affect a business?
7. What are the advantages of batch processing?
8. What are the advantages of computerised accounting?
9. What are the disadvantages?
10. What is an accounting suite?
11. What are the advantages of integrated software?
12. What sort of data is input into a sales ledger system?
13. What is the open item method of processing?

5: Completing ledger accounts

Answers to quick quiz

1. The narrative is required for audit and control, to show the purpose and authority of the transaction.
2. False. The error must be capable of correction by double entry.
3. The trial balance.
4. There will be a debit balance on the account.
5. There are five types, summarised as: complete omission, posted to wrong account, compensating errors, errors of principle, posting errors.
6. Bank account numbers and bank sort codes are two examples, but also account numbers designated by suppliers of goods or services to the business.
7. Batch processing is faster than transaction processing and checks on input can be made using control totals.
8. The packages can be used by non specialists, large amounts of data can be processed very quickly, it is more accurate and data can be rapidly analysed into useful formats.
9. The initial time and cost of installation, the need for security, the need for a system of coding, the lack of audit trail and the resistance of staff to use it.
10. It is a set of several modules.
11. One entry in a ledger will update the others, data for specific reports is automatically extracted and the workload is subsequently reduced.
12. Amendments and transaction data.
13. This method credits payments against specific invoices.

Answers to activities

Answer 5.1

(a) The balance on the suspense account is DR £9,800. Opening stock is a missing debit entry and a sales return is a missing credit entry to the debtors control account.

(b) The following journal will clear the suspense account:

	Dr	CR
Opening stock	10,000	
Debtors control account		200
Suspense account		9,800
	10,000	10,000

Answer 5.2

(a) The relevant books of prime entry are the cash book, the sales day book and the purchase day book.

CASH BOOK (RECEIPTS)

Date	Narrative	Total £	Capital £	Sales £	Debtors £
May 1	Capital	5,000	5,000		
May 13	Sales	200		200	
May 16	Clip	700			700
May 24	Hill	200			200
		6,100	5,000	200	900

Part A: Introduction to transaction accounting

CASH BOOK (PAYMENTS)

Date May	Narrative	Total £	Fixtures and fittings £	Creditors £	Rent £	Delivery expenses £	Drawings £	Wages £
1	Folder Fitments Ltd	2,000	2,000					
19	Staple	650		650				
20	Rent	200			200			
21	Delivery expenses	50				50		
30	Drawings	200					200	
30	Wages	320						320
31	Green	300		300				
		3,720	2,000	950	200	50	200	320

SALES DAY BOOK

Date	Customer	Amount £
May 4	Clip	700
May 11	Hill	580
May 18	Nailor	360
		1,640

PURCHASE DAY BOOK

Date	Supplier	Amount £
May 2	Staple	650
May 9	Green	300
May 17	Kaye	800
		1,750

(b) and (c)

The relevant ledger accounts are for cash, sales, purchases, creditors, debtors, capital, fixtures and fittings, rent, delivery expenses, drawings and wages.

CASH ACCOUNT

	£		£
May receipts	6,100	May payments	3,720
		Balance c/d	2,380
	6,100		6,100

SALES ACCOUNT

	£		£
Balance c/d	1,840	Cash	200
		Debtors	1,640
	1,840		1,840

PURCHASES ACCOUNT

	£		£
Creditors	1,750	Balance c/d	1,750

DEBTORS ACCOUNT

	£		£
Sales	1,640	Cash	900
		Balance c/d	740
	1,640		1,640

CREDITORS ACCOUNT

	£		£
Cash	950	Purchases	1,750
Balance c/d	800		
	1,750		1,750

CAPITAL ACCOUNT

	£		£
Balance c/d	5,000	Cash	5,000

FIXTURES AND FITTINGS ACCOUNT

	£		£
Cash	2,000	Balance c/d	2,000

RENT ACCOUNT

	£		£
Cash	200	Balance c/d	200

DELIVERY EXPENSES ACCOUNT

	£		£
Cash	50	Balance c/d	50

DRAWINGS ACCOUNT

	£		£
Cash	200	Balance c/d	200

WAGES ACCOUNT

	£		£
Cash	320	Balance c/d	320

(d) TRIAL BALANCE AS AT 31 MAY 20X7

Account	Dr £	Cr £
Cash	2,380	
Sales		1,840
Purchases	1,750	
Debtors	740	
Creditors		800
Capital		5,000
Fixtures and fittings	2,000	
Rent	200	
Delivery expenses	50	
Drawings	200	
Wages	320	
	7,640	7,640

Answer 5.3

This is a significant digit code. The digits are part of the description of the item being coded. '1' in 100000 clearly represents fixed assets, the '2' in 100200 represents plant and machinery etc.

Answer 5.4

The main advantage of computerised accounting systems is that a large amount of data can be processed very quickly. A further advantage is that computerised systems are more accurate than manual systems.

Part A: Introduction to transaction accounting

Lou's comment that 'you never know what is going on in that funny box' might be better expressed as 'lack of audit trail'. If a mistake occurs somewhere in the system it is not always possible to identify where and how it happened.

Answer 5.5

A **file** is made up of **records** which are made up of **fields**

Answer 5.6

The purchase ledger will consist of individual records for each supplier account. Just as for customer accounts, some of the data held on record will be *standing* data, and some will be *variable* data. Standing data will include:

- Account number
- Name
- Address
- Credit details
- Bank details (eg method of payment)
- Cash discount details, if appropriate

Variable data will include:

- Transaction date
- Transaction description
- Transaction code
- Debits
- Credits
- Balance

Part B

Recording and accounting for cash transactions

Chapter 6 Receiving and checking money

Chapter topic list

1 Control over receipts
2 Remittance advices
3 Receipts given to customers
4 Ways in which customers pay
5 Cash: physical security considerations
6 Cheques
7 Receipt of cheque payments
8 Receipt of card payments
9 EFTPOS
10 Other receipts

The following study sessions are covered in this chapter

			Syllabus reference
4	(g)	Describe the procedures and documentation relating to the use of debit and credit cards	3a
5	(a)	Describe the general procedures for dealing with cash, cheques, credit and debit card receipts and payments	3a
	(b)	Identify the documentation accompanying receipts	3a
	(c)	Recognise the importance of accurately recording all receipts	3c
	(k)	Describe the key procedures for ensuring safety, security and, where appropriate, confidentiality over the handling of cash and cheques	3b
	(l)	Explain the correct procedure to cope with unusual situations: exceeded limits on debit or credit cards, or discrepancies between receipts and supporting documents	3a

Part B: Recording and accounting for cash transactions

1 CONTROL OVER RECEIPTS

> **Exam alert**
> Cash transactions are given more emphasis than credit and payroll transactions. This is because you cannot understand credit transactions, which involve receiving and paying money at a later date, without understanding cash transactions.

1.1 In any business controls over cash **receipts** are fundamental if the company is to keep a healthy cash position. **Control over cash receipts** will concentrate on three main areas.

   (a) Receipts must be **banked promptly**.
   (b) The **record of receipts must be complete**.
   (c) The loss of receipts through **theft or accident** must be prevented.

The difference between these three controls can be demonstrated with an example.

1.2 EXAMPLE: CONTROL OVER CASH RECEIPTS

Suppose that your company sells goods for £10,000 during the month of April to XYZ & Co. You receive a payment of £10,000 by cheque along with a remittance advice which shows exactly which invoices the cheque covers.

   (a) You examine the cheque to ensure it is valid and completed correctly and you pay it in to the company account within 24 hours as company policy dictates (**banked promptly**).

   (b) A colleague records the cheque details and compares the amount of the cheque to the remittance advice (**checking for completeness**). Usually the payment would also be checked against the total amount owed by the customer as part of the completeness check.

   (c) The segregation of duties between the person who banks the money and the person who records it is considered to be a very good control to prevent **theft and accidental loss**. We will look at **segregation of duties** again later. Most cheques are now pre-printed crossed and can only be paid into the account of the payee. This helps to protect against loss and theft.

2 REMITTANCE ADVICES

2.1 Documents which are used to record transactions in the books of account of the company are called **source documents**. Source documents were covered in detail in Chapter 1 of this text.

2.2 When a **cheque** arrives from a trade (ie business) customer it is usually accompanied by a **remittance advice**.

> **KEY TERM**
> A **remittance advice** shows which invoices a payment covers.

2.3 The paying company may send out its own remittance advices with its payment. However, it is common now for the **receiving** company to send a statement which has a **detachable remittance advice** as shown here. The paying business or individual will mark off those invoices which are covered by the particular payment. This tear-off advice will then be returned by the paying company, although it may send its own remittance advice as well.

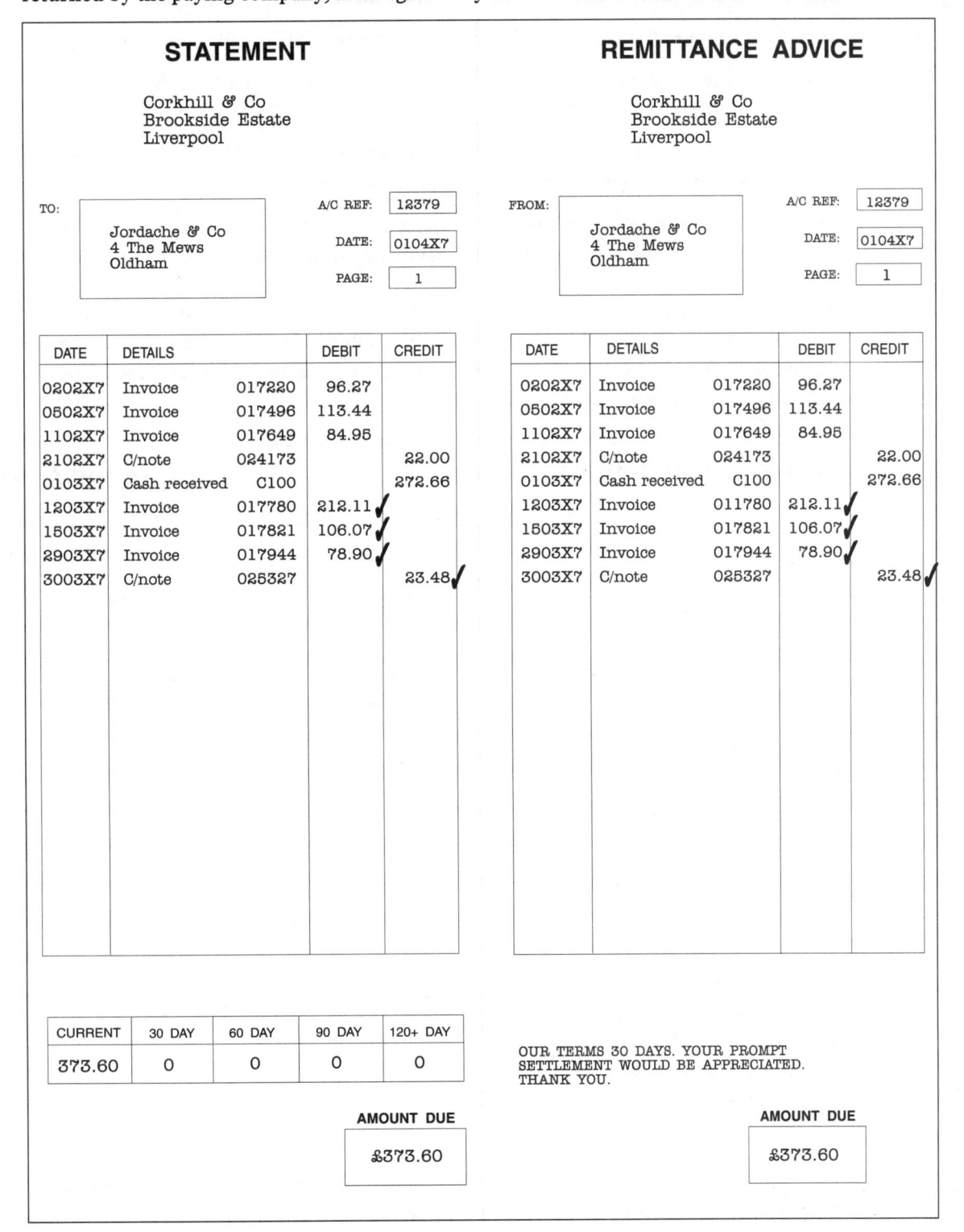

STATEMENT

Corkhill & Co
Brookside Estate
Liverpool

TO: Jordache & Co
4 The Mews
Oldham

A/C REF: 12379
DATE: 0104X7
PAGE: 1

DATE	DETAILS		DEBIT	CREDIT
0202X7	Invoice	017220	96.27	
0502X7	Invoice	017496	113.44	
1102X7	Invoice	017649	84.95	
2102X7	C/note	024173		22.00
0103X7	Cash received	C100		272.66
1203X7	Invoice	017780	212.11 ✓	
1503X7	Invoice	017821	106.07 ✓	
2903X7	Invoice	017944	78.90 ✓	
3003X7	C/note	025327		23.48 ✓

CURRENT	30 DAY	60 DAY	90 DAY	120+ DAY
373.60	0	0	0	0

AMOUNT DUE

£373.60

REMITTANCE ADVICE

Corkhill & Co
Brookside Estate
Liverpool

FROM: Jordache & Co
4 The Mews
Oldham

A/C REF: 12379
DATE: 0104X7
PAGE: 1

DATE	DETAILS		DEBIT	CREDIT
0202X7	Invoice	017220	96.27	
0502X7	Invoice	017496	113.44	
1102X7	Invoice	017649	84.95	
2102X7	C/note	024173		22.00
0103X7	Cash received	C100		272.66
1203X7	Invoice	011780	212.11 ✓	
1503X7	Invoice	017821	106.07 ✓	
2903X7	Invoice	017944	78.90 ✓	
3003X7	C/note	025327		23.48 ✓

OUR TERMS 30 DAYS. YOUR PROMPT
SETTLEMENT WOULD BE APPRECIATED.
THANK YOU.

AMOUNT DUE

£373.60

Part B: Recording and accounting for cash transactions

Procedures to compare receipt with remittance advice

2.4 The member of staff who records the receipt should compare it with the remittance advice sent by the paying company, using the following procedures.

Step 1. Check that the amounts shown on the **remittance advice add up** to the total.

Step 2. **Compare** the **total** with the amount of the **receipt** (usually a **cheque**).

Step 3. If there is a **disagreement** between the two amounts, mark on the remittance advice the amount received and calculate the **difference**.

Step 4. Send the cheque to be **banked** and then **record the receipt** (we will discuss **banking receipts** in Chapter 7 of this text and **recording receipts** in Chapter 8).

Step 5. Send the marked up remittance advice to the **sales ledger department** (where amounts which are owed to the business by individual customers are dealt with).

2.5 If there are differences between the amount received and the amount shown on the remittance advice these will be dealt with by the **sales ledger department** (the department that deals with customers who buy on credit). The sales ledger department will contact the customer and resolve any query.

REMITTANCE ADVICE				JORDACHE & CO	
To: Corkhill & Co Brookside Estate Liverpool				4 The Mews Oldham	
Account Ref: **01NIN**		Date: **0504X7**		Page: **1**	
DATE	DETAILS		INVOICES	CREDIT NOTES	PAYMENT AMOUNT
12.3.X7	Invoice	017780	212.11		212.11
15.3.X7	Invoice	017821	106.07		106.07
29.3.X7	Invoice	017944	78.90		78.90
30.3.X7	Credit note	025327		23.48	-23.48
			397.08	23.48	373.60

2.6 On the statement shown in Paragraph 2.3 the customer has marked off a total of £373.60 (remember to deduct the credit notes). The example above shows the remittance advice Jordache & Co would prepare itself.

Retail receipts

2.7 Payments (using cash, cheques and card vouchers) by **shop or retail customers** are not accompanied by any supporting documentation from the customer. The business selling the goods creates its own 'remittance advice' by recording the receipt on a cash register's till roll or on a manually written receipt voucher (described in the next section).

3 RECEIPTS GIVEN TO CUSTOMERS

> **KEY TERM**
>
> A **receipt** is a document given by the seller to the buyer when goods change hands in exchange for payment. It may be a till receipt, a written receipt or some other form of receipt.

Till receipts

3.1 **Cash registers** or '**tills**' are used mainly in retail shops where the money is handed over directly by the customer when the transaction takes place, in the form of cash, cheques and card vouchers (discussed later in this chapter). Most shops have electronic cash registers, often registering the details of items sold using bar code readers, which operate as follows.

- Store full price information on all stocks
- Record the value of the sale of each item
- Calculate the total value of the sale if more than one item is sold
- Calculate the required change to give to a customer once the operator has keyed in how much money has been handed over
- Issue a till receipt showing the entire transaction
- Sum up the transactions of the day at closing time

3.2 The cash register is acting as part of the **control over calculating and giving change** to customers. There are a number of potential errors in giving change, each of which will affect the customer directly and the business indirectly.

Potential error in giving change	Effect	Controlled by
Calculating and giving **too little change**	Customer annoyance - loss of goodwill	Cash register
Calculating and giving **too much change**	Loss of money by business	Cash register
Physically taking **incorrect amount** from till	Either of the above	Making sure staff are careful, well trained and numerate

3.3 Each till **receipt** will show some or all of the following.

(a) The name of the selling company or business
(b) The date (and possibly the time) of the transaction
(c) The price of each of the goods purchased
(d) The total value of goods purchased
(e) The VAT number (if applicable) of the selling company or business
(f) The amount tendered (given) by the customer
(g) The amount of change given to the customer
(h) The name of the assistant and/or cashier
(i) The till number

Part B: Recording and accounting for cash transactions

Written receipts

3.4 Where a cash register is not used then a **written or typed receipt** may be required. The same information should appear as that which appears on the till receipt, although it is often easier to enter more detailed information about the goods sold on a written receipt.

3.5 Some goods sold have a **unique registration or code number** to make them identifiable. Unique code numbers are often assigned to goods which are sold under guarantee (the supplier will repair or replace the goods for free within the time period specified in the guarantee). The code number is used by the supplier to make sure that the correct goods are being repaired or replaced, and not something that was bought elsewhere. Examples of such goods are electrical goods and cameras. The shop will usually keep a copy of the receipt by using carbon paper to write through onto another piece of paper.

Clarence's Cameras Ltd 14 The View Brighton	Date: 17.7.X7		**No. 78**
	List Price	VAT rate	Total
1 × Pencos 38 SL Camera ref: 34782938	372.00	17½%	372.00
1 × 35mm lens Pencos ref: 4983297	89.00	17½%	89.00
VAT @ 17½% Total	461.00		461.00 80.68 £ 541.68

Evidence of payment other than in cash

3.6 When a customer pays by some means other than cash, he may obtain some evidence of payment which is **not** a receipt. We will discuss each of these methods of payment in more detail later on in this chapter, here they are listed only briefly.

Method of payment	Evidence of payment
Credit card	The customer will receive a copy of the **signed credit card voucher** and there will be a record of the transaction on the **customer's monthly credit card statement** (which is important when a credit card has been used to buy things over the telephone).
Debit card	As with credit cards, the customer receives a copy of the signed **debit card voucher** and a record will appear on the **customer's bank statement**.
Cheque	The payment will appear on the **customer's bank statement**. The customer may have his **cheques returned** to him after they have cleared through the banking system (although this is rare).
Banker's draft, postal orders etc	The **issuing bank** or post office will hold records of the items issued.

Use of receipts in business trading

3.7 When companies trade with each other on a **credit basis** (goods are ordered and received before being paid for), **it is very unusual to issue a receipt**. For instance, ABC & Co have an account with XYZ Ltd. ABC buys £1,000 in goods in June 20X4. The terms of the trading agreement are to pay for the goods within 30 days of the end of the month in which the goods were sent, in this case payment is due on 30 July 20X4. ABC & Co pay the bill on time, sending a remittance advice. They get no receipt for their cheque for £1,000. The only acknowledgement of the payment is that the next statement of their account will show the cash receipt deducted from the balance outstanding.

3.8 We will look in more detail at cash registers in Chapter 8.

4 WAYS IN WHICH CUSTOMERS PAY

Types of receipt from customers

4.1 In the last section, when we mentioned a 'receipt', we were referring to the document given **to the purchaser by the seller** when goods changed hands. In this section we use the term receipt in a different sense.

> **KEY TERM**
>
> A **receipt** refers to the act of the **seller accepting payment** and to **the payment** itself once it has been accepted.

Methods of payment and their preparation are discussed in Chapter 9 of this text. In this chapter we will look at the most common forms of receipt.

- Cash
- Cheque
- Plastic cards

4.2 Generally, the way a company receives money will depend on the type of business it is in. Other forms of receipt include the following.

- Standing order
- Direct debit
- Mail transfer and telegraphic transfer
- BACS

Credit/cash sales

4.3 Some kinds of business make the bulk of their sales to customers on **credit** (they invoice customers). Others deal only with **cash sales**, in the sense that customers must pay for the goods on taking them, although the actual payment might be by cheque or card. The easiest way of distinguishing between these two types of business is as follows.

Type of sale	Typical business	Typical customer	Examples
Cash sale	Retailers	General public face-to-face as final consumer	Supermarkets Newsagents Chemists
Credit sale	Trading businesses	Other trading or retail businesses, who ultimately sell to general public as final consumer	Manufacturers of steel, gas, plumbing equipment, providers of training

4.4 The pattern of receipts experienced by these two types of business will be completely different.

(a) A **retail business** will get a fairly **steady flow of receipts** with perhaps more on Saturdays and late night shopping days.

(b) A **trading business** will get the bulk of its receipts on the date credit customers are due to pay. This is often the **end of the month**, although customers may be given different dates to pay to spread receipts more evenly over time.

5 CASH: PHYSICAL SECURITY CONSIDERATIONS

5.1 We all know what **money** looks like but what is it?

> **KEY TERM**
>
> **Cash** comprises the notes and coin which make up the legal tender of a country.

5.2 We will spend most of the rest of this section looking at the problems of **security** which concern organisations that deal with cash.

Forgery

5.3 There are frequent cases of **forgery of larger denomination notes** (£50, £20 and £10). It is advisable to examine all notes carefully before they are accepted, the metal thread incorporated into all these notes is difficult to duplicate. Even **small denomination notes and coins are forged**. London Underground Ltd was at one time forced to stop accepting 50 pence coins in ticket machines as some people were using 10 pence pieces wrapped in foil to fool the machines. Special marker pens and ultra-violet light detection equipment can now be used to check **bank notes**.

Theft

5.4 **Theft by staff.** This risk can be reduced by being careful about the people the business employs; their references should be checked properly and they should be monitored closely for their first few months of work.

Cash register security

5.5 The **cash register should be secure**, with keys needed to operate it. Staff should be trained to make them aware of the importance of keeping their keys safe and of not leaving the cash register open. Cash registers which are activated by different keys unique to each member of staff can give a **breakdown of sales by staff member**. This is another aid to preventing theft, as it will indicate staff who are not entering sales and pocketing the customer's money.

Safes

5.6 If possible, cash should be removed from the till regularly (so that there is only a relatively small amount in the till) and stored in a safer place. The ideal place would be a **safe**.

The safe should be in a place out of view of the customer. The number of **safe keys** should be kept to a minimum and access to the keys should be restricted.

Protective glass

5.7 Some businesses use **protective glass** (called a 'bandit screen') between the customer and the cashier to protect against theft and to ensure the safety of the cashiers. This measure is used in banks and building society branches, and also at petrol stations and many off licences after dark.

Strong box

5.8 Many retail outlets use a **strong box** at each cash register. When the cashier receives a large bank note, he or she will not place it in the cash register, but will put it down a chute or slot which leads to a strong box. The strong box will be built in to the counter under the cash register. The cashier can put money in but cannot take any out and of course customers cannot get into it. The money in the strong box can be removed at the end of the day.

Security guards and collections

5.9 Larger organisations will employ their own **in-house security staff**. As well as watching cashiers to check for theft, these security guards will accompany the staff who remove cash from the tills regularly during the day to take it to a safer location.

5.10 **External security firms** may be employed to collect money from the business premises and take it directly to the bank. This kind of firm uses trained staff and secured transport and is liable for the goods or money it carries.

Night safes

5.11 Where a business finds it impossible to bank money during normal banking hours, most banks will provide a key to their **night safe**. When the lid is unlocked and opened, it exposes only a small space in which the cash is deposited. Once the lid is closed the cash drops into a larger secure area within the bank. The bank issues boxes or wallets in which to put money and a press to mark the tags which close the boxes. Each press has a unique number on it which is allocated to one customer. In this way each box can be identified by the bank before it is opened and customers' deposits cannot be mixed up.

Frequent banking

5.12 In general, cash should be taken to the bank on a **regular and frequent basis,** this minimises the amount of money on the business premises. This may be particularly important if the amount of money the business can hold is limited under its insurance policy.

It is not a good idea to let the same person go to the bank every day at the same time. For security reasons it is better to **vary the member of staff** who takes the money to the bank and the **time of day it is taken**.

5.13 **Cash should never be sent by post,** if it is lost or stolen there is no way to trace or recover it.

Part B: Recording and accounting for cash transactions

6 CHEQUES

> **KEY TERM**
>
> A **cheque** is 'an unconditional order in writing addressed by a person to a bank, signed by the person giving it, requiring the bank to pay on demand a sum certain in money to or to the order of a specified person or bearer'.

6.1 **Cheques** and **card vouchers** are less easily exchanged by a thief, but the same security procedures should be maintained for cheques and card vouchers as for cash. **A cheque may be sent through the post,** as if it goes astray payment can be stopped.

6.2 **Cheques** are the most common receipt most businesses deal with and retail businesses will receive a high proportion of their revenue from the general public in the form of personal cheques (although these are gradually being replaced by card transactions - see below).

Cheque guarantee cards

6.3 When receiving a cheque which is *not* a company or business cheque, it is usual to accept the cheque only when it is supported by a **personal cheque guarantee card**. This card has on it a specimen of the account holder's signature and it will guarantee that a cheque written by the card holder will be **honoured** (cashed) by the bank **up to the amount** stated on the guarantee card. This is usually £50 although it is possible to obtain £100 and even £250 cheque guarantee cards.

6.4 If the cheque is written for an amount **greater** than that on the guarantee card then **the bank is not bound to honour it** although the cheque will normally be honoured if there are sufficient funds in the account and if the cheque is otherwise in order.

6.5 A typical cheque guarantee card looks like this.

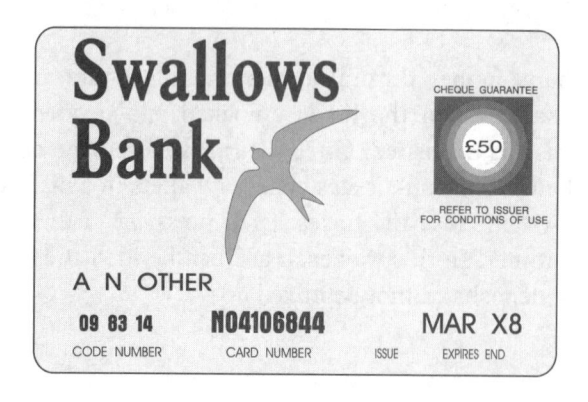

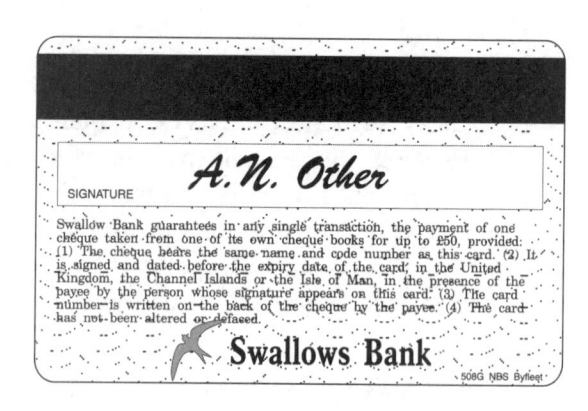

It shows many details that are on a cheque: sort code, account number and name, but it also has a **unique card number**. When the card is used to support a cheque this number will be written on the back of the cheque to prove to the bank that the cheque was guaranteed by a card.

7 RECEIPT OF CHEQUE PAYMENTS

7.1 It is best practice to follow these procedures when an individual customer pays by cheque supported by a cheque guarantee card.

Step 1. Examine the face of the cheque to ensure all the **details are correct**.
- **Date** (including the year)
- **Payee** name
- **Amount** in both words and figures

Step 2. Make sure that the cheque is **signed** by the drawer.

Step 3. **Compare the signature** on the cheque with that on the cheque guarantee card. It is unlikely that the match will be exact but it should be sufficiently close to avoid any doubt.

Step 4. **Check the details on the cheque guarantee card**.
- 'Expires end' date (has the card expired?)
- **Amount of the guarantee** (does it exceed the cheque amount?)
- **Name** agrees with that on the cheque
- **Other details** agree with the cheque (account number, sort code).

Step 5. **Copy details** from the cheque guarantee card on to the back of the cheque.
- **Card number**
- **Guarantee limit**
- **Expiry date**

7.2 Note that **only one guaranteed cheque can be used in one transaction.** A large number of cheques, each for an amount within the limit on the guarantee card, cannot be issued to make up one large aggregate amount.

7.3 Some businesses help their staff to make sure that all these checks are performed by using a **stamp** to list them on the back of the cheque. The cashier has to sign off or tick each check as it is performed.

7.4 Cheques received by a business through the **post**, from credit customers or individuals, will not be supported by cheque guarantee cards. Only Steps 1 and 2 above need be performed.

Cheques: security procedures

7.5 **Banks** recommend and carry out various security precautions with regard to cheques.

(a) Customers are asked to keep **cheque books and cards separate**, although this is not always easy or convenient, especially for women carrying handbags.

(b) The **number of cheques** in a book is kept to a minimum.

(c) Cheque cards are sent by **registered post** so that customers must sign for their receipt.

(d) The **card remains the property of the bank** and it can be withdrawn if it is being improperly used. New customers are often not issued with a cheque card until they have proved their reliability.

8 RECEIPT OF CARD PAYMENTS

8.1 **Plastic card payments** have become progressively more popular as methods of payment over the last few years. They are used **primarily by individuals,** rather than by companies (although companies do own credit cards which are generally allocated to members of staff

Part B: Recording and accounting for cash transactions

for their use to pay business expenses). Most retail outlets which accept credit and charge cards now use **EFTPOS** (Electronic Funds Transfer at Point of Sale). However, some small shops and restaurants still use manual processing which is described in this section. We will examine EFTPOS procedures in Section 9.

Plastic cards

8.2 A typical card would look like this and the letters (a) to (j) are explained below.

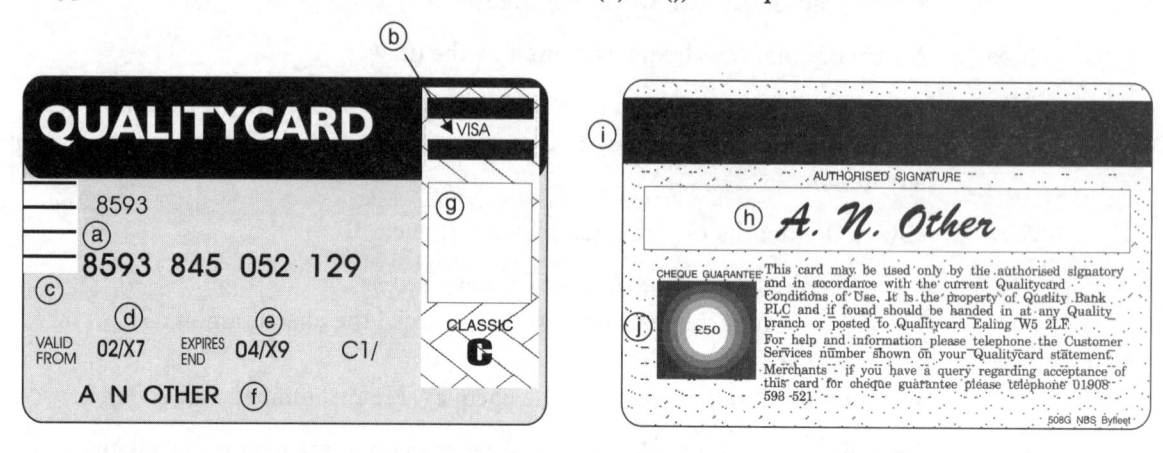

Feature		Explanation
(a)	Card number	Each card issued has a unique number allocated to it.
(b)	VISA	This is the type of credit card.
(c)	Qualitycard	This is the issuing company. There are many different issuing companies (mainly banks and building societies).
(d)	02/X7	This is the date from which the card can be used.
(e)	04/X9	This is the date on which the card expires.
(f)	A N Other	The name of the card holder is also on the front of the card.
(g)	Hologram	This is a special security device which seeks to prevent forgery of the card.
(h)	Signature strip	This holds the specimen signature of the card holder.
(i)	Magnetic strip	This black strip holds all the information on the card (except the signature) in code enabling a computer to read it.
(j)	£50	This is a cheque guarantee limit. Some cards double up as cheque guarantee cards.

The card number, the 'valid from' and 'expires end' dates, and the card holder name are all **raised lettering** so that when the card is imprinted onto a transaction voucher these details will appear on the voucher (see below).

8.3 There are two main types of card.
- Credit cards
- Debit cards

We shall look at each of them in turn.

Credit cards

8.4 A **credit card payment** involves three transactions and three parties (see below). Whilst credit is involved, for a supplier receiving payment in this way, credit card payments are treated as cash.

Transaction	Comments
Purchase of goods from a supplier by card holder	On producing his card to a **supplier** for goods and/or services, the **card holder** can obtain what he requires without paying for it immediately.
Payment of supplier by card issuer	The **supplier** recovers from the **card issuer** the price of goods or services less a commission which is the card issuer's profit margin.
Payment of card issuer by card holder	At monthly intervals the **card issuer** sends to the **card holder** a statement. The card holder may either settle interest-free within 28 days or he may pay interest on the balance owing after 28 days. He is required to pay a minimum of 5% or £5, whichever is the greater.

8.5 Card issuers often charge a flat yearly **membership fee** as well as charging **interest**.

8.6 The credit cards issued in the UK include **Visa** and **MasterCard** (Access). Most banks, building societies and finance houses issue either Visa or MasterCard credit cards, some issue both. American Express issues its own credit card (Optima).

8.7 Suppliers are allowed to charge more for goods purchased by credit card than the same goods purchased by cash or cheque. This reflects the **cost to the supplier** of accepting the credit card as payment. The card issuers charge the supplier a percentage of the supplier's credit card receipts (perhaps between ½% and 4%, depending on volume) for processing. **Differential pricing** of credit card purchases has not so far become widespread as it deters customers who wish to buy on credit.

8.8 Many card issuers issue special charity cards called **affinity cards** which are connected to a specific charity or cause. When a customer applies for and receives such a card, the issuer will donate, say £5, to the charity. Each time the card is used a small percentage of the purchase price of the item bought (say 0.25%) is also donated to the charity.

Accepting a credit card receipt

8.9 Credit card transactions can be accepted over the telephone or in person over the counter. If goods are ordered by credit card over the **telephone** then either the goods must be sent to the address of the cardholder, or the goods must be collected in person by the cardholder (for example, theatre tickets).

Part B: Recording and accounting for cash transactions

8.10 There are certain **security checks** that you must make before you can accept a credit card as payment.

Security check	Comments
Rub your thumb over the **signature panel**	It should be flush with the card, not raised (if it is not flush with the card then it may have been tampered with).
Compare the customer signature on the card with that on the voucher	They will not normally match exactly but the likeness should be close enough to leave no doubt.
Check whether the card is stolen against the warning lists regularly issued by the card issuing companies	These lists should be kept up to date and close to all tills where credit cards are accepted. Remember that there is currently a £50 reward for recovering a stolen credit card!
Check that the card is valid by the date	If the current date is past the expiry date, or if it is before the 'valid from' date, then the credit card is not valid. Also, if the 'valid from' date is the current month you should be wary as much fraud occurs on newly issued cards.
Check that the transaction does not exceed the business **floor limit**	When a credit card company allows a business to accept its cards as payment it will set a **floor limit** for the shop or business. Up to this limit the business can process all credit card transactions without any authority. The floor limit might be £100. If the purchase is above that amount then you must ring the credit card company to ask for **authorisation**. If there is no problem then the credit card company will give you an authorisation code which you need to enter in the relevant box. (See completed voucher below.)
Final checks	These are all worth checking, even for the second time. • Customer signature • Figures are correct • All details imprinted • Floor limit/authorisation code • Dated correctly

The telephone check system does not only exist for when a transaction is over the floor limit. A retailer can ring up if he is suspicious of the validity of the card and use a code to warn the credit card company that he is worried. The credit card company staff can then double check their records and they may also ask questions of the retailer and/or the customer to prove the identity of the customer.

Debit cards

8.11 **Debit cards** are designed for customers who like paying by plastic card but who do not always want credit.

(a) The customer **signs a voucher** at the point of sale

(b) This is then either **processed** through the credit card system (for example Barclays Connect card is a Visa card) or through an EFTPOS system (see below).

(c) The amount is **deducted directly from the customer's bank account**.

6: Receiving and checking money

8.12 If the debit card transaction has to be processed manually, then the voucher used is very similar to the vouchers used for credit card transactions.

9 EFTPOS

> **KEY TERM**
>
> **EFTPOS (Electronic Funds Transfer at Point of Sale)** makes possible the automatic transfer of funds from a customer's bank account to a retail organisation at the point in time when the customer purchases goods (or services) from it.

9.1 EFTPOS is an established system of payment for goods and services, in widespread use throughout the UK. The effect has been to reduce both the number of cheques written and the number of debit or credit card transactions processed manually.

The EFTPOS terminal

9.2 Most types of **credit card** and **debit card** can be processed through the EFTPOS terminal which sits on or by the retailer's counter. The terminal can read the magnetic strips on the backs of cards automatically.

9.3 The terminal allows businesses to capture card transactions **electronically,** which has many **advantages** over the manual system outlined above.

  (a) They do not **physically** have to take vouchers to the bank to get paid.

  (b) When a retailer carries out a transaction on the terminal it will automatically telephone the appropriate card company and seek **authorisation**, eliminating the need to ring them for approval of transactions above the floor limit.

  (c) At the same time the transaction will also be **accepted** by the card company for processing and subsequent payment to the retailer's account.

9.4 The terminal prints a **two part receipt** for the customer to sign that is used in place of the manual vouchers we discussed above. The **details of the card**, the **transaction amount** and the **supplier details** are all printed on the receipt. The customer receives the top copy of this receipt and the retailer keeps the bottom part for his records. Many outlets which have EFTPOS also have 'chip and PIN'. This involves the customer keying in his pin number rather than using his signature. As long as PIN numbers are safeguarded, this greatly reduces the risk of credit and debit card fraud.

Part B: Recording and accounting for cash transactions

9.5 The voucher produced by an EFTPOS sales transaction will look like this.

Retailer name	A.MERCHANT		
Retailer address	HIGH STREET		
	ANYTOWN		
Card issuer name	VISA		
Account number	4929000000014321		
Expiry date (mm/yy)	08X9		
	SALE	£25.25	Amount
	PLEASE KEEP THIS FOR		
	YOURS RECORDS		
	SIGNATURE		
	M. Stephens		
Authorisation code	AUTH CODE	12345	
Retailer message	THANKYOU		
Merchant number	M1234567		
Terminal ID	T06500015	R0019	Transaction number
Date	DATE 06/07/X7	07:25	Time

9.6 Note that, even though the terminal carries out most checks for you, you should still consider carrying out all the **checks in** Paragraph 8.10 as computers have been known to get it wrong!

9.7 There are a variety of further procedures, particularly for where the transaction is **not authorised** (the terminal can tell you to retain the card). Other types of transactions can also be processed, including **mail order** sales (where the card number is keyed in manually), **reversals** (ie returns) and the machine can also issue **duplicate receipts**.

9.8 The transaction will come back **not authorised** where the credit or debit card has been reported stolen. It may also be **not authorised** where the transaction would exceed the customer's credit limit on their card, although the credit card company may let the transaction through and suggest to the customer that their credit limit should be raised. If the transaction is not authorised due to exceeding the credit limit, you would explain to the customer that it has not been authorised and ask if they wish to use another means of payment.

9.9 The terminal will come with a **training card** for staff training and a **supervisor's card**, which has to be used in order to carry out certain transactions (for control purposes). Such transactions include refunds and report requests. These cards look like credit cards and they are 'wiped' through the terminal as normal credit cards are.

Reports

9.10 The reports which can be requested will usually include the following.

- Transactions processed through the terminal for **each card issuer** since the last report
- **'End of day' procedures**, which we will discuss in Chapter 7

10 OTHER RECEIPTS

10.1 We have examined the types of receipts which are dealt with by most businesses. There are some more **specialised kinds of receipts** which are used by certain businesses. They use these methods because it suits their particular business.

Banker's draft

```
┌─────────────────────────────────────────────────────────────┐
│  Quality Bank            Date_____20____    20-27-48N      │
│                          Branch _____              │
│                                                              │
│   On demand pay ─────────────────────────────── or order    │
│   ─────────────────────────────────────  £ _____         │
│   ─────────────────────────────── on account of this Office │
│                                                              │
│   To Quality Bank plc              ─────────── Manager      │
│   Head Office                                                │
│   London W5 2LF                    ─────────── Countersignature │
│        ⑉101131⑉  20⑉ 2748⑊  4731822 1⑉                      │
└─────────────────────────────────────────────────────────────┘
```

10.2 This is a method of payment which is available from banks on payment of a fee. Paying by **banker's draft** is common when a customer is buying property and needs a guarantee that the payment **cannot be dishonoured** in order to complete the purchase.

Standing orders and direct debits

10.3 These types of payment are described in more detail in Chapter 9. They are **regular payments** (usually monthly). The amount of a standing order can only be changed by the payer, but the amount of a direct debit can be changed by the receiver at will.

Activity 6.1

Imagine that you are employed in various different businesses, as detailed below. In each case, a customer or potential customer telephones you with a query about how a payment or payments may be made.

Task

State what you would say in response to the customer, making any assumptions about the policies of the businesses which you consider appropriate. You should explain your reasons as part of your response.

The customers' queries are as follows.

(a) *Business: electricity company*

'I am a domestic customer, and receive a bill from you each quarter. I want to continue to pay quarterly, but I don't want to go the trouble of writing out a cheque or making a special trip (for example to a bank or your office) to pay the bill. However, I do need to know how much the bill is going to be before I am due to pay it. What method of payment would you suggest?'

(b) *Business: house builder*

'If I buy one of your houses, I'll be getting a mortgage, and so some of the funds will be coming from my building society. However, some will be due from me when the sale is completed. How will that need to be paid?'

Part B: Recording and accounting for cash transactions

(c) *Business: mail order company*

'I want to place an order with you. I don't have a bank account, building society account or a credit card, so I suppose that I'll need to send you the amount due by cash through the post. Is that OK?'

(d) *Business: DIY retailer*

'I want to call in to your store to buy something costing £34 for a friend. I understand that you accept cheques supported by a cheque guarantee card. My friend has made out and signed the cheque and given me her cheque guarantee card. I'd like to bring the cheque and card in when I collect the goods.'

Key learning points

- Receipts have to be well **controlled** to ensure a good cash flow. There are three key features of control.
    - **Banking** (performed promptly and correctly)
    - **Security** (avoiding loss or theft)
    - **Documentation** (remittance advice)
- Trade customers usually send a *remittance advice* with their payment.
- **Till receipts** or **written** receipts should contain certain information.
- There are various ways a company can **receive money**. The main ones are:
    - Cash
    - Cheque
    - Credit or debit card
- **Holding cash** creates problems and careful security procedures are required.
- **Cheque guarantee cards** are issued to guarantee personal cheques up to a certain limit. Strict procedures should be followed when accepting a personal cheque as payment.
- **Strict procedures** should also be followed when accepting credit or debit cards as payment.
- **EFTPOS** is a means of allowing a transaction to be recorded immediately on customer bank accounts or credit card statements, while at the same time authorising the transaction.

Quick quiz

1. Control over cash receipts will concentrate on which three key areas?
2. What is the function of a remittance advice?
3. Why should cash be banked regularly?
4. Should cash be sent through the post in 'an emergency'?
5. Is it safe to send a cheque through the post?
6. What does EFTPOS stand for?
7. A banker's draft cannot be dishonoured. True or false?

Answers to quick quiz

1   Receipts should be banked promptly, correctly recorded and loss or theft should be prevented.

2   A remittance advice shows which invoices a payment covers.

3   To reduce the chance of it being lost/mislaid/stolen, and as part of general good business practice.

4   No. Never!

5   Yes. A cheque can be 'stopped' if it goes astray, and 'traced' if deposited by an unauthorised person.

6   EFTPOS = Electronic Funds Transfer at Point of Sale.

7   True.

Answer to activity

Answer 6.1

(a) 'You can pay by quarterly **direct debit**. You need to complete a direct debit mandate form which authorises us to debit amounts from your bank account. We will send you a bill in the usual way each quarter, and the amount due will be debited from your account 14 days after the date of the bill, so you'll know how much is to be debited well in advance. If an error is made, either the bank or ourselves must put it right.'

(b) 'Normally, any balance due to us when the sale is completed will be paid by **banker's draft** or by **BACS**. A banker's draft or BACS is considered to be as good as cash, and of course cash would be acceptable but it is unusual and not so convenient to pay such a large amount in cash.'

Tutorial note. A builder may accept a cheque for a *deposit* put down on a house, but is very unlikely to accept a cheque when the sale is 'completed', as that is when he must hand over the keys and there is a risk that the cheque could be dishonoured.

(c) 'We do not advise you to send cash through the post, as we cannot accept responsibility if it is lost. We suggest that you pay by **postal order**, obtained from your post office. The post office will charge a fee for this service.'

(d) 'In order to pay by a cheque supported by a **banker's card**, it is necessary for the person whose signature appears on the card to sign and date the cheque in the presence of the payee - in other words, in our store. This rule is a standard rule of all of the banks. Please therefore ask your friend to call in to make the payment herself, unless you wish to pay by some other means, such as cash.'

Chapter 7 Banking monies received

Chapter topic list

1. The banking system
2. The banker/customer relationship
3. Procedures for banking cash
4. Procedures for banking cheques
5. Procedures for banking plastic card transactions
6. Banking and EFTPOS
7. Banking other receipts

The following study sessions are covered in this chapter

			Syllabus reference
4	(a)	Describe the relationship between a bank and its customer	7a
	(b)	Outline the working of a central bank clearing system	7a
	(c)	Recognise the obligation owed by a bank to it's clients	7a
	(f)	Outline the purpose and format of paying in documents	3b
5	(f)	Understand procedures for banking cash receipts	3b
	(l)	Explain the correct procedure to cope with unusual situations: wrongly completed or out of date cheques	3a

7: Banking monies received

1 THE BANKING SYSTEM

1.1 This chapter is concerned with the **practical aspects of banking** the payments received by a business. Before dealing with these aspects, however, it would be useful to understand some background details about two areas.

(a) The **clearing bank system** and how it operates.
(b) The **legal relationship between the customer and the banker** (Section 2).

> **Exam alert**
>
> We refer to the UK banking system. Any questions on the central bank system in the examination will relate to the UK.

The banking system

1.2 The banking system in the UK consists of the following components.

(a) The **Bank of England** is the **central bank** which controls the banking industry.

(b) **Clearing** or **retail banks**. There are four major high street banks.
- Barclays
- Lloyds - TSB
- HSBC
- NatWest

(c) **Smaller retail banks**
- Co-operative Bank
- Yorkshire Bank
- Abbey National

The clearing system

> **KEY TERM**
>
> **Clearing** is the mechanism for obtaining payment for cheques.

1.3 Banks settle cheques and credits through the **clearing system**. Once the values of cheques passed between the banks at the end of a particular day's clearing have been determined, the resulting debts arising between the banks need to be settled.

For example, Lloyds may be asking for settlement of £20m worth of cheques drawn on Barclays bank paid in by its customers into their accounts at Lloyds branches. In turn, Barclays may have £25m worth of Lloyds cheques paid into branches of Barclays.

	£m
Lloyds owes Barclays	25
Barclays owes Lloyds	20
Net debt: Lloyds owes Barclays	5

In short, at the end of a day's banking, **banks owe money to other banks, and are owed money in return**. These debts are settled through accounts which the banks maintain at the Bank of England. The balances on these accounts are termed **operational balances**.

Part B: Recording and accounting for cash transactions

1.4 The diagram on the next page explains how the cheque clearing system operates.

1.5 The **cheque clearing system** follows the principles outlined below.

Step 1. The receiving bank branches **stamp their names and addresses** in addition to the crossings on the cheques, **sort the cheques** paid in by its customers into bundles of cheques drawn on each of the other banks which participate in the cheque clearing system. (The 'non-clearing' banks and building societies participate by using one of the clearing banks as their agent.)

Step 2. The bundles of cheques from each receiving bank branch are sent in, by special overnight delivery, to the **head office** of the bank to which the branch belongs.

Step 3. The head office delivers to the **Bankers Clearing House** the bundles of cheques (with covering lists) drawn on each of the other banks, or on non-clearing banks which they represent.

Step 4. The Bankers Clearing House distributes these cheques to the head offices of the relevant **paying banks**.

Step 5. The paying banks' head offices **process the cheques** using computers and distribute the cheques to the various branches of the banks on which the cheques are drawn.

1.6 The sequence of delivery to the Bankers Clearing House, exchange between bank head offices, and re-distribution down the chain to individual branches should be completed, as regards each cheque, within three working days.

1.7 If the paying bank **dishonours a cheque** (refuses to pay it, usually because the paying bank's customer has insufficient funds) delivered to the branch through the clearing system, it marks on the cheque the **reason for its refusal to pay** and returns it by post **direct** to the receiving bank branch from which it came.

The amount of the cheque will have been included in the total value of cheques passing from the receiving bank to the paying bank at the central clearing. The transaction between the receiving and paying banks is **cancelled** by the receiving bank branch sending in an **unpaid claim** for processing through the clearing system.

1.8 Since the total value of cheques payable by and receivable by each bank with regard to the other banks each day will not be equal, the banks' head offices **adjust the position between them by credits and debits in their respective accounts at the Bank of England.**

7: Banking monies received

The clearing system

Alpha, a customer of Barclays Bank, Penzance, writes a cheque to Beta. Beta is a customer of Lloyds TSB Bank, Stoke and pays the cheque into his branch at Stoke on Monday.

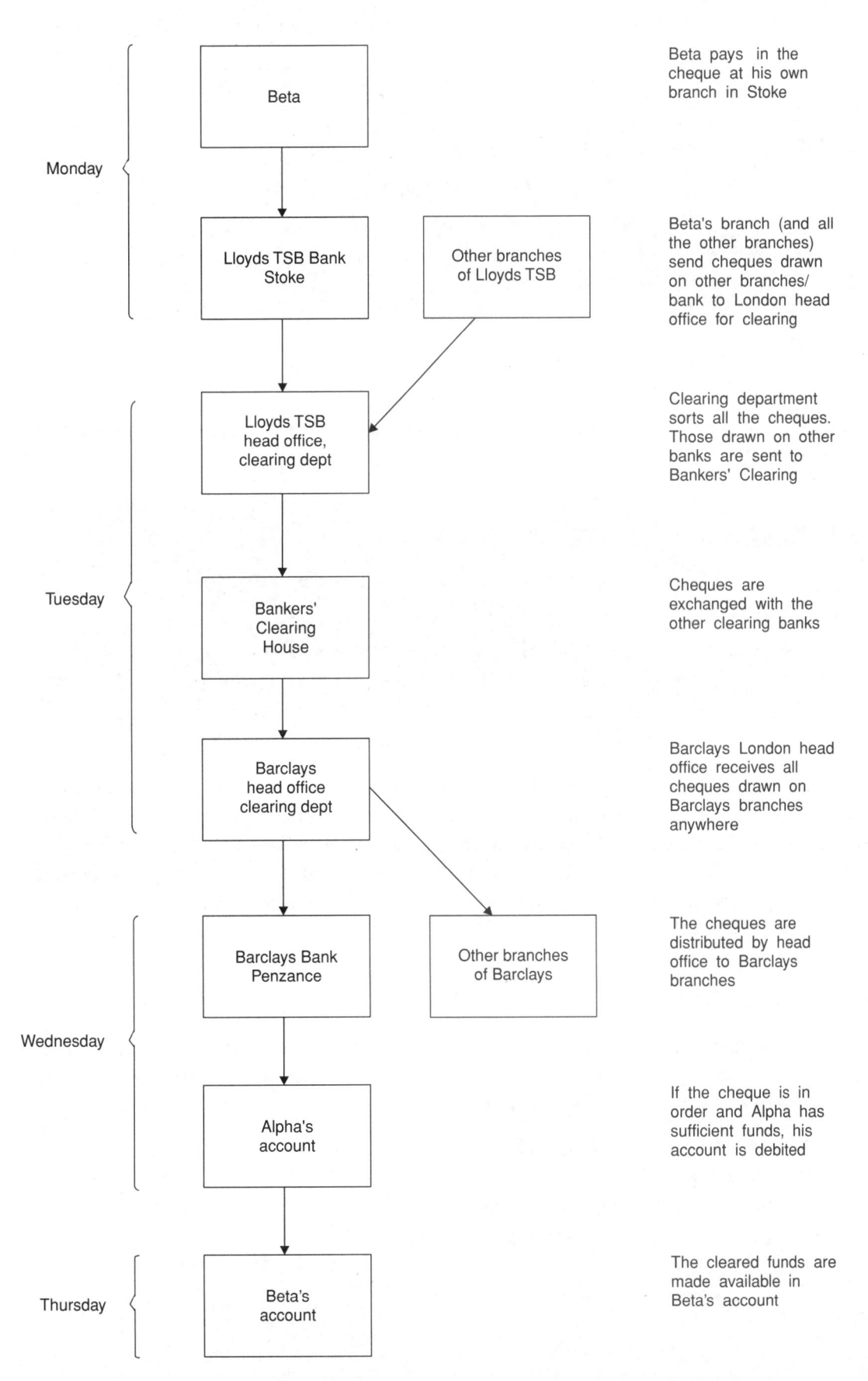

Monday

Beta → Beta pays in the cheque at his own branch in Stoke

Lloyds TSB Bank Stoke ← Other branches of Lloyds TSB → Beta's branch (and all the other branches) send cheques drawn on other branches/bank to London head office for clearing

Tuesday

Lloyds TSB head office, clearing dept → Clearing department sorts all the cheques. Those drawn on other banks are sent to Bankers' Clearing

Bankers' Clearing House → Cheques are exchanged with the other clearing banks

Barclays head office clearing dept → Barclays London head office receives all cheques drawn on Barclays branches anywhere

Wednesday

Barclays Bank Penzance → Other branches of Barclays → The cheques are distributed by head office to Barclays branches

Alpha's account → If the cheque is in order and Alpha has sufficient funds, his account is debited

Thursday

Beta's account → The cleared funds are made available in Beta's account

145

Part B: Recording and accounting for cash transactions

2 THE BANKER/CUSTOMER RELATIONSHIP

What is a banker?

2.1 The definition of a 'banker' has been decided by a combination of statute (laws passed by Parliament) and case law (results of situations where one person or company takes another person or company to court for the court to resolve a disagreement between the two parties).

> **KEY TERM**
>
> A **banker** is someone who will do the following.
> - Put money and cheques **received** on a customer's behalf into his account.
> - Take out all cheques and orders **paid** from the account by the customer.
> - **Keep accounts**, such as current accounts, which can be used for paying in or taking out on the customer's behalf.

What is a customer?

2.2 The term 'customer' or 'customer of a bank' is not defined in statute. However, case law has established the following definition.

> **KEY TERM**
>
> A person becomes a **customer** in respect of cheque transactions as soon as the bank opens an account for him in his name.
>
> In any other situation, for example when investment advice is given, a person becomes a **customer** as soon as the bank accepts his instructions and undertakes to provide a service.

2.3 It is important to know if a person is a customer because banks owe many **legal duties** to customers and can be **sued** if they do not carry out these duties adequately. There is also protection in law for a bank doing certain things for customers which would not apply if it did them for non-customers. For example, a bank might advance cash to a person presenting a credit card, who would not by virtue of this transaction alone become a customer.

The contractual relationships

2.4 The relationship between bank and customer arises from legal **contracts** between them which it is necessary to understand. There are **four** main types of contractual relationship which may exist between a banker and a customer.

- Debtor/creditor (see Paragraph 2.5)
- Bailor/bailee (see Paragraph 2.6)
- Principal/agent (see Paragraphs 2.7 and 2.8)
- Mortgagor/mortgagee (see Paragraph 2.9)

7: Banking monies received

Debtor/creditor relationship

2.5 If you lend a friend, Bill, some money, then you are said to be Bill's **creditor**. Bill owes you money and therefore he is your **debtor**. This relationship applies when a customer deposits money in a bank. At some point the bank will have to pay back the money to the customer, so the **customer is a creditor of the bank** whilst the **bank is the debtor of the customer**.

Exactly the converse is true if a customer has an overdrawn account at the bank: the debtor/creditor relationship is reversed.

The bank **does not hold the client's money in trust.** This would mean that they would have to give any profit made using the money to the client. Banks don't do this, over and above paying any agreed rate of interest to the customer.

The bailor/bailee relationship

2.6 This relationship exists where a bank offers a **safe deposit service** to customers, which allows use of the bank's strong room or safe. When it accepts the customer's property, the bank has the following obligations.

(a) To take '**reasonable' care to safeguard** it against damage and loss.

(b) To **redeliver** it to the customer or some other person authorised by him and not to deliver it to any other person. In law this type of arrangement is known as a **bailment**.

The customer is the bailor, the bank is the bailee.

Principal/agent relationship

> **KEY TERM**
>
> An **agency** relationship is one where one person (the **agent**) acts for another (the **principal**), usually for the purpose of doing business between the principal and a third party.

2.7 The use of an agent is often necessary as the principal does not have sufficient **specialist knowledge** to deal with the third party himself. An example of this is where an accountant deals with the Inland Revenue on behalf of a client, or where an employment agency finds a new employee or a temp for an employer.

2.8 The bank may act as **agent for its customers.** It may also employ agents (for example stockbrokers) to handle certain business, or it may have dealings with agents of its customers. A fairly common example of how the bank can act as agent is when the bank arranges insurance for the customer, the bank is acting as an insurance broker and is the agent of its customer.

Mortgagor/mortgagee relationship

2.9 This relationship arises when a customer asks a bank to give a loan secured by a charge or **mortgage** over the customer's assets such as property. The **customer**, or **mortgagor**, grants the **bank**, or **mortgagee**, a mortgage. **At the same time** the customer is the debtor, and the bank is the creditor for the amount of the loan. If the customer does not pay back the loan the bank can sell the asset or assets to recover its money.

2.10 Section summary

Contractual relationship	Transaction	Bank	Customer
Debtor/creditor	Customer deposits cash at bank	Debtor	Creditor
	Bank gives customer money on overdraft	Creditor	Debtor
Bailor/bailee	Customer stores property in bank's safest deposit facilities	Bailee	Bailor
Principal/agent	Bank arranges insurance for customer	Agent	Principal
Mortgagor/mortgagee	Bank lends money to customer with a mortgage on customer's property as its security	Mortgagee (Creditor)	Mortgagor (Debtor)

The fiduciary relationship

2.11 This type of relationship is **not contractual**. In a normal relationship between a bank and a customer, the bank can be in a position of exerting **undue influence** on the customer, perhaps forcing him to do something he does not really wish to do. The law recognises this and therefore expects the 'superior' party, in this case the bank, to act in good faith. This is said to be a **fiduciary** (or **special**) **relationship**.

The rights and duties of bankers and customers

The rights of bankers

2.12 Bankers' rights accrue on the basis of accepted legal or moral justice.

Rights of bankers	Comments
Making charges or commissions	If they are **reasonable** (this is apart from charging interest on overdrafts).
Using customers' money	As noted before, the money deposited is *not* held by the bank on trust and the bank can use it to **earn interest**.
Demanding repayment of overdrawn balances	All overdrafts are **repayable on demand**, unless separate terms state or imply otherwise.
Possessing a lien over securities	A **lien** is a right to retain possession of another's property to discharge a debt. This would *not* apply to items held in safe custody such as jewellery, but would apply to deposits of property as informal security for a loan.

7: Banking monies received

The duties of customers

2.13 On the basis of legal or moral justice, the following duties are owed to the bank by the customer.

Duties of customer	Comment
Ensuring that **fraud** is not facilitated when drawing cheques	Customers must be careful with their cheques in the sense that they should not do things like sign a blank cheque and then send it through the post. They must also tell the bank of any known forgeries.
Indemnifying the bank when it acts on the customer's behalf	'Indemnify' means 'secure against possible loss or damage'. The most common example of this is when the customer uses a cheque guarantee card to indemnify the bank against the possibility that the cheque he writes takes his account into overdraft. The customer is then obliged to repay the overdraft created on demand.

The duties of bankers = rights of customers

> **KEY TERM**
>
> A **duty** is a task or action which a person is bound to perform for moral or legal reasons.

2.14 The duties of a banker fall in the categories listed below. These duties may be said to represent the rights of customers as well as the duties of bankers. Customers' rights are supported by the **Banking Code** and the **Banking Ombudsman** schemes.

Duties of bankers	Comments
Honour a customer's **cheque**	The cheque must be correctly made out, there must be sufficient funds in the account and there must be no legal reason why the cheque cannot be paid (for instance, insolvency of the customer would bar payment of funds from his account).
Receipt of customer's funds	The funds must be credited to the customer's account.
Repayment on demand	There must be a written request for repayment from a customer, during normal bank opening hours and at the customer's branch or another agreed bank or branch.
Comply with customer's **instructions**	When there are sufficient funds, the bank must do as the customer requests.
Provide a **statement**	The banker must provide a statement showing transactions on a customer's account in a 'reasonable time' and also details of the balance of the account on request.
Confidentiality	As a general principle, a bank should keep in confidence what it knows about a customer's affairs. There are four recognised exceptions to this rule. (i) Disclosure may be **required by law,** for instance under

Part B: Recording and accounting for cash transactions

Duties of bankers	Comments
	the Drug Trafficking Offences Act 1986 and the Criminal Justice Act 1993.
	(ii) There may be a **public duty to disclose**, as when a customer trades with the enemy during a war.
	(iii) The **interest of the bank** may require disclosure, as when the bank sues the customer to recover what it is owed.
	(iv) The customer may have given **express or implied consent** (where, for instance, the customer asks a third party to obtain a 'bankers reference').
Advise of **forgery**	The bank must tell the customer when it becomes apparent that cheques bearing a forgery of the customer's signature are being drawn on his account.
Care and skill	Bankers are expected to use care and skill, partly for professional reasons but also to ensure the banks' statutory protection under some legislation.
Closure of accounts	Bankers have a duty to provide reasonable notice to a customer when the bank wishes to close the account. The period of notice should allow the customer to make other arrangements.

2.15 There is **no duty for the customer** to ensure that he keeps records of the account and he has **no duty to check the statements he gets from the bank**. This means that the onus is very much on the bank to ensure transactions are correctly applied to a customer's account. However, it is good business practice to monitor all bank accounts and **reconcile** the account back to your general ledger.

3 PROCEDURES FOR BANKING CASH

The paying-in slip

3.1 When a business or an individual wants to pay money into the bank, then normally a **paying-in slip** must be used. The bank treats this as a kind of summary document which 'totals up' the cash (or other forms of money) which is being banked.

3.2 A paying-in slip will look similar to the one shown here.

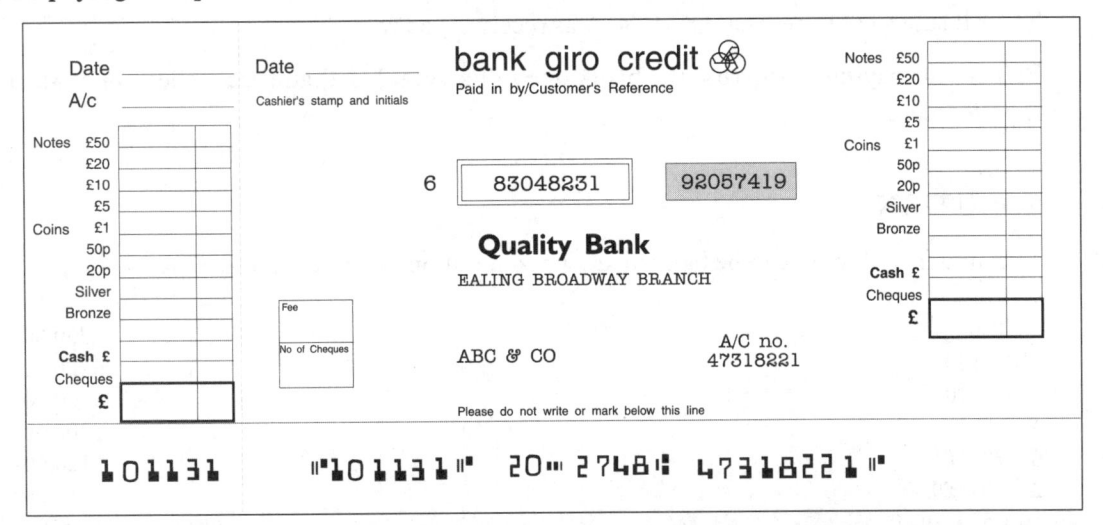

[Paying-in slip image showing Quality Bank, Ealing Broadway Branch, for ABC & Co, A/C no. 47318221]

> **KEY TERM**
>
> A **float** is the money kept in the till at the end of the day so that the next day there is some cash available to give change to customers.

Procedures for preparing a paying-in slip

3.3 The following procedures are good practice to follow when preparing money for banking.

Step 1. **Count the cash** as described above.

Step 2. **Add up**, on a separate piece of paper, how much cash you are banking.

Step 3. Compare the **calculated total** to the total according to the **cash register** (as we will discuss in Chapter 8 of this text).

Step 4. **Calculate any discrepancy** between the cash counted and the cash register total. If it is large then it should be investigated, but if it is small then it may be ignored, depending on company policy.

Step 5. Enter the **total for each denomination of note** in the appropriate place on the paying in slip.

Step 6. Add up the numbers again to check the total and **enter it in the 'total cash' box**.

3.4 EXAMPLE: BANKING CASH

You are preparing the day's takings for banking. When you have sorted and counted the notes you find you have the following.

(a) Five £50 notes
(b) 110 £20 notes
(c) 560 £10 notes
(d) 40 £5 notes
(e) Six bags each containing 20 £1 coins
(f) Two bags each containing 10 50p coins
(g) Ten bags each containing 50 20p coins
(h) Other silver worth £32.20
(i) Bronze worth 93p

Part B: Recording and accounting for cash transactions

The **float** left in the till was £34.90 at the end of yesterday and £43.62 at the end of today. The till summary states that £8,517.41 was received today.

Prepare the paying in slip (use the blank one in Paragraph 3.2) and reconcile cash banked to the till records.

3.5 SOLUTION

The amounts of money to be banked are worked out on a separate piece of paper.

	£
5 × £50	250.00
110 × £20	2,200.00
560 × £10	5,600.00
40 × £5	200.00
6 × 20 × £1	120.00
2 × 10 × £0.50	10.00
10 × 50 × £0.20	100.00
Other silver	32.20
Bronze	0.93
Total	8,513.13

The change in the **float** must be taken into account. If it had stayed the same then we would not need to make any adjustment. Here it has changed by £8.72 (£43.62 − £34.90). If we had not increased the float by that amount then we would have been able to put that money in the bank. So we should add it on to the money we are banking to compare it with what the till says we have taken.

	£
Money to be banked	8,513.13
Add increase in the float	8.72
	8,521.85
Receipts according to the till	8,517.41
Difference	4.44

This difference is very small and would be ignored (or **written off**). The business should set a limit, for instance £5, over which investigations are made. We will now complete the paying-in slip.

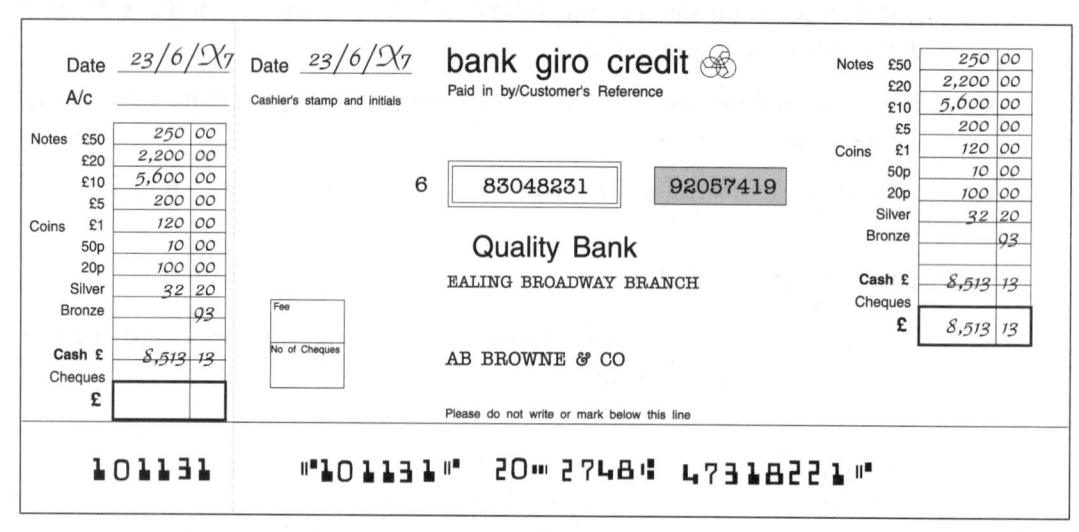

The paying-in slip is now ready to be taken to the bank with the money.

Security procedures when banking cash

3.6 We have already looked at some **security procedures** in Chapter 6. Generally, the points below should be considered and implemented where possible.

7: Banking monies received

(a) **Vary the time** of the visit to the bank and **vary which member of staff** takes the money there.

(b) If possible, **send more than one person**. This is particularly important when using the night safe. The banks advise that one person should drive and then watch over the other person who carries the money and puts it into the night safe.

(c) If very large amounts of cash are banked regularly then the business should consider employing a **security firm** to collect the money and deliver it to the bank.

(d) It is always wise to fill in the part of the paying-in slip which is retained by the customer of the bank (on the left hand side) so you have a **record** of paying the money into the bank. You can record the information elsewhere if you wish.

4 PROCEDURES FOR BANKING CHEQUES

4.1 The same paying-in slip is used for cheques as for cash, but this time we also need to look at the **back of the paying-in slip**.

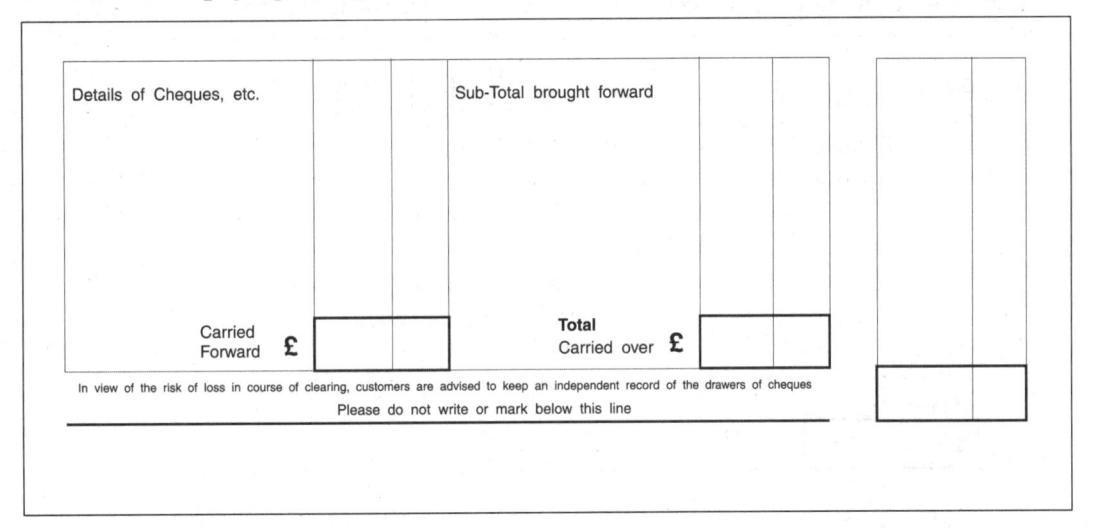

```
┌─────────────────────────────────────────────────────────────────────────────┐
│  ┌─────────────────────────┬───┬─────────────────────────┬───┐  ┌───────┐  │
│  │ Details of Cheques, etc.│   │ Sub-Total brought forward│   │  │       │  │
│  │                         │   │                          │   │  │       │  │
│  │                         │   │                          │   │  │       │  │
│  │                         │   │                          │   │  │       │  │
│  │                         │   │                          │   │  │       │  │
│  │                         │   │                          │   │  │       │  │
│  │       Carried       £   │   │    Total       £         │   │  │       │  │
│  │       Forward           │   │    Carried over          │   │  │       │  │
│  ├─────────────────────────┴───┴─────────────────────────┴───┤  └───────┘  │
│  │ In view of the risk of loss in course of clearing, customers are advised to keep an independent record of the drawers of cheques │
│  │                  Please do not write or mark below this line                                                                    │
└─────────────────────────────────────────────────────────────────────────────┘
```

4.2 The bank has to have a **list of the cheques** which you are paying in. The following details are required.

(a) The **drawer** (the person who signs the cheque)

(b) The **amount**

Part B: Recording and accounting for cash transactions

Activity 7.1

You are employed by Easter & Co and have the following amounts to pay in to the bank.

Cheques from	£	Cash
B Wyman	940.00	2 × £50 notes
Pacific Ltd	1,721.50	5 × £20 notes
S McManus	94.26	97 × £10 notes
A Singh	19.29	42 × £5 notes
P L Ferguson	57.37	804 × £1 coins
Dex Ltd	42.91	80 × 50p coins
M Green	12.50	120 × 20p coins
		£34.85 silver (10p/5p)
		£9.28 bronze (2p/1p)

Postal order from

S R Sykes   15.00

Task

Complete the paying-in slip and counterfoil below for presentation to the bank on 10 June 20X7.

7: Banking monies received

Returned/dishonoured cheques

4.3 After a cheque has been received and banked, the bank may find it necessary to return the cheque to you and to remove its amount from your bank account. This is because the cheque has been **dishonoured for payment**. The two main reasons the bank may give for dishonouring the payment are insufficient funds and stolen cheques.

Insufficient funds

4.4 There may **not be enough money in the customer's account to cover the cheque**. Normally the banks **will** honour a cheque in the following circumstances.

(a) The cheque is for an amount **lower than the cheque guarantee card limit**.

(b) There is evidence that a **check** was made between the cheque and the guarantee card (card number written on the back of the cheque).

4.5 When a cheque is dishonoured in this way, the cheque will be returned to you marked 'refer to drawer' and it is up to you to find your customer (the drawer) and obtain the money from him in some other way.

Stolen cheques and cheque guarantee cards

4.6 If a cheque is accepted where the cheque is stolen and the signature of the drawer is **forged**, then **the cheque is invalid and worthless** (see Chapter 6). Even if a cheque is accepted with a cheque guarantee card and all details appear to agree, a stolen and forged cheque is still worthless and it will be returned with 'cheque book and cheque guarantee card reported stolen, signatures differ', or something of a similar nature, marked on it.

Wrongly completed or out of date cheques

4.7 The bank will also return a cheque if it has been wrongly completed. The most common example of this is where the amount shown in words and figures do not match.

If the cheque has been dated for some date in the future, for instance next month, the bank will return it. Also, if a cheque is more than six months old the bank will not present it for payment. So bank your receipts promptly! In all of these situations, you will return the cheque to the drawer and request a replacement

5 PROCEDURES FOR BANKING PLASTIC CARD TRANSACTIONS

5.1 Card vouchers (for credit and debit cards) are **processed through the banking system**. Where the retailer processes transactions manually, he pays the vouchers into his bank account and his bank will present the vouchers to the card issuers for payment (so the card issuer pays the bank and the bank pays the retailer). We will consider the more straightforward situation with EFTPOS in Section 6.

5.2 Once again, the **same paying-in slip** is used to bank the card transactions, but other documents must be prepared first.

Card summaries

5.3 The card issuers require the business receiver of card transactions to **summarise all transactions on a summary voucher**. The summary voucher consists of an original or 'top

Part B: Recording and accounting for cash transactions

copy' and two copies with carbon paper in between. The bottom copy is the **processing copy,** on the back of it is a place to list the vouchers.

5.4 The **summary voucher** has to be imprinted with the retailer's plastic card. It contains all the relevant information about the business, including an account number. The summary voucher is imprinted from the card using the same machine as that used to imprint from customer cards.

5.5 Unlike cheques, **only the amount of the card transaction** needs to be entered on the back of the processing copy of the summary voucher - names are not needed.

5.6 EXAMPLE: BANKING CARD VOUCHERS

You are asked to bank all card transactions at the end of a working day. You receive all the card vouchers for the day and you obtain a summary voucher. The transaction vouchers are as follows.

	£		£
Sale	26.41	Sale	12.95
Sale	32.99	Sale	14.48
Sale	32.99	Sale	136.48
Sale	100.40	Sale	12.95
Sale	22.00	Sale	112.95
Sale	46.99	Sale	11.80
Sale	37.80	Sale	56.71
Sale	12.95	Refund	22.00

5.7 SOLUTION

Step 1. Enter the **amount of each transaction** on the back of the processing copy of the summary voucher. (Note that the transaction voucher amounts can be listed separately rather than on the summary voucher if there are a large number of vouchers.)

Step 2. Transfer the **total of the transactions** and the **number of vouchers** to the **front of the summary voucher** (the top copy, which will copy through to the two copies below, including the top of the processing copy).

Step 3. Imprint the **retailer card** details on the summary voucher.

Step 4. **Separate** the top two copies of the summary vouchers from the processing copy. Detach the processing copy from the individual transaction vouchers; these are sent to the card issuer with the summary voucher processing copy.

Step 5. The card issuer will provide a small transparent plastic wallet, or its equivalent, in which you put all the **processing copies.** Note that **only** the processing copies are sent to the card issuer.

7: Banking monies received

Back of processing copy

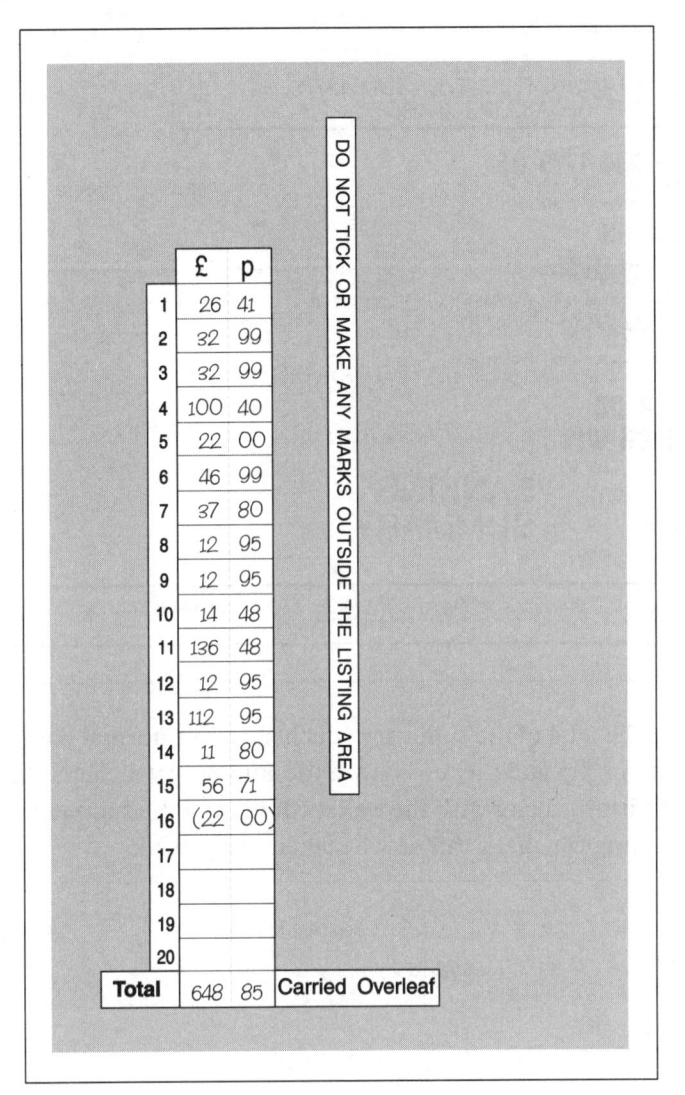

	£	p
1	26	41
2	32	99
3	32	99
4	100	40
5	22	00
6	46	99
7	37	80
8	12	95
9	12	95
10	14	48
11	136	48
12	12	95
13	112	95
14	11	80
15	56	71
16	(22	00)
17		
18		
19		
20		
Total	648	85

DO NOT TICK OR MAKE ANY MARKS OUTSIDE THE LISTING AREA

Carried Overleaf

Front processing copy

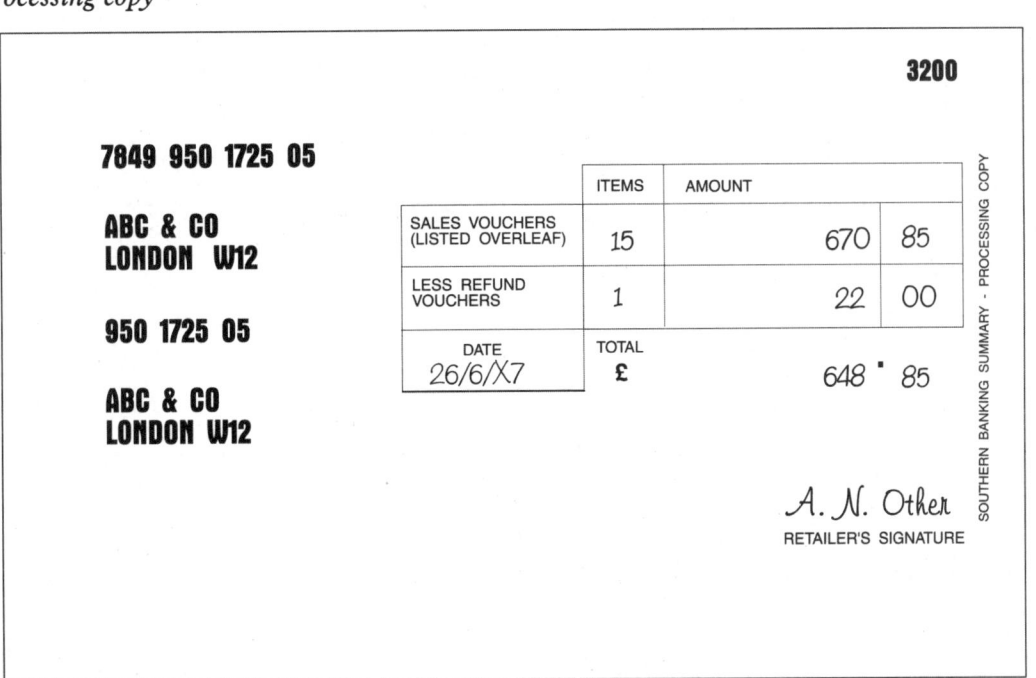

3200

7849 950 1725 05

ABC & CO
LONDON W12

950 1725 05

ABC & CO
LONDON W12

	ITEMS	AMOUNT	
SALES VOUCHERS (LISTED OVERLEAF)	15	670	85
LESS REFUND VOUCHERS	1	22	00
DATE 26/6/X7	TOTAL £	648	85

SOUTHERN BANKING SUMMARY - PROCESSING COPY

A. N. Other
RETAILER'S SIGNATURE

Part B: Recording and accounting for cash transactions

Top copy

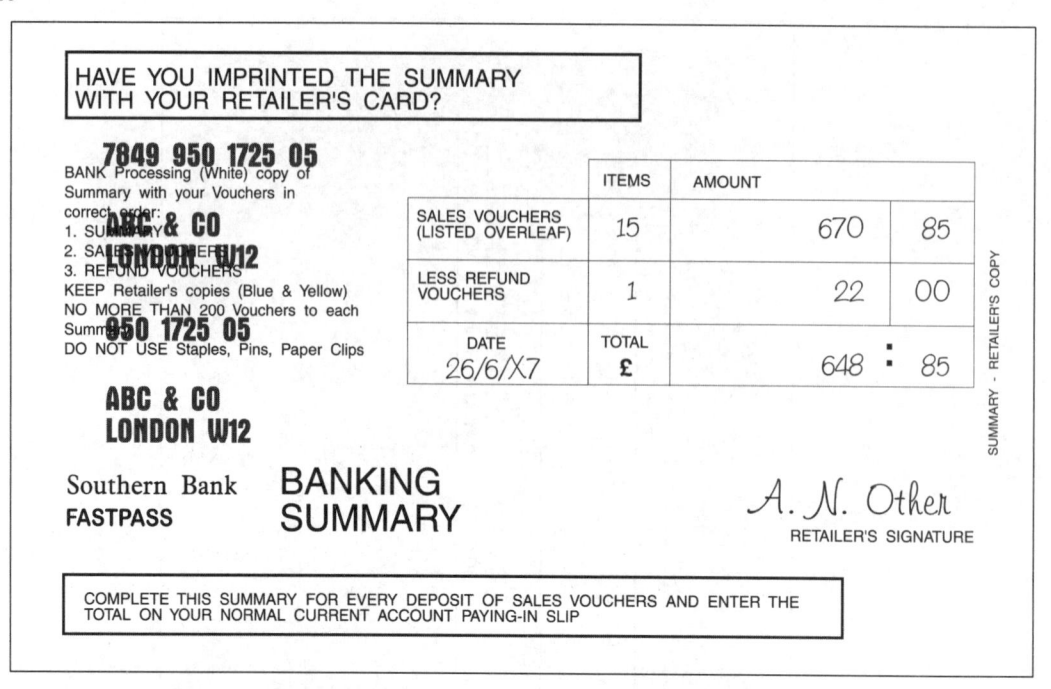

HAVE YOU IMPRINTED THE SUMMARY WITH YOUR RETAILER'S CARD?

7849 950 1725 05

BANK Processing (White) copy of Summary with your Vouchers in correct order:
1. SUMMARY
2. SALES VOUCHERS
3. REFUND VOUCHERS
KEEP Retailer's copies (Blue & Yellow)
NO MORE THAN 200 Vouchers to each Summary
DO NOT USE Staples, Pins, Paper Clips

ABC & CO
LONDON W12

950 1725 05

ABC & CO
LONDON W12

Southern Bank
FASTPASS

BANKING SUMMARY

	ITEMS	AMOUNT	
SALES VOUCHERS (LISTED OVERLEAF)	15	670	85
LESS REFUND VOUCHERS	1	22	00
DATE 26/6/X7	TOTAL £	648	85

A. N. Other
RETAILER'S SIGNATURE

COMPLETE THIS SUMMARY FOR EVERY DEPOSIT OF SALES VOUCHERS AND ENTER THE TOTAL ON YOUR NORMAL CURRENT ACCOUNT PAYING-IN SLIP

Step 6. Enter the total of the summary voucher on to a **normal paying-in slip**. The paying-in slip and the top copy of the summary voucher (which will be retained by the bank), along with the wallet containing the summary and transaction processing vouchers, can now be taken to the bank.

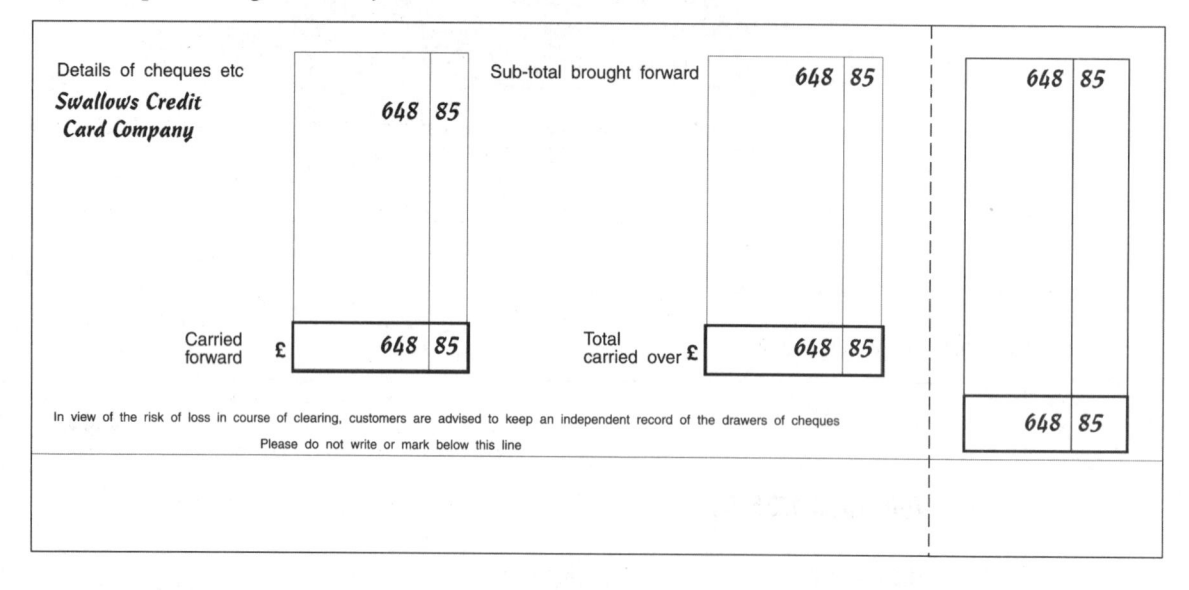

Details of cheques etc
Swallows Credit Card Company — 648 85

Carried forward £ 648 85

Sub-total brought forward — 648 85

Total carried over £ 648 85

648 85

648 85

In view of the risk of loss in course of clearing, customers are advised to keep an independent record of the drawers of cheques
Please do not write or mark below this line

7: Banking monies received

```
Date  26/6/X7    Date  26/6/X7         bank giro credit              Notes  £50
A/c   30595713   Cashier's stamp       Paid in by/Customer's Reference       £20
                 and initials                                                £10
                                                                             £5
Notes  £50                                                           Coins   £1
       £20                                                                   50p
       £10                6    83048231        92057419                      20p
       £5                                                            Silver
Coins  £1                       Quality Bank                         Bronze
       50p
       20p                     EALING BROADWAY BRANCH                Cash £
Silver                  Fee                                          Cheques  648 85
Bronze                                                               £        648 85
                        No of Cheques   ABC & CO    A/C no
Cash £                        1                     473181221
Cheques  648 85
£        648 85                Please do not write or mark below this line

        101129        101129        20   2748        473182221
```

Step 7. The second copies of the summary voucher and the transaction vouchers you have retained should be **filed together** in a way which makes an individual voucher easy to find. This is important as queries will arise from time to time.

Queries arising from card transactions

5.8 The most common types of problem which arise with card receipts are as follows.

Problem with card receipts	Action
Stolen cards	As a general rule it seems that, where a retailer has followed all proper security procedures (as discussed in Chapter 6) the card issuer will honour the transaction even if the card is stolen.
Transactions taking place **above the shop's floor limit**	The card issuer may refuse to honour the transaction as the retailer has been negligent is not obtaining authorisation.
Errors in completing the card voucher or in processing	Discrepancies which arise as a result of error can usually be dealt with quite quickly and efficiently by correspondence directly between the business and the card issuer.

Activity 7.2

Cholmley Sportswear is a retail shop which receives payment by cash, cheque and credit card. Each day's bankings are stored in a secure safe for banking on the following working day. Credit card vouchers are summarised daily on the bank's credit card summary.

The following summary relates to the week commencing Monday 27 November 20X7.

	Cash float at start of the day £	Cash/cheques for banking £	Cash float at end of the day £	Credit card sales vouchers £	Credit card refund £
Monday	24.16	684.08	37.05	104.28	-
Tuesday	37.05	504.27	12.60	202.96	-
Wednesday	12.60	691.41	19.40	124.17	37.26
Thursday	19.40	729.62	32.42	291.41	-
Friday	32.42	840.50	26.91	342.09	41.20

Part B: Recording and accounting for cash transactions

Tasks

(a) Prepare a schedule of each day's sales takings, showing cash/cheque sales and credit card sales separately for each day, and showing totals for the week.

(b) Three credit card sales vouchers and one credit card refund voucher were issued on Wednesday 29 November. Using the blank form below, complete for signature the retailer's banking summary for that day's credit card transactions.

```
┌─────────────────────────────────────────────────────────────────────┐
│  ┌───────────────────────────────────────┐                          │
│  │ HAVE YOU IMPRINTED THE SUMMARY        │                          │
│  │ WITH YOUR RETAILER'S CARD?            │                          │
│  └───────────────────────────────────────┘                          │
│                                                                     │
│  BANK Processing (White) copy of          ITEMS    AMOUNT           │
│  Summary with your Vouchers in                                      │
│  correct order:                      SALES VOUCHERS                 │
│  1. SUMMARY                          (LISTED OVERLEAF)              │
│  2. SALES VOUCHERS                                                  │
│  3. REFUND VOUCHERS                  LESS REFUND                    │
│  KEEP Retailer's copies (Blue & Yellow)  VOUCHERS                   │
│  NO MORE THAN 200 Vouchers to each                                  │
│  Summary                             DATE         TOTAL             │
│  DO NOT USE Staples, Pins, Paper Clips             £                │
│                                                                     │
│                                                                     │
│   First Region Bank     BANKING                                     │
│   FASTPASS              SUMMARY           RETAILER'S SIGNATURE      │
│                                                                     │
│  ┌─────────────────────────────────────────────────────────────┐    │
│  │ COMPLETE THIS SUMMARY FOR EVERY DEPOSIT OF SALES VOUCHERS   │    │
│  │ AND ENTER THE TOTAL ON YOUR NORMAL CURRENT ACCOUNT          │    │
│  │ PAYING-IN SLIP                                              │    │
│  └─────────────────────────────────────────────────────────────┘    │
└─────────────────────────────────────────────────────────────────────┘
```

(c) State what should be done with the banking summary you have prepared in (b).

---

6 BANKING AND EFTPOS

6.1 Where businesses use **EFTPOS** to process card receipts, there is no need to deposit the sale slips at the bank. The sales (and returns) are processed by the card issuers and credited **directly to the business bank account**, usually within two or three days. The narrative next to the bank account entry indicates the type of service (eg Switch, Visa and MasterCard).

Retention of documents

6.2 In the event of queries regarding individual transaction or bank account credits, the retailer will need to produce relevant copies of the receipts. It is therefore essential that all copy receipts are kept in a safe place, preferably in date order, for a **minimum period of 6 months** and sometimes even longer.

6.3 It is usually most convenient to attach the day's sales and refund slips (with the copy of the customer's signature) to the **end of day reconciliation** and then to keep these in date order.

7 BANKING OTHER RECEIPTS

7.1 Some receipts, by their very nature, require no action on the part of the business to have them paid into its bank account; these include **direct debits, standing orders, BACS payments** and **telegraphic transfers**. Other receipts which must be paid into the business's bank account and which are relatively rare in a business account are banker's drafts and bank giro credits.

Banker's drafts

7.2 **Banker's drafts** are paid into the bank by the business in the same manner as cheques.

Bank giro credits

7.3 Bank giro credits can be paid into a bank account by the **customer of the business**, in which case the amounts will appear automatically on the business's bank statement (see Chapter 9).

Key learning points

- You should note the important aspects of **banks, bankers and their relationship with their customers.**
  - How the clearing system works
  - Relationships between banker and customer
  - Rights and duties of banker and customer
- Banking procedures for various kinds of receipts should be fully understood and you should observe real transactions wherever possible.
- When **banking cash receipts**:
  - Cash must be properly counted and sorted
  - Notes and coins must be listed by denomination on the paying-in slip
- The details required on the paying-in slip when **cheques are banked** include.
  - Name of drawer (or endorser)
  - Amount of cheque
  - Total value of cheques banked
  - Number of cheques banked
- **Plastic card transactions** which are processed manually must be listed on a summary voucher for banking purposes. The processing copies are sent to the bank while the retailer retains two copies of each voucher (including the summary voucher).
- Credit, charge or debit card receipts via **EFTPOS** are credited directly to the retailer's bank account. He can agree the amounts received to the 'End of day' reconciliation produced by the terminal.

Quick quiz

1. What is 'clearing' in banking terms?
2. How long does a cheque take to clear?
3. What are the four types of relationship which may exist between a banker and customer?
4. What is a 'fiduciary relationship'?
5. How should coins be banked?
6. Which details from cheques should be included on the paying-in slip?
7. If you accept a stolen cheque in good faith, is it worth anything to you?
8. What happens if you accept a stolen credit card for an amount below your floor limit?

Part B: Recording and accounting for cash transactions

Answers to quick quiz

1. Clearing is the mechanism for obtaining payment for cheques.
2. Cheques take three working days to clear.
3. The relationships are: debtor/creditor, bailor/bailee, principal/agent, mortgagor/mortgagee.
4. A fiduciary relationship is one in which the superior party (the bank here) acts in good faith.
5. Coins should be banked in the plastic paying-in bags supplied by banks, with the correct number of coins as shown on the bag.
6. The drawer and the account should be noted on the paying-in slip.
7. No, you must pursue the person who forged the cheque to honour the debt.
8. If all security procedures have been followed, the issuer will usually honour the transaction.

Answers to activities

Answer 7.1

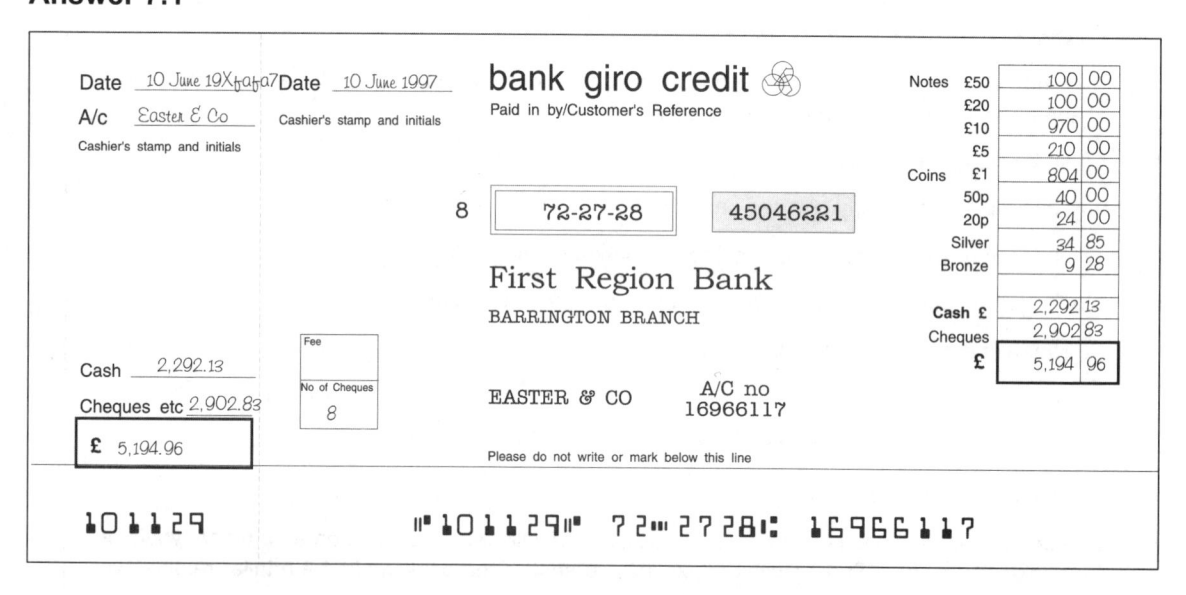

Bank giro credit — First Region Bank, Barrington Branch

Date: 10 June 19X7 / 10 June 1997
A/c: Easter & Co
Branch: 72-27-28   Ref: 45046221
A/C no: 16966117

Denomination	£	p
Notes £50	100	00
£20	100	00
£10	970	00
£5	210	00
Coins £1	804	00
50p	40	00
20p	24	00
Silver	34	85
Bronze	9	28
Cash £	2,292	13
Cheques	2,902	83
£	5,194	96

Cash: 2,292.13
Cheques etc: 2,902.83
£ 5,194.96
No of Cheques: 8

Details of cheques etc

Drawer	£	p
B Wyman	940	00
Pacific Ltd	1,721	50
S McManus	94	26
A Singh	19	29
P L Ferguson	57	37
Dex Ltd	42	91
M Green	12	50
Carried forward £	2,887	83

	£	p
Sub-total brought forward	2,887	83
Postal order	15	00
Total carried over £	2,902	83

Drawer	£	p
B Wyman	940	00
Pacific Ltd	1,721	50
S McManus	94	26
A Singh	19	29
P L Ferguson	57	37
Dex Ltd	42	91
M Green	12	50
R Sykes (Postal order)	15	00
	2,902	83

In view of the risk of loss in course of clearing, customers are advised to keep an independent record of the drawers of cheques.

Answer 7.2

(a)

Week beginning 27.11.X7	Cash/cheques takings £		Credit card takings £		Total takings £
Monday	696.97	(684.08 + 37.05 – 24.16)	104.28		801.25
Tuesday	479.82	(504.27 + 12.60 – 37.05)	202.96		682.78
Wednesday	698.21	(691.41 + 19.40 – 12.60)	86.91	(124.17 – 37.26)	785.12
Thursday	742.64	(729.62 + 32.42 – 19.40)	291.41		1,034.05
Friday	834.99	(840.50 + 26.91 – 32.42)	300.89	(342.09 – 41.20)	1,135.88
	3,452.63		986.45		4,439.08

(b)

```
HAVE YOU IMPRINTED THE SUMMARY
WITH YOUR RETAILER'S CARD?
```

BANK Processing (White) copy of Summary with your Vouchers in correct order:
1. SUMMARY
2. SALES VOUCHERS
3. REFUND VOUCHERS
KEEP Retailer's copies (Blue & Yellow)
NO MORE THAN 200 Vouchers to each Summary
DO NOT USE Staples, Pins, Paper Clips

	ITEMS	AMOUNT
SALES VOUCHERS (LISTED OVERLEAF)	3	124 : 17
LESS REFUND VOUCHERS	1	37 : 26
DATE 29.11.X7	TOTAL £	86 : 91

First Region Bank FASTPASS

BANKING SUMMARY

RETAILER'S SIGNATURE

COMPLETE THIS SUMMARY FOR EVERY DEPOSIT OF SALES VOUCHERS AND ENTER THE TOTAL ON YOUR NORMAL CURRENT ACCOUNT PAYING-IN SLIP

(c) As stated on the banking summary form, a summary should be completed for every deposit of sales vouchers and the total should be entered on the usual current account paying-in slip. The summary will be handed over at the bank with the credit card vouchers and the rest of the day's takings.

Chapter 8 Recording monies received

Chapter topic list

1   Controls over recording receipts
2   Cash registers
3   Cash received sheets (remittance lists)
4   Posting cash receipts to the general ledger

The following study sessions are covered in this chapter

			Syllabus reference
5	(e)	Record receipts in the cash book general ledger, sales ledger	3c
	(l)	Explain the correct procedure to cope with unusual situations: discrepancies between receipts and supporting documents	3e

8: Recording monies received

1 CONTROLS OVER RECORDING RECEIPTS

1.1 In practical terms, the first place that a receipt might be recorded is on a **cash register**, or on **cash received sheets** (see Section 2 in this chapter). For accounting purposes, however, the receipt is not recorded in the 'books' of the company until it has been entered in the **cash book**.

1.2 Recording receipts on cash received sheets or on cash registers is a method of **summarising cash transactions** which are then **recorded in summary form** in the cash book, which as we have seen in Chapter 4 is a **book of prime entry.**

1.3 The **controls** over recording receipts must be as good as controls over accepting and banking the money. If receipts are not recorded properly, how will we know whether we have received all the money that is due to us?

1.4 One of the main controls in this area is **segregation of duties**. As we saw in Chapter 6, this is where the **receiving and the recording functions are kept separate**. One person will receive, count and perhaps bank the money, while another person will record the money received. This is a way of avoiding theft, although collusion may occur between employees.

1.5 **Bank reconciliations** also help to control cash receipts (see Chapter 12).

2 CASH REGISTERS

2.1 We have looked at how the cash book works, but the cash book itself is not always the first place that receipts are recorded. Sometimes it is more practicable to **record receipts somewhere else** and then **summarise them to record them in the cash book**.

- Cash registers
- Cash received sheets or remittance lists (see Section 3 of this chapter)

2.2 **Cash registers** in some form have been in use for a long time in retail shops. They used to be mechanically operated, but today most are computerised. The more sophisticated and larger stores will have cash registers which are all connected to a central computer. The cash registers will update the computer automatically as a sale takes place, and each cash register can be updated for price changes.

Recording cash received by the register

2.3 The total of daily sales recorded by the cash register will be used in the following ways.

(a) To **check the amount of money** in the cash register at the end of the day against the summary, if there are any discrepancies they are investigated as in Chapter 7

(b) To **record receipts in the cash book**

2.4 The entry in the cash book will be the total amount of cash received. This will be analysed into sales and VAT, to facilitate **posting to the general ledger** (see Section 5).

Security and controls

2.5 We have seen how accurate a cash register can be and how well it can **control receipts**; but the cash register will only act as an effective control if it is used properly.

Part B: Recording and accounting for cash transactions

(a) **Access keys** should be given to the appropriate members of staff and they should be kept in a safe and secure place. A spare set should be kept by the person in authority.

(b) Staff should be **trained in the use of the cash register** and their work should be observed for a period.

(c) The maximum possible amount of **preset information** should be programmed into the cash register. This saves cashier time and reduces the risk of fraud.

(d) **Periodic information** produced by the cash register such as average sales proceeds per customer, average sales value of the items sold and sales by clerk or operator should be analysed carefully by the manager or owner, with perhaps a brief weekly or monthly report being written. All variations should be investigated.

3 CASH RECEIVED SHEETS (REMITTANCE LISTS)

3.1 Businesses which do not have a cash register still need to record money received from sales they have made. Very small shops or businesses will probably just write down on a piece of paper the money received as they sell something. (Note that 'cash' here means cash, cheques, cards or any other form of receipt.) This is a basic **cash received sheet**.

Acorn Antiques

Sales Takings 22 July 20X7

	£
Two Victorian chairs: cheque	45.00
One Victorian table: cheque	155.00
Two Watercolours: cheque	100.00
Bookshelves: cash	40.00
One Edwardian chair: cheque	55.00
Pair Chinese vases: credit card	360.00
Two sidetables: credit card	180.00
Total for day	£935.00

3.2 Larger non-retail companies may have **pre-printed cash received sheets** or **remittance lists** on which they record receipts as they arrive through the post.

CASH RECEIVED SHEET 7141 (b)			JOE'S BUILDING SUPPLIES LTD
DATE 10/4/X7		(a)	
NAME		ACCOUNT	AMOUNT
P Jones and Son	1	00437	169.00
S Car & Co	2	01562	62.70
H M Customs & Excise	3	00002	55.00
Moblem Ltd	4	02137	3,233.99
Lobells plc	5	05148	244.91
Cannery Whiff	6	02420	9,553.72
Lymping Ltd	7	09370	62.20
Yorker plc	8	09682	322.41
Mowley Ltd	9	01433	43.30
Regalia plc	10	03997	978.50
Herod & Sons	11	05763	71.40
Forman & Co	12	07211	4,288.52
Thatchers	13	04520	610.00
Eggary & Co	14	08871	4,823.50
Redwood & Sons	15	08759	420.68
TOTAL		10000 (c)	24,939.83 (d)

(a) **Account number.** This is the ledger account number of the customer in the **sales ledger**. When the details from the cash received sheet are entered into the accounting system, this code number will tell the system (whether it is manual or computerised) which customer has paid off all or part of his debt. For non-sales ledger receipts, the code of the account in the general ledger is substituted. In this case 00002 is the code for Customs & Excise refunding VAT.

(b) **Cash received sheet number.** Preprinted cash received sheets may be sequentially numbered. This is a control which helps to make sure that all receipts have been recorded, a check can be carried out to make sure all cash received sheets are present.

(c) **Bank account number (10000).** This is the ledger account number of the cash account in the general ledger.

(d) **Total receipts.** The money received is summarised here so only the totals need to be recorded in the cash book.

4 POSTING CASH RECEIPTS TO THE GENERAL LEDGER

Exam alert
To a large degree everything we have studied so far in this Interactive Text has been leading up to the moment when you can record cash received in the accounts of the business. An exam question is very likely to test this.

4.1 Back in Chapters 1 and 2 we saw that the aim of the accounting system was to document, summarise, record and present the financial transactions of a business. It is only when we **post the receipts side of the book to the cash (or bank) account in the general ledger that we can be said to have accounted for cash receipts.**

Part B: Recording and accounting for cash transactions

Book of prime entry	P O S	Ledger account
Cash book	T I →	Cash account
Summarises cash receipts	N G	Records cash receipts

4.2 Provided all the procedures have been followed correctly in preparing the cash book, posting it to the general ledger should be straightforward.

Step 1. **Add up** all the columns on the receipts side of the cash book.

Step 2. Check that the **totals of the analysis columns** (excluding the discount allowed memorandum column) add up to the total cash received column.

Step 3. **Identify general ledger accounts** which require posting by marking against cash book amount.

Step 4. Draw up a **posting summary** and post the general ledger.

Activity 8.1

Your employer, Quickpay Ltd, offers to its credit customers a 2½% discount for payment within 10 days of invoice. The company gives no trade or customer discounts. It operates a three-column cash book, with columns for discount, cash and bank.

At 30 June 20X7, the cash book figures totalled as follows.

Receipts side
Discount allowed	£237.65
Cash	£342.71
Bank	£15,842.65

Payments side
Discount received	£184.29
Cash	£232.40
Bank	£14,221.17

A new trainee has been asked to balance off the book, and has shown balances carried down as shown below.

Receipts

Date	Details	Discount	Cash	Bank
	Totals	237.65	342.71	15,842.65
	Balance carried down			1,621.48
		237.65	342.71	14,221.17
1 July X7	Balance brought down	53.36	119.31	

Payments

Date	Details	Discount	Cash	Bank
	Totals	184.29	232.40	14,221.17
	Balance carried down	53.36	119.31	
		237.65	342.71	14,221.17
1 July X7	Balance brought down			1,621.48

Task

Check and identify any errors in the new trainee's work.

4.3 EXAMPLE: POSTING THE GENERAL LEDGER FROM THE CASH BOOK

Suppose we wished to post Warren Miles's cash received for 1 September 20X7 to his general ledger. The relevant general ledger accounts are as follows.

CASH ACCOUNT — CA01

	£		£
1 Sept Balance b/d	900.00		

TOTAL DEBTORS — TD01

	£		£
1 Sept Balance b/d	51,795.00		

SALES — SA01

	£		£
1 Sept		Balance b/d	200,403.00

VAT — VAT01

	£		£
1 Sept		Balance b/d	35,070.00

FIXED ASSET DISPOSAL — DIS01

	£		£

DISCOUNT ALLOWED — DA01

	£		£
1 Sept Balance b/d	2,410.00		

Part B: Recording and accounting for cash transactions

4.4 SOLUTION

Step 1. The columns should be **added up** as follows (note that the 'total' columns total excludes the balance b/d - we do not want to double count).

WARREN MILES: CASH BOOK

RECEIPTS

Date	Narrative			Discount allowed	Total	Output VAT on cash sales	Receipts from debtors	Cash sales	Other
20X7									
01-Sep	Balance b/d				900.00				
	(a) Cash sale				80.00	11.91		68.09	
	(b) Debtor pays: Hay	SL96		20.00	380.00		380.00		
	(c) Debtor pays: Been	SL632			720.00		720.00		
	(d) Debtor pays: Seed	SL501		40.00	960.00		960.00		
	(e) Cash sale				150.00	22.34		127.66	
	(f) Fixed asset sale				200.00				200.00
				60.00	2,490.00	34.25	2,060.00	195.75	200.00
				TD01	CA01	VAT01	TD01	SA01	DIS01
				CR	DR	CR	CR	CR	CR
				DA01					
				DR					

Step 2. **Check the totals**

	£
Output VAT on cash sales	34.25
Receipts from debtors	2,060.00
Cash sales	195.75
Other receipts	200.00
Total cash received	2,490.00

Step 3. **Identify general ledger accounts**. We have marked the folio references for the general ledger accounts on the receipts page above.

- TD01   Total debtors
- CA01   Cash account
- VAT01   VAT account
- SA01   Sales
- DIS01   Disposal of fixed assets
- DA01   Discounts allowed

Step 4. Draw up the **posting summary** and post the general ledger.

			£	£
DEBIT	Cash account	CA01	2,490.00	
	Discounts allowed	DA01	60.00	
CREDIT	Total debtors	TD01		2,120.00
	VAT	VAT01		34.25
	Sales	SA01		195.75
	Disposal of fixed assets	DIS01		200.00

Being cash book receipts postings summary 1 September 20X7

Note that the credit to total debtors of £2,120 reflects £60 discounts allowed plus £2,060 received from them.

8: Recording monies received

	CASH ACCOUNT		CA01
	£		£
1 Sept Balance b/d	900.00		
1 Sept Cash book	2,490.00		

	TOTAL DEBTORS (Debtors control account)		TD01
	£		£
1 Sept Balance b/d	51,795.00	1 Sept Cash book	2,120.00

	SALES		SA01
	£		£
1 Sept		Balance b/d	200,403.00
		1 Sept Cash book	195.75

	VAT		VAT01
	£		£
1 Sept		Balance b/d	35,070.00
		1 Sept Cash book	34.25

	FIXED ASSET DISPOSAL		DIS01
	£		£
		1 Sept Cash book	200.00

	DISCOUNT ALLOWED		DA01
	£		£
1 Sept Balance b/d	2,410.00		
1 Sept Cash book	60.00		

4.5 Remember that the general ledger *is* the double entry system and therefore all debits and credits on the posting summary must be equal: the **total cash received** represents the **debit** entry in the **cash account.**

(a) The **total of each analysis column** represents the credit entries in the general ledger accounts when cash has actually been received.

(b) The **discounts allowed** total is **debited to the discounts expense account**, and **credited to the total debtors account**, where it reduces the total amount owed by debtors.

4.6 **Postings summary**

For cash sales:	£	£
DEBIT: Cash account (gross)	X	
CREDIT: Sales account (net)		X
VAT account		X

For cash sales with a discount allowed:	£	£
DEBIT: Cash account	X	
Discount allowed	X	
CREDIT: Sales account (net sales **plus** discount allowed)		X
VAT account		X

For receipts from debtors:	£	£
DEBIT: Cash account	X	
CREDIT: SLCA		X

Part B: Recording and accounting for cash transactions

(Remember that the sale and VAT were recorded when the invoice was sent out and a debtor was set up in the sales ledger control account.)

For receipts from debtors with a discount allowed:

		£	£
DEBIT:	Cash account	X	
	Discount allowed	X	
CREDIT:	SLCA (cash received **plus** discount allowed)		X

For receipts from the sale of fixed assets:

		£	£
DEBIT:	Cash account	X	
CREDIT:	Fixed asset disposal account		X

Note that capital items are not included in sales, as they would give an inaccurate picture of the profit made by way of trade. For example, a business is doing badly and sells some valuable land. If this were included in sales, it would give a totally inaccurate picture of the business's trade.

4.7 We will return to the payment side of Warren Miles's cash book in Chapter 10.

Activity 8.2

Green Bottles Ltd manufactures glass and plastic containers of various colours which it sells to other companies in the food and drinks industry. All monies received are entered on cash received sheets which record details in separate columns, headed as follows.

(a) *Date*

(b) *Name*, showing the name of the firm or person from whom the money is received

(c) *Account number*, showing

    (i) for sales ledger receipts, the account number of the customer in the sales ledger
    (ii) for other receipts, the code for the ledger account to be credited

(d) *Amount*

In the week commencing 20 April 20X7, the post includes the items listed below. All cheques received were accompanied by a remittance advice.

20.4.X7   A cheque for £492.70 from Jill's Kitchen Co.
            A cheque for £242.98 from G Edwards & Son.
            A credit note for £124.40 from a supplier, Extrans Ltd.

21.4.X7   A cheque for £892.76 from Crystal Water Co.
            A VAT repayment cheque of £487.50 from HM Customs & Excise.
            A cheque for £500 from Green Gourmet Co, being part payment against invoice No 17201 which was for a total amount of £1,024.20.

22.4.X7   A cheque for £1,700.00 from BRM Motors in payment for a secondhand motor vehicle.
            A cheque for £1,920.70 from Jennan Tonic Ltd.

23.4.X7   A cheque for £400 from Oliver's Organic Foods.
            A debit note for £92.00 from Fender Foods plc.
            A cheque for £3,208.00 from Parkers Preserves Ltd.

24.4.X7   A cheque for £4,920.75 from Pennine Springs Ltd
            A statement of account from British Telecom plc, showing a balance of £382.44, to be paid by direct debit.

The following is a list of sales ledger account numbers.

	Account number		Account number
Crystal Water Co	C101	Jill's Kitchen Co	J211
Denny's Ltd	D024	Oliver's Organic Foods	O301
G Edwards & Son	E102	Parkers Preserves Ltd	P002
Fender Foods plc	F108	Pennine Springs Ltd	P004

Green Gourmet Co	G105	Spring Bottlers plc	S003
Jennan Tonic Ltd	J110	West, Key & Eiss	W402

The following list shows certain nominal ledger account codes.

Cash	1000
Value added tax	1600
Motor vehicle disposals	1720
Telephones	1924

Tasks

(a) Draw up and total the cash received sheet for the week, using the blank sheet below.
(b) State how you would expect the cash receipts to be recorded in the cash book.

Cash received sheet   *Number* ....

Date	Name	Account No	Amount
			£
	Total	100	

Computerisation of receipts recording

4.8 Increasingly cash books are being maintained in computerised form either as a spreadsheet, or a cashbook software package that works with the computerised general ledger.

4.9 Computerised accounting is the same in principle as manual accounting. A computerised cashbook will either be printed out and manual journal entries prepared to post to the general ledger, or will have a computerised posting routine to post these entries automatically.

4.10 In a computerised accounting system, it is normal for receipts from trade debtors (who have balances owing on the sales ledger) to be **posted directly to the individual account on the computerised sales ledger.** At the end of the posting for a period (day or week, or even a month), the computer will produce a **posting summary**. An example is shown below.

SALES LEDGER POSTING SUMMARY 31 MARCH 20X7

	DR	£	CR	£
Sales	Total debtors	117.50	Sales	100.00
Output VAT			VAT	17.50
Cash received	Cash	90.00	Total debtors	90.00
		207.50		207.50

Part B: Recording and accounting for cash transactions

4.11 In some computer systems the sales ledger and general ledger are **interfaced** so they are connected and can update each other. If so, posting the sales ledger and the summary amounts can take place automatically. If the two systems are **not interfaced** then the posting will be input by the computer operator to the bank account in the general ledger.

4.12 The posting of the sales receipts to the sales ledger might be done from **cash received sheets** (remittance lists). A minimum amount of information would be posted.

Date	Customer account number	Details	Reference number	Total amount £
28.03.X7	37482	Receipt	469	349.57

The amount would be included in a total which would be posted to the bank account automatically.

4.13 It is not necessary to **summarise the receipts** before posting them to the sales ledger, each one could be entered individually. This method is often easier and saves time inputting into the computer. Sometimes a computer spreadsheet is used to provide a posting summary: when all the posted cash receipts are listed on it, it will automatically produce the posting entries.

4.14 **Miscellaneous receipts** will include sales of fixed assets, refunds from suppliers and perhaps VAT refunds from HM Customs & Excise. Such receipts do not normally appear in the sales ledger as it is unlikely that the supplier has an account on the sales ledger. In this case the receipt can be recorded directly in a cash book (either manual or computerised) and the cash book will update the general ledger either automatically or through manual journals.

Key learning points

- **Controls over the recording of cash receipts** include the following.
  - Segregation of duties
  - Bank reconciliations
- **Analysed cash books** show how much money has been received and paid, and what each amount was for, by placing it in the correct column. A cash book is a daybook or book of prime entry.
- **Cash registers** can be very useful in the control of cash receipts. They are accurate and they can be used to collect different kinds of sales information.
- **Cash received sheets**, or remittance lists are used to collect receipts ready for recording.
- **Computerised accounting systems** follow the same principles as manual systems.

Quick quiz

1. What is 'segregation of duties' when dealing with cash receipts?
2. The cash book reflects the movement of notes and coins through the business. True or false?
3. Why is a discount allowed column required in the cash book?
4. Is it easier for the operator if the computerised sales ledger and general ledger are interfaced?

Answers to quick quiz

1. The receiving and recording functions are kept separate to avoid theft.
2. False. The cash book records movements through the business bank account. Notes and coins are recorded in the petty cash book.
3. The discount allowed column shows why the full amount of a debt has not been received, for clearing the total amount in the sales ledger.
4. Yes, because journals updating the general ledger do not have to be manually prepared.

Answers to activities

Answer 8.1

The new trainee has made three errors.

(a) It is incorrect to try to balance the two discount columns. The discounts allowed shown on the receipts side of the cash book are an expense of the business, representing the cost of allowing discounts for early settlement. Discounts received, from the payments side of the cash book, represent a benefit to the business, gained from making early payment to suppliers. Therefore, discounts received and discounts allowed need to be treated separately and not 'netted off' against each other.

(b) The cash balance brought down should be £110.31 and not £119.31.

(c) The bank balance brought down should be £1,621.48 DR and not £1,621.48 CR, ie it is on the wrong side of the cash book. The added up totals of each side of the bank column would then be £15,842.65.

Part B: Recording and accounting for cash transactions

Answer 8.2

(a)

Cash received sheet		Number	
Date	Name	Account No	Amount
20.4.X7	Jill's Kitchen Co	J211	492.70
20.4.X7	G Edwards & Son	E102	242.98
21.4.X7	Crystal Water Co	C101	892.76
21.4.X7	H M Customs & Excise	I600	487.50
21.4.X7	Green Gourmet Co	G105	500.00
22.4.X7	BRMMotors	I720	1,700.00
22.4.X7	Jennan Tonic Ltd	J110	1,920.70
23.4.X7	Oliver's Organic Foods	O301	400.00
23.4.X7	Parkers Preserves Ltd	P002	3,208.00
24.4.X7	Pennine Springs Ltd	P004	4,920.75
	Total	1000	14,765.39

(b) The cash receipts will be recorded on the debit side of the cash book, probably on a single line showing the cash received sheet number.

Chapter 9 Authorising and making payments

Chapter topic list

1. Controls over payments
2. Cheque requisition forms
3. Expenses claim forms
4. The timing and methods of payments
5. Payments by cash
6. Payments by cheque
7. Bank Giro credits (credit transfers)
8. Payments by banker's draft (payable order)
9. Payments by standing order and direct debit
10. Documentation to go out with payments

The following study sessions are covered in this chapter

			Syllabus reference
4	(d)	Understand the content and format of a cheque	3d
	(e)	Prepare a cheque prior to despatch	3d
	(h)	Describe other services offered by banks – interbank transfers, payable orders, automated credit systems, standing orders, direct debits, credit transfers	3d
5	(b)	Identify the documentation accompanying payments	3d
	(d)	Identify the main ways to ensure that only authorised payments are made	3d

Part B: Recording and accounting for cash transactions

1 CONTROLS OVER PAYMENTS

1.1 Controls over payments by a business must be **strict**. This should apply to all payments, from the smallest to the largest. The need for controls should be fairly obvious: if any business allowed some of its employees to pay out its money without needing to obtain permission, the scope for cheating and dishonesty would be very wide.

1.2 There are three main steps in applying controls over payments.

Step 1. Obtaining **documentary evidence** of the reason why the payment is being made and the amount of the payment. In the case of payments to suppliers, the documentary evidence will be a supplier's invoice (or statement).

Step 2. **Authorisation** of the payment, which means giving formal 'official' approval to make the payment.

Step 3. **Restricting the authority to actually make the payment** to certain specified individuals.

The difference between Steps 1, 2 and 3 can be illustrated with an example.

1.3 EXAMPLE: CONTROLLING A PAYMENT

Suppose that a company buys goods costing £5,000.

Step 1. It will receive an invoice from the supplier. This is the **documentary evidence** of the reason for and amount of the payment.

Step 2. The invoice will be approved by the purchasing director. This approval is the **authorisation of the payment**.

Step 3. At some time later, the payment will be made to the supplier, probably by cheque. For a payment of £5,000, perhaps only the finance director or managing director will be permitted to sign the cheque, and so the **authority to make the payment** would be limited to these two people.

Authorisation

1.4 Every payment must be approved by an **authorised person**. This person will often be a manager or supervisor in the department that initiated the expense, but every organisation has its own system.

- **Which individuals** can authorise particular expenses
- The **maximum amount** of expenditure that an individual can authorise

1.5 As just one illustration, the authorisation/approval limits on spending in a company with three departments and a head office might be as follows.

9: Authorising and making payments

	Departments			Head Office
Limit on expenditure	Purchasing Authority	Production Authority	Sales Authority	Authority
No limit	Chairman or Managing Director	Chairman or Managing Director	Chairman or Managing Director	Chairman or Managing Director
£25,000	Purchasing director Chief accountant	Production director Chief accountant	Sales director Chief accountant	Chief accountant
£5,000	Grade 1 manager, Purchasing	Grade 1 manager, Production	Grade 1 manager, Sales	Grade 1 manager, head office
£1,000	Grade 2 manager, Purchasing	Grade 2 manager, Production	Grade 2 manager, Sales	Grade 2 manager, head office
£100	Supervisor, Purchasing	Supervisor, Production	Supervisor, Sales	Supervisor, head office

1.6 When a person authorises a payment, he or she should evidence this approval by putting a **signature** or **recognisable initials** on the appropriate document (invoice, cheque requisition form, expenses claim form, or similar document) and ideally also the date.

1.7 Without the signature or initials of an authorised person, the accounts department should **refuse to make the payment**, and should send the document back for the approval to be properly given.

1.8 Some companies use a **sticker** or **stamp** which they put on invoices received.

```
        INVOICE PAYMENT
          APPROVED BY

     Name ................................

     Dept ................................

     Date ................................

                    Initials ..............
```

This makes it easier later for the accounts department to check that the invoice has been properly authorised for payment.

2 CHEQUE REQUISITION FORMS

2.1 Documentary evidence of the reason for a payment, and the amount of the payment, are usually provided by a **supplier's invoice**. There will be some occasions, however, when a payment by cheque is required to pay for an item without evidence.

(a) The invoice has **not yet been received**, and although an invoice/receipt will follow later, payment is required now.

(b) There will be **neither an invoice, nor a receipt**.

Part B: Recording and accounting for cash transactions

2.2 The documentary evidence of the reason for and the amount of the payment can be obtained from the person who wants the payment to be made, by asking him or her to fill in a **cheque requisition form**.

> **KEY TERM**
>
> A **cheque requisition form** is simply a form requesting that a cheque should be drawn to make a payment.

2.3 A cheque requisition form is an **internal document** for use within the business, and so there is no standard design. We will use an example to show the information which would normally appear on the form.

2.4 **EXAMPLE: CHEQUE REQUISITION FORM**

The advertising manager of ABC Ltd wants to put an advertisement into the local weekly newspaper. The newspaper wants payment of £470 (£400 + VAT at 17½%) in advance, and has sent a fax letter requesting this amount. A receipt will be sent later with confirmation that the advertisement has been inserted and paid for.

The advertising manager will fill in a **cheque requisition form**.

2.5 **SOLUTION**

ABC LIMITED
CHEQUE REQUISITION FORM

DATE 17 June 20X7

Please draw a cheque on the company's account.

PAYABLE TO Popular Newspapers Plc

AMOUNT £470

REASON 2 column 5 inch ad in 20 June edition of Morning Herald newspaper

General ledger code (if known) 201/A01101

Please tick as appropriate

Invoice/receipt to follow ✓

No invoice or receipt

Other evidence attached ✓ Fax letter

Send cheque to A Davies, Ad Manager, for sending on to Popular Newspapers ASAP

Signature A Davies

Department 15

Telephone (extension) x326

2.6 This is what should be done when preparing a cheque requisition form.

Action	Comment
The form must be **signed** by a person who can **authorise** the payment.	This might be the advertising manager personally or his/her superior.
The **general ledger code** is needed to record the payment in the accounts.	A code will be written on the form either by the advertising manager or by someone in the accounts department.
Supporting documentation should be attached.	In this case the fax requesting payment.
The **cheque**, when it has been prepared and signed, will be sent to the person authorising payment.	This will be the advertising manager. In some organisations, the accounts department will only send the cheque to the payee direct.
An **invoice/receipt** may follow.	Some organisations may insist on this

2.7 You might wonder what payments could possibly be made where an invoice or receipt will not be obtained eventually. There are few such cases: one example would be a requisition by the company secretary for a cheque payable to Companies House to make the company's annual return to the Registrar of Companies. This is a payment required by law, for which no receipt or invoice is provided.

3 EXPENSES CLAIM FORMS

3.1 In many organisations, employees will make **payments out of their own pocket for items of business expense**, and then claim back the money from their organisation. Expenses for which payments might be claimed include the following.

- Money spent by the employee on **business travel**
- The cost of **newspapers or magazines** that the employee buys for business use
- Part or all of the employee's **domestic telephone bill**
- **Petrol**
- **Car service and repair bills** (for company cars)

KEY TERM

Expenses paid by an employee for which the employee wants reimbursement should be itemised on an **expenses claim form**.

3.2 Proof should be given of the existence and the amount of the expense, and this can be given by attaching **receipts**. If there is insufficient supporting evidence, the company may refuse to reimburse the expense.

Step 1. The claimant will submit the completed and signed form (normally to his or her superior) for **approval and authorisation** before it is sent on to the accounts department. The person approving the claim will check that it does not exceed any limits which have been set.

Step 2. **Receipts/bills/invoices** should be attached to the form.

Step 3. The **general ledger codes** will be entered on the form after it has been submitted to the accounts department for payment, although on some such forms these codes might be preprinted.

Step 4. The **separation of payments into the net amount and the VAT element** might also be done in the accounts department, although in the illustration below it has been done by the individual making the expenses claim.

3.3 Companies often use two different expense claims forms.

(a) One form would be for expenses that will be included in the employee's **gross pay for tax purposes**, and on which

   (i) the employee could be liable for income tax

   (ii) both the employer and employee will be liable for National Insurance contribution payments

These expenses include petrol, payments towards the employee's domestic telephone bill and 'round sum allowances' (regular payments of a standard amount) such as a monthly payment towards newspapers and magazines for managerial staff.

(b) The other form would be for all other expense items for which the employer and employee **will not be liable for National Insurance** (reimbursement for business trips etc).

4 THE TIMING AND METHODS OF PAYMENTS

When should payments be made and who to?

4.1 Suppliers submitting invoices will usually grant a **period of credit** to a customer.

(a) 'Net 30 days' on an invoice means that payment is due 30 days from the date of the invoice.

(b) Similarly 'net 60 days' and 'net 90 days' allow 60 and 90 days respectively from the date of the invoice.

(c) Some suppliers specify the latest date for payment on the invoice (such as 'Payment due by 30 November 20X7').

(d) If the invoice is not paid by the specified date then it becomes **overdue**, and reminders and telephone calls may be received from the supplier.

Who decides?

4.2 Decisions about who should be paid and when are made by a **senior person** in the company, perhaps the chief accountant. To help the decision-making an accounts clerk might be required to draw up a list of unpaid invoices.

- Overdue
- Outstanding for longer than a certain period of time, say two months
- Soon due to be paid.

4.3 **Miscellaneous payments** not made to trade suppliers will be paid at various dates during the month as they fall due, whereas **trade bills tend to be paid at the end of the month**.

Methods of payment

4.4 The methods that a business uses to **make payments** for goods and services, wages and salaries, rent and rates and so on are broadly the same as the methods of **receiving payments**. However, a business is likely to use some methods of payment much more often than others, and the following are most commonly used.

- Cheques
- BACS (especially for salaries and wages)
- Internet payments

4.5 **Other payment methods** are as follows.

- Cash
- Banker's draft
- Standing order
- Direct debit
- Company credit card or charge card
- Mail transfer and telegraphic transfer
- Internet payments

4.6 In this chapter, we shall look at the procedures for making payments by each of these methods. Small payments by cash will be dealt with separately in Chapter 11 on **petty cash**.

> Payments of **wages and salaries** are dealt with in Part D of this Interactive Text and are not described here.

5 PAYMENTS BY CASH

5.1 **Cash payments** are used for the following.

- For **small payments** out of petty cash (see Chapter 11)
- Sometimes for **wages** (wages payments are dealt with in Part D)

5.2 Using cash to pay large amounts of money to suppliers ought to be very rare indeed.

(a) Cash needs to be kept **secure**: it is easily stolen.

(b) Cash can get **lost in the post**.

(c) It will be difficult to keep **control over cash** if it is used often for making payments.

(d) Unless a supplier issues a **receipt**, there will be no evidence that a cash payment has been made. This is bad for record keeping.

Not surprisingly, the use of cash to make large payments to suppliers is sometimes associated with shady or dishonest dealers in backstreet or underworld businesses.

6 PAYMENTS BY CHEQUE

6.1 The most common method of payment by businesses (excluding wages and salary payments) is by **cheque**. Most companies and government agencies or departments use computer-produced cheques.

Part B: Recording and accounting for cash transactions

6.2 Cheques are for payments out of a **current account** at a bank. The accounts department of a company will be provided with cheque books for its current account by its bank, each book containing perhaps 50 crossed cheques.

6.3 An individual in the accounts department will be responsible for the **safekeeping of the cheque book(s)**. They should be kept under lock and key, perhaps in a **safe** and at the very least in a **locked drawer**. Cheque books, or individual cheques from a book, might be stolen by someone who intends to use them fraudulently. The person responsible for safekeeping may also be responsible for ordering new cheque books when the old ones run out.

Signatures on business cheques

6.4 A bank will not permit a payment by cheque from a customer's account unless it has been **properly signed**.

  (a) For company cheques, only certain **specified individuals** within the company will be permitted to sign a cheque on behalf of the company, and the names and signatures of these individuals must be supplied to the bank on a **bank mandate form** or in a bank mandate letter.

  (b) In many cases, cheques above a certain value must contain **two authorised signatures**.

  (c) Authorised signatories for company cheques are selected by the company itself, but might consist of the chairman, all the directors and the chief accountant or financial controller.

Procedures for preparing cheques

6.5 The starting point for preparing cheques for payments to suppliers or other creditors is deciding when to write cheques and **which payments to make**.

Steps	Action	Comment
Step 1.	Prepare list of payments	Instructions will be given to the accounts clerk to prepare a **list of all the payments that are due** (see Paragraph 4.2 above).
Step 2.	Payments authorised, sufficient funds available	A company cannot write and send off cheques unless it has enough money in its bank account to cover the payments (or it has a suitable overdraft facility), and so the decision about when to pay and who to pay will normally come from a manager in the accounts department, possibly the **chief accountant** once he has seen the list.
Step 3.	Check invoices to be paid	The accounts clerk will find the invoices appearing on the payment time list in the unpaid invoices file, and check that (a) The invoice has been **properly authorised** for payment (b) A **general ledger code** for the expense or purchase item has been written on the invoice (if not, an appropriate general ledger code should be written on now) (c) Any **remittance advice** is kept with it

9: Authorising and making payments

Steps	Action	Comment
Step 4.	Prepare the cheques	The accounts clerk will use the information on the invoice to **write the cheque**. A memorandum or record of the details of the cheque should be written on the **counterfoil**.
		• The name of the person/organisation to whom the cheque is payable
		• Amount
		• Date
		• Any other helpful details
		All cheques are now pre-printed '**crossed**' ie with two lines drawn across them and "Account payee" printed between the lines. This means that they can only be paid into the account of the person or organisation whose name appears on the cheque. This safeguard prevents lost or stolen cheques from being cashed.
Step 5.	Attach invoice to cheque, sign	The cheque should be attached to the invoice and remittance advice, and submitted for signature by an **authorised person** (or persons).
Step 6.	Mark invoice PAID	The invoice should be stamped PAID, with the date of payment written inside or beneath the stamp, and (ideally) the cheque number should be added too.
		Here is an example of a cheque for £1,520.75 made payable to J R Hartley Ltd and crossed 'A/c payee'. It has been prepared on 6 January 20X7 and is a payment of invoice 12345. Cheques over £1,000 need two authorised signatures.

```
6 Jan  20 X7            Southern Bank              6 Jan  20 X7
To                                                          20-27-48
   J R Hartley           CHISWICK BRANCH                SOUTHERN BANK PLC
                    17 HIGH ROAD, LONDON W4 6RG
Invoice  12345                                                   or order
                     Pay   H. V. Stern Ltd
                     One thousand and five hundred and twenty pounds 75p   £  1,520-75
                                                            A/c
                                                           payee        FOR ABC LTD
 This   £ 1,520.75                                            S J Knott
 Cheque              Cheque No.   Branch No.   Account No.   A J Bridges

  "101129"          "101129"  20"2748"  30595713"
```

Step 7.	Send cheque off to payee with remittance advice	The cheque should be sent to the payee, together with the **remittance advice**. This can now be detached from the invoice and posted off with the cheque. If there isn't a remittance advice, some form of covering letter will be required to explain to the payee what the cheque is for.

> **Exam alert**
> A multiple choice question might show a cheque and ask you to choose a reason why it may not be authorised for payment.

Part B: Recording and accounting for cash transactions

> The **accounting procedures** for recording the payment in the accounts ledgers will be described in the next chapter.

6.6 As we saw in Chapter 6, it is quite usual for regular suppliers to a company to send a monthly **statement of account** to a customer, listing all the unpaid invoices and unsettled credit notes, and showing the total amount payable by the customer to the supplier. Many companies try to reconcile their ledger balances with the statement from the supplier, so that they can be sure that all invoices are recorded.

Discounts for early settlement

6.7 As you saw earlier in this text, if a cash discount is received it must be deducted from the payment to be made.

6.8 EXAMPLE: CASH DISCOUNT

The supplier will indicate the availability of the **cash discount** on each invoice, but the method of showing the discount will vary from one supplier to another. Here is just one example.

```
                    CHIPPIES LTD
                     Jewel House
                    Richmans Road
                   LONDON SE1N 5AB
```

Invoice Number: 123456
Tax Point: 01/08/X7
Account Number: 3365

INVOICE

CUSTOMER
Table Tops Ltd
112 Peters Square
Weyford
Kent CR2 2TA

Telephone Number 01427 123 4567
VAT Registration Number 457 4635 19
Northern Bank plc Code 20-25-43
Account Number 957023

Item Code	Description	Quantity	Unit Price	Net Amount
13579A	Tables	30	250.00	7,500.00
	Delivery	1	100.00	100.00

SALES VALUE:	7,600.00
VAT AT 17.5%:	1,296.75
AMOUNT PAYABLE:	8,896.75

Terms of payment are 30 days net. A cash discount of 2.5% is available for payment within 7 days.

Settlement discount of £190.00 for payments by 8th August 20X7	
Amount payable	8,896.75
Less discount	190.00
Amount payable if payment made by the month of August 20X7	8,706.75

Note that, as explained in Chapter 1, VAT is calculated on the **sales value net of discount** regardless of whether or not the discount is taken.

6.9 SOLUTION

If Table Tops Ltd's chief accountant decides to take the cash discount, a cheque should be written and despatched not later than 8 August. The amount of the cheque will be £8,706.75.

	£
Sales value plus VAT, no discount	8,896.75
Less discount	190.00
Cheque amount	8,706.75

The counterfoil of the cheque could include a note to indicate that a 2.5% settlement discount has been taken. The invoice will be stamped PAID with the date and cheque number, and an extra note to indicate that the 2.5% discount has been taken would be useful.

If payment is delayed beyond 8 August, the **full amount of the invoice** (£8,896.75) would be payable.

6.10 If a **credit note** is due against the invoice, or has already been received, it should be deducted **before** the cash discount is calculated.

Advantages and disadvantages of paying by cheque

6.11 Cheques are widely used in business to pay for supplies and other expenses. It is worth thinking briefly about the advantages and disadvantages of using cheques as a method of payment.

Advantages of cheque payments	Disadvantages of cheque payments
Cheques are **convenient to use** for payments of any amount (provided sufficient money is in the bank, or the organisation has a large enough overdraft facility).	There are **security problems** with keeping cheques safe from theft and misuse (forged signatures), although cheques are certainly more secure than cash as a method of payment.
The cheque **counterfoil** and cheque number can be used to provide a useful method for tracing past payments whenever any queries arise.	Cheques can be a **slow method of payment,** and a supplier might insist on a different method that is more prompt and reliable, such as standing order.
They are commonly used and **widely accepted**.	

Lost cheques

6.12 Cheques can get **lost in the post**. The loss of the cheque will not become apparent until the supplier writes to you or telephones your office demanding payment.

(a) You should **check on the supplier's** account in the purchase ledger, to see that a payment by cheque has been made.

(b) If a cheque has been sent to the supplier, and the date on which it was sent is not recent (if recent it might still be in the post), the cheque has probably been **lost or misdirected**.

6.13 There are actions you should take when it appears a cheque has been lost.

Step 1. Confirm that the cheque has **not gone through your bank account**. You can do this by checking the most recent bank statements or by telephoning the bank.

Step 2. Check the details of the **name and address of the supplier** to which the cheque was sent, and the name of any particular person to whom the letter was addressed.

6.14 One of three things will probably have happened.

Circumstances	Action to take
The cheque **has gone through your bank account**, and the supplier has been paid.	The error is in the supplier's records, and you should give the supplier (in writing or by telephone) the details of the payment (the date of the cheque, your bank, branch, sort code, cheque number and bank account number).
The cheque has been sent to the supplier, but to the **wrong person** in the supplier's organisation.	You should inform the relevant member of staff at the supplier, and he will retrieve the cheque.
The cheque has either been sent to the **wrong address** or has been **lost in the post**.	If this appears to be the case, you should take measures to **stop the 'old' cheque** and prepare a new one.

Stopping cheques

6.15 Businesses need to stop payments of cheques it has drawn more often than you might imagine. Some might even have a special form for sending stop instructions to its bank. Usually a cheque has to be stopped because it has physically been lost in transit to the supplier, or by the supplier.

6.16 It might sometimes happen that a payment has been made to the wrong person, or that the recipient of the cheque has forgotten to bank it until it is **out of date**. A cheque is out of date after 6 months. In the latter case, the bank should not pay the cheque anyway, but the cheque should be stopped as a precaution against the bank paying it in error.

6.17 To **stop a cheque from being paid** if it is subsequently presented to the bank for payment you should carry out the following.

Step 1. **Telephone** your bank saying that you want the cheque to be stopped.

Step 2. Confirm this instruction **in writing**.

An example of a form that a company might use to do this is shown below. The accounts clerk will fill in the form, which will then be signed by a person who is an authorised signatory for cheques.

Note: The bank will make a charge for stopping a cheque.

ABC

3, The Mews

Barking

The Manager
Bank
6 Hill Road
Barking

DATE: _23 July 20X7_

Dear Sir

ABC ACCOUNT NO 2467890

We wish to confirm our request by telephone that the payment of the cheque detailed below is stopped.

Cheque No _009372_

Dated _3 July 20X7_

Amount £ _4,276.83_

Payee _A & P Plumb_

We have inspected our statements up to number _493_ inclusive and the cheque is not listed on them.

We have drawn a replacement cheque no: _00 9406_

Your faithfully

M. P. Green

FOR ABC

6.18 If the cheque has been stopped because it was **lost**, the supplier still has the right to be paid. A new cheque should be prepared and signed.

Step 1. The authorisation to prepare the cheque should come from a designated person within the organisation, perhaps the **chief accountant** who is likely to be the person who has signed the form instructing the bank to stop the original cheque.

Step 2. The supplier's invoice will have been stamped PAID, with the date and cheque number. It should now be **altered** to indicate that the old cheque has been stopped, and the date and number of the **replacement cheque** should be added.

Step 3. The **counterfoil of the old cheque** should be amended to record 'STOPPED' and the date on which this occurred.

Step 4. The **counterfoil of the new cheque** should refer to the supplier's invoice and indicate that it is a replacement cheque.

Step 5. The replacement cheque should be **sent to the supplier**, with supporting documentation (covering letter and/or remittance advice).

Part B: Recording and accounting for cash transactions

7 BANK GIRO CREDITS (CREDIT TRANSFER)

7.1 Bank giro credits (**credit transfers**) were mentioned in Chapter 7 as a means by which payments might be **received** from customers. Bank giro credits can also be used by businesses to **make payments**. A business can pay a supplier using giro credits by filling in a bank giro credit transfer form and handing this together with the payment (cheque or cash) over the counter at a bank. There might be a **fee** to pay to the bank for this service.

7.2 Banks find that there are often problems when bills are paid this way as the information entered on the transfer form is often wrong. This is why they issue **preprinted forms** whenever possible. (This is what most utility companies do on a preprinted strip attached to their invoices, the customer simply fills in the date and the amount of the payment, signs it and pays it in at a bank branch.) Alternatively, a bank credit form can be sent by post with the payment to the supplier.

7.3 In practice, bank giro credits are rarely used by businesses to pay suppliers, except in cases where the supplier sends an invoice with a detachable preprinted bank giro credit transfer paying-in slip as shown below.

7.4 The following suppliers use their own preprinted bank giro credit transfer forms.

- BG (British Gas) and BT
- Electricity companies
- Water companies

7.5 Bank giro credit transfers are sometimes used by small companies to pay monthly salaries.

YOUR ACCOUNT NUMBER	YOU CAN PHONE US ON		AMOUNT TO PAY
083.7793/084.821	020-7733-5611		492.30

G Girobank PAYMENT SLIP **Bank Giro Credit**

	Customer account number	Credit account number	Amount	By transfer from Girobank a/c no
135 205	083.7793/084.821	834 0963	£ 492.30	

Standard fee payable at PO counter

Cashier's Stamp and Initials

Signature _____ Date _____

CASH

CHEQ £

94-92-17 **Swallows Bank plc**
Head Office Collection Account

ABC & CO LTD
18 THE MEWS
DERBY

W WESTERN ELECTRICITY

Items Fee   Please do not write or mark below this line or fold this payment slip

N9287304958712 +000082913 0

9287304958712O B0298374912 82 X

8 PAYMENTS BY BANKER'S DRAFT (PAYABLE ORDER)

8.1 A supplier might sometimes ask a customer to pay by **banker's draft**. Unlike company cheques, a banker's draft **cannot be stopped or cancelled after it has been issued**, and so when a supplier receives the draft, payment is guaranteed. Banker's drafts are not used for small value items, but might be used when a large payment is involved, such as for the purchase of a company car.

8.2 EXAMPLE: PAYMENT BY BANKER'S DRAFT

As an example, suppose that one of your directors wants to buy a car from Fittipaldi Motors Ltd. The cost will be £33,334.45.

Step 1. You might be required to prepare an **application for a banker's draft** to be provided by your bank to pay the car supplier, who is insisting on this method of payment. Although applications for a banker's draft can be made by letter, banks also provide standard forms that can be used instead. A standard form is shown below as it would possibly be filled in by the accounts clerk of the company in this example.

Step 2. **Signatures (probably two) of authorised officials** of the company will be required.

Step 3. The form, once signed, should be **sent to the bank**.

Step 4. The bank will **return the form to the company, together with the draft** (shown below).

Step 5. The form should be signed to **acknowledge receipt of the draft** and then sent back to the bank.

Step 6. The draft will then be sent or taken to the **car supplier**, who will release the car to the company.

Application for Inland Draft
To Swallows Bank Plc

EDGWARE Date 3.6.X7

Kindly supply a crossed Draft. *Marked 'account payee'*

Payable to FITTIPALDI MOTORS LTD

£ 33,334.45 amount in words Thirty three thousand, three hundred and thirty four pounds - 45p

*Please debit my/our account no

| 8 | 2 | 3 | 7 | 4 | 1 | 6 |

*~~Herewith cash to cover~~

*~~Herewith cheque to cover~~

Charges (if any) to be ~~*deducted~~ / charged to me/us   *Delete as necessary

Signature(s) JP MacHugh   B Clive

Name(s) J P MACHUGH   B CLIVE

Address (if not a customer)

I/We acknowledge receipt of the above mentioned draft numbered 123455

_____ Signature

(To be signed by an authorised person in the company and returned to the bank)

Swallows Bank
Swallows Bank Plc
Head Office
London EC3V 1AB

15-14-12T

Date 4th June 20X7

Fittipaldi Motors Limited

the sum of *Thirty Three Thousand Three Hundred and Thirty Four Pounds and Forty Five Pence only*

£ 33,334 - 45

NOT NEGOTIABLE

For Swallows Bank Plc
EDGWARE BRANCH
BR Dowding
SV Pritchard

⑈123455⑈ 15⑈ 1412⑈ 000345 6⑈

9 PAYMENTS BY STANDING ORDER AND DIRECT DEBIT

9.1 **Standing orders** and **direct debits** were described in Chapter 6 on receiving payments. Here, we are looking at them from the point of view of a business **making payments**.

Standing orders

9.2 Standing order payments might be used by a business to make regular payments of a fixed amount.

  (a) **Hire purchase (HP) payments** to a hire purchase company (finance house), where an asset has been bought under an HP agreement.

  (b) **Rental payments** to the landlord of a building occupied by the business.

  (c) Paying **insurance premiums** to an insurance company.

9.3 Although the supplier (the HP company, landlord, or insurance company) might request payment by standing order, **it is up to the paying business to ask its bank to set up a standing order arrangement.**

9.4 The business must specify the following to its bank.

  (a) That it would like a standing order arrangement for **regular payments** from its account
  (b) The **fixed amount** of each payment
  (c) The **frequency** of each payment and the due date
  (d) **Banking details of the supplier** to which the payments should be made

  If the business subsequently needs to alter the amount of each payment, or to stop future payments, it must send the relevant instructions to the bank **in writing**.

9.5 A standing order request could be sent in a letter, but banks also supply standard forms that can be used instead. These are called **Standing Order Mandates**. The chief accountant of a company, or a director, will need to sign the request form, since the form will require the signature of someone who is an authorised cheque signatory and whose signature the bank can recognise. It is quite possible, however, that an accounts clerk might be asked to prepare a standing order request form for signature.

9.6 EXAMPLE: STANDING ORDER MANDATE

ABC Ltd buys some office furniture on hire purchase, arranging to make regular monthly payments of £240.25 to the hire purchase company, whose banking details are as follows.

HP company	Smooth Finance Ltd
Bank of HP company	Barminster Bank plc
	Richmond-upon-Thames branch
	Sort code 22-33-44
Bank account number	11742538

ABC Ltd banks at the Weyford branch of Lowlands Bank plc, 5 High Street, Weyford, Kent CR1 1GG, account number 36274859.

The first payment is to be made on 15 June 20X7 and the final payment on 15 May 20X9.

9.7 SOLUTION

A Standing Order Mandate would be prepared for signature by the chief accountant, or managing director (or other authorised individuals) as follows.

Standing Order Mandate

TO _LOWLANDS_ BANK

Address _5 HIGH STREET, WEYFORD, KENT_

Please pay

Bank	Branch Title (not address)	Sorting Code Number
BARMINSTER	RICHMOND-UPON-THAMES	22-33-44

for the credit of

Beneficiary's Name	Account Number
SMOOTH FINANCE LIMITED	11742538

the sum of

Regular amount in figures	Regular amount in words
£ 240-25	TWO HUNDRED AND FORTY POUNDS & 25 PENCE

commencing

Date and Amount of First Payment		and thereafter every	Due Date and Frequency
15 JUNE 20X7	£ 240-25		15TH OF EACH MONTH

*until

Date and Amount of Last Payment		*until you receive further notice from me/us in writing and debit my/our account accordingly.
15 MAY 20X9	£ 240-25	

quoting the reference _OFFICE FURNITURE_

This instruction cancels any previous order in favour of the beneficiary named above, under this reference.

Special instructions:

Account to be debited	Account Number
ABC LIMITED	3 6 2 7 4 8 5 9

Signature(s) _____ Date _____

*Delete if not applicable

9.8 The **reference** that is quoted, here 'Office furniture' has been used, will appear on ABC Ltd's bank statements. It helps to supply a reference that will identify the standing order payment on the bank statement.

A reference is not essential, and is only supplied at the choice of the customer. Alternatively, some form of reference number might be quoted, such as the supplier's code in ABC Ltd's purchase ledger, or the invoice number, or any similar type of reference for identification.

Direct debits

9.9 Direct debits, like standing orders, are used for **regular payments**. They differ from standing orders in the following ways.

(a) It is the **person who receives the payments who initiates each payment,** and informs the paying bank of the amount of each payment.

(b) Payments can be for a **variable amount** each time, and at irregular intervals, as well as for fixed amounts at regular intervals.

British Gas
South Midlands

British Gas plc (South Midlands)
Gas Payment Plan
Freepost
Coringham CV6 3TT

**Gas Payment Plan
Direct Debit Instruction**

Instructions to your Bank/Building Society to pay direct debits

Please complete parts 1 to 5 to instruct your Bank/Building Society to make payments directly from your account.

When completed please return the form direct to us.

1. The Manager

   WESTLAKE Bank/~~Building Society~~

   (Full Address of your Bank/Building Society)

   3 Great Way, Dudentry
   South Midlands
   DD1 1BC

2. Name of account holder(s)

   LARKSPUR LIMITED

3. Bank/Building Society Account Number

   3 5 1 4 9 7 5 5

4. Sort-Code

   62 – 31 – 95

   Originator's Identification Number
   916258

   Instruction Number
   Branch use only

   Account Reference Number

   00137200123468

   ┌─────────────────────────────────┐
   │ Revenue Officer   │
   │ British Gas plc South Midlands │
   │ PO Box 78   │
   │ Coringham CV6 3TT   │
   └─────────────────────────────────┘

   After completion the Bank/Building Society branch should detach this part of the form and return it to the address above.

   I/We would like to start a Gas Payment Plan and have completed a Direct Debit Mandate

   Please send the whole form to the reply address overleaf

5. Your instructions to the Bank/Building Society and signature

- I/We instruct you to pay direct debits from my/our account at the request of British Gas South Midlands.
- The amounts are variable and may be debited on various dates.
- I/We understand that British Gas South Midlands may change the amounts and dates only after giving prior notice.

   British Gas South Midlands
   Account Reference Number

   00137200123468

- I/We will inform the Bank/Building Society in writing if I/We wish to cancel this instruction.
- I/We understand that if a debit is paid which breaks the terms of the instruction, the Bank/Building Society will make a refund.

   Signature(s)   Date
   R. C. Watson   8/9/X7
   J. Keats   8/9/X7

- Banks/Building Societies may decline to accept Direct Debits from some types of account.

FOR BANK/BUILDING SOCIETY USE ONLY

Branch Title _____

Sort Code

A/c no.

A/c name

(maximum 18 characters)

Direct debits in respect of our customer's instruction under the reference number quoted should be made out as above.

Standing Order mandate cancelled.
Last payment made on _____
Standing Order mandate not traced _____

For _____ Bank/Building Society
Manager _____ Date _____

03/09/97 DIST. 24

LARKSPUR LTD
12 BONNY STREET
DUDENTRY
SOUTH MIDLANDS DD1 2ER

00137200123468

Part B: Recording and accounting for cash transactions

9.10 Payments by direct debit **might** be made by some companies for regular bills such as telephone, gas, electricity and water bills. The company being paid by direct debit will inform the payer of the amount and date of each payment in a printed statement.

9.11 If a company decides that it wants to pay some of its bills by direct debit, it must fill in a **Direct Debit Instruction**. This will be sent back to the supplier, not to the bank, and the supplier will then make arrangements through its own bank to set up the direct debit payments.

9.12 An example of a Direct Debit Instruction is shown on the previous page. It has been completed by the customer, Larkspur Ltd, and it is ready to send back to British Gas.

9.13 Large sums of money may be paid by telegraphic or interbank transfer. On receipt of written instructions the bank will transfer the funds directly to the bank account of the payee anywhere in the world.

9.14 Many companies now use internet banking and are able to pay suppliers and employees by online transfer. The funds normally arrive in the payee's account two working days after they are debited from the transferor's account.

Activity 9.1

Libra Ltd has to make the following payments.

(a) £6.29 for office cleaning materials bought from a nearby supermarket.

(b) £231.40 monthly, which represents hire purchase instalments on a new van. The payments are due to Marsh Finance Ltd over a period of 36 months.

(c) £534.21 to Southern Electric plc for the most recent quarter's electricity and standing charge. A bank giro credit form/payment counterfoil is attached to the bill. There is no direct debiting mandate currently in force.

(d) £161.50 monthly for ten months, representing the business rates payable to Clapperton District Council, which operates a direct debiting system.

(e) £186.60 to Renton Hire Ltd for a week's hire of a car on company business by the Sales Director from Edinburgh Airport. The Sales Director must pay on the spot, and does not wish to use a personal cheque or cash.

(f) £23,425.00 to Selham Motors Ltd for a new car to be used by the Finance Director. Selham Motors will not accept one of the company's cheques in payment, since the Finance Director wishes to collect the vehicle immediately upon delivering the payment in person and Selham Motors is concerned that such a cheque might be dishonoured.

Task

Recommend the method of payment which you think would be most appropriate in each case, stating your reasons.

10 DOCUMENTATION TO GO OUT WITH PAYMENTS

10.1 So far, we have concentrated in this chapter on the payment itself, but when a payment is made, it is usual to send out another document with the payment to inform the recipient as to what the payment is for and who it is from. This document might be any of the following.

(a) A **remittance advice**, either created by the customer or is part of the statement sent by the supplier

(b) An **order form** for payments which are sent with the order itself

(c) A copy of a **pro-forma invoice** where this has been provided by the supplier for payments with an order

(d) A **bank giro credit form** for telephone, electricity and other similar bills

(e) A **covering letter** explaining what the payment is for, when other forms of documentation do not exist

Remittance advices

10.2 We looked at remittance advices in Chapter 6. Remember that the **remittance advice** should include the following.

- The name and address of the customer
- The name and address of the supplier
- The customer's account number or code (as specified by the supplier) and/or the supplier code (as specified by the customer)
- The invoice number(s)
- The invoice amount(s)
- The invoice date(s)
- The date of payment
- The total amount of the payment

10.3 We have also referred to the fact that there might be **two** remittance advices.

(a) One remittance advice might be sent with the **supplier's statement**. This might be a separate form, or a tear-off slip on the statement itself.

(b) A second remittance advice might be prepared by the **customer's accounts department**, and sent to the supplier with the payment (with a copy kept for reference).

10.4 The example below is of a remittance advice **prepared** by ABC Ltd's accounts clerk for the payment of three invoices less a credit note. The total payment is £1,185.50.

ABC Ltd
112 Peters Square
Weyford
Kent CR2 2TA
Telephone: 01329 456272

REMITTANCE ADVICE

Rapid Supplies Ltd
63 Canterbury Road
Weyford
Kent CR3 6UX

Supplier code
603

Date of payment
8/9/X7

Invoice/ credit note date	Details	Invoices £	Credit notes £	Payment amount £
3/8/X7	Invoice 062074	375.80		375.80
10/8/X7	Invoice 063015	405.20		405.20
15/8/X7	Credit note CR2752		120.00	(120.00)
24/8/X7	Invoice 063240	524.50		524.50
	Total payment			1,185.50

Part B: Recording and accounting for cash transactions

Note. The supplier code is the code used by ABC Ltd to identify Rapid Supplies Ltd in its own accounting system.

10.5 This remittance advice will be sent to the supplier with a cheque for £1,185.50, and a copy of the remittance advice will be kept in the accounts department of ABC Ltd. In addition, if the supplier sent remittance advices with each invoice and credit note, these should also be sent back with the payment. In this example, the letter posted to the supplier would contain the following.

- A cheque
- ABC Ltd's own remittance advice, prepared by its accounts clerk
- The remittance advice(s) from Rapid Supplies Ltd

Activity 9.2

Penumbra Ltd is due to pay (or claim credit in the case of credit notes) the following items in respect of two creditors. The date shown is the date of the invoice or credit note.

Feathers Ltd (Ref F011)

		Goods	VAT	Total
		£	£	£
30.3.X7	Invoice 07114	74.40	13.02	87.42
6.4.X7	Credit note CR084 (re invoice 07101)	142.25	24.89	167.14
7.4.X7	Invoice 07241	248.71	43.52	292.23
9.4.X7	Invoice 07249	724.94	126.86	851.80
14.4.X7	Invoice 07302	141.17	24.70	165.87
22.4.X7	Credit note CR087 (re invoice 07241)	101.24	17.72	118.96
22.4.X7	Invoice 07487	421.00	73.68	494.68
28.4.X7	Credit note CR099 (re invoice 07114)	74.40	13.02	87.42
7.5.X7	Invoice 07714	98.94	17.31	116.25

The Furniture People (Ref F017)

		Goods	VAT	Total
		£	£	£
2.4.X7	Invoice 734282	3,742.28	654.90	4,397.18
23.4.X7	Invoice 735110	6,141.04	1,074.68	7,215.72
27.4.X7	Invoice 735192	842.92	147.51	990.43
27.4.X7	Invoice 735204	1,241.70	217.30	1,459.00
4.5.X7	Credit note 274221 (re invoice 732118)	942.41	164.92	1,107.33

The creditors' addresses are as follows.

Feathers Ltd, 247 Marconi Road, Chelmsford, Essex CM1 4PQ
The Furniture People, 4 Kane Street, Northampton NN3 4SR

The procedures manual of Penumbra Ltd specifies the following cheque signatories.

Cheque signatories

C Taylor	Financial Controller
R Hare	Financial Accountant
J Mackie	Finance Director
B Mitchell	General Manager
J Knight	Managing Director
S Lukes	Chairman

Two signatures are required on all cheques.

Cheques up to £1,000	Any two signatories
Cheques up to £10,000	Any two directors
Cheques over £10,000	Chairman or managing director, plus one other director

Tasks

(a) Prepare remittance advices for the payments to be made today (2 June 20X7) to each of the two creditors. You should use the blank forms provided below.

9: Authorising and making payments

(b) Show the total of the payments to be made.

Penumbra Limited

**42 Braintree Road
Bishop's Stortford
Herts CM23 9XY**

Telephone: 01279 33942
Fax: 01279 33920

*Feathers Limited
247 Marconi Road
Chelmsford, Essex CM1 4PQ*

REMITTANCE ADVICE

Supplier account number

Date of payment:

Invoice/ credit note date	Details	Invoices £	Credit notes £	Payment amount £
....	....	....	....	....
....	....	....	....	....
....	....	....	....	....
....	....	....	....	....
....	....	....	....	....
....	....	....	....	....
....	....	....	....	....
....	....	....	....	....
....	....	....	....	....

Penumbra Limited

**42 Braintree Road
Bishop's Stortford
Herts CM23 9XY**

Telephone: 01279 33942
Fax: 01279 33920

*The Furniture People
4 Kane Street
Northampton NN3 4SR*

REMITTANCE ADVICE

Supplier account number

Date of payment:

Invoice/ credit note date	Details	Invoices £	Credit notes £	Payment amount £
....	....	....	....	....
....	....	....	....	....
....	....	....	....	....
....	....	....	....	....
....	....	....	....	....
....	....	....	....	....
....	....	....	....	....
....	....	....	....	....
....	....	....	....	....

Activity 9.3

Carrying on from Activity 9.2, you establish that the following cheque signatories are available in the office today and tomorrow: R Hare, B Mitchell, S Lukes and C Taylor. J Knight is expected back in the office tomorrow.

Tasks

(a) Complete cheques for the payments to be made, using the crossing 'A/c payee'.

(b) State what action you will take to get each of the cheques signed.

(c) State what you would do to the invoices and credit notes now that they have been paid, giving reasons.

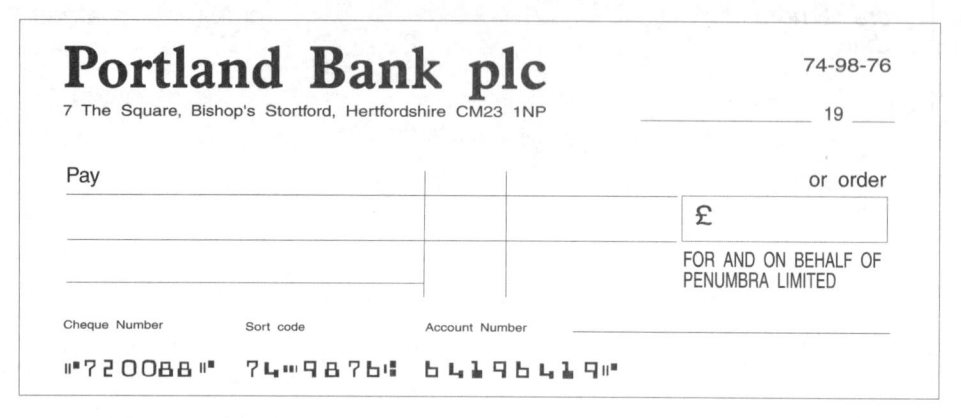

Portland Bank plc
7 The Square, Bishop's Stortford, Hertfordshire CM23 1NP
74-98-76
_____ 19 ___

Pay _____ or order
£ _____
FOR AND ON BEHALF OF PENUMBRA LIMITED

Cheque Number Sort code Account Number
⑈720088⑈ 74⑈9876⑈ 64196419⑈

Portland Bank plc
7 The Square, Bishop's Stortford, Hertfordshire CM23 1NP
74-98-76
_____ 19 ___

Pay _____ or order
£ _____
FOR AND ON BEHALF OF PENUMBRA LIMITED

Cheque Number Sort code Account Number
⑈720089⑈ 74⑈9876⑈ 64196419⑈

Key learning points

- It is very important to apply **controls over payments**.
    - Documentation (invoice, statement, cheque request form, expenses claim form)
    - Authorisation of the expenditure item (passing it for payment)
    - Authorised signatures for cheques and payment instructions to banks
- **Cheque requisition forms** are used when primary documentation such as an invoice has not been received. Cheque requisition forms help to ensure authorisation and recording of payments.
- It is important to establish **proper authorisation procedures**, with each person in authority having written limits.
- A business will use a variety of **methods to make payments**. Ignoring payroll (wages and salaries) and petty cash, the most common and convenient methods of payment are by **cheque** and by **BACS**.
- As far as the use of **cheques** is concerned, you should know how to do the following.
    - Prepare a cheque for payment
    - Deal with lost cheques
    - Stop cheques
- **Direct debits** are not often used for payments by businesses, but might occasionally be used for convenience.
- The **timing of payments** may depend on credit terms offered by suppliers, including **discounts** for prompt payment.
- A business should send proper **explanatory documentation** with all payments to avoid confusion. Copies of the relevant documents should be filed in such a way that the documents are easy to retrieve (see Chapter 10).
- The **accounts department** must:
    - Make all payments and send these to suppliers with associated documentation (remittance advices and so on)
    - Have a system for being able to trace each payment in the event of subsequent queries (for example by writing the invoice number on the cheque counterfoil and the cheque number on the invoice, and stamping invoices PAID with the date of payment)
    - Keep a filing system for paid and unpaid invoices, standing orders, credit card company statements and any other documentation
    - Record payments in the accounts (this aspect of payments is the subject of the next chapter)

Quick quiz

1. What are the three main steps in applying controls over payments?
2. When might documentary evidence not be available for a payment?
3. What is a cheque requisition form?
4. What is an expenses claim form used for and by whom?
5. Which methods of payment are most commonly used by businesses?
6. Should cash be sent by post?
7. What should you do to stop a cheque?
8. What is the main difference between a standing order and a direct debit?
9. What is the document most usually sent with a payment by a business?

Part B: Recording and accounting for cash transactions

Answer to quick quiz

1. The three steps are: obtaining documentary evidence, authorisation of payments, restricting authority to make payments.

2. When an invoice has not been received or there will be no invoice or receipt there will be no documentary evidence.

3. A cheque requisition form is an internal document requesting that a cheque be drawn for payment.

4. Employees will use an expenses claim form to obtain reimbursement for expenses for which they have paid.

5. Cheques and BACS are the most common.

6. No. It might get lost and there would be no proof of the amount sent and no means of retrieving it.

7. Telephone the bank saying you want the cheque stopped and then confirm the instruction in writing.

8. Standing orders are always for the same amount whereas direct debit can be for a different amount each time it is paid.

9. A remittance advice is usually sent with a payment.

Answers to activities

Answer 9.1

(a) **Recommended method: cash**

This is a small business payment which should be paid out of petty cash for the sake of convenience.

(b) **Recommended method: standing order**

A standing order is convenient for regular fixed payments. Once the standing order instruction is made, the bank will ensure that all payments are made on the due dates and will stop making payments at the date specified in the instruction. Some finance companies may insist on a standing order being set up, as it is convenient for them to receive instalments regularly without having to issue payment requests or reminders.

(c) **Recommended method: by cheque at the bank**, accompanied by the bill and completed bank giro credit form. The bank clerk will stamp the bill as evidence that the payment was made.

Paying by cheque is safer than paying by cash and is more usual for such a large payment. Handing the cheque over at the bank will be convenient and evidence of payment will be obtained.

If the payment is made at a bank other than that at which Libra holds an account, the bank receiving the payment will probably make a small charge for processing it.

An alternative method is to send a crossed cheque by post, enclosing the payment counterfoil.

(d) **Recommended method: direct debit mandate**

The direct debit mandate will allow the Council to debit the amounts due direct from Libra's bank account on the due dates. The mandate will be effective until it is cancelled. The Council must inform Libra in advance of the amounts it will be debiting.

(e) **Recommended method: credit card or charge card**

Payment by credit card or charge card avoids the need to pay immediately by cash or cheque. The amount paid will appear on the monthly statement for the card used. If the Sales Director's personal card is used, he will claim payment later from the company, which may pay him by cheque or with his monthly salary payment.

(f) **Recommended method: banker's draft**

A banker's draft cannot be stopped or cancelled once it is issued. Being effectively like a cheque drawn on the bank itself, it is generally accepted as being as good as cash. It is therefore most likely to be accepted by Selham Motors.

Answer 9.2

(a)

Penumbra Limited
42 Braintree Road
Bishop's Stortford
Herts CM23 9XY
Telephone: 01279 33942
Fax: 01279 33920

REMITTANCE ADVICE

Supplier account number: **7011**

Date of payment: **2 June 20X7**

Feathers Limited
247 Marconi Road
Chelmsford, Essex CM1 4PQ

Invoice/credit note date	Details	Invoices £	Credit notes £	Payment amount £
30.3.X7	Invoice 07114	87.42		87.42
6.4.X7	Credit note CR084		167.14	(167.14)
7.4.X7	Invoice 07241	292.23		292.23
9.4.X7	Invoice 07249	851.80		851.80
14.4.X7	Invoice 07302	165.87		165.87
22.4.X7	Credit note CR087		118.96	(118.96)
22.4.X7	Invoice 07487	494.68		494.68
28.4.X7	Credit note CR099		87.42	(87.42)
7.5.X7	Invoice 07714	116.25		116.25
Total payment				1,634.73

Penumbra Limited
42 Braintree Road
Bishop's Stortford
Herts CM23 9XY
Telephone: 01279 33942
Fax: 01279 33920

REMITTANCE ADVICE

Supplier account number: **7017**

Date of payment: **2 June 20X7**

The Furniture People
4 Kane Street
Northampton NN3 4SR

Invoice/credit note date	Details	Invoices £	Credit notes £	Payment amount £
2.4.X7	Invoice 734282	4,397.18		4,397.18
23.4.X7	Invoice 735110	7,215.72		7,215.72
27.4.X7	Invoice 735192	990.43		990.43
27.4.X7	Invoice 735204	1,459.00		1,459.00
4.5.X7	Credit note 274221		1,107.33	(1,107.33)
Total payment				12,955.00

Part B: Recording and accounting for cash transactions

(b) The total payments to be made are as follows.

	£
Feathers Ltd	1,634.73
The Furniture People	12,955.00
Total	14,589.73

Answer 9.3

(a)

Portland Bank plc
7 The Square, Bishop's Stortford, Hertfordshire CM23 1NP
74-98-76
Date: 2 June 19 X7

Pay: Feathers Limited or order
One thousand, six hundred and thirty-four pounds 73   £1,634.73
A/c payee
FOR AND ON BEHALF OF PENUMBRA LIMITED

Cheque Number   Sort code   Account Number
720088   74-9876   64196419

Portland Bank plc
7 The Square, Bishop's Stortford, Hertfordshire CM23 1NP
74-98-76
Date: 2 June 19 X7

Pay: The Furniture People or order
Twelve thousand, nine hundred and fifty-five pounds only   £12,955.00
A/c payee
FOR AND ON BEHALF OF PENUMBRA LIMITED

Cheque Number   Sort code   Account Number
720089   74-9876   64196419

(b) The cheque to Feathers Ltd requires the signatures of two directors. The cheque to The Furniture People requires the signature of the Chairman or the Managing Director and that of one other director. I would take the cheques for signature (together with invoices and any other supporting documentation) to S Lukes (Chairman). However, neither of the other two directors (J Knight and J Mackie) are in today, but I would ask J Knight, who is in tomorrow, to sign the cheque as early as possible.

(c) I would stamp the invoices to indicate that payment of the invoice has been approved and made, and on what date. In some firms, a sticker may be used for this purpose. This procedure provides a record of the approval of the payment for later reference and may help to prevent an invoice being paid twice in error.

Chapter 10　Recording payments

Chapter topic list

1　Controls over recording payments
2　The cash book: recording payments
3　Posting cash payments to the general ledger
4　Returned cheques
5　BACS

The following study sessions are covered in this chapter

Syllabus reference

5　(c)　Recognise the importance of accurately recording all payments　　3c

　　(e)　Record payments in the cash book, general ledger, purchase ledger　　3c

Part B: Recording and accounting for cash transactions

1 CONTROLS OVER RECORDING PAYMENTS

1.1 If an unauthorised payment is made and not recorded in the cash book, then it will be discovered when a **bank reconciliation** takes place. This is because, during the reconciliation, a comparison is made between what is in the cash book and what has passed through the bank account. We will see in detail how it is done in Chapter 12.

Fraud

1.2 Someone who makes an **unauthorised payment** (to himself or a third party) will want the payment to be recorded, but the **nature of the payment to be hidden**, because of the bank reconciliation. It is therefore necessary to ensure that the following procedures are in place.

(a) All payments are **authorised** correctly.

(b) Proper checks are made against supporting documentation.

(c) The person who writes out the cheques is not be the same person who records the payments in the cash book or remittance lists (**segregation of duties**).

(d) At the end of each day, a list of the payments for that day is submitted to a senior member of staff to check for **unusual payments**. He or she will investigate all payments which are unusual.

(e) A **minimum number of cheque books** is in use at any time, preferably only one.

1.3 Of course, it is always possible that someone might organise an unauthorised payment (a theft), and disappear before the inevitable discovery, but most frauds are carried out over a period of time and involve relatively small individual amounts. Most people could not carry out a one-off fraud large enough to warrant leaving their job (and becoming unemployable).

Completeness

1.4 It is necessary to ensure that **all** payments have been recorded. Once again, if a payment has not been recorded by accident, then this will become apparent when a bank reconciliation takes place. It may only be discovered, however, when the payment clears through the bank account. Before then it will not appear in the cash book or on the bank statement. To ensure completeness the following controls should be in place.

(a) Regular **bank reconciliations** should take place.

(b) Cheques should be issued **in sequence** and, where possible, only one cheque book should be used at a time.

(c) A **sequence check** should be carried out on the cheques entered in the cash book by someone other than the person who normally records them. This will ensure that no cheques are missing.

(d) Regular (probably weekly) examinations should be made of the bank statements to ensure that all payments by **direct debit and standing order** have been recorded in the cash book (along with bank interest and charges).

Activity 10.1

At Ferdi's Furniture plc, among the procedures in operation over the recording of payments are the following.

(a) Only one company cheque book is to be in use at any one time.

(b) Numbers of all cheques are to be entered in the cash book even where the cheque is cancelled.

(c) All cancelled cheques are to be retained.

(d) The tasks of writing cheques and writing up the cash book are to be carried out by different people.

(e) Authorised details of all standing orders and direct debits are to be filed and the details of any such payments are to be agreed to the file before being transferred from bank statements in to the cash book.

Task

Comment on the reasons for each of the above procedures.

2 THE CASH BOOK: RECORDING PAYMENTS

2.1 We have looked at the receipts role of the cash book in some detail in Chapters 4 and 8. Here we will examine the practical aspects of recording payments in the payments side of the cash book.

2.2 To help control the business, we **analyse the cash book** into different types of payment. Different businesses will do this in different ways depending on several factors.

- **How many categories** of purchases they have
- **How often** they purchase goods in each category
- The way the business is **split up** into separate segments
- How **complicated** the cash book may become

2.3 In the example shown in section 3 on pages 210 and 211, there are columns for two different types of purchases and columns for other sundry expense and capital payments.

2.4 There are some important points to note from this example.

Discounts received are recorded in a separate column, a memorandum column which is not part of the cash book balance. This is the same as we saw for **discounts allowed** on the receipts side in Chapter 4 Section 4.10 and Chapter 8 section 4.6.

2.5 The accounting entries for payments to creditors where a discount is received would be as follows. A £10 discount is received on a debt of £100.

	£	£
DEBIT Purchase ledger control a/c	90	
CREDIT Cash		90
DEBIT Purchase ledger control a/c	10	
CREDIT Discount received		10

The discount received column in example 3.3 below shows how **discounts received** are recorded in a memorandum column which is not part of the cash book balance.

The discount received column is required in order to show why the **full amount of a debt** is not being paid to the customer.

The list of creditors payable of the company will be recorded in the **purchase ledger**. The individual discounts received will be posted to the discount account and the individual creditors' balances thus clearing the **total** debt.

Part B: Recording and accounting for cash transactions

Type of payment	Treatment in the cash book
Cash purchases	The columns for cash purchases are analysed by type of purchase because this is the first record of the purchases in the accounts.
Payments to creditors	These are not analysed and come under a single column. The analysis is made in the purchase day book when the credit purchase is made, not when cash is paid.
VAT	Input VAT on purchases made on credit will have been recorded in the purchases day book and so will not appear in the cash book. **VAT on cash purchases** must be recorded in the cash book as it is **not** recorded elsewhere in the accounts.
Cancelled cheques	These should be entered in the cash book, even if they were never used, to allow a complete sequence check, and to make sure the cheque does not pass through the account. **Unused cheques** should be spoiled but retained.
Extent of analysis	This cash book is analysed in quite a lot of detail. This is not always necessary, but it makes things easier when it comes to posting to the ledger accounts as only the totals need to be posted.
Non-cheque payments	The **standing orders, direct debits** and other similar items have been entered at the end of the page, even though some of the transactions are dated earlier in the month. This is acceptable and it shows that this information is being extracted from the bank statements only monthly. The validity of all standing orders and direct debit payments should be checked against a **control list**. This list would be a complete record of all current standing orders and direct debits; it should be maintained by a responsible person.

Activity 10.2

State whether each of the two statements below is TRUE or FALSE.

(a) Cheque payments are recorded in the cash book only when they have been presented at our bank because it is only then that payment is made from our bank account.

(b) Standing order payments made by the bank should normally be entered in the cash book, but not where they represent payments in advance for goods or services not yet received.

Activity 10.3

You are involved in training some new members of staff at your firm on the recording of payments.

Task

Explain briefly each of the following terms.

(a) Cancelled cheque
(b) Stopped cheque
(c) Paid cheque
(d) Bank reconciliation statement

3 POSTING CASH PAYMENTS TO THE GENERAL LEDGER

3.1 As with cash receipts, which we saw in Chapter 8, it is only when we **post the payments side of the cash book to the cash (or bank) account in the general ledger that we can be said to have accounted for cash payments.**

3.2 The same steps apply to posting the payments side.

Step 1. Add up all the columns.

Step 2. Check that the analysis columns (excluding the discount received memorandum column) add up to the total cash paid column.

Step 3. Identify the general ledger account by marking against the cash book account.

Step 4. Draw up the posting summary and post the general ledger.

3.3 EXAMPLE: POSTING THE GENERAL LEDGER

Suppose we wished to post Warren Miles's cash payments for 1 September 20X7, which look like this.

WARREN MILES CASH BOOK

PAYMENTS

Date	Narrative			Discounts received	Total	Input VAT on cash purchases	Payments to creditors	Expenses	Fixed assets
20X7									
01-Sep	(g) Creditor paid: Ferdie	PL543		10	130.00		120.00		
	(h) Creditor paid: Kiera	PL76		20	330.00		310.00		
	(i) Telephone expense				400.00			400.00	
	(j) Gas expense				280.00			280.00	
	(k) Plant & machinery purchase				1,500.00				1,500.00
	(l) Cash purchase: Stationery				97.00	14.45		82.55	
					2,737.00	14.45	430.00	762.55	1,500.00
	Balance c/d				683.00				
					3,420.00	14.45	430.00	762.55	1,500.00

The entries for Kiera and Ferdie should reflect discounts received of £10 and £20 respectively. Why were £330 and £130 paid out?

Part B: Recording and accounting for cash transactions

3.4 SOLUTION

Warren Miles's amended payment side looks like this.

WARREN MILES: CASH BOOK

PAYMENTS

Date	Narrative	Ref.	Discount received	Total	Input VAT on cash purchases	Payments to creditors	Expenses	Fixed assets
20X7								
01-Sep	(g) Creditor paid: Ferdie	PL543	10.00	120.00		120.00		
	(h) Creditor paid: Kiera	PL76	20.00	310.00		310.00		
	(i) Telephone expense			400.00			400.00	
	(j) Gas expense			280.00			280.00	
	(k) Plant & machinery purchase			1,500.00				1,500.00
	(l) Cash purchase: stationery			97.00	14.45		82.55	
			30.00	2,707.00	14.45	430.00	762.55	1,500.00
			DR01	CA01	VAT01	TC01	XP01	FA01
			CR	CR	DR	DR	DR	DR
			TC01					
			DR					

Let us follow through the steps.

Step 1. **Add up the columns** (see above)

Step 2. **Check the totals**

	£
Input VAT on cash purchases	14.45
Payments to creditors	430.00
Expenses	762.55
Fixed asset purchases	1,500.00
	2,707.00

Step 3. **Identify the general ledger account.** We have marked the references for the general ledger account on the payment page above.

    TC01   Total creditors

    CA01   Cash account

    VAT01 VAT account

    XP01   Expenses

    FA01   Fixed assets

    DR01   Discounts received

Step 4. Draw up the **posting summary** and post the general ledger.

			£	£
DEBIT	Total creditors	TC01	460.00	
	VAT	VAT01	14.45	
	Expenses	XP01	762.55	
	Fixed assets	FA01	1,500.00	
CREDIT	Cash	CA01		2,707.00
	Discounts received	DR01		30.00

Cash book payments posting summary on 1 September 20X7

Note that the discounts received have been debited to total creditors.

Now we can post to the ledger:

CASH ACCOUNT   CA01

		£			£
1 Sept	Balance b/d	900.00	1 Sept	Cash book	2,707.00
1 Sept		2,490.00			

TOTAL CREDITORS   TC01

		£			£
1 Sept	Cash book	460.00	1 Sept	Balance b/d	42,972.00

EXPENSES   XP01

		£		£
1 Sept	Balance b/d	170,249.00		
1 Sept	Cash book	762.55		

VAT   VAT01

		£			£
1 Sept	Cash book	14.45		Balance b/d	35,070.00
			1 Sept	Cash book	34.25

FIXED ASSETS   FA01

		£		£
1 Sept	Cash book	1,500.00		

DISCOUNTS RECEIVED   DR01

	£			£
		1 Sept	Cash book	30.00

Computerisation of payments recording

3.5 In Chapter 8 we looked at the implications of a computerised cash book in relation to cash receipts in the general ledger cash account. The implications are the same for recording payments in a computerised cash book, but we should also look at the use of the **purchase ledger function which can record and issue cheques at the same time**.

3.6 In a computerised purchase ledger, the option would exist to produce computer-printed cheques. The computer would offer the following menu on screen in relation to payments.

```
                    PURCHASE LEDGER
                    AUTOMATIC PAYMENTS
    FILE SECURITY ...................................................................  1
    PROVISIONAL PAYMENTS LIST ..........................................  2
    TEMPORARY PAYMENT AMENDMENTS .............................  3
    AUTOMATIC PAYMENTS RUN .............................................  4
    LIST OF REMITTANCES .......................................................  5
    LIST OF CREDIT TRANSFERS .............................................  6
    REMITTANCE ADVICE NOTES .............................................  7
    CHEQUES ............................................................................  8
    CREDIT TRANSFERS ...........................................................  9
    PURGE CHEQUE/CREDIT TRANSFER FILE ........................ 10
    EXIT    < RETURN >
    PLEASE SELECT A FUNCTION
```

Part B: Recording and accounting for cash transactions

3.7 In sophisticated systems, cheques will automatically be produced from the 'payments list' held on file. This is done by dating each payment on the list. If the date matches today's date, then a cheque will be printed for it.

3.8 Once a selection is made from the menu above, then the relevant information can be keyed in. When the 'cheques' option is chosen, the operator can key in all the relevant details to appear on each cheque.

3.9 When the purchase ledger is instructed to prepare a cheque it will be given certain information.

- The **supplier's code number** on the purchase ledger
- The **amount** to be paid
- The **date** the cheque is to be paid if it is not the current date

There might be a 'proforma' cheque on screen which prompts the operator to give all this information.

3.10 The purchase ledger program will perform various tasks at the same time.

(a) The **cheque will be printed out** ready to sign.

(b) The balance on that creditor's account in the **purchase ledger** will be updated. This usually means that the amounts covered by the payment will be removed from the balance (see Paragraph 3.13 below).

(c) The **cash book,** or the **cash account** in the general ledger, will automatically be updated to reflect the issue of the cheque. This might be done in summary at the end of the day or at the end of each cheque run which is a group of cheques printed out together (see Paragraph 3.14 below).

(d) The purchase ledger may also update the **total creditors account** in the general ledger.

3.11 The cheques must be printed on **special blank cheque paper** which will be obtained from the bank. All the details which the bank needs for processing will be on the cheques already (particularly the magnetically treated numbers on the bottom of the cheque).

3.12 Many purchase ledgers will produce a **remittance advice attached to the cheque,** as the illustration in Section 4 demonstrates.

Recording in the purchase ledger and cash book

3.13 A purchase ledger system, when instructed that a payment has taken place, will **update the relevant supplier account** in the purchase ledger. Some will automatically remove all the oldest invoices in the balance until the amount of money paid is used up. This may not be correct, perhaps some old invoices are in dispute. In these cases the ledger account would be updated item by item by a clerk using a VDU screen to see the account. Alternatively, items which are in dispute may be marked in a special way in the account. This would stop the computer removing them from the account when a payment taken place.

Recording in the cash book

3.14 Cheques will usually be printed in batches or runs for convenience, on a periodic basis, perhaps weekly. It is usual to obtain a **printed list of the cheques issued as a record.** The total amount paid will be shown on the printout.

(a) If a manual cash book is kept, then this total would be entered in the cash book.

Date	Details	Cheque Nos	Total	Purchases
12.7.X2	Purchase ledger cheques	000375-87	£4,276.14	£4,276.14

(b) A **computerised cash book** will be updated automatically. The print outs of the cheque runs should still be kept in case any query arises as they are probably the only detailed list of the contents of all the cheques.

4 RETURNED CHEQUES

4.1 In this section the **returned cheques** we are referring to are cheques which have been drawn by the business, paid, processed by the bank and then returned to the business.

4.2 Banks will return cheques to both individuals and businesses on request, although they charge for the service. The cheque will have been processed and have the following markings.

(a) A 'crossing stamp' on the front identifying which bank and branch it was paid in at

(b) Encoded along the bottom with the amount the cheque is made out for in magnetic ink to allow automatic reading and sorting by machines in the banking system.

Advantages of receiving returned cheques

4.3 These are the main advantages of receiving returned cheques.

(a) The returned cheques act as an extra guard against fraud as the account holder can **check the signature, the amounts and the payee on the cheque** (someone might have altered the words and numbers after it had been signed).

(b) This also provides an **extra guard against the bank.** The bank may have processed a cheque which had the wrong signatures or was not completed correctly. It is much easier for the company to prove this happened if it actually holds the cheque.

Disadvantages of receiving returned cheques

4.4 It is comparatively rare now for individuals or banks to have cheques returned, there are several reasons.

(a) The bank will charge for this service and costs may become very high, the **cost will outweigh the benefit**.

(b) If a business is of any size, it will draw quite **large numbers of cheques**. The filing and storing of returned cheques can become difficult and costly.

(c) The number of **queries** surrounding payments where holding the returned cheque would be useful is very low. As long as the other controls we have considered are in place, then keeping returned cheques should not be necessary.

Part B: Recording and accounting for cash transactions

CATS-R-GO
27 THE MEWS, WEXFORD, KENT
TELEPHONE: 01272 932 178

REMITTANCE ADVICE

Dogs & Co Ltd
Blandford House
Woolford

SUPPLIER CODE
00732
DATE
31/03/x7

DATE	DETAILS	INVOICES	CREDIT NOTES	PAYMENT AMOUNT
2/3/x7	Invoice 27352	472.89		472.89
4/3/x7	Invoice 27591	124.44		124.44
11/3/x7	Invoice 28667	331.02		331.02
31/3/x7	Credit note 44372		229.47	- 229.47
				£698.88

CATS-R-GO LTD 04-27-92
Southern Bank
ARCHWOOD BRANCH
247 THE AVENUE, ARCHWOOD, LONDON W12 2WP

Date	Reference	Pay to the order of
31/03/x7	00732	Dogs & Co Ltd

| THOUSANDS | | | £HUNDREDS | £TENS | £UNITS | | Amount |
HUNDREDS	TENS	UNITS					
Nil	Nil	Nil	Six	Nine	Eight	£	***698.88

Amount of pounds in words, pence as in figures

A/C PAYEE ONLY

Per Pro Cats-R-Go Ltd

⑈101129⑈ 04⑈2792⑈ 30595713⑈

5 BACS

5.1 BACS stands for **Bankers Automated Clearing Services**. It is a company owned by the high street banks which operates the electronic transfer of funds between accounts within the banking system. It acts as an automated clearing system. When a business uses BACS, it sends information (which will be input into the books of the business) to BACS for processing.

5.2 Many different businesses use BACS, even small businesses can do so because their bank will help to organise the information for BACS. The most important advantage of the BACS system is that it operates with **very reduced amounts of paperwork**. Large amounts of paperwork cause expense, delay and can lack a great deal in the way of security.

5.3 BACS is used for processing any of the following.

- Standing orders
- Direct debits
- Salaries (monthly)
- Wages (weekly)
- Some one-off payments

> **Exam alert**
> An MCQ might give four methods of payment for a particular transaction with BACS as one of them and ask you to select the most appropriate.

Procedures for using BACS

5.4 If, for example, a company wished to pay the salaries of its staff using BACS then the procedure would be as follows.

Step 1. The company produces a file with the details of each member of staff to be paid.

- Full name
- Amount to be paid
- Bank/branch number
- Bank account number

The file is sent to the BACS processing computer centre. It can be sent on magnetic tape (discouraged by BACS), floppy disk or digitally on an ISDN line.

Step 2. The files are submitted to the computer which sorts the information into that required for certain banks on certain dates. The information can then be read into each bank's computer system direct for processing.

Step 3. On the day specified by the company.

(a) The salary due to each member of staff is credited to their account.
(b) The company's account is debited with the total amount paid.

Step 4. All BACS items are recorded on archive disks so that the user (the company) has a record in case any query arises.

Step 5. The business's records will be updated with the same information as that which was sent to BACS.

Part B: Recording and accounting for cash transactions

Activity 10.4

Terry Mayne runs a shop which sells suitcases, bags and umbrellas. He is not registered for VAT. His cash book analyses receipts into the three categories of sales, and analyses payments under the heading of cash purchases, creditors, wages and rent.

During the week commencing 25 March 20X7, the following transactions take place.

25 March	Balances brought forward are £142.50 in cash and a favourable bank balance of £272.00.
25 March	Paid a creditor, British Gas plc, £142.70 by cheque number 300179.
26 March	Cash sales of £241.00, made up of suitcases £159.10, bags £27.50 and umbrellas £54.40.
26 March	Paid cash of £250.00 into the bank.
26 March	Paid Goliath Luggage Ltd £290.00 by cheque no. 300181. Cheque no. 300180 was completed for £390.00 in error and was therefore cancelled.
27 March	Cash sales of £192.40, made up of suitcases £82.40, bags £42.20 and umbrellas £67.80.
27 March	Bought a secondhand cash register for £95.00 in cash.
28 March	Paid wages of £172.00 in cash.
28 March	Cash sales of £201.00, made up of suitcases £160.00 and umbrellas £41.00.
28 March	Paid Sian Asia Ltd £64.00 in cash for umbrellas.
28 March	Paid a creditor, Bolton Bag Co, £172.00 by cheque no. 300182.
28 March	Paid for cleaning materials costing £17.80 in cash.
29 March	Paid shop rent of £242.00 by cheque no. 300183.
29 March	Paid wages of £121.00 by cheque no. 300184.
29 March	Cash sales of £191.80, made up of suitcases £92.85, bags £32.44 and umbrellas £66.51.
29 March	Paid cash of £200.00 into the bank.

Tasks

(a) Draw up Terry Mayne's cash book for the period and enter the above transactions in it.

(b) Balance the cash book at the end of the week and carry down the cash and bank balances to the following week.

10: Recording payments

Key learning points

- Controls over recording payments are important to avoid fraud and to ensure completeness.
- The bank reconciliation is the most important control (see Chapter 12).
- Analysis of payments in the cash book will help to control the expenditure of the business.
- Posting the payments side of the cash book to the general ledger follows the same procedures as the receipts side.
    - Add up the cash book columns
    - Check that the analysis columns add up to the total
    - Identify relevant general ledger accounts
    - Draw up the posting summary and post to the general ledger
- Receiving returned cheques is not necessarily of great value for control purposes, although some businesses may find it useful.
- In a computer system, updating the purchase ledger for payments will usually cause the cash book to be automatically updated.
- BACS is a useful method of making and recording payments, it can save a business time.

Quick quiz

1. What procedure would identify an unauthorised payments not entered in the cashbook?
2. What other controls will help to prevent fraud involving payments?
3. Discounts received are shown in a memorandum column in the cash book. True or false?
4. What useful function is possible using a computerised purchase ledger?
5. What are the advantages of receiving returned cheques?
6. What does BACS stand for?

Answers to quick quiz

1. The bank reconciliation.
2. Other controls include: authorisation of payments, supporting documentation, segregation of duties, checks for unusual payments, one cheque book in use.
3. True. The column is there so that the total amount owed to creditors can be posted to the purchase ledger, not just the amount paid.
4. A computerised purchase ledger can issue computer-printed cheques.
5. Returned cheques are both a check against fraud and a check against mistakes by the bank.
6. Bankers Automated Clearing Services.

Answers to activities

Answer 10.1

(a) As a matter of physical security, using only **one cheque book** at a time minimises the risk that a cheque book will fall into the wrong hands. Cheque books which have not yet been started should be locked securely in a safe, as should the current cheque book when it is not in use.

Using only one cheque book at a time also makes it simpler to keep a check on the sequence of cheques being issued. Cheques will be issued and entered in the cash book consecutively.

Part B: Recording and accounting for cash transactions

(b) Entering the number of all cheques in the cash book even if **cancelled** makes it easier to check that all payments by cheque have been entered. It also means that the cash book will provide a record of all cheques in case of later queries or when checking the bank statement with the cash book.

(c) If cancelled cheques are not retained, anyone carrying out checks (for example, an internal or external auditor) cannot be sure what has happened to cheques which are recorded as having been cancelled. There is a risk that someone has taken the cheque with the intention of misusing it even though it has been recorded as cancelled. **Retaining cancelled cheques** provides conclusive evidence that the cheque has not fallen into the wrong hands.

(d) This is an example of **segregation of duties**. It will be less tempting for an employee to act dishonestly if he knows that related aspects of transactions which he deals with are handled by somebody else.

(e) Payments by **standing order or direct debit** will probably appear on the bank statement before they are entered into the cash book. But it is not acceptable simply to transfer the details of payments made from the bank statement to the cash book, since the wrong payments may have been made by the bank as the result of some error. The bank may have made a payment even though the standing order or direct debit mandate has been cancelled, or the company may have failed to cancel a mandate which should have been cancelled. It is therefore a good idea to check that any standing order or direct debit payments which *have* been made *should* have been made before the details are entered in the cash book.

Answer 10.2

Both (a) and (b) are FALSE.

The cash book records money received by the business and money paid by the business.

The name 'cash book' is still used even though money may be in the form of cheques or other media. Indeed, funds may be transferred electronically between different people's and business's bank accounts.

We record cheque payments in the cash book as soon as possible after we issue the cheques: (a) is therefore false. Payments could be very difficult to keep track of if we waited until the cheque was presented before recording the payment.

A standing order is a payment like any other, and needs to be recorded in the cash book regardless of whether we have yet received the benefit of what the payment is for, (b) is therefore also false.

Answer 10.3

(a) When a cheque is being written by hand, the writer may make an error. A computer-printed cheque might similarly have been printed incorrectly. Rather than making an alteration (which must be signed by the cheque signatories), it is generally better to **cancel** the cheque. The writer may do this by writing a line through the whole cheque and writing the word 'CANCELLED' across it.

There may be a good reason for cancelling a cheque even if it has been completed correctly. For example, it may be decided before the cheque is sent that a different amount should be paid to the supplier.

(b) Payment of one of our cheques may be **stopped** after it has been sent out by issuing an instruction to our bank. This instruction tells the bank not to pay the cheque, and when a collecting bank attempts to clear the cheque our bank will decline to honour it. A reversing entry will need to be made in the cash book.

It will not often be necessary to stop a cheque. If it is discovered that a cheque has been lost in the post, then stopping payment is a sensible precaution against the possibility that someone will attempt to present the cheque fraudulently. Most banks will accept a stop instruction by telephone, although this should be confirmed in writing to the bank. The bank will generally make a charge for stopping a cheque.

(c) A **paid cheque** is one which has been debited to the drawer's bank account. The paid cheque will either be retained by the drawer's bank or sent to the drawer.

(d) The bank balance per the cash book and the balance shown on the bank's statement at any particular time may be different mainly because of timing differences, such as cheques which have been issued and recorded in the cash book but have not yet been presented to the bank. A **bank reconciliation statement** lists the items which account for this difference.

Answers 10.4

Receipts

Date	Details	Cash	Bank	Suitcases	Bags	Umbrellas
20X7		£	£	£	£	£
25 March	Balances b/d	142.50	272.00			
26 March	Sales	241.00		159.10	27.50	54.40
26 March	Cash		250.00			
27 March	Sales	192.40		82.40	42.20	67.80
28 March	Sales	201.00		160.00		41.00
29 March	Sales	191.80		92.85	32.44	66.51
29 March	Cash		200.00			
29 March	Balance c/f		245.70			
		968.70	967.70	494.35	102.14	229.71
1 April	Balance b/d	169.90				

Payments

Date	Details	Cash	Bank	Cash purchases	Creditors	Wages	Rent
20X7		£	£	£	£	£	£
25 March	British Gas plc 300179		142.70		142.70		
26 March	Bank	250.00					
26 March	Cancelled cheque 300180						
26 March	Goliath Luggage Ltd 300181		290.00		290.00		
27 March	Purchase-cash register	95.00		95.00			
28 March	Wages	172.00				172.00	
28 March	Purchases-umbrellas	64.00		64.00			
28 March	Bolton Bag Co 300182		172.00		172.00		
28 March	Purchases-cleaning materials	17.80		17.80			
29 March	Rent 300183		242.00				242.00
29 March	Wages 300184		121.00			121.00	
29 March	Bank	200.00					
29 March	Balance c/f	169.90					
		968.70	967.70	176.80	604.70	293.00	242.00
1 April	Balance b/d		245.70				

Chapter 11 Maintaining petty cash records

Chapter topic list

1. The purpose of petty cash
2. Security and control of petty cash
3. The imprest system
4. Petty cash vouchers
5. The petty cash book
6. Recording and analysing petty cash transactions
7. Recording petty cash transactions: VAT
8. Topping up the float, balancing off and posting petty cash

The following study sessions are covered in this chapter

			Syllabus reference
5	(g)	Recognise the types of transaction likely to be paid out of petty cash	3e
	(h)	Account for petty cash using imprest and non-imprest methods	3e
	(i)	Exercise control over petty cash and recognise how control can be maintained – security of cash, authorised personnel and reconciliations	3e
	(j)	Record petty cash claims	3e
	(l)	Explain the correct procedure to cope with unusual situations: unauthorised claims for payment, insufficient supporting evidence or claims exceeding authorised limits	3e

11: Maintaining petty cash records

> **Chapter 11 scenario - Top Toys Ltd. This scenario applies to all the activities in this chapter.**
>
> You are the petty cashier at Top Toys Ltd. An imprest of £150 is operated for petty cash, with a limit of £25 applying to individual petty cash payments. The imprest float is made up at the end of each week.
>
> The office procedures manual states that you may authorise payments of up to £10, provided they are supported by receipts. Requests for larger sums and for payments which are not supported by receipts must be referred to the Administration Manager.

1 THE PURPOSE OF PETTY CASH

1.1 In every business, there will be a number of small expenses that have to be paid for in notes and coins, instead of by cheque or by other methods of payment. To make these payments, a supply of cash has to be kept on the business premises. This cash is called **petty cash**.

What items are paid for out of petty cash?

1.2 Petty cash payments should be for **small** items of expense for which payment in notes and coin is required.

  (a) Different organisations have different rules about what can be paid for out of petty cash. Many businesses specify in writing what can be paid for out of petty cash, and what items should be paid for by cheque or other payment method. They also specify **who** can receive money out of petty cash.

  (b) Not all businesses have a policy of providing an official list of allowable items for petty cash, and they rely instead on an informal system of judgement by the petty cash officer or his supervisor.

1.3 Here are some typical expenses, limits and recipients for payments out of petty cash.

Typical expense to be paid for	Typical maximum amount	Who directly receives the cash?	Who ultimately receives the cash?
Travel expenses of employee on official business	5.00	Employee	Travel company
Weekly milk bill	10.00	Milkman	Milkman
Items from local shop,			
eg tea, coffee	5.00	Employee	Shop
emergency stationery	5.00	Employee	Shop
stamps	5.00	Employee	Shop
Monthly office window cleaner	20.00	Window cleaner	Window cleaner

> **Exam alert**
>
> A possible MCQ might be 'Which one of the following items would/would not be paid out of petty cash?'. This is tested in Activity 11.1 below

Part B: Recording and accounting for cash transactions

Who gets paid out of petty cash?

1.4 You can see from the table in Paragraph 1.3 that payments out of petty cash for expenses are made to either of the following persons.

(a) To **employees** (to reimburse them for money they have spent out of their own pocket)

(b) Directly to **suppliers**, such as the milkman or window cleaner

Sometimes, employees will ask for petty cash to pay for items that have not yet been purchased, perhaps because they do not have enough cash themselves to make the payment first and to claim the money back later.

Watch out for: PAYE and NIC for casual labour

1.5 When petty cash is used to pay for casual labour, such as the weekly costs of an office cleaner, the Inland Revenue will want to know. Your organisation could be liable to pay **National Insurance Contributions** (NICs) and **income tax** for this person, on top of paying cash 'wages'.

1.6 Payments out of **petty cash for casual labour** should therefore be **sanctioned by an office manager**, who should then take the necessary measures to satisfy Inland Revenue requirements. You would certainly need to keep details of the name and address of the person receiving the cash wage.

Activity 11.1

Would you say that the items, amount and recipient below are acceptable for petty cash payments at Top Toys Ltd?

Expense item	Amount	Direct recipient	Acceptable?
Portable air conditioning unit	£75.99	Steve Gray, office manager	
Coffee filters for office coffee machine	£2.99	Asif Sultan, PA	
Bunch of flowers for Valentine's day	£18.00	Nick King, Sales	
Bus ticket to Plastics Today conference	£2.60	Nick King, Sales	

2 SECURITY AND CONTROL OF PETTY CASH

The petty cashier

2.1 Looking after petty cash should be the responsibility of one individual, who might be called the **petty cash officer** or **petty cashier**, although a 'deputy' or 'stand-in' will be required for the times when the petty cashier is absent.

(a) The petty cashier has to make sure that the cash is **held in a safe place**.

(b) He or she will **make the actual payments of cash**.

(c) He or she must ensure that all **payments are properly authorised** and are being made for valid reasons.

The petty cash box

2.2 Petty cash must be kept **secure**. It is usual to keep it in a lockable box or tin, and to keep the box or tin a locked drawer. Some organisations put their petty cash box in an office safe. The keys to the petty cash box and desk drawer are held by the petty cashier.

2.3 No one should be allowed access to the petty cash box except the petty cashier, the petty cashier's 'stand-in' or 'deputy' and the office supervisor. In some offices, you will find that more individuals than these can access cash in the petty cash tin, but this is a poor office procedure because it encourages a lack of proper control and security for cash.

Why are only small items paid for out of petty cash?

2.4 Petty cash should not be used for large expenses, such as office furniture, large restaurant bills or aeroplane tickets because of **security**.

(a) A large amount of cash would be an obvious target for theft.

(b) An organisation should always try to monitor and control its spending, and to authorise all payments properly. It is not always easy to exercise a sufficient degree of control over petty cash, and a system of payments from petty cash for large items could easily lend itself to abuse, dishonesty and error.

Limiting the size of petty cash payments

2.5 There should be a **maximum limit** to the amount of any individual payment. It might be a rule for an organisation, for example, that there should be a £40.00 limit on any individual petty cash payment. Requests for larger payments should be refused by the petty cashier, and the individual asking for the cash should be told to obtain the amount required by another method.

(a) If the individual is an employee of the organisation, he or she should submit an **expenses claim** or **cheque request form**.

(b) An external supplier (such as the milkman or window cleaner) might be asked to submit **invoices**, and make any request for payment by cheque through the accounts department staff that handle these payments.

Authorisation and authorisation limits

2.6 Payments out of petty cash should be **properly authorised by the appropriate person.**

(a) The petty cashier might be permitted to authorise individual payments up to a certain limit, say £20.00, but only perhaps if the person being paid is able to provide a receipt for the expense item.

(b) For payments in excess of the petty cashier's authorisation limit, the authorisation should be made by the petty cashier's supervisor (or perhaps other nominated individuals), provided that the size of the payment is within the maximum limit permitted for petty cash items, say £40.00.

(c) In exceptional cases, a petty cash payment in excess of the maximum limit might be permitted, subject to authorisation by a nominated senior person in the organisation.

Part B: Recording and accounting for cash transactions

Receipts

2.7 In most cases, a request for payment out of petty cash should be supported by a **receipt**, giving proof of purchase of the item for which the petty cash payment is being claimed. The receipt might simply be a till roll, showing the name of the shop or supplier from which the purchase was made and the amount of the payment. It is good practice to write down the nature of the item purchased on the till roll or receipt, if it does not show the information already.

VAT receipts

2.8 If there is an amount for VAT in a payment, and the VAT can be claimed back from Customs & Excise, the receipt must be a **VAT receipt**, showing these details.

- The total payment
- The VAT paid
- The supplier's name, address and VAT registration number
- The date of the transaction

Note that it is acceptable *not* to have the VAT shown separately, the person claiming the petty cash, or the petty cashier, can calculate the VAT element.

No available receipts

2.9 Payments out of petty cash will sometimes be requested by individuals **who do not have a receipt** to back up their request for cash. Travelling expenses might be an example, employees are not always obliged to provide proof of a taxi, bus or train fare. In these cases, the payment should be sanctioned by an authorised person, perhaps by the supervisor or manager of the individual who is asking for the cash.

Activity 11.2

Nick King suggests to you that it would be a much more convenient procedure for him if you could leave an amount of money, say £30, in a 'kitty box' by Reception, so that employees who are short of cash for parking meters, phones or bus fares could 'dip in' without all 'that receipt fuss'. Outline for him why this is not such a good idea.

3 THE IMPREST SYSTEM

KEY TERM

The **imprest system** is a system in which there is a maximum amount of money in petty cash, the imprest amount. The imprest amount varies from one organisation to another, and might be enough to make petty cash payments for about one month.

3.1 Let us suppose that the imprest amount for petty cash in company A is £500.00. At the start of one month, let us also suppose that the petty cash box contains this maximum amount of £500.00. Over time, as payments are made out of petty cash, the amount of cash left in the petty cash box will diminish, and eventually the petty cashier will decide that petty cash needs to be 'topped up' again to the imprest amount of £500.00.

3.2 Topping up petty cash

Topping up petty cash might occur whenever the need arises. Alternatively, it might be done regularly, once each week or once each month. In order to top up petty cash to the imprest amount, cash will be drawn from the bank. The amount of cash that is drawn should equal the amount of petty cash payments since the petty cash was last topped up. We will cover the procedure for topping up in Section 8 of this chapter.

3.3 EXAMPLE: TOPPING UP THE IMPREST

		£
1 May	Imprest amount	1,000.00
1-31 May	Petty cash payments (total of 57 receipts)	(826.40)
31 May	Petty cash in tin at month end	173.60
31 May	Top up drawn from bank	826.40
31 May	Restored imprest amount	1,000.00

Activity 11.3

You have the following receipts in the petty cash box at 30 November. By how much should the balance in the box be topped up?

Date	Expense	Amount £
3 November	Tea bags	1.99
6 November	Light bulbs	5.99
11 November	Train fare	10.50
17 November	Teapot and cups	24.99
22 November	Desk lamp	19.99
25 November	Stamps book	10.00

4 PETTY CASH VOUCHERS

4.1 The petty cashier is responsible for keeping a record of all the payments that are made out of petty cash. The initial record of payment is the **petty cash voucher**.

4.2 A voucher must be prepared by the petty cashier whenever a payment is requested. (Blank vouchers are purchased in pads from stationery suppliers.) Once completed, the receipt(s) should be firmly attached to the voucher.

4.3 When completed, a voucher should contain the following details.

- **Details** of the payment (the purpose for which the payment has been made)
- The **amount** paid
- The **name and signature of the person receiving the cash**
- The **authorising signature** of the person who has authorised the payment
- The **date** of payment
- The **number** of the voucher (see Paragraph 4.6 below)
- The relevant **receipt(s)** stapled to it

Part B: Recording and accounting for cash transactions

Petty Cash Voucher

No 471
Date 16.4.X7

	AMOUNT	
	£	p
Postage stamps	5	80
Coffee	3	10
	8	90

Signature: *J. Smith*
Authorised by: *V. Brown*

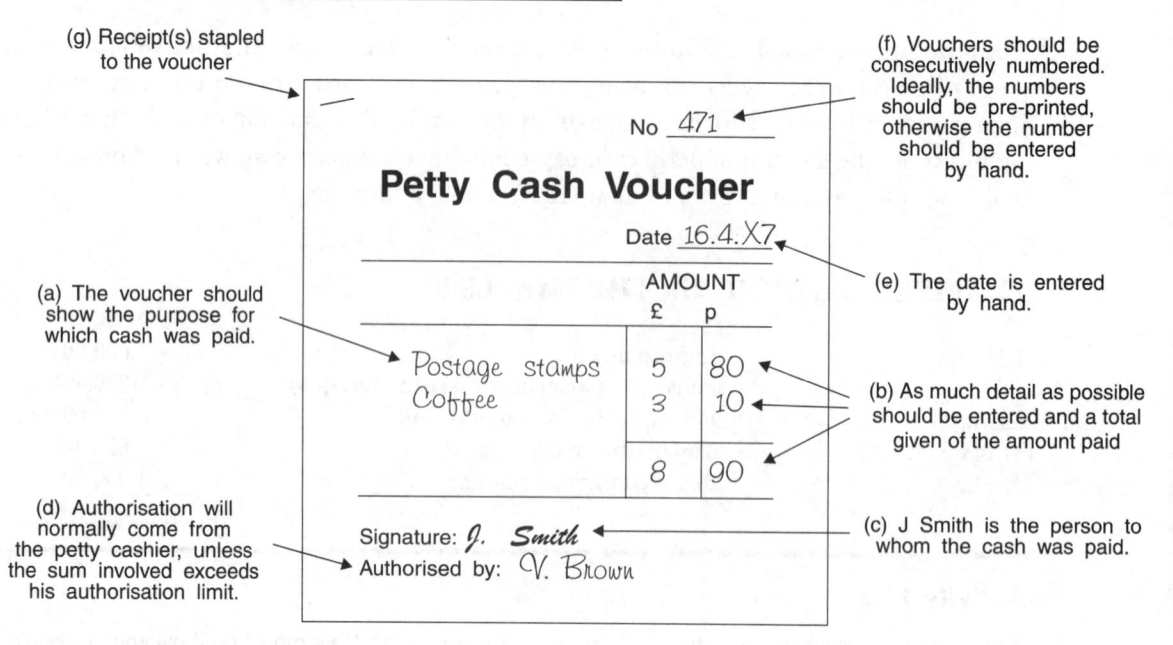

Annotations:
- (a) The voucher should show the purpose for which cash was paid.
- (b) As much detail as possible should be entered and a total given of the amount paid.
- (c) J Smith is the person to whom the cash was paid.
- (d) Authorisation will normally come from the petty cashier, unless the sum involved exceeds his authorisation limit.
- (e) The date is entered by hand.
- (f) Vouchers should be consecutively numbered. Ideally, the numbers should be pre-printed, otherwise the number should be entered by hand.
- (g) Receipt(s) stapled to the voucher

4.4 J Smith should be able to give the petty cashier a receipt for the coffee (in this case, a till roll from the shop or supermarket) and this should be attached securely to the petty cash voucher, probably by staple.

There should also be some evidence of purchase of the stamps (either a receipt from the shop or Post Office or a note from an office manager or supervisor confirming that the stamps have been obtained). Without this, the person claiming payment might have pocketed the cash or stamps himself.

4.5 EXAMPLE: PETTY CASH VOUCHERS

Suppose that the petty cash system in company B provides for a maximum individual payment of £100.00, and the petty cashier can authorise individual payments up to £25.00. Payments between £25.00 and £100.00 must be authorised by the accounts supervisor, R Greene. On 18 December 20X7 a petty cash claim is made for expenses for an office Christmas party, with receipts from a supermarket for food and drink totalling £82.56. Payment is to be made to the office manager, D Porter.

The petty cash voucher (here not yet given its sequential voucher number) would be made out as follows.

Petty Cash Voucher

No _____
Date 18.12.X7

	AMOUNT	
	£	p
Office party	82	56
	82	56

Signature: *D. Porter*
Authorised by: *R. Greene*

11: Maintaining petty cash records

Here the petty cashier writes out the voucher, but must ask the supervisor R Greene to authorise the payment and sign the voucher.

Voucher numbers

4.6 Every petty cash voucher must be given a **unique voucher number**. It is normal to number them in sequence, starting at 1 and going on (into thousands or tens of thousands). Usually, vouchers are numbered in sequence for each year, starting at 1 with the first voucher each year.

(a) This allows vouchers to be traced from the petty cash book to where they are **filed**.

(b) It allows a **completeness check** to make sure no vouchers are missing or not entered in the petty cash book.

4.7 The voucher's number should be inserted either when the payment is made, or when the petty cashier uses the vouchers to write up the petty cash book. More about this later.

4.8 When a voucher has been prepared and signed, and the cash payment has been made, the completed voucher must be attached securely to the relevant receipts(s) and put in the petty cash box. It should be kept in the petty cash box until petty cash is next 'topped up' to the imprest amount.

Activity 11.4

On Monday 14 December 20X7 you receive the following requests for reimbursement. The last voucher used the previous week was numbered 100.

(a) The receptionist, Mrs T Scott, produces a receipt for postage stamps purchased for office use to the value of £6.25.

(b) The sales manager produces a receipt for £7.50 in respect of a return rail ticket, purchased in order to visit a customer.

Task

Using the blank petty cash vouchers provided, complete vouchers for the above two items. Ignore VAT.

No _____	No _____
Petty Cash Voucher	**Petty Cash Voucher**
Date _____	Date _____
AMOUNT £ p	AMOUNT £ p
Signature:	Signature:
Authorised by:	Authorised by:

Part B: Recording and accounting for cash transactions

Petty cash payments for expenses not yet incurred

4.9 There will be occasions when someone needs petty cash to go out and buy an item, because he or she does not have enough cash to buy the item first and then claim back from petty cash.

(a) **Payments in advance** must be authorised by a supervisor or office manager.

(b) The petty cashier should write out a petty cash voucher, but insist that the person who is given the cash should provide a **receipt** and give back any change as soon as possible.

(c) When the voucher and the change are eventually received, the petty cashier should **alter the voucher** to show the exact amount of the payment.

4.10 EXAMPLE: PETTY CASH PAYMENTS FOR EXPENSES NOT YET INCURRED

Suppose that a director of company C needs money to pay for a taxi and asks for £20.00 from petty cash on 5 July 20X7. The payment might be sanctioned by the accounts supervisor, T Roberts. The next day, the director returns with a taxi cab receipt for £15.50 and gives back change of £4.50.

The petty cash voucher should be prepared initially as follows (the voucher has not yet been numbered).

On 6 July the original voucher is altered by the petty cashier.

Petty Cash Voucher

No _____

Date 5.7.X7

	AMOUNT	
	£	p
Taxi fare	20	00
	20	00

Signature: *P. Perkins (Director)*
Authorised by: *T. Roberts*

```
                    No _____

         Petty Cash Voucher
                    Date 5.7.X7
                    ───────────
                      AMOUNT
                      £     p
         ─────────────────────────
          Taxi fare      2̶0̶    0̶0̶
                         15    50

                         2̶0̶    0̶0̶
                         15    50

          Signature: P. Perkins (Director)
          Authorised by: T. Roberts
```

The change is put back in the petty cash box, together with the amended voucher and (attached to the voucher) the receipt. Alternatively, if the advance was insufficient and, say, a further £5 was required, then either a new voucher should be prepared or the old voucher should clearly show that the **adjusted figures have been authorised**. This is obviously more important when the figures are adjusted **upwards rather than downwards**.

Checks on petty cash and vouchers

4.11 Each week, the petty cashier will probably write out a large number of petty cash vouchers and make a large number of payments. For security and control reasons, there ought to be **regular checks** on the float, perhaps once a week.

		£
	Notes and coins in petty cash box	X
plus	total value of vouchers in the petty cash box	X
equals	imprest amount	X

4.12 If the amount of cash in petty cash plus the value of the vouchers does **not** equal the imprest amount, something must have gone wrong, and the petty cashier should inform his or her supervisor immediately.

The following are possible reasons for the discrepancy.

(a) A **mistake** in the amount of cash paid out, eg the petty cashier might have paid out £10.00 for a voucher of only £9.80, leaving a 20p shortage of cash

(b) **Theft** from the petty cash box

IOUs and petty cash

4.13 In some organisations, some individuals are permitted to borrow money from petty cash for a day or so, but they must of course pay the money back.

When someone borrows cash, he or she must put an **IOU** into the petty cash box. An IOU might look like this.

> I owe petty cash £10.00
>
> J. Smith
> 15/10/X7

4.14 For the purpose of petty cash, **IOUs are equivalent to cash**, so that at any time the following holds true.

		£
	Notes and coins in petty cash box	X
plus	Total value of IOUs	X
plus	Total value of vouchers in the petty cash box	X
equals	Imprest amount	X

4.15 When the borrowed money is returned to petty cash, the IOU is thrown away. It is not considered good practice to allow borrowing from petty cash by members of staff. However, it does happen and therefore must be properly controlled.

Receiving money into petty cash

4.16 Occasionally, **money is put into petty cash**. This does not happen often, but some situations when this might arise are as follows.

  (a) An employee of the organisation might use some of the office's postage stamps, to put on personal letters. He or she will pay for the stamps by giving the cash to the petty cashier.

  (b) Similarly, employees might be expected to pay for any private telephone calls that they make from an office telephone.

  (c) Very occasionally, perhaps when the petty cash float is running low, the money received from a cash sale might be used to boost petty cash.

4.17 When money is paid into petty cash in this way, the petty cashier should insert a **voucher for the money received**. For example, if C Trickey takes some stamps from the office to post his own letters, and gives £1.10 to the petty cashier, a voucher might be written as follows.

```
                              No _____

              Petty Cash Voucher
                              Date 17.9.X7
                              AMOUNT
                                £      p

   Cash received for sale    1     10
   of postage stamps to
   C Trickey

                              1     10

   Signature: V. Brown (Petty cashier)
   Authorised by:
```

4.18 Practice varies, but it is likely that vouchers for cash received (receipts) will **not** be given sequential numbers. It would be good practice and improve control over petty cash to have a numbering system for receipts, but as it is not common, we shall not number receipts in this chapter.

4.19 If a check is made on the imprest amount after money has been paid into petty cash in this way then the following should apply.

		£
	Notes and coins in petty cash box	X
plus	total value of IOUs	X
plus	total value of vouchers for payments out of petty cash	X
less	total value of vouchers for receipts of cash into petty cash	(X)
equals	imprest amount	X

Activity 11.5

On Tuesday 15 December 20X7, you receive the following requests for reimbursement.

(a) The new office clerk presents bus tickets for amounts totalling £3.60 to support a request for payment for his first week's travel to work.

(b) Ten new printer cartridges have been received costing £5.50 each. An invoice has been sent with the goods and a receipt will be issued on payment.

(c) The office caretaker asks for £5 to pay as a gratuity to the refuse collectors, as has been customary in previous years.

(d) A clerk says that the administration manager asked him to purchase coffee, tea and sugar for the office kitchen. The receipt shows a total cost of £15.40.

Task

Using the blank petty cash vouchers provided, complete vouchers for any of the above items which you are able to authorise. Indicate what action you would take in respect of any requests for which you have not completed vouchers.

5 THE PETTY CASH BOOK

5.1 Next we need to **account for petty cash**, that is, to make an accounting record of cash put into the petty cash box and of payments out of the petty cash book. To do this, we need to write up the **petty cash book,** which you will remember is a book of prime entry.

5.2 **The purposes of the petty cash book**

- **Provide an accounting record** of every petty cash transaction
- Allow for **posting petty cash expenses to the general ledger**

5.3 The petty cash book is a bound book with a large number of columns on each double page.

Left hand side: debit side	Right hand side: credit side
Used to record **cash receipts** into the petty cash box. This will consist of about two to four columns, although practice will vary from one petty cash book to another.	Used to record and analyse **cash payments**. The number of analysis columns can be quite large, but is typically between four and six, with practice varying from one petty cash book to another.

There is a column in the **middle** for showing the **date of each transaction**.

5.4 Each petty cash transaction, for cash in or cash out, is recorded on a **separate line** in the petty cash book. An example of a double page in a petty cash book is illustrated on the next page (although the actual lines across the page are not shown here).

5.5 Each double page in the petty cash book should record all petty cash transactions from the time that petty cash is topped up to its imprest amount to the next time that it is topped up.

This means that, as the petty cashier writes up the petty cash book over time, at the start of each new double page the amount of cash in the petty cash box should be the **imprest amount**.

5.6 This can be shown as a 'balance brought down' or '**balance b/d' on the receipts side** of the book. For example, if the imprest amount for company D is £250.00, and cash has just been drawn on 29 May 20X7 to bring the money in petty cash up to this amount, the petty cashier should start a new double page in the petty cash book by making the following entries in the receipts side.

Details	Net receipt £	VAT £	Total £	Date 20X7
Balance b/d			250.00	29 May

6 RECORDING AND ANALYSING PETTY CASH TRANSACTIONS

6.1 The petty cashier must record and analyse all the payments from petty cash, using the vouchers and supporting receipts. **Writing up the petty cash book** should be done fairly regularly, depending on how often petty cash is used in the organisation.

(a) Typically, a petty cashier will write up the petty cash book every two to four weeks.

(b) The book *must* be written up whenever cash is drawn from the bank to top up the money in petty cash, which might be about every month or six weeks.

Part B: Recording and accounting for cash transactions

PETTY CASH BOOK

Receipts				Payments							
Details	Net receipt £	VAT £	Total £	Date	Details	Voucher No	Total £	Analysis of payments			
								Travel £	Postage £	Stationery £	Repairs £	Sundry £	VAT £

Recording petty cash payments

6.2 The petty cashier transfers details of **payments** from the vouchers in the petty cash box into the book, on the right side of the double page. There will be a batch of several vouchers, and it is at this stage that the vouchers will normally be given their **sequential number**.

For example, if there are 20 vouchers in the petty cash box and the number of the last voucher written up in the petty cash book is, say 963, the 20 vouchers should be numbered 964-983.

6.3 Entries in the petty cash book are listed in **both** of the following orders.

- Voucher number order
- Date order

This means that **the vouchers must first of all be sorted into date order before they are given their sequential number.**

Columns on the payment side

6.4 The payments side of the petty cash book (the **credit** side) will have the following columns.

(a) One column will show the **total payment** on a voucher.

(b) One column will show the **voucher number**.

(c) Several columns will be used as **analysis columns** to analyse each payment. The headings for each column will be decided by the organisation's accounts management, but there will be a column for most of the regular expenditures out of petty cash.

- Postage
- Travel
- Entertainment
- Stationery
- Office administration and maintenance

(d) One column will be for **sundry items**. Sundry items are all the payments which cannot be classified into the other columns.

(e) There should be a '**Details**' column. This is used to explain (in some detail where appropriate) the reason for the petty cash payment. **All sundry items** ought to be explained, to keep a record of why the payment was made.

(f) One column will be for **value added tax** (VAT). VAT is covered in Chapter 1 of this text, although some aspects of VAT in relation to petty cash are mentioned in Section 7 of this chapter.

Writing up the payments side

6.5 Entering the details of petty cash expenses in the book should normally be a fairly simple process.

Step 1. Vouchers in the batch are taken one at a time, in date order/voucher number order. The petty cashier writes the following in the appropriate columns.

- The date on the voucher (which is the date of the payment)
- The voucher number
- The total amount paid

Part B: Recording and accounting for cash transactions

Step 2. The petty cashier must then **analyse the payment**. Analysis simply means explaining how much of the payment was made for each of the reasons in the analysis column.

(a) If a payment of £8.75 was made to reimburse an employee for a rail ticket for travel on official business, the total payment of £8.75 will be entered in both the 'total' column and the 'travel' analysis column in the petty cash book.

(b) If there is a payment of £9.20 to an employee who has spent £8.00 on postage stamps and £1.20 on newspapers for the office, the 'total' entry will be £9.20, with £8.00 in the postage analysis column and £1.20 in the office administration analysis column or sundry column (depending on office procedures for analysing expenditure on newspapers).

6.6 EXAMPLE: WRITING UP PETTY CASH BOOK PAYMENTS

The following four vouchers were taken from the petty cash box by the petty cashier, and numbered in sequence 1461 to 1464.

No 1461

Petty Cash Voucher

Date 22.2.X7

	AMOUNT £	p
Postage	15	20
	15	20

Signature: *B Travis*
Authorised by: *Admin Manager*

No 1462

Petty Cash Voucher

Date 24.2.X7

	AMOUNT £	p
Coffee	5	50
Biscuits	3	50
	9	00

Signature: *P Sayles*
Authorised by: *Office Manager*

No 1463

Petty Cash Voucher

Date 1.3.X7

	AMOUNT £	p
Taxi fare	6	40
	6	40

Signature: *R Olney*
Authorised by: *Petty Cashier*

No 1464

Petty Cash Voucher

Date 5.3.X7

	AMOUNT £	p
Bus fares	1	35
Payment to charity collectors	10	00
	11	35

Signature: *P Sayles*
Authorised by: *Office Manager*

11: Maintaining petty cash records

There are four analysis columns in the petty cash book.

- Travel
- Postage
- Stationery
- Sundry items

6.7 SOLUTION

The petty cash book should be written up as follows. (You would normally see a VAT column here, but we deal with this in Section 7.)

Date	Details	Voucher no	Total £	Analysis of payments			
				Travel £	Postage £	Stationery £	Sundry £
20X7							
22.2	Stamps	1461	15.20		15.20		
24.2	Coffee, biscuits	1462	9.00				9.00
1.3	Taxi	1463	6.40	6.40			
5.3	Bus fares, payment to charity	1464	11.35	1.35			10.00

Activity 11.6

Assume that items (c) and (d) in Activity 11.5 above have now been duly authorised on vouchers 103 and 104 respectively.

Task

Write up the payments side of the petty cash book below to reflect the authorised petty cash expenditure on 14 and 15 December 20X7.

Date	Details	Voucher no	Total £	Analysis of payments			
				Travel £	Postage £	Stationery £	Sundry £
20X7	December						

Part B: Recording and accounting for cash transactions

Recording receipts of money into petty cash

6.8 If there have been some receipts of money into petty cash, these should be recorded on the left-hand side (**debit** side) of the petty cash book.

Columns on the receipts side

6.9 The receipts side of the petty cash book (the **debit** side) will have the following columns.

(g) A column for the **total receipt** on a voucher
(h) A column for **VAT**
(i) A column for the **net receipt**
(j) A **details** column

6.10 Suppose, for example, that the imprest amount in a company's petty cash system is £400, and that when the petty cashier writes up the petty cash book, there is a receipt voucher amongst the vouchers in the petty cash box. This is for the receipt of £4.70 from an employee for a personal telephone call that he made to Italy on 12 August 20X7. The £4.70 payment is a net payment of £4.00 plus 70p for VAT at 17½%, and the employee has been given a copy of the receipt voucher for this amount.

6.11 The receipt would be recorded in the petty cash book as follows (and the opening balance is also shown).

Details	Net receipt £	VAT £	Total £	Date
Balance b/d			400.00	20X7 1.8
Telephone	4.00	0.70	4.70	12.8

7 RECORDING PETTY CASH TRANSACTIONS: VAT

7.1 VAT is covered in Chapter 1 of this text. In this section we will look at VAT only as it affects petty cash.

7.2 In some petty cash systems, the VAT element in any petty cash payments or receipts is ignored completely, on the grounds that there is not a large amount of money involved, and so accounting for the VAT in petty cash transactions is more trouble than it is worth. Strictly, however, the VAT element in petty cash transactions should be accounted for separately, but **only if the transaction is accompanied by a supporting VAT receipt**.

> **KEY TERM**
>
> A **VAT receipt** is a receipt showing the following.
> - The total payment
> - The VAT paid
> - The supplier's name, address and VAT registration number
> - The date of the payment

11: Maintaining petty cash records

7.3 To account for VAT in the payments side of the petty cash book there should be an **analysis column for VAT**.

(a) The total payment column will show the payment **inclusive** of VAT.

(b) The amount of VAT paid will be entered in the VAT column.

(c) The amount entered in the analysis column for the expense item will be the total amount **net of (less)** VAT.

7.4 EXAMPLE: PETTY CASH PAYMENTS INCLUDING VAT

Here are two receipts for payments that include a VAT element. A claim from petty cash is made separately for each. How would these be recorded as petty cash vouchers and how would they be recorded in the petty cash book?

```
XYZ Ltd
3 High Street, Kingston

VAT Reg No. 228 4135 62
Date 20/4/X7
                                £
Electric plugs and fuses    22.00
VAT @ 17.5%                  3.85
Total                       25.85
```

```
ABC Ltd
14 Low Street, Richmond

VAT Reg No. 221 4685 27
Date 22/4/X7

Paid £42.30 for stationery,
inclusive of VAT @ 17.5%
```

7.5 SOLUTION

In the case of receipt number 2, the actual amount of VAT is not shown, and you will need to work it out.

$$\text{VAT} = \frac{\text{VAT\%}}{(100\% + \text{VAT\%})} \times \text{total payment}$$

$$\text{Payment exclusive of VAT} = \frac{100\%}{(100\% + \text{VAT\%})} \times \text{total payment}$$

In this example, VAT is $17\frac{1}{2}\%$ and so

(a) VAT payment $= \dfrac{17\frac{1}{2}\%}{(100\% + 17\frac{1}{2}\%)} \times £42.30$

$= \dfrac{17.5}{117.5} \times £42.30$

$= £6.30$

(b) The payment *exclusive* of VAT is (£42.30 − £6.30) = £36.00, or

$$\frac{100}{117.5} \times £42.30 = £36.00$$

Note. For ease of calculations in future you should note that $17\frac{1}{2}/117\frac{1}{2}$ is equivalent to the fraction 7/47.

Part B: Recording and accounting for cash transactions

The vouchers for the payments might be prepared as follows. (It is assumed that the petty cashier can authorise the smaller payment but not the larger one.)

```
                    No 371
         Petty Cash Voucher
                        Date 20.4.X7
                         AMOUNT
                          £     p
   Plugs and fuses      22    00
   VAT                   3    85
                        ─────────
                        25    85

   Signature:    J. Smith
   Authorised by: V. Brown (Petty cashier)
```

```
                    No 372
         Petty Cash Voucher
                        Date 22.4.X7
                         AMOUNT
                          £     p
   Stationery           36    00
   VAT                   6    30
                        ─────────
                        42    30

   Signature:    R. Greene
   Authorised by: D. Nuttall (Supervisor)
```

These expenses would be entered in the petty cash book shown below. Here, our petty cash book only shows analysis columns for (a) stationery, (b) sundry items, and (c) VAT, in order to keep the illustration as simple as possible.

Date	Details	Voucher no	Total £	Analysis of payments		
				Stationery £	Sundry £	VAT £
20X7						
20.4	Plugs and fuses	371	25.85		22.00	3.85
22.4	Stationery	372	42.30	36.00		6.30

Activity 11.7

The following further petty cash vouchers were processed during the remainder of the week ending 18 December 20X7.

Petty Cash Voucher — No 105
Date 16.12.X7

	£	p
Stationery	10	81
	10	81

Signature: SM Body
Authorised by: Admin Manager

Petty Cash Voucher — No 106
Date 17.12.X7

	£	p
Sundry expenses	5	17
	5	17

Signature: T Scott
Authorised by: Petty Cashier

Petty Cash Voucher — No 107
Date 17.12.X7

	£	p
Repairs	22	09
	22	09

Signature: A Person
Authorised by: Administration Manager

Petty Cash Voucher — No 108
Date 17.12.X7

	£	p
Stationery	4	23
	4	23

Signature: NE Body
Authorised by: Petty Cashier

Petty Cash Voucher — No 109
Date 17.12.X7

	£	p
Sundry expenses	2	82
	2	82

Signature: Anne Onymus
Authorised by: Petty Cashier

Petty Cash Voucher — No 110
Date 18.12.X7

	£	p
Sundry expenses	6	58
Stationery	1	41
	7	99

Signature: C Happe
Authorised by: Petty Cashier

Part B: Recording and accounting for cash transactions

All of the expenses listed on vouchers 105 to 110 included VAT at 17.5%, and VAT receipts were presented in each case.

Task

Make appropriate entries in the petty cash book (payments side) on the next page, to record petty cash vouchers 105 to 110.

Activity 11.8

During the week beginning 14 December 20X7 the following cash sums were received in the office of Top Toys and banked by you, the petty cashier.

15.12.X7   Cash sale: £29.14 (including VAT at 17½%)
16.12.X7   £1.88 received from a member of staff to pay for personal telephone calls
18.12.X7   Cash sale: £13.16 (including VAT at 17½%)

Task

Write up the petty cash book (receipts side) on the next page for the week beginning 14 December 20X7.

---

8 TOPPING UP THE FLOAT, BALANCING OFF AND POSTING PETTY CASH

8.1 Whenever the imprest float is **topped up** by drawing more cash from the bank, the petty cash book must be **balanced off** to complete one double page and start the next. The balances must then be **posted** to the general ledger.

8.2 The following steps should be followed. Below we look at each of the steps in more detail, using the illustrative data from the petty cash book shown on the following page, and completed following Paragraph 8.7.

Step 1. Total the payment columns in the PCB. **Cross-cast** to total column.

Step 2. Check **amount left** in petty cash box.

		£
	Notes and coins in petty cash box	X
plus	IOUs	X
plus	payment vouchers	X
less	receipt vouchers	(X)
equals	imprest amount	X

All discrepancies, however small, should be investigated and discussed with the petty cashier's supervisor.

Step 3. Prepare **cheque requisition** for the difference between the imprest amount and the amount in the petty cash box.

		£
	Imprest amount	X
less	Cash in petty cash box	(X)
	Cheque requisition	X

Step 4. **Draw cash from bank**, specifying the notes and coins required, and place in box. Enter amount on left-hand (debit) side of petty cash book.

PETTY CASH BOOK

Receipts

Details	Net receipt £	VAT £	Total £
Balance b/d			150.00

Payments

Date	Details	Voucher No	Total £	Travel £	Postage £	Entertainment £	Office supplies £	Sundry £	VAT £
20X7									
14.12	Postage	101	6.25		6.25				
14.12	Travel	102	7.50	7.50					
15.12	Sundry	103	5.00					5.00	
15.12	Sundry	104	15.40					15.40	

Analysis of payments

Part B: Recording and accounting for cash transactions

Step 5. **Balance off PCB**, so completing the double page in the book and starting the next one.

Step 6. Ensure that the balancing off is **checked by the accounts supervisor**, who should sign and date the balanced off pages. This shows that the correct amount of cash has been drawn.

Step 7. **Post the totals** on the balanced off petty cash book to the general ledger.

8.3 EXAMPLE: TOPPING UP THE IMPREST

The imprest amount is £250, and at the end of March the petty cashier decides to top up the float in the petty cash box.

Step 1. **Add up the payments** in the total column and also the payments for each analysis column. These figures should **cross-cast** so that the sum of the payments for each analysis column should be equal to the payments in the total column.

These figures are shown on the next page.

Cross-cast check

	£
Travel	28.65
Postage	6.60
Entertainment	81.30
Office supplies and maintenance	56.40
Sundry	12.30
VAT	9.87
Total payments	195.12

Step 2. Check the amount of **cash left** in the petty cash tin. If there are no discrepancies, the cash in the box should amount to £55.98.

		£
	Imprest amount	250.00
plus	receipts	1.10
		251.10
less	total payments	195.12
equals	cash in box	55.98

Step 3. The **amount of cash** needed to top up the petty cash to the imprest amount can be calculated in either of two ways.

Method 1	£	*Method 2*	£
Imprest amount	250.00	Total payments	195.12
Cash in the box	(55.98)	Less receipts	(1.10)
Cash needed	194.02	Cash needed	194.02

A **cheque requisition form** should be prepared by the petty cashier for the amount of cash needed to top up the imprest float. In this example, the cheque requisition should be for £194.02.

Each organisation will have its own format for a cheque requisition form. An example of a completed form is given on page 246.

PETTY CASH BOOK

Receipts				Payments			Analysis of payments				
Details	Net receipt £	VAT £	Total £	Date	Details	Voucher No	Total £	Travel £	Postage £	Entertainment £	Office supplies £	Sundry £	VAT £

Details	Net receipt £	VAT £	Total £	Date	Details	Voucher No	Total £	Travel £	Postage £	Entertainment £	Office supplies £	Sundry £	VAT £
Balance b/d			250.00	20X7									
				5.3	Light bulbs	635	19.27				16.40		2.87
				8.3	Taxi fares	636	49.50	25.00		24.50			
				12.3	Entertainment	637	56.80			56.80			
				14.3	Window cleaner	638	47.00				40.00		7.00
				20.3									
Sale of postage stamps	1.10	—	1.10	21.3									
				22.3	Stamps	639	6.60		6.60				
				24.3	Magazines	640	12.30					12.30	
				29.3	Bus fares	641	3.65	3.65					

Part B: Recording and accounting for cash transactions

Cheque requisition

DATE: 31/3/X7

PAYABLE TO: Cash

AMOUNT: £194.02

DETAILS: Petty cash imprest float

SIGNED: Petty cashier

AUTHORISED BY: Accounts supervisor

Step 4. The cheque should then be prepared, taken to the **bank** and cashed. The cash should be put into the petty cash float.

NEWROSE INTERNATIONAL
1 Bower street, The Garden, W4 9EG   22 29 48

NEWROSE INTERNATIONAL   STAG BANK
                                 Forest Lane, The Dell

Date	Pay to the order of			Amount
31/03/X7	Cash			**** 194.02

Hundred Thousands	Ten Thousands	Thousands	Hundreds	Tens	Units
************	************			One	Nine	Four

Amount of pounds in words   Pence as in figures

Per Pro NEWROSE INTERNATIONAL

A Rose

⑃101127⑃ 22⑃2948⑃ 50195733⑃

When the cheque is cashed, the petty cashier should decide the **denomination** of notes and coins in which he or she would like the money. Since petty cash is for small payments, the petty cashier might decide to ask for the £194.02 to be made up as follows.

	Number	£
£20 notes	3	60.00
£10 notes	7	70.00
£5 notes	10	50.00
£1 coins	9	9.00
50p coins	6	3.00
20p coins	5	1.00
10p coins	4	0.40
5p coins	7	0.35
2p coins	10	0.20
1p coins	7	0.07
		194.02

The receipt of the money into petty cash must be recorded in both of the following books.

(a) The cash book (as a cheque payment)

11: Maintaining petty cash records

(b) The petty cash book (as a receipt)

In the petty cash book, the entry should include a reference to the corresponding folio number or entry number in the cash book for the cash withdrawal from the bank (CB 324 in this example).

Step 5. The left-hand (debit) side of the petty cash book is completed as follows.

(a) Enter the details of the **cash receipt**.

(b) **Total** the columns for receipts.

(c) On the payments side, insert an entry in the total column for the amount of cash in petty cash. This **balance carried down** is the imprest amount.

(d) Check the column totals and payments side of the book. The **total for receipts**, including the balance brought forward, **must be equal to the total for payments plus the balance carried down**. (If there is a discrepancy, something is wrong, and it could just be an error in adding up the columns. The first thing to do would be to check the arithmetic again.)

(e) Show the balance brought down, which should be the **imprest amount**, on the next page of the petty cash book.

These entries are shown following Paragraph 8.7.

Step 6. The petty cashier should now ask the accounts supervisor to check the entries on the page. The supervisor will probably already have checked the amount of cash in the petty cash box when the cheque requisition form was authorised. The check that is carried out now should be to ensure the following.

(a) The columns have been properly added up and cross-cast.

(b) The analysis of payments seems correct.

(c) There are vouchers for all the payments, attached in most cases to receipts, and the amount on each voucher corresponds with the amount shown in the petty cash book.

If the supervisor is satisfied, he or she should sign the page, and show the date on which his or her check was made.

Step 7. The accounting entries for the page of the petty cash book are not yet complete. The final step is to **post** the petty cash payments (and receipts) to the appropriate accounts in the general ledger. This can be done by drawing up a **posting summary** of the totals from the petty cash book. The ledger codes show where in the general ledger the amounts have been posted. In this example, A041 is the petty cash account, the 'E' accounts are expenses and the 'R' account is revenue or income.

	Account	Dr £	Cr £
Petty cash	A041	1.10	195.12
Travel	E151	28.65	
Postage	E153	6.60	
Entertainment	E155	81.30	
Office supplies	E164	56.40	
Sundry expenses	E180	12.30	
VAT	E247	9.87	
Sundry income	R302		1.10
		196.22	196.22

Every item of petty cash expense (or income) should be allocated to an expense account (or income account) in the general ledger. Each of these accounts will have its own unique code. There should be a separate account for each of the expenditure items for which there is an analysis column in the petty cash book. There will normally be an account for sundry income and an account for sundry expenses, as well as accounts for travel, entertainment, postage, VAT and so on.

Study the completed petty cash book on the following page and make sure that you can follow through each and every entry. The circled numbers refer to the steps outlined above.

Non-imprest methods

8.4 Some companies do not operate a strict imprest system. For example, they may reimburse petty cash with £100 whenever the float gets low. This is quite acceptable as long as the float is balanced and the petty cash book is correctly written up.

Drawing cash against a crossed cheque

8.5 Did you spot that the cheque in Step 4 above is made out to cash and yet is also a **crossed cheque**? When we discussed cheques earlier, we saw that crossed cheques should **normally** only be paid into another bank account. The bank may ignore the instruction of the crossing, however, under certain circumstances.

If the drawer (or some representative well known to the bank, such as the petty cashier of a company customer) **presents a crossed cheque for payment in cash**, banks can ignore the crossing on the grounds that there is no risk of the money passing to a person not entitled to it.

This is an example of practical business and banking needs overriding the rules relating to cheques and banking. (Note that most personal banking customers are also allowed to cash cheques on production of, and up to the limit of, a cheque guarantee card.)

Archive records

8.6 When a page in the petty cash book has been written up and the imprest float carried forward as the opening balance at the start of the next page, all the completed vouchers and receipts in the petty cash box must be **taken out of the box.**

8.7 The vouchers must not be thrown away, but kept for **at least seven years**. It must be possible for an auditor to find any voucher for which an entry has been made in the petty cash book. The petty cashier must therefore have a system of keeping used vouchers in an archive record.

11: Maintaining petty cash records

PETTY CASH BOOK

Receipts

Details	Net receipt £	VAT £	Total £
Balance b/d			250.00
Sale of postage stamps	1.10	—	1.10
Ledger code A041 ⑦	1.10 ⑤	④	
Cash book folio CB324 ④		⑤	194.02
			445.12
Ledger code	R302 ⑦		

Payments

Date	Details	Voucher No	Total £	Travel £	Postage £	Entertainment £	Office supplies £	Sundry £	VAT £
20X7									
5.3	Light bulbs	635	19.27				16.40		2.87
8.3	Taxi fares	636	49.50	25.00		24.50			
12.3	Entertainment	637	56.80			56.80			
14.3	Window cleaner	638	47.00				40.00		7.00
20.3	Stamps	639	6.60		6.60				
21.3	Magazines	640	12.30					12.30	
22.3									
24.3	Bus fares	641	3.65	3.65					
29.3			195.12 ①	28.65 ①	6.60 ①	81.30 ①	56.40 ①	12.30 ①	9.87 ①
31.3	Balance c/d ⑦	Ledger code A041	250.00	⑤					
			445.12	⑤					
				5153 ⑦	5153 ⑦	5153 ⑦	1913 ⑦	0813 ⑦	3247 ⑦

249

Part B: Recording and accounting for cash transactions

8.8 Although practice will vary, the normal system for **holding archive records** is as follows.

(a) The vouchers for a page of the petty cash book (with attached receipts) should be stapled together in number sequence.

(b) Until the accounts for the year to which these vouchers relate have been audited, the vouchers should be kept in box files (or other containers) in the petty cashier's office. These box files should be clearly labelled to show the numbers of the vouchers inside and the time period that these vouchers cover.

(c) After the annual audit, the box files can be moved to a more long-term and remote storage location.

Key learning points

- Petty cash is used to make **small payments** with notes and coins. The cash must be kept **safe**, in a **locked box or tin**, and its **security is the responsibility of a petty cashier**. Payments must be properly **authorised**, and all transactions should be supported by **receipts** and **vouchers**.

- There is usually an **imprest system** for petty cash, whereby a certain amount of cash is held in the box, say £200. At regular intervals or when cash runs low, vouchers are added up and recorded, and the total of the vouchers is used as the amount by which to top up the imprest to £200 again.

	£
Cash in box	X
Total of vouchers = top-up	X
Imprest amount	X

- All **payments** out of petty cash must be **properly authorised** and evidenced by a **voucher**, signed by both the person receiving the payment and the person authorising it. Claims for payment must be supported by a **receipt** whenever possible.

- If there is **no receipt** to support a claim for payment, the petty cashier should refer the claim to his or her supervisor.

- At regular intervals, details of payments out of petty cash are recorded from the vouchers into the **petty cash book**. Vouchers should be in date order and **numbered sequentially** and they should be entered into the petty cash book in this order.

- When the **VAT element in petty cash expenditure** is recorded, there must be a VAT receipt as evidence of the payment, and an analysis column for VAT in the petty cash book.

- A **new page** in the petty cash book is started whenever the imprest float is topped up.

- When the **imprest float** is topped up, a sequence of procedures must be followed.

  ○ The total expenses and analysis columns in the book should be added up, and these totals checked to ensure that they cross-cast.

  ○ The amount of cash in the petty cash tin must be counted, and a check made to ensure that the amount needed to top up petty cash to the imprest amount equals the total of voucher payments (minus any receipts).

  ○ A cheque requisition form must be prepared and authorised. When the cheque is written, it should be cashed at the bank. The petty cashier must specify the number of each denomination of notes and coins that he or she wants to make up the total.

  ○ The cash withdrawal is entered in the cash book and the petty cash book (receipts side).

  ○ The total receipts in the petty cash book must be added up. This should be equal to the total expenses (including balance carried down).

  ○ The page of the petty cash book should be checked by the accounts supervisor. The balance brought down, which is the imprest amount, is then carried forward to the next page of the petty cash book.

Key learning points (cont'd)

- A posting summary of items on the page of the petty cash book can be prepared, as a preparatory stage in posting the expenses/income details to the general ledger.
- The petty cashier must remove the completed vouchers from the petty cash box when a page of the petty cash book has been completed, and transfer them to an 'archive' file.

Quick quiz

1. Why do organisations need petty cash?
2. Who is responsible for the safety and security of the petty cash box?
3. What is the nature and purpose of the imprest system?
4. (a) What details are shown on petty cash vouchers?
   (b) What information is usually only added to petty cash vouchers when the petty cash book is about to be written up?
   (c) What should be attached to a petty cash voucher?
5. What items are recorded on the left-hand side of the petty cash book? And what on the right?
6. Why might money be received into petty cash?
7. On what grounds could you ignore the VAT element of petty cash vouchers?
8. State the 7 steps for topping up, balancing off and posting petty cash.

Answers to quick quiz

1. Because small items of expense need to be paid for out of notes and coins.
2. The petty cashier, a 'deputy' in his or her absence.
3. The imprest system is designed to keep control of petty cash. The imprest amount is the maximum amount in the petty cash box, payments are made out of this and vouchers created for the payments. The difference between the amount of cash in the petty cash box and the imprest amount is the amount that needs to be paid in to 'top up'. It should also be the sum total of the vouchers.
4. (a) Purpose of payment, amount paid, name and signature of recipient, name and signature of person authorising payment, date of payment.
   (b) Voucher number
   (c) Receipt
5. Receipts of money into petty cash (debit side). Payments of money from petty cash (credit side).
6. Payments from employees for personal use of company property, cash sales (rarely)
7. If it were company policy to do so.
8.
   1. Cast and cross-cast columns in petty cash book
   2. Count cash and vouchers in petty cash box
   3. Calculate amount of, and prepare, cheque requisition and cheque
   4. Specifying notes and coins required, cash cheque at bank and put cash in box, enter in petty cash book
   5. Balance off petty cash book
   6. Check balancing off
   7. Post totals to general ledger

Part B: Recording and accounting for cash transactions

Answers to activities

Answer 11.1

Expense item	Amount	Direct recipient	Acceptable?
Portable air conditioning unit	£75.99	Steve Gray, office manager	No
Coffee filters for office coffee machine	£2.99	Asif Sultan, PA	Yes
Bunch of flowers for Valentine's day	£18.00	Nick King, Sales	No
Bus ticket to Plastics Today conference	£2.60	Nick King, Sales	Yes

Answer 11.2

Reasons for not adopting the 'kitty box' suggestion

1   An open box at reception is not a safe place physically for cash - it could easily get lost or stolen.

2   'Dipping in' means that the designated authorised person (the petty cashier) is not making the payment, nor can it be ensured that the expenditure is authorised and for a valid reason.

3   A float of £30 in the kitty box would mean that, in theory, £30 could easily be taken and spent on one item of expenditure, in breach of the £25 limit on individual items of petty cash expense.

4   Usually petty cash can only be paid out against a receipt. The 'kitty box' suggests that payment can be made without a receipt. This is only permissible with the authority of the individual's manager.

Answer 11.3

	£
Imprest amount	150.00
Total of receipts	73.46
Top-up required	73.46

Answer 11.4

Petty Cash Voucher No 101
Date 14.12.X7

	AMOUNT	
	£	p
Stationery	6	25
	6	25

Signature: *T Scott*
Authorised by: *Petty Cashier*

Petty Cash Voucher No 102
Date 14.12.X7

	AMOUNT	
	£	p
Sundry expenses	7	50
	7	50

Signature: *A Manager*
Authorised by: *Petty Cashier*

Answer 11.5

I am not able to complete vouchers for any of the items in this exercise.

(a) I would refuse reimbursement. The cost of an employee's daily travel to work is not an expense of the business.

(b) This request exceeds the £25.00 limit applying to petty cash disbursements. I would refuse the request: the bill will be paid from the main bank account.

(c) No receipt will be available and the request should therefore be referred to the Administration Manager.

(d) The sum exceeds my £10.00 authorisation limit and should be referred to the Administration Manager.

Answer 11.6

Date	Details	Voucher no	Total £	Analysis of payments		
				Travel £	Postage £	Sundry £
20X7						
14.12	Postage	101	6.25		6.25	
14.12	Travel	102	7.50	7.50		
15.12	Sundry	103	5.00			5.00
15.12	Sundry	104	15.40			15.40

Answers 11.7 and 11.8

See over.

Part B: Recording and accounting for cash transactions

PETTY CASH BOOK

Receipts					Payments						
Details	Net receipt £	VAT £	Total £	Date	Details	Voucher No	Total £	Travel £	Postage £	Analysis of payments			
										Stationery £	Repairs £	Sundry £	VAT £
Balance b/d			150.00	20X7 14.12	Postage	101	6.25		6.25				
Cash sale	24.80	4.34	29.14	14.12	Travel	102	7.50	7.50					
				15.12	Sundry	103	5.00					5.00	
				15.12	Sundry	104	15.40					15.40	
Telephone	1.60	0.28	1.88	16.12	Stationery	105	10.81			9.20			1.61
				17.12	Sundry	106	5.17					4.40	0.77
				17.12	Repairs	107	22.09				18.80		3.29
				17.12	Stationery	108	4.23			3.60			0.63
				17.12	Sundry	109	2.82					2.40	0.42
Cash sale	11.20	1.96	13.16	18.12	Sundry	110	7.99			1.20		5.60	1.19
Cash book			43.08		Balance c/d	-	150.00						
	37.60	6.58	237.26				237.26	7.50	6.25	14.00	18.80	32.80	7.91
Balance b/d			150.00	21.12									

Chapter 12 Bank reconciliations

Chapter topic list

1 Bank reconciliations
2 The bank statement
3 Procedures for performing a bank reconciliation
4 Reconciliations on a computerised system

The following study sessions are covered in this chapter

			Syllabus reference
9	(a)	Recognise the need to reconcile the cash book with the bank statement periodically	7a
	(b)	Identify the main reasons for any discrepancies between the cash book and the bank statement such as errors, unanticipated receipts and payments and timing differences	7a
	(c)	Correct cash book errors and/or omissions	7a
	(d)	Reconcile the corrected cash book balance with the bank statement through adjustments for uncleared and uncredited cheques	7a

Part B: Recording and accounting for cash transactions

1 BANK RECONCILIATIONS

> **KEY TERM**
>
> The **cash book** of a business is the record of how much cash the business believes that it has in the bank.

1.1 In the same way, you might keep a private record of how much money you think you have in your own personal account at your bank, perhaps by making a note in your cheque book of the income you receive and the cheques you write. If you do keep such a record you will probably agree that when your bank sends you a bank statement from time to time the amount it shows as being the balance in your account is rarely exactly the same as the amount that you calculated as being your current balance.

Why is a bank reconciliation necessary?

1.2 Why might your own estimate of your bank balance be different from the amount shown on your bank statement? There are three common explanations.

Cause of difference	Explanation
Errors	Errors in calculation, or in recording income and payments, are as likely to have been made by yourself as the bank. These **errors must be corrected**.
Bank charges or bank interest	The bank might deduct interest on an overdraft or charges for its services, which you are not informed about until you receive the bank statement. **These should be accounted for in your records**.
Timing differences	(a) **Cheques recorded as received** and paid-in but not yet 'cleared' and added to your account by the bank. Although your own records show that some cash has been added to your account, it has not yet been acknowledged by the bank, although it will be in a very short time when the cheques are eventually cleared.
	(b) **Payments made by cheque** and recorded, but not yet banked by payee.
	Even when it is banked, it takes a day or two for the banks to process it and for the money to be deducted from your account.
	The timing differences should be listed and used to reconcile the cash book to the balance on the bank statement.

> **KEY TERM**
>
> A **bank reconciliation** compares the balance of cash in the business's records to the balance held by the bank. Differences between the balance on the bank statement and the balance in the cash book will be errors or timing differences, and they must be identified and satisfactorily explained.

1.3 You must be certain of the following.

(a) All transactions have been **correctly treated** by yourself and the bank.

(b) Cheques are not written when there are **insufficient funds** in your account because a receipt has not cleared at the bank.

1.4 If you do keep a personal record of your cash position at the bank, and if you do check your periodic bank statements against what you think you should have in your account, you will be doing exactly the same thing that the bookkeeper of a business does when he or she performs a bank reconciliation.

2 THE BANK STATEMENT

2.1 It is common practice for a business to issue a monthly **statement** to each credit customer.

- The balance the customer owed on his account at the beginning of the month
- New debts incurred by the customer during the month
- Payments made by the customer during the month
- The balance the customer owes on his account at the end of the month

> **KEY TERM**
>
> A **bank statement** is sent by a bank to its short-term debtors and creditors (customers with bank overdrafts and customers with money in their accounts) itemising the balance on the account at the beginning of the period, receipts into the account and payments from the account during the period, and the balance at the end of the period. These statements may be produced monthly, weekly or even daily depending on the volume of transactions going through the account.

2.2 You should be clear on one point. If a customer has money in his account, **the bank owes him that money,** and the customer is therefore a **creditor** of the bank (hence the phrase 'to be in credit' means to have money in your bank account). This means that if a business has £8,000 cash in the bank, it will have a debit balance in its own cash book, but the bank statement, if it reconciles exactly with the cash book, will state that there is a credit balance of £8,000 in the bank's 'creditors account'. (The bank's records are a 'mirror image' of the customer's own records, with debits and credits reversed.)

Part B: Recording and accounting for cash transactions

What does a bank statement look like?

2.3 An example of a bank statement is shown below. Nearly all bank statements will look something like this.

```
                    Northern Bank                      CONFIDENTIAL

        200 BROMFORD AVENUE      Account    ABC & CO.           SHEET NO    52
        LONDON                              4 THE MEWS
        E11 8TH                             LONDON  E4 2P2          (d)

                    Telephone
        20X7        0181 359 3100   Statement date  13 JUN 20X7 (a)   Account no   9309823 (b)
```

Date	Details		Withdrawals	Deposits	Balance (£)
(c) 11 MAY	Balance from Sheet no.	51 (d)			(f) 787.58
14 MAY		000059 (g)	216.81		570.77
22 MAY		000058	157.37		413.40
24 MAY		000060	22.00		391.40
29 MAY	LION INSURANCE	DD (i)	87.32		
	CATS238/ 948392093	DD	1,140.10		
	LB HACKBETH CC	SO (j)	54.69		
	COUNTER CREDIT 101479 (h)			469.86	
	INTEREST (l)		9.32		
	CHARGES (k)		30.00		460.17 O/D
13 JUN	Balance to Sheet no.	53			(f) 460.17 O/D

(e) **Key**
SO Standing Order DV Dividend CC Cash &/or Cheques Auto Withdrawals { AC Automated cash PY Payroll Interest -
EC Eurocheque TR Transfer CP Card Purchases { DD Direct Debit OD Overdrawn see over

2.4 We have discussed nearly all of the items which appear here in the earlier chapters on receipts and payments. The following points refer to the circled letters on the bank statement.

Letter	Item	Explanation
(a)	**The statement date**	This indicates that only transactions which have passed through your account **up to this date** (and since the last statement date) will be shown on the statement.
(b)	**Account number**	This number is required on the statement, particularly if the bank's customer has **more than one account**.
(c)	**Date**	This shows the date any transaction **cleared** into or out of your account. It is not normally the date that you performed the transaction as it takes three or more days for the bank to process a transaction.
(d)	**Sheet number**	Each bank statement received will have a number. The numbers run in **sequential order**, this helps to keep them in order and it immediately shows if a statement is missing.

Letter	Item	Explanation
(e)	Key	Not all bank statements will have a key to the abbreviations they use but it is helpful when one is provided. Note the following.
		• **Dividends** can be paid directly into a bank account if the shareholder has instructed the company in which he holds shares to do so.
		• **Automated cash** is a withdrawal from an automated teller machine - unusual for a business.
		• **Card purchase** is a purchase by debit card, again unusual for a business.
(f)	Balance	Most statements show a balance as at the end of each day's transactions.
(g)	Cheque numbers	The number is the same as that which appears on the individual cheque. Numbers are necessary to help you to **identify items** on the statement: you could not do so if only the amount of the cheque appeared.
(h)	Paying-in slip numbers	The need for these numbers is the same as for cheques.
(i)	Direct debit payments and receipts	The **recipient** of the direct debit payment is usually identified, either in words or by an account number.
(j)	Standing order payments and receipts	Again, the recipient is identifiable.
(k)	Charges	The charges which the bank levies are based on the **number of transactions** (cheques, receipts and so on) which have been processed through your account in a given period (usually a quarter).
(l)	Interest	Interest is charged on the amount of an **overdrawn balance** for the period it is overdrawn. On personal accounts, banks may pay interest to customers who do not go overdrawn.

Activity 12.1

The bank statement of Tip Top Trading Ltd for the month of February 20X7 is shown below.

Task

You are required to explain briefly the shaded items on the statement.

Part B: Recording and accounting for cash transactions

Northern Bank   CONFIDENTIAL

Weatherfield Branch
Weatherfield
Manchester M26

Account: Tip Top Trading Ltd
3 Barnes Street
Clapham SW6

SHEET NO 72

Telephone 0161 728 4213

20X7   Statement date 28 February 20X7   Account no 01140146

Date	Details		Withdrawals	Deposits	Balance (£)
	Balance brought forward				1,057.62
1 Feb	Cheque	800120	420.00		637.62
4 Feb	Cheque	800119	135.40		
7 Feb	Bank giro credit:	Manic Motors		162.40	664.62
9 Feb	Cheque	800121	824.70		160.08 OD
10 Feb	Credit	107428		400.00	239.92
16 Feb	Cheque	800122	123.25		116.67
18 Feb	Credit	107429		600.00	716.67
21 Feb	Direct debit:	Standish Ltd	121.00		595.67
23 Feb	Bank giro credit:	Bord & Sons		194.60	790.27
24 Feb	Credit	107430		300.00	1,090.27
25 Feb	Cheque	800123	150.00		940.27
28 Feb	Bank charges		15.40		924.87
28 Feb	Balance to Sheet no.	73			924.87

3 PROCEDURES FOR PERFORMING A BANK RECONCILIATION

3.1 The **cash book and bank statement will rarely agree at a given date**. Several procedures should be followed to ensure that the reconciliation between them is performed correctly.

Step 1. **Identify the cash book balance and the bank balance** (from the bank statement) on the date to which you wish to reconcile.

Step 2. **Add up the cash book** for the period since the last reconciliation and identify and note any errors found.

Step 3. Examine the bank statements for the same period and identify those **items which appear on the bank statement but which have not been entered in the cash book.**

- Standing orders and direct debits (into and out of the account)
- Dividend receipts from investments
- Bank charges and interest

Make a list of all those found.

Step 4. Identify all reconciling items due to **timing differences**.

(a) Some **cheque payments** made by the business and entered in the cash book have not yet been presented to the bank, or 'cleared', and so do not yet appear on the bank statement. It is usually best to mark off cheques in the cash book as they clear through the bank on a daily or weekly basis. In this way it will always be easy to identify unpresented cheques when a reconciliation takes place.

(b) **Cheques received**, entered in the cash book and paid into the bank, but which have not yet been cleared and entered in the account by the bank, do not yet appear on the bank statement.

Proforma bank reconciliation

3.2 If the procedures described here are followed, the bank reconciliation should look as it does below. The number of reconciling items will depend on the volume of transactions the company undertakes.

ADJUSTED CASH BOOK BALANCE

	£	£
Cash book balance brought down		X
Add: correction of understatement	X	
receipts not entered in cash book (standing orders, direct debits)	X	
		X
Less: correction of overstatement	X	
payments/charges not entered in cash book (standing orders, direct debits)	X	
		(X)
Corrected cash book balance		A

BANK RECONCILIATION

	£
Balance per bank statement	X
Add cheques paid in and recorded in the cash book but not yet credited to the account by the bank (**outstanding lodgements**)	X
Less cheques paid by the company but not yet presented to the company's bank for settlement (**uncleared cheques**)	(X)
Balance per cash book	A

3.3 EXAMPLE: BANK RECONCILIATION (1)

At 30 September 20X7 the debit balance in the cash book of Wordsworth Ltd was £805.15. A bank statement on 30 September 20X7 showed Wordsworth Ltd to be in credit by £1,112.30.

On investigation of the difference between the two sums, the following items were established.

(a) The cash book had been undercast by £90.00 on the debit side.
(b) Cheques paid in not yet credited by the bank amounted to £208.20.
(c) Cheques drawn not yet presented to the bank amounted to £425.35.

We need to show the correction to the cash book and show a statement reconciling the balance per the bank statement to the balance in the cash book.

Part B: Recording and accounting for cash transactions

3.4 SOLUTION

BANK RECONCILIATION

	£	£
Cash book balance brought down		805.15
Add correction of undercast		90.00
Corrected balance		895.15
Balance per bank statement		1,112.30
Add cheques paid in, recorded in the cash book, but not yet credited to the account by the bank	208.20	
Less cheques paid by the company but not yet presented to the company's bank for settlement	(425.35)	
		(217.15)
Balance per cash book		895.15

3.5 The reconciling items noted here will often consist of several transactions which can either be listed on the face of the reconciliation or listed separately. In particular, there may be a **great many outstanding cheques** if this is a busy business account.

3.6 You can see here that the reconciliation falls into **two distinct stages**.

- Correct the cash book
- Reconcile the bank balance to the corrected cash book balance

Activity 12.2

The cash book of Tip Top Trading Ltd for February 20X7 is set out below.

CASH BOOK

Receipts				Payments				
Date 20X7	Details	Cash £	Bank £	Date 20X7	Details	Cheq no	Cash £	Bank £
1/2	Balances b/d	167.75	922.22	1/2	Rent	800120		420.00
3/2	Manic Motors		162.40	4/2	R F Lessing	800121		824.70
3/2	Sales	780.75		4/2	Wages		124.20	
10/2	Transfer from cash		400.00	10/2	Transfer to bank		400.00	
11/2	Sales	522.70		11/2	British Gas plc	800122		123.25
16/2	Sales	122.08		18/2	D Waite	800123		150.00
18/2	Transfer from cash		600.00	18/2	Wages		124.20	
24/2	Sales	242.18		18/2	Transfer to bank		600.00	
24/2	Transfer from cash		300.00	23/2	S Molesworth	800124		207.05
28/2	Warley's Ltd		342.50	24/2	Transfer to bank		300.00	
				25/2	Fogwell & Co	800125		92.44
				28/2	Balance c/d		287.06	909.68
		1,835.46	2,727.12				1,835.46	2,727.12
	Balance b/d	287.06	909.68					

Task

Using the information from the bank statement (Activity 12.1), complete the cash book entries for the month. (The transactions to be entered are those which appear on the bank statement but are not to be found in the cash book as shown above.) You do not need to reproduce the whole of the cash book given above.

The following additional information is available. The difference between the opening bank balance at 1 February per the cash book of £922.22 and the opening balance at 1 February per the bank statement of £1,057.62 CR is explained by the cheque number 800119 which was recorded in the cash book in January and presented on 7 February.

Activity 12.3

Prepare a bank reconciliation statement for Tip Top Trading as at 28 February 20X7 using the information given in Activities 12.1 and 12.2.

Timing and frequency of the bank reconciliation

3.7 When and how often a company's bank reconciliation is performed depends on several factors.

Factor	Considerations
Frequency and volume of transactions	The more transactions there are, then the greater the likelihood of error.
Other controls	If there are very few checks on cash other than the reconciliation, then it should be performed quite often (other checks would include agreeing receipts to remittance advices).
Cash flow	If the company has to keep a very close watch on its cash position then the reconciliation should be performed as often as the information on cash balances is required. Most companies appear to be satisfied with a reconciliation at the end of each month but, if a company is very close to its overdraft limit, then a weekly reconciliation might be necessary.
Number of bank accounts	If, for some reason, a company has several bank accounts, all of which are used regularly, then it may be impractical, or even impossible, to perform reconciliations very often.

Activity 12.4

At your firm, Precision Products Ltd, a new trainee has been asked to prepare a bank reconciliation statement as at the end of October 20X7. At 31 October 20X7, the company's bank statement shows an overdrawn balance of £142.50 DR and the cash book shows a favourable balance of £24.13.

You are concerned that the trainee has been asked to prepare the statement without proper training for the task. The trainee prepares the schedule below and asks you to look over it.

	£
Balance per bank statement (overdrawn)	142.50
Overdraft interest on bank statement, not in cash book	24.88
Unpresented cheques (total)	121.25
Cheque paid in, not credited on bank statement	(290.00)
Error in cash book*	27.00
	25.63
Unexplained difference	(1.50)
Balance per cash book	24.13

*Cheque issued for £136.00, shown as £163.00 in the cash book.

The trainee says that he was not able to reconcile the difference completely, but was pleased that he was able to 'get it down' to £1.50. He feels that there is no need to do any more work now since the difference remaining is so small. He suggests leaving the job on one side for a week or so in the hope that the necessary information will come to light during that period.

Part B: Recording and accounting for cash transactions

Tasks

(a) So that you can show the trainee how a bank reconciliation ought to be performed, prepare:

    (i) a statement of adjustments to be made to the cash book balance
    (ii) a corrected bank reconciliation statement as at 31 October 20X7

(b) Explain to the trainee why it is important to prepare bank reconciliations regularly and on time.

Activity 12.5

You have been asked to prepare the monthly bank reconciliation as at 30 November 20X6 for your company Mentor Trading Ltd. The company's bank statement shows a credit balance of £1,698.50 and the cash book an overdrawn balance of £460.50.

During your investigation you discover the following:

- Overdraft interest of £24.60 in the bank statement, has not been posted to the cash book
- Cheques issued amounting to £1600.40 have not yet appeared on the bank statement
- A cheque received for £1906.00 was posted in the cheque book for £1609.00
- Bank charges of £25 were incorrectly posted to the wrong side of the cash book
- A cheque for £120.60 was paid in, but has not yet been credited on the bank statement
- An intercompany bank transfer in favour of Mentor Trading for £456.80 was made direct to the bank but not recorded in the cash book.

Tasks

(a) Prepare

    (i) a statement of adjustments to be made to the cash book balance
    (ii) a bank reconciliation statement as at 30 November 20X6

(b) Give two of the most common reasons why the cash book balance and the bank balance may differ.

Exam alert

The Pilot Paper contained a simple bank reconciliation question requiring a calculation of the bank balance. The 'distracters' (incorrect answers) tended to show figures that would have been calculated if items had been added instead of subtracted or vice versa.

4 RECONCILIATIONS ON A COMPUTERISED SYSTEM

4.1 In essence there is **no difference between reconciling a manual cash book and reconciling a computerised cash book**.

Computer controls over cash

4.2 In theory many of the same errors could occur in a computerised cash book as in a manual one. However, the computer will have **programme controls** built in to prevent or detect many of the errors.

Error	Programme control
Casting	Computers are programmed to add up correctly; this will avoid the errors of overcasting and undercasting which occur with manual cash books.

Error	Programme control
Updating from ledgers	In a computer system, the bank account will tend to be a secondary account which is updated from the sales ledger, purchase ledger, and any other relevant ledger. When money is received from debtors, it will be posted to the sales ledger. The computer will then automatically update the bank account in the nominal ledger to reflect the receipt of the money. This means that receipts and payments are unlikely to be confused.
Combined computer and manual cash books	Many organisations, even those with remarkably sophisticated computer systems, will normally maintain a manual cash book. This cash book will reflect transactions generated by the computer system (for instance cheque payments from the purchase ledger), and it will also reflect transactions initiated outside the computer system ('one-off' events such as the purchase of capital assets). The manual transactions will also be entered on to the computer. Thus the 'bank account' in the ledger runs in tandem with the manual cash book. When a bank reconciliation is due to take place, the first job might be to make sure that the computer bank account and the cash book balances are in agreement.

Key learning points

- A **bank reconciliation** is a comparison between the bank balance recorded in the books of a business and the balance appearing on the bank statement.

- The comparison may reveal **errors** or **omissions** in the records of the business, which should be corrected by appropriate adjustments in the cash book.

- Once the cash book has been corrected it should be possible to reconcile its balance with the bank statement balance by taking account of **timing differences**: payments made and cheques received which are recorded in the cash book but have not yet cleared through the bank account and have not, therefore, appeared on the bank statement.

Quick quiz

1. What are the three main reasons why a business's cash book balance might differ from the balance on a bank statement?
2. What is a bank reconciliation?
3. What is a bank statement?
4. Why are cheque numbers shown on the bank statement?
5. What are the two parts of a bank reconciliation statement?

Answers to quick quiz

1. Reasons for disagreement are: errors, bank charges or interest, timing differences (for amounts to clear).

2. A bank reconciliation compares the balance of cash in the business's records to the balance held by the bank.

3. A bank statement is a document sent by a bank to its short-term debtor and creditor customers, itemising transactions over a certain period.

Part B: Recording and accounting for cash transactions

4   Cheque numbers aid identification of the transaction, the amount would not be enough.

5   (a) The adjustment of the cash book balance
    (b) The reconciliation of the cash book balance to the bank statement

Answers to activities

Answer 12.1

(a) **Statement number 72.** The bank numbers each statement page issued for the account. Transactions from 1 March 20X7 onwards will be shown on statement number 73, and so on. Numbering the statements in this way allows the customer to check that none of its bank statements are missing.

(b) **Bank giro credit.** The bank giro credit system enables money to be paid in to any bank for the credit of a third party's account at another bank. Manic Motors has paid in £162.40 for the credit of Tip Top Trading's account at Northern Bank. A bank giro credit may take around two or three days for the banks to process.

(c) **£160.08 OD.** This shows that there is a debit balance (an overdraft) of £160.08 at the bank on 9 February 20X7. Tip Top Trading is at that point a *debtor* of the bank, the bank is a *creditor* of Tip Top Trading.

(d) **Direct debit.** Standish Ltd must have authority (by means of a direct debit mandate signed on behalf of Tip Top Trading Ltd) to make a direct debit from its account.

This arrangement allows payments to be made to a third party without a cheque having to be sent.

(e) **Bank charges.** The bank may make various charges to cover its costs in providing bank services to the customer. The bank will be able to explain how its charges are calculated.

Answer 12.2

CASH BOOK

Receipts Date 20X7	Details	Cash £	Bank £	Payments Date 20X7	Details	Cash £	Bank £
	Balances b/d	287.06	909.68	21 Feb	Standish		121.00
23 Feb	Bord & Sons		194.60	28 Feb	Bank charges		15.40
				28 Feb	Balances c/d	287.06	967.88
		287.06	1,104.28			287.06	1,104.28

Answer 12.3

Tutorial note. In the solution below, we have worked from the cash book balance to the bank statement balance rather than vice versa. However, the reconciliation may be done either way round.

TIP TOP TRADING LIMITED
BANK RECONCILIATION STATEMENT AS AT 28 FEBRUARY 20X7

	£	£
Balance at bank as per cash book (see Answer to Activity 12.2)		967.88
Add unpresented cheques		
800124	207.05	
800125	92.44	
		299.49
		1,267.37
Less credit in cash book, not on bank statement (Warleys Ltd)		(342.50)
Balance at bank as per bank statement		924.87

Answer 12.4

(a) (i) CASH BOOK

	£		£
Uncorrected balance b/d	24.13	Overdraft interest	24.88
Error in cash book	27.00	Balance c/f	26.25
	51.13		51.13

(ii) PRECISION PRODUCTS LIMITED
BANK RECONCILIATION STATEMENT AS AT 31 OCTOBER 20X7

	£
Balance as per bank statement (overdrawn)	(142.50)
Less unpresented cheques (total)	(121.25)
	(263.75)
Add cheque paid in, not yet credited on bank statement	290.00
Balance as per cash book	26.25

(b) Three reasons why bank reconciliation statements should be prepared regularly and on time are as follows.

(i) The company's records should be updated for items such as bank charges and dishonoured cheques so that managers are not working with an incorrect figure for the bank balance.

(ii) Errors should be identified and corrected as soon as possible, whether they are made by the company or by the bank.

(iii) Checks should be made on the time delay between cheques being written and their presentation for payment, and to check the time taken for cheques and cash paid in to be credited to the account. A better understanding of such timing differences will help managers to improve their cash planning.

Answer 12.5

(a) (i) Correcting the Cash book

CASH BOOK

DR   CR

	£		£
Correction of transposition error in posting cheque	297.00	Balance b/fwd	460.50
		Overdraft interest not posted	24.60
		Cancel incorrect posting of bank charges	25.00
Transfer from intergroup company	456.80	Bank charges recorded	25.00
		Bal c/fwd	218.70
	753.80		753.80

(ii) Bank reconciliation statement as at 30 November 20X1

	£
Balance as per bank statement	1,698.50
Less: cheques issued not yet cleared	(1,600.40)
	98.10
Add: cheque paid in not yet on bank statement	120.60
	218.70

(b) The most common differences between the cash book and the bank statement are timing differences and errors. The most common timing differences are due to unpresented cheques. These are cheques which have been issued by the company and recorded in the cash book but have not at the date of the bank reconciliation reached its bank.

Part C
Recording and accounting for credit transactions

Chapter 13 Sales and sales returns day books

Chapter topic list

1 What is the sales day book?
2 What is the sales returns day book?
3 Entering sales transactions in the day books
4 Coding data
5 Posting the day book totals

The following study sessions are covered in this chapter

			Syllabus reference
6	(f)	Record transactions in a sales day book and sales returns day book	4a
	(g)	Code sales and customer records and data	4a

Part C: Recording and accounting for credit transactions

> **Chapter 13 scenario - Gourmet Supplies Ltd.** This scenario applies to all the activities in this chapter.
>
> Gourmet Supplies Ltd is a wholesaler of crockery, glassware, electrical appliances and sundry other goods for the kitchen and home.
>
> Sales are classified into the following categories:
>
> C   Crockery
> G   Glassware
> E   Electrical appliances
> X   Sundry
>
> All of the company's supplies are standard-rated for VAT purposes. The standard rate of VAT is 17½%.

1 WHAT IS THE SALES DAY BOOK?

> You were introduced to the idea of the sales and purchase day books in Part A of this Text. In Part C on credit transactions we expand your knowledge further.

The need for the sales day book

1.1 A business will obviously want to make sure that it **receives the money due for all of the sales which it makes**.

- Raise invoices for all of the goods and services which it sells on credit
- Issue invoices to the right customer
- Keep track of the invoices and credit notes which it has raised

1.2 In other words, **the business will need records which show the following details**.

- **When and how much** money is due to the business
- **Total sales** made over a certain period of time

The business will therefore need to have some way of **recording** and **summarising** the contents of the invoices and credit notes, which are called 'source documents'.

The function of the sales day book

> **KEY TERM**
>
> The **sales day book** is used to keep a list of all the invoices and credit notes sent out to customers each day. One alternative name for this list is the sales journal, you may also come across other names for a listing which serves the same purpose.

1.3 Since a transaction is recorded in the sales day book before being recorded elsewhere, the sales day book is sometimes referred to as a **'book of prime entry'** or a **'primary record'**.

1.4 The term 'book' is used because that is the form which these records generally used to and sometimes still do take. It is worth bearing in mind that books of prime entry are often not actual books, but are rather files hidden in the memory of a computer. **Nevertheless, the principles of how transactions are recorded remain the same whether the records used are computerised or manual.**

1.5 Example: sales day book

An extract from the sales day book of Supershod Shoe Supplies appears as follows.

Date	Invoice number	Customer	Net total £	VAT £	Gross total £
10.1.X7	20247	S Jones	172.00	30.10	202.10
	20248	Abbey Supplies Ltd	84.50	14.78	99.28
	20249	Cook & Co	292.70	51.22	343.92
	20250	Texas Ltd	172.00	30.10	202.10
	20251	Dinham Shoes	74.75	13.08	87.83
	20252	Mentor Ltd	272.05	47.60	319.65
		Totals	1,068.00	186.88	1,254.88

1.6 The items listed in the day book should follow an **unbroken numerical sequence**, usually by invoice number. Numbers of **spoiled invoices** should be entered too, with blanks in the 'amounts' columns and/or a note as cancelled under 'customer', so that it is clearly recorded that no invoice with that number has been raised.

Activity 13.1

Task

Complete and total the proforma sales day book from Gourmet Supplies Ltd on page 277 in respect of the following transactions. The customer's name follows the invoice number.

17/3/X7   Invoice I2060 - Kirby Kitchenware

Product description	Amount (inc VAT) £
Bostonware plates	68.15
Wine glasses	72.85
	141.00

17/3/X7   Invoice I2061 – Boddington Kitchens Ltd

Product description	Amount (inc VAT) £
Electric toasting forks	42.03
Electric salt/pepper mills	30.92
Glassware	65.00
Sundry items	13.67
	151.62

17/3/X7   Invoice I2062 - Invoice form spoiled

17/3/X7   Invoice I2063 - Placesetters Ltd

Product description	Amount (inc VAT) £
Electric salt/pepper mills	30.92
Glassware (various)	40.50
Tablemats (sundry)	32.69
	104.11

Part C: Recording and accounting for credit transactions

18/3/X7   Invoice I2064 - Anston Mayne

Product description	Amount (inc VAT) £
Wine glasses	141.00

18/3/X7   Invoice I2065 - Nye & Co

Product description	Amount (inc VAT) £
Plates 9"	48.62
Saucers 5"	10.45
	59.07

18/3/X7   Invoice I2066 - Dindins Ltd

Product description	Amount (inc VAT) £
Electric plate cleaners	37.10
Sundry	8.88
	45.98

18/3/X7   Invoice I2067 - Major John Design

Product description	Amount (inc VAT) £
Crockery (various)	45.30
Glassware (various)	45.30
	90.60

Further information

Customer account numbers are as follows.

Anston Mayne	A01
Boddington Kitchens Ltd	B09
Dindins Ltd	D06
Fuller Crockery	F03
Kirby Kitchenware	K02
Major John Design	M09
Nye & Co	N04
Placesetters Ltd	P11

Tutorial note. You can ignore the rounding rules for VAT in this exercise.

GOURMET SUPPLIES - SALES DAY BOOK								
Date	Invoice No.	Customer No.	Total	C	G	E	X	VAT
			TOTAL					

Part C: Recording and accounting for credit transactions

2 WHAT IS THE SALES RETURNS DAY BOOK?

> **KEY TERM**
>
> The **sales returns day book** is a chronological listing of sales returns. It records the value of goods returned to the business by buyers, dealt with by the issue of credit notes.

2.1 Example: sales returns day book

An entry from the sales returns day book of Supershod Shoe Supplies looks like this.

Date	Credit note number	Customer	Net total £	VAT £	Gross total £
10.1.X7	C2214	Pediform Ltd	29.40	5.14	34.54

2.2 Some sales returns day books may have a column headed with something like 'goods returned', so that a **description of the goods returned** can be entered into the returns day book as well.

2.3 There might be no separate sales returns day book, with returns being entered as **figures in brackets in the sales day book** instead.

3 ENTERING SALES TRANSACTIONS IN THE DAY BOOKS

3.1 (a) In a **manual system of accounting**, which might be used by a small business, writing up the sales day book will probably involve writing out the details of each invoice - each transaction - by hand. The details of credit notes can similarly be written directly into the sales returns day book.

   (b) In a **computerised sales ledger**, transaction details will probably be entered onto the system using a keyboard and VDU (visual display unit).

Analysing sales

3.2 As well as the kinds of information which we showed in the example from the sales day book shown earlier (the date, the invoice number, the name of the customer, the net total, VAT and the gross total), it is common for the **net value of the sales** made to be analysed into different categories in the day book. This is because it can be helpful for a business to have information about the amount of **sales of different types** which it is making.

3.3 In a manual day book, we can achieve this analysis by adding more columns to the sales day book. For example, the transactions which we used as examples in Paragraphs 1.5 and 2.1 above might be analysed into columns headed 'Boot sales' and 'Shoe sales'.

3.4 Rather than set this out as if an analysed sales day book had been written out in full by hand, we shall look at how an analysis might be prepared using a **computer spreadsheet**.

A spreadsheet model

3.5 You may already be familiar with spreadsheets. The use of spreadsheets is covered in detail in your later studies. Here we illustrate a **simple use of spreadsheets**, and some introductory details are given in case you are unfamiliar with them.

3.6 A spreadsheet is basically a **grid** - like the grid on a large sheet of 'analysis paper' - which is held in the memory of a computer. There are **columns** which are generally headed with the letters of the alphabet and **rows** which are generally given numbers in sequence. The spreadsheet can be used like a large sheet of paper on which information can be written by keying it in through a keyboard to a VDU. Each position on the spreadsheet (given by where a column and a row meet, eg A1, C4, G7) is called a 'cell'.

3.7 Example: analysed sales day book using a spreadsheet

Suppose that we wanted to analyse our sales transactions (at sales value excluding VAT) into the following types.

GB	Gents' boots
LB	Ladies' boots
GS	Gents' shoes
LS	Ladies' shoes
A	Shoe polish/accessories

Once we have keyed in the information on each invoice, our sales day book spreadsheet model might look like this. Note that the totals of columns F to J come to the total of column C (the sales net of VAT), not column E.

	A	B	C	D	E	F	G	H	I	J	K
1	Supershod Shoe Supplies					Credit sales			Date:	101X7	
2	Invoice	Cust	Net	VAT	Gross	GB	LB	GS	LS	A	
3	No	No	£	£	£						
4	20247	J042	172.00	30.10	202.10		95.45		76.55		
5	20248	A009	84.50	14.78	99.28					84.50	
6	20249	C124	292.70	51.22	343.92				292.70		
7	20250	T172	172.00	30.10	202.10			172.00			
8	20251	D249	74.75	13.08	87.83	74.75					
9	20252	M201	272.05	47.60	319.65	94.20		72.42	105.43		
10											
11											
:											
24	Total		1,068.00	186.88	1,254.88	168.95	95.45	244.42	474.68	84.50	

3.8 Although spreadsheets can be very useful, it is important to recognise them for what they are. If a spreadsheet has been **set up incorrectly**, or if data has been **entered incorrectly** without any check being carried out on its accuracy, then the **spreadsheet may contain errors**. Just because a spreadsheet has been produced using a computer, it does not follow that it is going to be free of errors.

Sales ledger packages

3.9 As with a manual sales day book, a sales day book spreadsheet can be updated by each individual invoice being entered by somebody. Many businesses operate computerised accounting packages, however, with one part which deals with sales transactions (generally called a 'sales ledger package'). We now look at how this can affect the entering of sales transactions.

3.10 It may be that a computerised sales ledger system involves entering sales transactions in a similar way to that described for the spreadsheet model we looked at above.

Step 1. Sales invoices are typed out.

Step 2. The details on invoices are keyed into the computer using a keyboard and VDU.

Step 3. One of the 'reports' which the computer is able to produce might be a listing of sales invoices and credit notes for a particular day. This listing might be similar to the spreadsheet we looked at earlier.

3.11 Most businesses would want to save themselves the duplicated work of preparing invoices and then keying in the invoice details. This saving can be made by a sales ledger **package which will produce invoices itself**.

Step 1. Certain information will be input, such as the date, the customer number, product codes and quantities.

Step 2. The computer package will use this information to produce invoices.

Step 3. The package will collect the information on the invoices and credit notes needed to create the sales day book.

3.12 In some computer systems, a **system for recording stocks of goods held** is combined (or 'integrated') with **the system for processing sales orders**.

Step 1. The details of goods which a customer orders are keyed in and recorded by the Sales Order Processing (SOP) system, which can then produce an order acknowledgement form to send out to the customer.

Step 2. When the goods are despatched or sent out to the customer, details of this despatch can be keyed in to the computer together with the number of the order which is being satisfied.

Step 3. The computer will then produce a sales invoice, using the information it already has about the order.

Step 4. Reports may be produced of sales and returns made on a particular day or in a particular period to give the information which a 'traditional' sales day book would contain.

4 CODING DATA

Codes

4.1 Before we look at how details of sales transactions from the sales day book can be posted in the company's accounting records, we need to take a brief look at the importance of coding in transaction processing. Coding is, arguably, at the heart of transaction processing, and the integrity of the information derived from it.

4.2 Whenever a transaction arises, it must be coded. **Codes** are used because they can **identify** items more concisely and precisely than written descriptions and so help to **classify** items into groups for recording data.

> **KEY TERM**
>
> A **code** is defined as a system of symbols designed to be applied to a classified set of items to give a brief accurate reference, facilitating entry, collection and analysis.

4.3 Coding saves time in copying out data because **codes are shorter** than longhand descriptions. For this reason, and also to save storage space, computer systems make use of coded data.

Coding in the sales ledger

4.4 The **sales ledger** consists of individual accounts for each credit sale customer. Each customer is allocated an account and identified by a unique code number. If there were two customers with the same name, with a unique code, these would be distinguished. In addition to customer account numbers other examples of codes in a sales system can incorporate the following important information:

- sales invoice numbers

    a sequential coding of invoices can ensure completeness and help eliminate errors such as missing invoices, or goods not invoiced

- product code numbers

    as well as a customer identification number, a code can incorporate a product identification. For example customer Smith may be buying more than one type of product from the company such as pianos and string instruments. Separate identification of the products will enable the transaction to be correctly posted not just in the sales ledger but also in all relevant accounts in the nominal ledger.

4.5 Various coding systems (or combinations of them may be used when designing codes to offer the flexibility the company requires. These are described below:

Sequence codes

4.6 **Sequence codes** make no attempt to classify the item to be coded. It is simply given the next available number in a rising sequence. New items can only be inserted at the end of the list and therefore the codes for similar items may be very different.

4.7 Sequence codes are suitable for document numbering eg invoice numbers but rarely used when flexibility for different sub-groups is required.

Block codes

4.8 **Block codes** provide a different sequence for each different group of items. For example for a particular firm, customers may be divided up according to area:

South East	code numbers 10,000-19,999
South West	code numbers 20,000-29,999
Wales	code numbers 30,000-39,999

4.9 The coding of customer accounts is then sequential within each block.

Significant digit codes

4.10 **Significant digit codes** incorporate some digit(s) which is (are) part of the descriptions of the item being coded. An example is:

```
5000    Electric light bulbs
5025    25 watt
5040    40 watt
5060    60 watt
5100    100 watt
etc
```

Hierarchical codes

4.11 **Hierarchical codes** are allocated on the basis of a tree structure where the interrelationship between the items is of the paramount importance. A well known example is the Universal Decimal Code used by most libraries. For example:

```
5           Business
5 2         Finance
5 2 1       Cost accounting
5 2 1.4     Standard costing
5 2 1.4 7   Variance analysis
5 2 1.4 7 3 Fixed overhead variances
```

Faceted codes

4.12 **Faceted codes** are made up of a number of sections, each section of the code representing a different feature of the item. For example in a clothing store there might be a code based on the following facets.

| Garment type | Customer type | Colour | Size | Style |

4.13 If SU stood for suit, M for man and B for blue, a garment could be given the code SU M B 40 17. Similarly ND F W 14 23 could stand for woman's white nightdress size 14, style 23. On of the great advantages of this system is that the type of item can be recognised from the code.

4.14 Faceted codes may be entirely numeric. For example, a large international company may allocate code numbers for each sale representative on the basis that:

Digit 1   Continent (eg America –1, Europe –2)
Digits 2/3 Country (eg England – 06)
Digit 4   Area (eg North – 3)
Digits 5/6 Representative's name (eg Mr J Walker – 14)
The code number may be expressed as 2/06/3/14.

Coding in the accounts ledger

4.15 An accounts general ledger will consist of a **large number of coded accounts**. For example, part of a general ledger might be as follows:

Account code	Account name
100200	Plant and machinery (cost)
100300	Motor vehicles (cost)
300000	Total debtors
400000	Total creditors
500130	Wages and salaries

500140	Rent and rates
500150	Advertising expenses
500160	Bank charges
500170	Motor expenses
500180	Telephone expenses
600000	Sales
700000	Cash

4.16 A business will choose its own code for its general accounts. The codes given in the above table are purely imaginary.

5 POSTING THE DAY BOOK TOTALS

5.1 We have seen above how details of sales transactions may be entered in a sales day book. We mentioned at the beginning of the chapter that a business will want, among other things, to make sure that it receives the money due from all of the sales that it makes. It needs records to show when it should ask for the money due to it following a credit sale. Can the sales day book achieve that objective on its own?

Personal accounts for debtors

5.2 The answer is no. A listing of sales transactions in chronological order, such as the sales day book shows, would not meet these needs of a business of any size at all.

(a) For many businesses, the chronological record of sales transactions might involve very large numbers of invoices per day or per week.

(b) The same customer might appear in several different places in the sales day book, for purchases he has made on credit at different times. So at any point in time, a customer may owe money on several unpaid invoices.

What we need is a way of showing **who** owes **what** amount to the business and **when**.

5.3 This need is met by maintaining '**personal accounts**'. For sales, there will be personal accounts for each individual debtor maintained in the **sales ledger**.

(a) Each individual sales transaction is entered in the sales day book(s) and needs to be recorded in the personal sales ledger account of the customer.

(b) We will see below that day book totals need to be posted to the total debtors and sales accounts in the general ledger.

Personal accounts are sometimes called 'memorandum accounts' to indicate that the recording of transactions in these accounts is **not** part of the double entry. The **general ledger** accounts to which the double entry postings are made are sometimes called 'impersonal accounts'.

Recording the double entry

5.4 The transactions entered in the sales day book need to be recorded in the 'double entry' system of bookkeeping. (The principles of double entry bookkeeping were explained in Part A of this Interactive Text.)

Part C: Recording and accounting for credit transactions

5.5 Before we can record the double entry, the sales day book must be **totalled** and **ruled off**, to include all transactions since the book was last ruled off. In our examples in Paragraphs 1.5 and 3.7 the day books have already been ruled off and totalled.

5.6 Remember that a business will have a **cash account** as part of its double entry, posted from the cash book. This is the general ledger account in which receipts and payments of cash are recorded. Clearly no entries can be made in the cash account when a credit transaction first takes place, because initially no cash has been received or paid. Where then are the details of the transaction entered?

5.7 The solution is to use the debtors control account. (Total debtors)

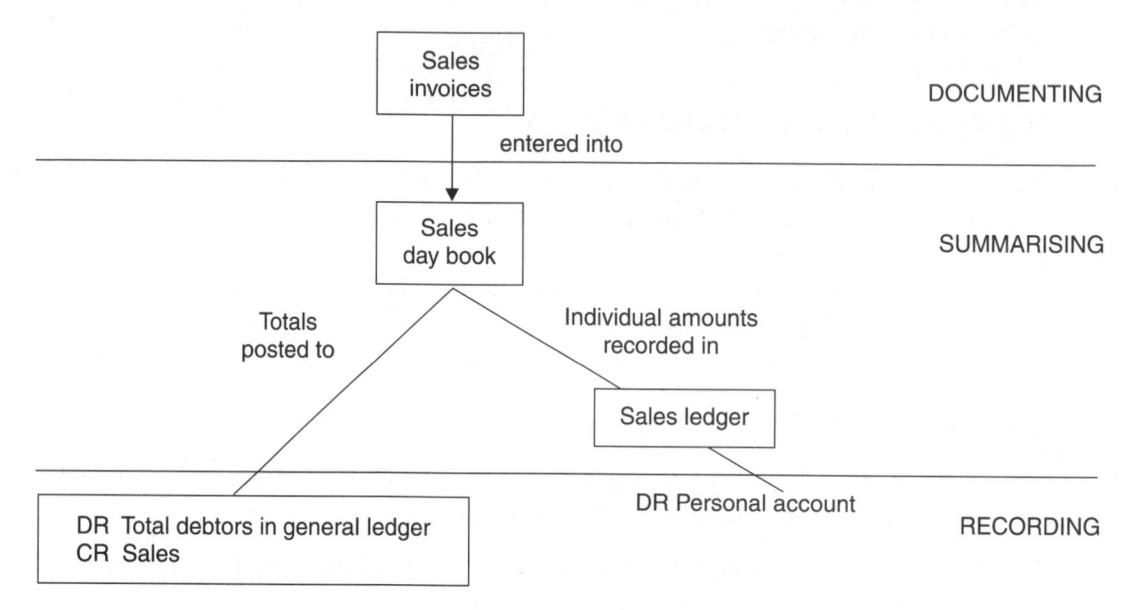

```
                    Sales
                   invoices                          DOCUMENTING
                      |
                 entered into
                      ↓
                    Sales
                   day book                          SUMMARISING
                   /      \
            Totals        Individual amounts
           posted to       recorded in
              /                 \
             /              Sales ledger
            /                    |
           /              DR Personal account
    DR Total debtors in general ledger               RECORDING
    CR  Sales
```

The double entry

5.8 Remembering basic double entry rules, we can see that the sales summarised in the sales day book are transactions having two aspects.

- An increase in our **asset** (debtors)
- An increase in **income** (sales)

> **KEY TERM**
>
> A **debtors control account**, or '**sales ledger control account**', is maintained in the general ledger to record in total the amounts which are posted to the debtors' individual personal memorandum accounts in the sales ledger.

5.9 For sales made to credit customers the entries made will be a **debit** to the debtors control account and a **credit** to the sales account.

- The **debtors control account** records an **asset** - the debts owed by the customers.
- The **sales account** records **income** - the amount of sales which the business is making.

5.10 We can show the basic double entry as follows.

		£	£
DEBIT	Total debtors account	X	
CREDIT	Sales account		X

5.11 We do not need to record each sales transaction separately in the general ledger. We make use of day book totals to summarise the transactions.

VAT

5.12 Looking back at the transactions in Paragraph 3.7, you can see that value added tax (**VAT**) is charged on the sales. As you know, the business must account to HM Customs & Excise for the output VAT it collects. In order to keep track of the amount it owes to or is owed by Customs and Excise, the business keeps a Value Added Tax Account (perhaps called a VAT Control Account) in the general ledger.

5.13 The VAT which customers owe to the business is included in the overall amount owed (total debtors), but the other side of the entry for the amounts of VAT invoiced to customers is an **increase in the liability of the business to pay over VAT to HM Customs & Excise**. The double entry will have this form (we'll show actual figures a little later).

		£	£
DEBIT	Total debtors account	X	
CREDIT	VAT account		X
	Sales account		X

Sales returns day book

5.14 The double entry arising from posting of totals from a **sales returns day book** will be rather like a mirror image of the posting of sales which we have just looked at. When goods are returned, we want to 'reverse' the transaction (or part of it) as it was shown in the books when we recorded the sale. The double entry will take the following form.

		£	£
DEBIT	VAT account	X	
	Returns account (or sales account)	X	
CREDIT	Total debtors account		X

Sales

5.15 Earlier we saw how sales can be analysed into different categories in the sales day book. Rather than maintaining a single account in the general ledger for sales, a business may split the sales into a number of general ledger accounts so that it has **a record in the general ledger of the amounts of the different types of sales.**

5.16 Example: double entry recording of sales

Using the example in Paragraph 3.7, the double entry for Supershod Shoe Supplies would look like this.

		£	£
DEBIT	Total debtors account	1,254.88	
CREDIT	VAT control account		186.88
	Sales - gents' boots account		168.95
	Sales - ladies' boots account		95.45
	Sales - gents' shoes account		244.42
	Sales - ladies' shoes account		474.68
	Sales - shoe polish/accessories account		84.50

As ever, the total amount posted to the debit side equals the total amount posted to the credit side (check this).

Part C: Recording and accounting for credit transactions

The posting summary

5.17 How then will we carry out the postings for the sales made by Supershod Shoe Supplies on 10 January 20X7?

(a) Use a double entry posting summary for the general ledger accounts, and post the sales ledger memorandum accounts straight from the individual invoices in the sales day book.

(b) Use a double entry posting summary for the general ledger, and use it to post the sales ledger too.

5.18 Supershod Shoe Supplies uses a posting summary to deal with the sales ledger postings as well as the general ledger (double entry) postings. Here is the posting summary for the 10 January 20X7 sales day book, and the sales returns day book shown in Paragraph 2.1 (which, you are informed, was of gents' boots).

SUPERSHOD SHOE SUPPLIES
General ledger posting summary

Account name	Account code	General ledger Dr		General ledger Cr	
Total debtors	60400	1,254	88	34	54
Sales - GB	01010			168	95
Sales - LB	01020			95	45
Sales - GS	01030			244	42
Sales - LS	01040			474	68
Sales - A	01050			84	50
Returns - GB	01110	29	40		
VAT	70700			186	88
VAT	70700	5	14		
TOTALS		1,289	42	1,289	42

Posted by ...C.F......   Date ......10/1/X7......

5.19 The total of the **debits** posted to the general ledger must equal the total of the **credits** posted to the general ledger. If these two columns do not add to the same figures, whoever is completing the form knows that they must have made some error and will look for the error before going any further.

Note that each general ledger account has an account code to identify the correct account to be posted.

13: Sales and sales returns day books

5.20 The **sales ledger postings** to be made from the sales day book are as follows.

Ref	A/c name	A/c code	Debit £	Credit £
20248	Abbey S	A009	99.28	
20249	Cook & Co	C124	343.92	
20251	Dinham	D249	87.83	
20247	S Jones	J042	202.10	
20252	Mentor	M201	319.65	
C2214	Pediform	P041		34.54
20250	Texas Ltd	T172	202.10	
			1,254.88	34.54

5.21 Check that you can see where the various figures come from and how they reflect the form of double entry of transactions which we have looked at above. Note also the following points.

- There is an account code for each customer, which is what will be used to identify the correct account to which a sales ledger posting should be made.

- The debit and credit totals posted to the individual sales ledger accounts are the same as the amounts posted to the total debtors account as shown at the top of the columns of postings to the general ledger in Paragraph 5.18 above.

5.22 Once the general ledger and the sales ledger postings have been keyed in to Supershod's computerised accounts package, the general posting summary is **filed for future reference**.

Activity 13.2

Task

Complete the general ledger posting summary form below with the double entry required to record the sales on 17 and 18 March 20X7 as detailed in Activity 13.1.

	GOURMET SUPPLIES LIMITED				
	General ledger posting summary				
JNL ENTRY	Date .... Prepared by .... Authorised by				
No.	Account	Code	DR £ p	CR £ p	
	Totals				

Part C: Recording and accounting for credit transactions

Further information

The following is a list of account codes.

Sales C	2010
Sales G	2020
Sales E	2030
Sales X	2040
Sales returns C	2310
Sales returns G	2320
Sales returns E	2330
Sales returns X	2340
VAT control account	4000
Creditors ledger control account	0310
Debtors ledger control account	0210

Activity 13.3

On 24 March 20X7, the sales returns day book of Gourmet Supplies Ltd records the fact that credit notes were issued to Anston Mayne and Major John Design in respect of all the purchases they made on 18 March 20X7 (as recorded in Activity 13.1).

Task

Using the account codes given in Activity 13.2, complete the general ledger posting summary form below with the double entry required to record the issue of these credit notes.

GOURMET SUPPLIES LIMITED

General ledger posting summary

JNL ENTRY

Date ....
Prepared by ....
Authorised by ....

No.	Account	Code	DR £ p	CR £ p
Totals				

286

Activity 13.4

(a) The closing balance at the end of an accounting period for Gourmet Supplies Ltd's VAT control account is £12,572.50 CR.

    (i) This means that £12,572.50 is owed by .... to .... (complete the blanks).

    (ii) Does the balance represent an asset or a liability for Gourmet Supplies Ltd?

        Asset / Liability   (circle the correct answer)

(b) The closing balances on the nominal ledger accounts below are credit or debit balances, as indicated. Indicate by circling the correct answer whether the balances represent an asset to the business, a liability of the business, an expense item or revenue earned.

Account	Credit or debit balance				
Sales	CREDIT	Asset	Liability	Expense	Revenue
Sales returns	DEBIT	Asset	Liability	Expense	Revenue
Debtors' ledger control account	DEBIT	Asset	Liability	Expense	Revenue
Discounts allowed	DEBIT	Asset	Liability	Expense	Revenue
Cash	CREDIT	Asset	Liability	Expense	Revenue

Cash sales

5.23 Note that if a cash sale is made, say of ladies' shoes, **this will not pass through the sales ledger** nor the **debtors control account** in the general ledger, and the double entry can be completed in this form.

		£	£
DEBIT	Cash account	X	
CREDIT	VAT account		X
	Sales - ladies' shoes account		X

Key learning points

- The **sales day book** lists the invoices raised by a business when it supplies goods or services on credit. The **sales returns day book** lists the credit notes raised when goods are returned. The sales day book and the sales returns day book are '**books of prime entry**': transactions are recorded in them before being recorded elsewhere.

- **How transactions are entered in the books of prime entry depends upon the accounting system which is used** by the business. Details will be entered from invoices in some systems. In others, information about which orders have been despatched will be entered and the invoices and primary records of sales will be generated by computer from this information.

- **Sales may be analysed** into different categories, according to the information needs of the business and its system of accounting. A **spreadsheet** could be used as a model to produce an analysed sales day book.

- The day book totals for sales and returns are posted to the **nominal ledger debtors control account**, the **VAT control account** and the **sales account**. The amounts owed by individual debtors are entered in the **sales ledger personal accounts** (where these are maintained as **memorandum accounts** separate from the nominal ledger).

Quick quiz

1. What is the purpose of the sales day book?
2. What is the purpose of the sales returns day book?
3. Why do businesses maintain personal accounts in the sales ledger?

Part C: Recording and accounting for credit transactions

4 What is another name for the 'debtors control account'?

5 What is the function of this account?

6 A cash sale will be shown in the sales ledger. True or false?

Answers to quick quiz

1 To record credit sales on a daily basis.

2 To record returns of credit sales on a daily basis.

3 To show who owes what to the business at any given time. This information is not in the sales day book or the debtors control account.

4 The sales ledger control account, or the 'total debtors account'.

5 To record in total the amounts posted to the debtors' individual memorandum accounts in the sales ledger.

6 False. The sales ledger only records credit sales.

Answers to activities

Note. **Answer 13.1 is on the next page.**

Answer 13.2

GOURMET SUPPLIES LIMITED

General ledger posting summary

JNL ENTRY

Date: 18 March 20X7
Prepared by: CCA Technician
Authorised by: ....

No.	Account	Code	DR £ p	CR £ p
	Debtors' ledger control account	0210	733.38	
	Sales C	2010		146.82
	Sales G	2020		310.34
	Sales E	2030		119.97
	Sales X	2040		47.01
	VAT control account	4000		109.24
	Totals		733.38	733.38

Answer 13.1

GOURMET SUPPLIES - SALES DAY BOOK

Date	Invoice number	Customer number	Total	C	G	E	X	VAT
17/3/X7	12060	K02	141-00	58-00	62-00			21-00
17/3/X7	12061	B09	151-62		55-32	62-09	11-63	22-58
17/3/X7	12062	Cancelled						
17/3/X7	12063	P11	104-11		34-47	26-31	27-82	15-51
18/3/X7	12064	A01	141-00		120-00			21-00
18/3/X7	12065	N04	59-07	50-27				8-80
18/3/X7	12066	D06	45-98			31-57	7-56	6-85
18/3/X7	12067	M09	90-60	38-55	38-55			13-50
		TOTAL						

Answer 13.3

GOURMET SUPPLIES LIMITED

General ledger posting summary

JNL ENTRY
Date: 24 March 20X7
Prepared by: CCA Technician
Authorised by: ....

No.	Account	Code	DR £ p	CR £ p
	Debtors' ledger control account	0210		231.60
	Sales Returns C	2310	38.55	
	Sales Returns G	2320	158.55	
	VAT control account	4000	34.50	
Totals			231.60	231.60

Answer 13.4

(a) (i) £12,572.50 is owed by Gourmet Supplies Ltd to HM Customs & Excise.

(ii) The credit balance on the VAT control account represents a liability for Gourmet Supplies Ltd.

(b)

Account	Credit or debit balance?	Answer
Sales	CREDIT	Revenue
Sales returns	DEBIT	Expense
Debtors' ledger control account	DEBIT	Asset
Discounts allowed	DEBIT	Expense
Cash	CREDIT	Liability

Chapter 14 The sales ledger

Chapter topic list

1. Personal accounts for credit customers
2. Recording transactions in the sales ledger
3. The age analysis of debtors and other reports
4. Bad debts

The following study sessions are covered in this chapter

			Syllabus reference
6	(h)	Recognise and describe authorisation procedures	4b
	(i)	Record sales:	
		(i) maintain a manual general and sales ledger	4b
		(ii) prepare, reconcile and understand the purpose of customer statements	4b
	(j)	Communicate efficiently and effectively with customers	4b
7	(a)	Explain the benefits and costs of offering credit facilities to customers	4b
	(b)	Understand the purpose of and prepare an aged debt analysis	4b
	(c)	Understand the purpose of credit limits	4b
	(d)	Recognise the existence and impact of bad debts	4b
	(e)	Record the accounting treatment of bad debts	4b

Part C: Recording and accounting for credit transactions

1 PERSONAL ACCOUNTS FOR CREDIT CUSTOMERS

The need for personal accounts

1.1 We have seen how the sales day book provides a chronological record of the invoices and credit notes sent out by a business to credit customers. In addition to keeping a chronological record of invoices, a business needs a record of how much money each individual credit customer owes, and what this total debt consists of. The need for a **personal account** for each customer is thus a practical one.

(a) A customer might telephone, and ask how much he currently owes. Staff must be able to **tell the customer the state of his account.**

(b) It is a common practice to send out **statements** to credit customers at the end of each month, showing how much they still owe, and itemising new invoices sent out and payments received during the month.

(c) The managers of the business will want to keep a check on the **credit position of an individual customer,** and to ensure that no customer is exceeding his **credit limit** by purchasing more goods.

(d) Perhaps most important is the need to **match payments against debts owed.** If a customer makes a payment, the business must be able to set off the payment against the customer's debt and establish how much he still owes on balance and which particular items are left unpaid.

1.2 **Authorisation**

A business supplying goods on credit has to ensure as far as possible that it will receive payment for those goods. There are three main authorisation procedures which will generally be in place.

(a) Allowing a customer to have a credit account will require authorisation and this will probably require references from suppliers with whom he already has a credit account, and maybe also a reference from his bank.

(b) The customer's credit limit must be authorised, and this will depend upon the information supplied in (a).

(c) Before goods are despatched to a customer, the order may need to be authorised by the credit control dept. If the customer has invoices overdue for payment, it may be decided that no further orders can be accepted until payment is received.

The sales ledger

1.3 **Debtors are people or organisations who owe money to the business.**

> **KEY TERM**
>
> The **sales ledger** contains the individual personal accounts showing what each individual debtor of the business owes. (It is sometimes called the **debtors ledger**.)

1.4 Sales ledger accounts are written up as follows.

DEBIT   When invoices are entered in the **sales day book**, they are subsequently also made in the **debit** side of the relevant customer account in the sales ledger.

CREDIT When entries are made in the **cash book** in respect of payments received from customers, or in the **sales returns day book** for goods returned, they are made in the **credit** side of the relevant customer account.

1.5 The entries recorded in a customer's personal account can be represented by a 'T'-account, as follows.

CUSTOMER ACCOUNT   CU01

On the debit side	£	On the credit side	£
Invoices sent out inc VAT	X	Sales returns (credit notes) inc VAT	X
		Payments received	X
		Discounts allowed	X

1.6 Each customer account is given a reference or code number (CU01 above). This reference can be used in the sales day book. In a manual ledger, a page in the sales ledger would normally be allocated for each account in the ledger.

1.7 Here is an example of how a sales ledger account can be laid out.

COOK & CO   A/c no: C124

Date	Details	£	Date	Details	£
1.1.X7	Balance b/d	250.00			
10.1.X7	Sales - SDB 48				
	(invoice 0249)	343.92	11.1.X7	Balance c/d	593.92
		593.92			593.92
11.1.X7	Balance b/d	593.92			

- The **debit** side of this personal account shows amounts owed by Cook & Co.
- When Cook pays some of the money it owes it will be entered into the cash book (receipts) and subsequently recorded in the **credit** side of the personal account.

For example, if Cook had paid £250 on 10 January 20X7, it would appear as follows.

COOK & CO   A/c no: C124

Date	Details	£	Date	Details	£
1.1.X7	Balance b/d	250.00			
10.1.X7	Sales - SDB 48		10.1.X7	Cash	250.00
	(invoice 0249)	343.92	11.1.X7	Balance c/d	343.92
		593.92			593.92
11.1.X7	Balance b/d	343.92			

The opening balance owed by Cook & Co on 11 January 20X7 is now £343.92 instead of £593.92, because of the £250 receipt which came in on 10 January 20X7.

Personal accounts as memorandum accounts

1.8 As we have seen, in manual systems of accounting and in **some** computerised accounting systems, the personal accounts of customers **do not form part of the double entry system of bookkeeping**. This is because the personal accounts include details of transactions which have already been summarised in day books and posted to ledger accounts. For example, sales invoices are recorded in sales and total debtors general ledger accounts, and payments received from debtors are recorded in the cash and total debtors accounts. **The personal**

Part C: Recording and accounting for credit transactions

accounts of customers do not then form part of the double entry system: if they did, transactions would be recorded twice over.

Integrated sales ledger

1.9 But in some computerised systems, **the sales ledger is 'integrated' with the general ledger**. Instead of being maintained as memorandum accounts reflecting the various customer balances making up the total debtors account in the general ledger, individual customers' accounts effectively do form part of the double entry system, and there is **no separate total debtors or debtors control account**. This means that the general ledger posting summary and the sales ledger postings that we saw in Chapter 13 Paragraphs 5.18 and 5.20 could effectively be combined as follows.

SUPER SHOD SHOE SUPPLIES
General ledger posting summary

Account name	Account code	Ref	Dr £	Dr p	Cr £	Cr p
Abbey S	A009	20248	99	28		
Cook & Co	C124	20249	343	92		
Dinham	D249	20251	87	83		
S Jones	J042	20247	202	10		
Mentor	M201	20252	319	65		
Pediform	P041	C2214			34	54
Texas Ltd	T172	20250	202	10		
Sales GB	O1010				168	95
Sales LB	O1020				95	45
Sales GS	O1030				244	42
Sales LS	O1040				474	68
Sales A	O1050				84	50
Returns GB	O1110		29	40		
VAT	70700				181	74
TOTALS			1,284	28	1,284	28

Posted by ......*C.F*...... Date ......*10/1/X7*......

Businesses not needing a sales ledger

1.10 You might think that all but the very smallest businesses will need to maintain a sales ledger. **But even some very large businesses have no credit sales at all.**

(a) Chains of supermarkets which make all of their sales by cash, cheque or plastic card.

(b) Other businesses, such as a defence contractor selling only to a government, may not sell to enough different organisations to make it worthwhile to operate a sales ledger.

2 RECORDING TRANSACTIONS IN THE SALES LEDGER

2.1 Let us now look at a more detailed example of how sales ledger accounts are produced from entries in the **sales and sales returns day books** and from details of cash received from the **cash book**.

14: The sales ledger

2.2 In a computerised system, transactions may be input directly to customer accounts in the sales ledger ('**transaction processing**') or alternatively stored as a **transaction file** to form a part of the next updating run.

2.3 EXAMPLE: SALES LEDGER TRANSACTIONS

Hawkins & Co started trading at the beginning of April. During April, the sales day book and the sales returns day book of Hawkins & Co showed the following transactions.

Sales day book

Date	Name	Invoice ref	Net total £ p	VAT £ p	Gross total £ p
2 April	Turing Machinery Ltd	2512	250.00	43.75	293.75
4 April	G Wright	2513	300.00	52.50	352.50
9 April	G Wright	2514	725.00	126.87	851.87
9 April	Turing Machinery Ltd	2515	620.00	108.50	728.50
10 April	Simpsons Ltd	2516	85.00	14.87	99.87
24 April	Simpsons Ltd	2517	1,440.00	252.00	1,692.00
25 April	Simpsons Ltd	2518	242.00	42.35	284.35
25 April	G Wright	2519	1,248.00	218.40	1,466.40
30 April	Totals		4,910.00	859.24	5,769.24

Sales returns day book

Date	Name	Credit note	Net total £ p	VAT £ p	Gross total £ p
23 April	G Wright	0084	220.00	38.50	258.50
25 April	Turing Machinery Ltd	0085	250.00	43.75	293.75
30 April	Totals		470.00	82.25	552.25

During May, the following payments for goods sold on credit were received.

Payments received

		£ p
7 May	Turing Machinery Ltd	728.50
14 May	G Wright	352.50
14 May	Simpsons Ltd	99.87

We need to show the entries as they would appear in the sales ledger accounts to reflect the above transactions.

2.4 SOLUTION: SALES LEDGER TRANSACTIONS

Sales ledger

TURING MACHINERY LTD

Date	Details	£ p	Date	Details	£ p
2 April	Invoice 2512	293.75	25 April	Credit note 0085	293.75
9 April	Invoice 2515	728.50	7 May	Cash book	728.50

G WRIGHT

Date	Details	£ p	Date	Details	£ p
4 April	Invoice 2513	352.50	23 April	Credit note 0084	258.50
9 April	Invoice 2514	851.87	14 May	Cash book	352.50
25 April	Invoice 2519	1,466.40			

Part C: Recording and accounting for credit transactions

SIMPSONS LTD

Date	Details	£ p	Date	Details	£ p
10 April	Invoice 2516	99.87	14 May	Cash book	99.87
24 April	Invoice 2517	1,692.00			
25 April	Invoice 2518	284.35			

Note how, in this example, we show the sales ledger accounts as **'T'-accounts**, with debits on the left and credits on the right. This is how ledger accounts are usually shown in ledger books in manual accounting systems and the 'T'-account format helps to show the logic of double entry principles.

2.5 However, many computerised accounting systems use a **single-column format**, with **debit** items making up the balance being shown as **negative** and **credit** items being shown as **positive**.

For example, the entries in G Wright's account in the sales ledger might appear as follows in a single-column format.

Sales ledger	A/c name: G Wright	Dr(–)/Cr(+)
4 April	2513	– 352.50
9 April	2514	– 851.87
23 April	0084	+ 258.50
25 April	2519	–1,466.40
14 May	Cash book	+ 352.50

2.6 So far we have recorded Hawkins and Co's transactions in the sales ledger memorandum accounts, but not in the double entry system of the general ledger. In this example, we shall assume that the cash book forms a part of the double entry (rather than being a book of prime entry from which a separate cash account is prepared).

2.7 EXAMPLE: POSTING TRANSACTIONS TO THE GENERAL LEDGER

The **payments received** will be posted as debits in the **cash account**.

CASH BOOK/ACCOUNT (IN THE GENERAL LEDGER)

Date	Details	£ p			£ p
7 May	Turing Mach. Ltd	728.50			
14 May	G Wright	352.50			
14 May	Simpsons Ltd	99.87			

Sales income excluding VAT will be **credits** in the **sales account**.

SALES ACCOUNT

Date	Details	£ p	Date	Details	£ p
			30 April	Sales day book	4,910.00

Sales returns excluding VAT will be **debits** in the **sales returns account**.

SALES RETURNS ACCOUNT

Date	Details	£ p			£ p
30 April	Sales returns day book	470.00			

VAT on sales and **sales returns** will be **credits** and **debits** respectively in the **VAT account**.

VAT ACCOUNT

Date	Details	£ p			£ p
30 April	Sales returns day book	82.25	30 April	Sales day book	859.24

To complete the double entry in the general ledger accounts, we need to post the **total amounts owed** and the **payments received** as the result of credit sales transactions in the period to the **debit** and **credit** side respectively of **total debtors account** in the general ledger.

TOTAL DEBTORS ACCOUNT

Date	Details	£ p	Date	Details	£ p
30 April	Sales day book total	5,769.24	30 April	Sales returns day book total	552.25
			7 May	Cash book	728.50
			14 May	Cash book	452.37
			31 May	Balance c/d	4,036.12
		5,769.24			5,769.24
1 June	Balance b/d	4,036.12			

Note that in this case the two amounts of cash received on 14 May have been added together to give the **daily total** posted to the total debtors account.

2.8 Section summary

	Source	DR	CR
Sales ledger (memorandum a/c)	SDB	Sales (inc VAT)[1]	
	SRDB		Sales returns inc VAT[2]
	CB		Cash received[3]
General ledger (double entry)	SDB	Total debtors (inc VAT)[1]	
	SDB		Sales
	SDB		VAT
	Invoices		
	CB		Total debtors (inc VAT)[3]
	CB	Cash account	
	Cash received		
	SRDB		Total debtors (inc VAT)[2]
	SRDB	Returns account	
	SRDB	VAT	
	Credit notes issued for goods returned		

The total entries in the sales ledger memorandum accounts will equal the correspondingly numbered entries in the general ledger shown above.

2.9 It should be clear to you that you would normally expect to find that the total debtors account has a **debit balance** overall. We will be looking at it in more detail in Chapter 17.

2.10 Sometimes it is easier to see how accounting entries are made by looking at a diagram of the process. The chart on the following page illustrates the process of **sales ledger postings** which we have examined above.

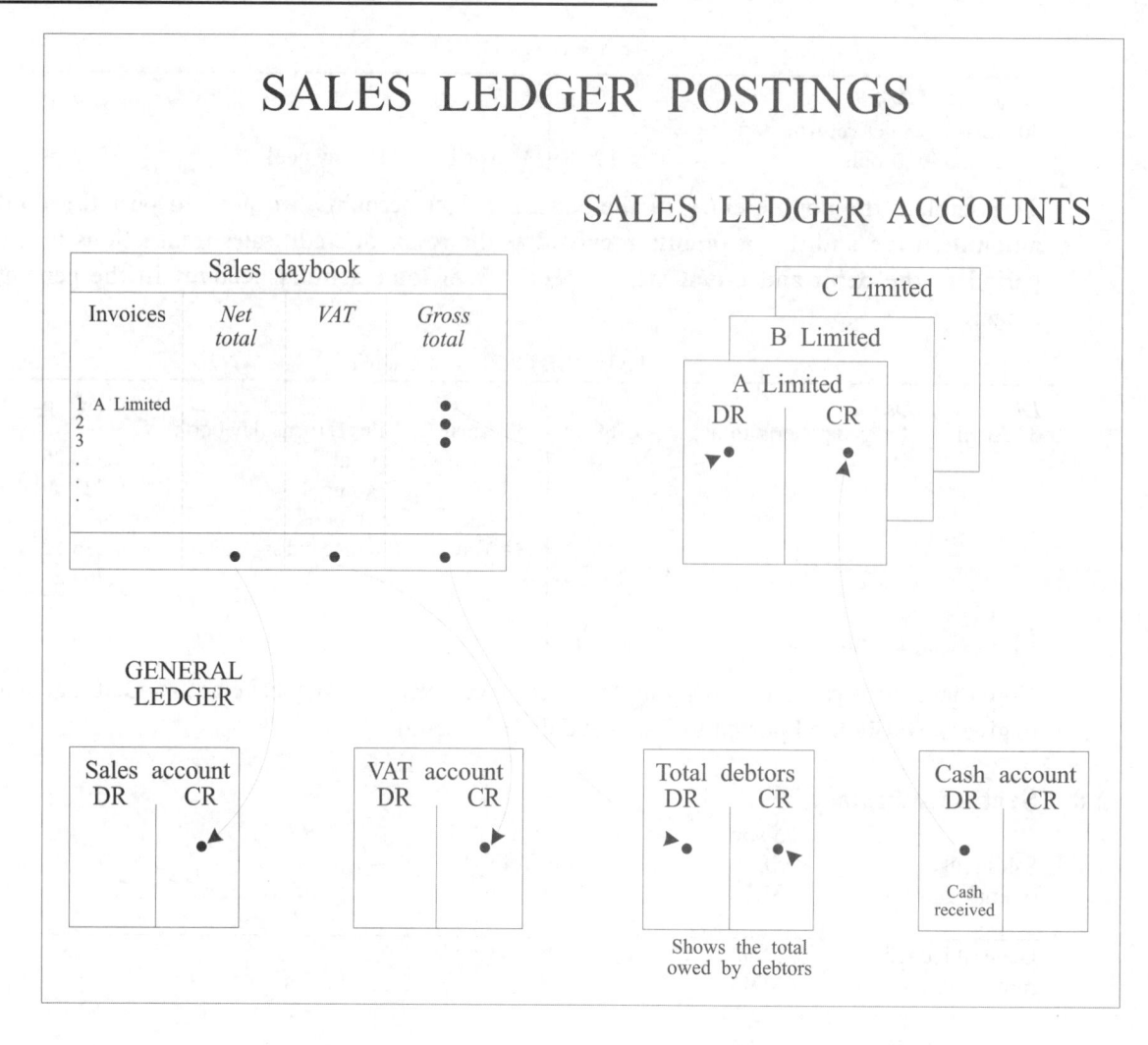

SALES LEDGER POSTINGS

[Diagram: Sales daybook (with columns Invoices, Net total, VAT, Gross total; rows 1 A Limited, 2, 3) posts to Sales Ledger Accounts (A Limited, B Limited, C Limited) and to the General Ledger accounts: Sales account (CR), VAT account (CR), Total debtors account (DR from sales, CR from cash — "Shows the total owed by debtors"), and Cash account (DR – Cash received).]

Checking the sales ledger recording

2.11 Having recorded the sales invoices, credit notes and cash received, we can now check the accuracy of the amounts recorded in the sales ledger memorandum account. This can be done by working out the total of the balances on individual sales ledger accounts and comparing this with the total balance on the general ledger total debtors account.

2.12 In the example of Hawkins & Co, we have balanced the postings to the total debtors account. The balance is £4,036.12. If this balance does not agree with the total of individual account balances, an **error or errors must have been made**. Check this for yourself by balancing the sales ledger accounts in the example.

Discounts allowed and posting to the sales ledger

2.13 We have looked at discounts allowed on sales in Chapter 4 Section 4. We have seen, that

(a) a memorandum column recording the discount allowed is kept in the cash book which has nothing to do with actual monies received.

(b) the discount allowed is posted as a DEBIT to a discounts allowed account and as a CREDIT to the trade debtor and the debtors control account

(c) the cash received and discount allowed accounting entries would ensure that the total debt is cleared.

2.14 EXAMPLE

Pet supplies makes a sale for £1,000 worth of goods to Janice. A 10% discount will be allowed if Janice settles within 10 days. Assuming that Janice settles within 10 days, record the journal entries in the supplier's books.

2.15 SOLUTION

	£	£
DEBIT Trade debtors	1,000	
CREDIT Sales		1,000
Being sale of £1,000 to Janice		
DEBIT Cash	900	
CREDIT Trade debtors		900
Being cash received from Janice in full settlement of the debt, within 10 days of sale		
DEBIT Discount allowed	100	
CREDIT Trade debtors		100

Being discount allowed to Janice for early settlement

Activity 14.1

The company you work for, Hinge and Bracket, has only recently begun to sell goods on credit in a big way. Up until now, the company has run one set of books: the nominal ledger. Every transaction has been entered in the nominal ledger. This is proving unwieldy - it is becoming difficult to chase individual debtors as all the amounts they owe are jumbled together in one account.

In outline only, show a way of accounting for credit transactions which would get round this problem.

Activity 14.2

You are presented with the following transactions from the sales day book and sales returns day book for 1 January 20X7.

SALES DAY BOOK					
Date	Customer account	Invoice number	Goods value £.00	VAT (17½%) £.00	Total £.00
1/1/X7	001	100	72.34	12.66	85.00
1/1/X7	030	101	83.53	14.62	98.15
1/1/X7	001	102	14.46	2.53	16.99
1/1/X7	132	103	17.20	3.01	20.21
1/1/X7	075	104	104.77	18.33	123.10
1/1/X7	099	105	30.40	5.32	35.72
1/1/X7	001	106	64.97	11.37	76.34
Total 1/1/X7			387.67	67.84	455.51

Part C: Recording and accounting for credit transactions

SALES RETURNS DAY BOOK						
Date	Customer account	Credit note	Invoice reference	Goods value £.00	VAT (17½%) £.00	Total £.00
1/1/X7	099	C44	89	301.03	52.68	353.71

Tasks

(a) Post the transactions to the sales ledger accounts provided below.

(b) Set out the double entry for the transactions shown.

(c) Comment on any unusual items resulting from your work in (a) and itemise any additional procedures which you consider necessary. Is there anything which should be brought to your supervisor's attention?

CUSTOMER NAME: Arturo Aski

ACCOUNT 001

ADDRESS: 94 Old Comedy Street, Vaudeville, BR, W. Meds

CREDIT LIMIT: £2,200

Date	Description	Transaction Ref	DR		CR		Balance	
			£	p	£	p	£	p
	Brought forward 1/1/X7						2,050	37

14: The sales ledger

CUSTOMER NAME: Maye West

ADDRESS: 1 Vamping Parade, Holywood, Beds, HW1

CREDIT LIMIT: £1,000

ACCOUNT 030

Date	Description	Transaction Ref	DR £	DR p	CR £	CR p	Balance £	Balance p
Brought forward 1/1/X7							69	33

CUSTOMER NAME: Naguib Mahfouz

ADDRESS: 10 Palace Walk, London NE9

CREDIT LIMIT: £1,500

ACCOUNT 075

Date	Description	Transaction Ref	DR £	DR p	CR £	CR p	Balance £	Balance p
Brought forward 1/1/X7							—	

Part C: Recording and accounting for credit transactions

CUSTOMER NAME: Josef Sveik

ADDRESS: 99 Balkan Row, Aldershot

CREDIT LIMIT: £700

ACCOUNT 099

Date	Description	Transaction Ref	DR £	DR p	CR £	CR p	Balance £	Balance p
	Brought forward 1/1/X7						353	71

CUSTOMER NAME: Grace Chang

ADDRESS: Red Dragon Street, Cardiff, CA4

CREDIT LIMIT: £1,200

ACCOUNT 132

Date	Description	Transaction Ref	DR £	DR p	CR £	CR p	Balance £	Balance p
	Brought forward 1/1/X7						1,175	80

3 THE AGE ANALYSIS OF DEBTORS AND OTHER REPORTS

The age analysis of debtors

3.1 It is important for a business to know what customer sales ledger balances are made up of so that **disagreements** with the customer and other queries can be resolved quickly. There also needs to be a way of knowing whether some of the invoices are **long overdue** so that those invoices can be followed up with the customer.

3.2 If a sales ledger consists of a large number of accounts, it would be a laborious and time-consuming process going through the details of each account to look for items which ought to be followed up. A lot of time can be saved by summarising the 'age' of the items in the various sales ledger accounts in a single schedule. This is achieved by what is called an **age analysis of debtors**.

> **KEY TERM**
>
> An **age analysis of debtors** breaks down the debtor balances on the sales ledger into different periods of outstanding debt.

What does the age analysis look like?

3.3 An age analysis of debtors will look very like the schedule illustrated below. The analysis splits up the total balance on the account of each customer across different columns according to the dates of the transactions which make up the total balance. Thus, the amount of an invoice which was raised 14 days ago will form part of the figure in the column headed 'up to 30 days', while an invoice which was raised 36 days ago will form part of the figure in the column headed 'up to 60 days'. (In the schedule below, 'up to 60 days' is used as shorthand for 'more than 30 days but less than 60 days'.)

HEATH LIMITED

AGE ANALYSIS OF DEBTORS AS AT 31.1.X8

Account number	Customer name	Balance	Up to 30 days	Up to 60 days	Up to 90 days	Over 90 days
B004	Brilliant Ltd	804.95	649.90	121.00	0.00	34.05
E008	Easimat Ltd	272.10	192.90	72.40	6.80	0.00
H002	Hampstead Ltd	1,818.42	0.00	0.00	724.24	1,094.18
M024	Martlesham Ltd	284.45	192.21	92.24	0.00	0.00
N030	Nyfen Ltd	1,217.54	1,008.24	124.50	0.00	84.80
T002	Todmorden College	914.50	842.00	0.00	72.50	0.00
T004	Tricorn Ltd	94.80	0.00	0.00	0.00	94.80
V010	Volux Ltd	997.06	413.66	342.15	241.25	0.00
Y020	Yardsley Smith & Co	341.77	321.17	20.60	0.00	0.00
Totals		6,745.59	3,620.08	772.89	1,044.79	1,307.83
Percentage		100%	53.7%	11.4%	15.5%	19.4%

3.4 An age analysis of debtors can be prepared manually or by computer. **Computerisation does make the job a lot easier.**

How is the age analysis used?

3.5 As already suggested, the age analysis of debtors may be used to **help decide what action to take about older debts**. Going down each column in turn starting from the column furthest

Part C: Recording and accounting for credit transactions

to the right and working across, we can see that there are some rather old debts which ought to be investigated.

(a) **Correspondence** may of course already exist in relation to some of these items.

(b) Perhaps some older invoices are still **in dispute**.

(c) Perhaps some debtors are known to be in **financial difficulties**. (If there are newer invoices also for customers who could be in financial difficulties, we should perhaps be asking whether we ought to be continuing to supply goods to these customers.)

3.6 We can see from the above age analysis of Heath Ltd's debtors that the relatively high proportion of debts over 90 days (19.4%) is largely due to the debts of Hampstead Ltd. Other customers with debts of this age are Brilliant Ltd, Nyfen Ltd and Tricorn Ltd.

3.7 As well as providing information on the state of individual debtors' accounts, the age analysis of debtors may be used to give us a broader picture of the total debtors of the business. If there seems to be a high percentage of debts which are older than the usual payment terms allowed by the business, we may question whether the **credit control department**, one of whose jobs is to chase up slow payers, is performing its role properly. It is vital to contact debtors where there are old unpaid debts. Sometimes it can happen that the invoice was simply mislaid or they did not receive it, or they thought it was paid. If they are having trouble paying it, get a firm commitment from them regarding when they will make payment. If the accounts department are not co-operating, contact the person who placed the order.

3.8 Sometimes, a **column listing customer credit limits** will appear on the age analysis of debtors. This will make it easy to see which customers (if any) have exceeded or are close to exceeding their current credit limit.

Other computerised reports

3.9 **Computerisation of sales ledger processing** also allows a number of other reports to be printed out from the information held on the ledger, such as those outlined in the remainder of this section below. Access to sales ledger reports will probably be restricted, so that reports can only be obtained by authorised staff members whose password will allow them access.

Sales day book

3.10 **Sales day book listings** provide a way of keeping track of all of the items entered in the sales ledger. Typically, the information listed will include the following.

- The date of the item
- The account reference
- A transaction reference (eg invoice number)
- Type of transaction (eg invoice, credit note or adjustment)
- Net total before VAT
- VAT
- Gross total

If the sales ledger is not integrated with the general ledger then the sales day book listings can be used as a **posting summary** to the general ledger.

Statements of account

3.11 **Statements of account** are sent to customers at the end of each month to tell them how much they owe the organisation, with details of the transactions involved.

3.12 At any time in the month, it will be possible to obtain for internal use a printout of the same details as are included in a **statement of account**. This may be needed from time to time to check details of transactions.

VAT analysis

3.13 If the rates of VAT (or other purchase taxes, in other countries) applying to the goods and/or services which a firm sells vary, then this report will show how much **output tax** has been invoiced at each of the different rates which apply. Even if different rates do not apply, in the European Union regulations require that statistics are submitted in **EU Intrastat** to show how much VAT-able supplies were made to other EU countries.

Sales analysis

3.14 Sales analysis reports allow the organisation to **analyse sales** in any way that it wants. The types of analysis required must be provided for when the system is set up for use by the organisation. (This is called the **configuration of the system**.) Among the more useful types of analysis could be those by product type, by area, by customer, or by sales representative.

3.15 EXAMPLE: SALES ANALYSIS

Purestream Water Filters Ltd produces water filters for domestic and industrial applications. When it bought a computerised sales ledger package two years ago, it configured the system so that transaction codes take the form product type / product number / sales representative / invoice number. Thus, DOM/220/RKP/33141 refers to a transaction for the sale of a domestic water filter, model number 220, sold by the sales representative with initials RKP on invoice number 33141.

Purestream can now easily get a printout run off of sales by product type, by product number or by sales representative. Other distinctions might be reflected in the account number. For example, if accounts for all sales in Scotland are prefixed with an 'S', it will be a straightforward matter for the computer to summarise all sales made in Scotland in any period.

An analysis of **sales by sales representative** might look like the illustration below.

```
Purestream Water Filters Ltd - Sales ledger
Sales ledger analysis
08-MAR-X7                                    Page 1
SALES REP                                         £
AB                                           463.80
KL                                         1,314.55
AMM                                          454.60
RN                                         1,123.65
RKP                                          881.70
Total                                      4,238.30
```

List of customer accounts

3.16 A **list of customer accounts** summarises all debtors' accounts on the ledger. It will usually be possible to select for analysis all the accounts which have exceeded their credit limit.

Part C: Recording and accounting for credit transactions

Lists such as this present **more selectively** information which is included in the full age analysis of debtors which was discussed earlier.

Customer mailing lists

3.17 The list of customer names and addresses held on the sales ledger is likely to be a **powerful marketing tool**, and may well be more up-to-date than mailing lists maintained on separate database packages for marketing purposes. If the firm wants to send a mailshot to all customers, or more selectively to all customers with turnover above say £20,000 per year, then the appropriate name/address labels can easily be printed out.

4 BAD DEBTS

4.1 For some debts on the ledger, there may be little or no prospect of the business being paid, usually for one of the following reasons.

(a) The customer has gone **bankrupt.**

(b) The customer is **out of business.**

(c) **Dishonesty** may be involved.

(d) Customers in another country might be prevented from paying by the unexpected introduction of **foreign exchange control** restrictions by their country's government during the credit period.

4.2 For one reason or another, therefore, a business might decide to give up expecting payment and to **write the debt off as a 'lost cause'**.

Bad debts written off: ledger accounting entries

4.3 For bad debts written off, there is a **bad debts account** in the general ledger. The double-entry bookkeeping is fairly straightforward. When it is decided that a particular debt will not be paid, the customer is no longer called an outstanding debtor, and becomes a bad debt.

DEBIT   Bad debts account (expense)
CREDIT   Total debtors account

A **write off of any bad debt will need the authorisation of a senior official in the organisation.**

4.4 EXAMPLE: BAD DEBTS WRITTEN OFF

At 1 October 20X7 a business had total outstanding debts of £8,600. During the year to 30 September 20X8, the following transactions took place.

(a) Credit sales amounted to £44,000.

(b) Payments from various debtors amounted to £49,000.

(c) Two debts, for £180 and £420 (both including VAT) were declared bad. These are to be written off.

We need to prepare the total debtors account and the bad debts account for the year.

4.5 SOLUTION: BAD DEBTS WRITTEN OFF

TOTAL DEBTORS ACCOUNT

Date	Details	£	Date	Details	£
1.10.X7	Balance b/d	8,600		Cash	49,000
	Sales for the year	44,000	30.9.X8	Bad debts	180
			30.9.X8	Bad debts	420
			30.9.X8	Balance c/d	3,000
		52,600			52,600
	Balance b/d	3,000			

BAD DEBTS

Date	Details	£	Date	Details	£
30.9.X8	Debtors	180	30.9.X8	Balance	600
30.9.X8	Debtors	420			
		600			600

4.6 In the sales ledger, personal accounts of the customers whose debts are bad will be **taken off the ledger**. The business should then take steps to ensure that it does not sell goods to those customers again.

Bad debts and VAT

4.7 A business can claim relief from VAT on the following bad debts.
- **At least six months old** (from the time of supply)
- **Written off** in the accounts of the business

Both conditions must be satisfied.

4.8 VAT bad debt relief is accounted for as follows:

DEBIT	VAT account	17.5	
	Bad debts	100.0	
CREDIT	Total debtors		117.5

4.9 EXAMPLE: BAD DEBTS AND VAT

If both the debts written off in Paragraph 4.5 were inclusive of VAT, the accounts would look as follows.

TOTAL DEBTORS ACCOUNT - no change

BAD DEBTS

Date	Details	£	Date	Details	£
30.9.X8	Debtors	153.19	30.9.X8	Balance	510.64
30.9.X8	Debtors	357.45			
		510.64			510.64

VAT ACCOUNT (part)

Date	Details	£	Date	Details	£
30.9.X8	Debtors	26.81			
30.9.X8	Debtors	62.55			

Part C: Recording and accounting for credit transactions

Key learning points

- The **sales ledger contains the personal accounts** of credit customers of the business. An account must be kept for each customer so that the business always has a full record of how much each customer owes and what items the debt is made up of.

- A customer's account in the sales ledger will normally show a debit balance: the customer owes money to the business and is therefore a debtor of the business.

- It is common for customers' personal accounts to be maintained separately from the nominal (or 'impersonal') ledger, as 'memorandum' accounts. Sales ledger postings then do not form part of the double entry in the system of bookkeeping being used. Instead, a total debtors' or sales ledger control account is maintained in the nominal ledger to keep track of the total of the amounts which make up the entries in the individual personal accounts.

- The age **analysis of debts** is useful to a credit controller wishing to decide on which debts to chase up. It also provides a general guide as to whether the debts of a business are being collected quickly enough. Various other useful reports may be printed out from a **computerised sales ledger package**.

- Some debts may need to be written off as 'bad debts' because there is no real prospect of them being paid.

Quick quiz

1. What does the sales ledger contain?
2. In manual accounting systems the personal accounts of customers do not form part of the double entry system. True or false?
3. How might you check the accuracy of the amounts recorded in the sales ledger?
4. What is the function of an age analysis of debtors?

Answers to quick quiz

1. The personal accounts of customers.
2. True.
3. Work out the total of the balances on the individual sales ledger accounts and compare this with the total balance on the debtors control account.
4. It breaks down the debtor balances in the sales ledger into different periods of outstanding debt.

Answers to activities

Answer 14.1

Tutorial note. If you could not begin to answer this question, you have not really got the point of the chapter! There is no point learning the mechanics of a process unless you know what it is *for*.

The situation describes one of the basic reasons for setting up a sales ledger system.

Your answer should have mentioned that you would keep a set of inter-related record books, rather than just the nominal ledger. The key record books which you would require are as follows.

(a) The *nominal ledger* (as at present), where the double entry of a transaction is recorded. However, instead of posting individual amounts due from debtors on each invoice to a single account in this ledger, you should consider setting up a separate sales ledger to record the detail and simply post a monthly total to the sales ledger control account in the nominal ledger.

(b) The *sales ledger*, which is a memorandum ledger divided into individual customer accounts. This will enable you to keep track of your dealings with each customer. You might also have suggested the use of a sales day book.

(c) A *sales day book* is used as the book of prime entry for recording the details of sales invoices raised by the company. (A book of prime entry is a book where entries are made straight from source documents, rather than posted from other records. The purpose of the whole process described here is largely to prevent the use of the nominal ledger as a book of prime entry.)

A thorough solution to this exercise might have identified *how* and *when* postings are made to each of the above books.

(a) As soon as invoices are raised (daily/weekly), details are posted to the sales day book.

(b) From the sales day book, the total of each invoice is posted to the relevant customer's account in the sales ledger.

(c) When cash is received in settlement of debts, it is recorded as cash received in the cash book (a book of prime entry) and posted to the credit of individual accounts in the sales ledger. The sales ledger will show the balance outstanding from each customer, together with a transaction history, which may be useful.

(d) At the end of each accounting period, the nominal ledger can be updated. This will involve the following procedures.

   (i) A debit to the sales ledger control account from the gross sales total in the SDB.

   (ii) A credit to the VAT control account (or output VAT account) from the VAT total in the SDB.

   (iii) A credit to the sales (revenue) account from the net sales total in the SDB.

   (iv) A debit to the cash account from the cash received total in the cash book.

   (v) A credit to the sales ledger control account from the cash received total in the cash book.

(e) Finally, to ensure that you have not missed anything, you must check that the following.

   (i) The closing balance in the cash book agrees with the cash account balance in the nominal ledger.

   (ii) The total of the individual account balances in the sales ledger agrees with the sales ledger control account balance in the nominal ledger.

Part C: Recording and accounting for credit transactions

Answer 14.2

(a)

CUSTOMER NAME: Arturo Aski
ACCOUNT 001
ADDRESS: 94 Old Comedy Street, Vaudeville, 1BR, W. Meds
CREDIT LIMIT: £2,200

Date	Description	Transaction Ref	DR £	DR p	CR £	CR p	Balance £	Balance p
Brought forward 1/1/X7							2,050	37
1/1/X7	Inv	100	85	00			2,135	37
1/1/X7	Inv	102	16	99			2,152	36
1/1/X7	Inv	106	76	34			2,228	70

CUSTOMER NAME: Maye West
ACCOUNT 030
ADDRESS: 1 Vamping Parade, Holywood, Beds, HW1
CREDIT LIMIT: £1,000

Date	Description	Transaction Ref	DR £	DR p	CR £	CR p	Balance £	Balance p
Brought forward 1/1/X7							69	33
1/1/X7	Inv	101	98	15			167	48

CUSTOMER NAME: Naguib Mahfouz

ADDRESS: 10 Palace Walk, London NE9

CREDIT LIMIT: £1,500

ACCOUNT 075

Date	Description	Transaction Ref	DR £	DR p	CR £	CR p	Balance £	Balance p
Brought forward 1/1/X7								
1/1/X7	Inv	104	123	10			123	10

CUSTOMER NAME: Josef Sveik

ADDRESS: 99 Balkan Row, Aldershot

CREDIT LIMIT: £700

ACCOUNT 099

Date	Description	Transaction Ref	DR £	DR p	CR £	CR p	Balance £	Balance p
Brought forward 1/1/X7							353	71
1/1/X7	Inv	105	35	72			389	43
1/1/X7	Cred	C44			353	71	35	72

Part C: Recording and accounting for credit transactions

CUSTOMER NAME:	*Grace Chang*				ACCOUNT
ADDRESS:	*Red Dragon Street, Cardiff, CA4*				132
CREDIT LIMIT:	£1,200				

Date	Description	Transaction Ref	DR		CR		Balance	
			£	p	£	p	£	p
Brought forward 1/1/X7							1,175	80
1/1/X7	Inv	103	20	21			1,196	01

(b) *Double entry*

The sales ledger (ie the list of credit-related transactions analysed by customer) is a memorandum account.

So, the *double entry* from the sales day book and sales returns day book (which you should be able to recall from Session 13) is as follows.

				£	£
(i)	DEBIT	Sales ledger control account		455.51	
	CREDIT	Sales			387.67
		VAT control account			67.84
				455.51	455.51
(ii)	DEBIT	Sales returns		301.03	
		VAT control account		52.68	
	CREDIT	Sales ledger control account			353.71
				353.71	353.71

(c) *Additional items*

(i) Did you check the sales return to the original invoice?

(ii) More importantly, did you notice that Arturo Aski (customer 001) has now exceeded his credit limit? How can this have slipped through the net?

(1) The customer may have told the person who took the order that a cheque was 'in the post'.
(2) The invoice might have been given the incorrect account code.
(3) The person receiving the order might not have checked the customer's credit status.
(4) The credit limit may have been raised, but you have not yet been told about it.

In any case, the matter should be referred to your boss for checking.

(iii) Grace Chang has an outstanding balance of £1,196.01. When she next makes an order, the account must be checked to see that she has reduced the balance outstanding, as it is near her credit limit. In any case, you may wish to monitor the account to ensure that she is not having cashflow problems (and therefore represents a risk to you). If her business is expanding and she is settling debts promptly (which you will be able to ascertain by looking at the ledger history), it may be appropriate to review her credit limit.

Chapter 15 Purchase and purchase returns day books

Chapter topic list

1. What is the purchase day book?
2. What is the purchase returns day book?
3. Entering purchase transactions in the day books
4. Coding data
5. Posting the day book totals

The following study sessions are covered in this chapter

			Syllabus reference
8	(d)	Record transactions in a purchase day book and a purchase returns day book	5a
	(e)	Code purchases and supplier records and data	5a

Part C: Recording and accounting for credit transactions

1 WHAT IS THE PURCHASE DAY BOOK?

1.1 A business needs to keep track of **all of its purchase transactions** together so that it knows how much it owes to particular suppliers at any one time.

   (a) A business will probably receive a number of invoices (with perhaps some credit notes) from many of its suppliers each month. It will be simpler in administrative terms if the business allows the amount it owes to the supplier to build up and then **to make a single payment** to each supplier monthly rather than to pay the supplier separately for each invoice.

   (b) The business is not likely to want to pay suppliers' invoices immediately on receipt of each invoice. A supplier's terms of business will probably allow the business some time to pay (say, 30 days or perhaps 60 days). It makes sense for the business to take advantage of these terms and **to pay close to the end of the credit period** of credit which the supplier allows.

   (c) A business will want to keep a **record of the total purchases** which it makes in each period (for example, each month, each quarter or each year).

1.2 Taking advantage of suppliers' allowed periods of credit will help the 'cash flow' position of the business because the business will be able to hold on to the money due to the supplier for longer. If the business pays its suppliers earlier than it needs to, it may incur either of the following.

   - Pay more interest on the larger bank overdraft it will need
   - Lose interest on a positive amount of cash instead of an overdraft

1.3 The first step in the process of record-keeping which meets the needs discussed above is the **recording of the source documents** - the suppliers' invoices and credit notes - in the **purchase day book**.

The function of the purchase day book

1.4 If you understand the function of the sales day book which we discussed in Chapter 13, then you should have little difficulty in understanding what the purchase day book does.

> **KEY TERM**
>
> The **purchase day book** is used to keep a list of all of the invoices received from suppliers of goods and services to the business. Like the sales day book, it is a 'book of prime entry' or a 'primary record' and not a ledger account.

We shall look later in the chapter at how the information collected in the purchase day book is posted in the ledger by the double entry system of bookkeeping.

> **Exam alert**
>
> As well as numerical questions, you may be asked about the *function* of the day books. Try Activity 15.1 below.

15: Purchase and purchase returns day books

Activity 15.1

(a) Which one of the following would you expect to see in a purchase day book?

    (i) Cash payments
    (ii) Invoices received from suppliers
    (iii) Cash purchases
    (iv) Personal accounts
    (v) Purchase ledger control accounts

(b) What is the double entry for posting invoices for goods received on credit?

(c) What is a debit note?

1.5 EXAMPLE: PURCHASE DAY BOOK

An extract from a purchase day book might look like the example below, for Megatype Printers Ltd.

Date	Ref	Supplier name	Supplier a/c no	Total before VAT £	VAT £	Invoice total £
10.1.X7	1423	V Princely	4009	152.00	26.60	178.60
	1424	Grantcroft Ltd	5020	28.00	4.90	32.90
	1425	Midnorth Electric plc	4010	116.80	20.44	137.24
	1426	Hartley & Co	5008	100.00	17.50	117.50
	1427	Cardright Ltd	3972	278.00	48.65	326.65
				674.80	118.09	792.89

1.6 The purchase invoices for any one day will be from lots of different suppliers and they are therefore not sequentially numbered. Some organisations assign **sequential numbers to purchase invoices** (using a stamp or a sticker) as Megatype Printers Ltd has (1423 – 1427). This can help to ensure that all purchase invoices are included in the records.

2 WHAT IS THE PURCHASE RETURNS DAY BOOK?

2.1 You should by now have no difficulty in saying what the purchase returns day book is. Just as customers may return goods to us, for which we will issue a credit note, we may return goods to suppliers and will expect to be issued with credit notes by the supplier.

KEY TERM

The **purchase returns day book** lists credit notes received in respect of purchase returns in chronological order.

Columns in the purchase returns day book will record similar details to those in the purchase day book illustrated in Paragraph 1.5 above.

2.2 Do goods have to be accepted back by the supplier?

(a) A business might return goods to suppliers if they are **faulty** or **damaged** and would expect a credit note for them.

(b) Goods which have been purchased on a '**sale or return**' basis will be returned if they cannot be sold.

(c) If goods have been ordered by the business and are in good condition but are **surplus to the requirements** of the purchasing business, it is up to the supplier whether he agrees to accept them as returns and to issue a credit note.

2.3 Quite often a business will not keep a separate purchase returns day book but will record credit notes for goods returned as a negative in the purchase day book.

Activity 15.2

Which of the following cases would you classify as a purchase return by your business? (*Hint:* there may be more than one right answer.)

(a) Goods purchased from you by a customer and returned.

(b) You have been billed twice, by accident, for a single amount of goods, and you return the superfluous purchase invoice.

(c) You have been delivered some goods which are faulty and you send them back. You have posted the invoice received in respect of the goods.

(d) A customer sends back some sub-standard goods to you.

(e) A supplier sends back some goods to you which you have delivered there by mistake, thinking the supplier was in fact a customer.

(f) An item of stock is damaged in a fire at your warehouse and, because you cannot use it any more, you have to go back to the original supplier and order a replacement.

(g) You question an invoice because you have been billed for items which you have not ordered, and which you have not received.

(h) You have been delivered a quantity of goods in excess of your requirements. The supplier agrees that you can return them.

3 ENTERING PURCHASE TRANSACTIONS IN THE DAY BOOKS

3.1 The writing up of the purchase day book and the purchase returns day book will be a similar procedure to the writing up of the sales day book and the sales returns day book which was discussed in detail in Chapter 13.

(a) In a completely **manual system** of accounting, invoice details will be entered in the purchase day book and credit note details in the purchase returns day book, by hand.

(b) In a system of accounting which uses a **computerised purchase ledger** module, entering purchase invoices will be done by entering details onto the computer records, probably through a keyboard and visual display unit. In a menu-based system, entering purchase invoices will be one of the options offered in the purchase ledger menu system.

Analysis of purchases

3.2 As well as the details shown in the purchase day book above at Paragraph 1.5 (the date, a transaction reference number, supplier name, supplier account number, the net total before VAT, VAT and the gross total) many purchase day books have further columns which split the purchases into different categories.

3.3 EXAMPLE: ANALYSING PURCHASES

We may add appropriate columns to the information from the purchase day book at Paragraph 1.5.

First of all, we need further information on the purchases. Megatype Printers Ltd makes purchases of raw materials for stock which include paper, card and ink. The company wants to analyse its other purchases into 'electricity' and 'other' categories. The purchases made on 10 January 20X7 consisted of the following.

Ref	Supplier name	Supplier a/c no	Details
1423	V Princeley	4009	Paper
1424	Grantcroft Ltd	5020	Ink
1425	Midnorth Electric plc	4010	Electricity
1426	Hartley & Co	5008	Desk fans for administrative office
1427	Cardright Ltd	3972	Card

The invoices might be analysed in the purchase day book or equivalent computer listing as follows (we have omitted the column for supplier name, which can be identified from the supplier account number).

PURCHASE DAY BOOK
Date: 10.1.X7

Ref	Supplier	Net total £	VAT £	Gross total £	Paper £	Card £	Ink £	Electricity £	Other £
1423	4009	152.00	26.60	178.60	152.00				
1424	5020	28.00	4.90	32.90			28.00		
1425	4010	116.80	20.44	137.24				116.80	
1426	5008	100.00	17.50	117.50					100.00
1427	3972	278.00	48.65	326.65		278.00			
		674.80	118.09	792.89	152.00	278.00	28.00	116.80	100.00

Note that the analysis columns show amounts *exclusive* of VAT.

3.4 How a purchase is analysed will depend upon the nature of the business and what forms its stock. In another kind of business than printing, for example a television and hi-fi shop, purchases of paper would not be treated as purchases of stocks since paper is not something which that business trades in. It is probable that paper purchased by such a business is for office use, and its cost will then be shown as office expenses or administrative expenses.

3.5 Some businesses keep separate day books for stock purchases and for expenses. The latter type of day book may be called the **expenses day book**.

3.6 Some businesses may wish to analyse purchases for stock so that they know how much of different kinds of item the business is purchasing.

3.7 In Chapter 13, we looked at how a spreadsheet model could be used to create the analysis of information desired in the sales day book.

(a) **A spreadsheet is** created in exactly the same way to produce a purchase day book.

(b) Alternatively, an analysed sales day book and an analysed purchase day book might both be facilities which are available in a **computerised accounting package**. The principles by which the package software presents the information will be very similar to that of a spreadsheet.

4 CODING DATA

4.1 In Chapter 13 we have dealt with the importance of coding and looked at types of codes and how these can be used in the context of a sales system. You may look back to Chapter 13 to refresh your memory if necessary.

Coding in the purchase ledger

4.2 Supplier invoices will have the supplier code on, but they will need to be allocated relevant codes by the purchasing company.

In a purchase system, the most obvious examples of codes are as follows:

- Supplier account number
- Product or service number
- Purchase invoices sequence number

4.3 The supplier account coding will be a method for allocating a unique number to each supplier so that even if two suppliers have the same name, these can be distinguished. The supplier account may be set up so that the location of the supplier can be identified. This would be relevant where one supplier may be supplying from more than one location.

4.4 The product or service code would identify the type of product or service as a particular supplier may supply more than one type of product. Identifying the different products via separate codes will enable to company to build controls when posting the general ledger. For example, via the use of appropriate codes, controls can be incorporated in a general ledger system to ensure that product purchases are posted in the correct product stock accounts.

4.5 A sequential numbering of purchase invoices, may be adopted in addition to the above coding system to ensure completeness and help prevent fraud.

5 POSTING THE DAY BOOK TOTALS

5.1 We have seen above how the details of purchase transactions are entered into the purchase day book. We have not gone into as much detail as with the sales day book which was dealt with in Chapter 13, because the processes involved in writing up the two different day books for sales and purchases are very similar. Look back to Chapter 13 if you are unclear as to the necessary procedures and the use of the day books.

5.2 In this section, we look at the recording of the information in the purchase ledger and the **posting** of it from the purchase day book to the purchase ledger and the general ledger. This step is very important for you to understand from an accounting point of view. It is, however, very similar indeed to what we saw for sales.

Recording transactions in personal accounts for creditors

5.3 Early in this chapter, we explained the need to keep a record of all the purchase invoices which a business receives so that it has a **cumulative record of what it owes to each supplier,** and then we went on to see how the purchase and purchase returns day books are used to list all of the invoices and credit notes (respectively) which the business receives.

5.4 Why do the day books not meet the needs of the business for a cumulative record of what it owes to suppliers? The answer is that they do not because they provide only a listing of purchases transactions in **chronological order**. For a business of some size, the chronological record could involve large numbers of purchase invoices and credit notes each day or each week. It will not be practicable, for all but the very smallest businesses, for firms to work out from the day books alone how much they owe any particular supplier.

5.5 As on the sales side of the business where we have a sales ledger in which individual 'personal' accounts are maintained for each individual debtor, so on the purchases side of the business, the **purchase ledger** (or 'creditors ledger' or 'bought ledger') **will contain personal accounts for each trade creditor or supplier of the business.**

5.6 As each purchase transaction is recorded in the day books, it is also entered in the personal purchase ledger account of the supplier concerned. The personal accounts maintained in the purchase ledger are **memorandum** accounts, not a part of the double entry system, except in some computerised accounting systems which integrate the purchase ledger with the general ledger.

Posting totals to the general ledger: double entry recording of purchases

5.7 In the general ledger a **total creditors account** (or 'purchase ledger control account') will be maintained to record **in total** the amounts which are posted individually to the creditors' personal accounts in the purchase ledger.

5.8 If a business purchases something on credit from a supplier, the double entry will be as follows.

(a) A **credit** to the total creditors account (the 'control account')

(b) A **debit** to either (i) or (ii) below

   (i) Purchases, or expenses, depending on whether the item is a purchase for stock or an expense (such as office stationery, electricity, sundry expenses)

   (ii) Fixed assets (if the item is capital expenditure)

5.9 We can show the basic double entry as follows.

		£	£
DEBIT	Purchases/expenses account	X	
CREDIT	Total creditors account		X

5.10 There will be a different **expense ledger account** for each expense category shown in the profit and loss account of the business and also for capital expenditure on fixed assets.

VAT and purchases

5.11 In most businesses part of the amount due to the creditors is input VAT which the suppliers charge to the purchasing business. While the VAT which the business owes to suppliers is a part of the total amount the business owes to its creditors, the other side of the double entry in respect of the amounts of VAT invoiced by suppliers is a **decrease** in the liability of the business to pay over VAT to HM Customs & Excise and so a debit to the VAT (control) account in the general ledger.

5.12 The double entry will therefore have the following form.

		£	£
DEBIT	Purchases/expenses account	X	
	VAT account	X	
CREDIT	Total creditors account		X

Part C: Recording and accounting for credit transactions

5.13 When we wish to record our return of goods which have been recorded as purchases, we want to 'reverse' the transaction (or the relevant part of the transaction) as it was recorded in the books when we recorded the purchase. The form of the double entry for purchase returns (credit notes received) will be as follows.

		£	£
DEBIT	Total creditors account	X	
CREDIT	VAT account		X
	Purchases/expenses account		X

5.14 EXAMPLE: POSTING PURCHASES AND RETURNS

Show the double entry ledger postings for the purchases made by Megatype Printers Ltd on 10 January 20X7. As well as the purchases shown at Paragraph 1.5, you are additionally informed that the following credit note (in respect of damaged paper) is shown in the purchase returns day book of Megatype Printers Ltd for 10 January 20X7.

RDB07

Ref	Supplier a/c no.	Net total £	VAT £	Gross total £
C014	4009	30.00	5.25	35.25

5.15 SOLUTION: POSTING PURCHASES AND RETURNS

Firstly we shall show the posting summary for the purchases. Check that you can see how the necessary information is derived from the analysed day book shown at Paragraph 3.3.

		£	£
DEBIT	Paper account	152.00	
	Card account	278.00	
	Ink account	28.00	
	Electricity account	116.80	
	Other expenses account	100.00	
	VAT account	118.09	
CREDIT	Total creditors account		792.89
		792.89	792.89

And now the purchase return.

		£	£
DEBIT	Total creditors account	35.25	
CREDIT	VAT account		5.25
	Paper account		30.00
		35.25	35.25

Megatype Printers Ltd might use a posting summary like the one we illustrated in Chapter 13 when we looked at the posting of sales transactions. The completed posting summary is shown below.

15: Purchase and purchase returns day books

MEGATYPE PRINTERS LIMITED
Nominal ledger postings sheet

Account name	Account code	Nominal ledger Dr £	p	Cr £	p
Total creditors	70100	35	25	792	89
Paper	02400	152	00		
Electricity	03215	116	80		
Other expenses	03428	100	00		
Paper returns	02401			30	00
VAT	70200	118	09	5	25
Card	02500	278	00		
Ink	02600	28	00		
TOTALS		828	14	828	14

Posted by ......A.B......   Date ......10/1/X7......

What records are to be made in the purchase ledger? Using the details from the analyses shown at Paragraph 3.3 on purchases and at Paragraph 5.14 on purchase returns, we have the following postings to make.

Ref	Account name	Account code	Debit £	Credit £
1423	V Princeley	4009		178.60
1424	Grantcroft Ltd	5020		32.90
1425	Midnorth Elec plc	4010		137.24
1426	Hartley & Co	5008		117.50
1427	Cardright Ltd	3972		326.65
C014	V Princeley	4009	35.25	
			35.25	792.89

Suppliers' accounts as part of the double entry

5.16 In some computer-based accounting systems, there will be a separate account for each supplier in the general ledger. In such an integrated system, there will be no need for a creditors control account. The individual suppliers' accounts will form part of the double entry rather than being 'memorandum' accounts. We discuss the creditors control account in the general ledger in more detail in Chapter 17.

Part C: Recording and accounting for credit transactions

Activity 15.3

You work for Bodgett DIY. You receive the following invoices from suppliers on the morning of 23 November 20X7. Each invoice has already been given a reference by one of your fellow workers for Bodgett DIY's own accounting system.

Tasks

(a) Post the invoices to the purchase day book, using the sheet provided on Page 326.

(b) Set out the *double entry* for these transactions, assuming that totals are posted to the general ledger at the end of each working day. Use the *account postings* form provided on Page 327.

Supplier account codes

Macin	1310
Payper, Overr, Crackes	1510
Pitiso Tools	1550
Throne Bathware	2010

Nominal ledger account codes

VAT	0694
Total creditors (purchase ledger control account)	0730
Tool purchases	4000
Painting and decorating purchases	5000
Bathroom items purchases	6000

To: Purchase ledger
Bodgett's DIY
Broad Street
Stornaway
ORKNEY

PITISO TOOLS
Zhivago House
Lawrence Street, Edinburgh
Phone: 01939 72101

SALES INVOICE
No: 21379
Date: 21/11/X7
Tax point: 21/11/X7

Stock code	Item	Quantity	£ p	£ p
0105	Hammer drills	20	70.00	1,400.00
0210	Hacksaw	10	5.00	50.00
0340	Electric screwdriver	15	7.00	105.00
0560	Hammers (10 in)	7	1.50	10.50
0791	Vices - metal	4	3.95	15.80
				1,581.30
		VAT 17 ½%		276.72
		TOTAL PAYABLE		1,858.02

Delivery
- as above

Bodgett's reference number 712

Pitiso Tools Ltd Registered Office: Zhivago House, Lawrence Street, Edinburgh
Reg No: 322 1014   VAT: 8 752 121

MACIN

Macin (UK) Ltd
Northern Region
Convention Street
GLASGOW

(Phone 01838 89414)
VAT reg 3 894 1210

To: Purchase Ledger
Bodgett's DIY Superstore
Broad Street
STORNAWAY

Invoice No: 84/Q

Customer No: BODG 1

Date/tax point: 21/11/X7

Terms: 28 days

Items ordered	Quantity	Unit price £ p	Total £ p
Paint stripper PYB75	200 tins	4.00	800.00
White gloss paint DUL10	400 x 1 litre	12.00	4,800.00
Primer SX91	800 x 0.5 litre	5.00	4,000.00
Wallpaper paste 'STICKO-2000'	500 packets	3.50	1,750.00
Total			11,350.00
VAT @ 17½%			1,986.25
Total payable			13,336.25

Bodgett's reference number: 713

Reg office: Water Street, Rainham, Essex
Reg no: 528 1000

Part C: Recording and accounting for credit transactions

THRONE Bathware

Habsburg Street
Windsor
BERKS
01421 374911

VAT reg 4 139 7210

SALES INVOICE

No: 4963
Date/tax point: 21/11/X7

Purchase Ledger
Bodgett's DIY Superstore
Broad Street
STORNAWAY

Item	£ p	Quantity	£ p
Wash basin 12 x 15	25.90	2	51.80
Kitchen sink 'Excelsior'	31.20	3	93.60
Steel taps	7.40	7	51.80
Gold plated taps	60.50	6	363.00
Baths	200.20	4	800.80
Micro-whirlpool bath	250.10	1	250.10
'Luxor' shower units	70.30	5	351.50
'Standard' shower units	50.30	4	201.20
Total			2,163.80
VAT @ 17 ½%			378.66
Total including VAT			2,542.46

Bodgett's reference number: 714

Reg office: Habsburg Street, Windsor, Berks
Reg no: 7000

Bodgett DIY
Broad Street
Stornaway
ORKNEY

Delivery if different

PAPER, OVERR, CRACKES HOME FURNISHINGS

Plastery House, Rachman Street, Inverness
Phone: (01563) 810372

SALES INVOICE: 0711		DATE/TAX POINT: 21/11/X7		
Item	Code	Quantity	£ p	£ p
Towel rails for bathroom	B121	1	16.90	16.90
Wallpaper 4 x 20 metres	H272	10	8.50	85.00
Wallpaper 4 X 40 metres	H274	15	16.25	243.75
Curtain rails 'A'	H351	10	20.00	200.00
Curtain rails 'B'	H352	12	35.00	420.00
				965.65
Value Added Tax				17½ %
				168.98
Total payable				1,134.63

Bodgett's reference number: 715

VAT registration no: 345 5678

Part C: Recording and accounting for credit transactions

Bodgett Purchase day book analysis — Page 41

Date	Ref	Supplier	Supplier account	Total	VAT	Purchase cost	Tools	Painting & decorating	Bathroom items			
23/11/X7												
Total for 23/11/X7												

ACCOUNT POSTINGS			DR	CR
Account code	Ref		£ p	£ p

DATE

Posted by ....

Activity 15.4

Tasks

(a) Enter the details supplied below into the *purchase returns day book* of Bodgett DIY for 23 November 20X7, using the sheet provided on page 329.

(b) Write the necessary double entry on the account postings form provided on page 330.

Items to be entered to purchase returns day book

1. A consignment of bathroom units from Dothelot DIY was found to be infested with woodworm. It was billed on invoice 7912, and the purchase day book reference is 613. The amount is valued at £176.25 inclusive of VAT.

2. Some paint stripper bought from C and R Builders Merchants Wholesalers plc had to be returned because it did not comply with the safety standards specified by Bodgett's DIY a while before. The amount was £221 excluding VAT. This was on supplier invoice 794, purchase day book reference 612.

3. Some items of bathroom equipment from The House Foundation had to be returned as they were leaking. The value of the goods returned, excluding VAT, was £959.59. This was found on supplier invoice 91113, purchase day book reference 627.

Part C: Recording and accounting for credit transactions

Dothelot, C and R, and The House Foundation will be sent debit notes number 64, 65 and 66 respectively dealing with these items.

Account numbers in Bodgett's accounting system are as follows.

Purchase ledger account codes

C and R	7211
Dothelot	8523
The House Foundation	6644

General ledger account codes

Purchases returns (bathware)	6050
Purchases returns (painting and decorating)	5050
Purchases returns (tools)	4050
VAT	0694
Total creditors	0730

Tutorial note. Remember the VAT rounding rules.

15: Purchase and purchase returns day books

	A	B	C	D	E	F	G	H	I	J	K	L	M
1			Bodgett Purchase returns day book									Page 5	
2	Date	Debit note ref	Supplier	Supplier account	Total	VAT	Purchase return total	Tools	Painting & decorating	Bathroom items	Purchase ref		
3													
4													
5	23/11/X7												
6													
7													
8													
9													
10													
11													
12													
13													
14	Total for 23/11/X7												

ACCOUNT POSTINGS			DR	CR
Account code	Ref		£　p	£　p

DATE

Posted by ....

15: Purchase and purchase returns day books

> **Key learning points**
>
> - The purchase day book lists the invoices received by a business from its credit suppliers. The purchase returns day book lists the credit notes received when goods are returned to suppliers. The purchase day book and the purchase returns day book are 'books of prime entry': transactions are recorded in them before being recorded elsewhere.
>
> - An expenses day book may be kept to record expense purchases, as distinct from purchases for stock. Alternatively, all purchases of goods and services may be recorded in the same place.
>
> - Purchases and expenses may be analysed into different categories in the day books. As with the sales day books, a computer spreadsheet might be used to produce an analysed purchase day book.
>
> - The day book totals for purchases and purchase returns are posted to the nominal ledger total creditors account, the VAT control account and the relevant purchases and expense accounts.
>
> - Expenses accounts will include capital expenditure (fixed assets) accounts as well as accounts for recording business expenses such as administrative expenses. The amounts owed to individual creditors are **entered in the purchase ledger personal accounts** (where these are maintained as **memorandum accounts** separate from the nominal ledger).

Quick quiz

1. What is the purchase day book used for?
2. What does the purchase returns day book do?
3. What is the double entry for a credit purchase?
4. What is the double entry where the credit purchase includes VAT?
5. What is the double entry for purchase returns with VAT?

Answers to quick quiz

1. To keep a list of all the invoices received from suppliers of goods or services to the business.

2. It lists credit notes received in respect of purchase returns in chronological order.

3. | | | |
   |---|---|---|
   | DEBIT | Purchases | |
   | CREDIT | Creditors | |

4. | | |
   |---|---|
   | DEBIT | Purchases (VAT exclusive amount) |
   | DEBIT | VAT |
   | CREDIT | Creditors (VAT inclusive amount) |

5. | | |
   |---|---|
   | DEBIT | Creditors (VAT inclusive) |
   | CREDIT | Purchase returns/Purchases (VAT exclusive) |
   | CREDIT | VAT |

Answers to activities

Answer 15.1

(a) Answer: (ii). The purchase day book is a book of prime entry in which purchases made on credit are recorded first of all.

Tutorial note. How invoices received are recorded varies from system to system. In most manual systems, purchase day book *totals* only (for example daily totals) are posted to the nominal ledger purchases account. In some computer systems, a separate purchase day book is not maintained. Instead invoices are posted individually to the nominal ledger.

Part C: Recording and accounting for credit transactions

(b) DEBIT   Purchases (Profit and Loss Account)
CREDIT   Creditors (Balance Sheet)

(The creditors account might be referred to as the purchase ledger control account.)

(c) A *debit note* is issued to someone when you wish them to reduce your liability. A debit note has the effect of telling the supplier that you think you owe him less. (You have *debited* his credit balance in your books.) It is an indication that you expect him to make a corresponding credit entry in respect of your account in his *sales* ledger.

Answer 15.2

Situations (c) and (h) would be reflected in a purchase returns day book. These are situations in which you have returned goods to the supplier. Items (a) and (d) refer to sales you have made, not your purchases. Item (b) is a different sort of dispute. You have received no goods, and you have not entered the invoice to your accounts. Item (g) is similar to item (b), reflecting over-zealous invoicing by a supplier. Item (e) is just an error, but refers to a delivery *you* have made. Item (f) is just bad luck! The goods were in perfectly good condition when you received them, and you are ordering more.

Answer 15.3

(a)

Bodgett Purchase day book analysis — Page 41

Date	Ref	Supplier	Supplier account	Total	VAT	Purchase cost	Tools	Painting & decorating	Bathroom items
23/11/X7	712	Pitiso Tools	1550	1,858.02	276.72	1,581.30	1,581.30		
	713	Macin	1310	13,336.25	1,986.25	11,350.00		11,350.00	
	714	Throne Bathware	2010	2,542.46	378.66	2,163.80			2,163.80
	715	Payper, Overr, Crackes	1510	1,134.63	168.98	965.65		948.75	16.90
Total for 23/11/X7				18,871.36	2,810.61	16,060.75	1,581.30	12,298.75	2,180.70

(b)

ACCOUNT POSTINGS			DR	CR
Account code	Ref		£ p	£ p
4000	PDB41	Tools purchases	1,581.30	
5000	PDB41	Painting & decorating purchases	12,298.75	
6000	PDB41	Bathroom	2,180.70	
0694	PDB41	VAT	2,810.61	
0730	PDB41	Creditors (PLCA)		18,871.36
		TOTAL	18,871.36	18,871.36

DATE 23/11/X7

Posted by _____

Tutorial note. If you decided that the curtain rails purchased from Paper, Overr, Crackes were for shower curtains and therefore came under the Bathroom category, the relevant totals would be:

    Painting and decorating   £11,678.75
    Bathroom   £2,800.70

Answer 15.4

(a)

	A	B	C	D	E	F	G	H	I	J	K	L	M
1	Bodgett Purchase returns day book												Page 5
2	Date	Debit note ref	Supplier	Supplier account	Total	VAT	Purchase return total	Tools	Painting & decorating	Bathroom items	Purchase ref		
3													
4													
5	23/11/X7	64	DotheLot	8523	176.25	26.25	150.00			150.00	613		
6		65	C and R	7211	259.67	38.67	221.00		221.00		612		
7		66	Foundation House	6644	1,127.51	167.92	959.59			959.59	627		
8													
9													
10	Total for 23/11/X7				1,563.43	232.84	1,330.59		221.00	1,109.59			
11													
12													
13													
14													

(b)

ACCOUNT POSTINGS			DR	CR
Account code	Ref		£ p	£ p
6050	PRDB5	Bathware purchase returns		1,109.59
5050	PRDB5	Painting & decorating purchase returns		221.00
0694	PRDB5	VAT		232.84
0730	PRDB5	Creditors	1,563.43	
		TOTAL	1,563.43	1,563.43

DATE 23/11/X7

Posted by _____

Chapter 16 The purchase ledger

Chapter topic list

1 Personal accounts for suppliers
2 Recording transactions in the purchase ledger
3 Payments to suppliers
4 The age analysis of creditors and other reports
5 Contra entries with the sales ledger

The following study sessions are covered in this chapter

Syllabus reference

8 (f) Record purchases
  (i) maintain a manual general and purchase ledger   5b
  (iii) understand the purpose of and prepare an aged creditors analysis   5b
  (iv) prepare, reconcile and understand the purpose of supplier statements 5b
 (g) Communicate efficiently and effectively with suppliers   5b

Part C: Recording and accounting for credit transactions

1 PERSONAL ACCOUNTS FOR SUPPLIERS

The need for personal accounts

1.1 We have seen how the purchase day book provides a chronological record of the invoices and credit notes received by a business from all its credit suppliers, for each of which a personal account is maintained in the purchase ledger.

1.2 There are various reasons why a business needs to maintain a **personal account** for each supplier.

(a) A supplier might telephone, asking for **payment of the full balance due to him**. Staff of the business will need to check that the balance claimed is correct and that it is now due for payment.

(b) It is common for businesses to **receive statements of account** from their suppliers monthly. The business needs to maintain its own records of how much it owes to a supplier so that it can check that the supplier's statement is correct.

(c) The business needs to maintain a **complete record** of the items making up the balance it owes so that it can make **appropriate payments** on an appropriate regular basis to suppliers.

(d) The business will not usually want to pay each of a supplier's invoices separately: it will generally be much easier to make **monthly payments** covering a number of invoices which have become due.

> **KEY TERM**
>
> The personal accounts showing how much is owed to each credit supplier of the business are contained in the **purchase ledger**.

The purchase ledger

1.3 Purchase ledger accounts are written up as follows.

(a) When entries are made in the **purchase day book** (for suppliers' invoices received), they are also made on the **credit** side of the relevant supplier account in the purchase ledger.

(b) Entries made in the **purchase returns day book** (credit notes received) are entered on the **debit** side of the suppliers' ledger account.

(c) When entries are made in the **cash book** in respect of payments made to suppliers, they are also made on the **debit** side of the relevant supplier account.

(d) Discounts received for prompt payment (cash discounts) are entered on the **debit** side.

1.4 The entries recorded in a supplier's personal account can be represented by a 'T'-account, as follows.

SUPPLIER ACCOUNT

On the debit side		*On the credit side*	
Payments made	X	Invoices received	X
Purchase returns	X		
Discounts received	X		

1.5 An example of how a purchase ledger account may be laid out is shown below.

BUNTER & CO   PL32

Date 20X7	Details	£	Date 20X7	Detail	£
15 March	Cash	150.00	15 March	Balance b/d	200.00
16 March	Balance c/d	365.00	15 March	Invoice rec'd PDB 37	315.00
		515.00			515.00
			16 March	Balance b/d	365.00

Debit balances in the purchase ledger

1.6 You should be able to see that if we pay more than £365 to Bunter & Co, we will be left with a net debit balance on Bunter & Co's personal account, instead of the credit balance we normally expect to see for a creditor. If, for example, we pay £375, there will be a net debit balance of £10. Being a debit balance, this will indicate that the creditor then owes us the balance of £10.

1.7 **Debit balances** in the purchase ledger are unusual, but they can sometimes arise. Perhaps you can think of some of the situations in which they might occur.

- An **overpayment** of the creditor's balance might be made in error.
- A **credit note** might be received after full payment has been made of the balance.

1.8 If debit balances are arising on purchase ledger accounts frequently, some **investigation** may be called for. The occurrence of debit balances could indicate that procedures in the purchase ledger department need to be improved.

Organisations not needing a purchase ledger

1.9 Maintaining a separate purchase ledger may be a waste of time for those organisations which make very few credit purchases. Examples of such organisations could include small shops, clubs and associations. Such organisations may also make few sales on credit, and may have no need to maintain either a purchase ledger or a sales ledger. What credit sales or purchases there are will be passed through **general ledger accounts**.

Trade creditors

1.10 Although the purchase ledger contains the personal accounts of creditors for the supply of both goods and services, it will not normally contain balances for **all** types of creditor. The purchase ledger will, however, normally cover all of the **trade creditors** of the business.

KEY TERM

Trade creditors consist of those liabilities which are related to the trade of the business.

1.11 Trade creditors include those businesses and organisations which supply the business with goods for the **trading stocks** of the business (the 'raw materials' of the business) as well as suppliers of other goods such as **office supplies** and services, such as the telephone company, the electricity company, and the garage which repairs the vehicles owned by the business.

Part C: Recording and accounting for credit transactions

Other creditors

1.12 **Other creditors** will not normally be recorded in the purchase ledger and the balances owed should instead be recorded in general ledger accounts for the purpose. Examples of 'other creditors' which you are most likely to come across are the following.

   (a) **Liabilities to pay wages and salaries.** (For example, suppose that a company pays its employees monthly on the last day of each month, and its year-end accounting date is 30 March. At the accounting date, the company will owe to its employees almost a full month's pay, and this must be shown as a creditor in the balance sheet at the accounting date).

   (b) **Taxes** and other amounts which are collected by the business on behalf of third parties. The main examples are VAT, which is due to HM Customs & Excise, and Pay-As-You-Earn (PAYE) which represents income tax deducted from employees' pay and is due to the Inland Revenue.

   (c) Amounts payable for *goods and services* which are *not* directly related to the main trade of the business, for example amounts payable for the purchase of **fixed assets**.

1.13 Some items of **overhead expenditure**, for example rent, may be processed in the purchase ledger along with trade creditors in some businesses, or may in other businesses be separately processed as other creditors.

1.14 Excluded from the above list of 'other creditors' are certain special categories of creditor which need to be shown separately in the balance sheet of the business.

   (a) **Corporation tax**, which a company must pay (to the Inland Revenue) on its profits.

   (b) **Bank loans and overdrafts**. Bank loans will be recorded in general ledger accounts for the purpose, while if a business has an overdraft on its current account, this will show up as a credit balance in the bank section of the cash book.

1.15 Of course, any of the types of account which we have mentioned in this section of the chapter would be expected to show a **credit balance**, indicating that the business owes money to the organisation or person concerned.

Activity 16.1

(a) What is the status of a trade creditor in the accounts of a business?

   (i) An asset
   (ii) A liability
   (iii) An expense
   (iv) An item of revenue

(b) Which of the following accounts are not normally found in a purchase ledger of *trade* creditors?

   (i) Depreciation provision
   (ii) Personal accounts for suppliers of subcomponents
   (iii) Inland Revenue
   (iv) Customs & Excise for VAT
   (v) Suppliers of raw materials stocks
   (vi) Bank overdraft
   (vii) Long-term bank loan
   (viii) Share premium
   (ix) Telephone expenses
   (x) Drawings
   (xi) Proprietor's capital

2 RECORDING TRANSACTIONS IN THE PURCHASE LEDGER

2.1 In Chapter 14, we looked at how sales ledger accounts can be recorded with individual entries from the day books and the cash book, using figures from a fictitious example. If you followed that example, then you should be able to work out how the recording of individual items will be made to the purchase ledger as well. The process is the same in principle but is like a mirror image of the sales ledger example.

2.2 As with the processing of sales ledger transactions, in a computer-based system supplier ledger accounts might be updated directly (**transaction processing**) or stored on a **transaction file** for a later updating run.

Recording purchases and cash paid

2.3 The chart below shows how entries are made in purchase ledger accounts from the purchase day book (invoices) and the cash account (cash paid). It also shows related postings from the purchase day book and indicates how the creditors control account (or purchase ledger control account) fits in.

(a) **Individual invoices**, representing the amounts owed to individual creditors in respect of each invoice, are **credited** to the **individual creditors' purchase ledger accounts**.

(b) **Totals of batches of invoices** are **credited** to the **creditors control account**, which forms a part of the **double entry system**.

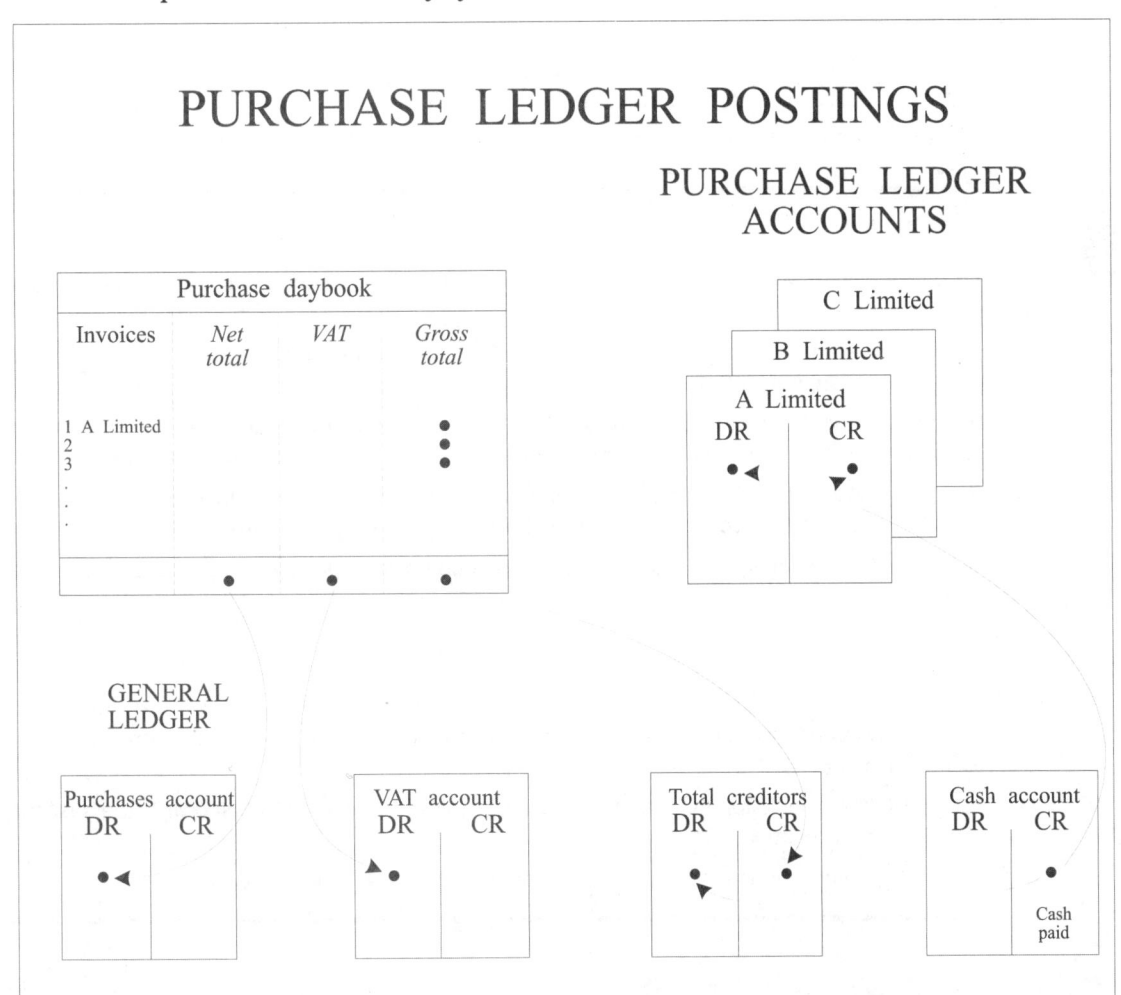

PURCHASE LEDGER POSTINGS

PURCHASE LEDGER ACCOUNTS

Purchase daybook			
Invoices	Net total	VAT	Gross total
1 A Limited			•
2			•
3			•
.			
.			
	•	•	•

C Limited
B Limited
A Limited
DR	CR
• ◄	▼ •

GENERAL LEDGER

Purchases account		VAT account		Total creditors		Cash account	
DR	CR	DR	CR	DR	CR	DR	CR
• ◄		▲ •		• ▼	► •		• Cash paid

Part C: Recording and accounting for credit transactions

(c) The net amount of purchases (or expenses) **excluding VAT** are **debited** to the **purchases** (or **expenses**) account.

(d) The **VAT** element can be set against VAT on sales for a VAT-registered business, and so is **debited** to the **VAT account**, reducing the amount shown as owed to HM Customs & Excise.

2.4 In some businesses, the cash book is a book of prime entry from which summaries are taken and recorded in a control account for cash maintained in the general ledger. In the chart above, we illustrate a business in which there is a single cash account (cash book) which itself forms part of the double entry.

Posting purchase returns

2.5 You should be able to see how recordings and postings (of credit notes received) are made from the purchase returns day book. The purchase ledger account and general ledger accounts to which postings are made will be the same as for the purchase day book, but the postings will be on the opposite side in each case.

Discounts received

2.6 Some businesses will account for **cash discounts received** from creditors in a similar way to that illustrated for discounts allowed in section 2 of Chapter 8. There will be a 'memorandum' discounts received column in the cash book which will be used to debit the individual creditor's accounts and to make the appropriate general ledger entries for total discounts received.

		£	£
DEBIT	Creditors control account	X	
CREDIT	Discounts received		X

Activity 16.2

Cosmo runs a picture framing business. You are given the following information about his transactions during January 20X6.

1. There is a balance of £1,200 in the bank. This is also reflected in the cash book as a debit balance brought forward.

2. On 10 January 20X6 Cosmo purchased £400 worth of glass from Quentin plc. The terms of the sale included a clause that he would receive a 10% discount if he paid within 3 weeks.

3. On 15 January 20X6 Cosmo purchased paper, card and frames worth £2,000 from W Honor Soper. He would receive a discount of £200 if settling by 31 January 20X6.

4. Cosmo take advantage of the cash discount offered and pays both creditors before the 31 January 20X6.

Task

Prepare

(a) the journal entries to reflect the above transactions in the cash book and the purchase ledger control account.

(b) Cosmo's cash book for the period 1 January to 31 January 20X6 showing the discount in memorandum column.

(c) Cosmo's purchase ledger control account showing the postings for January.

Retention of records

2.7 All purchase invoices and credit notes should be retained and filed after processing in case of query (from the supplier, the management or from the auditors).

3 PAYMENTS TO SUPPLIERS

3.1 Payments to suppliers are best made on a **regular periodic basis**, say monthly, as a matter of administrative efficiency. It is important to bear in mind that your suppliers need to collect cash due to them in the same way that your business does. For purposes of cash management (maximising your available cash) you will not want to pay supplier invoices until the end of the allowed credit period. However, in the interests of keeping a good relationship with your suppliers you should pay them when payment is due and let them know if there is a problem, for instance an invoice in dispute.

Methods of payment

3.2 You should be aware that different methods of payment to suppliers are available.

Method	Comments
Cash	An unusual method for a business to use to pay its suppliers, although it will be used for small non-credit 'petty cash' purchases.
Cheque	Still the commonest method of payment.
Interbank transfer	An increasingly common means of making payments to suppliers, for example using the 'BACS' (Bankers Automated Clearing Services) system. The system can save administrative time since, instead of making out individual cheques and sending each by post, details of a full payment run to the suppliers of the business can be submitted to the business's bank on computer tape or disk, and the funds are then transferred to suppliers' bank accounts electronically through the bank clearing system. There may also be savings in bank charges from using BACS.

Selecting items for payment

3.3 Deciding when and who to pay is a key function of a business's management and only a senior person should decide.

All systems	Computerised purchase ledger system
The items for payment may be selected manually.	A **'suggested payments' listing** may be produced, 'suggesting' how much should be paid to which suppliers, based on information on settlement days and any discounts which may be offered. A payments listing of this sort generated by computer will normally need to be checked through manually in case there are any reasons to make a different payment from that 'suggested'.
If **queries** on any invoices are to be raised with the suppliers, there needs to be procedures to ensure that the invoice is not paid until the query has been settled.	There may be a facility to 'flag' items which should not be paid for the time being. For example, the invoice may be placed **'in dispute'**, and the fact indicated in the reference used for the disputed invoice. The 'dispute' designation will need to be 'released' when the dispute has been settled so that the item can be paid in the normal way.

Part C: Recording and accounting for credit transactions

All systems	Computerised purchase ledger system
It may be desirable to take the full period of credit from each supplier.	The number of days before settlement can be recorded for each supplier. This indicates the time period before payment is to be made. A computerised purchase ledger which offers the option of making automatic payments will automatically list all items which are now due to be paid. This list will *exclude* the following. (a) Items which have not yet reached their settlement date (b) Items which are 'in dispute'

Computer cheques and remittance advices

3.4 A computerised purchase ledger system may offer the option of **printing cheques for payments to suppliers.** Special cheque stationery will be required for the printer. A remittance advice will normally be sent with each payment to tell the recipient what the payment is for. This too may be produced by a computerised purchase ledger system.

REMITTANCE ADVICE

KT Electronics
4 Reform Road
Wokingham
Berkshire

R&B Sound Services Ltd
Belton Estate
Peterborough
PE4 4DE

Account number: 427424

30/06/X7
Your ref: RBS/2011

Date	Details	Amount/£
08/05/X7	Invoice 202481	624.60
21/05/X7	Invoice 202574	78.40
24/05/X7	Credit note C40041	(62.20)
	Payment enclosed for	640.80

Checks over payments

3.5 You can appreciate that it is important for a business to have **procedures to ensure that only valid payments are made** - in other words, only the payments which *should* be made by the business.

Procedure	Effect
Authorisation of payments by an **appropriate official**, who should be a senior employee or director of the organisation.	The bank will pay the cheque as requested.
Cheques will need to be **signed** by the authorised **cheque signatories** which are recognised by the bank as authorised to sign cheques.	For cheques produced by a computerised purchase ledger system, the password restrictions should limit the value of cheques which different users can authorise.
Details and appropriate supporting documents for each payment should be presented to the person who must sign each cheque (say the general manager). '**Appropriate supporting documents**' may consist of the suppliers' invoices which are to be paid, authorised by an appropriate staff member, together with the goods received note or other document recording receipt of the goods invoiced.	Documents supporting payments are reviewed by people who are independent of the preparation and processing of the documents. The person carrying out this review will check for any unusual items which might deserve further investigation.

3.6 Automatic payment methods in a large organisation may include **mechanical signature of payments selected by computer**. If such a system is used, there is not the same check on individual payments as is appropriate to smaller businesses. To replace this lack of check on individual payments, an organisation using such methods will need to have strong checks over whether purchase ledger balances are correct to ensure that the wrong payments are not made.

3.7 If automated electronic payments methods such as **BACS** are used, there will need to be special procedures to ensure that all payments included on the tape submitted to BACS are properly authorised.

3.8 Sometimes, the usual payment method may need to be bypassed. For example, as mentioned earlier, computer selection of payments may need to be overridden in order to make a special **manual payment** of a different amount. Proper checks will need to be applied to such cases, and high level authorisation should be obtained.

4 THE AGE ANALYSIS OF CREDITORS AND OTHER REPORTS

The age analysis of creditors

4.1 An **age analysis of creditors** may be produced in a very similar way to the age analysis of debtors which we looked at in Chapter 14.

Part C: Recording and accounting for credit transactions

> **KEY TERM**
>
> The **age analysis of creditors** will consist of a listing of creditors' balances analysed between different 'ages' of debt represented by different items in the balance, measured in months (usually).

4.2 The age analysis of creditors serves to highlight any supplier accounts which are **long overdue**, for whatever reason. The totals of the age analysis indicate the **age 'profile'** of creditors' accounts. Information about this profile might be of use to business managers who might want to ask whether the business would do better by changing the profile, for example paying creditors a little later in order to improve the cash flow position of the business. However, the age analysis of creditors is not likely to be as important in a business as the age analysis of debtors, which as we have seen is an extremely useful aid to debt collection and credit control.

Other reports

4.3 Other reports which a computerised purchase ledger package is able to print out will be very similar to those produced from a sales ledger package, the more important of which were outlined in Chapter 14.

Activity 16.3

What, briefly, is the significance of a *creditors* age analysis?

Activity 16.4

Can you list the main types of report other than the age analysis of creditors discussed above?

4.4 As with sales ledger reports, access to purchase ledger reports will normally be restricted by **password**.

5 CONTRA ENTRIES WITH THE SALES LEDGER

5.1 Sometimes, a business might both **purchase goods from** and **sell goods to** the same person on credit.

(a) **Purchases** will be entered in the **purchase day book** when invoices are received, and an entry subsequently recorded in the supplier's individual account in the purchase ledger.

(b) **Credit sales** will be entered in the **sales day book** when invoices are sent out, and an entry subsequently recorded in the customer's individual account in the sales ledger.

5.2 Even though the supplier and the customer are one and the same person, he will have a **separate account in each ledger**. For example, if A owes B £200 for purchases and B owes A £350 for credit sales, the net effect is that B owes A £150. However, in the books of A

- There would be a creditor in the purchase ledger - B - for £200
- There would be a debtor in the sales ledger - B - for £350

5.3 Now, if A and B decide to settle their accounts by **netting off** their respective debts (and getting B to write a single cheque for the balance), settlement would be made **in contra**.

16: The purchase ledger

5.4 The contra entries in the accounts of A would be to set off the smaller amount (£200 owed to B) against the larger amount (£350 owed by B).

(a) In the sales ledger and purchase ledger

DEBIT	Creditor's account (B) purchase ledger - to clear	£200	
CREDIT	Debtor's account (B) sales ledger - leaving balance of £150		£200

(b) In the general ledger

DEBIT	Total creditors	£200	
CREDIT	Total debtors		£200

5.5 **The contra entries must be made in both the personal accounts of B and also in the total creditors and debtors accounts in the general ledger.**

Activity 16.5

You are the purchase ledger clerk for a company providing financial services, and the date is 28 August 20X7. The company operates a non-integrated purchase ledger system.

The purchase ledger account for a supplier called Kernels Ltd shows the following.

		(Debit)/Credit £	Balance £
01.08.X7	Balance b/f		76.05
01.08.X7	Invoice 20624	42.84	118.89
07.08.X7	Cash	(76.05)	42.84
16.08.X7	Invoice 20642	64.17	107.01
16.08.X7	Invoice 20643	120.72	227.73
16.08.X7	Invoice 20642	64.17	291.90
21.08.X7	Cash	(400.00)	(108.10)
22.08.X7	Invoice 20798	522.18	414.08
24.08.X7	C91004	42.84	456.92
27.08.X7	Invoice 21114	144.50	601.42
27.08.X7	Invoice 21229	42.84	644.26

The following facts came to light.

(a) Kernels Ltd's invoice 21201 for £97.40, dated 23 August 20X7, was misposted to the account of MPV in the purchase ledger.

(b) The cash payment of £400.00 made on 21 August 20X7 relates to another creditor, ASR Ltd.

(c) Item C91004 dated 24 August 20X7 is in fact a credit note.

(d) Invoice 20642 has been posted to the account twice.

(e) Kernels Ltd has a balance of £37.50 in the sales ledger, which is to be set off against its balance in the purchase ledger.

Task

Draw up journal entries for the above items and write up the Kernels Ltd's account accordingly, posting the journal entries to the account.

The journal entries should distinguish between nominal account adjustments and memorandum *account adjustments.

Part C: Recording and accounting for credit transactions

Key learning points

- The **purchase ledger contains the personal accounts of suppliers (trade creditors)** of the business. The suppliers' personal accounts provide the business with a full record of how much it owes to each supplier and of what items the debt consists.

- A **supplier's account** in the purchase ledger will **normally show a credit balance**: the supplier is owed money by the business and is therefore a creditor of the business. Other creditors which a business may have include the tax authorities, banks and employees (for any wages and salaries due).

- **Payments to suppliers** should be organised according to the periodic procedures of the business. **Checks and authorisation** are necessary in order to ensure that only valid payments are made. Payment methods vary, and the checks necessary will differ according to the payment methods used.

- The **age analysis of creditors** shows the age 'profile' of creditors' balances on the purchase ledger. It indicates how quickly the business is paying off its debts. A computerised purchase ledger will also allow a number of other reports to be printed out as necessary.

- **Contra entries 'net off'** amounts due to and from the same parties in the purchase ledger and sales ledger respectively.

Quick quiz

1. What does the purchase ledger contain?
2. What are trade creditors?
3. Give two examples of 'other creditors'.
4. What does the age analysis of creditors do?
5. What does settlement 'in contra' mean?

Answers to quick quiz

1. The personal accounts showing how much is owed to each credit supplier of the business.
2. Liabilities relating to the trade of the business, eg purchases of goods for re-sale.
3. (i) Wages and salaries
   (ii) VAT
4. Lists creditors' balances analysed between different 'ages' of debt.
5. An amount due from a customer in the sales ledger is set off against a target amount owed to the same person in the purchase ledger, or *vice versa*.

Answers to activities

Answer 16.1

(a) A creditor is a *liability* of a business. A creditor is owed money, or its equivalent, by a business.

(b) *Trade creditors* are those with whom you do business to carry on your own business. They supply you with materials, goods and services to enable you to carry out your own trade or profession and they offer you a credit period also. Items (ii), (v) and (ix) are trade creditors, by this definition.

The other creditors mentioned, although creditors are not *trade* creditors. While taxation paid to the Inland Revenue and Customs & Excise is used to provide the necessary infrastructure for the business, it is a legal obligation, based on the profits of a business, not payment for a service.

16: The purchase ledger

A bank overdraft is not a trade creditor. A bank supplies funds which are used to run a business on a day to day basis. A bank can also provide long-term capital, say to finance the purchase of a fixed asset.

Answer 16.2

(a) Journal entries

			£	£
(i)		DR Purchases	400	
		CR Creditors		400
		Being purchases from Quentin plc.		
(ii)		DR Purchases	2,000	
		CR Creditors		2,000
		Being purchases from W Honor Soper.		
(iii)		DR Creditors (Quentin plc)	360	
		CR Cash		360
		Being cash payment to Quentin plc.		
(iv)		DR Creditors	40	
		CR Discount received		40
		Being 10% discount received from Quentin plc.		
(v)		DR Creditors (W Honor Soper)	1,800	
		CR Cash		1,800
		Being cash payment to W Honor Soper.		
(vi)		DR Creditors	200	
		CR Discount received		200
		Being £200 discount received from W Honor Soper.		

(b)

Cash book

DR		CR		
			Discount received	
Bal b/d	1,200	Payment to Quentin plc	40	360
Bal c/d	960	Payment to W Honor Soper	200	1,800
	2,160			2,160
		Bal b/d		960

(c)

Purchase ledger control a/c

DR		CR	
Cash to Quentin	360	Purchases from Quentin plc	400
Discount received	40	Purchases form W Honor Soper	2,000
Cash to W Honor Soper	1,800		2,400
Discount received	200		
	2,400		

349

Part C: Recording and accounting for credit transactions

Answer 16.3

Put simply, you may feel that delaying payment of creditors for as long as possible is the most astute commercial option. However consider the following.

(a) You may end up losing discounts
(b) You may lose supplier goodwill
(c) You may lose the facility to buy on credit

A creditors' age analysis may indicate that you cannot pay your debts, or that you are delaying payment longer than is necessary.

Answer 16.4

The list will probably include the following.

(a) Day books
(b) Supplier account statement of transactions and current balance
(c) Remittance advices
(d) VAT analysis
(e) Purchases analysis
(f) List of supplier accounts
(g) Mailing list of suppliers' names and addresses

Answer 16.5

Journal 28 August 20X7

		Debit £	Credit £
(a)	*Memorandum account adjustment (JNL 1)*		
	Purchase ledger - MPV Ltd	97.40	
	Purchase ledger - Kernels Ltd		97.40
	Being correction of misposting of invoice (Kernels' ref 21201)		
(b)	*Memorandum account adjustment (JNL 2)*		
	Purchase ledger - ASR Ltd	400.00	
	Purchase ledger - Kernels Ltd		400.00
	Being correction of misposting of 21/8 cash payment to ASR Ltd		
(c)	*Nominal account journal (JNL 3)*		
	Purchase ledger control account (£42.84 × 2)	85.68	
	Purchases		85.68
	Being correction of misposting of Kernels Ltd credit note C91004		
(d)	*Nominal account adjustment (JNL 4)*		
	Purchase ledger control account	64.17	
	Purchases		64.17
	Being correction of double posting of invoice 20642		
	Memorandum account adjustment (JNL 5)		
	Purchase ledger - Kernels Ltd	85.68	
		64.17	
	Being adjustment to reflect JNL 3 and JNL 4		
	(*Note*. As the memorandum account does not form part of the double entry, it does not necessarily have to balance.)		
(e)	*Nominal account adjustment (JNL 6)*		
	Purchase ledger control account	37.50	
	Sales ledger control account		37.50
	Being double entry to reflect contra between Kernels Ltd's sales ledger and purchase ledger accounts.		

Memorandum account adjustment (JNL 7)
Purchase ledger - Kernels Ltd   37.50
Sales ledger - Kernels Ltd   37.50

Being adjustment to reflect JNL 6

KERNELS LIMITED

20X7			£	20X7			£
28/08	Misposted credit note	JNL5	85.68	27/08	Balance b/d		644.26
28/08	Misposted invoice	JNL5	64.17	28/08	Misposted invoice	JNL1	97.40
28/08	Contra	JNL7	37.50	28/08	Misposted cash	JNL2	400.00
28/08	Balance c/d		954.31				
			1,141.66				1,141.66
				28/08	Balance b/d		954.31

Chapter 17 Control accounts

Chapter topic list

1 Internal check
2 Control accounts
3 Control account reconciliations

The following study sessions are covered in this chapter

			Syllabus reference
11	(a)	Understand the need for internal checks	7b
	(b)	Complete postings to control accounts and understand the link to books of prime entry	7b
	(c)	Understand the need for individual debtors and creditors accounts and understand the link to books of prime entry	7b
	(d)	Explain the purpose of control accounts (i) as a check on the accuracy of entries in the individual accounts (ii) to establish a total of debtors and creditors at any time (iii) to identify errors in the completion of the day book and in posting the totals from books of prime entry (iv) as an internal check; the control account should be administered by someone other than the person who completes the day books	7b
	(e)	Perform a basic control account reconciliation	7b
	(f)	Identify errors which would be highlighted by performing a control account reconciliation	7b

1 INTERNAL CHECK

What is internal check?

> **KEY TERM**
>
> **Internal check** is concerned with the maintenance of accounting records. Internal checks, sometimes known as internal controls, ensure that transactions to be recorded and processed have been authorised, that they are all included and that they are correctly recorded and accurately processed.

Types of internal check

1.1 You have already met some types of internal check in earlier chapters. Examples are as follows.

(a) A **trial balance** is a type of internal check. If a trial balance does not balance, you know that an error has been made. As you may remember, a trial balance will not pick up every error.

(b) **Bank reconciliations,** discussed in Chapter 12, are a check on the accuracy of the cash book.

(c) **Control account reconciliations.** Below is a brief reminder of control accounts which you met earlier in your studies. The balance on the control account should ideally be the same as the total of the sales or purchase ledger balances. In practice, it rarely is. However, it should reconcile (see Section 3 of this chapter).

(d) **Segregation of duties** is another form of internal check. For example, the person preparing a cheque should not be the person who signs it.

(e) **Authorisation**. All transactions should require authorisation or approval by an appropriate responsible person. The limits for these authorisations should be specified.

2 CONTROL ACCOUNTS

What are control accounts?

2.1 A control account is an account in the nominal ledger in which a record is kept of the total value of a number of similar but individual items. Control accounts are used chiefly for debtors and creditors.

Activity 17.1

You met control accounts in Chapter 4 of this Interactive Text. *Without looking*, define a **debtors control account** and a **creditors control account.**

2.2 Control accounts can also be kept for other items such as goods, wages and salaries.

2.3 Control accounts are part of the double entry system. Daybooks and cashbooks are totalled periodically (say once a month) and the appropriate totals are posted to the control accounts. The individual entries in cash and day books will have been entered one by one in

Part C: Recording and accounting for credit transactions

the appropriate personal accounts contained in the sales and purchase ledger. These personal accounts are not part of the double entry system: they are memorandum only.

> **Exam alert**
>
> You covered accounting for debtors and creditors in Chapters 4, 14 and 16. If you are at all unsure about where control accounts fit into the overall picture, look back to these chapters.

Entries in control accounts - a reminder

2.4 Typical entries in the control accounts are listed below. Reference "Jnl" indicates that the transaction is first lodged in the journal before posting to the control account and other accounts indicated. References SRDB and PRDB are to sales returns and purchase returns day books.

SALES LEDGER (DEBTORS) CONTROL

	Folio	£		Ref.	£
Opening debit balances	b/d	7,120			
Sales	SDB	52,500			
Dishonoured bills or cheques	Jnl	1,000	Cash received	CB	52,450
			Discounts allowed	CB	1,250
			Returns inwards from debtors	SRDB	800
			Bad debts	Jnl	300
			Closing debit balances	c/d	5,820
		60,620			60,620
Debit balances b/d		5,820			

Note. Opening credit balances are unusual in the debtors control account. They represent debtors to whom the business owes money, probably as a result of the over payment of debts or for advance payments of debts for which no invoices have yet been sent. In these unusual circumstances where opening credit balances exist, these should be brought forward as separate credit balances and not netted off against the debit balances.

BOUGHT LEDGER (CREDITORS) CONTROL

		£			£
Cash paid	CB	29,840	Opening credit balances	b/d	8,300
Discounts received	CB	100	Purchases and other expenses	PDB	31,100
Returns outwards to suppliers	PRDB	60			
Closing credit balances	c/d	9,400			
		39,400			39,400
			Credit balances	b/d	9,400

Note. Opening debit balances in the creditors control account are unusual but may occur in certain circumstances. They would represent suppliers who owe the business money, perhaps because debts have been overpaid or because debts have been prepaid before the supplier has sent an invoice. Where there are opening debit balances, these should be carried down as separate debit balances and not netted of against the credit balances.

2.5 Posting from the journal to the memorandum sales or purchase ledgers and to the nominal ledger may be effected as in the following example, where N Horrocks has returned goods with a sales value of £100.

Journal entry	Folio	Dr £	Cr £
Sales	NL 21	50	
To debtors' control	NL 6		50
To N Horrocks (memorandum)	SL 13	-	50

Return of electrical goods inwards.

Activity 17.2

A creditors control account contains the following entries.

	£
Bank	79,500
Credit purchases	83,200
Discounts received	3,750
Contra with debtors control account	4,000
Balance c/f at 31 December 20X8	12,920

There are no other entries in the account. What was the opening balance brought forward at 1 January 20X8?

Reasons for having control accounts

2.6 The reasons for having control accounts are as follows.

(a) They provide a **check on the accuracy** of entries made in the personal accounts in the sales ledger and purchase ledger. It is very easy to make a mistake in posting entries, because there might be hundreds of entries to make. Figures might get transposed. Some entries might be omitted altogether, so that an invoice or a payment transaction does not appear in a personal account as it should.

   (i) Compare the total **balance on the debtors control account** with the **total of individual balances** on the personal accounts in the sales ledger

   (ii) Compare the total **balance on the creditors control account** with the **total of individual balances** on the personal accounts in the purchase ledger

   It is possible to identify the fact that errors have been made.

(b) The control accounts could also assist in the **location of errors**, where postings to the control accounts are made daily or weekly, or even monthly. If a clerk fails to record an invoice or a payment in a personal account, or makes a transposition error, it would be a formidable task to locate the error or errors at the end of a year, say, given the hundreds or thousands of transactions during the year. By using the control account, a comparison with the individual balances in the sales or purchase ledger can be made for every week or day of the month, and the error found much more quickly than if control accounts did not exist.

(c) Where there is a separation of clerical (bookkeeping) duties, the control account provides an **internal check**. The person posting entries to the control accounts will act as a check on a different person whose job it is to post entries to the sales and purchase ledger accounts.

(d) To provide debtors' and creditors' balances more quickly for producing a trial balance or balance sheet. A single balance on a control account is obviously **extracted more simply and quickly** than many individual balances in the sales or purchase ledger. This means also that the number of accounts in the double entry bookkeeping system can be kept down to a manageable size, since the personal accounts are memorandum accounts only and the control accounts instead provide the accounts required for a double entry system.

2.7 However, particularly in computerised systems, it may be feasible to use sales and purchase ledgers without the need for operating separate control accounts. In such a system, the sales or purchase ledger printouts produced by the computer constitute the list of individual balances as well as providing a total balance which represents the control account balance.

3 CONTROL ACCOUNT RECONCILIATIONS

3.1 The control accounts should be **balanced regularly** (at least monthly), and the balance on the account agreed with the sum of the individual debtors' or creditors' balances extracted from the sales or bought ledgers respectively. It is one of the sad facts of an accountant's life that more often than not the balance on the control account does not agree with the sum of balances extracted, for one or more of the following reasons.

(a) An **incorrect amount** may be **posted** to the control account because of a miscast of the total in the book of prime entry (ie adding up incorrectly the total value of invoices or payments). The nominal ledger debit and credit postings will then balance, but the control account balance will not agree with the sum of individual balances extracted from the (memorandum) sales ledger or purchase ledger. A journal entry must then be made in the nominal ledger to correct the control account and the corresponding sales or expense account.

(b) A **transposition** error may occur in posting an individual's balance from the book of prime entry to the memorandum ledger, eg the sale to N Horrocks of £250 might be posted to his account as £520. This means that the sum of balances extracted from the memorandum ledger must be corrected. No accounting entry would be required to do this, except to alter the figure in N Horrocks's account.

(c) A transaction may be recorded in the control account and not in the memorandum ledger, or vice versa. This requires an entry in the ledger that has been **missed out** which means a double posting if the control account has to be corrected, and a single posting if it is the individual's balance in the memorandum ledger that is at fault.

(d) The sum of balances extracted from the memorandum ledger may be **incorrectly extracted** or **miscast**. This would involve simply correcting the total of the balances.

Example: agreeing control account balances with the sales and bought ledgers

3.2 Reconciling the control account balance with the sum of the balances extracted from the (memorandum) sales ledger or bought ledger should be done in two stages.

(a) Correct the total of the balances extracted from the memorandum ledger. (The errors must be located first of course.)

17: Control accounts

	£	£
Sales ledger total		
Original total extracted		15,320
Add difference arising from transposition error (£95 written as £59)		36
		15,356
Less		
Credit balance of £60 extracted as a debit balance (£60 × 2)	120	
Overcast of list of balances	90	
		210
		15,146

(b) Bring down the balance before adjustments on the control account, and adjust or post the account with correcting entries.

DEBTORS CONTROL

	£		£
Balance before adjustments	15,091	Petty cash - posting omitted	10
		Returns inwards - individual posting omitted from control account	35
Undercast of total invoices issued in sales day book	100	Balance c/d (now in agreement with the corrected total of individual balances in (a))	15,146
	15,191		15,191
Balance b/d	15,146		

Activity 17.3

The total of the balances in a company's sales ledger is £800 more than the debit balance on its debtors control account. Which one of the following errors could by itself account for the discrepancy?

A   The sales day book has been undercast by £800
B   Settlement discounts totalling £800 have been omitted from the nominal ledger
C   One sales ledger account with a credit balance of £800 has been treated as a debit balance
D   The cash receipts book has been undercast by £800

Activity 17.4

The balance on the creditors control account of Haldane Ltd as at 31 December 20X6 was £110,000. A review of the individual creditors' accounts revealed the following:

	£
Total on list of credit balances in the creditors' ledger	106,280

List of debit balances in the creditors' ledger:

	£
Glenn Ltd account	670
Hewson Ltd account	3,000
	3,670

1. The debit balance on Glenn Ltd account was caused by a transposition error when posting a payment as £1,£1,968 instead of £1,298.

2. The purchase day book has been added incorrectly overstating the total by £600.

3. Purchases of £3,800 had not been posted to Hewson's personal account in the creditors ledger.

4. Discounts received of £1,340 had been posted to the personal accounts concerned but not to the control account.

Part C: Recording and accounting for credit transactions

5. A bad debt of £980 written off Jim Birch's account in the debtors' ledger had been incorrectly posted to the creditors' control account.

Tasks

(a) Make the necessary corrections to the creditors' control account.
(b) Make the necessary corrections to the creditors' ledger, ensuring that the revised control account balance agrees with the adjusted list of balances in the creditors' ledger.

Key learning points

- A control account is an account in the general ledger in which a record is kept of the total value of a number of similar but individual items.

- Controls accounts have various uses.
  - Check accuracy of entries made in the personal accounts
  - Assist in the location of errors
  - Internal check where there is separation of bookkeeping duties
  - A balance can be extracted quickly for producing a trial balance or balance sheet

- For various reasons, the balance on the control account may not agree with the sum of the individual debtors or creditors balances extracted from the sales or purchase ledger.

Quick quiz

1. What is a control account?
2. What does the balance on the creditors control account represent?
3. A dishonoured cheque is a credit entry in the debtors control account. True or false?
4. How might a credit balance arise in the debtors control account?
5. Why might the balance on the debtors control account not agree with the total of the individual debtors' balances?
6. When may a control account act as an internal check?

Answers to quick quiz

1. An account in which a record is kept of the total value of a number of similar but individual items.

2. The total amount owed by the business to its creditors.

3. False. Cash received is a credit entry, therefore a dishonoured cheque must be a debit.

4. A customer may return goods or overpay his balance.

5. (i) There may be a transposition error in posting an individual's transaction from the book of prime entry to the memorandum ledger.

   (ii) The day book could be miscast.

   (iii) A transaction may be omitted from the control account or the memorandum account.

   (iv) The total may be incorrectly extracted.

6. Where there is separation of bookkeeping duties. The person posting entries to the control account will act as a check on a different person whose job it is to post entries to the sales and purchase ledger accounts.

17: Control accounts

Answers to activities

Answer 17.1

- A **debtors' control account** is an account in which records are kept of transactions involving all debtors in total. The balance on the debtors control account at any time will be the total amount due to the business at that time from its debtors.

- A **creditors' control account** is an account in which records are kept of transactions involving all creditors in total, and the balance on this account at any time will be the total amount owed by the business at that time to its creditors.

Answer 17.2

	£	£
Amounts due to creditors at 1 January (balancing figure)		16,970
Purchases in year		83,200
		100,170
Less: cash paid to creditors in year	79,500	
Discounts received	3,750	
Contra with debtors control	4,000	
		87,250
Amounts still unpaid at 31 December		12,920

Answer 17.3

A The total of sales invoices in the day book is debited to the control account. If the total is understated by £800, the debits in the control account will also be understated by £800. Options B and D would have the opposite effect: credit entries in the control account would be understated. Option C would lead to a discrepancy of 2 × £800 = £1,600.

Answer 17.4

		£
(a)	Balance per creditors' control account	110,000
	Less: Overstatement of purchase day book totals	(600)
	Less: Discounts received not posted to control a/c	(1,340)
	Less: Bad debt written off, incorrectly posted to the creditors' control account	(980)
	Creditors' control account – adjusted balance	107,080

(b)	Adjustments to the list of balances in the creditors' ledger	DR	CR
	Total credit balances in the creditors' ledger		106,280
	Total debit balances in the creditors' ledger	(3,670)	
	Adjust for transposition error in Glenn Ltd's account	670	
	Adjust for invoice of £3,800 not posted in Hewson's personal account	3,800	
			800
	Total per list of balances in the creditors' ledger		107,080

Part D
Payroll

Chapter 18 Recording payroll transactions

Chapter topic list

1. The nature of payroll
2. Gross pay and basic pay
3. Overtime, bonus payments and commissions
4. Payroll administration and documentation
5. Payroll deductions
6. Payment methods
7. Updating records

The following study sessions are covered in this chapter

			Syllabus reference
10	(a)	Understand payroll systems	6a
	(b)	Understand the duties of employers in relation to taxes, state benefit contributions and other deductions	6a
	(c)	Record hours worked; time sheets, clock cards	6a
	(d)	Calculate gross wages for employees paid by hour, by output (piecework) and salaried workers	6a
	(e)	Define and calculate bonuses, overtime and commissions given the details of each scheme	6a
	(f)	Describe the documentation required for recording various elements of wages and salaries	6a
	(g)	Recognise the need for payroll to be authorised and identify appropriate authorisation, security and control procedures	6a
	(h)	Make other deductions from wages – trade union subscriptions, payroll saving, pension contributions and payroll giving	6a
	(i)	Identify various methods for making payments to employees	6a
	(j)	Account for payroll costs and payroll deductions	6a

Part D: Payroll

1 THE NATURE OF PAYROLL

Payroll and the employee

1.1 If you keep an eye on what goes on in your bank account, you will notice that the items of income (which are few and far between) are vastly outnumbered by the outgoings. The principal credit entry on your bank statement is your salary or wage, every month (or week).

1.2 Your salary determines what you can afford, what you can borrow, and what you can save, both for yourself and your dependants. So, if you expect a net payment of £540 per month and plan accordingly, imagine how concerned you would be if you only received £450. All your plans would be thrown into disarray, if you're unlucky you might run up an overdraft with the expense of bank charges and interest which that entails, or you might end up delaying settling some of your bills.

1.3 The credit entry to the bank statement, or the jangle of coins in the wages packet, is the final result of a long process of recording and calculation. This is often referred to as payroll processing and payroll accounting.

> **KEY TERM**
>
> A **payroll** is a list of employees and what they are to be paid. Being on the payroll of an organisation means that you are selling your labour to it for an agreed price: you are in paid employment, and your employer benefits from your skills and your time.

1.4 If you are employed as a payroll clerk, officer, or supervisor, what you do as your daily job has a direct and immediate impact on the life and happiness of every individual on the payroll.

Payroll and the employer

1.5 From the employer's point of view, too, the wages and salaries bill is of great importance. It is one of the largest items of expenditure an employer has to incur.

1.6 The payroll function is one of the pillars of an organisation's system for analysing and controlling costs, and assessing the organisation's economic efficiency.

Payroll and the government

1.7 As a payroll officer, or whatever title you might have if your job involves payroll work, you probably do not consider yourself as part of the government's tax collecting system. However, as we shall see in more detail later, this is effectively what you are.

1.8 Most people have to pay some of what they earn to the government as **taxation**, which pays for general social benefits (eg the Health Service, parts of the Education system). In the UK, people also pay **National Insurance** (NI) contributions. In practice, NI is similar to a tax: when originally introduced, it was a state-run insurance scheme, and so paying your NI contribution was like paying the instalments on an insurance policy.

1.9 People pay tax on what they earn, as **Income Tax**. This tax is collected by the employer when the employee is paid. The same is true for National Insurance. The system is called **PAYE (Pay As You Earn)**.

18: Recording payroll transactions

> **KEY TERM**
>
> **PAYE** is the system whereby the employer collects tax on behalf of the government as the employee is paid.

Employer's legal responsibilities to collect PAYE

1.10 **Employer's duties**

(a) Operate the PAYE system for all covered by it.

(b) Maintain the necessary records.

(c) Pay the Income Tax and National Insurance collected from employees to the Inland Revenue every month (in most cases).

(d) Let the Inland Revenue, or staff from the Department of Social Security or the Contributions Agency, inspect the records.

(e) Submit end of year returns.

(f) Give employees payslips detailing tax and NI deducted and to give them an annual statement (P60).

(g) Maintain for three years, at the minimum, after the end of a tax year, the records relating to that year.

Activity 18.1

All an employee's income is assessed to tax through the PAYE system.

True ☐   False ☐

Activity 18.2

It is the employee's duty to ensure that the correct deductions are made from his or her income and that the correct PAYE records are kept.

True ☐   False ☐

1.11 The **main requirements of** a **payroll processing** and accounting system are as follows.

1.12 **Accuracy** is very important.

- People get paid what they are owed
- The government receives what it is legally entitled to
- The employer's cost information is appropriate

The employer's cost information probably does not need to be accurate to the nearest penny, but the wages paid and tax collected do.

In an organisation with a large number of employees, slicing 10p off everyone's pay entitlement (a so-called Salami fraud) could net a criminal a considerable amount of money. For example, if there were 10,000 employees in an organisation and each was defrauded of

Part D: Payroll

10p per month, this would provide the fraudster with £1,000 each month. This might seem far-fetched to you, but there have been a number of frauds discovered by examining payslips which were only a few pence out.

1.13 **Timeliness**

(a) The employees do not suffer stress caused by being short of cash

(b) Employee morale does not suffer because of the fear that the employer has not got the money to pay their wages

(c) The Inland Revenue's requirements for prompt payment are satisfied

Management information may not be required quite so quickly, but there will be internal management information requirements which have to be satisfied within certain deadlines.

1.14 **Security**

(a) Payroll data relating to employees is kept confidential and is only disclosed to those authorised by the employee, or to those who have a legal right to see it

(b) Cash and cheques are not stolen, and the payroll system is safe from fraud

1.15 Payroll is an important function.

(a) Employees depend on the timeliness and accuracy of the processing

(b) The government has a direct interest in the collection of taxes and social security benefits through the payroll system

(c) The wages and salaries bill is a large component of an enterprise's total costs

2 GROSS PAY AND BASIC PAY

2.1 At the end of every payroll period we have to work out the gross pay for each employee.

> **KEY TERM**
>
> **Gross pay** is what an employee earns. It is not what the employee actually receives in cash or by transfer to the bank account.

2.2 Here is an example which shows how the two can differ.

	£
Basic pay etc: what your work has earned for you	1,000
Other pay (includes statutory sick pay, statutory maternity pay, holiday pay etc)	200
Gross pay	1,200
Less deductions	
Income Tax	(140)
National Insurance	(100)
Other deductions (eg pension scheme)	(50)
Net pay: what you take home or what goes into your bank account	910

2.3 Deductions are covered later in this chapter.

2.4 There are several ways to calculate an employee's earnings.

- The same amount every month
- On an hourly rate
- On a performance basis (eg per unit of output)

2.5 In addition there are other ways of remunerating employees.

(a) **Overtime** means that employees receive more for working extra hours.

(b) **Bonus schemes** are used so that employees can benefit from improvements in the overall performance of all or part of the enterprise which employs them.

2.6 **Basic pay** is often the largest element in the earnings calculation.

> **KEY TERM**
>
> **Basic pay** is the rate for the job, and is what you expect to receive for a normal period's work, irrespective of overtime and so forth.

There are a number of ways of calculating basic pay, and these are described below.

Basic pay: Fixed rate per period

2.7 Your contract of employment might state that you are to be paid, say, £9,000 per annum, that you will enjoy four weeks leave, and that you are expected to work a 35 hour week.

2.8 You are being paid, here, a fixed rate per annum of £9,000. Usually this annual amount will be divided into twelve equal monthly payments. Most employers pay at the end of the calendar month.

2.9 **EXAMPLE: BASIC SALARY**

Your contract of employment states that you are to receive an annual salary of £9,000. You join on 1 January 20X2. You are told that the first three months of your employment are a probationary period, and that from 1 April 20X2 your annual salary will increase by 10%. You are informed on 20 May 20X2 that everyone in the company is to receive a pay rise: yours works out at £600 per year in addition to the 10% rise you have already received, effective from 1 July 20X2.

Task

(a) What will be your basic pay for each of the following months?

  (i) January 20X2
  (ii) May 20X2
  (iii) July 20X2

(b) (i) At 31 December 20X2, how much basic pay would you have received since 1 January 20X2?

  (ii) Assuming no further rises, how much basic pay could you expect to receive in the 12 months to 31 March 20X3?

Part D: Payroll

2.10 SOLUTION

(a) (i) £9,000/12 = £750

(ii) £9,000 + (10% × £9,000) = £9,900, your new annual salary.

So, £9,900/12 = £825

(iii) £9,900 + £600 is £10,500, your latest annual salary.

So, £10,500/12 = £875

(b) (i) Remember that an annual salary is effectively a rate per month, and so your increases will not be backdated.

January	£750
February	£750
March	£750
April	£825
May	£825
June	£825

July to December £875 per month for 6 months

You have therefore earned (3 × £750) + (3 × £825) + (6 × £875) which comes to a total of £9,975 in the 12 months to 31 December 20X2.

(ii) In the 12 months to 31 March 20X3:

20X2	
April	£825
May	£825
June	£825

July to December £875 per month for 6 months

20X3	
January	£875
February	£875
March	£875

So, in total you will have received three months at £825, and nine months at £875 giving a total of £10,350.

Basic pay: Hourly rate

2.11 Some workers get paid a rate per hour. If you work 40 hours at £5 per hour then your basic pay will be £200.

2.12 High day-rate schemes aim to stimulate greater productivity (ie amount of output per hour) through higher pay. Employees are paid a higher hourly rate than that offered by most other employers in the hope that this will make them more productive.

Piecework

2.13 In a piecework scheme, wages are calculated by the following formula.

Wages = Units produced × Rate of pay per unit

Suppose, for example, an employee is paid £2 for each unit produced.

Weekly production	Pay
	(40 hours)
Units	£
40	80
50	100
60	120
70	140

As his output increases, the wage increases.

2.14 However, it is common for pieceworkers to be offered a guaranteed minimum wage, so that they do not suffer loss of earnings when production is low through no fault of their own.

2.15 EXAMPLE: PIECEWORK

Penny Pincher is paid 50p for each towel she weaves, but she is guaranteed a minimum wage of £60 for a 40 hour week. In a series of four weeks, she makes 100, 120, 140 and 160 towels. What was her pay each week?

	Output	Pay
	Units	£
1	100	60 (minimum wage)
2	120 × 50p	60
3	140 × 50p	70
4	160 × 50p	80

There is no incentive to Penny Pincher to produce more output unless she can exceed 120 units in a week. The guaranteed minimum wage in this case might be too high to provide an incentive.

2.16 Sometimes an employee may make several different types of product, some of which take longer than others. In this case, it is not possible to add up the units for payment purposes. Instead a standard time allowance is given for each unit to arrive at a total of piecework hours for payment.

2.17 EXAMPLE: PIECEWORK HOURS

An employee is paid £3 per piecework hour produced. In a 40 hour week the employee produces the following output.

	Piecework time allowed per unit
15 units of product X	0.5 hours
20 units of product Y	2.0 hours

What is the employee's pay for the week?

2.18 SOLUTION

Piecework hours produced:

Product X	15 × 0.5 hours	7.5 hours
Product Y	20 × 2.0 hours	40.0 hours
Total piecework hours		47.5 hours

Therefore the employee's pay = 47.5 × £3 = £142.50 for the week.

Differential piecework

2.19 Differential piecework schemes offer an incentive to employees to increase their output by paying higher rates for increased levels of production.

Up to 80 units per week, rate of pay per unit = £1.00
80 to 90 units per week, rate of pay per unit = £1.20
Above 90 units per week, rate of pay per unit = £1.30

Employers must make it clear whether they intend to pay the increased rate on all units produced, or on the extra output only.

Piecework schemes generally

2.20 Piecework schemes enjoy fluctuating popularity. They are occasionally used by employees as a means of increasing pay levels when other means are not available to them, but they are frequently condemned as a means of driving employees to work too hard to earn a satisfactory wage.

A further disadvantage of piecework schemes is that careful inspection of output is necessary so that quality does not suffer as employees try to increase the quantity produced.

3 OVERTIME, BONUS PAYMENTS AND COMMISSIONS

KEY TERM

Overtime pay is payment for work done in excess of an employee's hours at basic rate pay.

3.1 Generally speaking, you get a higher rate per hour. The employment contract of an hourly paid worker might specify that overtime is paid at time and a half. This means that the worker is paid half as much again for an hour of overtime as an hour paid at basic rate.

3.2 For example, if an hour at basic rate is £4, how much is an hour of overtime at time and a half?

The payment per hour of overtime is £4 + (£4 × 50%) = £6 per hour.

3.3 Sometimes there are a number of overtime rates offered. For example, a contract may specify the following rates.

(a) 40 hours at a basic rate of £4 per hour

(b) The first ten hours overtime at time and a half (ie £6)

(c) Overtime over and above ten hours at double time (basic rate times two, in this case £8 per hour)

3.4 EXAMPLE: OVERTIME

Marguerite Yourcenar works in a library. She is paid on an hourly basis. Her basic rate for the 35 hours she normally works a week is £6 per hour. The first five hours overtime are paid at time and a quarter. Any more overtime hours worked are paid at time and a half.

In the week ended 3 August 20X2 she worked a total of 47 hours.

Task

For the week ended 3 August 20X2 calculate Marguerite Yourcenar's basic pay and the overtime payments she receives, showing how each is made up.

3.5 SOLUTION

		£
Basic pay is	35 hours at £6 per hour	210.00
Overtime	5 hours at [£6 × 1.25 =] £7.50 per hour	37.50
Overtime	7 hours at [£6 × 1.50 =] £9.00 per hour	63.00
Total	47 hours	310.50

Overtime payments for employees on fixed annual salaries

3.6 Marguerite Yourcenar was an hourly-paid worker, and the calculation of her overtime payment was a fairly simple matter of assessing how many hours she worked at basic rate, and how many at the two overtime rates.

3.7 Overtime payments are also paid to staff who receive a fixed annual salary divided into equal monthly instalments. The hourly rate for overtime could be set out in the employment contract.

3.8 It may, of course, be the employer's policy not to pay overtime at all. Staff might be expected to work extra hours, as a matter of professionalism when the situation requires. This is particularly true of more senior employees and managers.

Activity 18.3

Alphonse is an hourly paid employee. His basic rate is £5 per hour for daytime shifts, £7.50 per hour for nighttime shifts, £7.50 per hour for overtime (ie hours worked in excess of 40 hours a week) except weekends when the rate is always £10 per hour.

How much would he earn, assuming an 8-hour day.

(a) For a 40 hour week of daytime shifts with no overtime?
(b) For a 40 hour week if one day is worked on Saturday?
(c) For a 40 hour week of nightshifts and an additional four hours overtime?

Activity 18.4

Boris is a pieceworker, and is paid £5 per widget produced. However, he gets a guaranteed minimum wage of £30, and if he works more than 50 hours a week he gets £2 per hour as overtime. If he produces over 60 widgets per week he gets £6 per widget over 60. How much would he earn in each of the following weeks?

(a) In the week ending 13/3/X1 Boris made 50 widgets and did 4 hours of overtime.
(b) In the week ending 20/3/X1 he produced one widget.
(c) In the week ending 27/3/X1 he produced 6 widgets.
(d) In the week ending 3/4/X1, Boris produced 70 widgets, and worked 6 hours overtime.

Part D: Payroll

> **KEY TERM**
>
> A **bonus** is an extra payment made to an employee (or a group of employees) as a reward for results achieved.

3.9 Offering a **bonus** is intended to motivate employees to work harder and to reach or exceed some target (normally of sales or productivity). In a sales department, a bonus might be paid to all individuals in a sales team if the sales for a period exceed the budget. Or, it might be paid to factory workers who produce more within a certain period than budgeted, so that the profit for the extra effort is shared between employer and employees.

3.10 EXAMPLE: BONUS SCHEMES

Carrot and Stick plc is a company which uses a variety of bonus schemes to motivate its employees.

(a) Senior managers get a bonus based on how well the company is doing as a whole. Their bonus is a percentage of their salary. For example if the company increases its annual profits by 1% then they get a bonus of 1% of their salary, paid on 30 June.

(b) The sales force, which has 100 members, gets a bonus paid on the last day of the month, based on the value of sales per month. If the value of sales (excluding VAT) is over £35 million in a particular month, 1% of the excess is divided equally between the members of the sales force.

(c) Factory workers receive a bonus based on productivity. They normally produce 1,000 units an hour. If they produce more than this amount per hour, then they get a payment of 10p per worker for every extra unit produced.

(d) All employees get a one-off bonus, in addition to any others, of £30 if Carrot and Stick plc's profits in the year to 31 March exceed £127.5 million. This is paid on 30 June.

(e) Weekly workers are given an extra one week's wages if their performance at work has merited them a Grade 1 assessment by their bosses for four consecutive weeks.

In the year ended 31 March 20X2, Carrot and Stick plc had made a profit of £130 million, a 3% increase over the year ended 31 March 20X1. This was £5 million more than anticipated. In the week ended 30 June 20X2 the factory staff produced 100 units more than usual. In the month of June 20X2, the value of sales excluding VAT was £36 million.

Task

Calculate the bonuses which will be paid in the following cases.

(a) David Eadwood, Senior Manager Finance Department, earns £30,000 per year. What bonuses will he receive on 30 June 20X2 for the year?

(b) Bernadette Larney, Assistant Sales Executive, earns £18,000 per year. What bonuses does she receive in the month ending 30 June 20X2?

(c) Stan Takhanov is a factory worker with a Grade 1 assessment in the four weeks ended 30 June 20X2. He earns £150 per week. What bonuses will he receive in the four weeks ended 30 June 20X2?

3.11 SOLUTION

(a) *David Eadwood*

	£
£30,000 × 3% profit increase is	900
One-off bonus	30
Total bonuses for the year ended 30 June 20X2	930

(b) *Bernadette Larney*

	£
Sales bonus [£36m-£35m ×1%]/100 sales staff	100
One-off bonus	30
Total bonuses in the month ended 30 June 20X2	130

(c) *Stan Takhanov*

	£
Grade 1 assessment bonus (ie one week's wage)	150
Extra production bonus 100 units at 10p	10
One-off bonus	30
Total bonuses in the four weeks ended 30 June 20X2	190

Commission

> **KEY TERM**
>
> **Commission** is a payment made to an employee (or agent) based on the value of something (usually sales) the employee (or agent) has generated.

3.12 This definition sounds complicated, but the examples below will show you how simple most commission schemes are.

3.13 It is not unheard of for **commission** to form the bulk of an employee's earnings, especially if that employee works in a selling capacity.

3.14 **Commission is usually based on the sales achieved**. (Note that the basis for calculating commission will in almost all cases exclude VAT.) Some examples are given below.

(a) Commission can be a **straight percentage** of all sales (eg 10% so that if you make £1,000 of sales you get £100, for £100,000 you get £10,000 etc).

(b) Commission can be on a **sliding scale,** so that more valuable contracts earn the salesperson greater commission (eg on contracts up to £5,000 a 5% commission is given, on contracts over £5,000 a 7.5% commission is given and so on).

(c) Commission can **increase with the total volume of sales**. For example, on total sales up to £100,000 a 5% commission is earned: if the target is exceeded, then a 7.5% commission is paid on the excess (ie all sales over £100,000).

3.15 EXAMPLE: COMMISSION

The Bubbly Shampoo Company Ltd sells crates of Bubbly Shampoo for £100 each. The company employs two sales staff. Each is paid commission, but on a different basis.

Part D: Payroll

(a) Michele Thuselah receives no commission on the first hundred crates of Bubbly Shampoo she sells a week, 10% commission on crates sold in excess of 100 but below 200, 15% on crates sold in excess of 200 but below 300 and 20% on crates sold in excess of 300. She receives her commission at the end of the month in which the sale is made. She receives a basic annual salary of £9,000 per year.

(b) Jerry O'Boam receives a basic salary of £4,500 per year and a straight 7.5% commission on all he sells.

From 2 August 20X2, Michele sold 120 crates in the first week, 340 in the second week, 30 in the third week and 95 in the fourth week. She made no sales on 1 August, 30 August or 31 August. In the same month, Jerry sold 500 crates.

Task

What are Michele's and Jerry's earnings, both basic salary and commission, in the four weeks from 2 August to 29 August 20X2?

3.16 SOLUTION

Michele			£
Basic salary	£9,000/12		750.00
Commission:	Week 1	20 × £100 × 10%	200.00
	Week 2	100 × £100 × 10%	1,000.00
		100 × £100 × 15%	1,500.00
		40 × £100 × 20%	800.00
	Week 3	None, as fewer than 100 crates sold	
	Week 4	None, as fewer than 100 crates sold	
Total earnings for August			4,250.00

Jerry	£
Basic salary £4,500/12	375.00
Commission 500 × £100 × 7.5%	3,750.00
Total earnings for August	4,125.00

Activity 18.5

Cassandra works for a company which pays bonuses and commission. Her basic pay is £900 per month, but at the end of the month she receives commission of 5% of the sales she made in the previous month (so that at the end of May she will be paid the commission for April for example). If her sales exceed £10,000 in any quarter (ie three month period from 1 January to 31 March, 1 April to 30 June, 1 July to 30 September, 1 October to 31 December) she gets a one-off bonus of £1,000. These are paid in the month after the quarter.

Here are her sales figures for the first six months of 20X2.

Month	£
Jan	5,000
Feb	4,000
March	3,000
April	2,000
May	3,000
June	4,000

Her sales in December 20X1 were £5,000.

What will be included in her gross pay at the end of each month from January to June inclusive?

Activity 18.6

Dilys is a salaried worker, who also receives overtime of £10 per hour for hours worked over 156 a month, and a productivity bonus of 5% of her basic monthly salary if the quality of her work exceeds expectations.

Her salary was £12,000 per year, payable in equal monthly instalments. This has been increased to £15,000, by agreement on 1 May, backdated to 1 January.

In May she worked 175 hours, and produced work of better quality than standard.

What will she receive as gross pay in May?

4 PAYROLL ADMINISTRATION AND DOCUMENTATION

Personnel department

4.1 The personnel department is responsible for recruiting and engaging employees. The personnel department holds certain basic data relating to the employees.

(a) A **personnel record card** might be completed for each employee. An example of a personnel record card is provided on the page after next. Note that there might be other information recorded as well, and so what is provided on the face of the card is not an exhaustive list.

(b) A **record of attendance card** might also be kept by the personnel department to review the number of days off work taken because of sickness, or the amount of leave taken, as holiday or for special reasons (eg bereavement). An example of such a card is provided on the page following the personnel record card.

This information might be held on computer, in which case the record will appear as a number of screens. The data held will, however, be the same. The main computer screen might be as follows.

```
A COMPANY PERSONNEL SYSTEM

Name: A Chappe

         Main Menu        Press

      1  Personal details
      2  Job and salary
      3  Training
      4  Exit
```

4.2 The personnel department may be involved in setting wage and salary levels, but is not usually involved in the day to day payroll process.

Part D: Payroll

Payroll function

4.3 The payroll function may be performed by a separate department, or by staff within the accounts department.

4.4 The role of the payroll department, or the payroll function comprises the following.

- Calculation of gross pay
- Calculation of tax, national insurance and other deductions
- Preparing payslips
- Making appropriate returns to external agencies such as the Inland Revenue
- Making up wages, or preparing tapes for bank transfer
- Distributing payslips
- Preparing payroll statistics.

Documentation – salaried employees

4.5 The personnel records held in the personnel department document how much each salaried employee is to be paid, and for what periods.

4.6 All the personnel department has to do is tell the payroll department how much the employee is to be paid, and the date from which the rate of pay is effective.

4.7 The payroll department will receive instructions from the personnel department relating to salary increases, or other alterations to an employee's pay.

Documentation - hourly paid employees

4.8 Hours of attendance can be recorded in a register in which employees note their times of arrival or by the use of a **time recording clock** which stamps the time on a card inserted by the employee. (Other similar automated schemes of time recording exist.)

Attendance cards are the basis for payroll preparation. Pre-printed blanks are used, allowing for the entry of gross wages and all deductions giving a net end figure.

(a) For time workers, the gross wage is the product of time attended and rate of pay. We then add overtime premium and bonus.

(b) For piece workers, gross wages are normally obtained as the product of the number of good units produced and the unit rate. We then add any premiums, bonuses and allowance for incomplete jobs.

4.9 Job time booking can also be done manually or by the use of a time recording device. The method adopted will depend on the size of the organisation and the nature of the work.

4.10 The records required might be one or several of the following.

(a) **Daily time sheets.** These are filled in by the employee to indicate time spent on each job. The total time on the time sheet should correspond with time shown on the attendance record.

(b) **Weekly time sheets.** These are similar to daily time sheets but are passed to the cost office at the end of the week, although entries should be made daily to avoid error.

(c) **Job cards.** Cards are prepared for each job. The time spent on the job by each employee is noted on the card.

PERSONNEL RECORD CARD

NUMBER:
NAME: OTHER, A.N.

PERSONAL DETAILS

SURNAME	OTHER	SEX	Nationality	British
FORENAMES	ALBERT NEIL	(M) F	Social Security Number	WD 48 47 41C

ADDRESS: 94 Bootsale House, Antique Street, Old Sarum, MERSEY OS2
Telephone: 900 738 9521

Date of Birth	1 June 1959
Marital Status	Single (Married) Separated Divorced Widowed
Dependants	3
Disabilities	None
Pension Scheme Eligible	1989 January
Joined	1989 January

ADDRESS 1ST CHANGE: 17 Newton Close, Brookeside, MERSEY ME1
Telephone: 1000 111 2221

ADDRESS 2ND CHANGE:

Professional Qualifications
Accounting Technician 1989

Educational Details
Higher Education
A levels: Economics (C)
BTec: Computer Services
Telephone:

GCSE	n/a
O levels	3
CSEs	4
Other	City & Guilds Photography

IN EMERGENCY CONTACT
Name: Other, Noreen Olga — Wife
Address: 17 Newton Close, Brookeside, MERSEY ME1
Telephone (h): 1000 111 2221
Telephone (wk): 1000 999 8887

EMPLOYMENT HISTORY

Years of Service (12 months to 31 December)
1 2 3 4 5 6 7 8 9 10 11 12 13 14 15 16 17 18 19 20 21 22

FROM	TO	TITLE	DEPT	REASON	PAY
1/1/88	31/3/88	Junior Clerk	Sls Ledger	1st job here	£6,500
1/4/88	30/6/88			Probation period over	£7,000
1/7/88				Annual payrise 5%	£7,350
1/89		Senior Clerk	Pur Ledger	Got AAT Quals & promoted	£9,000
7/89				10% pay rise	£9,900
7/90				10% (8% + 2% merit)	£10,890
12/90		Asst Technician	Payroll	Transfer	£10,890

Training History

Course Code		
0713/1	Induction to new employees	

Special Details

Leave Entitlement   20 days

Part D: Payroll

NAME: A.N OTHER **DEPT:** 072 **N.I REF:** WD 48 47 41 C **LEAVE ENTITLEMENT:** 20

	1	2	3	4	5	6	7	8	9	10	11	12	13	14	15	16	17	18	19	20	21	22	23	24	25	26	27	28	29	30	31
JAN																															
FEB																															
MAR																															
APR																															
MAY																															
JUNE																															
JULY																															
AUG																															
SEPT																															
OCT																															
NOV																															
DEC																															

Illness: I Leave: L Training: T *Note overleaf:* (1) The reasons for special leave (eg bereavement).
Industrial Accident: IA Unpaid Leave: UL Jury Service: J (2) Ensure training is noted on personnel card.
Maternity: M Unpaid Leave: SL

RECORD OF ATTENDANCE

(d) **Route cards**. These are similar to job cards, except that they follow the product through the works and carry details of all operations to be carried out.

4.11 Timesheets and job or route cards can take many different forms, some of which involve computerised systems of time-recording. The following examples may help to indicate the basic principles of recording labour costs of production work.

Time Sheet No........................							
Employee Name.................. Clock Code....................... Dept................							
Date........................... Week No...............................							
Job No.	Start Time	Finish Time	Quantity	Checker	Hours	Rate	Extension

The time sheet will be filled in by the employee, for hours worked on each job (job code) or area of work (cost code). Idle time, lunch breaks etc, should also be recorded.

4.12 A job card will be given to the employee, showing the work to be done and the expected time it should take. The employee will record the time started and time finished for each job. Breaks for tea and lunch may be noted on the card, as standard times, by the production planning department. The hours actually taken and the cost of those hours will be calculated by the accounting department.

JOB CARD					
Employee No.. Date.......................................					
Name... Department code.....................					
Job No.	Standard time (hours)	Time started	Time finished	Hours taken	Cost
345	2				
348	1 1/2				
349	2 1/2				
352	1 3/4				
Tea break (morning)... (afternoon).............................					
Lunch break (afternoon)...					
Idle time reference no...					
Signed by.. Date.......................................					
Verified by (foreman).................................... Date.......................................					

Part D: Payroll

Timesheets and salaried staff

4.13 You might think there is little point in salaried staff filling a detailed timesheet about what they do every hour of the day, as they are paid a flat rate every month. However, in many enterprises they are required to do so. There are a number of reasons for this.

(a) You should have remembered from the last chapter that payroll data is used to create management information about product costs, and hence profitability.

(b) The timesheet information may have a direct impact on the revenue the enterprise receives (see below.)

(c) Timesheets are used to record hours spent, and so support claims for overtime when this is paid to salaried staff.

4.14 On the following page is the type of timesheet which can be found in large firms in the service sector of the economy: examples would be a firm of solicitors, a firm of accountants and a firm of management consultants.

18: Recording payroll transactions

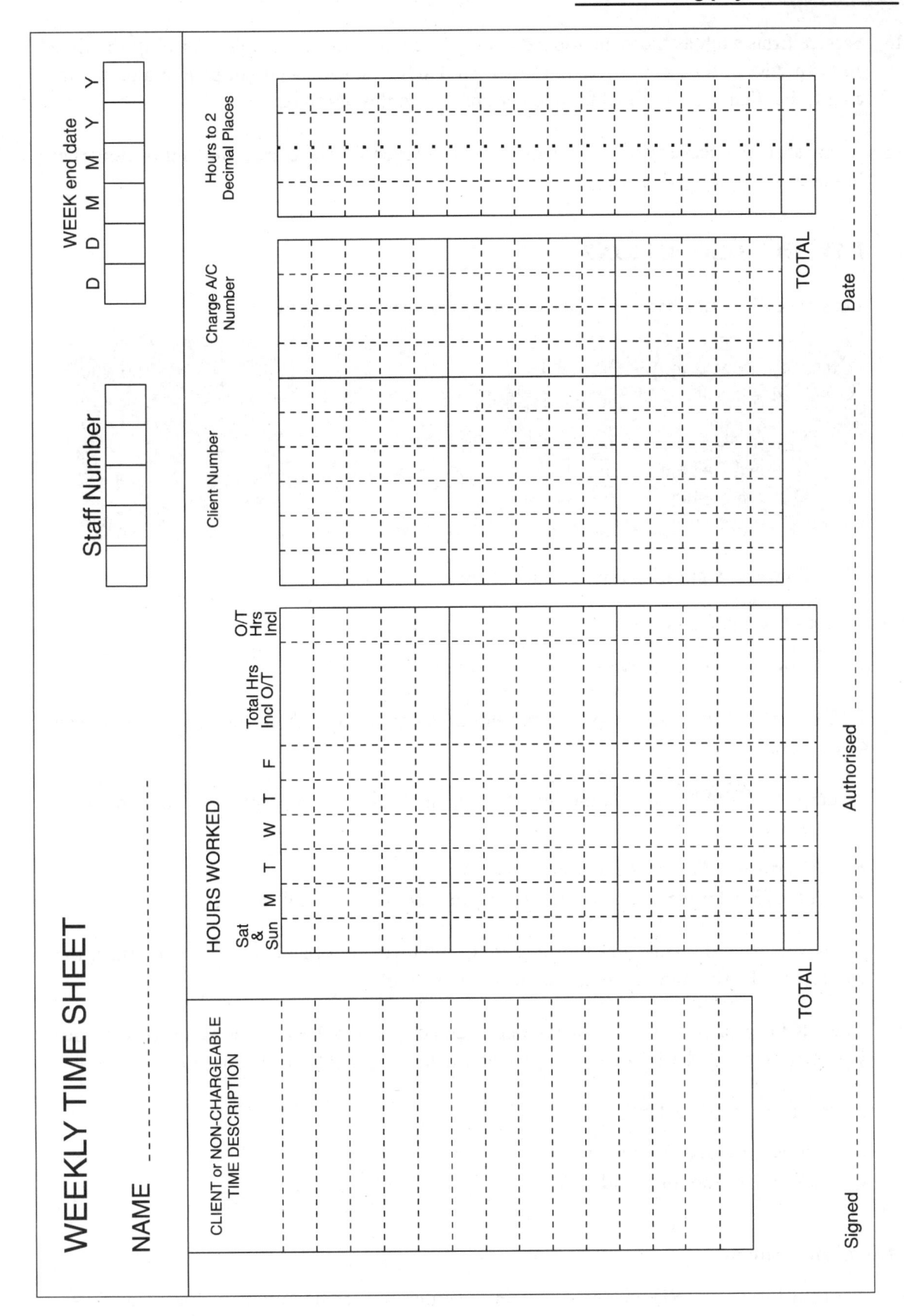

WEEKLY TIME SHEET

NAME _____

Staff Number ☐☐☐☐☐

WEEK end date
D D M M Y Y
☐☐☐☐☐☐

CLIENT or NON-CHARGEABLE TIME DESCRIPTION	Client Number	Charge A/C Number	Hours to 2 Decimal Places

HOURS WORKED							
Sat & Sun	M	T	W	T	F	Total Hrs Incl O/T	O/T Hrs Incl

TOTAL _____ TOTAL _____

Signed _____ Authorised _____ Date _____

4.15 Service firms such as those mentioned above are chiefly in the business of selling the time and expertise of their employees to clients. So if an employee spends an hour at a particular client, the client will be billed for one hour of the employee's time.

4.16 A timesheet is necessary so that clients will be charged for the correct amount of time that has been spent doing their work.

5 PAYROLL DEDUCTIONS

5.1 Let's have a look at a basic computation to see where everything fits in.

	£
Gross pay (what your work has earned you)	1,000
Other (includes statutory sick pay, statutory maternity pay, holiday pay etc)	200
	1,200
less Income Tax (PAYE)	(140)
National Insurance (NI)	(100)
Other deductions	(50)
Net pay	910

5.2 We will now look at various types of deductions

Income tax - the PAYE system

5.3 PAYE covers all the employees of an organisation.

5.4 PAYE does not cover self-employed people. If you are unsure about the difference, re-read Chapter 1.

5.5 Under the UK PAYE system, the Inland Revenue deals with employers through a network of tax offices.

- A particular **Tax Office** to deal with each employer
- A **PAYE reference number** (an identity number for the employer)

5.6 Employees have the same Tax Office as their employer, and the Tax Office will attach the employer's identity number to its records for each employee.

5.7 The UK **tax year** runs from 6 April in one calendar year to 5 April in the following calendar year. For example, the 2001/2002 tax year runs from 6 April 2001 to 5 April 2002.

5.8 Each tax year is divided into

- weeks, for weekly paid staff
- months, for monthly paid staff

National Insurance

5.9 National Insurance (NI) imposes a system of compulsory contributions for each employee, borne in part by the employee and in part by the employer, to fund the following benefits.

- Unemployment benefit
- Income support
- The state pension scheme, and the State Earnings Related Pension scheme
- The National Health Service

5.10 Employees' National Insurance contributions are **one of the deductions from salary** in arriving at net pay. **Employers also pay National Insurance**.

5.11 National Insurance payments are known as National Insurance Contributions (NICs)

5.12 The total amount remitted each period by the employer to the collecting authorities in NICs comprises the following.

(a) NICs payable by the employee, which form part of the deductions from gross pay.

(b) NICs payable by the employer, which have nothing to do with what goes into the employee's pay packet or cheque or bank transfer, but which are an additional cost to the employer.

> The total cost of wages and salaries in the profit and loss account is:
>
> Gross wages + employer's NIC

Give As You Earn (GAYE)

5.13 The simplest way of giving to charity is a gift out of taxed income. Putting a coin in a collecting box, or making a telephone donation by credit card (eg in response to a television feature) is an example of this.

5.14 However, although simple these are the most costly ways of giving to charity. Some other ways of charitable giving can ensure that the Inland Revenue forks out a bit too.

What is GAYE?

5.15 GAYE stands for Give As You Earn. This is sometimes referred to as **payroll giving**. It is entirely voluntary, so an employee can never be required to join a GAYE scheme.

5.16 In a GAYE scheme, an employee is allowed to set aside a portion of his or her gross salary for charitable donations. This portion of gross salary is not taxed, although both employer's and employee's NICs are still payable on this amount.

5.17 The employer pays the amounts collected to 'an approved agency charity' such as the Charities Aid Foundation.

5.18 Apart from paying the money to the agency charity, all the payroll office has to do is ensure that the correct deductions from gross pay are made according to the employee's instructions, and that the correct entries are made on the deductions working sheet.

5.19 The employer can deduct 5% of the donation to cover administration costs, but many choose not to.

5.20 EXAMPLE: GAYE

Gene Rowse earns a gross salary of £12,600 a year, payable in equal monthly instalments. The company which employs him, Tea and Sympathy Ltd, operates a payroll giving scheme. Gene contributes £50 per month from his gross pay.

Part D: Payroll

Tasks

(a) What is his gross pay?

(b) What will be entered in column 2 of the P11 for month 1?

(c) Fill in columns 2, 3, 5, 6, and 7. Assume for the purposes of this question, that his total free pay in month 1 is £275.00.

(d) Assuming NICs are payable on the basis that Gene Rowse is liable for Class 1 Not contracted out NICs, fill in columns 1a, 1b and 1c. The tables give the following figures.

Earnings £	Total NICs £	Employee's NICs £
997	180.60	78.70
1,001	181.41	79.10
1,049	191.10	83.90
1,053	191.91	84.30

5.21 SOLUTION

Month	Pay in the month	Total pay to date	Total free pay to date	K codes Total additional pay to date	Total taxable pay to date	Total tax due to date	K codes Tax due at end of current period	K codes Regul. limit	Tax deducted in the month	K codes Tax not deducted owing to the regul. limit
	2	3	4a	4b	5	6	6a	6b	7	8
1	1,000.00	1,000.00	275.00		725.00	161.00			161.00	

Earnings on which employee contribs payable	Total of employee and employer contribs payable	Employee contribs payable	Earnings on which employee contribs at cont-out rate payable	Employee contribs at cont-out rate	Statutory sick pay incl in column 2	Statutory materiality pay incl in column 2	Statutory maternity pay recovered	Month
1a	1b	1c	1d	1e	1f	1g	1h	
1,050	191.01	83.90						1

Workings

(a) His gross pay is £12,600 pa divided into twelve months or £1,050 per month.

(b) His pay in the week or month will be only £1,000 for the purposes of income tax.

	£
Gross pay	1,050
less GAYE (£600/12 months)	50
Per P11 Column 2	1000

(c) Free pay has been given in the question, so taxable pay is pay to date less free pay to date. This works out at £725. Tax on £725 is per Table B and the subtraction tables.

(d) GAYE is irrelevant as far as NICs are concerned, so there is no deduction. Using NIC monthly Table A for the next lower figure to £1,050 gives us the figures shown.

5.22 From this we can deduce that a donation of gross pay of £50 a month means that the effect on Gene's net pay is only £38 per month.

	£
Tax on taxable pay of £725	161.00
Tax on £775	173.00
Tax saved	12.00

So, although Gene is giving £50 per month out of his gross pay, he is saving £12 in tax by so doing. Thus, the gift is only really costing him, in net pay terms, £50 - £12 = £38. The charity gets the full £50.

5.23 At the end of every month, the employer fills in a form listing GAYE donations, which is sent to the agency.

The employees' NI numbers, payroll numbers, donations and names must be included.

5.24 An example of a monthly return is provided on the next page.

Part D: Payroll

INSTRUCTIONS FOR SUBMITTING DONATIONS

1. Quote your CONTRACT NUMBER and PAYROLL NAME on all documentation.
2. Check that the Employee identification number on each Charity Choice Form is correct.
3. Check that the Employee identification number which you quote on your monthly deduction list is also the same on the Charity Choice form.
4. Send us the completed TOP SECTION of the Charity Choice form AND keep a copy or the yellow carbonated copy on your file for future reference.
5. Please arrange for your monthly lists to be in this format or PHOTOCOPY FREELY and write or type the information required.
6. Please arrange for your monthly lists to show the MONTH OF DEDUCTION where possible.
7. Please submit donations by cheque. Other means of payment should be agreed with Give As You Earn prior to any change.
8. Please arrange for all Give As You Earn documentation to come to us in one monthly packet.
9. Use this as an example of the format needed for computer printouts.
10. It will help us if we could have both these numbers. If this poses a problem, please submit one or the other (see * overleaf).

GIVE AS YOU EARN EMPLOYEE DONATIONS   PAYLISTING/DEDUCTION STATEMENT

CONTRACT NUMBER: EMPLOYER NAME:
MONTH OF DEDUCTION: EMPLOYER ADDRESS:
PAYROLL NAME/ID/CODE:

*NI NUMBER AND *PAYROLL NUMBER	DONATION	NAME	STARTER/ LEAVER

NOTE:
*see Note 10 overleaf

PAGE TOTAL
OPTIONAL 5% ADMIN
REMITTANCE ENCLOSED   MUST AGREE WITH ENCLOSED CHEQUE

PTO....

18: Recording payroll transactions

5.25 **Sharesave payments** are deductions from net pay linked to share options. They do not affect payroll calculations. Sharesave is also called Save As You Earn (SAYE).

5.26 Sharesave schemes are run by the employer with the co-operation of a building society or bank. The employer deducts an agreed sum from the net pay of the employee and deposits it in a building society or bank, perhaps via BACS.

5.27 **Trade Union contributions** are often deducted from earnings, if the employee is a member of a union.

5.28 Where company has a pension scheme which employees contribute to, the payroll department will deduct **pension contributions** from employees' pay, maintain records of those contributions and report them to the pension fund administrators.

5.29 Contributions to company pension schemes can come from two sources.

- The employer only (a so-called non-contributory pension scheme)
- The employer and the employee (called a contributory pension scheme)

5.30 Contributions are based on the employee's pensionable earnings. In a typical contributory scheme, the employee might contribute 6% of his or her pensionable earnings. The employer might then contribute a further sum calculated as, say, 10% of the employee's pensionable earnings.

5.31 What are pensionable earnings? Pensionable earnings are often different from gross pay for the following reasons.

(a) Pensionable earnings for the year may be earnings defined at a particular date (eg 1 January each year). Pension contributions would not increase until 1 January the following year, even if, say, there had been a pay rise in June.

(b) Pensionable earnings may exclude bonuses and commission. If included, these might be averaged over three years.

(c) There is an earnings cap for final salary, by which the maximum lump sum and pension payment is calculated. In 2000/01 this cap was £91,800. The maximum lump sum is the cap × 1.5, and the maximum yearly pension is the cap × 2/3. For employees earning more than this amount, it may not be worth their while paying contributions on the excess through the company scheme.

5.32 EXAMPLE: CONTRIBUTIONS

Authentic Instruments Ltd runs a company pension scheme for all its employees, contributing a sum equal to 10% of each employee's gross salary into the scheme. Each employee has to contribute 5% of his or her gross salary to the scheme.

- Horatio Arpsichord earns £15,000 per annum.
- Letitia Ute earns £21,000 per annum.

Task

In a typical month how much will

(a) Horatio and Letitia earn gross?

(b) Horatio and Letitia contribute, out of salary, to the company pension scheme?

Part D: Payroll

(c) Authentic Instruments Ltd contribute to the company pension scheme on Horatio's and Letitia's behalf?

5.33 **SOLUTION**

	Horatio £	Letitia £
(a)	1,250.00	1,750.00
(b)	62.50	87.50
(c)	125.00	175.00

6 PAYMENT METHODS

6.1 Paying people who work for a large organisation can be a costly and time consuming exercise. Payroll processing must satisfy the following requirements.

- **Accurate** (to the penny)
- **On time** (to the day)
- **Secure**, both in terms of the data it contains and the cash

6.2 As with any other payment, payroll payments should be controlled by strict procedures, and subject to the correct level of authorisation. It may be helpful to refresh your memory and read the payment control and authorisation procedures outlined in chapter 9.

6.3 The specific controls required will depend on the payment method used.

(a) Reconcile the payroll system to both the bank statement and the general ledger.

(b) Have different staff members responsible for preparing the payroll and actually authorising payment.

6.4 No matter how an employee is paid he or she has a legal right to a payslip.

> **KEY TERM**
>
> A **payslip** must by law show:
>
> - An employee's gross pay
> - Deductions from gross pay and what they are
> - Net pay

6.5 The contents of a typical payslip are shown below.

Compulsory disclosures (unless aggregated fixed deductions)	**Not compulsory but usually disclosed**
The employer's name	The employee's tax code
The employee's name	NICs to date (ie in the current tax year)
Gross pay, showing how made up	The employee's payroll number
Additions to and deductions from pay	The employee's National Insurance number
Employee's pension contributions, if any	
Statutory Sick Pay, if any	The method of payment
Statutory Maternity Pay, if any	

18: Recording payroll transactions

Compulsory disclosures (unless aggregated fixed deductions)	Not compulsory but usually disclosed
Tax paid to date (ie in the current tax year)	
Tax in the period	
NICs for the period	
Date	
Net pay	
The method of payment for each segment of net pay, if they are paid in different ways	

6.6 There is no standard appearance of a payslip, but you might find that yours looks something like the example below.

120 MR A.N. OTHER		EXAMPLE LTD		
NI No: WE123456C Tax Code: 433L Pay By: EFT		Date: 21/02/00 Tax Period: Mt 11		
DESCRIPTION			AMOUNT	THIS YEAR
01 BASIC SALARY			1,350.00	
02 OVERTIME			10.00	
	TOTAL PAY	>>>	1,360.00	14,960.00
INCOME TAX - PAYE			213.29	2,347.11
EMPLOYEE'S NI (EMPLOYER 121.88) TABLE A			107.40	1,181.40
SEASON TICKET LOAN			40.00	
(HOL PAY ACCRUED 0.00)	TOTAL NET PAY	>>>	999.31	

6.7 The payslip can be made up either manually or by computer. In some payroll systems, the payslip is merely one of several computer generated reports.

Cash payments

6.8 **Cash payment** still occurs occasionally in the cases of part time employees, temporary staff and casual staff. Employers have largely abandoned cash payment for the following reasons.

(a) Counting notes and coins is a time consuming exercise, and requires more payroll staff than would otherwise be the case.

(b) Employees have to count their pay when they receive it, and sign for the amount. This might involve a long queue on a Friday afternoon, or whenever, when most employees would rather be elsewhere (if not at work!).

(c) The notes and coins required to make up an employee's pay have to be worked out in detail, before they are ordered from the bank.

(d) The handling and transport of large amounts of cash pose security problems every payday.

6.9 However, you might be involved in paying cash wages, so this is described below.

Part D: Payroll

Ordering money

6.10 As stated above, the cash required to pay an employee has to be worked out in detail before the bank can be told. To do so, a coinage analysis sheet might be prepared for each employee. An example is given below.

MONARCH BUILDERS LTD													
NAME	NET WAGE		£50	£20	£10	£5	£2	£1	50p	20p	10p	5p	2p	1p
	£	p												
L Bourbon	178	41	3	1		1	1	1		2				1
C Windsor	99	63	1	2		1	2		1		1		1	1
N Romanov	121	15	2	1				1			1	1		
F Habsberg	156	21	3			1		1		1				1
A Osman	174	51	3	1			2		1					1
R Rajah	180	62	3	1	1				1		1		1	
M Incah	79	90	1	1		1	2		1	2				
VALUE	990	43	£800	£140	£10	£20	£14	£3	£2	£1	30p	5p	4p	4p
NUMBER	—		16	7	1	4	7	3	4	5	3	1	2	4

6.11 Where employees are paid in cash, it is quite common for a breakdown of the notes and coin with which the employee is paid to be added to the documentation. Sometimes it will be printed on the payslip next to, or after, the figure for net pay.

6.12 A very simple example follows for an employee who received £156.98 net pay for a week.

Notes/Coins		£
£50	× 2	100.00
£20	× 2	40.00
£10	× 1	10.00
£5	× 1	5.00
£1	× 1	1.00
50p	× 1	0.50
20p	× 1	0.20
10p	× 2	0.20
5p	× 1	0.05
2p	× 1	0.02
1p	× 1	0.01
Net pay		156.98

6.13 The individual would be required to count the money and then sign for it.

6.14 Additional problems arise if an employee is unable to collect his or her wage packet (eg because of illness). Then, the unclaimed wages packet might have to be held in a safe until it is collected. If the employee sends someone else to collect the wages, the employee should send written authority naming the person collecting the wages, and that person should provide proof of identity.

6.15 It is not uncommon for casual workers to be paid out of **petty cash**. The practice is outside the main payroll system, and can be a source of confusion if the payee's status is uncertain. If personnel are paid out of petty cash, then the payroll department should be notified so that a payslip can be drawn up, and the necessary deductions made.

6.16 Because of the cost in time and inconvenience of cash payment, employers are increasingly using other methods of payment.

(a) Giving employees a cheque which they themselves present to the bank.

(b) Using BACS or BACSTEL to transfer the amount automatically between bank accounts.

6.17 A cheque is the **simplest form** of cashless pay. The cheque will display the name of the employee, and the amount to be paid which will agree exactly to the payslip.

6.18 The problem with cheque payments is that so much time is spent preparing them. For example, if you worked for an organisation with one thousand monthly paid employees, it might take a great deal of time to write out each cheque by hand and have them signed or stamped. Moreover, while the security problems with cheques are less than with cash, there is still the possibility of theft or fraud. Obviously, any organisation must keep a chequebook, but this can be a problem when it comes to be treated as just another part of the stationery.

6.19 Some of the effort of writing out a cheque can be spared if they are printed beforehand, so that only the signature is necessary. Printing the cheque can be the final run of the normal payroll processing. In fact, some organisations have an arrangement whereby the cheque is the second half of a perforated sheet of paper which has the pay slip on top. The employee receives both, tears off the cheque and takes it to the bank. An example is given over the page. The cheques must be numbered in sequence, and must be kept under **strict control**.

6.20 Even though the use of cheques, particularly for monthly paid staff, is diminishing as automated payment systems take over, they will still be used for exceptional circumstances.

- An employee leaving part way through the month
- A new employee joining during the month
- Advances of salary

Part D: Payroll

EMPLOYEE	NAME	CODE	MONTH	BLOGGS AND CO	
0152	A. WORKER	438L	11		21/2/X9

Narrative	Amount		Year To Date	
	£	p	£	p
BASIC PAY	1,000	00	11,000	00
GROSS PAY	1,000	00	11,000	00
INCOME TAX	138.75		1,526.24	
NICs	77.76		855.36	
NET PAY	783.49			

Any Bank
449 SOMEWHERE ROAD, LONDON W5 2LF

21 2 20 X9

20-27-48
SOUTHERN BANK PLC

Pay   A. WORKER   or order

SEVEN HUNDRED AND EIGHTY-THREE POUNDS AND FORTY-NINE PENCE

ACCOUNT PAYEE

£ 783-49

Authorised signature   *Any Body*
Authorised signature   *Some Body*

Bloggs and Co

Cheque No.   Branch No.   Account No.
⑈101129⑈   20⑈2748⑆   30595713⑈

6.21 Many companies now use some form of **automated payment system**. This means that instead of filling up pay packets with cash, or signing large numbers of cheques which the employees take to their various banks, the whole operation is done speedily and automatically through the banking system.

> **KEY TERM**
>
> The payroll department prepares the payroll on magnetic disk or tape, then sends it to the BACS service run by the clearing banks. **BACS** stands for Bankers' Automated Clearing Service. BACS then automatically transfer the funds from the employer's banks accounts to the employees'.

6.22 BACS is a company jointly owned by the UK high street banks, the Bank of England and some of the building societies. If an employer wishes to use the BACS service this can be arranged through the employer's bank.

6.23 BACS handles large volumes of payments and collections from customers.

- Standing orders
- Direct debits
- Direct credits
- Salaries

6.24 BACS is a computer-based system so to input data to it magnetic media must be used. You have probably come across floppy disks and/or magnetic tapes in your normal work. These are the principal media for input to the BACS system. BACS publish a detailed guide as to the exact specifications of the disk or tape. This need not concern you here: your information systems department, or perhaps even your bank, will sort this out for you.

6.25 The employer sends to the bank a BACS disc or tape with the following information.

- The employee's full name
- The exact amount to be paid (ie the net pay on the pay slip)
- The bank and branch number
- The employee's bank account number

6.26 The amount of time required by the bank to process the payment varies. Typically the bank will require the information 2 to 3 days before payment is made.

6.27 The Inland Revenue and DSS now accept payment by BACS. These payment instructions can be added to the monthly BACS tape or disk.

6.28 So far, it is assumed that the payment information is coded on to a disk or tape which is sent to the processing centre. **BACSTEL** is a service by which it is possible to transmit the information over the telephone system. Similar schemes are now available with some banks through on-line banking services, via the **Internet**. Companies with **on-line banking** can of course make their own direct payments into their employees accounts.

7 UPDATING RECORDS

7.1 Once the employees have been paid, a **record of each payment** has to be maintained on a cumulative basis.

7.2 Here are a few examples.

(a) Records of gross pay and employer's NICs can explain how an organisation's total labour cost is made up. Keeping records for individual employees is necessary so that their costs can be correctly allocated to the right departments.

(b) If your employer operates an occupational pension scheme then records of contributions have to be maintained, as the employee's benefits may depend on them. Bad record keeping now can adversely affect employees not just in the present but in future decades.

(c) If an employee has borrowed money from a company, the repayments should be noted down so that it is clear when the loan has been repaid.

7.3 Employee records should, therefore, be updated with the same data that is found on the payslip.

7.4 You will also want to ensure that there is a reconciliation between gross pay as calculated and net pay as paid. The document sometimes used for this, in manual systems, is a wages analysis book. An example is shown on the next page.

7.5 The accounting records must also be updated. In an integrated computerised accounting system these updates can be automated which reduces both the volume of work and the possibility of errors.

18: Recording payroll transactions

WAGES ANALYSIS BOOK - WEEKLY PAYROLL
PAGE 13

PAYMENT DATE: 12/7/20X8

PAYE WEEK 14

	Employee	No	1 Gross Pay £ p	2 Tax £ p	3 Employee's NICs £ p	4 Trade Union contributions £ p	5 Sharesave £ p	6 Other	7 Other	8 Net pay £ p	9 cheque no.
1	Brown F	010	250 -	51 25	19 93	2 00				176 82	100783
2	Holmes S	011	210 -	43 05	15 93	2 00	10 00			139 02	100784
3	Maigret G	012	230 -	46 00	17 93	2 00				164 07	100785
4	Marlowe P	013	210 -	43 05	15 93	2 00				149 02	100786
5	Marple M	014	150 -	17 75	9 93	2 00	20 00			100 32	100787
6	Poirot H	015	275 -	55 00	22 43	2 00				195 57	cash
7	Smiley G	016	140 -	16 50	8 93	2 00				112 57	100788
8	Watson J	017	230 -	43 05	17 93	2 00	5 00			162 02	100789
9	Wimsey P	018	220 -	45 10	16 93	2 00				155 97	100790
10											
11	TOTAL		1,915 -	360 75	145 87	18 00	35 00			1,355 38	
12											

395

Part D: Payroll

Key learning points

- The **payroll function** in an organisation is important.
    - The employer's **obligations to pay wages** are carried out
    - The employer's **obligations as a tax collector** are undertaken efficiently

- A person's wage packet or pay cheque is that person's net pay for a period.
    - Gross pay
    - Less tax, National Insurance and other deductions

- **Gross pay** is the pay for the employee's work done in a period.
    - Basic pay
    - Overtime
    - Commission, bonuses, profit related pay and so forth
    - Backpay

- **Overtime** comprises **hours worked over a standard working week**. The overtime rate can be based on the hourly rate, or can be fixed by mutual agreement with hourly paid or salaried staff.

- **Commission** is often paid to employees who have succeeded in making a sale. It is normally a **percentage** of the value of the sale.

- **Bonuses** may be paid to employees if an agreed target is reached, or for any reason determined by management. Bonuses can take many forms.

- There are a number of documents associated with payroll preparation.
    - **Timesheets** record the hours spent by each employee on each job, or doing the work of each client.
    - **Attendance** records are used by the personnel department to determine the reasons for absence from work, and to administer the granting of annual leave.
    - **Other personnel record documentation** includes cards to record a person's career progress.

- **Give As You Earn** allows certain payments to charities to be deducted from a person's gross pay before income tax is calculated. However, GAYE payments are not deducted from gross pay in NIC calculations.

- **Sharesave** payments are deductions from net pay to a building society or bank.

- Payments into a **pension scheme** are another important payroll deduction.

- For the employee the **payslip** is second in importance only to the actual money received. Certain things must be on a payslip.

- Payments are usually made either by cheque or increasingly by BACS.

- Cash payments have reduced due to the following reasons.
    - Security problems
    - Extra time and effort compared to other payment methods

Quick quiz

1. What are the three main requirements for payroll processing?
2. What are the three main ways of calculating basic pay?
3. What is an overtime premium?
4. If personnel are paid wages out of petty cash, no PAYE or NI is due. True or false?

5   Unless BACS is used, much of the payroll department's time is spent signing cheques. True or false?

6   What does BACS stand for?

7   What is the cost of wages and salaries in the profit and loss account made up of?

Answers to quick quiz

1   Accuracy, timeliness and security.

2   (a) The same every month
    (b) Hourly rate
    (c) Performance basis (eg per unit of output)

3   The extra amount paid for overtime hours on top of the basic rate.

4   False

5   True

6   Bankers' Automated Clearing Service

7   Gross wages plus employer's NIC

Answers to activities

Answer 18.1

False. The employer only deals with income arising from the employment. If the employee, say, received interest on a deposit account, this would not be taxed directly, through his or her employer's payroll system, although it might be reflected in the tax code. However, lower rate tax on such income may be deducted at source.

Answer 18.2

False. Although the employee owes the tax, it is the employer's legal duty to ensure the correct working of the PAYE system. Any underpaid tax under PAYE is collected from the employer, who may then try to recover it from the employee.

Answer 18.3

(a) 40 hours × £5 =   200

(b) 32 hours × £5 =   160
     8 hours × £10 =   80
                                        240

(c) 40 hours × £7.50 =   300
     4 hours × £7.50 =   30
                                        330

Answer 18.4

                                         £
(a) 50 widgets × £5 =   250
     Overtime 4 hours × £2 =   8
                                        258

(b) Guaranteed minimum   £30

Part D: Payroll

(c) 6 widgets × £5 =   £30

(d) 1st 60 widgets × £5 =   300
Next 10 widgets × £6 =   60
6 hours overtime × £2 =   12
   372

Answer 18.5

		£
End of		
January	£900 + 5% × £5,000 (December)	1,150
February	£900 + 5% × £5,000 (January)	1,150
March	£900 + 5% × £4,000 (February)	1,100
April	£900 + (5% × £3,000) + £1,000 bonus (Total sales Jan-March exceed £10,000)	2,050
May	£900 + 5% × £2,000 (April)	1,000
June	£900 + 5% × £3,000 (May)	1,050

Answer 18.6

	£
Basic salary £15,000/12	1,250.00
Overtime (175 − 156) × £10	190.00
Quality bonus 5% × £1,250	62.50
	1,502.50
Back pay Jan – April (£15,000 − £12,000) × 4/12	1,000.00
	2,502.50

Question Bank

Question bank

1   A trade discount is best described as

    A   A reduction in the amount of money demanded from a customer

    B   An optional reduction in the amount of money payable by a customer

    C   A reduction by the supplier of the amount payable by a customer in return for prompt payment

    D   An offer by the supplier to reduce the amount demanded on the invoice if certain conditions are fulfilled

2   A cash discount is best described as

    A   A reduction in the amount of money demanded from a customer

    B   An optional reduction in the amount of money payable by a customer

    C   A reduction in the amount of money demanded from a customer as shown on the supplier's invoice because of the customer's large re-order quantities

    D   A reduction in the amount demanded from a customer as shown on the invoice as certain conditions have been fulfilled

3   The double-entry system of bookkeeping normally results in which of the following balances on the ledger accounts?

	Debit balances	Credit balances
A	Assets and revenues	Liabilities, capital and expenses
B	Revenues, capital and liabilities	Assets and expenses
C	Assets and expenses	Liabilities, capital and revenues
D	Assets, expenses and capital	Liabilities and revenues

4   A business commenced with capital in cash of £1,000. Stock costing £800 is purchased on credit, and half is sold for £1,000 plus VAT, the customer paying in cash at once.

    The accounting equation after these transactions would show:

    A   Assets £1,775 less Liabilities £175 equals Capital £1,600

    B   Assets £2,175 less Liabilities £975 equals Capital £1,200

    C   Assets £2,575 less Liabilities £800 equals Capital £1,775

    D   Assets £2,575 less Liabilities £975 equals Capital £1,600

5   Net profit was calculated as being £10,200. It was later discovered that capital expenditure of £3,000 had been treated as revenue expenditure, and revenue receipts of £1,400 had been treated as capital receipts.

    The correct net profit should have been

    A   £5,800

    B   £8,600

    C   £11,800

    D   £14,600

6   A credit balance on a ledger account indicates

    A   An asset or an expense

    B   A liability or an expense

    C   An amount owing to the organisation

    D   A liability or a revenue

Question bank

7   Which ONE of the following is not a book of prime entry?

   A   The petty cash book
   B   The sales returns day book
   C   The sales ledger
   D   The cash book

8   A book of prime entry is one in which

   A   The rules of double-entry bookkeeping do not apply
   B   Ledger accounts are maintained
   C   Transactions are entered prior to being recorded in the ledger account
   D   Subsidiary accounts are kept

9   A credit balance of £917 brought down on Y Ltd's account in the books of X Ltd means that

   A   X Ltd owes Y Ltd £917
   B   Y Ltd owes X Ltd £917
   C   X Ltd has paid Y Ltd £917
   D   X Ltd is owed £917 by Y Ltd

10 Rent paid on 1 October 20X2 for the year to September 20X3 was £1,200, and rent paid on 1 October 20X3 for the year to 30 September 20X4 was £1,600.

   Rent payable, as shown in the profit and loss account for the year ended 31 December 20X3, would be

   A   £1,200
   B   £1,600
   C   £1,300
   D   £1,500

11 An error of commission is one where

   A   A transaction has not been recorded
   B   On side of a transaction has been recorded in the wrong class of account, such as fixed assets posted to stock
   C   An error has been made in posting a transaction
   D   The digits in a number are recorded the wrong way round

12 Where a transaction is entered into the correct ledger accounts, but the wrong amount is used, the error is known as an error of

   A   Omission
   B   Original entry
   C   Commission
   D   Principle

Question bank

13 A remittance advice is

    A   A document showing which invoices a payment covers

    B   A till receipt

    C   A document given by the seller to the buyer when goods change hands in exchange for payment

    D   A document issued by the seller to evidence delivery of goods

14 EFTPOS is best described as

    A   A system of payment for goods and services via electronic funds transfer at point of sale

    B   A system of electronic payment by debit card

    C   A system of electronic payment by credit card

    D   An electronic system that a business can use to monitor its cash receipts

15 A fiduciary relationship is

    A   A contractual relationship

    B   A special relationship recognised in law even though it may not be contractual where one party is in a position to exert undue influence on another and must therefore be shown to act in good faith

    C   Not recognised in law unless it is contractual

    D   Between principal and agent

16 Cash received sheets (remittance lists) are best described as

    A   Documents used to record money received from sales made

    B   Documents used to record customer discounts

    C   Documents used to reconcile the bank balance with the cash book

    D   Documents used to record refunds from suppliers

17 A cheque requisition form is

    A   A form requesting that a cheque should be drawn to make payment

    B   A list of cheques issued on a particular day

    C   A request for cheque payment authorisation when amounts payable are over a certain limit

    D   A form requesting payment by cheque when the supporting documentary evidence is missing

18 Which of the following are the most effective controls in helping to prevent fraud involving payments (i) a bank reconciliation independently prepared and authorised (ii) using BACS to effect payments (iii) authorisation of payments (iv) segregation of duties

    A   (ii)

    B   (i) and (ii)

    C   (i), (iii) and (iv)

    D   (ii) and (iv)

19 An organisation restores its petty cash balance to £500 at the end of each month. During January, the total column in the petty cash book was recorded as being £420, and hence the imprest was restored by the amount. The analysis columns, which had been posted to the nominal ledger, totalled only £400. This error would result in

    A   No imbalance in the trial balance

    B   The trial balance being £20 higher on the debit side

Question bank

C The trial balance being £20 higher on the credit side

D The petty cash balance being £20 lower than it should be

20 Your cash book at 31 December 20X3 shows a bank balance of £565 overdrawn. On comparing this with your bank statement at the same date, you discover the following:

(a) A cheque for £57 drawn by you on 29 December 20X3 has not yet been presented for payment

(b) A cheque for £92 from a customer, which was paid into the bank on 24 December 20X3, has been dishonoured on 31 December 20X3.

The correct bank balance to be shown in the balance sheet at 31 December 20X3 is

A £714 overdrawn

B £657 overdrawn

C £473 overdrawn

D £53 overdrawn

21 The cash book shows a bank balance of £5,675 overdrawn at 31 August 20X5. It is subsequently discovered that a standing order for £125 has been entered twice, and that a dishonoured cheque for £450 has been debited in the cash book instead of credited.

The correct bank balance should be

A £5,100 overdrawn

B £6,000 overdrawn

C £6,250 overdrawn

D £6,450 overdrawn

22 A business had a balance at the bank of £2,500 at the start of the month. During the following month, it paid for materials invoiced at £1,000 less trade discount of 20% and cash discount of 10%. It received a cheque from a debtor in payment of an invoice for £200, subject to cash discount of 5%.

The balance at the bank at the end of the month was

A £1,970

B £1,980

C £1,990

D £2,000

23 When a trial balance was prepared, two ledger accounts were omitted:

Discounts received   £6,150
Discounts allowed   £7,500

To make the trial balance balance, a suspense account was opened. What was the balance on the suspense account?

A Debit   £1,350

B Credit £1,350

C Debit   £13,650

D Credit £13,650

Question bank

24 Your firm's cash book at 30 Aril 20X8 shows a balance at the bank of £2,490. Comparison with the bank statement at the same date reveals the following differences:

	£
Unpresented cheques	840
Bank charges	50
Receipts not yet credited by the bank	470
Dishonoured cheque not in cash book	140

The correct balance on the cash book at 30 April 20X8 is

- A £1,460
- B £2,300
- C £2,580
- D £3,140

25 Your firm's bank statement at 31 October 20X8 shows a balance of £13,400. You subsequently discover that the bank has dishonoured a customer's cheque for £300 and has charged bank charges of £50, neither of which is recorded in your cash book. There are unpresented cheques totalling £2,400. Amounts paid in, but not yet credited by the bank, amount to £1,000. You further discover that an automatic receipt from a customer of £195 has been recorded as a credit in your cash book.

Your cash book balance, prior to correcting the errors and omissions, was:

- A £11,455
- B £11,960
- C £12,000
- D £12,155

26 Your firm's cashbook shows a credit bank balance of £1,240 at 30 April 20X9. upon comparison with the bank statement, you determine that there are unpresented cheques totalling £450, and a receipt of £140 which has not been passed through the bank account. The bank statement shows bank charges of £74 which have not been entered in the cash book.

The balance on the bank statement is

- A £1,005 overdrawn
- B £930 overdrawn
- C £1,475
- D £1,550

27 Which of the following is NOT a valid reason for the cash book and bank statement failing to agree?

- A Timing difference
- B Bank charges
- C Error
- D Cash receipts posted to creditors

28 The bank statement at 31 December 20X1 shows a balance of £1,000. The cash book shows a balance of £750 in hand. Which of the following is the most likely reason for the difference.

- A Receipts of £250 recorded in cash book, but not yet recorded by bank
- B Bank charges of £250 shown on the bank statement, not in the cash book
- C Standing orders of £250 included on bank statement, not in the cash book
- D Cheques for £250 recorded in the cash book, but not yet gone through the bank account

Question bank

29 The cash book balance at 30 November 20X2 shows an overdraft of £500. Cheques for £6,000 have been written and sent out, but do not yet appear on the bank statement. Receipts of £5,000 are in the cash book, but are not yet on the bank statement. What is the balance on the bank statement?

- A £1,500
- B £500 in hand
- C £1,500 in hand
- D £500 overdrawn

30 The sales account is

- A Credited with the total of sales made, including VAT
- B Credited with the total of sales made, excluding VAT
- C Debited with the total of sales made, including VAT
- D Debited with the total of sales made, excluding VAT

31 Write-off a bad debt will result in:

- A An increase in liabilities
- B A decrease in working capital
- C A decrease in net profit
- D An increase in net profit

32 If a purchase return of £48 has been wrongly posted to the debit of the sales returns account, but has been correctly entered in the supplier's account, the total of the trial balance would show

- A The credit side to be £48 more than the debit side
- B The debit side to be £48 more than the credit side
- C The credit side to be £96 more than the debit side
- D The debit side to be £96 more than the credit side

33 A company received an invoice from ACB Ltd, for 40 units at £10 each, less 25% trade discount, these being items purchased on credit and for resale. It paid this invoice minus a cash discount of 2%. Which of the following journal entries correctly records the effect of the whole transaction in the company's books?

		Debit £	Credit £
A	ABC Ltd	300	
	Purchases		300
	Cash	292	
	Discount allowed	8	
	ABC Ltd		300
B	Purchases	300	
	ABC Ltd		300
	ABC Ltd	300	
	Discount allowed		8
	Cash		292
C	Purchases	300	
	ABC Ltd		300
	ABC Ltd	300	
	Discount allowed		6
	Cash		294

	D	ABC Ltd	400	
		Purchases		400
		Cash	294	
		Discount allowed	106	
		ABC Ltd		400

34 You are given the following information:

Debtors at 1 January 20X3
Debtors at 31 December 20X3
Total receipts during 20X3 (including cash sales of £5,000)

Sales on credit during 20X3 amount to:

- A £81,000
- B £86,000
- C £79,000
- D £84,000

35 A supplier sends you a statement showing a balance outstanding of £14,350. Your own records show a balance outstanding of £14,500.

The reason for this difference could be that

- A The supplier sent an invoice for £150 which you have not yet received
- B The supplier has allowed you £150 cash discount which you had omitted to enter in your ledger
- C You have paid the supplier £150 which he has not yet accounted for
- D You have returned goods worth £159 which the supplier has not yet accounted for

36 The sales ledger control account at 1 May had balances of £32,750 debit and £1,275 credit. During May, sales of £125,000 were made on credit. Receipts from debtors amounted to £122,500 and cash discounts of £550 were allowed. Refunds of £1,300 were made to customers. The closing balances at 31 may could be

- A £35,175 debit and £3,000 credit
- B £35,675 debit and £2,500 credit
- C £36,725 debit and £2,000 credit
- D £36,725 debit and £1,000 credit

37 The debit side of a trial balance totals £50 more than the credit side. This could be due to

- A A purchase of goods for £50 being omitted from the creditor's account
- B A sale of goods for £50 being omitted from the debtor's account
- C An invoice of £25 for electricity being credited to the electricity account
- D A receipt for £50 from a debtor being omitted from the cash book

38 The sales ledger control account had a closing balance of £8,500. It contained a contra to the purchase ledger of £400, but that had been entered on the wrong side of the control account.

The correct balance on the control account should be

- A £7.700 debit
- B £8,100 debit
- C £8,400 debit
- D £8,900 debit

Question bank

39 Your purchase ledger control account has a balance at 1 October 20X8 of £34,500 credit. During October, credit purchases were £78,400, cash purchases were £2,400 and payments made to suppliers, excluding cash purchases, and after deducting cash discounts of £1,200, were £68,900. Purchase returns were £4,700.

The closing balance was:

A £38,100

B £40,500

C £47,500

D £49,900

40 At the end of the month, an organisation needs to accrue for one week's wages. The gross wages amount to £500, tax amounts to £100, employer's national insurance is £50, employees' national insurance is £40, and employees' contributions to pension scheme amount to £30. The ledger entries to record this accrual would be

A	Debit wages expense	£500	Credit national insurance creditor	£90
			Credit income tax creditor	£100
			Credit pension scheme creditor	£30
			Credit wages accrued	£280
B	Debit wages expense	£550	Credit national insurance creditor	£90
			Credit income tax creditor	£100
			Credit pension scheme creditor	£30
			Credit wages accrued	£330
C	Debit wages expense	£500	Credit wages accrued	£500
	Debit national insurance expense	£90		
	Debit income tax expense	£100		
	Debit pension scheme expense	£30		
D	Debit wages expense	£330	Credit wages accrued	£550
	Debit national insurance expense	£90		
	Debit income tax expense	£100		
	Debit pension scheme expense	£30		

Answer Bank

Answer bank

1	A	A reduction in the amount of money demanded from a customer
2	B	An optional reduction in the amount of money payable by a customer
3	C	DR Assets and expenses/CR Liabilities, capital and revenues
4	D	

	£
Assets	
Opening cash	1,000
Cash received £(1,000 + 175 VAT)	1,175
Closing cash	2,175
Stock £(800-400)	400
	2,575
Liabilities	
Opening liabilities	-
VAT creditor	175
Purchase stock	800
Closing liabilities	975
Capital	
Opening capital	1,000
Profit on sale of stock £(1,000 - 400)	600
Closing capital	1,600

5	D	£10,200 + £3,000 + £1,400 = £14,600
6	D	A liability or a revenue
7	C	The sales ledger
8	C	Ledger accounts are posted from books of prime entry
9	A	Y is a creditor of X
10	C	$(9/12 \times £1,200) + (3/12 \times £1,600)$
11	C	A is an error of omission, B is an error of principle, D is a transposition error
12	B	The posting is correct, but the wrong amount has been used
13	A	A remittance advice normally accompanies a cheque
14	A	EFTPOS can be done with debit or credit cards
15	B	A bank has this relationship with its customer
16	A	Remittance lists simply record money received
17	A	A form requesting that a cheque should be drawn
18	C	Fraudulent payments can be made using BACS
19	C	Think of the double entry. Bank has been credited by £420 but expenses only debited by £400
20	B	£(565)o/d - £92 dishonoured cheque = £(657) o/d
21	D	The question refers to the figure to be shown in the balance sheet

	£	£
Balance per cash book		5,675
Reversal – Standing order entered twice	125	
Adjustment – Dishonoured cheque (450 x 2)		900
Entered in error as a debit		
Bank overdraft	6,450	
	6,575	6,575

Answer bank

22 A

	£	£
Opening bank balance	2,500	
Payment (£1,00 - £200) x 90%		720
Receipt (£200 - £10)	190	
Closing bank balance		1,970
	2,690	2,690

23 A These are the postings that clear the suspense account:

Suspense account

Opening balance	1,350	Discounts allowed	7,500
Discounts received	6,150		
	7,500		7,500

24 B

	£
Cash book balance	2,490
Adjustment re charges	(50)
Adjustment re dishonoured cheque	(140)
	2,300

25 B

	£	£
Bank statement balance b/d	13,400	
Dishonoured cheque	300	
Bank charges not in cash book	50	
Unpresented cheques		2,400
Uncleared banking	1,000	
Adjustment re error (2 x 195)		390
Cash book balance c/d		11,960
	14,750	14,750
Cash book balance b/d	11,960	

Alternative approach:

	£	£
Cash book balance b/d	11,960	
Dishonoured cheque		300
Bank charges not in cash book		50
Unpresented cheques	2,400	
Uncleared banking		1,000
Adjustment re error (2 x 195)	390	
Bank statement balance c/d		13,400
	14,750	14,750
Bank statement balance b/d	13,400	

26 A

	£	£
Cash book (the cash book has a credit balance)		1,240
Unpresented cheques	450	
Uncleared deposit		140
Bank charges		75
Bank overdraft	1,005	
	1,455	1,455

27 D Provided that the cash receipts have been correctly posted to the cash book, then the fact that they have incorrectly been posted to creditors instead of cash sales and debtors will not affect the bank reconciliation.

28 D All the other options would have the bank account £250 less than the cash book.

Answer bank

29	B		£	£
		Cash book		500
		Unpresented cheques	6,000	
		Uncleared deposit		5,000
		Bank balance		500
			6,000	6,000

30 B The VAT element of the invoices will go to the VAT account in the balance sheet.

31 C This will be debited to bad debts in the profit and loss account.

32 D Debits will exceed credits by 2 x £48 = £96.

33 C Trade discounts are not included in the cost of purchases.

34 C Credit sales = £80,000 - £10,000 + £9,000 = £79,000.

35 B All other options would lead to a *higher* balance in the supplier's records.

36 C Debits total £32,750 + £125,000 + £1,300 = £159,050. Credits total £1,275 + £122,550 + £550 = £124,325. ∴ Net balance = £34,725 debit.

37 A The other options would make the credit side total £50 more than the debit side.

38 A £8,500 – (2 x £400) = £7,700.

39	A		£
		Opening balance	34,500
		Credit purchases	78,400
		Discounts	(1,200)
		Payments	(68,900)
		Purchase returns	(4,700)
			38,100

40 B The cost to the business consists of gross wage plus employer's NI.

List of key terms and index

List of key terms

These are the terms which we have identified throughout the text as being KEY TERMS. You should make sure that you can define what these terms mean, go back to the pages highlighted here if you need to check.

Accounting system, 9
Age analysis of creditors, 346
Age analysis of debtors, 303
Agency, 147
Asset, 35

BACS, 393
Balance sheet, 48
Bank reconciliation, 256
Bank statement, 257
Banker, 146
Basic pay, 367
Batch processing, 105
Bonus, 372
Books of prime entry, 59

Capital, 37
Capital expenditure, 53
Capital income, 54
Cash, 130
Cash book, 65, 256
Cash discount, 17
Cash transaction, 4
Cheque, 132
Cheque requisition form, 180
Clearing, 143
Commission, 373
Compensating errors, 99
Computer programs, 106
Control account, 81
Control totals, 105
Credit note, 13
Credit transaction, 4
Creditor, 41
Creditors ledger, 80
Current assets, 50
Current liabilities, 50
Customer, 146

Data controllers, 29
Debtor, 41
Debtors ledger, 79
Discount, 16
Double entry bookkeeping, 43
Drawings, 39
Duty, 149

EFTPOS, 137
Error of omission, 97
Error of principle, 98
Error of transposition, 97
Errors of commission, 98
Expenses claim form, 181

Fixed asset, 49
Float, 151

General ledger, 69
Gross pay, 366
Gross profit, 51, 52

Imprest system, 224
Internal check, 353
Invoice, 10

Journal, 92
Journal voucher, 93

Liability, 35
Long-term liabilities, 51

Module, 109

Net assets, 38
Net profit, 51, 52

Overtime pay, 370

PAYE, 365
Payroll, 364
Personal accounts, 79
Petty cash book, 69
Posting, 70
Profit, 34
Profit and loss account, 51, 52, 53, 54
Purchase day book, 64, 314
Purchase ledger, 80, 338
Purchase returns day book, 64, 315

List of key terms

Receipt, 127, 129
Remittance advice, 124
Retention policy, 28
Revenue expenditure, 53
Revenue income, 54

Sales day book, 62, 272
Sales ledger, 79, 292
Sales ledger control account, 282
Sales returns day book, 63, 276
Source documents, 59
Suspense account, 100

Total creditors account, 82
Total debtors account, 81, 282
Trade creditor, 41
Trade creditors, 339
Trade debtor, 41
Trade discount, 17
Trading account, 52
Trial balance, 94

VAT, 19
VAT receipt, 238

Index

Accounting equation, 37, 48
Accounting systems, 106
Accuracy, 365, 366
Acknowledgement, 5
Active file, 27
Advantages and disadvantages of paying by cheque, 187
Age analysis of creditors, 345
Age analysis of debtors, 303
Agency, 147
Allowance, 19
Analysed cash book, 65
Analysis of purchases, 316
Archive records, 248
Attendance cards, 376
Audit trail, 107
Authorisation, 178, 223
Authorised signatures, 184
Automatic payment methods, 345
Automatic payments, 211

BACS, 183, 215, 387, 393
Bad debt relief, 307
Bad debts, 306
Bad debts and VAT, 307
Bailor/bailee relationship, 147
Balance sheet, 356
Balancing ledger accounts, 95
Balancing the cash book, 66
Bank charges, 256
Bank giro credits, 190
Bank of England, 143
Bank reconciliations, 165, 206, 256, 261
Bank statements, 69, 257, 258
Banker, 146
Banker's draft, 128, 139, 161, 183. 191
Banking
System, 143
Banking and EFTPOS, 160
Banking cash, 150
Banking cheques, 153
Banking plastic card transactions, 155
Basic pay, 367
Basic pay: Fixed rate per period, 367
Basic pay: Hourly rate, 368
Books of prime entry, 92, 165
Bought ledger, 319
Business, 34

Cancelled cheques, 208
Capital, 37, 51

Cash, 150, 183
Cash account, 282
Cash book, 80, 165, 207
Cash cycle, 50
Cash discount, 16, 186
Cash flow, 314
Cash payment, 389
Cash received sheets, 165, 166
Cash registers, 123
Cash sale, 287
Central bank, 143
Charge cards, 133
Checks on petty cash, 229
Checks over payments, 345
Cheque books, 184
Cheque guarantee card, 132
Cheque requisition forms, 179
Cheque signatories, 345
Clearing or retail banks, 143
Clearing system, 143
Coding, 103. 104, 107, 108
Coding data, 103, 318
Coinage analysis sheet, 390
Commission, 373
Companies Act 1985, 49
Company credit card or charge card, 183
Compensating errors, 96
Completeness, 206
Computer cheques, 344
Computerisation of payments recording, 211
Computerised accounting, 106
Computerised cash book, 211
Computer-produced cheques, 183
Configuration of the system, 305
Contract law, 24
Control accounts, 81, 353, 355
Control list, 208
Control over receipts, 123
Controls over payments, 178
Controls over recording payments, 206
Correction of errors, 93
Costing module, 109
Costs, 364
Credit card transactions, 159
Credit card summaries, 155
Credit card vouchers, 155
Credit notes, 9, 13
Credit transfers, 190
Creditors, 35, 74
Creditors control account, 82
Creditors ledger, 319
Credits, 95
Crossed cheque, 248
Current assets, 35
Customer, 146
Customer mailing lists, 306

Index

Daily time sheets, 376
Data protection, 28
Data subjects, 29
Day book analysis, 77
Day book totals, 318
Debit note, 14
Debits, 95
Debtor/creditor relationship, 147
Debtors, 74, 110
Debtors control account, 81
Debtors ledger, 292
Deductions, 366
Delivery note, 5
Differential piecework, 370
Direct debit, 129, 139, 183, 194, 259
Direct debit Instruction, 196
Discounts, 16, 53, 68, 186
Discounts received, 342
Dishonoured for payment, 155
Document, 5
Documentation to go out with payments, 196
Double entry bookkeeping, 34, 96, 319
Double entry recording of sales, 282
Double entry system, 281
Doubtful debts, 306
Duality, 42
Duties of customers, 149

E & O E, 12
Earnings cap, 387
E-commerce, 14
EFTPOS, 123, 160
Electronic cash registers, 127
Employee, 366
Employer's legal responsibilities to collect PAYE, 365
Entity, 36
Errors, 93, 256
Errors of principle, 97
Errors of transposition, 97
Evidence of payment, 128
Ex works, 12
Exempt items, 20
Expenditure, 34, 52
Expenses claim forms, 181
Expenses day book, 317
External documentation, 5

Fiduciary relationship, 148
Fixed assets, 35, 49
Float, 152, 242
Floor limit, 136
FOB, 11
Forgery, 130
Format of a ledger account, 70

Fraud, 206
Frequency of the reconciliation, 263

Give As You Earn, 383
Giving change, 127
Goods received note, 7, 14
Gross pay, 366

High day-rate schemes, 368
HM Customs & Excise, 19, 283

Impersonal accounts, 79
Imprest system, 220, 224
Income, 34, 51
Income Tax, 365
Input, 104
Insufficient funds, 155
Integrated accounting, 110
Integrated software, 109
Internal check, 353, 355
Internal documentation, 7
Internet, 393
Invoice, 5, 9
IOUs, 229

Job card, 379
Journal, 92
Journal entries, 92
Journal vouchers, 93

Ledger account, 70
Ledger file, 111
Liabilities, 50
Limited companies, 36
Limited liability, 36
List of balances, 94
Lost cheques, 187

Mail transfer, 129
Mail transfer and telegraphic transfer, 183
Management reports, 109
Master files, 27
Memorandum accounts, 293
Methods of payment, 343
Mortgagor/mortgagee relationship, 147

National Insurance, 364, 383
National Insurance number, 382
Net pay:, 366
NICs payable by the employee,, 383
NICs payable by the employer, 383
Night safes, 131
Nominal ledger, 69, 114
Non-active file, 27

Index

Omission of a transaction, 96
Operational balances, 143
Other creditors, 340
Output, 104
Output VAT, 20
Overdraft, 314
Overhead expenses, 53
Overtime, 370
Overtime pay, 370

Password, 108
PAYE, 365
PAYE does not cover self-employed people, 382
Paying-in slip, 150, 155, 158
Payments
   by banker's draft, 191
   by cash, 183
Payments by cheque, 183
Payments to suppliers, 343
Payroll, 364
Payroll and the employee, 364
Payroll and the employer, 364
Payroll and the government, 364
Payroll department, 375
Periods of credit, 314
Permanent files, 27
Personal accounts, 79, 292, 338
Personal accounts for creditors, 318
Personal accounts for debtors, 281
Personnel record card, 375
Personnel records, 376
Petty cash, 220, 221, 391
Petty cash book, 65, 69, 220, 232, 235, 247
Petty cash vouchers, 220, 225
Petty cashier, 222
Piecework, 368
Posting document, 284
Posting from the day books, 77
Posting the ledgers, 60
Preparing cheques, 184
Principal/agent relationship, 147
Procedures on receipt of a cheque, 133
Processing, 104
Processing copies, 156
Profit, 34, 38
Profit and loss account, 52, 83
Pro-forma bank reconciliation, 261
Programme controls, 264
Purchase day book, 314
Purchase ledger, 113, 338, 341, 356
Purchase ledger control account, 319
Purchase order, 7
Purchase returns, 342
Purchase returns day book, 315
Purchases and returns, 320

Quotation, 5

Rebate, 19
Receipts, , 224
Receiving money into petty cash, 230
Reconciliations on a computerised system, 264
Record of attendance card, 375
Recording receipts, 165
Reference files, 27
Relationship between banker and customer, 146
Remittance advices, 197, 344
Retail receipts, 126
Retention periods, 28
Returned cheques, 213
Rights and duties of bankers and customers, 148
Route cards., 379

Safes, 131
Salami fraud, 365
Sales analysis, 62
Sales analysis reports, 305
Sales day book, 79, 80, 272
Sales ledger, 80, 281, 292
Sales ledger control account, 282 297
Sales ledger department, 126
Sales order, 12
Sales order document, 5
Sales order processing (SOP, 278
Sales returns day book, 276
Security, 366
Security and control of petty cash, 220, 222
Security guards, 131
Segregation of duties, 124, 165
Semi-active files, 27
Separate entity, 36
Settlement discount, 186
Smaller retail banks, 143
Spreadsheets, 276, 317
Staff schedules, 7
Standard rate, 19
Standing order, 129, 139, 183, 193, 215
Standing order mandates, 193
Statements, 113
Statements of account, 305
Stock lists, 7
Stock module, 109
Stolen cheques and cheque guarantee cards, 155
Stopping cheques, 188
Storage of information, 26
Strong box, 131
Summary voucher, 155, 156, 158
Supplier lists, 7

Index

Suspense account, 100

T accounts, 70
Tax Office, 382
Telegraphic transfer, 129
Temporary files, 27
Terms of business, 314
The legal relationship (banker/customer), 146
The Sale of Goods Act, 24
Theft, 130
Till receipts, 123, 127
Time sheets, 379
Timeliness, 366
Timing and methods of payments, 182
Total creditors account, 82
Trade creditors, 339
Trading and profit and loss account, 52
Transaction files, 27
Transaction processing, 295
Transposition error, 356
Trial balance, 94, 356
Types of receipt, 123

Unclaimed wages, 390
Undue influence, 148
Updating the payment record, 394

Variable data, 111
VAT, 83, 84, 238, 283, 342
VAT (Value Added Tax), 19
VAT account, 84
VAT analysis, 305
VAT in cash transactions, 84
VAT in credit transactions, 84
VAT return, 23
VDU, 277

Wages analysis book, 394
Weekly time sheets., 376
Written receipts, 128
Wrong account, 96

Zero-rate, 20

CAT Paper 1 – Recording Financial Transactions (6/05)

REVIEW FORM & FREE PRIZE DRAW

All original review forms from the entire BPP range, completed with genuine comments, will be entered into one of two draws on 31 January 2006 and 31 July 2006. The names on the first four forms picked out on each occasion will be sent a cheque for £50.

Name: _____ Address: _____

How have you used this Interactive Text?
(Tick one box only)
- ☐ Home study (book only)
- ☐ On a course: college _____
- ☐ With 'correspondence' package
- ☐ Other _____

Why did you decide to purchase this Interactive Text? *(Tick one box only)*
- ☐ Have used BPP Texts in the past
- ☐ Recommendation by friend/colleague
- ☐ Recommendation by a lecturer at college
- ☐ Saw advertising
- ☐ Other _____

Which BPP products have you used?
- ☑ Text ☐ Kit ☐ i-Pass ☐ i-Learn

During the past six months do you recall seeing/receiving any of the following?
(Tick as many boxes as are relevant)
- ☐ Our advertisement in *ACCA Student Accountant*
- ☐ Other advertisement _____
- ☐ Our brochure with a letter through the post
- ☐ Our website www.bpp.com

Which (if any) aspects of our advertising do you find useful?
(Tick as many boxes as are relevant)
- ☐ Prices and publication dates of new editions
- ☐ Information on Interactive Text content
- ☐ Facility to order books off-the-page
- ☐ None of the above

Your ratings, comments and suggestions would be appreciated on the following areas

	Very useful	Useful	Not useful
Introductory section (How to use this Interactive Text)	☐	☐	☐
Key terms	☐	☐	☐
Examples	☐	☐	☐
Activities and answers	☐	☐	☐
Key learning points	☐	☐	☐
Quick quizzes	☐	☐	☐
Exam alerts	☐	☐	☐
Question Bank	☐	☐	☐
Answer Bank	☐	☐	☐
List of key terms and index	☐	☐	☐
Structure and presentation	☐	☐	☐
Icons	☐	☐	☐

	Excellent	Good	Adequate	Poor
Overall opinion of this Interactive Text	☐	☐	☐	☐

Do you intend to continue using BPP products? ☐ Yes ☐ No

Please note any further comments and suggestions/errors on the reverse of this page. The BPP author of this edition can be emailed at marymaclean@bpp.com

Please return this form to: Mary Maclean, CAT Range Manager, BPP Professional Education, FREEPOST, London, W12 8BR

REVIEW FORM & FREE PRIZE DRAW (continued)

Please note any further comments and suggestions/errors below

FREE PRIZE DRAW RULES

1. Closing date for 31 January 2006 draw is 31 December 2005. Closing date for 31 July 2006 draw is 30 June 2006.

2. No purchase necessary. Entry forms are available upon request from BPP Professional Education. No more than one entry per title, per person. Draw restricted to persons aged 16 and over.

3. Winners will be notified by post and receive their cheques not later than 6 weeks after the relevant draw date.

4. The decision of the promoter in all matters is final and binding. No correspondence will be entered into.

CAT Order

To BPP Professional Education, Aldine Place, London W12 8AW
Tel: 020 8740 2211   Fax: 020 8740 1184
email: publishing@bpp.com   website: www.bpp.com
Order online www.bpp.com/mybpp

Mr/Mrs/Ms (Full name) _____
Daytime delivery address _____
Postcode _____
Daytime Tel _____ Email _____
Date of exam (month/year) _____

Occasionally we may wish to email you relevant offers and information about courses and products. Please tick to opt into this service. ☐

	6/05 Texts	2/05 Kits	2/05 Passcards	2/05 i-Learn CD	2/05 i-Pass CD	Learn Online
INTRODUCTORY						
Paper 1 Recording Financial Transactions	£19.00 ☐	£10.95 ☐	£6.95 ☐	£29.95 ☐	£19.95 ☐	£100.00 ☐
Paper 2 Information for Management Control	£19.00 ☐	£10.95 ☐	£6.95 ☐	£29.95 ☐	£19.95 ☐	£100.00 ☐
INTERMEDIATE						
Paper 3 Maintaining Financial Records	£19.00 ☐	£10.95 ☐	£6.95 ☐	£30.95 ☐	£19.95 ☐	£100.00 ☐
Paper 4 Accounting for Costs	£19.00 ☐	£10.95 ☐	£6.95 ☐	£30.95 ☐	£19.95 ☐	£100.00 ☐
ADVANCED CORE						
Paper 5 Managing People and Systems	£19.00 ☐	£10.95 ☐	£6.95 ☐	£30.95 ☐	£21.95 ☐	£100.00 ☐
Paper 6 Drafting Financial Statements	£19.00 ☐	£10.95 ☐	£6.95 ☐	£30.95 ☐	£21.95 ☐	£100.00 ☐
Paper 7 Planning, Control & Performance Management	£19.00 ☐	£10.95 ☐	£6.95 ☐	£30.95 ☐	£21.95 ☐	£100.00 ☐
ADVANCED OPTION						
Paper 8 Implementing Audit Procedures	£19.00 ☐	£10.95 ☐	£6.95 ☐	£30.95 ☐	£21.95 ☐	£100.00 ☐
Paper 9 Preparing Taxation Computations (FA2005)	£19.00 ☐†	£10.95 ☐	£6.95 ☐	£30.95 ☐	£21.95 ☐	£100.00 ☐
Paper 10 Managing Finances	£19.00 ☐	£10.95 ☐	£6.95 ☐	£30.95 ☐	£21.95 ☐	£100.00 ☐
INTERNATIONAL STREAM					3/05*	
Paper 1 Recording Financial Transactions	£19.00 ☐	£10.95 ☐	£6.95 ☐		£21.95 ☐	
Paper 3 Maintaining Financial Records	£19.00 ☐	£10.95 ☐	£6.95 ☐		£21.95 ☐	
Paper 6 Drafting Financial Statements	£19.00 ☐	£10.95 ☐	£6.95 ☐		£21.95 ☐	
Paper 8 Implementing Audit Procedures	£19.00 ☐	£10.95 ☐	£6.95 ☐		£21.95 ☐	
Learning to Learn Accountancy (7/02)	£9.95 ☐					
Business Maths and English (6/04)	£9.95 ☐					

*Available in March 2005
†Published in October 2005

SUBTOTAL £ _____

POSTAGE & PACKING

Study Texts/Kits
	First	Each extra	Online
UK	£5.00	£2.00	£2.00
EU**	£6.00	£4.00	£4.00
Non EU	£20.00	£10.00	£10.00

Passcards/Success CDs/i-Learn/i-Pass
	First	Each extra	Online
UK	£2.00	£1.00	£1.00
EU**	£3.00	£2.00	£2.00
Non EU	£8.00	£8.00	£8.00

Learning to Learn Accountancy/Business Maths and English
	Each		Online
UK	£3.00		£2.00
EU**	£6.00		£4.00
Non EU	£20.00		£10.00

Grand Total (incl. Postage) £ _____

I enclose a cheque for _____
(Cheques to BPP Professional Education)

Or charge to Visa/Mastercard/Switch

Card Number ☐☐☐☐ ☐☐☐☐ ☐☐☐☐ ☐☐☐☐

Expiry date _____   Start Date _____

Issue Number (Switch Only) _____

Signature _____

We aim to deliver to all UK addresses inside 5 working days; a signature will be required. Orders to all EU addresses should be delivered within 6 working days. All other orders to overseas addresses should be delivered within 8 working days. **EU includes the Republic of Ireland and the Channel Islands.

CAT Order

To BPP Professional Education, Aldine Place, London W12 8AW
Tel: 020 8740 2211   Fax: 020 8740 1184
email: publishing@bpp.com   website: www.bpp.com
Order online www.bpp.com/mybpp

Mr/Mrs/Ms (Full name)
Daytime delivery address
Postcode
Daytime Tel
Date of exam (month/year)
Scots law variant Y / N

Occasionally we may wish to email you relevant offers and information about courses and products. Please tick to opt into this service. ☐

POSTAGE & PACKING

Home Study Packages

	First	Each extra
UK	£6.00	£6.00
EU**	-	-
Non EU	£15.00	-
	£50.00	

I-Learn

	First	Each extra	Online
UK	£2.00	£1.00	£1.00
EU**	£3.00	£2.00	£2.00
Non EU	£8.00	£8.00	£8.00

Learning to Learn Accountancy/Business Maths and English

	Each		Online
UK	£3.00		£2.00
EU**	£6.00		£4.00
Non EU	£20.00		£10.00

Postage and packing not charged on free copy ordered with Home Study Course.

Grand Total (incl. Postage)

I enclose a cheque for £ ☐☐☐☐☐☐
(Cheques to BPP Professional Education)
Or charge to Visa/Mastercard/Switch
Card Number ☐☐☐☐☐☐☐☐☐☐☐☐☐☐☐☐
Expiry date ☐☐☐☐   Start Date ☐☐☐☐
Issue Number (Switch Only) ☐☐
Signature

	Home Study Package*	Home Study PLUS*	2/05 i-Learn CD	Learn Online
INTRODUCTORY				
Paper 1 Recording Financial Transactions	£100.00 ☐	£180.00 ☐	£29.95 ☐	£100.00 ☐
Paper 2 Information for Management Control	£100.00 ☐	£180.00 ☐	£29.95 ☐	£100.00 ☐
INTERMEDIATE				
Paper 3 Maintaining Financial Records	£100.00 ☐	£180.00 ☐	£30.95 ☐	£100.00 ☐
Paper 4 Accounting for Costs	£100.00 ☐	£180.00 ☐	£30.95 ☐	£100.00 ☐
ADVANCED CORE				
Paper 5 Managing People and Systems	£100.00 ☐	£180.00 ☐	£30.95 ☐	£100.00 ☐
Paper 6 Drafting Financial Statements	£100.00 ☐	£180.00 ☐	£30.95 ☐	£100.00 ☐
Paper 7 Planning, Control & Performance Management	£100.00 ☐	£180.00 ☐	£30.95 ☐	£100.00 ☐
ADVANCED OPTION				
Paper 8 Implementing Audit Procedures	£100.00 ☐	£180.00 ☐	£30.95 ☐	£100.00 ☐
Paper 9 Preparing Taxation Computations (FA2005)	£100.00 ☐	£180.00 ☐	£30.95 ☐	£100.00 ☐
Paper 10 Managing Finances	£100.00 ☐	£180.00 ☐	£30.95 ☐	£100.00 ☐
INTERNATIONAL STREAM				
Paper 1 Recording Financial Transactions	£100.00 ☐	£180.00 ☐		
Paper 3 Maintaining Financial Records	£100.00 ☐	£180.00 ☐		
Paper 6 Drafting Financial Statements	£100.00 ☐	£180.00 ☐		
Paper 8 Implementing Audit Procedures	£100.00 ☐	£180.00 ☐		
Learning to Learn Accountancy (7/02)	Free/£9.95 ☐			
Business Maths and English (6/04)	Free/£9.95 ☐			

SUBTOTAL £ ☐

We aim to deliver to all UK addresses inside 5 working days; a signature will be required. Orders to all EU addresses should be delivered within 6 working days. All other orders to overseas addresses should be delivered within 8 working days. *Home Study Courses include Texts, Kits, Passcards and i-Pass. You can also order one free copy of either Learning to Learn Accountancy or Business Maths and English per Home Study Package, to a maximum of one of each per person. Please indicate your choice on the form. **EU includes the Republic of Ireland and the Channel Islands.

READING SKILLS FOR THE SOCIAL SCIENCES

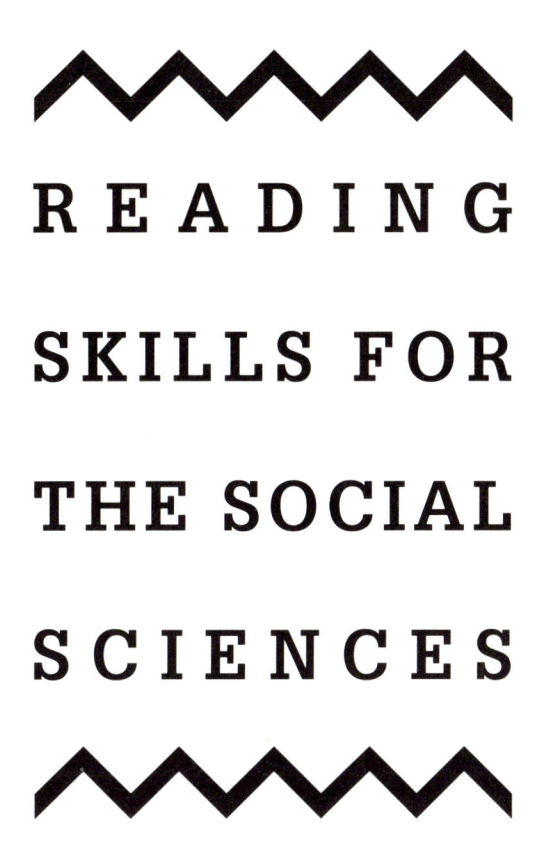

LOUANN HAARMAN
PATRICK LEECH
JANET MURRAY

OXFORD UNIVERSITY PRESS
1988

Oxford University Press
Walton Street, Oxford OX2 6DP

Oxford New York Toronto
Delhi Bombay Calcutta Madras Karachi
Petaling Jaya Singapore Hong Kong Tokyo
Nairobi Dar es Salaam Cape Town
Melbourne Auckland

and associated companies in
Berlin Ibadan

OXFORD is a trade mark of
Oxford University Press

ISBN 0 19 451230 4

© Oxford University Press 1988

All rights reserved. No part of this
publication may be reproduced, stored in a
retrieval system, or transmitted, in any form
or by any means, electronic, mechanical,
photocopying, recording, or otherwise,
without the prior permission of Oxford
University Press

This book is sold subject to the condition that
it shall not, by way of trade or otherwise, be
lent, re-sold, hired or otherwise circulated
without the publisher's consent in any form
of binding or cover other than that in which it
is published and without a similar condition
including this condition being imposed on
the subsequent purchaser.

Set by Pentacor Limited, High Wycombe, Bucks
Printed in Hong Kong

Acknowledgements

The authors wish to thank the many colleagues and students who experimented with this material in various stages of perfection, and in particular Rosa Maria Bollettieri Bosinelli and Wayne Harper, whose suggestions and encouragement have been extremely useful. A special thanks is also due to Cisella Rossetti who, with unfailing patience and ability, contributed in countless ways to the preparation of the many versions of this work which were used during the experimental phase.

The authors and publisher would like to thank the following for permission to reproduce copyright material:

Summit Books
Tavistock Publications
Yale University Press
University of Chicago Press
Columbia University Press
New Society
Psychology Today
MacGraw-Hill
New Statesman
Encyclopaedia Britannica
Transatlantic Perspectives
Public Opinion Quarterly
The Times Literary Supplement
Penguin Books
Cambridge University Press

Illustrations by:
Camera Press
Oxford Illustrators
Paul Robinson

CONTENTS

INTRODUCTION TO THE COURSE vi
THE SKILL AND PRACTICE OF READING vii

UNIT ONE — BOOK ADVERTISEMENTS 1

Approaching the text 2
Pre-reading questions
Skimming and scanning

Intensive reading 3
Text structure/language functions
Distinguishing the functions of description and evaluation

Language work 4
Discrimination of adjectives and adjectival suffixes
Lexical inference
Practising the use of lexis common to expository/evaluative prose

Vocabulary work and word building 8

Observations on text type 9

UNIT TWO — RESEARCH DIGEST (Brief research reports) 11

Approaching the text 12
Pre-reading questions
Scanning
Skimming for text structure

Intensive reading 13
Checking understanding
Information extraction (Document 2)
Information extraction (Document 3)

Language work 14
Identifying tense patterns
Checking understanding

Vocabulary work and word building 16

Observations on text type 17

UNIT THREE — ECONOMICS (Extracts from a textbook) 19

Approaching the text 21
Pre-reading questions
Skimming and scanning for contents
Pre-reading vocabulary work

Intensive reading 22
Previewing text organization/content
Explanations/examples of key terms

Language work 25
Vocabulary work
Modal verbs
Reutilization of key vocabulary

Vocabulary work and word building 28

Observations on text type 29

UNIT FOUR — 1917: THE RUSSIAN REVOLUTION (Book review) 31

Approaching the text 32
Pre-reading questions
Identifying reviewer's evaluation
Distinguishing text structure

Intensive reading 33
Reference
Checking understanding

Language work 35
Reutilization of selected lexis
Topic sentences and paragraph structure

Vocabulary work and word building 38

Observations on text type 39

UNIT FIVE — THE OVERSELLING OF CANDIDATES ON TELEVISION (Extended report)   41

Approaching the text   44
    Pre-reading questions
    Guided contact with introductory passage
    Skimming for general organization

Intensive reading   45
    Information extraction
    Introduction to note-taking

Language work   47
    The function of linkers
    Recognizing logical links in discourse
    Practising the use of selected linkers
    Lexical inference/Dictionary work

Vocabulary work and word building   51

Observations on text type   52

UNIT SIX — ASKING THE AGE QUESTION (Academic research report)   53

Approaching the text   56
    Pre-reading questions
    Identifying main points

Intensive reading   57
    Annotating bibliographical references
    Information extraction
    Checking understanding

Language work   58
    Textual devices and specialized terminology
    Lexis common to academic prose
    Reutilization of lexis

Vocabulary work and word building   61

Observations on text type   62

UNIT SEVEN — THE OTHER ECONOMY (Extended report)   63

Approaching the text   64
    Pre-reading questions
    Skimming for general organization
    Pre-reading vocabulary work

Intensive reading   66
    Guided note-taking
    Reference
    Checking understanding

Language work   69
    Discriminating examples, contrasts and further information

Vocabulary work and word building   70

Observations on text type   70

UNIT EIGHT — MOBILIZING THE MIDDLE CLASSES (Book review)   71

Approaching the text   74
    Pre-reading questions
    Identifying evaluation and description
    Distinguishing text structure

Intensive reading   75
    Reference
    Note-taking

Language work   76
    Lexis common to academic prose
    Distinguishing the function of linkers
    Practising the use of selected linkers

Vocabulary work and word building   79

Observations on text type   80

UNIT NINE — HUMAN AGGRESSION (Introduction to a book) 81

Approaching the text 83
    Predicting content

Intensive reading 83
    Identifying author's presentation of theme
    Discriminating units of information

Language work 85
    Revising modal meaning
    Use and function of modal verbs
    Recognizing logical links in discourse

Vocabulary work and word building 88

Observations on text type 89

UNIT TEN — INSIDE THE BLACK BOX (Preface to a book) 91

Approaching the text 94
    Skimming for general organization
    Skimming and scanning for chapter headings
    Pre-reading vocabulary work

Intensive reading 97
    Extracting author's main points
    Note-taking: identifying topics and point of view
    Checking understanding

Language work 99
    Practice with lexis marking topics and arguments

Vocabulary work and word building 100

Observations on text type 101

APPENDIX 1 — LEXIS COMMON TO ACADEMIC PROSE 103

APPENDIX 2 — PREFIXES AND SUFFIXES 105

KEY — TO WORKSHEETS AND PRE-READING QUESTIONS 107

INTRODUCTION TO THE COURSE

The material in this coursebook has been specifically designed for intermediate students of English whose language requirements centre on reading skills in the social sciences. The course (of about 80 hours) has two principal objectives: to develop those reading skills and strategies fundamental to efficient reading in a second language, with particular reference to academic prose; and to develop techniques for dealing with extended texts in the social sciences.

As regards the first objective, particular emphasis is given to the following abilities: to apply a variety of reading 'styles' (skimming, scanning, intensive and extensive reading) depending on the kind of text and reading purpose; to recognize aspects of text structure; to infer the meaning of unknown words; to understand lexis common to academic prose, aspects of textual cohesion and coherence, and other linguistic features typical of academic texts (e.g. the use of linkers and modal verbs). With respect to the second objective, practice is given in such study skills as information extraction and note-taking.

In order to make the student fully aware not only of the variety of factors which contribute to efficient reading, but also of the methodology and didactic objectives underlying the course, an introductory section entitled *The Skill and Practice of Reading* has been included. This section provides a general overview of the reading process and more specific comments with reference to reading academic prose.

The documents included in the ten didactic units are authentic texts representing a number of genres typical of academic prose (introductory chapters of books, book reviews, research reports, etc.), and deal with topics specific to or closely related to the field of the social sciences (politics, sociology, history, economics). In order to give the student guidance and practice in developing techniques to deal with extended texts, such as he or she[*] presumably will have to do in an authentic reading situation, materials of increasing length have been included.

The worksheets and other activities which accompany the texts fall into the following categories:

1 *Approaching the text*
   These activities are designed to guide initial contact with the document by activating prior knowledge of the subject matter or genre. During this phase the worksheets aim principally to encourage skimming and scanning of the text.

2 *Intensive reading*
   These exercises require a more careful processing of the text and may include the following: information extraction, inferring the meaning of words from context, work on text structure or reference, questions on content, note-taking activities.

3 *Language work*
   Here the worksheets require more specific work on lexis common to academic prose and other linguistic features of the text (e.g. linkers and modal verbs). Also included in this section is an exercise on word building designed to fix the student's knowledge of recurrent lexis (through translation) and build his store of vocabulary through practice in the formation of derivative words.

In the section *Observations on Text Type* at the end of each Unit, there is a summary of the principal characteristics of the genre represented by the document or documents of the didactic unit, including comments on its function, structure and typical linguistic features, where applicable.

The material in the Appendices includes:
1 a list of lexis drawn from the word building charts for each Unit;
2 a list of prefixes and suffixes common to academic prose;
3 a comprehensive key to the worksheets and pre-reading questions.

---

[*] Throughout, "he" should be taken to mean "he or she".

THE SKILL AND PRACTICE OF READING

1 The reading process

Though reading is often considered a passive skill, research in the field of psycholinguistics has demonstrated that it is actually a highly complex process of interaction between reader and text. For example, it has been shown that the reader does not decode text in his first language (L1) in an orderly, linear fashion, word after word, but rather that his eyes move rapidly over the page, going forward and backward as he perceives meaningful *groups* of words and relates these to the non-verbal information at his disposal (that is, to his knowledge of the world and of the topic of the written text), thereby deriving meaning from the text.

Reading, thus, can be seen as the *processing of information*. The reader brings to the text his own store of general information deriving from his native culture, education, personal experience, and, normally, some specific knowledge of the topic of the written text. (We very rarely pick up a text dealing with a subject we know nothing about.) At the same time, the reader also possesses a linguistic competence, including a knowledge of words (lexis), of how these words are deployed according to the linguistic system in order to form sentences (syntax), and of the rhetorical patterns and linguistic conventions which characterize different types of text. (News stories, poetry and research reports are all distinctly recognizable text types or *genres*.)

Furthermore, in an ideal situation, the reader approaches a text with a genuine *motivation* to read and a *reading purpose*. He may pick up a telephone book to find the number of a friend, or a textbook to prepare for an examination, or a novel for pleasure. Whatever the text, he will also have some *expectations* or *predictions* regarding its content, based both on graphic cues (headline, photographs, tables, etc.), and on his knowledge of the subject matter and regarding how the text is likely to be organized depending on its genre. As he reads, these predictions are confirmed (or not confirmed) by the text. The better the predictions, the faster the processing of text, since the mind is "prepared" for the information encountered and thus perceives meaning more readily. Depending on his reason for reading, he will utilize one or more specific reading *strategies* (see 2 below): he will search rapidly for his friend's name in the telephone book, or read the textbook carefully in preparation for the exam.

The text, in turn, is composed of more or less overlapping layers of lexis and syntactic structures deployed according to certain linguistic and rhetorical conventions, and organized in such a way as to convey meaning. The reader's capacity to apprehend the meaning of the text depends on 1) his ability to decode the lexical and syntactic signals of the text, 2) his knowledge of how these features combine to realize linguistic and rhetorical conventions, and 3) his ability to make full and efficient use of his reading skills and strategies. Learning to read well in a second language (L2) necessarily involves developing the ability to transfer to the L2 text the processing skills and strategies automatically brought into play when we read in our L1.

Below is a rough diagram of the reading process as it has been described here. In what follows, the various aspects of the process will be treated in further detail, with particular reference to reading in English as a second language.

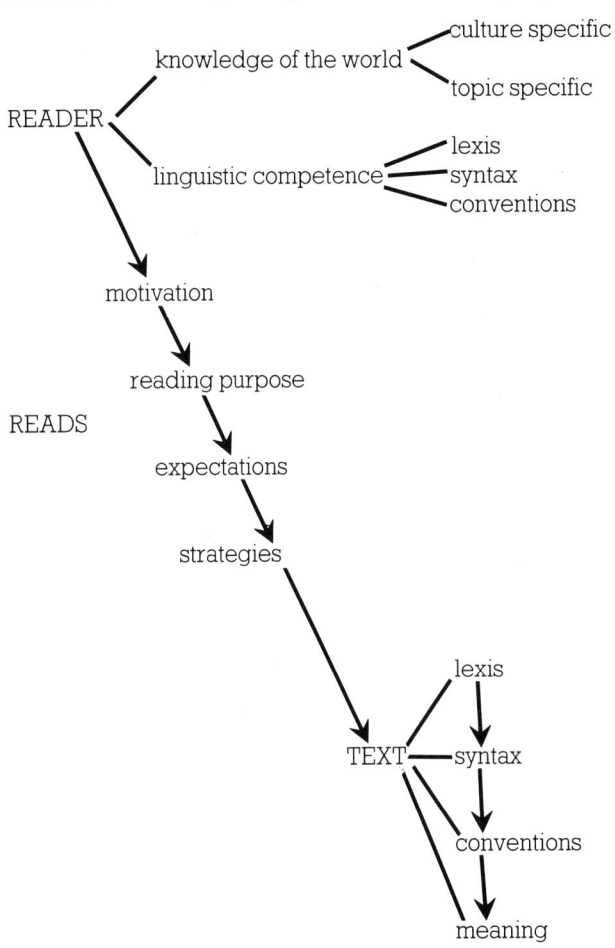

```
                          ┌── culture specific
         knowledge of the world
                          └── topic specific
READER
                          ┌── lexis
         linguistic competence ── syntax
                          └── conventions
         ↓
         motivation
         ↓
         reading purpose
READS
         ↓
         expectations
         ↓
         strategies
         ↓
                          ┌── lexis
         TEXT ─────────── syntax
                          ↓
                          conventions
                          ↓
                          meaning
```

2 Reading strategies

When we read in our own language we use – often unconsciously – a variety of reading strategies and techniques depending on the text and our reason for reading: for example, we would not normally read a newspaper and a textbook in the same way. There are four principal "styles" of reading:

Skimming involves moving our eyes rapidly over the page or pages in order to get a general idea of what the text is about, focusing on certain key words or phrases. Thus, after skimming a chapter in a textbook on Mexican history, we would be able to say, for example, that the particular chapter treats the rise and fall of the Aztec empire. When the reader already has some knowledge of the subject or the author, skimming the text may have more specific objectives, e.g. that of understanding the author's approach to his subject.

Scanning, instead, is the strategy we use when we seek specific pieces of information in a text, such as names, dates, statistics, or whether a particular topic is treated. Here our expectations are heightened by our awareness of certain lexical fields or other textual features which are likely to signal the presence of the information we are looking for. We might scan the chapter on the Aztec empire, for instance, in order to find out the historical period in which it flourished, the names and dates of important battles, the names of Aztec gods and rulers.

Intensive reading is the style we employ when we wish to have a very clear and complete understanding of the written text. This implies a careful decodification of the writer's discourse, usually with the aim of comprehending not only the literal meaning of the text, but also the writer's deeper purpose, his position, and other eventual textual subtleties such as irony for example. After applying such a reading style to our chapter on the Aztecs, we should be able to refer its contents in a complete and, if necessary, exhaustive manner to a friend or teacher, including remarks on the writer's position with respect to his material (e.g. whether or not he agrees with standard treatments of the subject, whether or not he presents his material clearly).

Extensive reading is the term used to describe the strategies called into play when we read longer texts either for pleasure or for information, and may involve the entire gamut of strategies, which the reader applies according to the individual text and his interest in its various parts. In our chapter on the Aztecs, we may be particularly interested in the writer's treatment of religion or military history. In this case, after skimming, we would scan to be sure these topics were dealt with, read rapidly and superficially sections treating, say, agriculture or trade, then read intensively the passages of particular interest.

Thus the reading style we apply to any given text should be a function of the type and content of the text on the one hand, and our reading purpose on the other. It is important to use these strategies appropriately and flexibly: obviously not all texts need to be read intensively, though language learners often apply only this strategy to texts in foreign languages. In reading English for academic purposes, for example, it will often suffice to have a general idea of whether certain information is contained in an article and, if so, where, so that is might be consulted at a later date. On the other hand, information which is of interest may be located quickly and selected passages focused upon for the purpose of extracting and annotating specific information. Practice in the use of the different reading strategies is given throughout this coursebook.

3 Aspects of the text

3.1. *Lexis*

Needless to say, meaningful reading cannot take place unless we know the meaning of words. Often, however, it is not necessary to understand all the words in a given text in order to grasp the main points expressed or even understand the text in its entirety. Sometimes, especially when we are familiar with the subject matter or when the text shows a high density of cognates (words having the same root in the native language and the foreign language), we can "make sense" of the text even without knowing some specific words or phrases. A variety of exercises on lexis appear throughout the coursebook, and below (in 4.1) we discuss some possible strategies for dealing with unknown words. Here we shall mention some basic lexical categories (content words and function words) and discuss two "classes" of words (linkers and modals) which, because of their high frequency and importance in academic prose, seem to merit particular attention.

3.1.1. *Content words*

In a very broad and simplistic sense, vocabulary items can be said to be either "content" (or "lexical") words (e.g. *run automobile, red, quickly*) or "function" words (e.g. *the, and, for, which*). Content words can change their grammatical class or their meaning by the addition of prefixes or suffixes (e.g. to govern, government, governor, governable, ungovernable). Each didactic unit ends with an exercise on word formation with the aim of familiarizing the student with these morphological features and of enlarging his stock of academic vocabulary.

3.1.2. *Function words*

Function words are determiners, intensifiers, auxiliary verbs and prepositions. They help to express the relationship between concepts; they are essential to cohesive and coherent discourse and in general must be learned. They are much more difficult to guess than content words, insofar as, signalling the relationship between concepts, they can determine the precise meaning of the content word.

a. *Linkers*

One of the most important kinds of function word, especially in academic prose, is the class of linkers, also known as conjunctions, connectors, link words etc.: for example, *however, although, furthermore*. They may be broadly classified in four types: additive, temporal, causal and adversative.[1] Whenever a text is dense in units of information, and where the writer is concerned to set out these units in such a way as to explain or describe a situation or process, argue a point or evaluate (i.e. when the prose is prevalently expository, argumentative or evaluative rather than narrative/sequential) we tend to find a high frequency of linkers. This is because the writer endeavours to achieve his purpose in writing (to explain, to argue etc.) as efficiently and effectively as possible by *overtly signalling* the relationships he has drawn, and intends the reader to draw, between units of information. Let us illustrate the importance of linkers with a very simple example:

> *John bought an expensive sports car.*
> *His wife left him.*

In the absence of an explicit linker, the reader cannot be certain of the relationship the writer/speaker wishes to draw between these two statements unless he has a very clear grasp of the preceding and possibly the following context, and indeed unless he has understood the purpose of the writer/speaker in presenting the units of information. The linkers that could be used to connect the two concepts change not only the relationship between them but also the overall meaning.

[1] See M. A. K. Halliday and R. Hasan (1976). *Cohesion in English*. London: Longman.

Additive e.g. John bought an expensive sports car *AND* his wife left him.

An additive linker could be used in the context of a list of events (not necessarily in chronological order) in which John was involved in a certain period.

Temporal e.g. John bought an expensive sports car *AFTER* his wife left him.

A temporal linker such as *after* would establish a sequence of events.

Causal e.g. John bought an expensive sports car *SO* his wife left him.

A causal linker would establish that one event determined the other. In this case (*so*), the second event is caused by the first (perhaps because John's wife did not like John spending a lot of money on a car). In the case of *because*, the first event would be determined by the second, that is, John bought the car in compensation for the fact that his wife left him.

Adversative e.g. John bought an expensive sports car *BUT* his wife left him.

An adversative linker here would indicate that John tried to make his wife stay with him by buying a sports car but that, contrary to his expectations, she left him in any case.

If the reader has closely followed the writer's "line of reasoning" or discourse, he will normally be able to recuperate the relationship the writer wishes to establish, even in the absence of linkers. Their presence, however, is a substantial help to the reader, for it renders these relationships explicit, facilitating the rapid and efficient processing of the text. It is thus important that the reader of a foreign language learn the meaning of linkers as soon as possible.

b. *Modal verbs*

Another class of words that the reader in a foreign language must master is that of modal verbs. They are formally different from other verbs[1], but this is of secondary importance for the *reader* who does not have to produce grammatically correct sentences. It is fundamental, however, to have a clear idea of their function and to be able to distinguish between the various meanings modal verbs can have in different contexts. In the table below the modal verbs are listed according to their most recurrent meanings in academic prose.[2]

---

[1] They do not have infinitive or participle forms or tenses (in the precise sense of the term); they do not take "do" in their negative or question forms; they do not have "-s" as a mark of the third person singular.

---

[2] In order to offer a clear and succinct presentation of modal verbs we have omitted many of the meanings and uses that are common to spoken discourse and social interaction. For a more complete presentation of modal verbs, see for example, Eastwood and Mackin, 1982, *Basic English Grammar*, Oxford.

MODAL	ABILITY/ POTENTIAL[1]	PROBABILITY/ POSSIBILITY[2]	OBLIGATION/ NECESSITY	OBLIGATION/ DESIRABILITY	ADVICE OR SUGGESTION	CONDITIONAL	FUTURE	PROHIBITION
must		√	√					√ must not
ought to		√		√	√			
should		√		√	√			
could	√	√			√	√		
may		√						
might		√			√			
can	√							√ cannot[3]
will							√	
would						√		

[1] Potential with inanimate subjects
[2] In this column the modals appear according to degree of probability expressed, from most probable (must) to least probable (might)
[3] *cannot* may also mean lack of ability/potential

3.2. *Conventions*

3.2.1. *Genre and global text structure*

Different genres or text types are characterized by different types of organization or text structure, usually depending on the function of the text. The more familiar we are with the particular characteristics and organization of the genre which we are reading, the better we are able to read the text. Let us illustrate this point with the example of the news story genre typical of British and American newspapers. The British or American reader is aware that the first one or two sentences of the article will include indications of who was involved, what happened, where, when and occasionally why. Successive paragraphs normally represent expansions of one or more of these elements in a descending order of importance and/or relevance with respect to the "fact" being reported. Familiarity with the characteristics of the genre provides the reader with a useful key to the rapid extraction of information. In the first place, his expectations regarding the *type* of information in the text are heightened. Moreover, his knowledge of the way in which information is likely to be organized permits him to apply reading strategies most appropriate to his reading purpose. A description of the various genres represented in this coursebook, their function and aspects of language typical of the genre, if any, appear after each didactic unit in which the genre is presented for the first time.

3.2.2. *Paragraph structure*

Just as the text as a whole shows a characteristic structure usually conforming to the distinguishing features of its genre, so each paragraph comprising the text can be analysed in terms of its internal structure. Familiarity with the pattern according to which most English paragraphs are developed greatly facilitates reading by allowing the reader to focus immediately on those parts of the paragraphs which are likely to carry forward the writer's discourse or in any case show a high density of *general* information. In English paragraphs, normally the first or second sentence presents the *topic* or central idea of the paragraph (*topic sentence*). Where the *topic sentence* is the second sentence, the first sentence is normally the *topic introducer*. Successive sentences are expansions of this particular topic, and the final sentence will usually refer backward to the topic considered and forward to the topic of the following paragraph.

4 Processing the text

4.1. *Lexical inference*

If reading is interrupted too often as the reader looks up unknown words in a dictionary, global comprehension of the text tends to be lost. The ability to *infer* the meaning of unknown words quickly and confidently is therefore an essential reading and study skill.

There are several reasons why practice in inferring the meaning of unknown words can improve reading competence. It will first of all sensitize the reader to the fact that it is often enough to appreciate the general meaning of a word or its possible negative or positive connotations to be able to continue reading and maintain the sense of the text.

One possible strategy for inferring the meaning of an unknown word is first to decide its word class (verb, noun, adjective etc.) by considering the position of the word in the sentence, its relationship to other words, and morphological markers (e.g. suffixes, tense markers etc.). Next, a possible meaning may be inferred by considering both the immediate syntactic context and the wider context, over several sentences if necessary. Checking that the class of the word inferred is appropriate, it may then be substituted for the unknown word and the sense of the entire sentence verified. (If you need to confirm your guess, scan the entries under the appropriate lexical heading and word class in a dictionary).

This procedure may appear lengthier and more time-consuming than using a dictionary, but it must be pointed out that most of the above operations can occur almost simultaneously and also that the reader, with practice, will become increasingly proficient in inferring meaning in this way.

Of course, if a complete phrase or sentence is not clear, it will be difficult to apply this strategy. In this case, the efficient reader will not stop, but will continue reading and in the light of what he reads should a) be able to decide whether the problematic phrase or sentence is important or not, and b) try to assign some meaning to it if he considers it important. Where no sense can be made of what appears to be a key phrase or sentence, obviously it will be necessary to consult a dictionary.

4.2 *Note-taking*

There are many possible reasons for taking notes. A reader may decide to take notes on a text in order to have a record of the writer's main ideas, to help him when revising for an examination and so on. It is not our aim here to *teach* note-taking as a study skill – the reader may already use a satisfactory note-taking system in his own language which he can adapt for note-taking in a foreign language. However, *practice* in taking notes is given on a range of text types (book reviews, research reports, introductions to books) with the aim not only of illustrating how the recording of information often depends on the genre and consequent organization of the text, but above all, of giving practice in the discrimination and annotation of key points in extended academic prose.

Taking meaningful notes which can be referred to later entails first discerning the *structure* of the text. This will enable the reader to identify the key points and ideas and the relationships between them. Thus, as the reader surveys the text prior to taking notes, he should look out for and graphically highlight important points and sections by numbering, underlining, boxing, etc. On the basis of this, he may then decide the best way of recording the information (in the form of a list, chart, table etc.).

"A well-documented and clearly argued volume, of undoubted value for the Western reader: I know of no better general textbook which may be recommended to students of the period, one which provides so much of the flavour of Soviet life. There are some fascinating pages devoted to literature and culture, foreign affairs and politics." — *Alec Nove, The Times Literary Supplement (London)*

"The authors have produced the first history of the USSR which combines the insights and knowledge of an insider with the distance and access to vital documentation of the foreigner. There is a wealth of new detail and the whole is remarkable for the freshness of attack. No one else yet has woven the whole story together in a great tapestry of a narrative that is sober, carefully documented, and very readable indeed. This will become a standard history to be kept in print for many years.

Anyone remotely concerned with Russia will have to read this book."
— *Edward Crankshaw, author of Russia and the Russians*

UTOPIA IN POWER
THE HISTORY OF THE SOVIET UNION FROM 1917 TO THE PRESENT
BY MIKHAIL HELLER AND ALEKSANDR M. NEKRICH

SUMMIT BOOKS
Simon & Schuster, Inc. · A G + W Company

New Books from Oxford

Britain's Shadow Economy
Stephen Smith

The shadow economy embraces not only the black economy of moonlighting, tax dodging, and scrounging, but also the wide range of ordinary, though productive, household activities such as washing-up, baby-sitting, and DIY improvements. This book takes a critical look at the whole of the shadow economy and makes new estimates of the scale and pattern of concealed incomes.

0 19 828569 8, Clarendon Press, Oxford   £19.50

The Decline of the British Economy
An Institutional Perspective
Edited by Bernard Elbaum and William Lazonick

'A distinguished contribution... The essays that it contains are coherent and thought-provoking... this is a fascinating new approach to the analysis and understanding of the decline of the British economy. It should be read.'
Peter L. Payne, *The Times Higher Education Supplement*

0 19 828494 2, Clarendon Press, Oxford   £25.00

For further details of these books contact: Academic Publicity, OUP, Walton Street, Oxford OX2 6DP. (Information on Oxford Journals can be obtained from the Journals Subscription Department, at the same address).

UNIT ONE

BOOK ADVERTISEMENTS

UNIVERSITY · OF · CHICAGO · PRESS

University Paperback
Policing Industrial Disputes
1893 to 1985
ROGER GEARY

The recent increase of violent confrontation in industrial disputes has led to renewed interest in the nature of industrial violence and the police tactics employed to counteract it. Roger Geary's study provides a fascinating and historically detailed account of the changing nature of industrial violence.
192 pages   Paperback 0 416 90200 6 £5.95

TAVISTOCK
11 New Fetter Lane, London EC4P 4EE.

Arab Politics
The Search for Legitimacy
Michael C. Hudson

The first systematic comparative analysis of political behavior throughout the entire Arab world, from Morocco to Kuwait. In an attempt to explain why the Arab world remains in ferment, Hudson discusses such crucial factors as Arab and Islamic identity, ethnic and religious minorities, the crisis of authority, the effects of Western imperialism, and modernization.

"Hudson has succeeded brilliantly in surveying and analyzing the entire range of contemporary Arab politics. . . . [He] focuses his vast knowledge of theory and historical data with valid and illuminating generalizations, perhaps the most basic one being that most if not all Arab countries lack an effective structure for full political participation."
—*Library Journal* $22.50

Yale
Yale University Press
New Haven and London

Sri Lanka
Ethnic Fratricide and the Dismantling of Democracy
S. J. TAMBIAH

A native Sri Lankan of Tamil origins, the distinguished social anthropologist S. J. Tambiah analyzes the causes of the conflict between majority Sinhalese Buddhists and minority Tamils that has wracked the island of Sri Lanka for almost forty years. In his view, recent social stresses rather than ancient religious and racial differences are the source of the trouble.
"An excellent and thought-provoking book."—Paul Sieghart, *Los Angeles Times Book Review.*
"Concise, informative, lucidly written. . . .a powerful case for the importance of pluralism."
—Merle Rubin, *Christian Science Monitor*
$17.95 cloth

Hegemony and Culture
Politics and Religious Change among the Yoruba
DAVID D. LAITIN

Since the early nineteenth century, eighty percent of the Yoruba of Nigeria have converted, in approximately equal numbers, to either Christianity or Islam; yet these sharp religious differences have not caused political division. Laitin explores the reasons for this "unnatural" religious toleration, focusing on the hegemonic role of the nineteenth-century British administration in Yorubaland. Moving between empirical and conceptual levels, he has produced a richly complex work that combines political science, anthropology, sociology, and social theory. $13.95 paper, $30.00 cloth

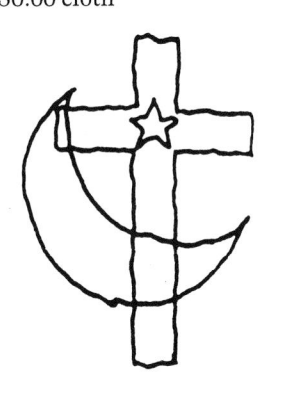

APPROACHING THE TEXT

▶ Look at the texts and answer the following questions:

1 What typographical features of the text characterize the genre *book advertisement*?

2 What are the five publishers represented?

3 Which books are published in Britain and which in America?

4 Which books are published in paperback?

5 Which are published in hardback (cloth) editions?

> The first operation we normally perform on texts when we read in our first language is to read them rapidly and superficially to get a general idea of their contents and/or to find specific information. You have just done the latter in order to answer the questions above. You will be given guided practice in performing these operations when you read in English. (See the introductory notes on reading, Section 2, for a description of the various reading strategies which may be applied to texts.)

WORKSHEET 1

Skimming and scanning

▶ Scan the seven book advertisements and complete the chart below with the following information where possible: author(s) or editor(s), title, sub-title, and subject area (e.g. history, sociology, etc.)

Author(s) or Editor(s)	Title of Book	Sub-title	Subject Area
	Utopia in Power		
Stephen Smith			
			economics
Roger Geary			
	Arab Politics		
S.J. Tambiah			

INTENSIVE READING

One useful way to approach a written text is through an examination of its structure or organisation, especially when the reader will subsequently need to take notes on what he has read. Discerning the structure or organization of a text involves understanding not only the writer's words, but the function of those words in context: to understand, that is, not only what the writer is *saying*, but what he is *doing*, e.g. making an example or comparison, formulating a definition or hypothesis, etc. (See the OBSERVATIONS at the end of this Unit.)

WORKSHEET 2

Text structure/language functions

▶ Below, beside the advertisement for *Arab Politics*, there is a "flow chart", or schematic summary, of the structure of the text. Read the text and divide it using a stroke (/) to indicate the position of the function.

▶ Now underline all the adjectives in the text. Which are descriptive and which are evaluative?

```
┌─────────────────────┐
│ General description │
└─────────┬───────────┘
          ▼
┌─────────────────────┐
│  Writer's purpose   │
└─────────┬───────────┘
          ▼
┌─────────────────────┐
│ Detailed description│
└─────────┬───────────┘
          ▼
┌─────────────────────┐
│     Evaluation      │
└─────────┬───────────┘
          ▼
┌─────────────────────┐
│   Exemplification   │
└─────────────────────┘
```

ARAB POLITICS*
The Search for Legitimacy
Michael C. Hudson

The first systematic comparative analysis of political behavior throughout the Arab world, from Morocco to Kuwait. In an attempt to explain why the Arab world remains in ferment, Hudson discusses such crucial factors as Arab and Islamic identity, ethnic and religious minorities, the crisis of authority, the effects of Western imperialism and modernization.

> "Hudson has succeeded brilliantly in surveying and analyzing the entire range of contemporary Arab politics. . . . (He) focuses his vast knowledge of theory and historical data with valid and illuminating generalizations, perhaps the most basic one being that most if not all Arab countries lack an effective structure for full political participation."
>
> — *Library Journal*

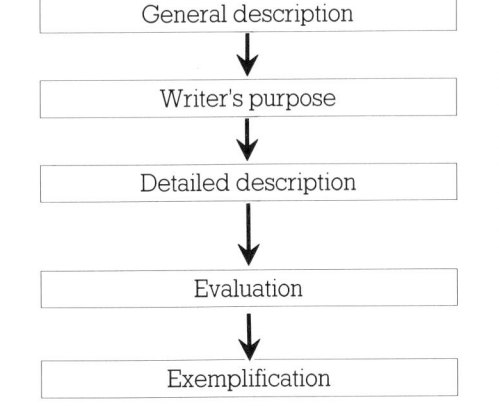

* Texts chosen for illustration do not necessarily reflect the views of the authors or OUP.

Notice that the language of description and evaluation in the book advertisement for *Arab Politics* is rather well balanced. Often, however, book advertisements tend to be either predominantly evaluative or predominantly descriptive, as in the remaining advertisements. (See Worksheet 3 below.)

3

WORKSHEET 3

Distinguishing the functions of description and evaluation

▶ Read the remaining book advertisements carefully and indicate on the table below whether they are predominantly descriptive of the contents of the book or predominantly evaluative of the book itself. *One* advertisement may be considered balanced.

	Predominantly descriptive	Predominantly evaluative
Utopia in Power		
Britain's Shadow Economy		
Decline of British Economy		
Sri Lanka		
Hegemony and Culture		
Policing Industrial Disputes		

Notice that different terms may be used to replace the word *book* (e.g. *contribution* in *The Decline of the British Economy*). This not only avoids repetition, but also permits aspects of meaning to be refined and elaborated.

▶ Find in the text as many terms as you can which are used to substitute or elaborate on the word *book*.

LANGUAGE WORK

Familiarity with suffixes as "markers" of a particular word class can be extremely useful when an unknown word is encountered. If unknown lexical items can be identified as adjectives, adverbs, nouns etc., the possibility of inferring meaning from context is substantially increased. (See the notes on reading, Section 3; appendix II; and the Word Building exercises at the end of each Unit.) In the exercise below practice is given in the recognition of adjectives and adjectival suffixes.

WORKSHEET 4

Discrimination of adjectives and adjectival suffixes

▶ Re-read the book advertisements and indicate on the table all adjectives which appear in the book titles and texts proper (excluding quantifiers, e.g. *some, many* etc.). Then write the adjectival suffix, if any, in the column provided, checking with your dictionary if necessary.

	adjectives	suffixes
Utopia in Power		
Britain's Shadow Economy		
The Decline of the British Economy		
Policing Industrial Disputes		
Sri Lanka		
Hegemony and Culture		

> Notice, in addition to the more common *adjective + noun* combination, the following ways of qualifying nouns:
> - *noun + noun* ("shadow economy", "police tactics"), where the noun functions as adjective
> - *noun + past participle* ("pages devoted to literature", "tactics employed"), where we may consider as deleted a relative pronoun + verb *to be* ("tactics *which are* employed")

WORKSHEET 5

Lexical inference

In the following exercise you are given practice in identifying a variety of word classes, and in inferring meaning from context. Be sure to read the section on lexical inference in the notes on reading, Section 4.1, before completing the exercise.

▶ Read the first book advertisement, *Poland in the 20th Century*, and underline the words you do not know. Most of these will be listed in the chart below. First, identify word class (noun, verb, adjective, adverb) and then infer a possible meaning by examining the immediate and general context carefully. Next, study the jumbled definitions and choose the one which fits best. An example has been given.

The staggering cost of capitulation

POLAND IN THE 20TH CENTURY

M. K. Dziewanowski. For centuries the Poles have struggled against the attempts of partitioning powers to Germanize or Russify them. This richly detailed history reaches back to the tenth century to expose the roots of political ideologies which have flourished in Poland and to explain better her paradoxical status: geo-politically part of the Communist orbit, culturally and economically tied to the West. $14.95

TWENTIETH-CENTURY CZECHOSLOVAKIA
The Meanings of Its History

Josef Korbel. A former member of the Czech diplomatic service here unravels two intertwining but contradictory themes in Czech history: fierce pursuit of human freedom and, on the other hand, a tendency to yield without struggle to foreign onslaught. A penetrating inside view that draws upon previously classified Communist documents and memoranda. $14.95

COLUMBIA UNIVERSITY PRESS
136 South Broadway, Irvington, New York 10533

	Word class	Definitions
1 struggled b	verb (past participle)	made great efforts
2 attempts __		
3 to expose __		
4 roots __		
5 flourished __		
6 tied __		

a sources, origins
b *made great efforts*
c grown vigorously, prospered
d acts of trying to do something
e attached, connected
f to uncover, make known

▶ Now read the book advertisement *Twentieth Century Czechoslovakia*. Follow the same strategy used above in order to infer the meaning of the words in the chart below, but this time write your guess in the appropriate column, then check with your dictionary, being careful to copy the correct definition for the function and meaning of the word as used in this text.

6

▶ Complete the chart by following the same procedure for three other words you did not know in these book advertisements.

	Word class	**Your guess**	**Dictionary definition**
1 former			
2 unravels			
3 pursuit			
4 yield			
5 onslaught			
6 draws upon			
7			
8			
9			

WORKSHEET 6

Practising the use of lexis common to expository/evaluative prose.

▶ Decide the word class of the missing words in the text below, then complete the hypothetical book advertisement by inserting an *appropriate* noun, verb or adjective from those listed. Consider carefully the meaning of each of the options with reference to the context: not all the alternatives are interchangeable. Take care to use the correct form of the verb.

Nouns	**Verbs**	**Adjectives**
synthesis	explain	profound
survey	survey	logical
topic	discuss	brilliant
study	study	important
history	present	comprehensive
concept	describe	invaluable
area	bring into focus	powerful
aspect	consider	sensitive
theme	explore	discussed
overview	illuminate	rigorous
discussion	introduce	incisive
analysis	analyze	considered
system	constitute	systematic

The Interpretation of Dreams is the first _____ _____ of dream psychology. In an attempt to _____ why dreams are _____ to the well-being of the mental processes, Sigmund Freud _____ a wide variety of common dreams. Among the topics _____ are the processes of dislocation and transference that occur in dreams. _____ and _____, the author succeeds in _____ some of the darker workings of the mind. This _____ work is the most _____ _____ of the psychology of the unconscious available. Published in paperback, *The Interpretation of Dreams* is _____ for all those who are seriously interested in dream psychology.

VOCABULARY WORK AND WORD BUILDING

▶ Find these words in the texts,* decide the word class, and write it and the translation of the word in the space provided.

▶ Then complete the table by forming other words using appropriate suffixes if necessary. Consult your dictionary.

VOCABULARY WORK			WORD BUILDING			
Word and Location	**Class**	**Translation**	**Noun**	**Verb**	**Adjective**	**Adverb**
analyzes (6)						
attempt (5)						
basic (5)						
conceptual (7)						
discusses (5)						
economy (2)						
effective (5)						
entire (5)						
equal (7)						
historically (4)						
industrial (4)						
informative (6)						
institutional (3)						
politics (5)						
productive (2)						
range (2)						
succeeded (5)						
surveying (5)						
value (1)						

* The book advertisements have been numbered as follows:

1 – *Utopia in Power*   3 – *The Decline of the British Economy*   5 – *Arab Politics*   7 – *Hegemony and Culture*
2 – *Britain's Shadow Economy*   4 – *Policing Industrial Disputes*   6 – *Sri Lanka*

These numbers appear in brackets after the words to be located.

8

OBSERVATIONS ON TEXT TYPE

BOOK ADVERTISEMENTS

Function:	To recommend the book to a potential reader.
Structure:	This will vary according to the length and nature of the advertisement, but will usually include one or more of the following: **a** general description – of the subject of the book **b** author's purpose – a brief consideration of what the author attempts to explain or demonstrate in the book **c** detailed description – of the contents of the book. This is often a list of the various topics discussed. **d** evaluation – positive evaluation as regards the worth and importance of the book **e** quotations from reviewers – containing positive evaluations from other sources (usually from well-known writers in the field or academic journals)
Aspects of language:	In texts of this kind, it is common to find evaluative language. This is particularly apparent in the author's choice of adjectives and adverbs. It is important to keep in mind that although adjectives can be broadly categorized into the functions of evaluation (e.g. *brilliant, important*, and so on) and description (*Arab, historical*), there are many cases in which these two functions overlap, particularly considering the function of the book advertisement.

NOTES

UNIT TWO

New Society
RESEARCH DIGEST

New Society 25 April 1986

What use is psychology?

1   Ordinary people who know nothing about psychology can predict the results of psychological experiments with reasonable accuracy on the basis of their own common sense. This finding that most hard-won psychological knowledge is in fact self-evident comes from John Houston, of the University of California at Los Angeles (*Psychological Reports,* vol. 57, No. 2, page 567).
2   Houston, a psychologist himself, placed a poster which read "Earn $5 by answering 21 questions about behaviour" in a local park on a Sunday afternoon. He got 50 respondents who had never read a book on experimental psychology or studied the subject, and they completed a questionnaire consisting of 21 questions each of which embodied a principle related to the working of the memory.
3   For example, they were asked how pigeons would behave if they expected food to be left on a particular windowsill because this had been so over a long period, and then found it empty one day. And they were asked which words in a word list were easiest to remember after they had been read aloud by someone else.
4   Of the 21 items, 16 were answered correctly more often than chance would have predicted. Older and better-educated people were more likely to be correct. But one question, where the correct experimentally verified answer seems to contradict common sense, received significantly more wrong answers than might have been expected by chance.
5   Houston concludes that psychology is, at least partly, "a system of self-evident information." But he points out that what psychology *does* offer is precise measurement of such phenomena and a theoretical explanation.

New Society 7 November 1986

Eating people is wrong

1   Attitudes to the Russians among Americans shifted dramatically immediately after the shooting down of the Korean civilian airliner in 1983, according to a very small study carried out by David Krus of Arizona State University (*Psychological Reports,* vol. 59, No. 1, page 3).
2   The attribution of atrocity to other nationalities has long been regarded as a very effective measure of attitude, and one of the most significant attributions of atrocity is the accusation of cannibalism.
3   A study of the popularity of other nationalities had been carried out shortly before the KAL incident. Krus then administered a modified version of his test to 39 students immediately after the incident.
4   The students were asked to read a fictitious passage which described a New Zealand airliner crashing en route to the South Pole. There were 264 passengers on board, representing 21 nationalities. When the rescue party arrived half the passengers were dead and had been partially eaten by the survivors. Which nationalities would be most likely to commit cannibalism in the period of hardship and starvation following the crash?
5   The Russian passengers were rated fifth most likely to eat human flesh before the shooting down of the airliner, but jumped to the top immediately afterwards. Not surprisingly, the English and white Americans were consistently seen as least likely to resort to cannibalism.

New Society 6 June 1986

Too relaxed to read?

1   Backward readers can be helped more by teaching them to read than by teaching them to relax, according to Christopher Sharpley, of Monash University, Australia, and Steven Rowland, of the Scot's School, Australia (*British Journal of Educational Psychology,* vol. 56, part 1, page 40).
2   Previous studies have suggested that backward readers experience stress caused by anxiety at failure, and that their learning can be improved by teaching relaxation.
3   This study involved 50 nine to eleven year old children, in five small primary schools, in four country towns in New South Wales. The children were divided into five groups. One group were taught to lower their muscle tension by using electromyographic biofeedback (which involves electrodes attached to a forearm and to a visual display dial); the second was given relaxation training; and the third had remedial teaching based on phonics and comprehension. In addition, one of two control groups had daily reading tests (as did the three experimental groups) and the other did not.
4   The children's accuracy, speed and comprehension in reading were measured for two weeks, then the different treatments were given for five weeks. The results showed that only the group which had received remedial teaching improved in reading accuracy. No group improved in reading speed—and this even *decreased* for the group which experienced biofeedback.
5   All the experimental groups showed gains in comprehension, as did the first control group, suggesting that this was an effect of increased reading practice.
6   The authors suggest that reducing stress may have worked against any improvement in reading (an optimum level of stress being necessary for successful learning), or that teaching the children to relax reduced the attention they gave to their reading.
7   So while relaxation may be of general benefit, reducing the symptoms of stress seems to be less helpful than reducing its cause—failure.

APPROACHING THE TEXT

These brief research reports appeared in a weekly magazine (*New Society*) addressed to an educated public. Though less detailed and specialistic than the examples of academic research reports given elsewhere in this coursebook, they are similar to the latter in the *type* of information they contain.

▶ Before reading the reports, indicate the *kinds* of information you would expect to find in a research report.

_____

_____

_____

WORKSHEET 1

Scanning

▶ Scan the reports in order to answer the following questions:

1 Which researcher paid his subjects to participate in his research?

2 Which study was carried out in Australia?

3 Which study made use of a questionnaire?

4 Which study involved dividing the subjects into groups?

5 Which study used the fewest subjects? How many?

Familiarity with the genre or text type which is being read is of considerable help in approaching any text. If the reader is aware of the kind of information which is likely to be found, and its probable position in the text, his expectations are heightened and he can process the information in the text more quickly and efficiently (see the notes on reading, Section 3). Throughout this coursebook practice will be given in recognizing the structure of a number of genres common to academic prose. Always refer to the OBSERVATIONS at the end of each Unit.

WORKSHEET 2

Skimming for text structure

▶ Skim each article and complete the flow charts below by inserting one of the following headings (indicating various *types* of information) in each box. Indicate also the paragraph or paragraphs which contain the information. (Headings have been inserted for the first report.)

Procedure – General assumptions (including previous work on the subject) – *Conclusions – Summary* (including researcher/s and publication) – *Results*

What use is psychology?	Eating people is wrong	Too relaxed to read?
Summary (par.)	(par.)	(par.)
Procedure (par.)	(par.)	(par.)
Results (par.)	(par.)	(par.)
Conclusions (par.)	(par.)	(par.)
		(par.)

12

INTENSIVE READING

WORKSHEET 3

Checking understanding

▶ Read carefully the research report "What use is psychology?" and answer the following questions.

1 What common characteristic did Houston's subjects have?

2 What common characteristic did his questions have?

3 How can the higher incidence of wrong answers to one of the questions be explained?

4 What use, then, is psychology, according to Houston?

WORKSHEET 4

Information extraction

▶ Read carefully the research report "Eating people is wrong" and complete the table below.

Title of research:	*Popularity of other nationalities (follow-up)*
Researcher and Affiliation:	
Published in:	
Purpose of research:	*To verify changes in attitude towards national groups*
When conducted:	
Procedure:	
Results:	

WORKSHEET 5

Information extraction

▶ Read carefully the research report "Too relaxed to read?" and complete the table below.

Phase 1 of experiment (2 weeks):
Procedure for all groups: _____

Phase 2 (5 weeks):

Group	Procedure	Results		
		Accuracy	Speed	Comprehension
				improved
			no improvement	
		no improvement		

Conclusions:
_____
_____
_____

LANGUAGE WORK

▶ In preparation for the following activity, re-read the three research reports and underline all the verbs.

> Note that the single sections of the reports are usually characterized by a particular verb tense. For example, the section regarding general assumptions will normally include verbs in the present tense, used to express "general truths" or describe a situation, or verbs in the present perfect, used in this case to imply present relevance of a past event. If a section regarding the purpose of the research is included, we are likely to find the infinitive of purpose (e.g. "*To determine* whether 'x' was true, a questionnaire was distributed . . .") or alternative linguistic forms ("*For the purpose of . . .*", "*In order to . . .*"). Sections on procedure and results will predictably make wide use of the past or past perfect tense, while comments and conclusions may include forms expressing possibility or probability ("'x' *may occur . . .*", "'y' *may have depended* on . . ."), or present or future tenses ("When 'x' is the case, 'y' *will occur . . .*"). Notice also the frequency of passive forms ("Subjects *were asked* to complete . . .", "50 questions *were answered . . .*").

14

WORKSHEET 6   **Identifying tense patterns**

▶ Complete the research report below by inserting the *appropriate* tense of the verbs in brackets. (Remember that certain tenses are recurrent in the different sections of a research report, as described above.) *Use one form expressing probability or possibility.*

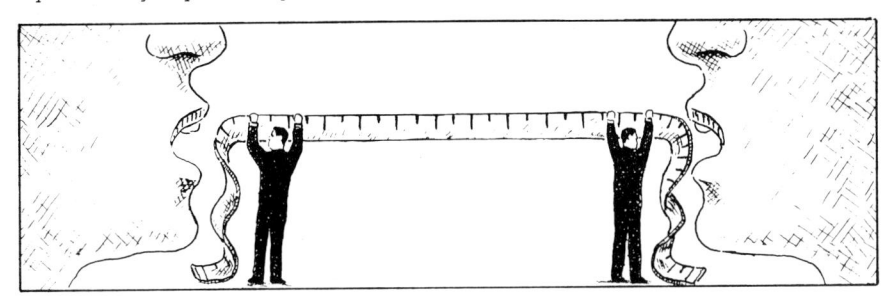

(converse)	When foreigners _____ in English, their bodies seem to do likewise. Researchers _____ for some time that Arabs,
(know)	
(prefer)	South Americans, and Eastern Europeans _____ close conversational encounters, while Asians, Northern Europeans and North Americans
(keep)	_____ their distance.
	In the most recent study, 35 Japanese and 31 Venezuelan students who
(study)	_____ English before coming to America, and 39 American
(talk)	students each _____ to someone from his or her own country
(tell)	about hobbies or sports. Half of the foreign students _____ to speak in their native language, the others to speak in English.
(ask), (talk)	The participants _____ to sit down when they _____,
(have to)	and _____ arrange their own chairs. Speaking their native
(perform)	languages, each group _____ as expected. The Venezuelans
(sit)	_____ closest (32.2 inches apart on average), the
(be)	Americans _____ in between (35.4 inches), and the Japanese
(place)	_____ their chairs farthest apart (40.2 inches). But the
(change)	spacing _____ dramatically for the foreign students speaking English. The Venezuelans sat an average of 7.9 inches farther away than their countrymen speaking Spanish — farther away, in fact, than the
(move)	Americans. The Japanese students _____ their chairs an average of 1.6 inches closer than the Japanese who were speaking Japanese.
	Why did the English-speaking Venezuelans choose such a large
(speculate)	distance? Perhaps, the researchers _____, because
(know)	they were not sure of the American "distance norms . . . They _____ the proper direction to move, but not how far." Why did the English-speaking Japanese make a smaller adjustment? The researchers
(suggest), (be)	_____ that this _____ due to the fact that they did not speak English as well as the Venezuelans.
(do)	The research _____ by Nan Sussman, a psychologist at the International Council on Education for Teaching, Washington, D.C., with Howard Rosenfield, a psychologist at the University of Kansas.
(appear)	A report _____ in *The Journal of Personality and Social Psychology*, Vol. 42, No. 1.

Adapted from an article in *Psychology Today*, July 1982.

WORKSHEET 7   **Checking understanding**

▶ Making reference to the text, decide whether the statements below are true or false.

1 Each of the participants spoke to someone from a different country.

2 All the foreign students spoke in English. _____
3 The participants positioned their own chairs. _____
4 The language spoken by each participant did not affect the result of the experiment. _____

VOCABULARY WORK AND WORD BUILDING

▶ Find the words in the text, decide the word class, and write it and the translation of the word in the space provided.

▶ Then complete the table by forming other words using appropriate suffixes if necessary. Consult your dictionary.

VOCABULARY WORK			WORD BUILDING			
Word and Location	**Class**	**Translation**	**Noun**	**Verb**	**Adjective**	**Adverb**
accuracy (1, par. 1)						
accusation (2, 2)						
administered (2, 3)						
anxiety (3, 2)						
behave (1, 3)						
comprehension (3, 3)						
concludes (1, 5)						
contradict (1, 4)						
correctly (1, 4)						
experimental (1, 2)						
measurement (1, 5)						
partially (2, 4)						
predict (1, 1)						
psychological (1, 1)						
questionnaire (1, 2)						
respondent (1, 2)						
significant (2, 2)						
theoretical (1, 5)						

The research reports have been numbered as follows:
1 – What use is psychology?   2 – Eating people is wrong   3 – Too relaxed to read?
These numbers and the paragraph number appear in brackets after the word to be located.

OBSERVATIONS ON TEXT TYPE

BRIEF RESEARCH REPORT

Function:	To summarize an extended research project for the general reader
Structure:	Although individual examples may deviate somewhat from the general model, the report normally includes the following sections: **a** brief summary – of the main points of the research, including researchers and place of publication **b** general assumptions – remarks or other background information where the author introduces the subject and may report the state of present knowledge or current beliefs regarding the subject of the research **c** purpose of the research – where the aim of the present investigation is explained **d** procedure or method – in which the various steps of the research project are explained, the subjects described and the means of gathering the data are set forth (e.g. through questionnaires, interviews, experiments and so on) **e** results of the research – including what new information, if any, emerged from the analysis of the data **f** conclusions/ comments – including general remarks regarding the findings of the research and their relevance in some larger context
Aspects of language:	In the research report we will tend to find language with a descriptive, not evaluative, function, and therefore a prevalence of nouns and verbs and a low density of adjectives. See page 14 for a discussion of recurrent tense patterns in research reports.

NOTES

UNIT THREE

CHAPTER 1
INTRODUCTION
...

Extracts from P.A. Samuelson and A. Nordhaus, 1985, *Economics*, New York: McGraw-Hill.

WHAT ECONOMICS IS

1 As a scholarly discipline, economics is only two centuries old. Adam Smith published his pathbreaking book *The Wealth of Nations* in 1776, a year notable also for the Declaration of Independence. It is no coincidence that both documents appeared the same year: Political freedom from the tyranny of monarchy was closely related to emancipation of prices and wages from the interfering hand of state regulation.

2 Adam Smith, of course, represented only a beginning. In more than a century and a half that elapsed between the appearance of *The Wealth of Nations* and the publication of John Maynard Keynes' *The General Theory of Employment, Interest and Money* (1936), economics went through many stages of development. Almost at the halfway point, there appeared the massive critique of capitalism by Karl Marx: *Das Kapital* (1867, followed by two posthumous volumes). More than a billion people, one-third of the world's population, live in countries where *Das Kapital* is economic gospel.

Definitions

3 On first encountering economics, people often want a short definition. In response to this demand, there is no shortage of supply. Here are a few popular definitions:

4 • Economics is the study of those activities that involve production and exchange among people.

5 • Economics analyzes movements in the overall economy—trends in prices, output, and unemployment. Once such phenomona are understood, economics helps develop the policies by which governments can affect the overall economy.

6 • Economics is the science of choice. It studies how people choose to use *scarce* or *limited* productive resources (land, labor, equipment, technical knowledge) to produce various commodities (such as wheat, beef, overcoats, concerts, roads, missiles) and distribute these goods to various members of society for their consumption.

7 • Economics is the study of how human beings go about the business of organizing consumption and production activities.

8 • Economics is the study of money, interest rates, capital and wealth.

9 The list is a good one, yet a scholar can extend it many times over. Why is it so long? Because, for a subject that encompasses so much and evolves so rapidly, it is always hard to compress into a few lines an exact description that will differentiate its boundaries from those of other disciplines. Economics certainly does involve all the elements stressed in these various definitions—and more.

10 Economists today agree on a general definition something like the following:

11 Economics is the study of how people and society choose to employ scarce resources that could have alternative uses in order to produce various commodities and to distribute them for consumption, now or in the future, among various persons and groups in society.

Measurement in Economics

12 We might conclude that economics talks about many of life's practical questions. But it does more than talk: Economics is vitally concerned with the *measurement* of important phenomena—unemployment, prices, incomes, and so forth.

13 One important example of such measurement occurs in macroeconomics. As we will see in Parts Two and Three of this text, *macroeconomics* studies the behavior of the economy as a whole—movements in overall prices or output or employment. *Microeconomics*, in a sense, looks at the economy through a microscope—studying the behavior of an economy's individual molecules, like firms or households.

14 Returning to measurement, one of the most important concepts in all economics is the *gross national product* (GNP). This, as Chapter 6 will discuss, represents the total dollar value of all goods and services produced each year in a nation. The GNP tells us much about the real economic performance of a country. It is the best available summary measure of the quantity of real goods and services—food, clothing, penicillin, ballet, baseball, and so forth—a country is capable of generating. It tells us much about a country's living standard, its health status, and its educational attainment.

...

ECONOMICS

ECONOMIC DESCRIPTION AND POLICY

15 Economics is used in two important ways today. The first is to describe, explain, and predict the behavior of production, inflation, incomes. But for many, the fruit of such labors is found in a second task—to improve economic performance.

16 Thus, we first attempt to describe the hardships of poverty. We then might prescribe the programs that could reduce the extent of poverty. Or we might start with an analysis of how higher energy taxes would lead to lower energy consumption. We might then conclude that the country should raise its gasoline taxes.

17 In each case, we are first engaging in positive economics, and then in normative economics.

Normative vs. Positive Economics

18 One of the central distinctions in a science like economics is between a value judgment and a factual statement. Here, we distinguish between positive and normative economics.

19 *Positive economics* concerns description of the facts, circumstances, relationships in the economy. What is the unemployment rate today? How does a higher level of unemployment affect inflation? How will a gasoline tax affect gasoline usage? These are questions that can be resolved only by reference to facts—they may be easy or tough questions, but they are all in the realm of positive economics.

20 *Normative economics* involves ethics and value judgments. How much inflation should be tolerated? Should taxation soak the rich to help the poor? Should defense spending grow at 3 or 5 or 10 percent a year? These are questions involving deeply held values or moral judgments. They can be argued about, but they can never be settled by science or by appeal to facts. There simply is no right or wrong answer about how high inflation should be, how much poverty is just, or how much defense we need. These issues are settled by political choice.

· · ·

THE METHODOLOGY OF ECONOMICS

21 How does economics progress? How does it move from a massive jumble of chaotic data to theories and economic laws on which our political leaders rely for advice? Economics proceeds as an evolutionary discipline, looking at data, developing hypotheses, testing them, and reaching a sometimes uneasy consensus on how the economy works. A textbook like this one, then, attempts to embody both the established wisdom and the hot controversies of today. In a decade or two, however, new facts will have toppled rotten old theories, and the subject will evolve further.

22 Let's look at some of the problems that arise in understanding economic issues.

Other Things Equal

23 The economic world is extremely complicated. There are millions of people and firms, thousands of prices and industries. One possible way of figuring out economic laws in such a setting is by *controlled experiments*. A controlled experiment takes place when everything else but the item under investigation is held constant. Thus a scientist trying to determine whether saccharine causes cancer in rats will hold "other things equal" and only vary the amount of saccharine. Same air, same light, same type of rat.

24 Economists have no such luxury when testing economic laws. They cannot perform the controlled experiments of chemists or biologists because they cannot easily control other important factors. Like astronomers or meteorologists, they generally must be content largely to observe.

25 If you are vitally interested in the effect of the 1982 gasoline tax on fuel consumption, you will be vexed by the fact that in the same year when the tax was imposed, the size of cars became smaller. Nevertheless, you must try to isolate the effects of the tax by attempting to figure out what would happen, if "other things were equal." You can perform calculations that correct for the changing car size. Unless you make such corrections, you cannot accurately understand the effects of gasoline taxes.

· · ·

APPROACHING THE TEXT

The texts presented in this Unit are extracts from *Chapter 1: Introduction* of an economics textbook.

▶ Drawing on your knowledge of this genre from your previous schooling, indicate below the purpose or purposes of a textbook, and some of its graphic or organizational characteristics.

_____
_____
_____
_____

WORKSHEET 1

Skimming and scanning for contents

▶ Skim and scan the extracts and place a tick beside the topics which are discussed in the texts.

1. ____ Definitions of field of study
2. ____ Some examples of how the study of economics can influence policy decisions
3. ____ Indication of importance of field of study
4. ____ Presentation and definitions of essential terminology
5. ____ Historical references to the development of the field of study
6. ____ The relationship of economics to other social sciences
7. ____ Some methodological principles and problems
8. ____ An overall discussion of the contents of the textbook

WORKSHEET 2

Pre-reading vocabulary work

▶ The words in the table overleaf all appear in the first section of the Introduction, "What Economics Is" in the paragraph indicated. (All except two are nouns.) Scan the text to find the context in which they are used, underline them, decide the word class, and write it in the first column.

▶ Then choose an appropriate definition for each word from the list below (there are more definitions than there are words), and write it in the second column. An example has been given.

a quantity of goods produced
b including everything
c business companies
d *payment for labour or services*
e general directions/tendencies
f a quantity which is obtainable or available
g classifies
h articles of trade
i values measured in relation to another amount
j not available in sufficient quantity
k a deficiency, insufficient quantity
l (possession of) a large amount of money or property
m unlimited

	Word Class	Definitions
1 wages (par. 1 _d_)	*noun*	*payment for labour or services*
2 shortage (par. 3 __)		
3 supply (par. 3 __)		
4 overall (par. 5 __)		
5 trends (par. 5 __)		
6 scarce (par. 6 __)		
7 commodities (par. 6 __)		
8 rates (par. 8 __)		
9 wealth (par. 8 __)		
10 output (par. 13 __)		
11 firms (par. 13 __)		

INTENSIVE READING

WORKSHEET 3

Previewing text organization/content

As you will have noted, the textbook genre is characterized by typographically prominent headings and sub-headings. Each of the extracts presented in this Unit has a general heading followed by a brief introduction to the topic to be considered in the section, and one or more subsections. Section headings and subsections for the three extracts are given below:

What Economics Is
1 Introduction
2 Definitions
3 Measurement in economics

Economic Description and Policy
1 Introduction
2 Normative vs. positive economics

The Methodology of Economics
1 Introduction
2 Other things equal

▶ Read the introductory paragraphs under each general heading (pars. 1–2; pars. 15–17; pars. 21–22) and choose from the list below an *appropriate* title for the introduction to each section, writing it in the space provided.

What Economics Is
- The contributions of some important economists to the development of the discipline
- Development of economics from Adam Smith to Karl Marx
- Some important theories in the development of economics as a discipline

Economic Description and Policy
- The behaviour of production, inflation, incomes
- Two major uses of economics
- The application of economics to problems of poverty and energy consumption

The Methodology of Economics
- Theories and economic laws
- Problems in understanding economic issues
- The method of economic analysis

▶ Now read the other parts of the text and insert the items below under the appropriate headings.

authors' definition – controlled experiments – GNP – macroeconomics – value judgements vs. factual statements – microeconomics – popular definitions

What Economics Is

1 Introduction: _____

2 Definitions: _____

3 Measurement in economics
_____

Economic Description and Policy

1 Introduction: _____

2 Normative vs. positive economics
_____

The Methodology of Economics

1 Introduction: _____

2 Other things equal
_____

WORKSHEET 4

Explanations/examples of key terms

There are a number of key terms in the text for which an explanation or definition is given. In some cases, instead of an explanation, an example or further clarification of the term is provided. For a few terms, both an explanation and an example are given.

▶ Complete the chart below with reference to the text.

Key term	Explanation/Definition	Examples/Further clarification
movements in overall economy (par. 5)		
		land, labor, equipment, technology, knowledge (par. 6)
commodities (par. 6)		
important (economic) phenomena (par. 12)		
macroeconomics (par. 13)		
	a study of economy through a microscope (par. 13)	
gross national product (par. 14)		
		food, clothing, penicillin, ballet, baseball (par. 14)
	description of facts, circumstances, relationships in the economy (par. 19)	
normative economics (par. 20)		
	everything but the item under investigation is held constant (par. 23)	

24

LANGUAGE WORK

WORKSHEET 5

Vocabulary work

▶ Find words in the section "Economic Description and Policy" which:

a) have a *similar* meaning to the following:

1 trend _____ (in par. 15)
2 output _____ (in par. 15)
3 wages _____ (in par. 15)
4 difficulties _____ (in par. 16)
5 (to) increase _____ (in par. 16)
6 petrol _____ (in par. 16)
7 resolved _____ (in par. 20)
8 problems _____ (in par. 20)

b) mean approximately the *opposite* of:

1 deflation _____ (in par. 15)
2 wealth _____ (in par. 16)
3 (to) raise _____ (in par. 16)
4 (to) finish _____ (in par. 16)
5 employment _____ (in par. 19)
6 easy _____ (in par. 19)
7 (to) decline _____ (in par. 20)
8 right _____ (in par. 20)

▶ Find words in "The Methodology of Economics" which match the following definitions (the definitions are in the same order as the words in the text).

Definitions	Words in text
1 very big	(in par. 21)
2 opinion about what to do	(in par. 21)
3 (to) express, include, comprise	(in par. 21)
4 the quality of having good sense, knowledge, judgement	(in par. 21)
5 understanding by thinking	(in par. 23)
6 a single unit in a list or group	(in par. 23)
7 (to) be or make different	(in par. 23)
8 extremely	(in par. 25)

The sections "Economic Description and Policy" and "The Methodology of Economics" present many examples of a very important and highly recurrent feature of academic prose, modal verbs (*can, will, must,* etc.). These words add a particular meaning to the principal verb, and their function may vary according to the context. See the notes on reading, Section 3.1.3 for a detailed presentation of modal meaning.

WORKSHEET 6

Modal verbs

▶ Underline all the modal verbs in "Economic Description and Policy" and "The Methodology of Economics" (some modals are used several times in the text). Look carefully at the context in which each modal verb is used, and assign it to one of the general categories below on the basis of its function in this text.

Meaning	Modal verbs
Ability/Potential	
Probability/Possibility	
Obligation/Necessity	
Obligation/Desirability	
Future	
Conditional	

▶ Now read the text below and insert an appropriate modal verb in the spaces provided, indicating in the margin the meaning of the modal chosen. An example has been given. (More than one answer is possible in several cases.)

The Technological Choices Open to Any Society: Society's Production-Possibility Frontier

Limitation of the total resources capable of producing different commodities means that society 1)_____ choose between relatively scarce commodities. This basic economic fact 2)_____ be illustrated simply. Here, we 3) _will_____ consider an economy with a limited number of people, technical knowledge, factories, limited tools, and a limited amount of land, water power and natural resources. In deciding WHAT 4)_____ be produced and HOW, the economy 5)_____ really decide how these resources are to be allocated among the thousands of different possible commodities. How much land 6)_____ be allocated for wheat growing? How many factories 7)_____ produce knives?

   The question 8)_____ be simplified further by assuming that only two economic goods are to be produced. For dramatic purposes, guns and butter 9)_____ be our example, although the same argument 10)_____ apply to any pair of goods – bread and wine, consumption and investment, and so forth.

Meaning

1 _____
2 _____
3 _future_____
4 _____
5 _____
6 _____
7 _____
8 _____
9 _____
10 _____

WORKSHEET 7   **Reutilization of key vocabulary**

▶ Choosing from the words listed below, complete the text "Prices and Inflation". Each word may be used only once. Read through the text before beginning the exercise.

averaged (v)	decline (n)	output (n)	rise (v)
consumer (n)	hyperinflation (n)	plus (adj)	variation (n)
controls (n)	overall (adj)	rate (n)	wages (n)

Prices and Inflation The third major macro-economic objective is to ensure *price stability with free markets*. Price stability means that prices neither _____ nor fall too rapidly; that the rate of inflation (measured as the rate of change of prices from one period to the next) be close to zero. The desire to maintain "free markets" is based on the political judgment in the United States that prices and _____ be set in decentralized private markets or bargaining rather than by government fiat. The desire for this form of organization is based on the economic judgment that free-market-determined prices are an efficient way of organizing _____ and keeping markets responsive to people's tastes.

The most common way to measure the _____ price level is the *consumer price index*, popularly known as the *CPI*. The CPI measures the cost of a fixed basket of goods (items like food, shelter, clothing, and medical care) bought by the typical urban _____ . The overall price level is often denoted by the letter *P*. The *rate of inflation* is the rate of growth or _____ of the price level, say, from one year to the next.

Figure 5–4 illustrates the _____ of inflation for the CPI from 1929 to 1984. Over this entire period, inflation _____ 3.2 percent. Note, however, that there was enormous _____ of inflation in different years, varying from *minus* 10 percent in 1932 to a high of _____ 14 percent in 1947.

The objective of price stability with free markets is more subtle than those concerning output and employment (a fuller treatment is provided in Chapters 12 and 13). It is clearly undesirable to impose an absolutely rigid set of prices, such as has sometimes been the case in communist countries, or during times of wartime price _____ in market economies. A frozen price structure would prevent the *invisible hand* of markets from allocating goods and inputs—there would be no efficient way to induce energy conservation or to discourage the production of horse-drawn buggies.

At the other extreme, we must avoid _____ _____, where the price level rises a thousand or a million percent a year. In such situations, as was seen in Weimar Germany of the 1920s, prices are useless. Those foolish or naive enough to hold on to currency become impoverished. An economy returns to barter.

▶ Figure 5–4 on inflation illustrates the points made in the preceding text. With reference to the figure, complete the accompanying explanation.

INFLATION

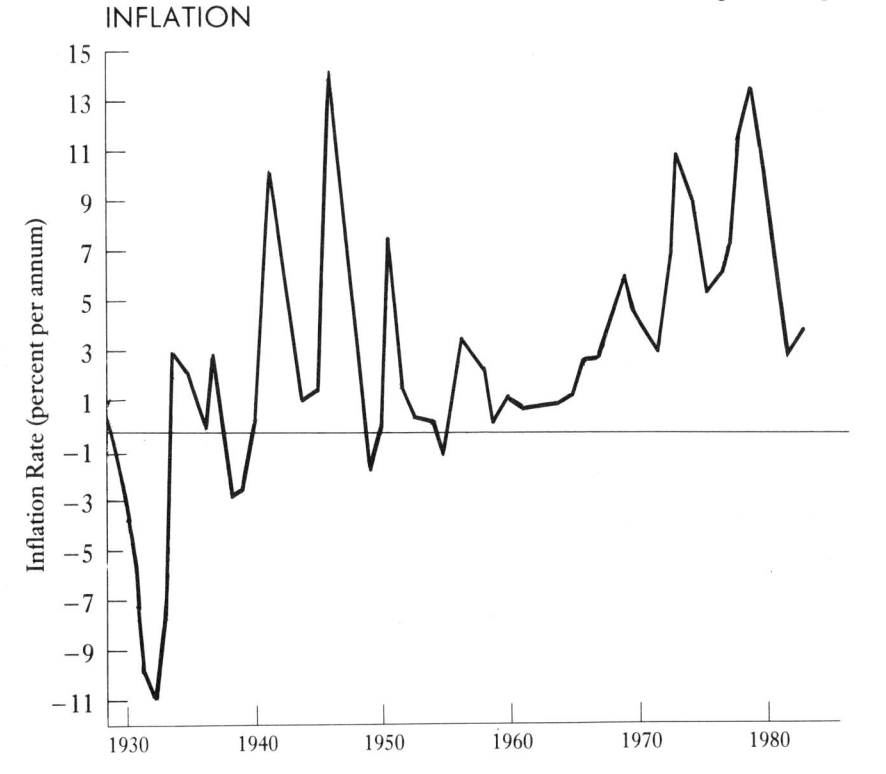

Figure 5-4 The rising trend of consumer price inflation, 1929–1984

This _____ shows the year-over-year increase in consumer prices as measured by the _____ _____ (CPI). During the Depression, prices actually _____. Since World War II, however, deflation (or falling _____) has been *rare*. Note the upward _____ of _____ from 1960 to _____, followed by the steep _____, or disinflation, after 1980 that resulted from recession, _____ unemployment, and falling oil prices. (Source: U. S. Department of Labor.)

VOCABULARY WORK AND WORD BUILDING

▶ Find the words in the text (paragraphs are given), decide the word class, and write it and the translation of the word in the space provided.

▶ Then complete the table by forming other words using appropriate suffixes if necessary. Consult your dictionary.

VOCABULARY WORK			WORD BUILDING		
Word and Location	**Class**	**Translation**	**Noun**	**Verb**	**Adjective**
affect (19)					
agree (10)					
attainment (14)					
available (14)					
choice (6)					
critique (2)					
differentiate (9)					
employ (11)					
involve (4)					
notable (1)					
occurs (13)					
performance (14)					
proceeds (21)					
rates (8)					
reference (19)					
related (1)					
rely (21)					
scholarly (1)					
shortage (3)					
statement (18)					

Given the regularity with which adverbs are formed from adjectives, from this Unit onwards the Word Building Chart will include only nouns, verbs and adjectives.

OBSERVATIONS ON TEXT TYPE — TEXTBOOK

Function:	To present in a clear and accessible way to a non-specialized reader an introductory and/or general overview of a given topic, either of a broad subject area (e.g. economics) or of a more specific aspect of a subject area (e.g. The History of Medieval Britain).
Structure:	In accordance with its aim of providing clear and comprehensive information on a topic, the textbook is organized in such a way as to facilitate use and consultation by the reader. We thus normally find clearly marked divisions into sections and subsections, summaries of the contents of each chapter, occasionally exercises or questions for discussion on the contents of the chapters, as well as charts, figures, tables, photographs etc.
Aspects of language:	In texts belonging to this genre, common features of language are: a) the frequent use of the simple present tense to describe or explain (history textbooks, however, will show a predictably higher use of past tenses), and modal auxiliaries (e.g. in the consideration of hypothetical situations, depending on the topic of the textbook) b) the introduction of key terminology and explanations or definitions of such c) frequent discourse markers or rhetorical questions which "guide" the reader through parts of the text (e.g. "Let's look at some problems...", "How does economics progress?").

NOTES

UNIT FOUR

Olga Semenova

In sadness

1917: The Russian Revolution and the Origins of Present-Day Communism
LEONARD SCHAPIRO *Temple Smith* £12.95

1 Leonard Schapiro was exceptionally well-qualified to write a book on 1917. A leading academic authority on the Bolsheviks (Professor at the LSE, author of *The Communist Party of the Soviet Union* etc.), he witnessed the Russian revolution as well. Schapiro completed *1917* in 1983, just before he died. His book is the distillation of a lifetime's teaching and reflection on the Russian revolution. It is both a concise and lucid narrative and a highly-charged piece of political analysis.

2 As narrative, *1917* fills a surprising gap in the literature on the subject. There are a large number of detailed studies of different aspects of the revolution, some of them brilliant works of scholarship. But no simple, comprehensive account of the two revolutions and the civil war exists. Schapiro's book is brief, but covers all the main points with absolute clarity. It also incorporates the conclusions of the most important recent research on the subject. The reader gets both an excellent introduction to the Russian revolution and an idea of how new material is causing thinking about it to change.

3 The value of Schapiro's analysis is more questionable. Schapiro was old and rigid, an adherent of the cold war/totalitarianism school. His interpretation of the Russian revolution is crude and unashamedly biased. He hates the Bolsheviks. He looks at the Russian revolution purely from the point of view of political power.

4 Schapiro's thesis goes roughly as follows. After the disintegration of the monarchy in February 1917, there was general support in the country for a broad-based socialist coalition. This quickly came to mean support for the Soviets, rather than for the Provisional Government. However, support for the Soviets did not mean support for the Bolsheviks, but for the 'traditional ideals of Russian socialism', represented by the SRs and, especially, the Mensheviks. The Bolsheviks were a small band of disciplined fanatics. They were able to seize power in October because no one organised to stop them. They held on to it by annihilating their opponents, ruthlessly manipulating public opinion and militarising the economy. Right up to 1924, they were 'a largely unpopular party'. The first choice of a majority of the population would have been 'some form of moderate socialism'.

5 While it is undoubtedly true that the Bolsheviks were unscrupulous in their choice of methods and that they were not supported by a majority of the population when they seized power, Schapiro's thesis is prejudiced, one-sided and out-dated.

'Disciplined fanatics . . . ruthlessly manipulating public opinion'? Molotov, Stalin and Lenin at the start of it all, working on *Pravda* in 1917

6 Schapiro's hostility to Leninism (which he sees as the precursor of Stalinism) leads him to maintain a position on the Bolsheviks which has been shown to be wrong. He presents them as an autocratically run and conspiratorial organisation, staffed by a group of men whose opinions were (with rare exceptions) uniform. Recent research, however, including that of Rabinowitch (whom Schapiro himself quotes), has shown that the Bolshevik party was not a homogeneus body, but a collection of committees. Each of these tended to run its own affairs independently and take initiatives of its own, regardless of the opinions and instruction of the Central Committee.

7 Other problems with Schapiro's work stem from the fact that he was an old-fashioned political historian. *1917* is based on the premise that it is possible to understand the Russian revolution purely in terms of political power, without reference to social or economic questions.

8 This, firstly, leads Schapiro into errors of interpretation. He concentrates exclusively on the mechanics of the Bolshevik seizure of power. This approach allows him to avoid discussing the appeal which the Bolsheviks' programme held for industrial workers and peasants. He seriously underestimates the degree of popular support which the Bolsheiks enjoyed: the strong power base which, by October, they had in the cities; and the enthusiasm generated by their land policy in the countryside, which was probably the crucial factor in their victory in the civil war.

9 Secondly, Schapiro's purely political orientation affects his choice of period. He picks the dates 1917–1924 because they delimit the transfer of political power. But, for any real understanding of the Russian revolution, one needs to go both further back and further forward. 1917 is not the right point at which to start. The events of that year make sense only if viewed in the context of the rapid industrialisation of Russia in the late 19th and early 20th centuries. 1924 is not a good place at which to stop, because the most dramatic changes resulting from the Bolshevik takeover — the social and economic transformation of Russia undertaken by Stalin — didn't happen until 1928–1933. Schapiro doesn't consider these events part of the Russian revolution. Most younger historians, however, would argue that they were and that a revolution should be defined as the period of upheaval, social and economic as well as political, which intervenes between the fall of an old regime and the firm consolidation of a new one. This is the approach taken by Sheila Fitzpatrick, in her recent appraisal of the Russian revolution, a work which forms an interesting contrast to Schapiro's.

10 Schapiro's enduring advantage over more modern historians, however, is that he lived in Petrograd as a boy (from 1917–1920). This has helped him to bring what is essentially just a well written text book to life. He has managed to breathe into it something of the feel of the time — the euphoria, excitement and suffering of revolutionary Russia.

New Statesman 20 April 1984

APPROACHING THE TEXT

▶ Answer the following questions before reading the main body of the text.
1 To which genre does this text belong? _____
2 What is the name of the reviewer? _____
3 What is the title and who is the author of the book? _____
_____
4 What does the caption to the photograph imply about the reviewer's attitude towards the book? _____
_____

WORKSHEET 1

Identifying reviewer's evaluation

▶ Read the first sentence of each paragraph and decide whether it presents an opinion of the book which is very favourable, favourable, neutral, unfavourable or very unfavourable. Underline the language used to convey the reviewer's opinion, then place a tick in the appropriate column.

par.	very favourable	favourable	neutral	unfavourable	very unfavourable
1					
2					
3					
4					
5					
6					
7					
8					
9					
10					

How would you classify the evaluation of the book as a whole? _____

In the preceding units your attention was drawn to the general organization of the texts. In some cases the development of the text may be relatively simple and straightforward, each paragraph having a particular function (as in the brief research report: *general assumptions, procedure,* etc.). In longer texts the writer may need or want to organize his discourse in a more complex manner, linking certain facts or steps in his exposition and following a line of argument through various stages. Thus some aspects may be developed at greater length than others. This is the case in the present book review. Below is an *outline* of the structure of the text. This format (showing by means of indentation the relationship between sections and subsections) represents one standard way of indicating the structure of a text. Note that headings in outlines often indicate the *functions* of the various sections of the text, especially in the major headings (i.e. what the author is *doing* – presenting, evaluating, discussing – not what he is *saying*). Increasingly specific subsections will indicate in more detail the actual arguments treated.

WORKSHEET 2 **Distinguishing text structure**

▶ Read the article rapidly and indicate the paragraph or paragraphs which comprise the following sections and subsections.

1 PRESENTATION OF THE BOOK AND AUTHOR (par. _____)
2 EVALUATION OF THE BOOK AS NARRATIVE (par. _____)
3 DISCUSSION OF SCHAPIRO'S POLITICAL ANALYSIS (par. _____)
— Presentation of Schapiro's thesis (par. _____)
— Criticism of Schapiro's thesis (par. _____)
— On the grounds that he was biased against the Bolsheviks (par. _____)
— On the grounds that he considers the revolution purely in terms of political power (par. _____)
— Leading to errors of interpretation (par. _____)
— Leading to an unsatisfactory choice of period (par. _____)
4 CONCLUSION: EVALUATION OF THE BOOK (par. _____)

INTENSIVE READING

All texts contain examples of reference, whereby words or phrases are referred to by others (e.g. *it, this, those* etc.) in order to avoid repetition and achieve a "tighter" and more economical text. Sometimes these words refer backwards in the text to concepts already mentioned (in this case the reference is called *anaphoric*). In other cases the reference is forward to words or phrases which follow in the text (in which case the reference is called *cataphoric*). In the text below are examples of both.

1   In March 1898 representatives of several illegal Marxist groups met in Minsk to found the Russian Social Democratic Workers' Party. Its leaders, however, were almost immediately arrested by the police, and the Social Democratic movement took
5   political shape among Russian exiles in Western Europe. At its second congress in 1903, held partly in Brussels and partly in London, appeared the rift between the followers of V. I. Ulyanov (Lenin) and the rest. Lenin maintained that the party should be confined to full-time "professional revolutionaries", while
10 others preferred as their aim a mass working-class party. Lenin took for his faction the name Bolshevik (derived from *bolshinstvo*, "majority"), because it had won a majority in the election of the party's key bodies. His opponents became known as Mensheviks (*menshinstvo*, "minority"). In fact, in the following
15 decade the factions within the movement were extremely fluid, and no single group for any length of time had clear majority support among the party membership.
    The various Populist illegal groups in Russia also made efforts to unite, and at a conference held in 1902 in Switzerland
20 they formed a Party of Socialist Revolutionaries (S.R.'s). This party's leadership came principally from the intelligentsia. Its aim was to appeal above all to the peasants, whereas the Social Democrats laid the main emphasis on the industrial working class. In practice it was hard to establish contact with
25 peasants, because of their scattered distribution and the ease with which the police could observe the entry of strangers into villages. Consequently the S.R.'s no less than the Social Democrats found their mass support in the cities.

Adapted with permission from "Russian History" in *Encyclopaedia Britannica*, 14th edn (1967), 19:797.

As you can see, in lines 3 and 5 the pronoun *its* replaces the previously named *Russian Social Democratic Workers' Party*. In line 10, *their* refers back to *others*, and in lines 11 and 13 *his* replaces *Lenin*. In line 12, *it* substitutes the previously mentioned *(his) faction*; in line 20 *they* replaces *the various Populist illegal groups*, and in lines 21 and 22 *This (party)* and *Its* refer back to *Party of Socialist Revolutionaries*. In line 24 *it* is cataphoric, referring forward to the phrase *to establish contact with peasants,* and in line 25 *their* substitutes the word *peasants*.

▶ Now read the whole text carefully.

WORKSHEET 3

Reference

▶ Underline the words listed below. Decide whether the reference is anaphoric or cataphoric, then write the words or phrases referred to in the space provided.

	Anaphoric	Cataphoric	Words or phrases referred to
1 This (par. 4, line 5)			
2 it (5, 1)			
3 these (6, 12)			
4 it (7, 4)			
5 This (8, 1)			
6 they (9, 19)			
7 This (10, 3)			

WORKSHEET 4

Checking understanding

▶ The following statements are *reformulations* of passages in the text. Find the relevant passages and decide whether the opinions presented would be those of Schapiro or those of Semenova. Place a tick in the appropriate column.

Opinion	Schapiro	Semenova
1 The Bolshevik party was a highly centralized organization controlled from the top by the Central Committee		
2 The Bolshevik party was a heterogeneous organization that was guided by the Central Committee but whose various sub-committees had a certain autonomy.		
3 The Russian revolution can be best understood by situating the political struggle within its social and economic context.		
4 The Bolshevik party had little concrete support amongst the peasantry.		
5 The events of 1928–33 cannot be considered part of the Russian revolution.		
6 A revolution is the process during which political power is transferred from one ruling group to another.		
7 To understand the Russian revolution it is necessary to analyse it in the context of the development of Russian industry in the later 19th and early 20th centuries.		

▶ Which of the following options best reflects the reviewer's *overall* judgement of *1917*?

1. It is prejudiced, one-sided and out-dated.
2. It provides a complete review of the historical period but an inadequate political analysis.
3. It is a concise and lucid narrative and a highly charged piece of political analysis.
4. It is essentially just a well written textbook.

▶ Why do you think the review is entitled "In Sadness"?

LANGUAGE WORK

WORKSHEET 5

Reutilization of selected lexis

▶ Below is a list of words common to academic prose that are used in the text. Find them and underline them. Look at the context in which they appear, decide their word class and meaning, checking in a dictionary if necessary. Then complete the synopsis of the book review of *1917* below by filling in the blanks with the appropriate item. (Use the correct verb form.) Each word can be used only once.

par. 1: both . . . and	par. 6: whose	par. 9: secondly
par. 2: main	own	to affect
par. 4: rather than	regardless of	as well as
however	par. 7: to stem from	between
up to	without	
largely	par. 8: firstly	par. 10: to manage to
par. 5: while	leads	
	to allow	

_____ most of the books on 1917 are detailed analyses of particular aspects of the Russian revolution, Leonard Schapiro _____ present a general account of the years _____ 1924, which is _____ simple _____ accurate, and _____ which a surprising gap in the literature on the subject would not have been filled. Schapiro's boyhood years in Petrograd (_____ 1917 and 1920), and his academic background _____ him to write about these events with authority. _____, his hatred of the Bolsheviks _____ his interpretation of the revolution, which is _____ biased and crude. He makes two principal errors. _____, his analysis of the Bolsheviks, _____ popular support he seriously underestimates, is inadequate. This position on the Bolsheviks, prejudiced _____ one-sided, _____ his hostility towards Leninism. _____, the fact that he was an old-fashioned political historian _____ him to assume that the Russian revolution can be understood in purely political terms, _____ social and economic factors. His reference to political criteria alone greatly conditions his choice of period (1917–1924); the _____ social and economic changes did not take place until the period 1928–1933. _____ a brilliant work of scholarship, *1917* is a well written textbook brought to life by Schapiro's _____ experience of the events.

In the preceding Units you have been introduced to features of the global organization of different text types, and have seen how familiarity with text structure can help the reader by allowing him to make better predictions about text content and development, to locate more rapidly specific types of information, etc. Similarly, English paragraphs, particularly in academic prose, are organized according to a relatively stable pattern; sensitivity to this pattern facilitates reading by allowing the reader to focus on those parts of the paragraph which are likely to carry forward the writer's line of reasoning or "discourse". (See also the notes on reading, Section 3.2.2.)

The first or second sentence in English paragraphs usually presents the TOPIC or central idea. (The *TOPIC SENTENCE* is sometimes preceded by a sentence which functions as a *TOPIC INTRODUCER*.) The rest of the paragraph expands the topic sentence, the last sentence usually referring back to the topic considered and forward to the topic of the following paragraph. In the first paragraph of *1917*, for example, the topic sentence (the first in the paragraph) is:

> Leonard Schapiro was exceptionally well qualified to write a book on 1917.

Successive sentences expand 1) Schapiro's qualifications, and 2) the book that he wrote. In other words, the paragraph answers the hypothetical questions (after reading the topic sentence), "Why was he well qualified?" (he was *a leading academic authority, Professor at LSE, he witnessed the Russian revolution*, etc.), and "What is this book?" (*the distillation of a lifetime's teaching, reflections on the Russian revolution,* etc.). Note also that the final sentence both draws a conclusion about the book (sending backward to the topic sentence), and prepares for the following paragraph: *it is a concise and lucid narrative* (developed in paragraph 2), and *a highly-charged piece of political analysis* (developed in the remainder of the article).

The following exercise aims to give practice in recognizing the function of topic sentences and to call attention to aspects of the internal structure and development of English paragraphs.

WORKSHEET 6

Topic sentences and paragraph structure

▶ Complete the text below by writing the appropriate topic sentence in the space provided.

Topic sentences

1 The most important problem for the regime was whether to continue the war, or, if not, how to get out of the war.

2 In Petrograd, the Russian capital, there were in March 1917 two separate authorities, both claiming to speak for the people, but neither of them representing more than a section of it: the Provisional Government and the Soviet (council) of Workers' Deputies.

3 It has often been argued by historians of a later epoch that the Western Allies were foolish not to have agreed to release Russia from its war obligations.

4 The fundamental question facing the new regime was that of legitimacy.

The Provisional Government and the First World War

_____

_____

_____

The former had been chosen on March 15 by the members of a duma elected four years earlier on a restricted franchise. Its leaders reflected the point of view of the more conservative members of the professional classes. The soviet represented primarily the working class of the capital, but could in a wider sense speak for the industrial workers of all Russia. It became a sort of parliament of Russian socialism, from the Socialist-Revolutionaries (S.R.) to the Bolsheviks.

The old legitimacy of the monarchy had been destroyed. It could be replaced only by the legitimacy of the will of the whole people of Russia, but this could be ascertained only by an elected Constituent Assembly. But Russia was at war with Germany, Austria-Hungary, and Turkey, and to hold such an election at that time seemed hardly possible, both because it would divert energies from the war effort and because so many citizens were away in the army. Consequently, the Provisional Government decided to wait for the end of the war so that completely free and comprehensive elections could be held. However, an immediate election would have caused less chaos than later occurred, and would have given the government the democratic legitimacy that it lacked.

The foreign minister, P. N. Milyukov, a convinced patriot, believed that the war was just, that it was being fought to liberate the peoples oppressed by Austria-Hungary and by Turkey, and that Russia should be rewarded for its part in the war by acquiring Constantinople, the Straits, and Turkish Armenia. The Socialists, however, were not interested in these aims and believed that the war should be ended "without annexations and without indemnities." But until the Germans were willing to make peace, the Russian fatherland still had to be defended. And in any case the new Russian leaders admitted that they could not make peace without their allies' consent.

But at the time it was inconceivable that the Western governments should do so. The release of the German divisions held on the Russian front might have made it possible for Gen. Erich Luddendorff finally to crush the West.

▶ Now, making reference to the completed text, indicate whether the following statements are true or false.
1 The leaders of the Provisional Government of Petrograd were more conservative than those of the Soviet Council. _____
2 Holding the elections after the end of the war would have resulted in less chaos because citizens who had been away in the army could have voted freely. _____
3 If the Russians had been allowed to withdraw from the war, as the Socialists wanted, the German army might have been able to overcome Western resistance. _____

VOCABULARY WORK AND WORD BUILDING

▶ Find the words in the text (paragraphs are given), decide the word class, and write it and the translation of the word in the space provided.

▶ Then complete the table by forming other words using appropriate suffixes if necessary. Consult your dictionary.

VOCABULARY WORK			WORD BUILDING		
Word and Location	**Class**	**Translation**	**Noun**	**Verb**	**Adjective**
avoid (8)					
biased (3)					
claiming (Worksheet 6)					
clarity (2)					
lacked (Worksheet 6)					
largely (4)					
leads (8)					
mechanics (8)					
purely (7)					
rewarded (Worksheet 6)					
studies (2)					
support (4)					
tended (6)					
wider (Worksheet 6)					
witnessed (1)					

OBSERVATIONS ON TEXT TYPE — BOOK REVIEW

Function:	To assess a book by describing its content and commenting on its theoretical assumptions, its consequent analysis and practical aspects such as accuracy of data, sources used and so on.
Structure:	Most book reviews will contain the following three items (sometimes these may be preceded by a discussion of the subject in general by the reviewer): **a** General description – of the book and/or the views or position of the author **b** Summary – of the main items discussed in the book and of the ideas put forward **c** Evaluation – of the overall usefulness or importance of the book The last category often includes an exposition of the reviewer's own views and a discussion of points raised as well as a positive or negative judgement.

NOTES

UNIT FIVE

The Overselling of Candidates On Television

Glimpses of political candidates, packaged for viewers as if they were soap or a headache remedy, are endemic on American television screens this campaign spring of 1984. Those carefully crafted pitches, flashing on and off in 30 or 60 seconds, add little or nothing to viewers' understanding of issues, but their staggering cost drains off as much as three-fourths of rapidly expanding campaign budgets. Other Western democracies conduct their elections at much lower cost and, in many cases, with higher voter participation. With the help of a Fund grant, the Committee for the Study of the American Electorate set out to discover how some of them deal with the largest cost item in U.S. campaigns—political advertising on television. This report is based on the Committee's findings.

1 WHEN THE SHOUTING FINALLY DIES DOWN after next November's national election, the accounting is likely to show that a single U.S. Senate race—for the seat now held by North Carolina Republican Jesse Helms—cost as much as $20 million. The magnitude of that figure, which is well over one-ninth of the total amount spent on all U.S. election campaigns in 1960, graphically illustrates what has happened to the cost of running for U.S. political office in the last two decades (see also Figures 1 and 2). This was the period in which television, firmly ensconced as the centerpiece of American communications, gradually became the primary mode of political campaigning.

2 That the purchase of television air-time is the principal cause of escalating campaign costs is no longer open to doubt. The Federal Election Commission does not require candidates to report their television expenditures as a separate item, so there are no exact figures on the proportion of increased campaign costs attributable to television. But careful scrutiny of a sampling of campaign expenditure reports shows that when television commercials are used in a campaign they eat up from two-thirds to three-fourths of all budgeted funds. A prime-time minute on network television costs $174,000 today, up from $40,000 in 1972, and local stations have increased their rates as much as fifteen-fold.

3 As more and more of every campaign dollar is poured into television advertising, less and less is available for more traditional modes of campaigning. These, however, are precisely the kinds of activities that involve people in the political process: organizing efforts, storefronts, rallies for interest groups and minorities, neighborhood coffee klatches, local political clubs, and personal appearances by the candidate. The more electronic politics becomes, the less it is involved with people. It is small wonder that voter turnout has sharply declined as citizens have been transformed from participants in the political enterprise to consumers of television messages, which all too often are no more than 30- or 60-second attacks on an opponent.

4 At the same time, media consultants and packagers are fast supplanting the political party as the point of access to the political ladder. This is to the detriment of the party's ability not simply to select and elect candidates but to devise a program and discipline membership toward its adoption. Now, it seems, all a candidate needs in order to enter the lists is money, a pollster, and a media adviser.

5 Despite frequent grumbling in the press and in the streets of America about the pernicious effects of the overselling of candidates on television, there appears to be a general perception that unlimited access to television air-time is part and parcel of democracy and that any restriction would constitute an infringement of free speech. How badly this misconstrues the prerogatives of democracy is indicated by the fact that some of the most advanced democracies in the world (see Figure 3) deny political candidates any opportunity whatsoever to place commercial messages on television.

When television commercials are used in a campaign, they eat up from two-thirds to three-fourths of all budgeted funds. Today, a prime-time minute on network television costs $174,000, up from $40,000 in 1972.

Transatlantic Perspectives, April 1984, by Elizabeth McPherson

41

Expenditures in Average Congressional Campaign

U.S. HOUSE OF REPRESENTATIVES: $40,000 (1972), $158,000 (1982)

U.S. SENATE: $360,000 (1972), $1 million plus (1982)

Figure 2

Total U.S. Campaign Expenditures

$175 million (1960), $425 million (1972), $1.2 billion (1980)

Figure 1

Other Advanced Democracies Have Acted To Restrict Television Campaigning

6 In a study commissioned by the Center for the Study of the American Electorate, Howard Penniman and Austin Ranney of the American Enterprise Institute (AEI) took a close look at six major democracies—Canada, France, the Federal Republic of Germany, Italy, the United Kingdom, and Venezuela—and found that only Venezuela permits the broadcast of political advertising on a scale comparable to that of the United States.

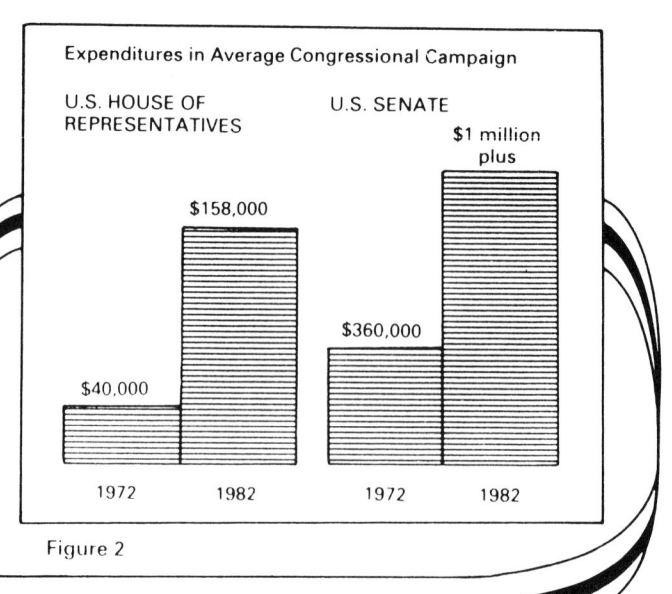

7 Like many other democracies, France, the Federal Republic of Germany, and the United Kingdom permit no political advertising on radio and television. This stand is supported by almost all parties and commentators. In France, report Penniman and Ranney, "not only is the American example never held up for emulation; it is often used as an example of how purchased political advertising can corrupt the political process." The British and Germans are equally chary of allowing the airwaves to be turned over to the political image-makers and manipulators. Writes journalist Tim Robinson from London: "Nothing annoys a British politician more than the allegation that he or she has become 'Americanized,' the euphemism for showiness."

8 Canada, on the other hand, allows television stations to sell some time for political advertising, but only to political parties, not individuals, and only within strict total time limits. In every general election, six and one-half hours of air-time is allocated between the parties according to a proportional formula agreed to among themselves. In the 1980 election, most of the time went to the two major parties, the Conservatives (143 minutes) and the Liberals (137 minutes), but minority parties got a share, including even the Communists, the Marxist-Leninists, and the Rhinoceros party (6 minutes each). In fact, however, because of the low ceiling on campaign spending imposed by Canadian law, none of the parties was actually able to purchase all of the time to which it was entitled.

9 Radiotelevisione Italiana, the government-owned television system which holds an exclusive right to nationwide broadcasting in Italy, has never sold time for political advertising. The unregulated private companies which provide local programming pick up advertising for individual politicians, but their role is minor, according to Penniman and Ranney.

10   Only in Venezuela, among the six countries studied, is televised political advertising of major importance, and it may be more expensive and more influential there than in any other country in the world, including the United States. A number of major American political consultants, including John Deardourff, David Garth, Joe Napolitan, and F. Clifton White, have been hired by one Venezuelan party or another to design and direct a media campaign. In 1978 the total expenditure for advertising by all parties was estimated at $150 million, of which at least 80 percent was spent on television. For a nation which mobilizes only five to six million voters in presidential elections, that may well have been a more lavish outlay per voter than has ever occurred elsewhere.

Free Time: A Better Alternative?

11   While five of the six democracies studied by Penniman and Ranney prohibit or strictly limit paid political advertising on television, none of them is opposed in principle to the broadcasting of partisan views. In fact, all six of these countries, by law or by practice, provide some free time on national television for party political broadcasts, in which the parties themselves decide the contents.

12   In French presidential elections the free time is given equally to all candidates regardless of their prospects for electoral success. Elsewhere, the more general practice is to allocate the time among the various parties in proportion to their electoral strength, as manifested either by their representation in the national parliament or by their share of the popular vote in the preceding general election.

13   In the Federal Republic of Germany, for example, the publicly-owned networks divvy up one to two hours of broadcast time among the parties, in segments of two and one-half minutes (*Wahlspots*). The leading parties, the Christian Democrats (CDU) and the Social Democrats (SPD), get the most spots, perhaps ten or eleven each, but fringe parties end up with one or two as well. The networks decide when the spots will be broadcast and in what order.

14   German law forbids the parties to design a spot presentation in such a way as to make it look like a bona fide newscast or documentary or anything other than what it is—a direct appeal by a party to the voters for their support. But the kind of tableau much favored by U.S. media consultants—the candidate apparently chatting with ordinary voters in the marketplace—turns up in German spots too. In fact, Penniman and Ranney report, the CDU made great use of this technique in the 1983 general election to emphasize its point that its leader, Helmut Kohl, is a true man-of-the-people.

15   France is the only one of the six countries studied that prohibits virtually all production materials or special effects in its free-time political broadcasts. As Monica Charlot reported after the French presidential election of 1974. "The style of the official campaign is direct, allowing no room for gimmicks or effects. Candidates cannot show films or conduct interviews in the street—or anywhere save in the studio. The amount of time a candidate may spend actually recording his broadcasts is severely limited, and although he may make more than one version of a broadcast, he may not piece together bits from successive recordings. He may only choose between recording A and recording B."

The Overselling Can Be Stopped

16   The AEI study, as briefly sketched above, describes three approaches that have succeeded in preventing the overselling of candidates on television in several of the world's most advanced democracies. They are, first, provision of free time for campaign messages, coupled with prohibition of political commercials (France, the Federal Republic of Germany, the United Kingdom); second, provision of free time, with limited purchased time available to political parties (Canada); and, third, mandated uniformity and simplicity of message format (France).

17   Penniman and Ranney made no attempt to assess the impact of these practices on campaign costs. Common sense tells us, though, that any one of the three approaches, if put into effect in the United States, would go a long way to reduce bloated campaign costs. The prospects for such reforms are nevertheless relatively dismal in the near term, because of the adamant opposition of the major television networks, which have so far fought off almost all attempts to regulate their sale of air-time.

18   Until the day when citizens and their representatives in government are willing to stand up to the networks and vigorously assert public ownership of America's airwaves, the best hope for reform may lie with placing restrictions more squarely on the candidates than on the networks. A modified version of the French formula for controlling the political-message format is now being considered in Congress. A bill introduced in the Senate by Senators Inouye and Rudman, and in the House by Representatives Conable and McHugh, would require that political advertising of ten minutes' duration or less be presented in a straightforward format without the distortion of special effects. Such a requirement would dramatically reduce both production costs and the opportunities for image manipulation.

19   Television may have served to bring politics into everyone's living room, but the price the American public has had to pay in terms of oversimplified and distorted images, limited access to the political marketplace, and disillusionment with the political process is probably too steep a price to continue paying for that privilege.

Some Democratic Nations Where There Are No Paid Political Messages on Television

Austria	Israel
Belgium	Nigeria
Denmark	Norway
France	Portugal
Federal Republic	Spain
of Germany	Sri Lanka
Greece	Sweden
Iceland	United Kingdom

Source: *The Europa Year Book 1983: A World Survey*

Figure 3

APPROACHING THE TEXT

▶ Look at the title of the text and the graphs and charts on the following pages.

What can be predicted about the content of the article?

What does the "overselling" of the title mean?

> When approaching a longer text such as this, after getting a general idea of its topic, it is useful to focus on any typographically prominent parts of the text (in this case, the introductory passage). In this way the reader can obtain a more precise idea of its contents by concentrating on whatever units of information are readily comprehensible without worrying about unknown words. The exercise below is designed to train the student in dealing with passages dense in unknown lexis by focusing on specific units of information. These units of information can be extracted *without* a careful decodification of the whole passage.

WORKSHEET 1

Guided contact with the introductory passage

▶ Write succinct answers to the following questions with reference to the introductory passage, underlining the relevant words or phrases.

1 How long are most political advertisements on T.V.?

2 According to the author are they helpful in increasing an understanding of the issues?

3 What proportion of campaign budgets do they represent?

4 Are campaign budgets increasing or decreasing?

5 How do campaign costs and voter participation in other Western democracies compare with American figures?

6 What organization conducted the study reported here?

7 What financial help was given to the research?

8 What was the purpose of the study?

> In Unit Four, you saw how the first sentence of every paragraph often states the principal idea treated in the paragraph. The reader can gain an overall impression of the structure and content of the passage by focusing on these topic sentences.

WORKSHEET 2   **Skimming for the general organization of the text**
▶ Skim the text, paying particular attention to the first sentence of each paragraph. Divide it according to the following headings:
General remarks: pars. _____
Results of study: pars. _____
Conclusions/Comment: pars. _____

▶ How does the structure of this report differ from the ones in Unit II? _____

▶ How can this be explained? _____

INTENSIVE READING

Texts used for study or research can often be read in a highly selective manner: it is often enough to find and note information relevant to the reader's purpose. The exercise below is thus intended to give the student practice in focusing attention on one specific aspect of a report (in this case, paid political advertising versus free time for political advertising on television). For comments on this flexible approach to reading, see the notes on reading, Section 2.

WORKSHEET 3   **Information extraction**
▶ The article makes a distinction between air-time which is *bought* for political advertising (paid political advertising), and air-time which is allocated *free of charge* (free time for advertising). Complete the table below with information relevant to each, reading paragraphs 1–15 (General remarks and Results of study).

Country	PAID POLITICAL ADVERTISING ON T.V.			FREE TIME FOR ADVERTISING ON T.V.			
	Yes	No	Other information (including cost)*	Yes	No	Method of Allocation	Restrictions/ Other information
USA							
France							
Germany							
UK							
Canada							
Italy	✓		RAI no: unregulated private companies for individuals, but role minor	✓		in proportion to electoral strength	
Venezuela							

* regarding countries where paid political advertising exists

45

> Intensive reading is usually accompanied by note-taking, or the annotation of the most important points under the general sections of the passage. This does *not* mean transcribing entire sentences of the text, but rather *discriminating* key points and summarizing them in concise notes. (See the notes on reading, Section 4.2). The exercise below is an introduction to this study skill.

WORKSHEET 4

Introduction to note-taking

▶ Below are notes for the first section of the text (General remarks, pars. 1–5). Find the relevant passage in the text for each item and underline it. Notice how the passages have been summarized in note form.

General remarks

- T.V. has become primary mode of political campaigning in U.S.
- Purchase of T.V. air-time = principal cause of rising campaign costs; commercials = ⅔ or ¾ of all funds.
- Less money is thus available for traditional modes of campaigning which involve people in pol. process.
- Possible explanation for decrease in voting: people are no longer participants in pol. process but consumers of a T.V. message.
- Growing power of media consultants; declining role of pol. party.
- General feeling in U.S.: restrictions on access to T.V. air-time = infringement of free speech; *BUT* many advanced Western democracies deny candidates any opportunity to televise pol. commercials.

▶ Now read paragraphs 16–19 (Conclusions/Comment) and complete the notes for this final section by ordering the following items and inserting them in the spaces provided below.

— Major T.V. networks however have opposed attempts to regulate sale of T.V. air-time
— Pol. advertising of 10 mins. or less in straightforward format without special effects would result in reduced production costs, reduced opportunities for image manipulation
— 3 possible ways to prevent overselling of candidates on T.V.
— Uniformity and simplicity of message format (France)

— Proposed bill: modified version of French formula for control of pol. message format
— Current possibilities for reform: placing restrictions on candidates, not on networks
— Free time + limited purchase time to pol. parties (Canada)
— *Impact on campaign costs not calculated in study, but such restrictions would obviously reduce costs if applied in U.S.*
— *Free time for campaign messages + prohibition of pol. commercials (France, Germany, U.K.)*

Conclusions/Comment

— _____

e.g. — _____

— _____

— _____

— *Impact on campaign costs not calculated in study, but such restrictions would obviously reduce costs if applied in U.S.*

— _____

— _____

— _____

LANGUAGE WORK

One of the most important classes of words in academic prose is that of *linkers* (or conjunctions, connectors, link-words, etc.). The function of linkers is to signal the precise relationship between concepts. They can be classified according to four categories (additive, temporal, causal, adversative) which are discussed in detail in the notes on reading, Section 3.1.2. Worksheet 5 is an introduction to the classification of linkers in this way.

WORKSHEET 5

The function of linkers.

▶ The following is a list of linkers. The first seven have been classified as additive, temporal, causal or adversative. The remaining linkers appear in the text. Study their function in the context in which they appear and tick the box which best describes their function.

Linker	Additive	Temporal	Causal	Adversative
also	✓			
consequently			✓	
for instance	✓			
hence			✓	
next	✓			
until		✓		
yet				✓
so (par. 2, line 5)				
but (2, 6)				
however (3, 3)				
despite (5, 1)				
while (11, 1)				
for example (13, 1)				
although (15, 9)				
first (16, 4)				

WORKSHEET 6

Recognizing logical links in discourse

▶ Complete the sentences below with the option which most logically follows the linker given. The first one has been done for you.

1 Some Americans seem to believe that restrictions on political advertising on television would constitute an infringement of the democratic process, but __a__

   a many advanced Western democracies deny or limit such television campaigning on their national networks.

   b the Committee for the Study of the American Electorate has investigated how other Western democracies conduct their elections.

2 Political advertising on television represents a form of persuasion only a little more than 30 years old, yet ___

   a it is now known as a "polispot", meaning a 30–60 second political commercial.

   b in that short period it has already developed distinct rhetorical modes and visual styles.

3 The polispot has grown to dominate U.S. political campaigns, especially in national presidential elections and in the large states. For example, ___

   a of the $29 million in federally allotted campaign funds that Reagan and Carter each spent in 1980, almost half went into political advertising, mainly on television.

   b in New York in 1982 a rich unknown named Lewis Lehrman spent close to $10 million to run for governor and almost won.

4 The polispot form has become very important in recent years. However, ___

   a little has been written in any orderly fashion about the role of political advertising and marketing in American politics.

   b it is changing the way political campaigns take place in America.

5 Academic research now suggests that people watching television pay attention principally to messages that reflect their pre-existing views. Consequently, ___

   a they are extremely susceptible to persuasion from candidates expressing political views different from their own.

   b the most attentive audience for a particular spot will be people who have already decided to vote for the candidate who appears in the spot.

WORKSHEET 7

Practising the use of selected linkers

▶ The following is a brief summary of "The Overselling of Candidates on Television". Insert an appropriate linker in the spaces provided, choosing from the linkers in the boxes beside each paragraph.

| NEXT |
| DESPITE |
| SO |
| UNTIL |
| BUT |
| ALSO |

Costs for the purchase of television air-time represent one of the major items in political campaign budgets, _____ the Federal Election Commission does not require candidates to report television expenses as a separate item, _____ we do not know exactly how much is spent on television advertising by political candidates.

| ALTHOUGH |
| HOWEVER |
| FOR EXAMPLE |
| SO |
| FIRST |
| DESPITE |

_____ the fact that Americans often complain about the quality of political advertisements on television, they seem to feel that restrictions on the use of air-time by political candidates would represent an infringement of free speech. _____, many advanced democracies do not permit the purchase of air-time for political campaigning.

| WHILE |
| ALSO |
| SO |
| NEXT |
| FOR INSTANCE |
| UNTIL |

France, Germany and the U.K., _____, permit no advertising on television. Italy _____ forbids the sale of air-time to political parties or candidates on the government-owned networks. _____ Canada does allow television stations to sell some time for political campaigning, such time may be bought only by political parties, not individual candidates.

| ALTHOUGH |
| BUT |
| HENCE |
| FIRST |
| NEXT |
| UNTIL |

_____ paid political advertising is not allowed, or strictly limited, in these Western democracies, free air-time is provided to political parties for the broadcasting of partisan views. This free time may be regulated in the following ways: _____, time may be allocated among political parties either equally (France) or according to the parties' prospects for success, where the leading parties get more time (Germany). _____, the content of the political broadcasts may be controlled in order to avoid the use of "gimmicks" or special effects (France and Germany), and _____ the advertisements are presented in a straightforward way as a direct appeal to voters. _____ such regulations can be put into effect in the U.S., production costs of political advertising on television will continue to represent a disproportionate part of campaign costs, and the opportunities for image manipulation will remain high.

49

Many words change their meaning according to the context in which they appear. Finding the correct meaning in the dictionary involves studying this context closely. For example, the verb *to set out* (line 8 of the introductory passage) has four common meanings:
- a. *to begin a journey*, e.g. "They set out for London at dawn."
- b. *to begin a course of action*, e.g. "She set out to reorganize the company."
- c. *to display or show*, e.g. "The women set out their chickens in the market place."
- d. *to declare, make known*, e.g. "The workers set out the reasons for the strike in a letter to *The Times*."

In the context of the introductory passage, *to set out* has the meaning of *to begin a course of action*. The following exercise gives practice in dealing with these potentially ambiguous definitions by making reference to the context in which the unknown words appear.

WORKSHEET 8

Lexical inference/Dictionary work

▶ Below is a list of words which appear in the introductory passage. Decide upon their word class and then try to infer their meaning by making reference to the immediate and larger context. Finally, check your guess with a dictionary.

	Word class	Your guess	Dictionary definition
1 glimpses			
2 pitches			
3 crafted			
4 flashing			
5 staggering			
6 drains off			
7 deal with			

VOCABULARY WORK AND WORD BUILDING

▶ Find the words in the text (paragraphs are given), decide the word class, and write it and the translation of the word in the space provided.

▶ Then complete the table by forming other words using appropriate suffixes if necessary. Consult your dictionary.

VOCABULARY WORK			WORD BUILDING		
Word and Location	**Class**	**Translation**	**Noun**	**Verb**	**Adjective**
allegation (7)					
allocated (8)					
assert (18)					
citizens (3)					
consultants (4)					
deny (5)					
devise (4)					
emphasize (14)					
expensive (10)					
influential (10)					
ownership (18)					
perception (5)					
prospects (12)					
provide (11)					
regulate (17)					

OBSERVATIONS ON TEXT TYPE — EXTENDED REPORT

Function:	To describe and comment upon a given topic, often drawing on a more specialized treatment of the subject.
Structure:	Although the structure of the extended report may vary depending on its length, the nature of the topic, and the kind of publication in which it appears, generally speaking we may find, as in the brief research report, sections dealing with general assumptions and/or background information; results of a research or other investigation of the problem; comments, conclusions or recommendations. Where the information has been gathered by means of field research, a section may also deal with procedure.
Aspects of language:	Language will be principally descriptive, although it may carry overtones of persuasion or argument, especially in the section dedicated to conclusions or recommendations.

Asking the Age Question: A Research Note

ROBERT A. PETERSON

1 One of the most frequently asked questions in public opinion polls and consumer surveys is the age question. However, despite its wide usage, there is a dearth of methodological research on how to best ask this question. Although a few studies have investigated the accuracy of answers to an age question (e.g., Weaver and Swanson 1974, Perry and Crossley 1950, Myers 1954), with few exceptions (e.g., Kerin and Peterson 1978) the question of how to best ask age so as to obtain the most accurate data has not been empirically addressed. In a classic book on question construction, Payne (1950:125–6) implied that asking the age question two different ways—"How old are you?" or "What is the date of your birth?"—would result in different and possibly inconsistent answers. Unfortunately, he provided no data to support this contention. Similarly, Parten (1950:169) merely suggested ways in which the age question could be posed, such as open-end (date of birth, direct age) or closed-end (categorical format).

2 Because the manner in which an age question is asked may influence *if* it will be answered as well as *how* it will be answered, the purpose of this research note is to report an experiment conducted to evaluate the results of asking age using four different question formats. Since validating or criterion age data were available, it was possible to compare the self-report of a study participant's age with his or her actual age, thus permitting an evaluation of the four question formats with respect to the accuracy of the respective age data obtained.

Research Method

3 In early 1982 telephone interviews were conducted with a statewide probability sample of 2,083 registered voters in a major southwestern state.[1] The interviews were conducted for a state agency and addressed various voting-related attitudes and opinions.

Abstract An experiment was designed to evaluate the accuracy of data obtained from asking age four different ways. Study participants consisted of 1,324 registered voters from a large southwestern state. Because criterion age data were available from a state agency, it was possible to compare each study participant's reported age with his or her actual age. The results indicated that all four question formats provided accurate data, but that refusal rates were different across the question formats.

Robert A. Peterson is Sam Barshop Professor of Marketing Administration and a Senior Research Fellow at the Institute for Constructive Capitalism, the University of Texas at Austin. This research was supported in part by the Institute for Constructive Capitalism, the University of Texas at Austin. The opinions expressed in this paper are those of the author and do not necessarily reflect the views of the Institute.

Public Opinion Quarterly Vol. 48:379–383

---

[1] This represented a response rate of 63.2 percent. Because of the nature of the sampling frame, some potential study participants were deceased, while others had moved from the state. Other nonresponse reasons included those typically associated with telephone interviews, namely, no telephone in the household, refusals, terminations, and unlocatable individuals.

4   Within this context, a split ballot (experimental) design was employed whereby approximately each quarter of the sample was asked age utilizing a different question format. Three open-end and one closed-end question formats were investigated:

How old are you?
What is your age?
In what year were you born?
Are you . . . 18–24 years of age, 25–34, 35–49, 50–64, 65 or older?

Each question format was drawn from previous research and was selected to be illustrative of one approach to asking age. The particular question format used when asking an individual study participant his or her age was randomly determined prior to the interview. Interviewers made no determination as to what age question format was employed for a specific study participant.

5   All interviews were conducted from a centralized, supervised interviewing location and began with an interviewer asking to speak to a prespecified individual. The interviewer then introduced himself/herself and stated who was conducting the study and asked for the potential study participant's cooperation. The questionnaire consisted of 20 questions, of which the age question was number 15.

6   Actual age data were available from the state agency for 1,324 of the individuals interviewed.[2] Therefore, following the completion of an interview it was possible to compare an individual's reported age with his or her actual age. This in turn permitted inferences as to which question format produced the most accurate age data as well as which format resulted in the lowest refusal rate or nonresponse rate.

Results

7   Table 1 contains the results of asking the four age questions. As can be seen from the table, 1,260 individuals answered an age question (an average of 315 per question format), while 64 (4.8 percent of the sample) refused to do so. To facilitate comparisons among the question formats, the response distributons for the three open-end questions were converted to that of the closed-end (categorical format) question.

8   The table reveals that each of the question formats produced accurate age data. Of the study participants asked the question "How old are you?" 98.7 percent reported accurate ages. The lowest percentage accuracy was obtained for the categorical question; 95.1 percent of the individuals responding to this question format provided

---

[2] Because the state agency age data were drawn from birth certificate records, they were considered to be factually accurate. Actual age data were not available for all individuals interviewed because of a multiyear processing backlog at the state agency. Since survey results were required prior to the availability of a complete age data file, it was only possible to analyze data for those individuals whose processing was completed. However, since processing order was essentially random, no systematic bias was introduced into the data. A comparison of the reported ages of individuals for whom there were actual age data and those for whom there were no age data revealed the latter were somewhat older (although not significantly so) than the former. Given the nature of the study, however, this difference does not detract from the conclusions.

Table 1. Actual and Reported Ages by Question Format

	Percentage Distribution							
	"How Old" Question		"What Is" Question		"Year Born" Question		Categorical Question	
Age Category	Actual	Reported	Actual	Reported	Actual	Reported	Actual	Reported
18–24	8.7	8.7	6.6	6.6	8.9	8.9	8.1	8.1
25–34	21.1	20.7	20.5	21.1	16.0	16.7	22.5	21.0
35–49	23.7	23.9	27.1	26.8	26.5	26.2	23.3	23.9
50–64	25.8	26.0	23.8	24.1	26.6	26.2	26.2	27.4
65 or older	20.7	20.7	22.0	21.4	22.0	21.6	19.9	19.6
N respondents answering age question	299		332		282		347	
% respondents reporting correct age	98.7		97.3		97.2		95.1	
N respondents refusing to answer age question	32		11		17		4	
% refusal rate[a]	9.7		3.2		5.7		1.1	

[a] Based upon total number of respondents asked question (e.g., 9.7 percent = 32 ÷ (299 + 32). Refusal rates for "How Old" question and categorical question, "Year Born" question and categorical question, and "How Old" question and "What Is" question are significantly different $p < .01$ using multiple-t comparisons.

accurate age data. Differences among the accuracy percentages were not statistically significant. Virtually the same number of study participants *understated* their age as *overstated* it when reporting an incorrect age for themselves. Moreover, there was no systematic relationship between reporting accuracy and age. Under- and over-reporting existed at all age levels. In most instances where inaccuracies existed, reported age differed from actual age by one category, either above or below the actual age category.

9   Table 1 also contains the number of study participants who were asked but refused to answer each of the four age questions. The largest percentage of study participants not answering an age question was found for the "How old are you?" question; 9.7 percent of the individuals asked this question refused to answer it. Simultaneously, only 1.1 percent of the study participants asked the categorial age question refused to answer it. Hence, there appears to be a relationship between the accuracy percentage and the refusal percentage (see footnote to Table 1).

Conclusions

10   While the results obtained in this investigation must be evaluated relative to the population sampled, the mode of data collection employed, and the sponsoring agency, comparisons between reported and actual ages for each of the question formats studied revealed uniformly high levels of reporting accuracy. Simultaneously, though, there were significant differences among the refusal rates associated with the question formats.

11   Unfortunately, perhaps, the present study does not provide unequivocal evidence as to the preferability of one age question format over another. The decision to use a particular age question format must take into account and "balance" its response accuracy and potential refusal rate. Ultimately, the "best" age question format will be a function of researcher and decision maker needs.

References

Kerin, Roger A., and Robert A. Peterson
  1978 "The effect of question form on age reports in a mail survey." Proceedings of the American Marketing Association 43:229–31.

Myers, Robert J.
  1954 "Accuracy of age reporting in the 1950 United States Census." Journal of the American Statistical Association 49:826–31.

Parry, Hugh J., and Helen M. Crossley
  1950 "Validity of responses to survey questions." Public Opinion Quarterly 14:61–80.

Parten, Mildred
  1950 Surveys, Polls, and Samples: Practical Procedures. New York: Harper & Brothers.

Payne, Stanley L.
  1951 The Art of Asking Questions. Princeton, NJ: Princeton University Press.

Weaver, Charles N., and Carol L. Swanson
  1974 "Validity of reported date of birth, salary, and seniority." Public Opinion Quarterly 38:69–80.

APPROACHING THE TEXT

▶ Skim the first page to find the following information:
1 Author's name: _____
2 Author's academic position and the academic institution in which he works:

3 One of the sources of financial aid given to this research:

4 Whose views are reported in this research note?

In a research report of an academic nature, the *abstract* is likely to contain not only the above information, but also the key points of the research itself. It is thus useful to read the abstract carefully before starting on the main body of the report. As has been noted in Unit Two, research reports can usually be divided up into the sections listed in Worksheet 1 below. Where the data has been obtained by field research, as in this case, the section *subjects* may also be found.

WORKSHEET 1

Identifying the main points of the research

▶ The following is a list of sections which are usually found in a research report. Check to see if they are contained in the abstract and mark with a tick if they are. Write the information given in the space provided.

▶ Now complete the final column by indicating the paragraphs in the text where information, or further information can be found.

	In abstract	**Information given**	**Pars. in text**
General Assumptions			
Purpose			
Procedure			
Subjects			
Results			
Conclusions			

INTENSIVE READING

WORKSHEET 2

Annotating bibliographical references

The purpose of any research is often closely linked to previous work carried out in the same field, and this is often summarized in the introduction to the research report.

▶ Read the first section of the text and fill in the following chart on previous research.

Author(s)	Date	Page ref.	Research/Previous Work	Comments
Weaver and Swanson				
	1978			
			Question construction	
				Mere suggestion; No data

▶ What is the difference between an "open-end" and a "closed-end" question, discussed by Parten? _____

▶ Where can other information about previous research (title, name of the review, etc.) be found? _____

WORKSHEET 3

Information extraction

▶ Read the section on **Research Method** and fill in the following table on procedure, making careful reference to the text and to footnotes 1 and 2. One of the answers must be calculated.

1 Potential sample	
2 Probability sample	
3 Sample on which the data are based	
4 No. of questions in the State Agency research	
5 No. of the "age question"	
6 Means of conducting interview	
7 Method of determining which of the four questions would be asked	

- What are the reasons for the difference between:
  a) the potential sample and the probability sample?

  b) the probability sample and the actual sample?

- Why is this information contained in the footnotes?

WORKSHEET 4

Checking understanding

- Read the **Results** section of the research. Making reference to both the written text and Table 1, decide whether the following statements are true or false. Underline the parts of the text and of the table which give you the answer. The letters correspond to the following question formats:
  - (a) = "How old" question
  - (b) = "What is" question
  - (c) = "Year born" question
  - (d) = categorical question – see table.

  1 If you ask question (a) you are likely to receive the correct reply.

  2 If you ask question (d) you are more likely to receive a refusal than if you ask questions (a), (b) or (c).

  3 The results of the research are statistically significant in terms of the variation in the percentage of correct answers to the four questions.

  4 The results of the research are statistically significant in terms of the variation in percentage of refusals to the four questions.

  5 You are most likely to receive a refusal if you ask question (a).

- Read the section **Conclusions** and answer the following questions:
  1 Does the study provide evidence as to the preferability of one type of question over another?
  2 How can this research help those people who "ask the age question"?
  3 What will the choice of the "best" question depend on?

LANGUAGE WORK

Consider the following sentence:

> "In the civilized world, a man is permitted to have only one wife. In many tribal communities, however, different kinds of polygamy, or multiple marriages, are commonly practised."

In this sentence, the word *or* functions to introduce an explanation of a term which may be unfamiliar to the native reader. These **reformulations** are especially frequent in specialist academic literature. It is thus important to learn how to look for explanations of unknown terminology in its immediate context, as in the exercise below.

WORKSHEET 5   **Recognition of textual devices used to explain, expand or reformulate specialized terminology**

▶ Read the sentences below and complete the table. The numbers refer to the paragraph and lines in the text, where applicable.

Sentence	Words explained or reformulated	Reformulation	Device used
1 *Parten merely suggested ways in which the age question could be posed, such as open-end (date of birth, direct age), or closed-end (categorical format). (par. 1, lines 13–15)*			
2 *Since validating or criterion reference data were available, it was possible to compare . . . (2, 5–8)*			
3 *The particular format was randomly determined before the interview, that is, no fixed pattern for asking the question was followed.*			
4 *Within this context, a split ballot (experimental) design was employed, whereby each quarter of the sample was asked age utilizing a different question format . . . (4, 1–3)*			
5 *Other non-response reasons included those typically associated with telephone interviews, namely, no telephone in the household, refusal etc. (note 1, 3–5)*			

WORKSHEET 6   **Lexis common to academic prose**

▶ Read the text rapidly to find the words for which the definitions are given below. The words appear in the text in the same order as the definitions. Use your dictionary to check meaning if necessary.

Abstract

a person who takes part in an activity _____

Introduction

par. 1 a survey of public opinion by questioning a representative selection of persons _____

a study undertaken to discover new facts or information _____

to make a careful study of something (past participle) _____

	to give or supply something needed or useful (past) _____
	an assertion, an argument _____
par. 2	to carry out/direct (past participle) _____
	able to be obtained/used _____
	to examine/judge the similarities or difference of persons or things _____
	exactness or correctness _____

Research Method

par. 3	a group of people or things representing a larger group _____
	ways of thinking, feeling or behaving _____
par. 4	without any plan, aim or purpose _____
	before _____
	relating to one particular thing _____

Results

par. 8	almost/very nearly _____

Conclusions

par. 10	important, having a special meaning _____
par. 11	having only one possible meaning _____

Footnote 2

to ask someone for opinions or information (past participle) _____

WORKSHEET 7

Reutilization of lexis common to academic prose

▶ Complete the summary of the imaginary research report below. Where there is a line (_____) insert one of the words defined in Worksheet 6 (some may be used more than once); where there are dots (. . . . .) insert any appropriate word. Be sure to read through the incomplete report before beginning.

The _____ of data regarding the . . . . of foreign workers employed illegally in Italy is not always dependable. In order to _____ this . . . ., a _____ project was _____ using a _____ of foreign workers from a variety of sectors, in twelve Italian cities.

The _____ were _____ using a _____ interviewing technique which has recently proved very . . . . The _____ produced some _____ results. For example, foreign workers are more likely to be given work illegally in the building and catering sectors, in agriculture and as domestic help, while this is . . . . to occur in other sectors.

Although the results of this . . . . cannot be considered _____, it is certainly _____ that in _____ all cities _____, the same industries abused foreign workers to the same extent, throughout Italy.

60

VOCABULARY WORK AND WORD BUILDING

▶ Find the words in the text (paragraphs are given), decide the word class, and write it and the translation of the word in the space provided.

▶ Then complete the table by forming other words using appropriate suffixes if necessary. Consult your dictionary.

VOCABULARY WORK			WORD BUILDING		
Word and Location	**Class**	**Translation**	**Noun**	**Verb**	**Adjective**
categorical (8)					
consumer (1)					
contention (2)					
detract (note 2)					
frequently (1)					
illustrative (4)					
implied (1)					
inferences (6)					
participant (abstract)					
prior (4)					
processing (note 2)					
refusal (6)					
respective (2)					
revealed (note 2)					
supervised (5)					
utilizing (4)					

61

OBSERVATIONS ON TEXT TYPE — ACADEMIC RESEARCH REPORT

Function:	To give a detailed report of a research project to a reader with a specialized knowledge of the subject (cf. Units Two and Five).
Structure:	The main outlines of a research report have been discussed in the *Observations* in Unit Two (summary, general assumptions, purpose, procedure, results, conclusions/comment). In longer reports of a more specialized nature such as this, however, the categories *purpose* and *results* may often include the following: – *purpose*: a brief survey of previous literature on the subject, with reference to the author, the date of publication and the relevant pages (for example, Payne, 1950: 125–126). In an authentic reading situation, a student researching into the topic under consideration can find full details of these works in the references section at the end of the article. – *results*: if the results are of a statistical nature, the information will often be given twice – once in the written text and once in numerical or tabular form. These are, of course, complementary in that the information given numerically in the table reinforces that given in the written text, while this is itself a condensation and summary of the full statistics given in tabular form.
Aspects of language:	Reports such as this which treat a specialized topic often use an accordingly specialized terminology. Some of the terms used may be unfamiliar or unclear to the native reader and so may need to be explained or reformulated in the text itself. The reader in a foreign language should learn to distinguish between words which he must guess or look up in a dictionary and specialist terms which are explained in the text, as well as to recognize the signals of such explanations or reformulations (*that is, namely* or parentheses, commas or dashes – see Worksheet 4).

New Society 17 October 1986

ANALYSIS

The other economy

Most discussions of the economy concern the official, taxed sector. But how important is the unofficial, untaxed sector and who gains from it, asks STEPHEN SMITH.

1 What do we mean by the economy of the country? In assessing a country's standard of living or comparing the standards of living of different countries it is common practice to use statistics of the Gross Domestic Product. The GDP measures incomes earned, and the goods and services produced, in the official "formal" economy. But this tends not to account for the mass of productive activity outside the formal economy—moonlighting, DIY, voluntary work and so forth, which may well not be reflected in the indicators of GDP. And since the balance between the shadow and formal economy varies from country to country, comparisons on the basis of GDP may be quite misleading.

2 The problems in assessing the economy of a single country are much the same. Our understanding of the distribution of income, and hence much of our thinking on poverty and inequality, derives from what we know about people's incomes from work in the formal economy. Is it possible that by relying on statistics of the formal economy alone, we may be misled about the extent of poverty in the UK?

3 In a research project at the Institute for Fiscal Studies we have been exploring the interaction of the formal and shadow economies. Two issues struck us as important. Firstly, does the shadow economy reinforce or offset the inequalities which are observed in the formal economy? Secondly, what scope does the shadow economy provide for households to compensate for a temporary decline in earnings and employment opportunities in the formal economy?

4 The wide range of activities in the shadow economy can be divided into two broad categories. There are monetary transactions concealed to avoid tax—people doing odd jobs for cash payment, a businessman failing to declare part of his turnover, and so forth—which, following popular usage, we have called the "black economy." Then there is a wide range of productive activities which do not involve monetary payment—housework, DIY, voluntary work—which we have simply called the "wider shadow economy." There are important similarities between activities in the black economy and some parts of the wider shadow economy—especially in the role that the tax system can play in encouraging alternatives to formal economy goods and services.

5 But there is the important difference that attempts are already made to adjust certain official statistics—most notably the national accounts—to include an estimated amount for the black economy. Productive activity in the rest of the shadow economy is almost entirely excluded from GDP by convention: official statistics are confined to measuring transactions where money changes hands. The amounts included in GDP for the contribution of the black economy are not large—they have generally been between 1 and 3 per cent of total GDP. And our own estimates do not suggest that it is much larger—perhaps in total some 3 to 5 per cent of GDP.

6 The black economy is, however, highly concentrated in particular areas. Certain types of taxpayer are in a better position than others to evade income tax. In particular, self-employed people have control over the amount of income they declare for tax in a way that most employee taxpayers, who pay tax through PAYE, do not. Through econometric analysis of employee and self-employed households' expenditure patterns, we found evidence of substantial under-declaration of income by householders where the head was self-employed. We estimated that on average self-employed households were failing to declare some 10 to 20 per cent of income for tax, making tax evasion by the self-employed much the largest part of the black economy. Second job earnings may also escape the PAYE net—but survey evidence suggests that incomes earned in second jobs may well be less than 1 per cent of incomes earned in main jobs.

Business 'off the books'

7 The kinds of business most involved in the black economy are likely to be smaller businesses selling labour-intensive services to private households and individuals—building, decorating, cab driving, for example. Larger businesses are likely to experience control and management problems if they try to conduct business "off the books" on a large scale; and the structure of the tax system—especially of VAT—means that it is a high value-added business where the greatest competitive pressures to trade "off the books" may arise.

8 Given this uneven distribution of the black economy across the economy, who benefits from it? On the face of it, it would seem that the people who work in the black economy, and do not pay the income tax or VAT that they are supposed to pay, are the gainers, and that the "honest taxpayers" are the losers. But in fact the answer is more complex than this. Each transaction in the black economy involves a buyer and a seller; the gains to be made for evading tax may accrue to either—or may be split between them. How the gains from evasion are divided between buyers and sellers of black economy goods and services depends on the prices at which they are sold. If customers get a discount off black economy work, or if black economy traders try to undercut the prices of formal economy traders to gain business, then some of the gains from tax evasion will flow to the customer.

9 Indeed, in sectors where black economy business forms a high proportion of the total, customers may receive all the gains from evasion, and the seller none. In parts of the building industry, for example, evading tax may be the price for business survival; competition from other black economy businesses may hand all the gains to customers.

10 Where the black economy is small, the gains from evasion are likely to be reaped by the businesses involved. This does not necessarily mean that they flow to the rich; the earnings of many self-employed people are surprisingly low. But we believe by far the largest part of the black economy to be concentrated in a relatively small number of areas—in building and decorating in particular. Here competitive pressures may transfer most of the gains to the customers, through a lower level of prices for these services. Typically the customers will be owner occupiers, and relatively well off. The black economy may well reinforce inequality.

11 How does the pattern of production in the wider shadow economy affect the relative living standards of different sections of the population? There are few households which do not perform some unpaid productive activity, but those households that can afford labour-saving domestic equipment may use their domestic labour time more productively than those who cannot.

12 The need for expensive equipment and materials may also prevent poorer households participating effectively in areas of shadow economy production such as DIY. The unemployed, whilst having plenty of free time, can rarely buy the materials and equipment necessary for home maintenance and home improvements.

13 It turns out that DIY is predominantly an activity of the comparatively well-off, home owners in particular. Some councils still discourage DIY maintenance by their tenants, and private tenants in furnished accommodation may often be forbidden even to redecorate their homes. In any event, home improvements bring no financial benefit to tenants—whilst owner occupiers not only reap the capital gains on their property, but can keep them tax free too. As with the black economy, there is thus little evidence that the wider shadow economy offsets inequalities observed in the formal economy. In some areas it may even reinforce them; the ability to gain from production in the shadow economy may partly be a function of success in the formal economy.

The IFS research project was reported in Britain's Shadow Economy, by Stephen Smith, published this week by Oxford University Press at £19.50. A comparative study based on this research, The Shadow Economy in Britain and Germany by Stephen Smith and Suzanne Wied-Nebbeling has also been published, by the Anglo-German Foundation, at £5.95. For details of household labour see J. Gershuny's Social Innovation and the Division of Labour.

APPROACHING THE TEXT

▶ Focusing exclusively on typographically prominent features of the text, answer the following questions:

1 What is the title of the text? _____
 Who is its author? _____
 What else has this author written? _____

2 In which publication did the article appear and under what general heading? _____

3 What predictions can you make about the content of the article on the basis of the title and subtitle?
_____
_____
_____

WORKSHEET 1

Skimming for the general organization of the text

▶ The article can be roughly divided into 4 sections as below. Read and underline the first sentence of each paragraph and indicate the paragraphs under each heading.

1 Introductory comments and statement of research objectives
  (pars. _____)

2 Classification of shadow economy activities; impact on official statistics
  (pars. _____)

3 Detailed discussion of aspects of the black economy (pars. _____)

4 Detailed discussion of aspects of the wider shadow economy
  (pars. _____)

WORKSHEET 2

Pre-reading vocabulary work

▶ The words in the chart all first appear in the text in the paragraph indicated. Decide their class and write it in the first column of the chart. Then look for the appropriate definition or explanation below and write it in the second column. An example has been given.

Definitions/Explanations

a families (economic units)
b to offer goods or services at a lower cost than competitors
c profits
d value-added-tax
e pay-as-you-earn
f working without an employer
g regular buyers
h kept secret, hidden
i do-it-yourself
j leading in a wrong direction

k depending on with confidence
l balance, compensate for
m range of possibilities, opportunities
n money obtained by working
o people who live in houses which they have bought
p rich, wealthy
q have enough money to buy something
r local governments
s people who pay money to live in a house or flat

| t | money received regularly, (usually payment for work) |

64

	Word class	**Definition/Explanation**
1 income (par. 1, line 6 ___)	noun	money received regularly (usually payment for work)
2 DIY (1, 10 ___)		
3 misleading (1, 16 ___)		
4 relying on (2, 7 ___)		
5 offset (3, 6 ___)		
6 scope (3, 8 ___)		
7 households (3, 9 ___)		
8 earnings (3, 10 ___)		
9 concealed (4, 4 ___)		
10 self-employed (6, 5 ___)		
11 PAYE (6, 8 ___)		
12 VAT (7, 10 ___)		
13 gains (8, 10 ___)		
14 customers (8, 16 ___)		
15 undercut (8, 18 ___)		
16 owner occupiers (10, 13 ___)		
17 well off (10, 14 ___)		
18 afford (11, 6 ___)		
19 councils (13, 3 ___)		
20 tenants (13, 4 ___)		

INTENSIVE READING

In Unit Five you were shown how parts of a text can be synthesized in note form. The following exercise aims to give you further practice in discriminating and annotating the principal points of a more complex text.

WORKSHEET 3

Guided note-taking

▶ Read the article carefully, and while reading complete the following by writing the appropriate information in the spaces provided.

(par. 1) 1 *Introductory comments and statement of research objectives*
  – economy: formal (measured by _____) + shadow
    (_____). Comparisons
    between countries based on GDP may be _____

(par. 2) – poverty and inequality calculated on formal economy incomes: valid?

(par. 3) – IFS project on _____ – 2 points:
  – _____
  – _____

(par. 4) 2 *Classification and description of shadow economy activities; impact on official statistics*
  – "black economy" = monetary transactions concealed to avoid tax,
    e.g. _____
    _____

  – "wider shadow economy" = _____
    _____, e.g.
    _____

  – similarities between black and wider shadow economies, especially
    in _____
    _____

(par. 5) – difference: attempts made to adjust official statistics to include amount for
    black economy, but _____
    _____ excluded from GDP

(par. 6) 3 *Detailed discussion of black economy:*
  – income tax evasion (self-employed vs. _____
    taxpayers)

(par. 7) – business "off the books": smaller vs. _____
    businesses – greatest competitive pressure to trade off the books
    in _____

(par. 8) – who benefits? Gains may accrue to _____:
(par. 9)   – where black economy forms high proportion of total, _____
(par. 10) – where _____
    gains to business

(par. 11)   4 *Detailed discussion of aspects of wider shadow economy:*
(par. 12)   – need for expensive equipment means poor households _____
(par. 13)   – DIY mainly practised by _____
            – activities in wider shadow economy thus _____

WORKSHEET 4 **Reference**

▶ Underline the word or words listed below in the text, and write the word, phrase or concept referred to in the space provided.

1 which (par. 4, line 7)	
2 it (5, 14)	
3 this (8, 9)	
4 either (8, 12)	
5 they (8, 16)	
6 none (9, 4)	
7 these services (10, 12)	
8 it (13, 15)	
9 them (13, 15)	

▶ The identification of what is referred to can sometimes be problematic, and may involve a detailed reading and synthesis of the surrounding text. To what exactly do the two phrases below refer?

10 the same (2, 2)	
11 this uneven distribution (8, 1)	

WORKSHEET 5

Checking understanding

▶ Check your understanding of the text by answering the following questions.

1 If figures are cited in a text, it is important to note *exactly* what these figures refer to. For example, *1–3%* (par. 5) refers to the usual estimated proportion of GDP represented by the black economy. Note exactly what the following percentages represent:

   a 3–5%: _____

   b 10–20%: _____

   c less than 1%: _____

2 In the following circumstances, is it the buyer or the seller who benefits from the black economy?

   a high competition between black economy traders: _____

   b high competition between black and formal economy traders _____

   c the building and decorating trade: _____

   d a small amount of black economy trading: _____

3 Indicate which of the following categories, according to the report, benefit from DIY and the wider shadow economy.

   a poorer households   YES/NO
   b the well off   YES/NO
   c council tenants   YES/NO
   d private tenants   YES/NO
   e owner occupiers   YES/NO

4 The article provides answers to a series of questions posed in the introduction to the discussion. Give a brief answer to each of them.

   a Is it possible that by relying on statistics of the formal economy alone, we may be misled about the extent of poverty in the UK? (par. 2)

   _____
   _____
   _____

   b Does the shadow economy reinforce or offset the inequalities which are observed in the formal economy? (par. 3)

   _____
   _____
   _____

   c What scope does the shadow economy provide for households to compensate for a temporary decline in earnings and employment opportunities in the formal economy? (par. 3)

   _____
   _____
   _____

LANGUAGE WORK

WORKSHEET 6 **Discriminating examples, contrasts and further information**

The common punctuation mark, the dash (—) is used frequently in the text. The dash has three different functions:
- to signal that an example or examples are being given
- to signal contrasting information
- to signal further information about the subject under discussion

▶ Complete the chart by indicating the function of the words or phrases set off by dashes (*example*, *contrast*, or *further information*). Note that insofar as *examples* may be considered *further information*, on some occasions the function might be ambiguous. An example has been given.

Words/phrases in text	Function
1 – moonlighting, DIY, voluntary work and so forth, ... (par. 1)	*example*
2 – people doing odd jobs for cash payment, a businessman failing to declare part of his turnover, and so forth – (par. 4)	
3 – housework, DIY, voluntary work – (par. 4)	
4 – especially in the role that the tax system can play in encouraging alternatives to formal economy goods and services. (par. 4)	
5 – most notably the national accounts – (par. 5)	
6 – they have generally been between 1 and 3 per cent of GDP. (par. 5)	
7 – perhaps in total some 3 to 5 per cent of GDP. (par. 5)	
8 – but survey evidence suggests that incomes earned in second jobs may well be less than 1% of incomes earned in main jobs. (par. 6)	
9 – building, decorating, cab driving, for example. (par. 7)	
10 – especially of VAT – (par. 7)	
11 – or may be split between them. (par. 8)	
12 – in building and decorating in particular. (par. 10)	
13 – whilst owner occupiers not only reap the capital gains on their property, but can keep them tax free too. (par. 13)	

VOCABULARY WORK AND WORD BUILDING

▶ Find the words in the text (paragraphs are given), decide the word class, and write it and the translation of the word in the space provided.

▶ Then complete the table by forming other words using appropriate suffixes if necessary. Consult your dictionary.

VOCABULARY WORK			WORD BUILDING		
Word and Location	**Class**	**Translation**	**Noun**	**Verb**	**Adjective**
assessing (1)					
broad (4)					
comparing (1)					
competitive (7)					
depends (8)					
estimates (5)					
extent (2)					
failing (4)					
gain (8)					
pattern (11)					
prevent (12)					
structure (7)					
supposed (8)					
surprisingly (10)					
system (7)					
typically (10)					

OBSERVATIONS ON TEXT TYPE

EXTENDED REPORT

(See Observations for Unit Five for *function, structure* and *aspects of language*).

Mobilizing the middle classes

Jeremy Noakes

RICHARD F. HAMILTON
Who Voted for Hitler?
664pp. Guildford: Princeton University Press.
£37.15 (paperback, £12.30).
0 691 09395 4

THOMAS CHILDERS
The Nazi Voter: The social foundations of Fascism in Germany, 1919–1933
367pp. University of North Carolina Press.
£27.20.
0 8078 1570 5

1 It is well known that the Nazis achieved power in January 1933 not by winning a parliamentary majority but rather through a backstairs intrigue involving an alliance with the traditional German élites. Nevertheless, the 37 per cent of the vote won by the NSDAP in the Reichstag election of July 1932 not only made it by far the largest party but would probably have been sufficient to give it victory under the British electoral system. Moreover, it was the Nazis' substantial electoral base which both obliged the German élites to take them seriously and indeed formed their most attractive feature for those élites. The questions of who voted for Hitler and why are therefore of central importance for an understanding of the Nazi takeover. The two books under review both make substantial contributions.

2 On the question of who voted Nazi, both authors take issue with the dominant explanation according to which it was the lower middle class who provided the mass electoral support for the Party. In his first section Richard F. Hamilton provides a powerful critique of some of the previous literature and the shaky evidence on which its thesis of lower-middle-class support was based. He then moves on to a detailed electoral analysis of a number of major cities through which he shows that the Nazis did best not so much in those districts where the lower middle class were present in large numbers, but rather in overwhelmingly upper-middle-class districts. Examples of these are Zehlendorf in Berlin (36.4 per cent compared with 28.6 per cent in the city as a whole) or Blankenese in Hamburg which with 53.8 per cent had the largest Nazi vote of any district in the city and compared with 33 per cent for the city as a whole. This conclusion is confirmed by an illuminating analysis of the vacation vote, for example on cruise liners. Moreover, the author provides a subtle and perceptive analysis of the political attitudes and behaviour of urban white-collar workers, suggesting that the more marginal ones tended to vote SPD rather than Nazi. He also points out that the conservative DNVP found some support in working-class districts whose voters, the equivalent of working-class Tories, then proved vulnerable to the Nazis.

3 It is true that the sample of cities is limited (twelve) and in some respects unrepresentative – there are none from Central or East Germany where some of the largest concentrations of Nazi urban votes were to be found (eg, Breslau and Chemnitz). It is also true that the data for most of the cities are limited, making it impossible to compare the voting behaviour and social structure of all the various districts with equal success. And one could quibble about the categorization of some of the districts. Nevertheless, Hamilton has clearly proved his main point. It is an important one and it has hitherto been overlooked. However, having said that, it could be argued that he makes too much of it. As he admits, the Nazi vote declined in an inverse ratio to the size of the community; the Nazis did best in communities of less than 25,000 and generally worst in big cities. Hamilton argues that the evidence from rural areas suggests that voting patterns here, too, did not follow class lines. Villages tended either to vote overwhelmingly Nazi or for other parties, often depending on the attitude of the local opinion leaders. Moreover, religion played a crucial role, Catholic rural areas proving strongly resistant to Nazism, thus providing, in other words, another instance where Nazi support cannot be related to a single class category.

4 All this is true, though not new. In my view, however, it still does not dispose of the lower-middle-class thesis. Because of his urban

emphasis, Hamilton focuses above all on the white-collar workers – in German sociological parlance the "new *Mittelstand*". He ably succeeds in demonstrating that many white-collar workers had more in common with the working-class milieu from which they sprang than with the bourgeoisie; and voted SPD. He has much less to say about the "old *Mittelstand*" – the butchers and bakers and candlestick-makers who formed the core group of Nazi support. Furthermore, he tends to equate the lower middle class with its most marginal members – the small shopkeeper or artisan barely keeping his head above water, the low-grade clerk or salesman – Hans Fallada's "little man". He is right in his assumption that Nazi support did not derive primarily from this group. If, however, one broadens the category of lower middle class to include the reasonably prosperous retailer or artisan – the moderately successful small-town pharmacist or master butcher and the peasant farmer with a middle-sized holding, and these were hardly *upper* middle class – then it seems to me that it is difficult not to locate the majority of Nazi support among the lower middle class.

5 To answer the question of *why* people voted Nazi Hamilton focuses on the roles of the Nazi political cadres and the local press. As far as the first is concerned, regional studies of the Nazi Party have provided clear evidence of the important role played by the local organization. However, Hamilton tends to exaggerate the importance of the military background of these cadres as the key to their success. The ex-officers tended to gravitate towards the SA, which had nothing but contempt for what it saw as the Party bureaucrats and generated much friction, although it is true that many leaders on the political side also had some military experience. Moreover, the success of the cadres must be understood in terms of the particular local contexts in which they were operating. They had little success in penetrating working-class or Catholic districts, and even in the Protestant rural areas, where they achieved their biggest success, they did not so much burst in on and sweep aside a moribund bourgeois conservative or liberal establishment as take over from other parties. These had for a time successfully mobilized rural support (eg, the Schleswig-Holstein Landespartei, the Hanoverian Guelphs, the Bavarian Bauernbund) but had for various reasons proved incapable of sustaining their momentum.

6 Second, while the local press may well have played an important role in creating a climate in which members of the upper middle class in the cities were persuaded to vote Nazi – and the author puts forward plausible grounds for why it should have been so effective, for example the newness of most party loyalties after the disruption of the 1918 revolution and the complexity of the options facing most voters under the multiparty system of Weimar – it seems doubtful whether its role could have been quite as decisive as he suggests. To understand why some cities proved more vulnerable than others to the Nazi appeal one would need to look much further than the local press: for example, at such questions as recent history, particularly during the period 1918–23 when sharp political polarization occurred in some cities, less so in others, at the nature and health of the local economy and the local labour market, and at the quality and prestige of its previous political representatives.

7 Finally, the book has a basic structural flaw. In his preface the author admits that he has tried to cater for the interests of both historians and social scientists, each of whom will find some parts of the book commonplace and others new. Unfortunately, the result is likely to satisfy neither. As a historian I found Hamilton's analysis of the party system too long and unproductive. His lengthy quotations from monographs could have been summarized and the reader referred to those works via the footnotes. Above all, however, I feel that with his attack on the lower-middle-class thesis he has to some extent set up an Aunt Sally which he then proceeds to knock down very effectively. For, as he himself admits, historians of the period have now produced a much more differentiated picture of the social bases of Nazi support than the old "centrist" thesis of the marginal lower middle class, which derived in fact largely from social science literature.

8 In his study Thomas Childers shows a much surer grasp of the historical context in which the Nazis were operating. Indeed his introductory chapter provides a masterly account of the sociology of German electoral politics between 1871 and 1924. Then, on the basis of a sophisticated use of a wide range of electoral statistics, he defines the characteristics of the Nazi voters with a greater degree of precision than has hitherto been possible. One of his most significant points is that the Nazi constituency was not socially static. It changed substantially over

time and in response to changing economic conditions. There was a core group among the old *Mittelstand* which predominated in the period 1924–8 and which, because of its long-standing discontent with the effects of modernization, proved vulnerable to the anti-modernist appeal of Nazism. At the same time, other groups, such as farmers and the upper middle class, were drawn in under the impact of economic crisis.

9   On the question of who voted Nazi, Childer's most significant findings are: first, that there was much less support for the Nazis among white-collar workers than had hitherto been thought – a point he first made in an important article some years ago and which Hamilton has now perceptively elucidated. Second, while the Party's membership tended to be younger than average, it found substantial electoral support among the older generation, many of whom were pensioners hit by the hyper-inflation of the early 1920s. Third, he concurs with Hamilton's thesis about widespread upper-middle-class support. Those who voted Nazi were not generally uneducated, economically devastated or socially marginal. Finally, in the last Weimar elections women appear to have surpassed men in the Nazi electorate. Nazi propaganda evidently had some success in persuading women that their limited degree of emancipation had merely produced greater exploitation while devaluing traditional feminine roles in the home.

10   To explain *why* people voted Nazi, Childers has concentrated on the content and techniques of Nazi propaganda, examining the appeal of the messages addressed to particular sections of the community and the methods used to put them across. He attributes their success to a large extent to the effectiveness of the Nazi propaganda machine. This is not a new thesis, but it is one which he has developed in more detail than has been done hitherto. Indeed, he has perhaps exaggerated the importance of the national propaganda apparatus. It was arguably the remarkable initiative shown by the local Party organization and the role of local opinion leaders which proved most crucial to Nazi success.

11   What then is the state of our knowledge of Nazi electoral support after the appearance of these two books and, one must add, the work of Jürgen Falter in Germany? Who did vote for Hitler? Despite being somewhat battered by the heavy critical artillery mounted against it by both authors, it seems to me that the lower-middle-class thesis still stands, though in a modified form. Thus, it is now clear that the basis of Nazi support was much broader than has hitherto been believed. The Party gained substantial numbers of votes both from the upper middle class and the working class. Moreover, the upwardly mobile white-collar worker voting Nazi for fear of proletarianization has been shown to be something of a myth. Nevertheless, although the Nazi Party's social basis was broader than that of any other German party, with the exception of the Centre with Catholicism as its bond, it was not a true *Volkspartei*. The working class was heavily under-represented and as a result the party's mass basis came inevitably largely from the lower middle class. This voted Nazi primarily because of its distaste for, and fear of the Left and all it stood for, and because the Nazis had persuaded it that they were the party who would deal with this threat most effectively. The Nazis were essentially a movement of middle-class integration – a *Sammelbewegung*. If asked, therefore, who were the typical Nazi voters I would still be inclined to quote Seymour Martin Lipset's famous verdict, which is a major target of both these books: "the ideal-type Nazi voter in 1932 was a middle-class self-employed Protestant who lived either on a farm or in a small community".

APPROACHING THE TEXT

▶ Answer the following questions without reading the main body of the text:
1. To which genre does this text belong?

2. What is the name of the reviewer?

3. What are the titles and who are the authors of the two books?

4. Which is the longest book?

5. Are either of the two books available in paperback?

6. Where did this review appear?

7. What predictions can be made about the content of the book review from its title?

WORKSHEET 1

Identifying evaluation and description in topic sentences

▶ Underline the first sentence of paragraphs 1–10 and decide whether they convey evaluative or descriptive comments on the part of the reviewer, putting a tick in the appropriate column. Where evaluative, decide whether the judgement is *critical* or *favourable*.

▶ Which words or phrases convey evaluation on the part of the writer?

	Descriptive	Evaluative (critical)	Evaluative (favourable)	Words conveying evaluation
par. 1				
2				
3				
4				
5				
6				
7				
8				
9				
10				

▶ What is the function of the questions which open paragraph 11?

WORKSHEET 2 **Distinguishing text structure**

▶ Skim the article and indicate the paragraph or paragraphs which comprise the following sections and subsections.

1 INTRODUCTION (par. _____)
2 DISCUSSION OF HAMILTON'S THESIS (par. _____)
   — Nature of Nazi electoral support (par. _____)
   — Reasons for Nazi electoral support (par. _____)
   — Concluding evaluation (par. _____)
3 DISCUSSION OF CHILDER'S THESIS (par. _____)
   — Nature of Nazi electoral support (par. _____)
   — Reasons for Nazi electoral support (par. _____)
4 GENERAL CONCLUSIONS (par. _____)

INTENSIVE READING

WORKSHEET 3 **Reference**

▶ The words below appear in the sentences you have underlined. Write the words or phrases they refer to in the space provided.

1 it (par. 1, line 1)	
2 it (3, 1)	
3 none (3, 3)	
4 it (6, 6)	
5 it (6, 10)	
6 its (6, 11)	
7 he (6, 12)	
8 them (10, 6)	

In order to take concise, clearly recorded notes, it is often useful to establish beforehand the global structure of the text, as you have done in Worksheet 2. The exercise which follows illustrates one way of recording the main points of the review. For comments on different note-taking techniques, see the notes on reading, Section 4.2.

WORKSHEET 4

Note-taking

▶ Now read carefully the introductory paragraph and the part of the text discussing Hamilton's book. Study the notes taken on Hamilton's book and underline the sentences which contain this information in the text.

▶ Now read the part of the text discussing Childer's book and Noakes' conclusions. Underline the relevant passages and transfer this information to the table in note form. Read the final paragraph carefully to decide how many points Noakes makes.

	Hamilton	**Childers**	**Noakes**
Who Voted Nazi?	1 *not lower middle class but upper middle class* 2 *the more marginal urban white-collar worker voted SPD not Nazi* 3 *some workers voted DNVP and later Nazi* 4 *more voters in communities under 25,000* 5 *villages voted normally one party, Nazi or other* 6 *Catholic rural areas resistant*	1 2 3 4	
Why?	1 *influence of Nazi political cadres (military background)* 2 *influence of local press*	1	

LANGUAGE WORK

WORKSHEET 5

Lexis common to academic prose

▶ In each of the following three groups, find the verb which has a completely different meaning from the other verbs and underline it, looking carefully at the contexts in which the verbs are used, and checking in a dictionary (some verbs do *not* appear in the text). Then write the dictionary definition for each of the verbs, being careful to copy the correct definition for the meaning they carry in *this* text.

1 to suggest that (par. 6) _____
  to deal with (par. 11) _____
  to argue that (par. 3) _____
  to put forward that (par. 6) _____

2 to quibble with (par. 3) _____
   to take issue with (par. 2) _____
   to disagree with _____
   to concur with (par. 9) _____

3 to focus on (pars. 4/5) _____
   to concentrate on (par. 10) _____
   to dwell on _____
   to elucidate (par. 9) _____

> In Unit Five you were introduced to the main functions of linkers. The exercise below is intended to consolidate the functions of other important linkers. Note that some of these may perform more than one function, depending on the context.

WORKSHEET 6

Distinguishing the functions of selected linkers

▶ The linkers listed below all appear in the text (paragraph and line are given). Look carefully at the context in which they are used and assign them to one of the four columns in the table, according to whether their function *here* is *additive, temporal, causal* or *adversative*.

nevertheless (1, 5)   hitherto (3, 14)   although (5, 13)
moreover (1, 10)   thus (3, 27)   for (7, 16)
indeed (1, 13)   though (4, 1)   because (11, 26)
therefore (1, 15)   furthermore (4, 14)
then (2, 9)   then (4, 27)

▶ The linkers which follow do *not* appear in the text. Check their meaning and use in a dictionary and add them to the table.

henceforth   similarly
likewise   yet

additive	temporal	causal	adversative

WORKSHEET 7

Practising the use of selected linkers

▶ The following is a passage comparing the seizure of power in Germany, Italy and Russia. Insert an appropriate linker in the spaces provided, choosing from the linkers in the boxes beside each section.

Totalitarian regimes 1917–1945: The seizure of power

The victory of National Socialism was consolidated in less than two years, between January 1933 and August 1934. _____ Germany was to have a one-party dictatorship. A comparison of events in Germany with those which ten years earlier in Italy and fifteen years earlier in Russia had led to the installation of totalitarian regimes, points up many differences.

NEVERTHELESS
HITHERTO
HENCEFORTH
THEN

For example, _____ the Bolshevik seizure of power was accomplished as rapidly as the others, it was the result of a planned coup d'état, and, _____, the revolutionary Soviet Government turned into a totalitarian dictatorship only after a considerably longer period.

THUS
ALTHOUGH
MOREOVER
FOR
HOWEVER
SIMILARLY

It is true that in all three cases we are dealing with the seizure of power by a violent minority. _____ it is clear that the intervals between the actual seizure of power and the definitive consolidation in one-party rule varies considerably. _____ we must distinguish between these two events and treat them separately.

FOR
SIMILARLY
THEREFORE
YET

_____, the preconditions in the three countries were also different. If we look at the case of Russia, _____, we must realize that the revolution took place against the background of an absolutist state and an agrarian, feudal society, _____ in Italy, the seizure of power occurred in different circumstances. Here, a parliamentary democracy was unable to cope with the explosive force of the transition to industrialism. Germany, on the other hand, was faced with the particular political and psychological problems of the unresolved defeat of 1918. A comparison of the circumstances in which the seizure of power took place, _____, highlights further differences between the transition to totalitarianism in these three countries.

BECAUSE
THEN
FURTHERMORE
WHILE
HENCEFORTH
FOR INSTANCE

VOCABULARY WORK AND WORD BUILDING

▶ Find the words in the text (paragraphs are given), decide the word class, and write it and the translation of the word in the space provided.

▶ Then complete the table by forming other words using appropriate suffixes if necessary. Consult your dictionary.

VOCABULARY WORK			WORD BUILDING		
Word and Location	**Class**	**Translation**	**Noun**	**Verb**	**Adjective**
achieved (1)					
alliance (1)					
assumption (4)					
derive (4)					
electoral (1)					
evidence (5)					
exploitation (9)					
feature (1)					
modernization (8)					
modified (11)					
obliged (1)					
persuaded (6)					
prosperous (4)					
representatives (6)					
resistant (3)					
sufficient (1)					

OBSERVATIONS ON TEXT TYPE

BOOK REVIEW

(See Observations for Unit Four for *function, structure* and *aspects of language*.)

UNIT NINE

HUMAN AGGRESSION
Anthony Storr

Penguin Books, 1971

Introduction

1 That man is an aggressive creature will hardly be disputed. With the exception of certain rodents, no other vertebrate habitually destroys members of his own species. No other animal takes positive pleasure in the exercise of cruelty upon another of his own kind. We generally describe the most repulsive examples of man's cruelty as brutal or bestial, implying by these adjectives that such behaviour is characteristic of less highly developed animals than ourselves. In truth, however, the extremes of 'brutal' behaviour are confined to man; and there is no parallel in nature to our savage treatment of each other. The sombre fact is that we are the cruellest and most ruthless species that has ever walked the earth; and that, although we may recoil in horror when we read in newspaper or history book of the atrocities committed by man upon man, we know in our hearts that each one of us harbours within himself those same savage impulses which lead to murder, to torture and to war.

2 To write about human aggression is a difficult task because the term is used in so many different senses. Aggression is one of those words which everyone knows, but which is nevertheless hard to define. As psychologists and psychiatrists use it, it covers a very wide range of human behaviour. The red-faced infant squalling for the bottle is being aggressive; and so is the judge who awards a thirty-year sentence for robbery. The guard in a concentration camp who tortures his helpless victim is obviously acting aggressively. Less manifestly, but no less certainly, so is the neglected wife who threatens or attempts suicide in order to regain her husband's affection. When a word becomes so diffusely applied that it is used both of the competitive striving of a footballer and also of the bloody violence of a murderer, it ought either to be dropped or else more closely defined. Aggression is a portmanteau term which is fairly bursting at its seams. Yet, until we can more clearly designate and comprehend the various aspects of human behaviour which are subsumed under this head, we cannot discard the concept.

3 One difficulty is that there is no clear dividing line between those forms of aggression which we all deplore and those which we must not disown if we are to survive. When a child rebels against authority it is being aggressive: but it is also manifesting a drive towards independence which is a necessary and valuable part of growing up. The desire for power has, in extreme form, disastrous aspects which we all acknowledge: but the drive to conquer difficulties, or to gain mastery over the external world, underlies the greatest of human achievements. Some writers define aggression as 'that response which follows frustration', or as 'an act whose goal-response is injury to an organism (or organism surrogate)'. In the author's view these definitions impose limits upon the concept of aggression which are not in accord with the underlying facts of human nature which the word is attempting to express. It is worth noticing, for instance, that the words we use to describe intellectual effort are aggressive words. We *attack* problems, or *get our teeth into* them. We *master* a subject when we have struggled with and *overcome* its difficulties. We *sharpen* our wits, hoping that our mind will develop a *keen edge* in order that we may better *dissect* a problem into its component parts. Although intellectual tasks are often frustrating, to argue that all intellectual effort is the result of frustration is to impose too negative a colouring upon the positive impulse to comprehend and master the external world.

4 The aggressive part of human nature is not only a necessary safeguard against predatory attack. It is also the basis of intellectual achievement, of the attainment of independence, and even of that proper pride which enables a man to hold his head high amongst his fellows. This is no new conception. The historian Gibbon, in a famous passage, displays a very similar idea of human nature to that which psychotherapists profess. Whereas the latter refer to sexual instincts

and aggressive instincts. Gibbon writes of 'the love of pleasure and the love of action':

> . . . To the love of pleasure we may therefore ascribe most of the agreeable, to the love of action we may attribute most of the useful and respectable qualifications. The character in which both the one and the other should be united and harmonized would seem to constitute the most perfect idea of human nature.

Gibbon recognizes quite clearly that the most deplorable manifestations of aggression share identical roots with valuable and essential parts of human endeavour. Without the aggressive, active side of his nature man would be even less able than he is to direct the course of his life or to influence the world around him. In fact, it is obvious that man could never have attained his present dominance, nor even have survived as a species, unless he possessed a large endowment of aggressiveness.

5   It is a tragic paradox that the very qualities which have led to man's extraordinary success are also those most likely to destroy him. His ruthless drive to subdue or to destroy every apparent obstacle in his path does not stop short at his own fellows; and since he now possesses weapons of unparalleled destructiveness and also apparently lacks the built-in safeguards which prevent most animals from killing others of the same species, it is not beyond possibility that he may yet encompass the total elimination of *homo sapiens*.

6   What follows are the reflections of a psychotherapist upon the aggressive component in human nature. The views which are put forward are anything but dogmatic. All psychotherapists suffer from the fact that, although their knowledge of a few people may be rather profound, their conclusions are necessarily drawn from a limited and highly selected sample of the population. Moreover, many of the theories which are available in the practice of psychotherapy are difficult to substantiate scientifically, because the psychotherapist is endeavouring to deal with the person as a whole. Psychologists working in laboratories can construct experiments in which, for example, aggressive emotions can be more or less separately aroused and studied; and the conclusions which they reach can be statistically expressed. The disadvantage of nearly all such experiments is that the situations upon which they are based are so restricted that they are far removed from life as it is lived. Aggression, for example, is inextricably mingled with fear and sex in many situations. It is very much to be hoped that, in time, there will be a *rapprochement* between the precise but limited viewpoint of the experimentalist, and the less defined but wider conceptions of the psychotherapist. In the meantime, we must do the best we can with incomplete and unproved hypotheses.

7   The present preoccupation of Western society with the problem of aggression is, of course, dictated by the fear of destruction by nuclear weapons which overhangs us all. The problem of war is more compelling than ever before in history. The complexities of the circumstances which provoke war are such that no one man and no one viewpoint can possibly comprehend them all. Anyone who promises a solution to a problem so perennial is too arrogant to be trusted; and no such solution will be put forward here. The author believes, however, that if stability in world affairs is ever to be achieved, the psychological point of view deserves equal consideration with the political, economic and other aspects. The study of human aggression and its control is, therefore, relevant to the problem of war although, alone, it cannot possibly provide a complete answer.

APPROACHING THE TEXT

In some genres the structure of the text is fairly standard. However, this is not the case with the *Introduction to a book*, in which the author can be more flexible in his approach, choosing to highlight the aspects he considers most important (see OBSERVATIONS for this Unit). The exercise below indicates the structure of this particular introduction and aims to give practice in predicting the content of the individual sections.

WORKSHEET 1

Predicting content

▶ The four general headings for the different sections of this *Introduction* are indicated below. The phrases summarize the contents of each paragraph. *Without making reference to the text*, put the phrases in the order in which you think they might appear. An example has been given.

a Possibility of self-destruction inherent in man's aggression

b The previous definitions of the concept of aggression: negative aspects

c *The advantages and disadvantages of a psychotherapist's approach*

d Statement of man's innate aggression.

e Elaboration of the concept of aggression in intellectual activity, supported by a quotation.

f The implications of the study of aggression for world affairs and the problems of war.

g Positive aspects of aggression: e.g. in intellectual activity.

1 *General statement of the subject*
   – _____

2 *Review of previous definitions of the subject*
   – _____

3 *Author's own reformulation of the subject*
   – _____
   – _____

4 *Relevance of the subject and statement of author's approach*
   – _____
   – *advantages and disadvantages of a psychotherapist's approach* (**c**)
   – _____

▶ Now skim the text to check your predictions, underlining the parts of the text which correspond to the phrases you have inserted.

INTENSIVE READING

An introduction to a book commonly focuses on the author's presentation of certain key terms. The exercise below is intended to draw attention to the presentation of the principal theme of the book – aggression – and to two important purposes of the introduction, to define and exemplify this theme.

WORKSHEET 2   **Identifying aspects of author's presentation of theme**

▶ Read the first two paragraphs and underline descriptions and examples of 1) man's aggressive behaviour, and 2) information and comments on the definition of the term *aggression*, and write them in the appropriate column.

	Descriptions/Examples of man's aggressive behaviour	**Information/Comments on definition of the term**
par. 1	– destroys members of own species	
par. 2	– red-faced infant squalling for the bottle	– term used in many different senses

▶ Now read the rest of the text carefully.

WORKSHEET 3   **Discriminating units of information**

One way of introducing a theme is by contrasting or comparing different aspects of it (see, for example, paragraph 1 where the author contrasts man's behaviour with that of animals). Paragraphs 3, 4, 5, 6 and 7 each present one or more "pairs" representing two aspects of a problem, which can be contrasted or compared. One of those in paragraph 3 is indicated in abbreviated form in the table on the following page.

▶ Complete the table with two examples for each of the paragraphs (except for paragraph 5, which has only one example).

	Information Pairs	
Par. 3	– *those forms of aggression which we all deplore*	*– those which we must not disown if we are to survive*
	–	/ –
	–	/ –
Par. 4	–	/ –
	–	/ –
Par. 5	–	/ –
Par. 6	–	/ –
	–	/ –
Par. 7	–	/ –
	–	/ –

LANGUAGE WORK

WORKSHEET 4

Revising modal meaning

▶ Below is a list of some modal verbs or their negative forms, and their location in the text. Underline them together with the principal verb and the subject. Then assign each modal verb to one of the general categories below, on the basis of its function in the text.

par. 1, line 1 – will
       line 13 – may
par. 2, line 15 – ought to
       line 17 – can
       line 19 – cannot
par. 3, line 3 – must not

par. 4, line 20 – would
       line 23 – could
par. 6, line 23 – must
par. 7, line 15 – cannot

Meaning	Modal verbs
Ability/Potential	
Probability/Possibility	
Obligation/Necessity	
Obligation/Desirability	
Future	
Conditional	
Prohibition	

WORKSHEET 5

Use and function of modal verbs

▶ Below is a synopsis of the introduction. Fill in the blanks with a suitable modal verb *or its negative form* and indicate in the margin the meaning of the modal chosen. More than one answer is possible in several cases.

Meaning

1 _____
2 _____
3 _____
4 _____
5 _____
6 _____

7 _____
8 _____

9 _____
10 _____
11 _____
12 _____
13 _____
14 _____

The concept of aggression has yet to be clearly defined. It is a concept which 1) _____ have numerous applications, some of which 2) _____ not always be relevant. However, even though the term "aggression" 3) _____ be applied more carefully, it is a term which we 4) _____ abandon. That human beings are the most aggressive creatures ever to have existed is a reality we 5) _____ ignore. But unfortunately, aggression 6) _____ always play a part in those worthy aspects of human endeavour, without which man 7) _____ survive. It is perhaps utopistic to state that man 8) _____ achieve what he wants through his positive qualities alone. Nevertheless, given the current state of the balance of power between the nations, man 9) _____ learn to control his aggression. He 10) _____ continue his egoistic battle to dominate the world, since in so doing, he 11) _____ destroy it, and himself in the process. Man 12) _____ be intelligent enough to realize that he 13) _____ control his aggression if he wishes, and that this 14) _____ mean the possibility of world peace.

As you have seen in previous Units, linkers fulfill the important function of signalling the logical development of a text. A writer may, however, not overtly signal the link between parts of the text, as for example, in paragraph 3 (lines 10–16) of the *Introduction*, where contrast between the definitions of aggression and the author's view is not explicitly marked:

"Some writers define . . . (*However*) In the author's view these definitions impose limits . . . ."

In the absence of an explicit linker, then, the reader must identify the logical links between sentences. The exercise below aims therefore to give practice in determining the function of unmarked sentences in extended discourse, with reference to an abbreviated version of the first two paragraphs of the text.

WORKSHEET 6

Recognizing logical links between parts of discourse

▶ In the text below, insert an appropriate linker where indicated. You may choose from the following list:

and
for example
for instance
indeed
in fact
even though
furthermore
moreover
likewise
similarly
yet
but
nevertheless
however

That man is an aggressive creature will hardly be disputed. _____, with the exception of certain rodents, no other vertebrate habitually destroys members of his own species. _____, no other animal takes positive pleasure in the exercise of cruelty upon another of his own kind. We generally describe the most repulsive examples of man's cruelty as brutal or bestial, implying by these adjectives that such behaviour is characteristic of less highly developed animals than ourselves. In truth, _____, the extremes of "brutal" behaviour are confined to man; and there is no parallel in nature to our savage treatment of each other. _____ we may recoil in horror when we read in the newspaper or history book of the atrocities committed by man upon man, we know in our hearts that each one of us harbours within himself those same savage impulses which lead to murder, to torture and to war.

To write about human aggression is a difficult task because the term is used in so many different senses. _____, aggression is one of those words which everyone knows, but which is nevertheless hard to define. As psychologists and psychiatrists use it, it covers a very wide range of human behaviour. _____, the red-faced infant squalling for the bottle is being aggressive; and so is the judge who awards a thirty-year sentence for robbery. _____, the guard in a concentration camp who tortures his helpless victim is obviously acting aggressively. When a word becomes so diffusely applied that it is used both of the competitive striving of a footballer and also of the bloody violence of a murderer, it ought either to be dropped or else more closely defined. Aggression is a portmanteau term which is fairly bursting at its seams. _____ until we can more clearly designate and comprehend the various aspects of human behaviour which are subsumed under this head, we cannot discard this concept.

VOCABULARY WORK AND WORD BUILDING

▶ Find the words in the text (paragraphs are given), decide the word class, and write it and the translation of the word in the space provided.

▶ Then complete the table by forming other words using appropriate suffixes if necessary. Consult your dictionary.

VOCABULARY WORK			WORD BUILDING		
Word and Location	**Class**	**Translation**	**Noun**	**Verb**	**Adjective**
able (4)					
acknowledge (3)					
aggressive (1)					
apparent (5)					
applied (2)					
characteristic (1)					
define (2)					
destroy (1)					
diffusely (2)					
human (title)					
hypotheses (6)					
impulses (1)					
intellectual (3)					
necessary (3)					
solution (7)					
threatens (2)					

OBSERVATIONS ON TEXT TYPE	INTRODUCTION	
Function:	To give a general presentation of the topic and of the organization or orientation of the book.
Structure:	Whereas the structure of some genres can be predicted fairly accurately (for example, a research report will inevitably include a section on *results* and almost certainly one on *procedure*) there is a much greater flexibility as to what an author includes in his introduction. The following is a list of common features, at least one or two of which are likely to appear: – general statement on the subject – review of previous knowledge or research in the area – statement of purpose – statement of approach – statement of relevance of the topic – definition of terminology – organization of the book There is also considerable flexibility as regards the order in which these features may occur, although the *general statement* and the comments on *organization*, if they appear, will probably come towards the beginning and towards the end respectively. This particular introduction is organized as follows: 1 General statement on the subject 2 Review of previous definitions of the subject 3 Author's own reformulation of the subject 4 Relevance of the subject and statement of the author's approach

NOTES

INSIDE THE BLACK BOX: TECHNOLOGY AND ECONOMICS

NATHAN ROSENBERG

Cambridge University Press, 1983

Preface

1 The central purpose of this book may be simply stated. Economists have long treated technological phenomena as events transpiring inside a black box. They have of course recognized that these events have significant economic consequences, and they have in fact devoted considerable effort and ingenuity to tracing, and even measuring, some of these consequences. Nevertheless, the economics profession has adhered rather strictly to a self-imposed ordinance not to inquire too seriously into what transpires inside that box.

2 The purpose of this book is to break open and to examine the contents of the black box into which technological change has been consigned by economists. I believe that by so doing a number of important economic problems can be powerfully illuminated. This is because the specific characteristics of certain technologies have ramifications for economic phenomena that cannot be understood without a close examination of these characteristics. Thus, I attempt to show in the following pages how specific features of individual technologies have shaped a number of developments of great concern to economists: the rate of productivity improvement, the nature of the learning process underlying technological change itself, the speed of technology transfer, and the effectiveness of government policies that are intended to influence technologies in particular ways.

3 The separate chapters of this book reflect a primary concern with some of the distinctive aspects of industrial technologies in the twentieth century: the increasing reliance upon science, but also the considerable subtlety and complexity of the dialectic between science and technology; the rapid growth in the development costs associated with new technologies, and the closely associated phenomena of lengthy lead times and the

high degree of technological uncertainty associated with precisely predicting the eventual performance characteristics of newly emerging technologies; the changing structure of inter-industry relationships, such as that between the makers of capital goods and their eventual users; and the changing characteristics of technology over the course of its own life cycle. Each of the chapters in Part II represents an attempt to identify some significant characteristics of specific advanced industrial technologies – or of the process by which such technologies have emerged and have been introduced into the economy. The chapters in Parts III and IV continue this examination against the backdrop of a concern with issues of public policy and with the implications of technology transfer in the international context.

4 The book opens with a broad survey, in Part I, of the historical literature on technical change. It attempts to provide a guide to a wide range of writings, including those by some social historians and social theorists as well as economic historians and economists, that illuminate technological change as a historical phenomenon. It should not be necessary to belabor two points: (1) that past history is an indispensable source of information to anyone interested in characterizing technologies, and (2) that both the determinants and the consequences of technological innovation raise issues that go far beyond the generally recognized domain of the economist and the economic historian. The first chapter discusses aspects of the conceptualization of technological change and then goes on to consider what the literature has had to say on (1) the rate of technological change, (2) the forces influencing its direction, (3) the speed with which new technologies have diffused, and (4) the impact of technological change on the growth in productivity.

5 A separate chapter is devoted to Marx. Marx's intellectual impact has been so pervasive as to rank him as a major social force *in* history as well as an armchair interpreter *of* history. And yet, curiously enough, I argue that Marx's analysis of technological change opened doors to the study of the technological realm through which hardly anyone has subsequently passed.

6 Part II is, in important respects, the core of the book. Each of its chapters advances an argument about some significant characteristics of industrial technologies, characteristics that are typically suppressed in discussions of technological change conducted at high levels of aggregation or lacking in historical specificity. Chapter 3 explores a variety of less visible forms in which technological improvements enter the economy. Each of these forms, it is argued, is important in determining the connections between technological innovations and the growth of productivity flowing from innovation. Chapter 4 explicitly considers some significant characteristics of different energy forms. It became a common practice in the 1970s, following the Arab oil embargo, to treat energy as some undifferentiated mass expressible in Btus which it was in society's interests to minimize. This chapter examines some of the complexities of the long-term interactions between technological change and energy resources. It emphasizes, in particular, the frequently imperfect substitutability among energy sources in industrial contexts and the consequent suboptimality of criteria for energy utilization that fail to take specific characteristics of different energy forms into account.

7 Chapter 5, "On Technological Expectations," addresses an issue that is simultaneously relevant to a wide range of industries – indeed, to all industries that are experiencing, or are expected to experience, substantial rates of technical improvement. I argue that rational decision making with respect to the adoption of an innovation requires careful consideration of prospective rates of technological innovation. Such a consideration will often lead to counterintuitive decisions, including slow adoption rates that, from other perspectives, may appear to be irrational. Expectations about the future behavior of technological systems and their components are shown to be a major and neglected factor in the diffusion of new technologies.

8 The last two chapters of Part II are primarily concerned with issues of greatest relevance to high-technology industries – industries in which new product development involves large development costs, long lead times, and considerable technological uncertainty (especially concerning product performance characteristics) and that rely in significant ways upon knowledge that is close to the frontiers of present-day scientific research. Chapter 6, "Learning by Using," identifies an important source of learning that grows out of actual experience in using products characterized by a high degree of system complexity. In contrast to learning by doing, which deals with skill improvements that grow out of the productive process, learning by using involves an experience that begins where learning by doing ends. The importance of learning by using is explored in some detail with respect to aircraft, but reasons are advanced suggesting that it may be a much more pervasive phenomenon in high-technology industries.

9 The final chapter in Part II, "How Exogenous Is Science?" looks explicitly at the nature of science–technology interactions in high-technology industries. It examines some of the specific ways in which these industries have been drawing upon the

expanding pool of scientific knowledge and techniques. The chapter also considers, however, a range of much broader questions concerning the institutionalization of science and the manner in which the agenda of science is formulated in advanced industrial societies. Thus, a major theme of the chapter is that, far from being exogenous forces to the economic arena, the content and direction of the scientific enterprise are heavily shaped by technological considerations that are, in turn, deeply embedded in the structure of industrial societies.

10 The three chapters constituting Part III share a common concern with the role of market forces in shaping both the rate and the direction of innovative activities. They attempt to look into the composition of forces constituting the demand and the supply for new products and processes, especially in high-technology industries. This analysis, in turn, has direct implications for government concern with accelerating the rate of innovative activity. Thus, policy considerations emerge as an important element of these chapters.

11 Chapter 8 examines the history of technical change in the commercial aircraft industry over a fifty-year period 1925–75. This industry has been, and remains, a remarkable success story in terms of both productivity growth and continued American success in international markets. For a variety of reasons, including the strategic military importance of aircraft and a concern with passenger safety, the federal government's role has been particularly prominent with respect to aircraft. This chapter evaluates the impact of government policies and considers the possible relevance of these policies to other industries. Chapter 9 examines the ongoing technological revolution embodied in very-large-scale integration. It points out that there are a variety of mediating factors that stand between an expanding technological capability and commercial success. The growth in circuit-element density, with the resulting dramatic improvement in the capability of a single chip, offers a great potential for the application of electronic techniques in many fields. The success of such applications will turn upon developments internal to the industry, but also upon the creation of mechanisms that will translate this new technological capability into tangible economic advantages. Chapter 10 focuses not upon an individual industry but upon a number of recent empirical studies of technical change. These studies, which share an emphasis upon the dominant role of market demand in the innovation process, have been widely cited as providing an adequate basis for a successful government innovation policy. It is argued that these studies are, analytically and conceptually, seriously incomplete. The chapter attempts to provide a more comprehensive framework for both analysis and policy formulation.

12 Finally, the two chapters of Part IV place the discussion of technological change in an international context, with the first chapter oriented toward its long history and the second toward the present and the future. Chapter 11 pays primary attention to the transfer of industrial technology from Britain to the rest of the world. This transfer encompasses a large part of the story of worldwide industrialization, because nineteenth-century industrialization was, in considerable measure, the story of the overseas transfer of the technologies already developed by the first industrial society. Particular attention is devoted to the conditions that shaped the success of these transfers, but a central concern is their eventual impact upon the technology-exporting country. The last chapter speculates about the prospects for the future from an American perspective, a perspective that is often dominated by apprehension over the loss of American technological leadership, especially in high-technology industries. By drawing upon some of the distinctive characteristics of high-technology industries, an attempt is made to identify possible elements of a future scenario. I am confident that the world economy of the 1990s will be powerfully shaped by the international distribution of technological capabilities; but it will also be shaped by economic and social forces that strongly influence the comparative effectiveness with which the available technologies are exploited. I also suspect that the world of the 1990s will be a good deal more complex – and more interesting – than the one currently depicted by the harbingers of The Japanese Challenge, just as the scenario presented in Jean-Jacques Servan-Schreiber's *The American Challenge*, published in 1968, bore little resemblance to the subsequent decade of the 1970s.

13 This book is, in many respects, a continuation of the intellectual enterprise that was embodied in my earlier book, *Perspectives on Technology*. Whereas in the introduction to that book I stated that my interest in coming to grips with technological change had had the effect of transforming an economist into an economic historian, I am now inclined to say that much of the content of the present book can be read as the musings of an economic historian who has stumbled – not entirely by accident! – into the twentieth century. For the benefit of economic historians who still think of themselves as young, and who take it for granted that to study history is to study some remote past, I must point out that the twentieth century is, by now, mostly history.

APPROACHING THE TEXT

WORKSHEET 1 **Skimming for the general organization of the text**

▶ Number the paragraphs of the text and divide it up according to the following outline:

1 INTRODUCTION TO THE BOOK AS A WHOLE (par. _____)
2 DETAILED PRESENTATION OF CONTENTS OF THE BOOK (par. _____)
   – in Part I (par. _____)
   – in Part II (par. _____)
   – in Part III (par. _____)
   – in Part IV (par. _____)
3 CONCLUDING REMARKS (par. _____)

WORKSHEET 2 **Skimming and scanning for chapter headings**

▶ Below is a list of the chapter headings of "Inside the Black Box". Scan the *Preface*, underlining all the sentences in which the various chapters are first mentioned and insert the appropriate heading in the *Table of Contents* on the following page.

Chapter Headings (jumbled)

- The international transfer of technology
- Technological interdependence in the American economy
- The influence of market demand upon innovation: a critical review of some recent empirical studies
- U.S. technological leadership and foreign competition
- The historiography of technical progress
- The economic implications of the VLSI revolution
- The effects of energy supply characteristics on technology and economic growth
- Technical change in the commercial aircraft industry 1925–1975
- Marx as a student of technology
- On technological expectations

Contents

Preface	page vii
Part I. Views of technical progress	
1	3
2	34
Part II. Some significant characteristics of technologies	
3	55
4	81
5	104
6 Learning by using	120
7 How exogenous is science?	141
Part III. Market determinants of technological innovation	
8	163
9	178
10	193
Part IV. Technology transfer and leadership: the international context	
11	245
12	280

WORKSHEET 3 **Pre-reading vocabulary work**
▶ Find the following words in the text, decide upon their word class and look closely at their immediate context. Then insert an appropriate definition from the list overleaf.

	Word class	Definition/explanation
1 transpiring (par. 1, line 2 __)		
2 ramifications (2, 5 __)		
3 backdrop (3, 16 __)		
4 to rank (5, 2 __)		
5 core (6, 1 __)		
6 undifferentiated (6, 12 __)		
7 suboptimality (6, 17 __)		
8 counterintuitive (7, 7 __)		
9 drawing upon (9, 4 __)		
10 pool (9, 4 __)		
11 exogenous (9, 9 __)		
12 embedded (9, 11 __)		
13 ongoing (11, 10 __)		
14 depicted (12, 23 __)		
15 harbingers (12, 23 __)		
16 coming to grips with (13, 4 __)		
17 musings (13, 7 __)		
18 stumbled (13, 7 __)		

Definitions/Explanations

a people who predict the coming of something
b to classify in order of importance
c continuing
d not treated as different
e described
f centre, most important part
g external, originating from outside a system
h happening, occurring
i moved or proceeded in an uncertain way
j background
k making use of, taking from
l implications, consequences
m firmly fixed in the surrounding structure
n thoughts, reflections
o understanding, dealing with on a fundamental level
p against one's instincts or intuition
q condition of being less than the best
r common fund or supply

▶ The following are examples of the technical terminology in this text. Look at the context in which they appear, choose appropriate definitions from the list below, and write them in the space provided. An example has been given.

1 lead times (3, 6 ___)	
2 capital goods (3, 10 ___)	
3 aggregation (6, 4 _d_)	*generality, inclusion of many different elements*
4 Btus (6, 12 ___)	
5 system complexity (8, 9 ___)	
6 very large scale integration (11, 10 ___)	
7 circuit element density (11, 13 ___)	

a the number of elements placed in each electronic circuit
b a unit of energy used to compare different sources of energy
c durable goods which are employed to produce other goods
d *generality, inclusion of many different elements*
e the number of interrelations between the elements of a given system
f the period in which a firm is the sole owner of a particular technology
g high functional interrelation between the elements of a given electronic circuit

INTENSIVE READING

When important parts of a text are particularly dense or complex, it may be useful to consider them in detail and extract the author's main points in order to clarify the progression of his argument. The exercise below is an example of this kind of operation applied to the first three paragraphs of Rosenberg's *Preface*.

WORKSHEET 4

Extracting author's main points

▶ Read the first three paragraphs carefully and insert the missing information below.

Background
- *Economists have:* 1
  2
  3
- *but have not:* 1

Purpose of book
- *immediate:*
- *ultimate:*
- *justification:*

- *aspects of technologies influencing developments of interest to economists:* 1
  2
  3
  4

Distinctive features of 20th century industrial technologies considered
  1 –
    –
  2 –
    –
    –
  3 –
  4 –

WORKSHEET 5

Note-taking: Identifying topics and author's point of view

In paragraphs 4–12 the author discusses the contents of each of the 12 chapters of his book, indicating the principal topic of each chapter and, for 9 of them, his main argument or point of view. Sometimes the author's views are clearly marked ("I argue that . . ."); elsewhere he uses other stylistic devices to convey that a personal opinion is being presented.

▶ Read carefully paragraphs 4–12 and underline all the words or phrases which signal the presentation of the topic and the author's argument. (These and other markers of topic and argument will be reutilized in Worksheet 7.) Then complete the table overleaf.

Chap.	Principal topic	Author's main argument/point of view
1		
2		
3	variety of less visible forms in which technological innovations enter economy	
4		
5		that rational decision-making re. adoption of innovation requires careful consideration of prospective rates of technical improvement
6		
7		
8		
9		
10		
11		
12		

WORKSHEET 6

Checking understanding

▶ Making reference to the text, decide whether the following statements are *true* or *false* representations of Rosenberg's views.

1 Accurate predictions regarding the future performance characteristics of newly-emerging technologies can be made without difficulty. (par. 7) _____

2 Anyone wishing to characterize modern technologies cannot do so without close reference to past events. (par. 4) _____

3 Significant characteristics of industrial technologies tend to be ignored in discussions of technological change. (par. 6) _____

4 Actual experience in using products with a high degree of system complexity is not a useful source of learning in high technology industries. (par. 8) _____

5 Technological considerations deeply embedded in the structure of industrial society do not usually influence the content and direction of scientific research. (par. 9) _____

6 Recent studies on the dominant role of market demand in the innovation process constitute a solid basis for government policy on innovation. (par. 11) _____

LANGUAGE WORK

WORKSHEET 7 **Practising with lexis used to present topics and arguments**

▶ Below is a list of topics which might be treated in the various chapters of a book on the growth of wealth in Western Europe. Match the principal argument of each chapter with the relevant topic. An example has been given.

Topics	Arguments
Chap. 1 _d_ The origins of Western European wealth in the High Middle Ages	**a** The strength of the link between the two from 1880 onwards should not conceal the fact that before this date, industrial technology had been mostly the product of artisan inventors.
Chap. 2 The growth of European trade and commerce from twelfth century Italy to 1750	**b** This was the most striking period of economic expansion so far, even though the Western economies' institutional foundation changed only modestly during this period.
Chap. 3 The period of the Industrial Revolution up to 1880	**c** The growth of Western economies has _not_ rested on their use of conspicuously large industrial enterprises but rather on their use of enterprises best suited to particular circumstances.
Chap. 4 The background to the development of the large business corporations	**d** European countries were not capable of maintaining sustained growth in the fourteenth century.
Chap. 5 The connection between science and industrial development	**e** This period saw the gradual development of a plural society in which the economic sphere in Europe eventually gained appreciable autonomy from political control.
Chap. 6 The diversity in the size and function of Western economic enterprises	**f** It was only after 1880 that Western industry began to turn increasingly away from the older modes of enterprise organization.

Below is a list of common verbs or phrases signalling the presentation of topics and arguments/points of view. Your attention has been drawn to some of these in Worksheet 4.

- to stress
- to be devoted to
- to maintain
- to consider
- to address

- to emphasize
- to evaluate
- to focus on
- to discuss
- to hold

- to explore
- to examine
- to speculate
- to look at
- to argue

▶ Rewrite the matched topics and arguments (the first one has been done for you) using an appropriate marker. Your completed text should form a brief summary of the contents of the book.

The origins of Western European wealth in the High Middle Ages _is considered_ in Chapter 1. _I argue that_ European countries were not capable of maintaining sustained growth in the fourteenth century.

VOCABULARY WORK AND WORD BUILDING

▶ Find the words in the text (paragraphs are given), decide the word class, and write it and the translation of the word in the space provided.

▶ Then complete the table by forming other words using appropriate suffixes if necessary. Consult your dictionary.

VOCABULARY WORK			WORD BUILDING		
Word and Location	**Class**	**Translation**	**Noun**	**Verb**	**Adjective**
capability (11)					
complexity (3)					
consequences (4)					
continuation (13)					
creation (11)					
distinctive (3)					
identify (3)					
improvement (2)					
individual (11)					
innovation (6)					
inquire (1)					
interaction (6)					
precisely (3)					
recognized (1)					
separate (3)					
specific (3)					
speculates (12)					
substitutability (6)					

OBSERVATIONS ON TEXT TYPE	PREFACE	
Function/ Structure:		See OBSERVATIONS on the *Introduction*, Unit Nine. This *Preface* has the same functional and structural characteristics as an introduction. It should be noted, however, that many prefaces limit themselves to a very brief discussion of the subject and of the organization of the book, and often include acknowledgements to various people and institutions that have made the book possible (colleagues, institutions that have provided funds etc.).

NOTES

APPENDIX 1

Lexis common to academic prose

The following is a list of words which occur frequently in all types of academic prose. They are given in the form in which they appear in the texts. (Unit and paragraph or text are given in brackets.) Further work on these words can be found in the *vocabulary work and word building* exercise at the end of the relevant Unit.

able (IX, 4)
accuracy (II, What use is psychology?)
accusation (II, Eating people is wrong)
achieved (VIII, 1)
acknowledge (IX, 3)
administered (II, Eating people is wrong)
affect (III, 19)
aggressive (IX, 1)
agree (III, 10)
allegation (V, 7)
alliance (VIII, 1)
allocated (V, 8)
analyzes (I, Sri Lanka)
anxiety (II, Too relaxed to read)
apparent (IX, 5)
applied (IX, 2)
assert (V, 18)
assessing (VII, 1)
assumption (VIII, 4)
attainment (III, 14)
attempt (I, Arab Politics)
available (III, 14)
avoid (IV, 8)

basic (I, Arab Politics)
behave (II, What use is psychology?)
biased (IV, 3)
broad (VII, 4)

capability (X, 11)
categorical (VI, 8)
characteristic (IX, 1)
choice (III, 6)
citizens (V, 3)
claiming (IV, Worksheet 6)
clarity (IV, 2)
comparing (VII, 1)
competitive (VII, 7)
complexity (X, 3)
comprehension (II, Too relaxed to read)
conceptual (I, Hegemony and Culture)
concludes (II, What use is psychology?)
consequences (X, 4)
consultants (V, 4)
consumer (VI, 1)
contention (VI, 2)
continuation (X, 13)
contradict (II, What use is psychology?)
correctly (II, What use is psychology?)
creation (X, 11)

critique (III, 2)
define (IX, 2)
deny (V, 5)
depends (VII, 8)
derive (VIII, 4)
destroy (IX, 1)
detract (VI, note 2)
devise (V, 4)
differentiate (III, 9)
diffusely (IX, 2)
discusses (I, Arab Politics)
distinctive (X, 3)

economy (I, Shadow Economy)
effective (I, Arab Politics)
electoral (VIII, 1)
emphasize (V, 14)
employ (III, 11)
entire (I, Arab Politics)
equal (I, Hegemony and Culture)
estimates (VII, 5)
evidence (VIII, 5)
expensive (V, 10)
experimental (II, What use is psychology?)
exploitation (VIII, 9)
extent (VII, 2)

failing (VII, 4)
feature (VIII, 1)
frequently (VI, 1)

gain (VII, 8)

historically (I, Policing Industrial Disputes)
human (IX, title)
hypotheses (IX, 6)

identify (X, 3)
illustrative (VI, 4)
implied (VI, 1)
improvement (X, 2)
impulses (IX, 1)
individual (X, 11)
industrial (I, Policing Industrial Disputes)
inferences (VI, 6)
influential (V, 10)
informative (I, Sri Lanka)
innovation (X, 6)
inquire (X, 1)
institutional (I, Decline of the British Economy)
intellectual (IX, 3)
interactions (X, 6)
involve (III, 4)

lacked (IV, Worksheet 6)
largely (IV, 4)
leads (IV, 8)

measurement (II, What use is psychology?)
mechanics (IV, 8)
modernization (VIII, 8)
modified (VIII, 11)

necessary (IX, 3)
notable (III, 1)

obliged (VIII, 1)
occurs (III, 13)

ownership (V, 18)
partially (II, Eating people is wrong)
participant (VI, abstract)
pattern (VII, 11)
perception (V, 5)
performance (III, 14)
persuaded (VIII, 6)
politics (I, Arab Politics)
precisely (X, 3)
predict (II, What use is psychology?)
prevent (VI, 12)
prior (VI, 4)
proceeds (III, 2)
processing (VI, note 2)
productive (I, Shadow Economy)
prospects (V, 12)
prosperous (VIII, 4)
provide (V, 11)
psychological (II, What use is psychology?)
purely (IV, 7)

questionnaire (II, What use is psychology?)

range (I, Shadow Economy)
rates (III, 8)
recognized (X, 1)
reference (III, 19)
refusal (VI, 6)
regulate (V, 17)
related (III, 1)
rely (III, 21)
representatives (VIII, 6)
resistant (VIII, 3)
respective (VI, 2)
respondent (II, What use is psychology?)
revealed (VI, note 2)
rewarded (IV, Worksheet 6)

scholarly (III, 1)
separate (X, 3)
settled (III, 20)
significant (II, Eating people is wrong)
solution (IX, 7)
specific (X, 3)
speculates (X, 12)
statement (III, 18)
structure (VII, 7)
studies (IV, 2)
substitutability (X, 6)
succeeded (I, Arab Politics)
sufficient (VIII, 1)
supervised (VI, 5)
support (IV, 4)
supposed (VII, 8)
surprisingly (VII, 10)
surveying (I, Arab Politics)
system (VII, 7)

tended (IV, 6)
theoretical (II, What use is psychology?)
threatens (IX, 2)
typically (VII, 10)

utilizing (VI, 4)

value (I, Utopia in Power)

wider (IV, Worksheet 6)
witnessed (IV, 1)

APPENDIX 2

The prefixes and suffixes listed below are recurrent in academic prose. The prefixes have been grouped according to meaning; the suffixes according to the grammatical classes of which they are markers.

PREFIXES

1 *the opposite, negation of something*
- a- (amoral)
- anti- (anti-modernist)
- counter- (counteraction/
- contra-   contradict)
- de- (devalue)
- dis- (disadvantage)
- il- (illegal)
- im- (impersonal)
- in- (inaccurate)
- ir- (irrelevant)
- non- (non-response)
- un- (unrepresentative)

2 *bad, wrong*
- mal- (malformation)
- mis- (misconstrue)

3 *quantity*
- bi-/tri- etc. (bilingual)
- cent- (centenary)
- dec- (decade)
- equi- (equivalent)
- macro- (macroeconomics)
- micro- (microeconomics)
- mono- (monolingual)
- multi- (multipurpose)

a lot, too much
- hyper- (hyperinflation)
- out- (outlive)
- over- (overselling)
- super- (superhuman)
- ultra- (ultramodern)

little, too little
- sub- (substandard)
- under- (underestimate)

4 *temporal*
- ex- (ex-president)
- fore- (forewarn)
- neo- (neo-Fascist)
- post- (post-war)
- pre- (pre-specified)

5 *to make or cause to be*
- be- (befriend)
- em- (embody)
- en- (enable)

6 *relations*
- co- (co-author)
- inter- (international)
- intra- (intramural)
- intro- (introduction)
- mid- (midway)
- semi- (semiprecious)
- trans- (transaction)
- vice- (vice-chairman)

7 *other important prefixes*
- pro-   in favour of   (pro-divorce)
- re-   again   (re-examine)
- self-   of or by oneself   (self-employed)

SUFFIXES

Nouns	Adjectives	Adverbs	Verbs
-ability (capability)	-able (capable)		
-age (shortage)			
	-al (social)		
-an (historian)	-an (Republican)		
-ance/-ence (importance)	-ant/-ent (important)		
-ary (library)	-ary/-ory (contemporary)		
-ate (electorate)	-ate (passionate)		-ate (formulate)
-ation (information)			
-cracy (aristocracy)			
-cy (efficiency)			
-dom (freedom)			
-ee (employee)			
	-en (golden)		-en (threaten)
-er/-ar/-or (employer)	-er[1] (larger)	-er[1] (faster)	
-ery (slavery)			
-ese (Japanese)	-ese (Japanese)		
	-est[2] (soundest)	-est[2] (closest)	
-ful (mouthful)	-ful (powerful)		
-hood (boyhood)			
-ics (economics)	-ic (historic)		
	-ical (political)		
			-ify (simplify)
	-ish (British)		
-ism (socialism)			
-ist (socialist)	-ist (socialist)		
-ite (Thatcherite)	-ite (Thatcherite)		
-ity/-ty (entirety)			
	-ive (comprehensive)		
			-ize/-ise (institutionalize)
	-less (helpless)		
	-ly (daily)	-ly (sharply)	
-ment (development)			
-ology/-logy (sociology)			
	-ous (famous)		
-ship (scholarship)			
	-some (awesome)		
-ster (pollster)			
	-th (nineteenth)		
-ure (failure)			
	-ward(s) (backward)	-ward(s) (forward)	
	-wide (nationwide)		

[1] *-er* is the marker of the *comparative* of short adjectives and adverbs.
[2] *-est* is the marker of the *superlative* of short adjectives and adverbs.

KEY

Where the answers have been given as examples in the text, they appear in the key in square brackets [ ].

UNIT ONE — BOOK ADVERTISEMENTS

PRE-READING

1 title of book, name of author, publishing house, price, number of pages etc.
2 Summit Books, University of Chicago Press, Yale University Press, Tavistock, Oxford (University Press)
3 Britain: *Shadow Economy*; *Decline of the British Economy*; *Policing Industrial Disputes*; *Arab Politics*[1]
America: *Utopia in Power*[2]; *Sri Lanka*; *Hegemony and Culture*; *Arab Politics*[1]
4 *Policing Industrial Disputes*; *Hegemony and Culture*
5 All books except *Policing Industrial Disputes*

[1] Note New Haven and London
[2] Simon and Schuster is an American publishing house.

WORKSHEET 1

Author(s) or Editor(s)	Title of book	Sub-title	Subject area[1]
Mikhail Heller Aleksandr M. Nekrich	[Utopia in Power]	The History of the Soviet Union from 1917 to the Present	history/politics/Soviet studies
[Stephen Smith]	Britain's Shadow Economy	—	economics/sociology
Bernard Elbaum William Lazonick (eds.)	The Decline of the British Economy	An Institutional Perspective	[economics]
[Roger Geary]	Policing Industrial Disputes 1893 to 1985	(1893 to 1985)[2]	industrial relations/politics
Michael C. Hudson	[Arab Politics]	The Search for Legitimacy	politics/Middle Eastern studies
[S. J. Tambiah]	Sri Lanka	Ethnic Fratricide and the Dismantling of Democracy	(social) anthropology
David D. Laitin	Hegemony and Culture	Politics and Religious Change among the Yoruba	sociology/political science/anthropology/social theory

[1] There may be some disagreement over the subject areas. Various possibilities are given.
[2] 1893–1985 may be accepted as a subtitle.

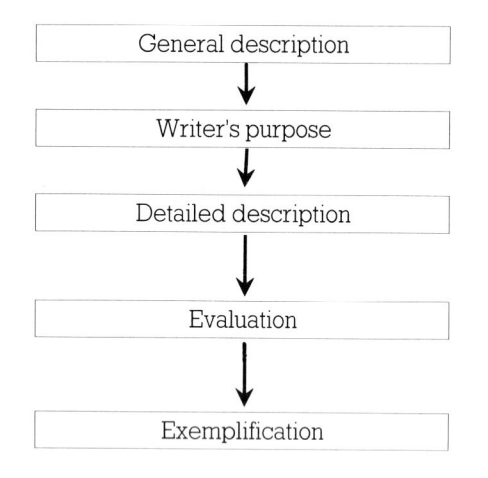

WORKSHEET 2

- General description
- Writer's purpose
- Detailed description
- Evaluation
- Exemplification

ARAB POLITICS
The Search for Legitimacy
Michael C. Hudson

The *first* (D/E[1]) *systematic* (D/E) *comparative* (D) analysis of *political* (D) behavior throughout the *Arab* (D) world, from Morocco to Kuwait./ In an attempt to explain why the *Arab* (D) world remains in ferment,/ Hudson discusses such *crucial* (D/E) factors as *Arab* (D) and *Islamic* (D) identity, *ethnic* (D) and *religious* (D) minorities, the crisis of authority, the effects of *Western* (D) imperialism and modernization./

"Hudson has succeeded brilliantly in surveying and analyzing the *entire* (D/E) range of *contemporary* (D) *Arab* (D) politics. . . . (He) focuses his *vast* (D/E) knowledge of theory and *historical* (D) data with *valid* (E) and *illuminating* (E) generalizations,/ perhaps the most *basic* (D/E) one being that most if not all *Arab* (D) countries lack an *effective* (D/E) structure for *full* (D/E) *political* (D) participation."
—*Library Journal*

[1] The aim of this exercise is to sensitize the students to the fact that some descriptive adjectives may assume *evaluative functions* depending on the immediate and wider context. For example, *first* is a descriptive adjective expressing chronology, but in the context of a book advertisement, it would also take on a positive, evaluative function.

WORKSHEET 3

(PE = predominantly evaluative, PD = predominantly descriptive)

▶ *Utopia in Power*, PE; *Britain's Shadow Economy*, PD; *Decline of the British Economy*, PE; *Sri Lanka*, balanced; *Hegemony and Culture*, PD; *Policing Industrial Disputes*, PD.
▶ volume, textbook, history (*Utopia in Power*); contribution (*Decline of the British Economy*); work (*Hegemony and Culture*); study (*Policing Industrial Disputes*). Also acceptable are: essays (*Decline of the British Economy*) and analysis (*Arab Politics*).

WORKSHEET 4

	adjectives	suffixes	
Utopia in Power	Well-documented; argued; undoubted; Western; better; general; Soviet; fascinating; devoted; foreign; first; vital; new; remarkable; whole; great; sober; documented; readable; standard; concerned	– ed; – al; – able	– er; – ing;
Britain's Shadow Economy	shadow; black; wide; ordinary; productive; household; DIY; critical; new; concealed	– ary; – al;	– ive; – ed
The Decline of the British Economy	institutional; distinguished; coherent; thought-provoking; fascinating; new; British	– al; – ent; – ish	– ed; – ing;
Policing Industrial Disputes	industrial; recent; violent; renewed; police; employed; fascinating; detailed; changing	– al; – ed;	– ent; – ing
Sri Lanka	ethnic; native; Tamil; distinguished; social; majority; Sinhalese; minority; recent; ancient; religious; racial; excellent; thought-provoking; concise; informative; written; powerful	– ic; – ed; – ity;[1] – ent; – ing	– ive; – al; – ese; – ous; – ative; – ful
Hegemony and Culture	religious; early; nineteenth; equal; sharp; political; unnatural; hegemonic; nineteenth-century; British; empirical; conceptual; complex; political; social	– ous; – th; – ic	– al; – ish;

[1] Note that –*ity* is a noun suffix, and that here the noun functions as an adjective. (See Box below Worksheet)

WORKSHEET 5
- ▶ [1b]; 2d; 3f; 4a; 5c; 6e
- ▶ (only the word class is given) 1 adj; 2 verb; 3 noun; 4 verb; 5 noun; 6 verb.

WORKSHEET 6

The following represents one possible version of the text.

The Interpretation of Dreams is the first comprehensive (adj.) study (noun) of dream psychology. In an attempt to explain (verb) why dreams are important[1] (adj.) to the well-being of the mental processes, Sigmund Freud explores (verb) a wide variety of common dreams. Among the topics discussed (adj. past part) are the processes of dislocation and transference that occur in dreams. Powerful (adj.) and incisive (adj.), the author succeeds in illuminating (verb) some of the darker workings of the mind. This brilliant (adj.) work is the most systematic (adj.)

analysis (noun) of the psychology of the unconscious available. Published in paperback, *The Interpretation of Dreams* is invaluable[1] (adj.) for all those who are seriously interested in dream psychology.

[1] Note that in these two cases, only one word from the list is possible either syntactically (*to* would not follow *invaluable*) or semantically, i.e. in final position this genre would require a highly evaluative adjective.

UNIT TWO RESEARCH DIGEST

PRE-READING   ▶   general assumptions; purpose; procedure/method; results; conclusions; comments; previous research; researchers; subjects; name of publication, etc.

WORKSHEET 1   1 John Houston   2 The study on backward readers *Too relaxed to read?*   3 *What use is psychology?*   4 *Too relaxed to read?*   5 *Eating people is wrong*, 39 subjects

WORKSHEET 2   WHAT USE IS PSYCHOLOGY?: Summary (par. 1); Procedure (par. 2, 3); Results (par. 4); Conclusions (par. 5)
EATING PEOPLE IS WRONG: Summary (par. 1); General assumptions (par. 2); Procedure (par. 3, 4); Results (par. 5)
TOO RELAXED TO READ?: Summary (par. 1); General assumptions (par. 2); Procedure (par 3, 4); Results (par. 4, 5); Conclusions[1] (par. 5–7)

[1] Note that the final sentence in *What use is psychology?* and the final paragraph in *Too relaxed to read?* may be considered as further comment on the conclusions of the report.

WORKSHEET 3
1 They had never read a book on experimental psychology or studied the subject.
2 Each embodied a principle related to the working of the memory.
3 The correct experimentally verified answer seemed to contradict common sense.
4 It offers a precise measurement of self-evident phenomena, and provides a theoretical explanation.

WORKSHEET 4

Title of research:	[Popularity of other nationalities (follow-up)]
Researcher and Affiliation:	David Krus, Arizona State University
Published in:	Psychological Reports, vol. 59, No 1, p. 3
Purpose of research:	[To verify changes in attitude towards national groups]
When conducted:	immediately after shooting down of KAL airliner in 1983
Procedure: (main points)	students read fictitious report of airline crash; rated which nationalities most likely to have committed cannibalism
Results:	Russians rated most likely after KAL crash (5th most likely before); white Americans and English consistently least likely

WORKSHEET 5

Phase 1 of experiment (2 weeks):
Procedure for all groups: Children's accuracy, speed and comprehension in reading were measured

Phase 2 (5 weeks):

Group	Procedure	Results		
		Accuracy	Speed	Comprehension
1	taught to lower muscle tension with electromyographic feedback + daily reading tests	no improvement	decreased	[improved]
2	relaxation training + daily reading tests	no improvement	[no improvement]	improved
3	remedial teaching based on phonics + comprehension + daily reading tests	improved	no improvement	improved
4	daily reading tests	[no improvement]	no improvement	improved
5	—	no improvement	no improvement	no improvement

Conclusions:
– improvement in comprehension may be effect of increased reading practice
– reducing stress may work against improvement in reading, since optimum level of stress is necessary for learning, *or* teaching to relax may reduce attention given to reading.

WORKSHEET 6

converse/have known/prefer/keep/studied/talked/were told/were asked/talked/had to/performed/sat/were/placed/changed/moved/speculate/know (knew[1])/suggest/may be (may have been[1])/was done/appeared

[1] Depending on whether emphasis is placed on the *general truth* of the assertion or on the *specific research results*, either the present or the past tense respectively may be used.

WORKSHEET 7

1 false   2 false   3 true   4 false

UNIT THREE   ECONOMICS

PRE-READING

purpose(s): to give an introductory/general overview of a subject area (e.g. economics) or of a more specific aspect of a topic (e.g. medieval history in Britain)
characteristics: charts, summaries, large headings, typographically prominent sections and subsections, figures, etc.

WORKSHEET 1

1 – 2 – 4 – 5 – 7

WORKSHEET 2

[1 (noun) d];   2 (noun) k;   3 (noun) f;   4 (adj.) b;   5 (noun) e;   6 (adj.) j;   7 (noun) h;   8 (noun) i;   9 (noun) l;   10 (noun) a;   11 (noun) c

WORKSHEET 3

What Economics Is

1 The contributions of some important economists to the development of the discipline
2 popular definitions/authors' definitions
3 microeconomics – macroeconomics – GNP

Economic Description and Policy

1 Two major uses of economics
2 value judgements vs. factual statements

The Methodology of Economics

1 The method of economic analysis
2 controlled experiments

WORKSHEET 4

Key term	Explanation/Definition	Example/Further clarification
[*movements in overall economy (par. 5)*]		trends in prices, output and unemployment
scarce or limited productive resources		[*land, labour, equipment, technology, knowledge (par. 6)*]
[*commodities (par. 6)*]		wheat, beef, overcoats, concerts, roads, missiles
[*important (economic) phenomena (par. 12)*]		unemployment, prices, incomes and so forth
[*macroeconomics (par. 13)*]	studies the behaviour of the economy as a whole	movements in overall prices, or output, or employment
microeconomics	[*a study of economy through a microscope (par. 13)*]	studies the behaviour of an economy's individual molecules, e.g. firms or households
[*gross national product (par. 14)*]	represents total dollar value of all goods and services produced each year in a nation	tells us much about the real economic performance . . . and its educational attainment
real goods and services		[*food, clothing, penicillin, ballet, baseball (par. 14)*]
positive economics	[*description of facts, circumstances, relationships in the economy (par. 19)*]	what is the unemployment rate today? . . . affect gasoline usage?
[*normative economics (par. 20)*]	involves ethics and value judgements	How much inflation should be tolerated? . . . or 10 percent a year?
controlled experiments	[*everything but the item under investigation is held constant (par. 23)*]	a scientist trying to determine whether . . . same type of rat

WORKSHEET 5

▶ **a** 1 behavior; 2 production; 3 incomes; 4 hardships; 5 raise; 6 gasoline; 7 settled; 8 issues/questions
  b 1 inflation; 2 poverty; 3 reduce/lower; 4 start; 5 unemployment; 6 tough; 7 grow; 8 wrong
▶ 1 massive; 2 advice; 3 embody; 4 wisdom; 5 figuring out; 6 item; 7 vary; 8 vitally

WORKSHEET 6[1]

▶ Ability/Potential: can, cannot
Probability/Possibility: might, may
Obligation/Necessity: must
Obligation/Desirability: should
Future: will
Conditional: would, could

▶ The following is one possible version of the completed text. Several answers are acceptable in all cases (changing the meaning slightly) except for the first, where *must* is the only option possible.

1 must, obligation/necessity;   2 may, probability/possibility;   [3 *will, future*];
4 should, obligation/desirability;   5 must, obligation/necessity;
6 should, obligation/desirability;   7 should, obligation/desirability;
8 can, ability/potential;   9 will, future;   10 might, probability/possibility

[1] Note that there may be a considerable range of nuances of meaning in modal verbs, depending on context and interpretation. This exercise aims to sensitize students to this range, also with reference to similar shades of meaning in the student's mother tongue.

WORKSHEET 7

▶ prices neither *rise* nor fall; prices and *wages* be set; organizing *output* and keeping markets; measures the *overall* price level; typical urban *consumer*; growth or *decline* of the price level; the *rate* of inflation; inflation *averaged* 3.2%; enormous *variation* of inflation; a high of *plus* 14%; wartime price *controls*; we must avoid *hyperinflation*

▶ This *figure* shows; the *consumer price index* (CPI); prices actually *fell*; falling *prices*; [has been *rare*]; upward *trend* of *inflation*; 1960 to *1980*; steep *decline*; *high* unemployment

UNIT FOUR 1917: THE RUSSIAN REVOLUTION

PRE-READING

1 book review;   2 Olga Semenova;   3 *1917: The Russian Revolution and the Origins of Present-day Communism*, Leonard Shapiro;   4 The reviewer is negative or at least dubious (because a question mark has been put after the quotation from the book).

WORKSHEET 1

Note that in some cases the distinction between *very unfavourable* and *unfavourable* is rather subjective.

▶ 1 very favourable;   2 favourable;   3 unfavourable;   4 neutral;
5 very unfavourable;   6 unfavourable or very unfavourable;
7 unfavourable;   8 unfavourable or very unfavourable;   9 unfavourable;
10 favourable

▶ unfavourable

WORKSHEET 2

1 PRESENTATION OF THE BOOK AND AUTHOR (par. 1)
2 EVALUATION OF THE BOOK AS NARRATIVE (par. 2)
3 DISCUSSION OF SCHAPIRO'S POLITICAL ANALYSIS
  (par. 3–9)
  — Presentation of Schapiro's thesis (par. 4)
  — Criticism of Schapiro's thesis (par. 5–9)
    — On the grounds that he was biased against the Bolsheviks
      (par. 6)
    — On the grounds that he considers the revolution purely in terms of
      political power (par. 7–9)
      — Leading to errors of interpretation (par. 8)
      — Leading to an unsatisfactory choice of period (par. 9)
4 CONCLUSION: EVALUATION OF THE BOOK (par. 10)

WORKSHEET 3

1 anaphoric, general support for a broad-based socialist coalition
2 cataphoric, that the Bolsheviks were unscrupulous ... power   3 anaphoric, committees   4 cataphoric, to understand the Russian revolution ... questions
5 anaphoric, 1917 is based on the premise that it is possible ... social or economic questions   6 anaphoric, these events   7 anaphoric, that he lived in Petrograd as a boy

WORKSHEET 4

▶ 1 Shapiro;   2 Semenova;   3 Semenova;   4 Shapiro;   5 Shapiro;
  6 Shapiro;   7 Semenova

▶ 2

▶ Perhaps Semenova is disappointed in the work of a fellow Russian scholar of such importance and prestige.

WORKSHEET 5

While most of the books; Shapiro *manages to* present; years *up to* 1924; *both* simple *and* accurate; *without* which a surprising gap; *between* 1917 and 1920; background *allow/ed* him; *However*, his hatred of the Bolsheviks *affects/ed* his interpretation; which is *largely* biased; *Firstly*, his analysis; Bolsheviks, *whose* popular support; prejudiced *as well as* one-sided, *stems from* his hostility; *Secondly*, the fact; historian *leads/led* him to assume; *regardless of* social and economic factors; the *main* social; *Rather than* a brilliant work; Shapiro's *own* experience

WORKSHEET 6

▶ 2 – 4 – 1 – 3

▶ 1 true;   2 false;   3 true

UNIT FIVE THE OVERSELLING OF CANDIDATES ON TELEVISION

PRE-READING

▶ Amount spent on TV campaigning in USA compared with other Western democracies; that too much money is spent on publicizing candidates.

WORKSHEET 1

1 30 or 60 seconds;   2 no (add little or nothing);   3 three-fourths;   4 increasing;   5 lower costs, higher voter participation;   6 Committee for the Study of the American Electorate;   7 a Fund grant;   8 to discover how some Western democracies deal with political advertising on television.

WORKSHEET 2

▶ General remarks: pars. 1–5; results of study: pars. 6–15; conclusions/comment: pars. 16–19.[1]

▶ The research procedure is not described.

▶ This research used documented evidence and not information gathered in the course of field research.

[1] Note that the function of par. 16 is to briefly summarize the most important results already given as a prelude to the conclusions. The subtitle *Overselling can be stopped* also indicates a comment.

WORKSHEET 3

Country	PAID POLITICAL ADVERTISING ON T.V.				FREE TIME FOR ADVERTISING ON T.V.			
	Yes	No	Other information[1] (including cost)	Cost	Yes	No	Method of Allocation	Restrictions/Other information[1]
USA	√		30 or 60 second spots, attacking opponents; no exact figures re. cost since TV expenditure not reported; low voter participation despite cost	⅔ – ¾ campaign budgets		√		
France		√			√		given equally to all candidates, regardless of prospects for success	all special effects prohibited; can only record in studio, and time limit on making spot; cannot edit different films to make one spot
Germany		√			√		publicly owned networks divide 1–2 hours time in proportion to electoral strength	networks decide when spots broadcast and in what order; German law forbids spot being designed to look like something it isn't
UK		√			√		in proportion to electoral strength[2]	
Canada	√		only to parties, not individuals, + within strict time limits (6½ hours) – ceiling on spending so low that parties cannot purchase all time		√		in proportion to electoral strength[2]	
Italy	[√]		[RAI no: unregulated private companies for individuals, but role minor]		[√]		[in proportion to electoral strength][2]	
Venezuela	√		more expensive and influential than anywhere else, but only 5 – 6 million voters in elections	1978: $120 million				

[1] Note that the Other information columns are to a certain extent free, although the answers given here are perhaps the most relevant.

[2] See par. 12, "Elsewhere . . . in proportion to their electoral strength", as in fact is the case in the UK, Canada and Italy.

WORKSHEET 4	**Section III: Conclusions/Comment**
	– 3 possible ways to prevent overselling of candidates on TV, e.g.
	  – Free time for campaign messages and prohibition of political commercials (France, Germany, UK)
	  – Free time + limited purchase time to pol. parties (Canada)
	  – Uniformity and simplicity of message format (France)
	[– *Impact on campaign costs not calculated in study, but such restrictions would obviously reduce costs if applied in US*]
	– Major TV networks however have opposed attempts to regulate sale of TV air-time
	– Current possibilities for reform: placing restrictions on candidates, not on networks
	– Proposed bill: modified version of French formula for control of pol. message format
	– Pol. advertising of 10 minutes or less in straightforward format without special effects would result in reduced production costs, reduced opportunities for image manipulation

WORKSHEET 5	so, causal; but, adversative; however, adversative; despite, adversative; while, adversative; for example, additive; although, adversative; first[1], additive [1] Note that words like *first, second, next, then* etc. in academic prose are very often used in the presentation of lists where their function is *additive*. Where these words are used to refer to events outside the text, their function is normally *temporal* (e.g. *First*, the Bolsheviks seized power, *next* they banned other political parties, *then* . . . etc.).
WORKSHEET 6	[1a]; 2b; 3a; 4a; 5b
WORKSHEET 7	campaign budgets, *but* the Federal Election Commission; separate item, *so* we do not know; *Despite* the fact that Americans often complain; *However*, many advanced democracies; the UK, *for instance*, permit no advertising; Italy *also* forbids the sale; *While* Canada does allow; *Although* paid political advertising; *first*, time may be allocated; *Next*, the content; and *hence* the advertisements; *Until* such regulations
WORKSHEET 8	(only the word class is given) 1 noun; 2 noun; 3 adj.; 4 verb; 5 adj.; 6 verb; 7 verb

UNIT SIX — ASKING THE AGE QUESTION

PRE-READING	1 Robert A. Peterson 2 Sam Barshop Professor of Marketing Administration and Senior Research Fellow, Institute for Constructive Capitalism, University of Texas at Austin. 3 Institute for Constructive Capitalism, University of Texas at Austin. 4 Those of the author, not necessarily those of the Institute.

WORKSHEET 1

	In abstract	Information given	Pars. in text
General Assumptions	—		1
Purpose	√	to evaluate the accuracy of data obtained from asking age 4 different ways	2
Procedure	(√)[1]	it was possible to compare each participant's reported age with his/her actual age	3–6
Subjects	√	1,324 registered voters from a large SW state	3, 6
Results	√	all question formats provided accurate data, but refusal rates different	7–9
Conclusions	—		10–11

[1] The sentence *Because criterion age data ... actual age* can be considered in only a very vague sense as *Procedure*. Even in abstracts description of the *Procedure* is usually more specific.

WORKSHEET 2

Author(s)	Date	Page ref.	Research/Previous Work	Comments
[*Weaver and Swanson*]	1974		Accuracy of answers to an age question	
Perry and Crossley	1950		Accuracy of answers to an age question	
Myers	1954		Accuracy of answers to an age question	
Kerin and Peterson	[*1978*]		How to best ask age to obtain most accurate data	empirically addressed
Payne	1950	125–6	[*Question construction*]	no data to support contention
Parten	1950	169	Question construction	[*mere suggestion; no data*]

▶ *open-end*: date of birth, direct age; *closed-end*: e.g. are you 18–35? (categorical format)

▶ in the references at the end of the report

WORKSHEET 3

▶ 1 3,296[1]; 2 2,083; 3 1,324; 4 20; 5 15; 6 by telephone; 7 random

[1] Potential sample = 2,083 divided by 0.632 = 3,295.880

▶ **a** non-response reasons: potential study participants deceased, moved from state, no telephone, refused, terminated, were unlocatable (see note 1 in text); **b** only possible to analyze data for those subjects whose processing was complete (see note 2 in text).

▶ It is not essential to an understanding of the main points of the text.

WORKSHEET 4

▶ 1 true; 2 false; 3 false; 4 true; 5 true.

▶ 1 no; 2 shows how decision to use particular question must consider both response accuracy and potential refusal rate; 3 on researcher and decision maker needs

WORKSHEET 5

Sentence	Words explained or reformulated	Reformulation	Device used
1	open-end, closed-end questions	date of birth, direct age categorical format	parentheses ( )
2	validating (data)	criterion reference data	... or ...
3	randomly determined	no fixed pattern for asking questions was followed	that is
4	split ballot (experimental)[1] design	each quarter of sample asked age using different question format	whereby
5	non-response reasons typically associated with telephone interviews	no telephone in household, refusals, etc.	namely

[1] Note that *experimental* in parentheses is not an explanation of the term *split ballot*, but simply gives further information regarding this particular split ballot design.

WORKSHEET 6

Abstract: participant   Par. 1: public opinion poll/consumer survey; research; investigated; provided; contention   Par. 2: conducted; available; to compare; accuracy   Par. 3: sample; attitudes   Par. 4: randomly; prior to; specific   Par. 8: virtually   Par. 10: significant   Par. 11: unequivocal   Footnote 2: interviewed

WORKSHEET 7   The words inserted where there are dots are not necessarily the only possible answers. Note, however, that *less likely* or *unlikely* in par. 2 are the only possible answers.

The __accuracy__ of data regarding the __percentage__ of foreign workers employed illegally in Italy is not always dependable. In order to __investigate__ __this situation__, a __research__ project was __conducted__ using a __sample__ of foreign workers from a variety of sectors, in twelve Italian cities.

The __participants__ were __interviewed__ using a __specific__ interviewing technique which has recently proved very __effective__. The __research__ produced some __significant__ results. For example, foreign workers are more likely to be given work illegally in the building and catering sectors, in agriculture and as domestic help, while this is __less likely/unlikely__ to occur in other sectors.

Although the results of this __study__ cannot be considered __unequivocal__, it is certainly __significant__ that in __virtually__ __all cities__ __investigated__, the same industries abused foreign workers to the same extent, throughout Italy.

UNIT SEVEN   THE OTHER ECONOMY

PRE-READING
1 *The Other Economy*, Stephen Smith; *Britain's Shadow Economy, The Shadow Economy in Britain and Germany.*
2 *New Society* 17 October 1986; Analysis.
3 That it deals mainly with the unofficial, untaxed sector of the economy and who benefits from it.

WORKSHEET 1   1 pars. 1–3;   2 pars. 4–5;   3 pars. 6–10;   4 pars. 11–13.

WORKSHEET 2   [1 (noun) t];   2 (noun) i;   3 (adj.) j;   4 (noun[1]) k;   5 (verb) l;   6 (noun) m;
7 (noun) a;   8 (noun) n;   9 (adj., past participle) h;   10 (adj.) f;   11 (noun) e;
12 (noun) d;   13 (noun) c;   14 (noun) g;   15 (verb) b;   16 (noun) o;
17 (adj.) p;   18 (verb) q;   19 (noun) r;   20 (noun) s.

[1] Verb forms function as nouns after prepositions, in this case *by*.

WORKSHEET 3

The following represents a very complete version of the notes. These can, of course, be more succinct.

(par. 1)   1 *Introductory comments and statement of research objectives*
- economy: formal (measured by <u>GDP</u>) + shadow (<u>moonlighting, DIY, voluntary work etc.</u>). Comparisons between countries based on GDP may be <u>misleading</u>.

(par. 2)   – poverty and inequality calculated on formal economy incomes: valid?

(par. 3)   – IFS project on interaction formal/shadow economies – 2 points:
- <u>does shadow economy reinforce or offset inequalities in formal economy?</u>
- what scope does shadow economy provide for households to <u>compensate for temporary decline in formal economy earnings?</u>

(par. 4)   2 *Classification and description of shadow economy activities; impact on official statistics*
- "black economy" = monetary transactions concealed to avoid tax, e.g. <u>people doing odd jobs for cash payment, businessman not declaring part of turnover etc.</u>
- "wider shadow economy" = <u>wide range of productive activities with no payment</u>, e.g. <u>housework, DIY, voluntary work</u>
- similarities between black and wider shadow economies, especially in <u>role tax system plays in encouraging alternatives to formal economy goods and services</u>

(par. 5)   – difference: attempts made to adjust official statistics to include amount for black economy, but <u>productive activity in rest of shadow economy excluded from GDP</u>

(par. 6)   3 *Detailed discussion of black economy:*
- income tax evasion (self-employed vs. <u>employee (PAYE)</u> taxpayers)

(par. 7)   – business "off the books": smaller vs. <u>larger</u> businesses – greatest competitive pressure to trade off the books in <u>high value-added business</u>

(par. 8)   – who benefits? Gains may accrue to <u>buyer and/or seller</u>

(par. 9)   – where black economy forms high proportion of total, <u>customer may</u> receive all gains, seller none

(par. 10)   – where <u>black economy is small</u>, gains to business

(par. 11)   4 *Detailed discussion of aspects of wider shadow economy:*

(par. 12)   – need for expensive equipment means poor households <u>cannot participate in areas of shadow economy production (e.g. DIY)</u>

(par. 13)   – DIY mainly practised by <u>comparatively well-off (esp. home owners)</u>
- activities in wider shadow economy thus <u>do not offset inequalities</u> observed in formal economy.

WORKSHEET 4

▶ 1 monetary transactions concealed to avoid tax; 2 the contribution of the black economy; 3 that the people who work in the black economy ... taxpayers are the losers; 4 buyer or seller; 5 black economy goods and services; 6 gains from evasion; 7 building and decorating; 8 wider shadow economy; 9 inequalities.

▶ 10 i.e. (the GDP) tends not to account for the mass of productive activity outside formal economy; 11 i.e. (between) self-employed people and employee taxpayers (par. 6), smaller businesses and larger (esp. high value added) businesses (par. 7).

WORKSHEET 5

1**a** estimation of contribution of black economy to GDP; **b** average amount of income not declared for tax purposes by self-employed; **c** income from second jobs relative to income from main jobs.
2**a** buyer; **b** buyer and seller; **c** buyer; **d** seller
3**a** no; **b** yes; **c** no; **d** no; **e** yes.
4**a** yes, poverty may be greater because shadow economy tends to reinforce inequalities; **b** in some areas it may reinforce them, little evidence that it offsets these inequalities; **c** little or none: need for expensive equipment and materials prevents poorer households participating effectively in areas of shadow economy production. Black economy, moreover, concentrated in particular areas.

WORKSHEET 6

[1 example]; 2 example; 3 example; 4 further information; 5 example/further information[1]; 6 further information; 7 further information; 8 contrasting information; 9 example; 10 example/further information; 11 contrasting information; 12 example/further information; 13 contrasting information

[1] Note that in the three cases which cover the functions both of *example* and *further information*, words such as *notably*, *especially* and *in particular*, giving emphasis to the importance of the example, are used.

UNIT EIGHT MOBILIZING THE MIDDLE CLASSES

PRE-READING

1 book review; 2 Jeremy Noakes; 3 *Who voted for Hitler?*, Richard F. Hamilton; *The Nazi Voter*, Thomas Childers; 4 *Who Voted for Hitler?* (664 pages); 5 Yes, *Who Voted for Hitler?*; 6 In the TLS (*Times Literary Supplement*); 7 that the middle classes voted for Hitler

WORKSHEET 1

▶ 1 descriptive; 2 descriptive; 3 evaluative (critical); 4 evaluative (critical); 5 descriptive; 6 evaluative (critical); 7 evaluative (critical); 8 evaluative (favourable); 9 evaluative (favourable)[1]; 10 descriptive

[1] Mention is made of Childer's *important* article and the fact that Hamilton has *perceptively elucidated* it.

▶ The author uses the questions to introduce his concluding comments, i.e. he asks the questions in order to answer them himself. Note that this is a common stylistic device in academic prose.

WORKSHEET 2

1 INTRODUCTION (par. 1)
2 DISCUSSION OF HAMILTON'S THESIS (par. 2–7)
— Nature of the Nazi electoral support (par. 2–4)
— Reasons for Nazi electoral support (par. 5–6)
— Concluding evaluation (par. 7)
3 DISCUSSION OF CHILDER'S THESIS (par. 8–10)
— Nature of the Nazi electoral support (par. 8–9)
— Reasons for Nazi electoral support (par. 10)
4 GENERAL CONCLUSIONS (par. 11)

WORKSHEET 3

1 that the Nazis ... German élites; 2 that the sample of cities ... Chemnitz; 3 cities; 4 local press; 5 whether its role could ... as he suggests; 6 local press; 7 Hamilton; 8 messages

WORKSHEET 4

	Hamilton	**Childers**	**Noakes**
Who Voted Nazi?	1 *not lower middle class but upper middle class* 2 *the more marginal urban white collar worker voted SPD not Nazi* 3 *some workers voted DNVP and later Nazi* 4 *more voters in communities under 25,000* 5 *villages voted normally one party, Nazi or other* 6 *Catholic rural areas resistant*	1 *much less support among white-collar workers than hitherto thought* 2 *substantial support amongst older generation e.g. pensioners* 3 *widespread upper-middle class support* 4 *women surpassed men in Nazi electorate*	1 *support largely from lower middle class, but basis of support wider than thought* 2 *substantial number of votes from upper-middle class and working class*
Why?	1 *influence of Nazi political cadres (military background)* 2 *influence of local press*	1 *effectiveness of Nazi propaganda machine*	1 *lower middle class distaste for, and fear of, Left* 2 *Nazis persuaded lower middle class that they were party who could deal with threat of Left most effectively*

WORKSHEET 5 The verbs which have a completely different meaning are: 1 to deal with; 2 to concur with; 3 to elucidate

WORKSHEET 6 Additive: moreover, indeed, furthermore, likewise, similarly;

Temporal: then (par. 2 line 9), hitherto, henceforth;

Causal: therefore, thus, then (4, 27), for, because;

Adversative: nevertheless, though, although, yet

WORKSHEET 7 *Henceforth* Germany was to have; *For example, although* the Bolshevik seizure; coup d'état, and, *moreover*, the revolutionary; *Yet* it is clear; *Therefore* we must distinguish; *Furthermore*, the preconditions; the case of Russia, *for instance*, we must realize; feudal society, *while* in Italy; took place, *then*, highlights further differences

Note: NSDAP = *Nationalsozialistische Deutsche Arbeiterpartei* (Nazi Party)
DNVP = *Deutschnationale Volksparteo* (People's party)
SPD = *Sozialdemokratische Partei* (Social Democratic Party)

UNIT NINE HUMAN AGGRESSION

WORKSHEET 1 1d; 2b; 3g, e; 4a, [c], f

WORKSHEET 2 Par. 1: *Description/Examples* [destroys members of own species]; pleasure in exercise of cruelty on another of own kind; cruelty brutal or bestial; no parallel in nature to our savage treatment of each other; cruellest, most ruthless species; atrocities committed by man

Par. 2: *Descriptions/Examples* [red-faced infant squalling for the bottle]; judge who awards 30-year sentence for robbery; guard in concentration camp who tortures victims; neglected wife who threatens or attempts suicide

Par. 2: *Information/Comments* [term used in many different senses]; word everyone knows but hard to define; covers wide range of human behaviour; so diffusely applied that it ought to be dropped or more closely defined; portmanteau term bursting at the seams

WORKSHEET 3

Information Pairs

Paragraph 3	– [those forms of aggression which we all deplore	/ – those which we must not disown if we are to survive]
	– a child rebelling against authority is being aggressive	/ – also manifesting drive towards independence
	– desire for power, in extreme form, has disastrous consequences	/ – drive to conquer difficulties underlies greatest of human achievements
Paragraph 4	– aggressive part of human nature *not only* safeguard against predatory attack	/ – *also* basis of intellectual achievement, of attainment of independence etc.
	– whereas psychotherapists refer to sexual instincts and aggressive instincts	/ – Gibbon writes of "love of pleasure" and "love of action"[1]
Paragraph 5	– very qualities which have led to man's extraordinary success	/ – those most likely to destroy him
Paragraph 6	– although psychotherapists' knowledge of a few people is profound	/ – conclusions drawn from limited and highly selected sample of population
	– rapprochement between precise but limited view of experimentalist	/ – less defined but wider conceptions of psychotherapist
Paragraph 7	– psychological point of view	/ – deserves equal consideration with the political, economic and other aspects
	– study and control of human aggression relevant to problem of war	/ – though alone, cannot provide a complete answer

[1] An alternative pair could be "love of pleasure"/"love of action"

WORKSHEET 4

Ability/Potential: can, could, cannot (par. 7)
Probability/Possibility: may
Obligation/Necessity: must
Obligation/Desirability: ought to
Future: will
Conditional: would
Prohibition: cannot (par. 2), must not

WORKSHEET 5

The following represents one possible version.
1 can, potentiality; 2 may, probability/possibility; 3 ought to, obligation/desirability; 4 must not, prohibition; 5 cannot, prohibition; 6 will, future; 7 cannot, ability; 8 can, ability; 9 must, obligation/necessity; 10 cannot, prohibition; 11 will, future; 12 ought to, obligation/desirability; 13 can, ability; 14 would, conditional

WORKSHEET 6

The following represents one possible version (except in the case of *Even though*). The function of the linker required is indicated.
Indeed (add.), with the exception; *Moreover* (add.), no other animal; In truth, *however* (adv.), the extremes; *Even though* (adv.) we may recoil; *In fact* (add.), aggression is one of those words; *For example* (add.), the red-faced infant; *Similarly* (add.), the guard in a concentration camp; *But* (adv.) until we can more clearly designate

UNIT TEN INSIDE THE BLACK BOX

WORKSHEET 1

1 INTRODUCTION TO THE BOOK AS A WHOLE (par. 1–3)
2 DETAILED PRESENTATION OF CONTENTS OF THE BOOK (par. 4–12)
  – in Part I (par. 4–5)
  – in Part II (par. 6–9)
  – in Part III (par. 10–11)
  – in Part IV (par. 12)
3 CONCLUDING REMARKS (par. 13)

WORKSHEET 2

Preface   *page vii*

Part I. Views of technical progress

1 The historiography of technical progress   3
2 Marx as a student of technology   34

Part II. Some significant characteristics of technologies

3 Technological interdependence in the American economy   55
4 The effects of energy supply characteristics on technology and
   economic growth   81
5 On technological expectations   104
6 [*Learning by using*]   120
7 [*How exogenous is science?*]   141

Part III. Market determinants of technological innovation

8 Technical change in the commercial aircraft industry
   1925–1975   163
9 The economic implications of the VLSI revolution   178
10 The influence of market demand upon innovation: a critical
   review of some recent empirical studies   193

Part IV. Technology transfer and leadership: the international context

11 The international transfer of technology   245
12 U.S. technological leadership and foreign competition   280

WORKSHEET 3

▶ 1 (adj.) h; 2 (noun) l; 3 (noun) j; 4 (verb) b; 5 (noun) f; 6 (adj.) d;
  7 (noun) q; 8 (adj.) p; 9 (verb) k; 10 (noun) r; 11 (adj.) g; 12 (adj.) m;
  13 (adj) c; 14 (adj.) e; 15 (noun) a; 16 (noun) o; 17 (noun) n; 18 (verb) i

▶ 1f; 2c; [3d]; 4b (British Thermal Units); 5e; 6g; 7a

WORKSHEET 4

Background
- *Economists have*
  1. long treated eco. phenomena as "inside a black box"
  2. recognized they have important consequences
  3. devoted energy to tracing/measuring these consequences
- *but have not:* 1. inquired too seriously into what transpires "inside"

Purpose of book
- *immediate:* to break open box and examine contents
- *ultimate:* to illuminate number of important eco. problems
- *justification:* specific characteristics of certain technologies have ramifications for eco. phenomena

- *aspects of technologies influencing developments of interest to economists:*
  1. rate of productivity improvement
  2. nature of learning process
  3. speed of technological transfer
  4. effectiveness of government policies on technology

Distinctive features of 20th century industrial technologies considered
1. – reliance on science
   (but)
   – complexity of science/technology dialectic
2. – growth in development costs of new technology
   – lengthy lead times
   – tech. uncertainty re. performance
3. – changing structure of interindustry relationships
4. – changing characteristics of a technology in its own life-cycle

WORKSHEET 5

Chap.	Principal topic	Author's main argument/point of view
1	conceptualization of technological change	—
2	Marx's analysis of technological change	that it has not been exploited (*opened doors . . . hardly anyone subsequently passed*)
3	[*variety of less visible forms in which technological innovations enter economy*]	each of these forms is important in determining connection between tech. innovation + productivity growth
4	some significant characteristics of different energy forms	the frequently imperfect substitutability among energy sources
5	technological expectations	[*that rational decision-making re. adoption of innovation requires careful consideration of prospective rates of technical improvement*]
6	the importance of learning by using	that learning by using may be more pervasive in high technology industries
7	nature of science/technology interactions in high technology	that scientific enterprise is heavily shaped by technological considerations
8	history of technological change in aircraft industry 1925–1975	—
9	ongoing technological revolution embodied in VLSI	the successful application of VLSI will turn upon internal developments but also on "translation" mechanisms[1]
10	a number of recent empirical studies of technological change	these studies are analytically and conceptually seriously incomplete
11	the transfer of industrial technologies from Britain to the rest of the world	—
12	prospects for the future from an American perspective	– that world economy of 1990s will be shaped by international distribution of tech. capabilities *and* social/economic forces which will influence effectiveness of technologies – that world of 1990s will be more complex than predicted

[1] Note that in this case the author's principal argument is not explicitly marked, but is recognizable from the phrase *success . . . will turn upon*. The sentence beginning *It points out that . . .* seems to mark here an assumption which is closely linked to the author's main argument.

WORKSHEET 6   1 false; 2 true; 3 true; 4 false; 5 false; 6 false

WORKSHEET 7

Topics	Arguments
Chap. 1 d The origins of Western European wealth in the High Middle Ages	**a** The strength of the link between the two from 1880 onwards should not conceal the fact that before this date, industrial technology had been mostly the product of artisan inventors.
Chap. 2 e The growth of European trade and commerce from twelfth century Italy to 1750	**b** This was the most striking period of economic expansion so far, even though the Western economies' institutional foundation changed only modestly during this period.
Chap. 3 b The period of the Industrial Revolution up to 1880	**c** The growth of Western economies has *not* rested on their use of conspicuously large industrial enterprises but rather on their use of enterprises best suited to particular circumstances.
Chap. 4 f The background to the development of the large business corporations	**d** European countries were not capable of maintaining sustained growth in the fourteenth century.
Chap. 5 a The connection between science and industrial development	**e** This period saw the gradual development of a plural society in which the economic sphere in Europe eventually gained appreciable autonomy from political control.
Chap. 6 c The diversity in the size and function of Western economic enterprises	**f** It was only after 1880 that Western industry began to turn increasingly away from the older modes of enterprise organization.

▶ Free

NOTES

NOTES